CW00950609

The Sound With The Pound

by

Manfred Kuhlmann

The Sound With The Pound

by

Manfred Kuhlmann

Published by
Mediaworld PR Ltd
Best Books Online

Copyright 2008
First paperback edition published in Great Britain
July 2009 by
Mediaworld PR Ltd
Best Books Online

All rights reserved.
No part of this publication may be reproduced, stored in a retrieval system or
transmitted in any form or by any means; electronic, mechanical, photocopying,
recording or otherwise without the prior permission of the publisher.

ISBN 978-1-906349-12-7

MUSICIAN'S FOREWORD

It was at a 'Beatles Convention' held in the Adelphi Hotel, Liverpool that Manfred fittingly asked me to write a foreword for his book. As we sat in the restaurant and I leafed through the manuscript, even I, a hardened Merseybeat veteran, was surprised at the details and the facts regarding many of the groups listed within, some of the more obscure groups, I had forgotten about and I found many of the rare photographs fascinating.

I know Manfred has taken many years to compile, research and obtain the many photos used in this book, a feat of endurance and tenacity.

The 1960's era is now many years past, memories fade, faces, facts and photographs are lost and dissipated with the passing of time, and I feel that this book will be the last of its kind, making it a permanent and fitting record and tribute to all the unknown and famous groups of a golden age, never to be forgotten.

Rock on always,

Johnny Guitar
'Rory Storm & the Hurricanes'

Johnny sadly died on 18ᵗʰ August 1999
A great guy and a real gentlemen who is
much missed by everyone.

Manfred Kuhlmann – The Liverpool-Bielefeld Connection

Manfred Kuhlmann´s hometown of Bielefeld sported a Star-Club subsidiary where all the Hamburg and Liverpool stars loved to play. Roy Orbison found his wife here. Manfred was born in the suburb of Schildesche on July 2nd 1952, and got the Beat bug forever, as he recalls vividly: "As a 13-year-old, I managed to sneak into the local Star-Club. The first act I saw there was Earl Royce & The Olympics. Other venues where young Kuhlman used to hang out were the 'Eisenhuette', and from 1967 onwards the 'Jaguar Club' in nearby Herford, where he was especially impressed by the Small Faces. But for Manfred, the real joy still lay in the club´s Liverpool sounds – his new champions were The Searchers! Other Merseybeat favourites became Ian & the Zodiacs, the Remo Four and Denny Seyton & the Sabres.

That same year, Kuhlmann won a Deejay competition, having become a regular disc jockey at the communication centre HOT in Bielefeld. Later, he deejayed in various renowned clubs in his area. So how did the beat fan and record spinner become a legendary promoter? In 1974, Manfred drove a truck when he saw a Searcher's poster on a roadside billboard – Mike Pender & Co had been booked into the 'Riverside-Club' in Detmold. He went – and was hooked: The Searchers sounded better than on record! Soon, he negotiated a reasonable fee, and persuaded fans to sign I.O.U.s for him – in case of an attendance disaster. No sweat: The Searchers rocked Bielefeld in September 1975, the fans raised the roof. Sold out - punters were turned away!

The HOT was to see more great concerts, featuring Gerry & the Pacemakers, Ian & the Zodiacs, Billy J. Kramer & The Dakotas, The Merseybeats, The Undertakers as well as The Swinging Blue Jeans and the Pete Best Band. Kuhlmann also established a long tradition of 'Oldie Nights', and for those, he managed to hire the famous concert venue Oetkerhalle. Here, The Tremeloes, Dave Dee Dozy Beaky Mick & Tich, The Troggs and The Hollies played to packed houses. So did US stars he brought over: Del Shannon, Percy Sledge, a moody but magnificent Wilson Pickett, the Mamas & Papas and Johnny & The Hurricanes.

Still, the challenge for Manfred lay in conquering Liverpool. Lee Curtis, who had found his way from Hamburg down to Bielefeld, invited our boy over: "If you´re ever round Liverpool way, Manfred, you can kip at my brother´s!" At Easter 1987 Kuhlmann boarded a Boeing and stayed at Joe Flammery´s, starting a series of visits to the Scouse scene. Dreams came true – like meeting the Beatles motivator Bob Wooler, spotting an ad for Karl Terry & The Cruisers in the 'Liverpool Echo', or visiting the Old Cavern club. Karl Terry & The Cruisers hit a spot in Manfred´s beat sensitivity and were often invited to play Germany, including Bielefeld, and in 1994 produced their only long player in Bielefeld. By then, Manfred had his own label, Merseyside Records, including a 'Beat Revival' with 11 local bands.

In 1990, after 15 years of managing bands, booking international stars, working as Radio-DJ, running his record label, and juggling turntables, Manfred Kuhlmann decided to put a lid on it all. A farewell gig for Merseyside Concerts, apart from local musos Barry & The Back Beats or the Thunderbirds, also starred Karl Terry & The Cruisers, The Undertakers and Beryl Marsden. But requests never stopped – and so for five more years Manfred got bands to Germany two or three times per season. In 1995, he finally got hitched – marrying his beloved Chérie, but still took up old habits: managing the Rock´n´Roll matadors The Rock-A-Teers, starting the 'Beat City' movement for more concerts by the big names in Beat, and re-establishing the 'Liverpool Club' in Buende, also founding today's very successful 'Beat Club ´66' in 2004.

Manfred Kuhlmann remains a local treasure, and of course he is *the* symbol of the Liverpool-Bielefeld connection. The book you are holding in your hands now? It´s the Liverpool Bible!

Uli Twelker, Good Times magazine

AUTHOR'S FOREWORD

Well, it's done. After more than ten years I have finished a book which has been overdue for at least the same length of time. You may ask why I've written a book about a scene and bands which are almost forgotten today, but the question really answers itself. It shouldn't happen that the pioneering groups that opened the doors for pop music in Europe in the early Sixties are one day forgotten. The bands mentioned in this book were the basis on which groups like the 'Beatles', 'Searchers' or 'Gerry & the Pacemakers' built their success, and which in the end led to the worldwide breakthrough of the Merseybeat, later simply called Beat music.

That's reason enough to keep their history alive in words and to pay them long overdue attention, even 45 years and more after it all started in Liverpool on the River Mersey. It's very difficult to find good information about this interesting and very important Merseybeat scene, although there are some books which are really good supplements to *The Sound with the Pound,* namely, *Let's Go Down The Cavern* and *Twist and Shout*, both written by popular Liverpool DJ Spencer Leigh, as well as *The Best Of Cellars* by Phil Thompson, a book that tells the history of the Cavern.

This book is the first extensive biography of the Merseyside music scene. In addition to the bands that achieved worldwide stardom, it also includes those groups that were only locally or nationally successful.

It is certainly somewhat unfair that not every group from this era is named. They were all important in some way and they all had a role to play, but because there were so many it is simply impossible to feature them all. To balance this unfairness a bit, I have compiled some line-up and band name lists that I came across while researching the featured individual band stories, sometimes including short versions of the stories of other groups they were connected with. In spite of the fact that the material is more than interesting, this biography required an awful lot of work and the research brought me my first grey hair! I have only written about Liverpool groups who released a record, made test recordings or demos (on acetate) which might be released one day, as well as the ones that had huge importance in the development of the Merseybeat. The complete discographies up to 1970 are featured for all these group stories. These are based on the British market and are completed with different foreign releases.

While I was searching for information I met some musicians of that era who expected me to change or manipulate history with this book. I did not want to do this because reality is not changeable by including a lot of mistakes and lies. The purpose of this book is to present history as it really was and so I researched as exactly as possible, just to take the bands out of the anonymity of Merseybeat and to take the musicians out of the anonymity of the band names. This biography will probably contain some mistakes, but after all, I am convinced that one cannot write such a book without accepting that risk.

I have written this book for all the people who are interested in the material as well as for all the musicians who were part of that unique era. Many of them gave me great help in completing the project. I want to specifically name *Bob Wooler*, the former disc jockey, compere and programme manager of the famous Cavern Club, whose importance on the scene was always underrated, even if he was sometimes accurately named as *Mr. Merseybeat, the Baron of Beat* or *Mr. Big Beat*. There are lots of groups which owe their careers to him and I personally owe him a lot more than mere thanks for all the information, interesting leads and contacts with lots of people who were involved in the scene. The title of this book was his idea, a play on words which was typical of him. Words cannot describe his enormous help and kindness.

Bob Wooler sadly died in 2002, before he could finish the promised foreword to my book, which he often referred to as the 'Merseybeat Bible' in various letters to me. Because of his hugely important role in developing the Liverpool Beat scene, and in as much as one person, he was as important as lots of the groups featured here, he should never be forgotten and that is why this book is dedicated to him whom I proudly called my friend.

Manfred Kuhlmann
Bielefeld/Schildesche
Germany, autumn 2007

ACKNOWLEDGEMENTS

Firstly I would like to thank my wife, Nelly, who everyone knows as Chérie, for her understanding and support while I was working on this book. Not forgetting her patience in accepting the enormous telephone bills and the travel costs for my numerous trips to Liverpool.

Many thanks also to my friends Armin Grants, Karl-Heinz 'Charly' Decker, Alfred Hebing, Holger Roggemann, Gerry Nolan, Dave Forshaw Karl Terry, John Wishart, Phil Eaves from Preston, Dave Lodge and Gina Hazlehurst for their great help. Wihout them the realisation of this book would not have been possible. Not forgetting my editor, Margaret Smith, for being so kind and patient with me when I continued to send corrections.

Also very special thanks to all the musicians who helped me with information about their groups and gave me photographs that had never been seen before. I simply cannot name them all as there were hundreds I have spoken to over the years, but I can confirm that the contact and time I spent with them was a great pleasure for me.

THE SOUND WITH THE POUND

When a new sound was born at the beginning of the Sixties in dozens of cellars in Liverpool, no one could foresee that this movement would cause a musical revolution which has not been equalled since the birth of Rock'n'Roll.

It is no accident that the harbour and industrial city of Liverpool, at the mouth of the River Mersey on the Irish Sea, was the starting point of a musical style known first as Merseybeat and later as Beat, which was the most important development in the history of European pop music. **Mike Evans**, born Liverpudlian and sax player with the **Clayton Squares** wrote about this in the foreword to the book *Beat in Liverpool* (Jürgen Seuss, 1965):

"The city in its character has lots in common with the New Orleans of the turn of the century. The prosperity of the harbour, grown with the profit of cotton and slavery in the cosmopolitan tradition for the life in Liverpool has the same dominating role as at that time the birthplace of Jazz."

It is said that the seamen who brought the first American Rock 'n' Roll and Rhythm & Blues records into the city were the originators of this musical revolution but most probably it was the American soldiers serving at the huge American Air Force base in Burtonwood that brought Rock 'n' Roll into Liverpool.

Whichever it was, within months an idea had developed into a boom which was to influence the youth around the world. Liverpool Skiffle groups, which had existed in huge numbers at the end of the Fifties, took on the American sound and gave it their own individual touch. Most of these groups changed their names and started to play this kind of music.

So the **Mars Bars** became **Gerry & the Pacemakers**, the **Raving Texans** developed into **Rory Storm & the Hurricanes**, the **Quarrymen** at first changed their name to the **Silver Beatles** and then

The Kirkbys at the Cavern

THE CAVERN

THE BIG TUESDAY SHOW, 30th JUNE
THE REDCAPS
THE ROAD RUNNERS
THE MARKFOUR
THE PILGRIMS
THE VIKINGS

Members: 3/-   Visitors: 4/-   7.30 p.m. start

MATHEW ST., LIVERPOOL

THE IRON DOOR CLUB

THURSDAY, April 23rd
THE REV. BLACK & THE ROCKING VICARS
SONNY WEBB & THE CASCADES
FRIDAY, April 24th
TONY D & THE SHAKEOUTS
THE VALKYRIES
LEE PAUL & THE BOYS
SATURDAY, April 25th
THE BLACKWELLS
THE PILGRIMS
THE CYMERONS
SUNDAY, April 26th
THE EXCHECKERS
THE PATHFINDERS
THE GRIMBLES
TUESDAY, April 28th
MIKE CADILLAC & THE PLAYBOYS
THE CASCADES

shortened it to **The Beatles**, the **Bluegenes** became the **Swinging Blue Jeans**, and so on and so on.

New clubs called 'Jive Halls' opened everywhere, or changed their programme from Jazz, Swing or

Skiffle to Rock'n'Roll and Beat, where these groups performed for less money. The fee for one evening

— MERSEYSCENE PROMOTIONS —
present
'21' BEAT SPECTACULAR
at the GRAFTON BALLROOM
West Derby Road
on FRIDAY 13th. MAY, 1966
21 FANTASTIC GROUPS
The Dennisons, Hideaways, Dark Ages, Fix, Aztecs, Georgies Germs, Kop, Solomons Mines, Jigsaw, Calderstones, Runaways, Heatwave, Dions, Keez, Kringin Nobs, Proffits, Lonely, Crescendos, Roadrunners Do-Does, Outrage
Star Comperes— BILLY BUTTLER plus SACREMENTO FRED
DANCING IN THE GOLDEN CAGES
The Go! Go! Kittens
7. p.m. to 12.30 a.m.   Admission 6/-   LICENSED BARS

at that time was around three to four English pounds. The best known clubs in Liverpool were the Cavern, the Iron Door, the Blue Angel, the Casbah, the Peppermint Lounge, the Sink, the Downbeat, the Grafton Ballroom and Hope Hall.

Outside the city centre there were ballrooms, church rooms and public halls like the Litherland Town Hall, the

The original Dominoes

Aintree Institute, the Orrel Park Ballroom, the Wilson Hall in Garston, the Majestic Ballroom in Birkenhead, the Tower Ballroom in New Brighton or the Jive Hive in Crosby.

Every day new, talented and hopeful groups were formed and at the climax of Merseybeat there must have been around 400 groups in and around Liverpool. There were **King Size Taylor & the Dominoes**, who claimed to have been the first Liverpool Rock 'n'Roll band, and **Cass & the Casanovas**, who always quarrelled with them for that title. Or were, in the end, **The Black Cats** the first, or even **Gus & the Thundercaps**?

In addition, there were **Rory Storm & the Hurricanes,** without doubt one of the local heroes in Liverpool; the **Chants**, the first Liverpool vocal

The Chants at the Cavern

Cass & The Casanovas

Gus & The Thundercaps

group consisting entirely of black singers; **Derry & the Seniors**, the first Liverpool group that played in Germany (Kaiserkeller, Hamburg) and also the first Liverpool group that had a

Johnny Tempest & The Tornadoes

record out - under the name **Howie Casey & the Seniors**. **Bob Evans & the Five Shillings**, who a little later became the legendary **Undertakers**; **Steve Bennett & the Syndicate**, the first Liverpool band to go to London in search of national stardom; the **Bobby Bell Rockers, Johnny Rocco & the Jets, Cliff Roberts' Rockers, Karl Terry & the Cruisers** and **Johnny Tempest & the Tornadoes**, who all, without exception, played Rock 'n' Roll only. Then there were **Tommy & the Metronomes**, the **Strangers**, the **Travellers**, **Danny & the Asteroids, Mark Peters & the Cyclones, Gene Day & the Jango-Beats, Carl Vincent & the Counts, Dee Young & the Pontiacs, Vinny & the Dukes, Rikki & the Red Streaks** and **Paul Valance & the Tremors**, just to name a few of the typical pioneering groups. Most of them were already popular and successful in Liverpool, while others came up with the **Beatles**, but not because of them. It should be pointed out that **The Beatles** were a product of the Merseybeat and not the other way round!

THE ASTEROIDS
BILL HENRY   STO 4378

Dee Young & The Pontiacs

Rikki & The Red Streaks

The Searchers

The **Beatles** recorded for the first time in their own right in October 1962, if the German recordings with **Tony Sheridan** were not considered. *Love Me Do* climbed up the charts to

No.17 in December of the same year. In March 1963, **Gerry & the Pacemakers** had the first chart-topper to come out of Liverpool with *How Do You Do It*, and from this moment on the Merseybeat's big international breakthrough was unstoppable.

The next No.1 hit came from the **Beatles** with their third release *From Me To You*, followed by the **Searchers** with *Sweets For My Sweet*, **Billy J. Kramer & the Dakotas** with *Bad To Me* (all No.1 hits), the **Fourmost** with *Hello Little Girl* (No.9), the **Swinging Blue Jeans** with *Hippy Hippy Shake* (No.2), the **Merseybeats** with *I think Of You* (No.5), **Cilla Black** with *Anyone Who Had A Heart* (No.1), and so on. In the meantime, the **Searchers**, **Gerry & the Pacemakers** and of course the **Beatles** had had more big hits.

As a result of this success, promoters from all over the world became interested in booking groups from Liverpool, just the suggestion 'from Liverpool' was a mark of quality at that time. So the problem arose that Liverpool promoters suddenly did not have enough of the established local groups for their events anymore, because these groups were booked nationally or even abroad.

HUBBLY
BUBBLY
BEAT
AT THE NEW
WITCH'S
CAULDRON CLUB
Wirral's Top Beat Centre
THURSDAY
DENIMS
FRIDAY
SCHATZ
SATURDAY
BO-WEEVILS
SUNDAY
MINUTES
62 ALBION STREET,
NEW BRIGHTON
(Back of Victoria Hotel)

This of course was the big chance for new and lesser known Liverpool groups to step into the spotlight and also for groups from other cities like Manchester (**Pete MacLaine & the Dakotas**, **Wayne Fontana & the Jets** and **Don Curtis & the Coasters**), Birmingham (**Gerry Levene & the Avengers**, **Brumbeats** and **Fortunes**), Stoke (**The Marauders**) or cities in the vicinity of Liverpool, like Chester, Crewe, Widnes, St. Helens, Wigan or Preston. Most of them became a steady part of Liverpool's Merseybeat scene and that is why they are also included in this book - with the exception of the Manchester, Stoke and Birmingham bands.

Sadly, although they recorded, not enough information could be obtained for the following Merseyside groups to write an individual account of them. That is why they are at least being named here, although this listing will probably be incomplete: **Geoff Stacey & the Wanderers** (*It Ain't Necessarily So* – Decca demo), **The Bo-Weevils** (*I'm A Lover Not A Fighter* on acetate),

Michael Cox

The **Sassenachs** (*That Don't Worry Me* – Fontana) and **The Roger James Four** (*Leave Me Alone* - Columbia).

Early chart success was brought to Liverpool by **Russ Hamilton** (*Rainbow* - 1957), the Rock 'n' Roll singer **Michael Cox** (*Angela Jones* - 1960) and the singer **Chris Morris** from the Birkenhead group **The Firecrests** who, under the name of **Lance Fortune**, had a top 10 hit with *Be Mine* in 1960 and who later continued to sing with **Dave Lee & the Staggerlees** from Manchester.

Johnny Gentle was another Liverpool singer from

Lance Fortune

Johnny Gentle with
George Harrison

the early days who should be mentioned here. He is mainly known for the fact that he was backed by the **Beatles** on certain dates, although he recorded four singles and an EP in his own right for Philips in 1959 and 1960. His final single *My Tears Will Turn To Laughter* was released under the name of **Darren Young** of Parlophone in 1963.

Undoubtedly the most important Liverpool artist of the early days was **Ronald Wycherley**, who had international fame under the name of **Billy Fury**. As he was part of the British Rock 'n' Roll scene, his individual story is not related in this book, and so he should be considered here, along with some information about his impressive career.

Billy Fury

In his successful years **Billy Fury** was backed by the **Four Kestrels**, the **Blue Flames**, the **Tornadoes**, who later had their own hit (*Telstar*) and by **The Gamblers** from Newcastle, who also recorded in their own right, but surprisingly never by a Liverpool group.

Billy Fury was one of the outstanding personalities in British show business and it is not only because he had a string of big hits, like *Maybe Tomorrow, Jealousy* and *Halfway To Paradise* amongst others, that he is still remembered and admired in England these days, especially in his hometown of Liverpool, but also because he was a very nice and likeable guy who did not change after becoming successful. His records mostly were Rock ballads in the American Highschool style, which he sang with a lot of feeling. From February 1959 until February 1983 his records were in the charts for a total of 281 weeks, and one must take into account that he took a recording break from September 1966 until September 1982.

He never had a real chart topper, but his best placement was at No.2 with *Jealousy* in

THE THREE BELLS

1961. Up to August 1966 he had 26 Top 40 hits, including 11 Top 10 hits. This is a record of success which deserves deep respect and which made him the most successful Decca artist of all time. He was the real pioneer of Liverpool's successful and popular music scene, but sadly died much too young on 28th January 1983, having been ill for many years with a hole in his heart.

Others, who were not part of the Merseybeat but part of Liverpool's more than interesting recording scene of the Sixties are the all girl groups: **Vernon's Girls** (*Lover Please*), the **Three Bells** (**Carol, Sue and Jean Bell** - *Somewhere In The Night*), who also appeared at the Star-Club in Hamburg, **The Ladybirds** (*I Wanna Fly*), **The Bowbells** (with **Nola York** - *Not To Be Taken*) and **The Breakaways** (*He's A Rebel*), who also sang backing vocals for other artists' records. The folk groups: **The Spinners** (*Dirty Old Town*), who for a long time were England's most popular folk band, as well as **Adam, Mike & Tim** (**Peter Sedgwick, Mike Sedgwick** and **Tim Sounders** - *Little Baby*). The country bands: **The**

Blue Mountain Boys (*Drop Me Gently*), who were an offshoot of the very popular **Hank Walters & the Dusty Road Ramblers**, who also cut a nice album in the early Seventies on the 'Liverpool Sound' label, **Phil Brady & the Ranchers** (later also **Phil Brady & the Ranch Set**), who as **The Ranchers** released the first single on the newly founded 'Cavern Sound' label (*An American Sailor At The Cavern*), the **Kentuckians** (*Pop a Top*), who also recorded an album, **The Foggy Mountain Ramblers** (*Lovin' Lady's Man*) and of course

the legendary **Hillsiders**, who are featured in this book in the continuation of the story of **Sonny Webb & the Cascades**. Comedy groups were **The Scaffold** (*Thank U Very Much*) and the **Liverpool Scene** (*The Baby*).

Most of Liverpool's recording Beat groups only had one or two hits or releases, and then disappeared again from the international scene. Maybe this was the reason why lots of superficial critics state that there was not much quality in the Merseysound, but this is definitely not true and in all honesty there were no differences in quality to earlier or later popular sounds, only that the idea was better.

When you listen to these records today and consider the unfavourable circumstances that they were recorded under, it is impossible to claim that this sound or these bands were of poor musical quality, or that all groups sounded the same. Such a statement could only be made by people who don't have the correct knowledge and do not give too much thought to what they are saying, writing or pilfering from other people.

For example the two **John Schroeder** produced albums 'This Is Merseybeat Vol.1' and 'Vol.2' were recorded at the Rialto Ballroom and the featured bands went on stage as they would for a normal live performance. It was recorded on a one-track machine and in one take without any chance to repeat the parts which were not too good. Bearing this in mind, these records are just fantastic! These days, bands record in special fully-mechanized recording studios on a 24-track machine with lots of special effects and overdubs.

However, it is not necessary to defend this music and musicians against some poor critics, who seem to have severe learning problems. Everyone can judge for themselves by listening to these records anyway. The most important feature of the Merseysound was doubtless the feeling and the atmosphere which was around that music and spread by it.

Never before was a generation on the international scene united and influenced by music as at that time. Screaming crowds of young people and fans who tried very hard to climb onto stages to get any little piece of their idols as a talisman or memento were a common feature. Compared with today it was more of a natural enthusiasm than manipulated mass hysteria.

Youth fashion was copied from their big idols - pointed shoes (Cuban heels), drainpipe trousers, frilled shirts and shoelace ties. Girls did their hair in the Farah Diba look, piled up like haystacks, and their stiletto heels left imprints behind in the wooden floors which can sometimes still be admired today. The boys' Beatle haircuts were the cause of the biggest trouble in lots of 'honourable' families.

In front of the live clubs, hundreds and thousands of people queued up and fought for the last tickets. Fainting fits during the live performances were the order of the day, because everything was so wild and exciting - and the air sometimes so bad.

The Big Three

Motion pictures were made which kept the music and atmosphere for all time. These included 'Ferry Cross The Mersey' with **Gerry & the Pacemakers**, **Earl Royce & the Olympics**, **The Black Knights**, **The Fourmost**, **The Blackwells**, **The Koobas** and **Cilla Black**, or the **Beatles** films 'A Hard Day's Night' and 'Help'.

The Dennisons
— Decca Records

Kennedy Street Enterprises Ltd.
Kennedy House,
14 Piccadilly, Manchester 1.
CENtral 5423

Another interesting aspect of the scene are the early live recordings like the album 'At The Cavern' with **Lee Curtis & the All Stars**, **Beryl Marsden**, the **Dennisons** and the **Big Three** (all from Liverpool), the **Fortunes** (from Birmingham), **the Marauders** (from Stoke), **Dave Berry & the Cruisers** (from Sheffield), **Heinz** and **Bern Elliott & the Fenmen** (from Essex).

Mark Peters & The Silhouettes

There was also the album 'Liverpool Today' with Liverpool groups like **Earl Preston's Realms**, the **Michael Allen Group** and **The Richmond**, the live recordings from the 'Iron Door' of **Freddie Starr & the Starr Boys** (*This Is Liverpool Beat*) and **The Liverpool Beats**(*This Is Liverpool*), who were identical with the Excheckers, as well as some German recordings of **The Swinging Blue Jeans** (*Live at the Cascade in Cologne*) or **The Searchers**, **King Size Taylor & the Dominoes** and **The Roadrunners** live at the Star Club in Hamburg.

Faron's Flamingos

Michael Allen

Bill Harry

A brilliant overall view of Liverpool's early Beat scene is given by the above mentioned Oriole albums 'This Is Merseybeat Vol.1 and Vol.2' with groups like **Earl Preston & the TTs**, **Faron's Flamingos**, **Rory Storm**

& the Hurricanes, **The Del Renas**, **Derry Wilkie & the Pressmen**, **The Nomads**, **Sonny Webb & the Cascades**, **Mark Peters & the Silhouettes**, **The Merseybeats** and **Ian & the Zodiacs** - all groups of the so-called 'pre-Beatles era'.

Dave Forshaw with the Merseybeats

Another important milestone in the development of Liverpool's Beat scene was the music paper *Mersey Beat*, edited by **Bill Harry**, which in the early years reported exclusively on the local groups, clubs and events. Not as important but also very interesting was another Beat paper called *Combo*, which was also published on Merseyside.

The most successful manager of this time without a doubt was **Brian Epstein**. Despite the fact that the Merseybeat was built up by lots of managers and promoters like **Ted Knibbs**, **Allan Williams**, **Dave Forshaw**, **Jim McIver**

DAVID FORSHAW ENTERPRISES
6 DALEY PLACE   BOOTLE 20   AINTREE 9654

SOLE MANAGEMENT FOR—
RICKY GLEASON AND THE TOPSPOTS
J.J. AND THE HI-LITES * THE CASUALS
THE LEE EDDIE 5 * THE PREMIERS
THE FOUR MUSKETEERS
ADAM & THE SINNERS * THE DIAMONDS
FROM MYSELF AND ALL GROUPS UNDER MY MANAGEMENT WE
WOULD LIKE TO WISH EVERYBODY 'ALL THE BEST' FOR THE
COMING SEASON.

and **Doug Martin** (Ivarmar Promotions), **Jim Ireland**, **Ralph Webster**, **Brian Kelly**, **George Blood**, **Jim Turner**, **Sam Leach**, **Gordon Brown**, **Joe Flannery** and most of all **Bob Wooler**, just to name some of the important ones, **Brian Epstein** became the most popular person of all after he had taken over the management of the Beatles, Gerry & the Pacemakers, Billy J. Kramer & the Dakotas, Tommy Quickly & the Remo Four, the **Fourmost** and **Cilla Black**. Without him only the Searchers, Swinging Blue Jeans, Merseybeats, Escorts, Mojos, Lee Curtis & the All Stars, Beryl Marsden, King Size Taylor & the Dominoes, Ian & the Zodiacs, Denny Seyton & the Sabres and the

Bob Wooler

Brian Kelly

Undertakers made an international breakthrough from the Liverpool scene.

But it would be wrong to call **Brian Epstein** the 'father of Merseybeat' because this accolade without a doubt belongs to **Bob Wooler**, who backed nearly every group in both word and deed, and who was something like the good spirit of the whole scene long before **Brian Epstein** appeared.

For some, he suggested their names (**Merseybeats** and **Four Mosts**, etc.), for some he suggested the right songs for record releases (*Hippy Hippy Shake)* by the **Swinging Blue Jeans**, and for others he helped to get recording contracts (**Masterminds**) or important gigs at the Cavern and other big venues, as well as big concerts.

He helped to build up an image for numerous bands, for some he wrote songs such as *Sidetracked* for **Phil Brady & the Ranchers** - a great song, or *I know* for **Billy J. Kramer & the Dakotas**, or he took over direct management (**The Clayton Squares**). His contribution to the history of Liverpool's Merseybeat is immense and worth a special book alone. Without him, the Beat scene would not have been the same!

Brian Epstein

Compared to him, **Brian Epstein** was more a businessman who knew how to make a profit out of the local talent. This is not meant negatively, as it was also a very important part of achieving a breakthrough. In 1967 he, allegedly, attempted suicide with tablets, but this is not proven even today and lots of insiders of that time talk about a terrible accident in relation to this.

However, the Merseybeat was already as good as dead in 1966. Not least to blame for this fall was the plague of talent seekers who descended upon Liverpool like a swarm of insects during the successful times and tempted all the more or less talented musicians away.

Also not too advantageous was the superior, dominating role of the **Beatles** as trendsetters, because from a certain time on every group that came out of Liverpool was expected to be like

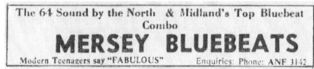

The 64 Sound by the North & Midland's Top Bluebeat
Combo
MERSEY BLUEBEATS
Modern Teenagers say "FABULOUS"   Enquiries: Phone: ANF 3142

them, what the groups could not be and let's face it, the majority of them did not want to be. The Merseybeat was probably the last naturally grown music scene in Europe. Later, more or less everything was manipulated by the music industry before it could strengthen itself.

Merseybeat was in many respects phenomenal. As well as the musical idealism, a lot of the famous Scouse sense of humour and a special kind of closeness to Liverpool can be found in it, which is also shown in lots of the bands' names.

Although there was no Liverpool group which included 'Liverpool' in its name, if the German releases of the **Pressmen** as **Liverpool Triumphs** and the **Excheckers** as **The Liverpool Beats** are not taken into account, a hint of the River Mersey can often be found in group names like **The Merseybeats** (later the **Merseys**), **The Mersey Four** or **The Mersey Five**, **The Mersey Monsters**, **The Mersey Bluebeats**, **Mike & the Merseymen**, **The Mersey Blues Preachers** or **The Mersey Gonks**. At this place the **Liverbirds** should not be forgotten. Imagination and the above mentioned humour can be found in names like **Johnny Apollo & the Spartans, Gerry Bach & the Beethovens, Pete Picasso & the Rock Sculptors, Ray Satan & the Devils, Rip Van Winkle & the Rip-It-Ups, Eddie Falcon & the Vampires, Johnny Autumn & the Fall Guys, Dave & the Devil Horde, Al Quentin & the Rock Pounders, Johnny Anger & the Wild Ones** or **Dino & the Wild Fires**.

Whatever might be thought about these names today, you get the feeling they were chosen with lots of love and imagination, which was characteristic for the scene of that time.

The Mersey Gonks

Well, what has happened to the previously well-known and sometimes very successful bands and their individual members? Some of them remained in the business, still playing in groups, working as session or studio musicians, going out on their own or became producers, and so on. Others switched to related parts of showbusiness like entertainment, comedy or film.

Here, to name a few, are especially big TV stars like **Faith Brown** (formerly **The Carrolls**), **Freddie Starr** (formerly with the **Midnighters**), plus **Lewis Collins** (of the **Mojos**), **Vince Earl** (in the Sixties with the **Talismen**), **Clive Hornby** (of the **Dennisons**) and **Ozzie Yue** (of the **Hideaways**). But detailed information about all this can be found in the individual group stories featured in this book.

Karl Terry & The Cruisers - 1978

Some groups still work as professionals, even if they all have had personnel changes over the years, like for example the **Searchers**, the **Merseybeats**, the **Pete Best Band**, the **Swinging Blue Jeans**, **Gerry & the Pacemakers**, the **Kirkbys** or **Karl Terry & the Cruisers**. These groups are still gigging in the clubs of England, mainly in the North, but some of them also tour on the European continent, in the United States and in Australia. Every now and then they release records, but chart success is very rare.

In 1978 **Karl Terry & the Cruisers** and **Faron's Flamingos** were featured on the revival compilation 'Mersey Survivors', together with other Liverpool groups like the **Dimensions**, **Pawns**, **Renegades**, **Groups Inc.** and the **Gibson James Band**, but these were more recording sessions than steady line-ups. The intro on this record is spoken by **Bob Wooler**, as it was on some other samplers from the Sixties.

The 'Merseycats' organisation is very important for Liverpool's Beat scene these days. It was formed in 1989 and has a lot of the original Merseybeat musicians as members. The 'Merseycats' promote concerts and other events for charity reasons only. Through the 'Merseycats' lots of groups and musicians came back onto the scene. The same is valid for the 'Merseycats' offshoots like 'New Brighton Rock', still going as the 'Cheshire Cats', 'Sounds Of The Sixties' or the 'Merseyside Rock 'n' Roll-Society'.

Some of the re-formed groups split up again for various reasons, like **Denny Seyton & the Sabres**, **Johnny Guitar & his Hurricanes**, **The Kansas City Five** or **Cliff Roberts'**

Johnny Guitar & his Hurricanes

Rockers. Some othes still perform fairly regularly, like **The Del Renas**, the original **Dominoes**, **The Mojos**, **The Four Originals**, **The Rainchecks**, **The Black Knights** or **Group One**.

With only a few exceptions, these groups do not play the normal circuit, but appear only for 'Merseycats', a fantastic idea, greatly appreciated by real Beat fans and of course also by those who benefit from 'Merseycats'.

In spite of all this activity, it is obvious that this formerly so successful and exciting Merseysound has lost its meaning for the public at large... Sadly! But lots of Beat fans can still be found worldwide who are interested in the Sixties bands from Liverpool who are still active on the scene. Sometimes these fans travel hundreds or thousands of miles to see their former idols live again. They come from the USA, Japan, Australia or all over the European continent and for them it is a real adventure to see and hear the stars of their youth performing again and to dance to the old and fondly remembered hits. Of course, this is a kind of nostalgia and a rooting in memories, but is this so bad and so hard to understand?

Those days in the unique Sixties were great and exciting, not only for the fans but, despite unfavourable circumstances, also for the bands that today are still playing their music, their sound - **THE MERSEYBEAT!!**

The Merseybeats - Today

THE ADDICTS

It was probably sometime in 1962 that this group was formed as a four-piece in Widnes, Lancashire, very close to Liverpool. From the beginning, the **Addicts** were a real beat group with their sound and their classic line-up that consisted of the following musicians:

Geoff Keeley	(voc/rg)
Steve Duggan	(lg/voc)
Paul Nash	(bg/voc)
Dennis Keeley	(dr)

For the two Keeley brothers it was probably their first group, while **Steve Duggan** and **Paul Nash** had formerly played with another group – **The Cadillacs** (formerly known as **Rocky Stone & the Pebbles**), who had been very popular locally as one of the pioneering groups in Widnes and its surrounding area.

The **Addicts** with their 'new sound' went the same successful way and became one of the busiest groups and very soon had a large following. It is hard to understand that in spite of this they did not appear too often in the city centre of Liverpool and its popular clubs.

Paul Nash left the group again and nothing was heard of him after that. His replacement was **Denny O'Neill**, who came from another local group, the name of that sadly got lost.

Nothing is known about any particular management or agency for the **Addicts** and so it is quite surprising that they were signed to Decca in 1963. In the following year they had their first record out with the **Geoff Keeley** original *That's My Girl,* coupled with *Here She Comes,* which most likely was also an original number.

The record received some good critical reviews in the music papers and opened the door for the **Addicts** to play the national circuit as professionals, but in the end the record was not spectacular enough to get into the charts. The quartet kept gigging around all over England but still didn't play too much in Liverpool. Their only recorded 'Cavern' appearance was in November 1964.

The **Addicts** were not given a second chance by Decca and no other recording contract was signed elsewhere but they managed to make a living out of their music until they broke up around 1967/68.

Steve Duggan and **Denny O'Neill** disappeared from the scene while **Geoff Keeley** and **Dennis 'Snowy' Keeley** became members of the **Michael Henri Group** in the late Sixties.

So what's left of the **Addicts**, besides a legendary name in their hometown of Widnes, is a nice beat record, worth looking out for . . . .

Discography:
That's My Girl / Here She Comes   **UK- Decca F.11902 / 1964**

ALBY & THE SORRALS

This group, successful on the local scene, was formed in 1960 in Liverpool under the name **The Cadillacs**. One of the original members was drummer **Trevor Morais**, who in 1961 joined **Robin & the Ravens**, which a little later became **Faron's Flamingos**. **Trevor Morais** later also played in famous groups like **Rory Storm & the Hurricanes**, **Ian Crawford & the Boomerangs** from Manchester and **The Peddlers**.

Shortly after he left, the **Cadillacs** changed their name to **The Sorrals** and when the group was joined by **Alby Ellis** in 1962, they called themselves **Alby & the Sorrals** and appeared with the following line-up:

Alby Ellis	**(voc)**
Keith Draper	**(lg/voc)**
Brian Cox	**(rg)**
Dave Foley	**(bg/voc)**
Pete Dobson	**(sax)**
Maurice Daniels	**(dr)**

Pete Dobson was a former member of the **Black Cats**, one of the important and very successful Liverpool pioneer groups.

By 1963 **Alby & the Sorrals** established themselves as one of the leading groups on Merseyside, but never had any national or international significance. But as they were one of England's Beat centre's successful groups, it can be taken for granted that some recording companies were interested in signing them. Despite this, they never released a record, although it is known that the group recorded the originals *Why* and *Foolin'* as demos in 1963.

Still, in 1963 the existence of the group started to shake when **Keith Draper**, **Brian Cox** and **Dave Foley** left to form the **Nocturns**. The rest of the group was then joined by new members and so **Alby & the Sorrals** were able to continue. When **Pete Dobson** also left in 1964, the group lost its 'saxy sound' which had been typical of it in the past.

That's why it is hard to understand that no new sax player was recruited to the line-up and instead an additional guitarist named **Brian Johnson**, a former member of the **Blue Country Boys**, joined. But soon **Alby & the Sorrals** disbanded totally. Of the former members only **Maurice Daniels** appeared again when he was a member of the little known **Coins**. All the other musicians seem to have left show business.

Discography
Why / Foolin'   UK - Demo (acetate) / 1963

STEVE ALDO & THE CHALLENGERS

This group was formed in Liverpool in the very early Sixties under the name **The Cossacks** and at first did not make any progress on the scene.

In August 1962, their name was changed to **The Challengers** and a little later the band became the backing group for singing brother and sister **Thomas** and **Patricia Quigley**. This connection lasted until July 1963 when **Thomas Quigley** became **Tommy Quickly** and teamed up with the **Remo Four**.

Tommy Quickly & the Remo Four were managed by **Brian Epstein** and released a string of good records, but only their great version of *Wild Side Of Life* became a chart success. That, however, is a different story. **Pat Quigley** at first also tried to start a solo career but then disappeared from the scene.

The Challengers then amalgamated with the coloured singer **Steve Aldo**, whose real name is **Edward Berrisford**. **Steve Aldo & the Challengers,** as they were named then, became very popular in the line-up were:

Steve Aldo	(voc)
Bob Gilmore	(lg)
Pete Wilson	(rg)
Ray Anderson	(bg)
John Bedson	(dr)

Steve Aldo

John Bedson who formerly had played with the **Four Clefs** and the short-lived **Roadrunners** was the replacement for original drummer **Ian Bailey**, who at that time disappeared from the scene.

Ray Anderson in the history is sometimes delivered as **Ray Dawson** and it is hard to determine what, in the end, was his right name. However, it can be taken for sure that it was one and the same person.

Steve Aldo & the Challengers were booked to appear at the Star Club in Hamburg in 1963, where they went down well and one of their live performances was recorded for an album which unfortunately was not released. During their stay in Hamburg, **Steve Aldo** fell out with some other group members and left the **Challengers**, who returned to Liverpool without him.

TO ALL OUR GOOD FRIENDS AND FANS ON MERSEYSIDE AND IN GERMANY, OUR SINCEREST BEST WISHES FOR CHRISTMAS AND THE NEW YEAR

JOHN ★ ROB ★ PETE ★ RAY & FRED

The **CHALLENGERS**
STA 6068

They at first continued as a four piece in 1963 and once again played the Star Club in Hamburg. The vocals were then shared by all band members. After that the group had some other vocalists, one of them was **Norby Del Rosa**, who came from the just disbanded **Mafia**.

The **Challengers** disbanded totally when **John Bedson** and **Bob Gilmore** left in March

1964 to join the **Harlems**, at that time the backing group for the very popular vocal group **The Chants**. It is sadly not known what happened to the other members after the split because the press at that time did not pay too much attention to the group although it certainly was a very good one.

Steve Aldo, in 1963, stayed in Hamburg and joined **King Size Taylor & the Dominoes** as an additional vocalist. He was also recorded for Polydor with this group by **Paul Murphy**, who, by the way, was a former member of **The Raving Texans** from Liverpool, a predecessor of **Rory Storm & the Hurricanes**.

Steve Aldo with **King Size Taylor & the Dominoes** recorded an album for Polydor which in the end also remained unreleased, but some of the recorded songs later appeared on different compilation albums - under the name **Boots Wellington & his Rubber Band.**

When **Steve Aldo** returned to Liverpool, he joined the **Nocturns** for a short spell and then became a member of the **Griff Parry Five**, who later developed into the **Steve Aldo Quintet** and released the single *Can I Get A Witness* under the name **Steve Aldo**.

After that, the singer put one more record out with **Arthur Alexander's** *Everyday I Have To Cry* under the title *Everybody Has To Cry*, but on this single he was backed by studio musicians. It certainly was not the **Challengers** who backed him as is so often stated. **Steve Aldo** later became a member of the **Fyx**, the **In Crowd** and he was finally backed by the **Fairies** for a time before he quit show business.

Discography

The **Challengers** never released a record, but **Steve Aldo & the Challengers** were recorded at a live performance in 1963 at the Star Club in Hamburg for an album which sadly never was released.
For recordings of **Steve Aldo,** please see the stories of **The Griff Parry Five** and **King Size Taylor & the Dominoes.**

The Challengers

DAVE ALLEN & THE EXOTICS

Reconstructing the story of this group was very difficult as it was hard to determine their place of origin – it could have been Wigan, Leigh or Liverpool. In the end it was all of them, plus Chester. **Dave Allen**'s real name is **Allan Parkinson**. He hailed from Leigh and started to play with the **Martinis** and after that was a member of the legendary **Beat Boys** from Wigan. When he left that group in 1964 he, with other members of the **Beat Boys**, formed the Rhythm & Blues group **The Rats**. Under the management of **John Jenkins** from Liverpool, they recorded two singles and became a steady part of the Merseybeat scene with lots of appearances at all the important venues.

When **John Jenkins** returned from holiday in Spain sometime in 1965, he had an interesting contract in his luggage, which guaranteed the group 3 weeks work in the sunny South, but he found the **Rats** had split up in the meantime. So he offered this contract to band leader **Allan Parkinson**, who already had adopted the stage name **Dave Allen** and who then looked for a new group to front to fulfil this contract.

In the end he amalgamated with the **Exotics** from Chester, but their drummer for some reason did not want to go to Spain and so he was replaced by Liverpudlian **Ian Broad** from **Rory Storm & the Hurricanes**, who had formerly played in other Liverpool groups like the **Five Stars**, **Gus Travis & the Midnighers** and the group which evolved from them **Freddie Starr & the Midnighters**, the **Seniors** and in London with **Heinz & the Wild Boys**.

So in 1965 **Dave Allen & the Exotics** went down to Spain with the following line-up:

Dave Allen	**(voc/g/harp)**
Ray Faulkner	**(lg/voc)**
Robert J. Hopkins	**(org/voc)**
Malcolm Rattrey	**(bg)**
Ian Broad	**(dr)**

Ray Faulkner had already appeared on the scene before when he was a member of **Vic Takes Four**. **Dave Allen & the Exotics** went down a bomb in Spain and were immediately signed by Spanish Hispavox.

A really great EP was released on that established label. Besides the two **Robert Hopkins** originals *The Monkey* and *She Walks*, it also included the **Chuck Berry** classic *Sweet Little Rock 'n Roller* and the Spanish version of the **Kinks** success *A Well Respected Man*, done as *Un hombre respectable*.

The record obviously sold very well and from this EP a single with *The Monkey* and *Sweet Little Rock 'n' Roller* was coupled out for the Italian market later in the year, where it was released on the Derby label. Through this **Dave Allen & the Exotics** came to Italy where they became very popular. On a holiday trip back to Liverpool, **Ian Broad** left and was replaced by the original **Exotics** drummer called **Dave**, whose surname sadly got lost with the passing of time. The group went back to Italy for a longer residence and a little later, for promotional reasons, changed their name to **Dave Allen & the Bigs**.

In 1967 **Dave Allen** left the group and continued as a solo singer in Italy under the name of

Al Torino. The group also stayed in Italy and continued as **The Bigs**, adding two sax players and becoming something of a showband. When **Ray Faulkner** left to live in Spain, it was **Al Torino**, a.k.a. **Dave Allen**, who arranged for his old mate **Malcolm Grundy** from the **Beat Boys** and the **Rats** to take over the lead guitar in the group, who continued to play successfully in Italy, but nothing is known of further records.

    Al Torino himself took part at the famous 'Knokke' Beatfestival in the Netherlands and was signed by the Dutch Decca label, where the single *Inside, Outside, Upside Down* was released. His A+R man for this record was none other than Liverpudlian **Wayne Bickerton**, who amongst others, had formerly played with the **Pete Best Four**. After that release **Al Torino** changed his name into **Guy Challenger**, returned to England and continued in the music business. He later emigrated to Spain and formed the Jazz group **East Coast Jazz**, which included **Ray Faulkner** again. When they disbanded, **Allan Parkinson**, under his real name again, continued to play as a solo artist in Spanish clubs, but he also took part in two **Beat Boys** reunion concerts in Wigan and Leigh in 2001 and 2002.

Discography

EP **DAVE ALLEN & THE EXOTICS**
- Un Hombre Respectable / Sweet Little Rock'n'Roller /
The Monkey / She Walks　　　　　　　　　　　　　ES- Hispavox HH 17-354 / 1965

The Monkey / Sweet Little Rock 'n' Roller　　　　　I – Derby DB 5144 / 1965

Al Torino - solo:
Inside, Outside, Upside Down / Can't Nobody Love You　　　　NL – Decca / 1967

THE MICHAEL ALLEN GROUP

This group came from the Birkenhead area on the west side of the river Mersey, or as the Liverpudlians like to say, 'from somewhere over the water'.

They were formed as the **Abstracts** and their singer **Michael Allen Mulloy** was only 15 years old when the group started gigging in 1963. They played a sort of Rhythm & Blues and rehearsed in the basement of the lead guitarist's home in Woodside.

The **Abstracts** very soon became popular on the local scene and also started to play the venues in Liverpool's city centre - in the line-up were:

Mike Mulloy	**(voc)**
John Thompson	**(lg)**
Jimmy	**(rg/lg)**
Gordon Didsbury	**(bg)**
Alan Westcot	**(dr)**

The surname of the rhythm guitarist sadly has been lost with the passing of time.

It seems for all the musicians it was their first group and in consideration of that their success was really notable. They had a large following on both sides of the river Mersey and were regularly booked at the Cavern. Therefore it is quite surprising that in late 1964 the group changed its name to **Mike Mulloy & the Mountwoods**, but this was only temporary for a few concerts.

On one of these concerts they were recorded and a little later the songs *Spectatin' The Blues* and *Parchment Farm* were cut on a highly interesting acetate at Marble Arch in London. This acetate shows **Mike Mulloy** as a good singer with a great feeling for the Blues and this was also recognized by **Bob Wooler**, who took the group under his wing. It was probably his idea to change the group's name again – this time to the **Michael Allen Group**.

John Thompson left and disappeared from the scene and the group was joined by their former roadie **Peter Bays** (org/p) and the sax-player **Derek Marl**. It was probably this line-up of the **Michael Allen Group** that, beside **Earl Preston's Realms** and the **Richmond Group,** was featured on the second live compilation from the Cavern, which was released on the Ember label with the title *Liverpool Today – Live At The Cavern* in 1965.

On this interesting album the **Michael Allen Group** played the songs; *Telegram, Evenin', I Can't Stand It* and *Trains And Boats And Planes*. The first three of these songs make it especially clear that the group had not really changed its musical style and still was a fine Rhythm & Blues band. In his spoken intro on that record, **Bob Wooler** named them as one of the 'new wave Liverpool attractions'.

A CHRISTMAS MESSAGE FROM CAVERN ARTISTES...

"We hope all our fans have a very happy time this coming Christmas. Thanks for your support during the past year and we look forward to seeing you in the New Year."

MICHAEL ALLEN GROUP
CLAYTON SQUARES
EXCELLES
HIDEAWAYS
KUBAS
NOTIONS
EARL PRESTON'S REALMS
ST. LOUIS CHECKS

SOLE REPRESENTATION:
CAVERN ARTISTES LTD.
8—12 MATHEW STREET,
1st North John Street Liverpool 1. CEN. 3676

The **Michael Allen Group**, although managed by the 'Cavern Artists Ltd.', sadly never had any success on the national scene, but today it is still remembered as one of the better Liverpool Rhythm & Blues groups. It was probably towards the end of 1965 that the group disbanded totally. After that it is only known that **Derek Marl** occasionally appeared with the **Secrets** but without being a steady member. He joined the **Times** who played in their own right but were also backing the **Signs**. In 1967 he became a member of the **Almost Blues** and in the Seventies he was with the successful recording group **Champagne**.

All the other musicians of the **Michael Allen Group** disappeared from the scene – with the exception of **Mike Mulloy**, who followed **Bob Wooler**'s advice and teamed up with the **Press Gang**, a group that was formed at Liverpool University and consisted of **James Trimmer** (g/voc), **Colin Jordan** (g), **John Rotherham** (p), **Ernie Hankin** (bg) and **David Mason** (dr). This group did not really take part in the Merseybeat scene but was playing universities all over the country.

John Rotherham was a great piano player and his secret love was Jazz music. So he parted from the **Press Gang** and together with **John Allcock** (bg) and **Barry Davenport** (dr) formed the **John Rotherham Trio**, which then was also joined by **Mike Mulloy**, who sang with them at various Jazz festivals. This line-up then later developed into the seven piece Rhythm & Blues band **Gravy Train** and continued on the scene for quite some time.

Mike Mulloy quit the band scene, went down to London and became a singing actor. He for example appeared in the musical '*Hair*' and in 1978 sang the part of Judas in '*Jesus Christ Superstar*', both with enormous success. After that he regularly appeared in the famous *Benny Hill Show* over a period of eight years. Today he is still living in London but is not in showbusiness anymore. He still sings from time to time, but just for fun.

Discography

as **Mike Mulloy & the Mountwoods**:
Parchment Farm / Spectatin' the Blues   **UK Recorded Sound Studios   acetate / 1964**

as **The Michael Allen Group**
Telegram   on **Liverpool Today - Live At The Cavern**   **UK- Ember NR 5028 / 1965**
Evenin'   on **Liverpool Toady - Live At The Cavern**   **UK- Ember NR 5028 / 1965**
I Can't Stand It   on **Liverpool Today - Live At The Cavern**   **UK- Ember NR 5028 / 1965**
Trains And Boats And Planes   on **Liverpool Today - Live At The Cavern**
                                                  UK- Ember NR 5028 / 1965

THE ALMOST BLUES

In early 1964 **Alan Peters**, **Mike Haralambos** and **John Beasley** formed one of the best Liverpool Rhythm & Blues outfits. Within a short time the **Almost Blues** established themselves as one of the city's leading groups with this sound, which was sadly still underrated at that time.

The very first line-up of the group only lasted until March 1964 and then the **Almost Blues** were joined by **Eddie Williams**, who came from the **Clayton Squares**. Under the name of **'Jerkin' George Paul** he took over the lead vocals, while former lead singer **Alan Peters** continued in the group as trumpet player. Additionally, the pianist named **'Bernie'** and the drummer, whose name was **'John'**, had left the group, which from that time on appeared in the following line-up:

Eddie Williams	**(voc)**
Mike Haralambos	**(g/voc)**
John Beasley	**(bg/voc)**
Alan Peters	**(voc/tr)**
John Weston	**(tr)**
Ray Fowlis	**(sax)**
Ronnie Wilson	**(dr)**

They were also joined as background vocalists by two girls named **Angela** and **Lena**, who called themselves **The Bluesettes**. This was not only an unusual but also a very interesting line-up, and it was really good, as can be heard on their great Unicord acetate with the songs *Jerk* and *Just Won't Do Right* which sadly were never released on vinyl. The song *Jerk*, by the way, was an original by the group, written by **Eddie Williams**.

When the **Bluesettes** left again, the **Almost Blues** were joined by **Angela Williams** as an additional singer, the sister of the lead vocalist. But this line-up only lasted until August 1965 and then **Eddie Williams** and his sister **Angela** left and disappeared from the scene. **Colin Areety** came in as their new lead singer, having formerly sung with the **In Crowd**.

In this line-up, the **Almost Blues** recorded the songs *Who Is Going To Pick Up The Pieces, Midnight hour, Try Me* and *Papa's Got A Brand New Bag* for EMI, which were not released.

In February 1966, the group went into the Abbey Road Studios again and recorded the song *Tell Daddy* for EMI, once again it was not released. But the connection with EMI continued and in the end this led to the departure of **Colin Areety** because there were disagreements about their musical style for further recordings. EMI wanted the **Almost Blues** to record *Cupid*, which a little later became a big hit for **Johnny Nash**, but **Colin Areety** did not want to sing it and so he left to join the **Dennisons**. After that he became a member of the **Fyx** and then appeared with the **Michael Henri Group** before he started a solo career.

In 1972 and 1973 he had record releases with *Poco Joe, I Don't Want To Be Right* and *Holy Cow* on Deram, all great records, especially *Holy Cow*, but none of them had any major success. He was active as a singer on the scene until he sadly died in 2007.

In 1968, **The Almost Blues** were joined by **Tommy Brown**, who had formerly sung with the **Valentinos**. At that time, founder member **Mike Haralambos** also left and was replaced by **Billy Faulkner**, a former member of **Vic Takes Four**. Two sax players named **Pete Harvey** and **Tommy Husky** joined the group as additional members.

Tommy Husky, a former member of the **Dee-Jays**, the **Nashpool** and **Earl Preston's Realms**, stayed for only a short time and then left to join the **Detours**. Later, he became very successful on the British Rockabilly scene and recorded a solo album in the Nineties. He was replaced in the **Almost Blues** by **Navo Nield**, while **John Rathbone** came in as the new drummer for the departing **Ronnie Wilson**. **John 'Jay' Rathbone**, sometimes also named **John Foskett**, was a former member of the **Masterminds**.

But that was still not the end of the personnel changes in the **Almost Blues** and the next to leave was **Billy Faulkner**, who was replaced by **John Hodgson,** who came from **Georgie's Germs**. Then **Graham Heatherington**, a new trumpet player, came in for the departing **John Weston**. In 1969 **John Rathbone**, was replaced by **Barry Robinson**, the former drummer of the **Heartbeats**, **Excerts** and **Georgie's Germs**. In this line-up the **Almost Blues** recorded the song *Lovitis* for EMI, but again it was not followed by a release, although once again it was an excellent recording.

Tommy Brown left again and **Alan Peters** switched back to lead vocals. The departing **Ray Fowlis, Pete Harvey, Navo Nield** and **Graham Heatherington** were only replaced by the two sax players **Graham Robertson** and **Derek Marl**, and so the group was restricted to a six-piece again, while it had been something like a little Rhythm & Blues orchestra before.

If all the steady changes in the line-up were taken into account, it is not really surprising that the **Almost Blues** never made a national breakthrough and probably disbanded totally in 1969. **Alan Peters** joined **Liverpool Scene** before he formed his own band **Tryptych**, which only existed for a short time. He then became a member of the internationally successful band **Supercharge**, before he again formed his own group with the unusual name of **29th & Dearborn**, who released one single and then disbanded again. Then he played with the **Opposition** and the **Love Ponies** before he formed **Lawnmower** which became quite a successful live act in the clubs of Liverpool and its surrounding areas.

Discography

The **Almost Blues** never had a record released but recorded the very good and interesting acetate
Jerk / Just Won't Do Right   UK – Unicord acetate / 1965

Other line-ups of the group from 1965 until 1969 recorded the following songs in the Abbey Road Studios for EMI: *Who Is Going To Pick Up The Pieces, Midnight Hour, Try Me, Papa's Got A Brand New Bag, Tell Daddy* and *Lovitis*, but for mysterious reasons none of these songs were ever released on vinyl.

THE BEAT BOYS

It can be debated here whether this group was more part of the Merseybeat or the Manchester scene. They hailed from Wigan in Lancashire, which is a little closer to Liverpool, but they obviously appeared regularly on both scenes, later maybe more often in Manchester when **Jack Abadie**, who owned the 'Twisted Wheel' became their manager, and of course the **Beat Boys** appeared there very often.

However, let's start at the beginning and that was the Wigan Skiffle / Rock 'n' Roll group **The Dominoes** most probably formed in 1957. This group, amongst others, also included a certain **Clive Powell** on piano and vocals, who left in late 1959 and found international stardom as **Georgie Fame**.

The line-up of the group kept changing and in 1960 the **Dominoes** leader **Ronnie Carr**, together with the remaining members **Kenny Fillingham** and **Eric Eastham**, formed the **Beat Boys**. After drummer **Eric Eastham** had left again, the group consisted of:

Allan Parkinson	(voc/g/harp)
Kenny Fillingham	(lg)
Malcolm Grundy	(rg)
Ronnie Carr	(bg/voc)
Ronnie Simms	(dr)

Allan Parkinson was a former member of the **Martinis**.

The **Beat-Boys** soon became very popular on the scene but that did not keep **Kenny Fillingham** from leaving to join **Vince Taylor & the Playboys** in 1962, with whom he probably went to France. **Gerry Kenny**, who also came from the **Martinis,** replaced him but left very soon again. **Malcolm Grundy** then took over the lead guitar and in as a new rhythm guitarist came **Geoff Bibby**.

This line-up was signed to Decca and **Joe Meek** produced their first single *Third Time Lucky* which was coupled with the **Ronnie Carr** original *That's My Plan*. A great record that sold very well but in the end failed to make the charts.

In 1964, **Micky Most** produced another **Ronnie Carr** original with *A Little Lovin'* and also the song *I'm Just A Rolling Stone* with them for Decca but these for mysterious reasons were not released. This was probably the reason that **Allan Parkinson** and **Malcolm Grundy** left the **Beat Boys**. They teamed up with former member **Gerry Kenny** to form the **Rats**, but this is another story in this book. **Allan Parkinson** later changed his name to **Dave Allen** and formed **Dave Allen & the Exotics**, but this again can be found in another story. **Malcom Grundy** also joined that group when it continued after the leaving of **Dave Allen** as **The Bigs** in Italy.

Back to the **Beat Boys**, who were joined by the returning **Kenny Fillingham** on lead guitar, while **Geoff Bibby** was replaced by keyboarder **George Twist**. For a short time they continued as the **Beat Boys** but then they started to work for **Don Arden** and became more a backing group for American Blues singers who toured England, for example **Screaming Jay Hawkins**, **Memphis Slim** and **Champion Jack Dupree**. For that reason and because they found out that there was another recording group of the same name, **The Beat Boys** became the **Blues Set**.

In 1966, the group was tired of continuously touring around and returned to their old name and to Wigan, where they became the resident band at the 'Sportsman' club. But this was only for one more year and when **Ronnie Simms** left to join **Jimmy Martin & the Martinis** and **George Twist** became a member of the **Sportsmen**.

Ronnie Carr and **Kenny Fillingham** formed the **New City Showband** in 1967 and after that their ways also separated, although they all stayed in the music business.

A 2001 **Beat Boys** reunion at the 'Monaco Ballroom' in Wigan saw the Sixties' members **Allan Parkinson** (voc/harp), **Ronnie Carr** (voc/bg), **Eric Eastham** (dr) and **Ronnie Simms** (perc) together on stage again.

Discography

| **Third Time Lucky / That's My Plan** | **UK - Decca F. 11730 / 1963** |

Unreleased tracks:
In 1964 Micky Most recorded the songs *A Little Lovin'* and *I'm Just A Rolling Stone* with the **Beat Boys** for **Decca**, but they did not come out on record.

THE BEAT BOYS decca records

THE BEATLES

The story of what later became the most popular and successful Beat band in the world can be traced back to 1956. At that time, **John Lennon** (voc/g) together with **Pete Shotton** (wb) and the other schoolmates **Nigel Whalley** (t-bass), **Ivan Vaughan** (bg), **Rod Davis** (bj), **Eric Griffiths** (g) and **Colin Hanton** (dr) formed the Skiffle group **The Quarrymen**. This name was chosen because all members were pupils of Quarry Bank High school in Liverpool.

In the same year, **Nigel Whalley** concentrated on managing the group and he was replaced by **Len Garry**, who joined as a second bass guitarist. Shortly after this, **Pete Shotton** and **Eric Griffiths** also left and were replaced by **Paul McCartney** and **George Harrison**, who both played guitar. **George Harrison** was a former member of the **Rebels**, where he had played together with his brother **Peter Harrison**. In 1958, this line-up probably recorded the demo *In Spite Of All The Danger* on acetate, which was coupled with *That'll Be The Day*.

In 1958 **Len Garry** and **Rod Davis** left the group, which a little later changed its name to **Johnny & the Moondogs**. After **Colin Hanton** and **Ivan Vaughan** had also left, **John Lennon**, **George Harrison** and **Paul McCartney** continued as a trio under various names, for example **The Rainbows**. At this time, **John Lennon** and **Paul McCartney** also appeared as a duo under the name **The Nurk Twins**, while **George Harrison** sometimes played with the **Les Stuart Quartet**.

In 1959, **Johnny & the Moondogs** consisted of **John Lennon** (voc/rg), **George Harrison** (lg/voc), **Paul McCartney** (voc/g) and **Ken Brown** (bg). **Ken Brown** was a former member of the **Les Stuart Quartet**, where he had met **George Harrison** who took him into **Johnny & the Moondogs**, who had no steady drummer at this stage. In the same year, **Ken Brown** joined the **Blackjacks** and was replaced by **Stuart Sutcliffe**, who couldn't really play the bass guitar, but who was a good friend of **John Lennon**. When, in 1960, **Tommy Moore** joined them on drums, the band changed their name to **The Silver Beatles**. This line-up did not last and in early 1961 **Tommy Moore** left again because of trouble with his girlfriend.

For a short time **Norman Chapman** played the drums but then went on to play with the **In Crowd** and was replaced by **Pete Best**, who had formerly played with the **Blackjacks**. It is said to have been the suggestion of **Brian 'Cass' Cassar** (later known as **Casey Jones**) to shorten the group's name to **The Beatles**, which was accepted by the musicians. Accordingly the first line-up that appeared under the name **The Beatles** consisted of:

John Lennon	**(voc/rg)**
George Harrison	**(lg/voc)**
Paul McCartney	**(voc/g)**
Stuart Sutcliffe	**(bg)**
Pete Best	**(dr)**

Initially, **Mona Best**, **Pete Best's** mother, looked after the interests of the band and then their management was taken over by **Alan Williams**. A little later, the **Beatles** went to Hamburg for the first time, where they were booked to play the 'Indra', which later became the 'Hit-Club'. After **Derry & the Seniors** and **Rory Storm & the Hurricanes**, the **Beatles** were the third Liverpool group to appear in Hamburg.

Howie Casey, at that time with **Derry & the Seniors**, was non too happy with the **Beatles** coming over as he feared that they were not good enough and would possibly spoil the chances of more Liverpool groups coming to Hamburg. Of course his doubts were exaggerated, but it is also true that the **Beatles** didn't have great musical quality at that time, a fact that can be heard very clearly on the early live tapes.

Derry & the Seniors were certainly more professional at

The original Beatles

that time, but in spite of this, it was the **Beatles** who started the Beat avalanche rolling over there. In 1961, **Bert Kaempfert** signed them as backing group for an album with **Tony Sheridan** on Polydor, for which the group's name was changed to **The Beat Brothers**. This name was given to other musicians that backed **Tony Sheridan** on later releases and also recorded some instrumental singles in their own right with a dominant saxophone sound. So it is not true that the **Beatles** were identical to the **Beat Brothers** in general. The single *My Bonnie* was taken from the above album, which led to **Brian Epstein** becoming aware of them and taking over the band's management.

After their return to Liverpool, the **Beatles** stage outfit, stage show and of course their musical transition into a really hard Rock'n'Roll group, caused a sensation on their hometown's scene. With the support of producer **George Martin**, **Brian Epstein** managed to obtain a recording contract with EMI, after Decca had turned them down. **Stu Sutcliffe** had meanwhile parted from the group to study in Hamburg, where he died of a brain haemorrhage in 1962.

In August 1962, **Pete Best** was replaced by **Ringo Starr**, whose real name is **Richard Starkey** and who had played before with the **Eddie Clayton Group**, the **Darktown Skiffle Group**, the **Raving Texans** which became **Rory Storm & the Hurricanes**. It was not that **Pete Best** wanted to leave, but he was sacked by the other members for mysterious reasons. It is more likely that it wasn't the 'others' but probably just one member, still active, and the obvious reason was jealousy.

This change is and will always be one of the most controversial points in the **Beatles** story and it is rubbish when it is stated that **Ringo Starr** was a better drummer or that **George Martin** was responsible for that change. But this is not the right place to go into it and therefore the advice for people who are interested in knowing the truth about it is 'better ask a real insider of that time and scene'. The advice for **Beatles** fans is 'don't do it'. **Pete Best** joined **Lee Curtis & the All Stars** who later became **The Pete Best Four** and **The Pete Best Combo**.

The **Beatles** new line-up had their biggest success with records like *Love Me Do, Please, Please Me*, *From Me To You, She Loves You, I Want To Hold Your Hand, A Hard Day's Night, I Feel Fine, Ticket To Ride, Help, We Can Work It Out* and lots of others, which all became worldwide hits. Most of their records were Lennon/McCartney compositions and this team also wrote very successfully for other Beat stars of that time like **Billy J. Kramer & the Dakotas**, the **Fourmost**, the **Applejacks**, **Peter & Gordon**, **Cilla Black** and **Tommy Quickly**.

Their motion pictures 'A Hard Day's Night' and 'Help' became bestsellers, although they lacked any sensible storyline. Their incredible, but at this stage deserved success, went to their heads and although they already were the most successful group, they wanted to be different to all the other groups. With a few exceptions like *Hey Jude, Yesterday, Lady Madonna* and *Let It Be*, this resulted in many trashy records being released. Songs like *Yellow submarine, I'm The Walrus, Ob-La-Di Ob-La-Da* and others would have brought an end to the careers of any other group, but the **Beatles** had enough fans unwilling to be critical and so they were the only group who could afford such escapades. Their songs had also lost the drive that once had carried all before them. Typical examples of this are songs like *Michelle* or *Girl,* which were no more than second or even third class pop songs. But of course they sold well and became big hits, although from the Rock 'n' Roll point of view the **Beatles** had taken a step backwards.

It is also quite hard to understand why 'Sgt. Pepper' is always claimed to be their best album, as some of their real Beat albums were a lot better. As to the enormous influence that this album apparently had on popular music at large, it has to be pointed out that these kinds of musical experiments were not new at all as lots of American groups had done similar things years before.

In 1970, the **Beatles** disbanded, not having performed live together for quite some time. All of the members started solo careers, which were more (**John Lennon** and **Paul McCartney**) or less (**Ringo Starr**) successful.

The always underrated **George Harrison** also released some very good records (*What Is Life*!!) and had some hits over the years. However, he gained real recognition for the first time in the Eighties, when he had his best time musically and ended up in a great project called **The Travelling Wilburys**.

On 8th December 1980, **John Lennon** was shot by a mentally disturbed fan in the hall of the Dakota building in New York and **George Harrison** died on 29 November 2001 of a cancerous brain tumour.

Single-Discography

As the **Beatles** have made so many records that were released all over the world in many variations and there were already books written about it, it is sensible to cut their discography down to the English market plus the early German solo recordings and of course the ones with **Tony Sheridan**.

Love Me Do / P.S. I Love You	**UK- Parlophone R 4949 / 1962**
Please Please Me / Ask Me Why	**UK- Parlophone R 4983 / 1963**
From Me To You / Thank You Girl	**UK- Parlophone R 5015 / 1963**
She Loves You / I'll Get You	**UK- Parlophone R 5055 / 1963**
I Want To Hold Your Hand / This Boy	**UK- Parlophone R 5084 / 1963**
Can't Buy Me Love / You Can't Do That	**UK- Parlophone R 5114 / 1964**
A Hard Day's Night / Things We Said Today	**UK- Parlophone R 5160 / 1964**
I feel fine / She's a woman	**UK- Parlophone R 5200 / 1964**
Ticket To Ride / Yes It Is	**UK- Parlophone R 5265 / 1965**
Help / I'm Down	**UK- Parlophone R 5305 / 1965**
We Can Work It Out / Day Tripper	**UK- Parlophone R 5389 / 1965**
Paperback Writer / Rain	**UK- Parlophone R 5452 / 1966**
Eleanor Rigby / Yellow Submarine	**UK- Parlophone R 5493 / 1966**
Strawberry Fields Forever / Penny Lane	**UK- Parlophone R 5570 / 1967**

All You Need Is Love / Baby, You're A Rich Man	UK- Parlophone R 5620 / 1967	
Hello Goodbye / I Am The Walrus	UK- Parlophone R 5655 / 1967	
Lady Madonna / The Inner Light	UK- Parlophone R 5675 / 1968	
Hey Jude / Revolution	UK- Parlophone R 5722 / 1968	
Get back / Don't Let Me Down	UK- Parlophone R 5777 / 1969	
The Ballad Of John & Yoko / Old Brown Shoe	UK- Parlophone R 5786 / 1969	
Something / Come Together	UK- Parlophone R 5814 / 1969	
Let It Be / You Know My Name	UK- Parlophone R 5833 / 1970	

(please note, that from *Get Back* on, all singles displayed the 'Apple' label)

Different German releases:

Cry For A Shadow / Why	G- Polydor	52275 / 1964	
Ain't She Sweet / Take Out Some Insurance On Me Baby	G- Polydor	52317 / 1964	
***Komm Gib Mir Deine Hand / Sie Liebt Dich**	G- Odeon	O 22671 / 1964	

(*please note that these were the German versions of *I Want To Hold Your Hand* and *She Loves You*)

Releases with **Tony Sheridan**:
Singles:

My Bonnie / The Saints	G - Polydor	24673 / 1961	
Why / Cry For A Shadow	G - Polydor	52275 / 1964	
Ain't She Sweet / Take Out Some Insurance On Me Baby	G - Polydor	52317 / 1964	
Skinny Minny / Sweet Georgia Brown	G - Polydor	52324 / 1964	

(please note that the instrumental *Cry For A Shadow* and the song *Ain't She Sweet* were recorded by the **Beatles** without Tony Sheridan)
EPs:

Ya Ya	G - Polydor	21485 / 1961
- Ya Ya (Pt. 1) / **Ya Ya** (Pt. 2) / **Sweet Georgia Brown / Skinny Minny**		
MY BONNIE	G - Polydor	21610 / 1964
- My Bonnie / Why / The Saints / Cry for a shadow		

- plus some tracks accompanying Tony Sheridan on his first three albums 'My Bonnie' (G-Polydor 237112 / 1962) 'The Beatles First' (G-Polydor Hi-Fi 46432 / 1964) and 'Meet the Beat' (G-Polydor J 74557 / 1965), which mostly were put out on single and EP (see above).

EP discography:

THE BEATLES' HITS	UK- Parlophone GEP 8880 / 1963
- From Me To You / Thank You Girl / Please Please Me / Love Me Do	
TWIST AND SHOUT	UK- Parlophone GEP 8882 / 1963
- Twist And Shout / A Taste Of Honey / Do You Want To Know A Secret / There's A Place	
THE BEATLES (No.1)	UK- Parlophone GEP 8883 / 1963
- I Saw Her Standing There / Misery / Anna / Chains	
ALL MY LOVING	UK-Parlophone GEP 8891 / 1964
- All My Loving / Ask Me Why / Money / P.S. I Love You	
LONG TALL SALLY	UK- Parlophone GEP 8913 / 1964
- Long Tall Sally / I Call Your Name / Slow Down / Matchbox	
Extracts from the film **A HARD DAY'S NIGHT**	UK- Parlophone GEP 8920 / 1964
- I Should Have Known Better / If I Fell / Tell Me Why / And I Love Her	
Extracts from the album **A HARD DAY'S NIGHT**	UK- Parlophone GEP 8924 / 1964
- Any Time At All / I'll Cry Instead / Things We Said Today / When I Get Home	
BEATLES FOR SALE	UK- Parlophone GEP 8931 / 1965
- No Reply / I'm A Loser / Rock 'n' Roll Music / Eight Days A Week	
BEATLES FOR SALE (No.2)	UK- Parlophone GEP 8938 / 1965
- I'll Follow The Sun / Baby's In Black / Words Of Love / I Don't Want To Spoil The Party	
THE BEATLES' MILLION SELLERS	UK- Parlophone GEP 8946 / 1965
- She Loves You / I Want To Hold Your Hand / Can't Buy Me Love / I Feel Fine	

YESTERDAY   UK- Parlophone GEP 8948 / 1966
- Yesterday / Act Naturally / You Like Me Too Much / It's Only Love
NOWHERE MAN   UK- Parlophone GEP 8952 / 1966
- Nowhere Man / Drive My Car / Michelle / You Won't See Me
MAGICAL MYSTERY TOUR   UK- Parlophone   MMT 1 / 1967
- Magical Mystery Tour / Your Mother Should Know / I Am The Walrus / The Fool On The Hill / Flying / Blue Jay Way

LP discography:
PLEASE PLEASE ME   UK - Parlophone PMC 1202 / 1963
- I Saw Her Standing There / Misery / Anna / Chains / Boys / Ask Me Why / Please Please Me / Love Me Do / P.S. I Love You / Baby It's You / Do You Want To Know A Secret / A Taste Of Honey / There's A Place / Twist And Shout
WITH THE BEATLES   UK - Parlophone PMC 1206 / 1963
- It Won't Be Long / All I've Got To Do / All My Loving / Don't Bother Me / Little Child / Till There Was You / Please Mr. Postman / Roll Over Beethoven / Hold Me Tight / You Really Got A Hold On Me / I Wanna Be Your Man / Devil In Her Heart / Not A Second Time / Money
A HARD DAY'S NIGHT   UK - Parlophone PMC 1230 / 1964
- A Hard Day's Night / I Should Have Known Better / If I Fell / I'm Happy Just To Dance With You / And I Love Her / Tell Me Why / Can't Buy Me Love / Any Time At All / I'll Cry Instead / Things We Said Today / When I Get Home / You Can't Do That / I'll Be Back
BEATLES FOR SALE   UK - Parlophone PMC 1240 / 1964
- No Reply / I'm A Loser / Baby's In Black / Rock 'n' Roll Music / I'll Follow The Sun / Mr. Moonlight / Kansas City / Hey - Hey - Hey - Hey / Eight Days A Week / Words Of Love / Honey Don't / Every Little Thing / I Don't Want To Spoil The Party / What You're Doing / Everybody's Trying To Be My Baby
HELP!   UK - Parlophone PMC 1255 / 1965
- Help / The Night Before / You've Got To Hide Your Love Away / I Need You / Another Girl / You're Going To Lose That Girl / Ticket To Ride / Act Naturally / It's Only Love / You Like Me Too Much / Tell Me What You See / I've Just Seen A Face / Yesterday / Dizzy Miss Lizzy
RUBBER SOUL   UK - Parlophone PMC 1267 / 1965
- Drive My Car / Norwegian Wood / You Won't See Me / Nowhere Man / Think For Yourself / The Word / Michelle / What Goes On / Girl / I'm Looking Through You / In My Life / Wait / If I Needed Someone / Run For Your Life
REVOLVER   UK - Parlophone PMC 7009 / 1966
- Taxman / Eleanor Rigby / I'm Only Sleeping / Love You To / Here, There And Everywhere / Yellow Submarine / She Said She Said / Good Day Sunshine / And Your Bird Can Sing / For No One / Doctor Robert / I Want To Tell You / Got To Get You Into My Life / Tomorrow Never Knows
A COLLECTION OF BEATLES OLDIES   UK - Parlophone PMC 7016 / 1966
- She Loves You / From Me To You / We Can Work It Out / Help / Michelle / Yesterday / I Feel Fine / Yellow Submarine / Can't Buy Me Love / Bad Boy / Day Tripper / A Hard Day's Night / Ticket To Ride / Paperback Writer / Eleanor Rigby / I Want To Hold Your Hand
SGT. PEPPER'S LONELY HEARTS CLUB BAND   UK - Parlophone PMC 7027 / 1967
- Sgt. Pepper's Lonely Hearts Club Band / With A Little Help From My Friend / Lucy In The Sky With Diamonds / Getting Better / Fixing A Hole / She's Leaving Home / Being For The Benefit Of Mr. Kite / Within You, Without You / When I'm Sixty-Four / Lovely Rita / Good Morning Good Morning / Sgt. Pepper's Lonely Hearts Club Band / A Day In The Life
THE BEATLES   UK- Parlophone PMC 7067 + 7068 / 1968
- Back In The USSR / Dear Prudence / Glass onion / Ob-La-Di, Ob-La-Da / Wild Honey Pie / The Continuing Story Of Bungalow Bill / While My Guitar Gently Weeps / Happiness Is A Warm Gun / Martha My Dear / I'm So Tired / Blackbird / Piggies / Rocky Raccoon / Don't Pass Me By / Why Don't We Do It In The Road / I Will / Julia / Birthday / Yer Blues / Mother Nature's Son / Everybody's Got Something To Hide Except Me And My Monkey / Sexy Sadie / Helter Skelter / Long, Long, Long / Revolution / Honey Pie / Savoy Truffle / Cry, Baby, Cry / Revolution / Good night

YELLOW SUBMARINE   UK - Parlophone PMC 7070 / 1969
    - Yellow Submarine / Only A Northern Song / All Together Now / Hey Bulldog / It's All Too Much / All You Need Is Love plus seven soundtrack instrumentals by the George Martin Orchestra
ABBEY ROAD   UK-Apple (Parlophone) PCS 7088 / 1969
    - Come Together / Something / Maxwell's Silver Hammer / Oh Darling / Octopus's Garden / I Want You / Here Comes The Sun / Because / You Never Give Me Your Money / Sun King / Mean Mr. Mustard / Polythene Pam / She Came In Through The Bathroom Window / Golden Slumbers / Carry That Weight / The End / Her Majesty

LET IT BE   UK-Apple (Parlophone) PCS 7096 / 1970
    - Two Of Us / Dig A Pony / Across The Universe / I, Me, Mine / Dig It / Let It Be / Maggie May / I've Got A Feeling / The One After 909 / The Long And Winding Road / For You Blue / Get back

BERNIE & THE BUZZ BAND

This Liverpool Soul group was formed in 1967 in the Toxteth area by singer **Bernie Wenton**, who had formerly sung with the **Sobells** and the **Triumphs**.

At this time, Liverpool's Merseybeat was no longer dominating the English music scene, and the Beat was changing into Rock on one hand and into Mainstream pop on the other.

But **Bernie Wenton** didn't want to take either of these directions, and so he decided for Soul music when he formed **Bernie & the Buzz Band**. This band included the following musicians:

Bernie Wenton	(voc)
Neil Ford	(lg)
Jan Schetheer	(bg)
Jeff Edmondson	(org)
Andy O'Hagan	(sax)
Dave O'Hagan	(sax)
Geoff Howard	(tr)
Jimmy Turner	(dr)

Neil Ford was a former member of the **Vaaveros** and **Johnny Ringo & the Colts**, while **Jeff Edmondson** had played before with **Them Calderstones**.

Andy O'Hagan and **Dave O'Hagan** both came from the **Times**, who were the backing group for the **Signs** and prior to this **Andy O'Hagan** had played with the **Dions**, formerly known as **Roy & the Dions**. All the others were experienced musicians too, but it is unknown which groups they had played in before.

As well as at the Liverpool venues, **Bernie & the Buzz Band** played a lot down in London, where **Noel Walker** became aware of them. He was working as a producer for the Decca sub label 'Deram' at that time and he managed to get the group signed by the recording company. This was in early 1968 and a little later he produced the first single with **Bernie & the Buzz Band**. The A-side was *Don't Knock It*, coupled with the **Sam & Dave** classic *When Something Is Wrong With My Baby*. This outstanding record sold quite well, but did not get near the charts.

Dave O'Hagan, **Andy O'Hagan**, **Geoff Howard** and **Jeff Edmondson** left the group, that was joined by **Alby Donnelly** (sax/fl) and **Nick Roman** (latin perc). **Alby Donnelly** had formerly played with the **Plainsmen**, the **Terry Hines Sextett** and the **Clayton Squares**. With this line-up, the group recorded *The House That Jack Built* (not to be confused with **Alan Price's** hit success) and a version of *Funky Broadway* for their next single. For unknown reasons it was never released, although *The House That Jack Built* did come out later on the Decca label, and was coupled with *Midnight Confessions* by the **Pete Kelly Solution** from Southport. This record was also unsuccessful and **Bernie & the Buzz Band** split up in late 1968 or early 1969.

Alby Donnelly went to Germany and found stardom with his group **Supercharge**, while **Neil Ford** stayed in the music business as a session guitarist and **Bernie Wenton**, together with his brothers **Willie** and **Bobby Wenton,** (both also vocalists) amalgamated with a group called **The Shuffler's Sound**. Following these changes, the group changed their name to **The Shuffler's Sound feat. the Buzz Brothers**.

Besides **Bernie**, **Willie** and **Bobby Wenton** (all voc), the line-up consisted of **Silver Chantry** (g), **Billy Good** (bg), **Ivor Alli** (org), **Mike Kearns** (sax) and **Alan Seff** (dr).

Silver Chantry later was replaced by **Willie Osu** on guitar, and then the band changed its name (probably to **Black Magic**) and became a real Rock band. After the split, **Mike Kearns** played with **Karl Terry & the Cruisers** and then joined **Gaz & the Groovers** who also went to Germany, where they changed their name to **Juke** and became a successful live act for years. **Mike Kearns** committed suicide in 1992.

Billy Good later played with the newly formed and very short-lived **Lee Curtis & the All Stars** and then joined the **Undertakers**, under the leadership of **Geoff Nugent**. He is still a member of that group and is also gigging as a solo performer in Liverpool clubs these days.

Bernie Wenton teamed up with **Alby Donnelly** in a band (was it already **Supercharge**?) and later, together with his brother **Willie Wenton**, sang backing vocals in **Chris Rea**'s band. **Bernie Wenton** later appeared quite often as an actor on British television until he sadly died in 2007.

All the other members of the **Shuffler's Sound** disappeared from the scene.

Discography

Don't Knock It / When Something Is Wrong With My Baby   **UK-Deram** **DM 181 / 1968**
The House That Jack Built / Pete Kelly's Solution: Midnight Confessions
                                                    UK-Decca   **22829 / 1968**

Bernie Wenton with brothers Willie and Bobby
and the Shufflers Sound

THE PETE BEST FOUR

The career of drummer and band leader **Pete Best** started in the late Fifties in Liverpool, when he was a member of a trio called **The Blackjacks**. In 1960 he replaced the departing **Tommy Moore** in the **Silver Beatles**, who a little later shortened their name to **The Beatles** and went to Hamburg.

When **Pete Best** was sacked from that band for (not really) mysterious reasons, he joined **Lee Curtis & the All Stars** who in the same month were voted second to the **Beatles** in the 'Mersey Beat's' popularity poll. **Pete Best** stayed with the group when **Lee Curtis** left to go to Germany with another backing band. He then took over the leadership and their first appearances were made as **Pete Best & the Original All Stars**.

Because **Lee Curtis'** new backing group also used the name of **The All Stars**, the **Original All Stars** changed their name into the **Pete Best Four** after lead guitarist **Frank Bowen** left and was replaced by **Tommy McGuirk**, a former member of **Gene Day & the Jango-Beats** and the **Aarons**. As a result of these changes the **Pete Best Four** from then on appeared with the following line-up:

Tony Waddington	**(g/voc)**
Tommy McGuirk	**(g/voc)**
Wayne Bickerton	**(bg/voc)**
Pete Best	**(dr/voc)**

Tony Waddington was a former member of the **Comets, Gene Day & the Jango-Beats, Steve Bennett & the Syndicate** and **Lee Curtis & the All Stars**. **Wayne Bickerton** had formerly played with the **Bobby Bell Rockers, Steve Bennett & the Syndicate** and with **Lee Curtis & the All Stars**.

In 1964 the **Pete Best Four** were signed by Decca and soon after had their first single released with the **Tony Waddington/Wayne Bickerton** original *Why Did I Fall In Love With You*, which was coupled with a good version of the **Eddie Hodges** success *I'm Gonna Knock On Your Door*. **Tony Waddington** and **Wayne Bickerton** later proved to be very talented songwriters, but sadly this single took them nowhere.

The **Pete Best Four** toured Germany again and besides the 'Star Club' in Hamburg, also played at the opening concert at the 'Star Club' in Bielefeld. Around the same time there was a single released under **Pete Best**'s name in the USA with the songs *Kansas City* and *Boys*, but this did not have any impact either.

Maybe because of their lack of success, the **Pete Best Four** disbanded in early 1965 after they had recorded some more of their own material, which was

Pete Best Four

only released later. **Tommy McGuirk** wanted to form a new group with **Denny Alexander**, with whom he had played together in the **Aarons**, but that did not work out and **Tommy McGuirk** disappeared for some time and later was a member of the **Everglades**.

Pete Best, **Tony Waddington** and **Wayne Bickerton** re-formed the group as the **Pete Best Combo** in the same year, together with the two sax players **Billy Burton** and **Trevor Baker**. **Billy Burton**, sometimes also known as **Bill Wesley**, was a former member of the **Few** which had developed from the **Cyclones**. In this line-up the **Pete Best Combo** recorded the song *Last Night* for the European market but it was not released.

The independent US producer **Bob Gallo** became interested in the group and got them to come to the United States where he recorded the band using the name **Peter Best**, and for the album he chose the title 'Best Of The Beatles'. The album was released on the Savage label in 1965 and included the song *Last Night* and, with the exception of *Shimmy Like My Sister Kate*, *Casting My Spell* and *Some Other Guy*, only featured songs by **Tony Waddington** and **Wayne Bickerton**. It could have been a really nice album had it been mixed and produced better. In any case, it was not successful but today it is a very rare and expensive collector's item. A further **Peter Best** single was released in the USA with the songs *If You Can't Get Her* and *The Way I Feel About You* on the 'Happening' label in 1965 but once again it wasn't a great success and so did not help the group at all.

The **Pete Best Combo** returned to Liverpool where it then broke up. **Trevor Baker** disappeared from the scene and **Billy Burton** at first played with the **Denims** and later with **Karl Terry & the Cruisers**, before he emigrated to South Africa. Sometime in the Nineties he returned to Liverpool and played again with **Karl Terry**, as well as with various other groups on the scene.

For a short time the **Pete Best Combo** was re-formed as a trio with **Pete Best**, **Tony Waddington** and **Wayne Bickerton**, but finally broke up again without having recorded anymore songs. **Tony Waddington** and **Wayne Bickerton** continued as a song-writing and producing duo and, as well as hits for the **Flirtations**, they also wrote all the early material for the **Rubettes**, including their million selling *Sugar Baby Love*. Besides this, **Wayne Bickerton** was a member of the great group **World of Oz**, who recorded a fantastic album and had hits with songs like *The Muffin Man* and *King Croesus* in the late Sixties.

Pete Best quit show business and went back to a normal day job, but around 1967/68 there was a single released by **Peter Best** on the Australian Columbia label with the title

Pete Best Combo

Want You. Now, it is hard to say if it was **Peter Best** from Liverpool or just another singer with the same name, but there is at least the possibility that this was a solo record by the former **Beatles** drummer and that is why it is mentioned here. The **David Mackay** production was zapped up a bit with an orchestral sound, but its rhythm was still Beat.

It might be of interest to collectors to know that in 1982, an album was released in the USA on the 'Phoenix 10' label with the title 'The Beatle That Time Forgot', which featured previously unissued Sixties recordings from the **Pete Best Combo**.

However, **Pete Best** was later assistant manager of the job centre in Liverpool and in 1988 he appeared on stage again for the first time, on the bill at the yearly 'Merseybeatle Convention' in Liverpool. It was announced as a concert by the **Pete Best Band**, but this group only came together for this one performance and, besides members of **Liverpool Express** (**Billy Kinsley**, etc.), included his younger brother **Roag Best** as second drummer, who normally played with **Watt 4**. It was an impressive performance and a lot of people later agreed that it was more than sad that this line-up did not stay together for further concerts.

In 1989 **Pete Best** sat in with the **Merseybeats** at a 'Merseycats' charity concert for their original drummer **John Banks**, who had died in 1988. Besides him, the line-up consisted of the Sixties original members **Tony Crane**, **Billy Kinsley** and **Aaron Williams**. He obviously enjoyed playing again, even if not with a steady band and on a regular basis. This line-up of the **Merseybeats** including **Pete Best** played some more concerts but only for the 'Mersey Cats'.

In 1990 **Pete Best** recorded the single *Heaven/Fool In Love* together with **Billy Kinsley** of the **Merseybeats** which was released as **Kinsley & Best** on the English Prestige Label. Shortly after, **Pete Best** and his brother **Roag** formed a new **Pete Best Band** who, with a frequently changing line-up, toured sporadically the United States again, as well as Canada, Japan and Germany.

Besides the two brothers, since 2002 the group has included the two guitarists **Phil Melia** (ex **Mojo Filter)** and **Tony Flynn** (ex **Crowded House**), as well as bassist **Paul Parry** (formerly with **Thunderboots**, **Pretenders** and the band of **Georgie Fame**).

This is a really great line-up with all the members sharing the vocals.

Single discography
as **The Pete Best Four**
Why Did I Fall In Love With You / I'm Gonna Knock On Your Door
                                      UK - Decca   F. 11929 / 1964
Different US releases:
as **Peter Best**:
Kansas City / Boys   US-Cameo Parkway C 391 / 1964
I'll Try Anyway / I Wanna Be There   US- Original Beatles Drummer Best   800 / 1964
as **Peter Best** (Best Of The Beatles):
Don't Play With Me / If You Can't Get Her   US- Happening   405 / 1964
If You Can't Get Her / The Way I Feel About You   US- Happening HA 1117 / 1965
I Can't Do Without You / Key To My Heart   US- Mr. Maestro   711 / 1965
Casting My Spell / I'm Blue   US- Mr. Maestro   712 / 1965

From that period in the late Eighties, a series of singles were released on the Collectables label. The last two were coupled with songs that Pete Best had recorded together with the **Beatles** for Polydor in Germany. They are:

I'll Try Anyway / I Don't Know Why I Do	US- Collectables	1516 / 1987
She's Not The Only Girl In Town / More Than I Need Myself	US- Collectables	1517 / 1987
I'll Have Everything Too / I'm Checking Out Now Baby	US- Collectables	1518 / 1987
How'd You Get To Know Her Name / If You Can't Get Her	US- Collectables	1519 / 1987
Rock 'n' Roll Music / Cry For A Shadow	US- Collectables	1520 / 1988
I'll try anyway / Why	US- Collectables	1524 / 1988

Peter Best solo:
Want You / Carousel Of Love   AUS-Columbia DO 5039 / 1967

Unissued tracks:
In 1964 the **Pete Best Four** recorded the song *Last night* as a follow-up single for Decca but this was not released. The song was later included on the US album of the **Pete Best Combo** but most probably not the original version.

LP discography:

as **Peter Best**:
BEST OF THE BEATLES   US - Savage   BM - 72 / 1965
- Last Night / Why Did You Leave Me Baby / Shimmy Like My Sister Kate / I Need Your Lovin' / Nobody But You / I Can't Do Without You / Casting My Spell / Wait And See / Some Other Guy / I'm Blue / She's Alright / Keys To My Heart

Beside this, in 1965, US producer **Bob Gallo** recorded some more songs with the **Pete Best Combo**, which were not released at that time, but in 1982 under the name of **The Pete Best Band** the following albums were released:
REBIRTH   US- PB Records   44 / 1981
- I Can't Do Without You / Off The Hook / She's Alright / I Need Your Lovin' / Why Did You Leave Me Baby / Shimmy Like My Sister Kate / I Wanna Be There / Everybody / Pete's Theme / Keys To My Heart
THE BEATLE THAT TIME FORGOT   US- Phoenix10   PHX 340 / 1982
- I'll Try Anyway / I Don't Know Why I Do / She's Not The Only Girl In Town / More Than I Need Myself / I'll Have Everything Too / I'm Checking Out Now Baby / How'd You Get To Know Her Name / If You Can't Get Her / Rock 'n' Roll Music

THE BIG THREE

This Liverpool trio originated from the group **Cass & the Casanovas** after **Brian 'Cass' Cassar** had left them. He later became famous in Germany under the name **Casey Jones**, where he had big hits like *Jack The Ripper, Don't Ha Ha* or *Yockomo*. His story can be followed under **Cass & the Casanovas** in this book.

The **Big Three** soon earned the reputation of being a 'band's band', admired by other musicians, due to their very good but also very hard Beat interpretations. But of course they were also loved by the public at large, a fact that is proven by their regularly high placing in the 'Mersey Beat's' popularity polls. The trio had a very high musical quality and originally consisted of:

Adrian Barber	**(lg/voc)**
Johnny 'Gus' Gustafson	**(voc/bg)**
Johnny 'Hutch' Hutchinson	**(dr/voc)**

Their amplifiers, which were constructed by **Adrian Barber** were of such interest to other bands, that he left to concentrate on building these so-called 'coffins'. His replacement in the **Big Three** was the great and imaginative guitarist **Brian 'Griff' Griffiths**, who came from the recently disbanded **Howie Casey & the Seniors**, originally known as **Derry & the Seniors**.

The group was signed to Decca and with their first release *Some Other Guy*, the **Big Three** became the third Liverpool group to enter the British charts, when the record climbed up to No.39 in 1963. But apart from this, *By The Way* (No. 24) and their outstanding live EP 'The Big Three Live At The Cavern' (No.6) became the group's only other chart successes. Very fine recordings like *I'm With You / Peanut Butter* and *If You Ever Change Your Mind / Gotta Keep Her Under Hand* were sadly only known by some fans, insiders and specialists, although they are real documents of the better part of Merseybeat history. But it is also true to say that the **Big Three** were far better live than in the studio, and just like **Rory Storm & the Hurricanes**, their exciting live sound was never caught on their records.

In 1964, **Johnny Gustafson** and **Brian Griffiths** left to form a trio under the name the **Seniors**, together with drummer **Ian Broad**, who had formerly played with **The Five Stars, Gus Travis & the Midnighters** and **Freddie Starr & the Midnighters**. But these **Seniors** were short-lived and broke up again after a German tour in 1964.

Johnny Gustafson joined the **Merseybeats** and **Brian Griffiths** was one of the founder

The Big Three

members of the **Griff Parry Five**, before both met up again in the **Johnny Gus Set**. Their replacements in the **Big Three** in 1964 were **Billy 'Faron' Ruffley** and **Paddy Chambers**, who both came from the recently disbanded **Faron's Flamingos**. But 'Faron' did not stay too long and was replaced by **Paul Pilnick**, who had formerly played with **Vince & the Volcanoes** and **Lee Curtis & the All Stars**. 'Faron' later emigrated to France where he was a member of **Blue Suede**, but in the Seventies returned to Liverpool. His story can be followed under **Faron's Flamingos**.

Paddy Chambers also left the **Big Three** in 1965 to join the **Eyes**. He later played with **Paddy, Klaus & Gibson** and the **Escorts**, before he became a member of groups like **Big John's Rock'n'Roll Circus**, **Sinbad** and **Paddy Chambers & the Java Jive**.

He was replaced by **John 'Brad' Bradley** (bg) and **Howie Casey** (sax), while **Paul Pilnick** took over on lead guitar. Both new members of the **Big Three** (they kept the name, though they were a four-piece now) came from the just disbanded **Krewkats**, who originally hailed from Birmingham, the hometown of the new bass guitarist.

Howie Casey, of course, was the former leader of **Howie Casey & the Seniors** and in the meantime had played with various Merseybeat groups, like **King Size Taylor & the Dominoes**. But this line-up only lasted until July 1965 when the first **Big Three** split occurred. At this time they had no recording contract and only played gigs on Merseyside. **Howie Casey** had a short spell with the **Griff Parry Five**, while **John Bradley** joined the **Jam Buttees**, but very soon both teamed up again to re-form the **Krew** - another story in this book.

Paul Pilnick followed **Lee Curtis** to Hamburg, where he joined the **All Stars** again, and was later a member of groups like **Stealer's Wheel**, **Badger**, **Sinbad**, **Deaf School** and **Jake**. The only remaining original member, **Johnny Hutchinson** joined the **Spidermen**, but in September 1965 he re-formed the **Big Three** with **Ray Marshal** (bg/voc), formerly with the **Mersey Four**, and **Barry Womersley** (g/voc), a former member of the **Diplomats** and the **Rhythm & Blues Inc.**.

This once again was a very good **Big Three** line-up, but they only gigged around the Liverpool area. It is not known exactly when the final line-up of the **Big Three** disbanded again, but it was probably in 1966.

Ray Marshall went back to Southport where he remained in the music business and was later the leader of **Ray Marshall & the All Stars**. **Barry Womersley** firstly became a member of the **Clayton Squares**, but only for a short time and then he joined **Jasmin T**, who recorded a great version of *Some Other Guy* in 1969. In the mid-Seventies he played with **Inner Sleeve**, and in 1977 had a solo single out before he disappeared from the scene for years and then re-formed his old group **Rhythm & Blues Inc.**, which still appears on the scene sporadically. **Johnny Hutchinson** quit show business and so a real Liverpool legend was lost.

In 1973 both former members **Johnny Gustafson** and **Brian Griffiths** re-formed the **Big Three** together with **Nigel Olson** (why not **Johnny Hutchinson**?), the former drummer with the **Spencer Davis Group** and **Elton John's** backing group. But the new **Big Three** only recorded the album 'Resurrection' in 1973, from which an EP with the songs *Let It Rock*, *Some Other Guy* and *If You Gotta Make A Fool Of Somebody* was coupled out. The first two numbers also came out as a single for the German market.

On this album, which was more Rock than Beat, the three musicians were supported by **Peter Robinson** (p), **Les Thatcher** (bj), **Henry Lowther** (horns), **Mick Grabham** (g) and **John Smith** (tuba). After that release, the name of the **Big Three** disappeared from the scene with the only exception being a concert for the 'Merseycats' in 1991, but this was a session and did not include **Johnny Hutchinson** or **Johnny Gustafson**.

Johnny Gustafson, who in the Sixties had formed a duo together with **John Banks** of the **Merseybeats** under the name of **Johnny & John** had also, in the meantime, played with **Quartermass, Hard Stuff** and **Roxy Music**. From 1975 until 1978 he occasionally appeared with the **Ian Gillan Band**, before he played with **Rowdy** and the **Rock Band**. Finally, he was a member of the **Pirates**.

Brian Griffiths emigrated to Canada where he still lives, but not playing guitar anymore. For collectors it might be interesting to know that in the mid-Eighties, an album was released on the Edsel label which featured the complete **Big Three** Sixties material.

Discography

Some Other Guy / Let True Love Begin	UK - Decca F.11614 / 1963
By The Way / Cavern Stomp	UK - Decca F.11689 / 1963
I'm With You / Peanut Butter	UK - Decca F.11752 / 1963
If You Ever Change Your Mind /Gotta Keep Her Under Hand	UK - Decca F.11927 / 1964

EP THE BIG THREE LIVE AT THE CAVERN	UK-Decca DFE 8553 / 1964
- What'd I Say / Don't Start Running Away /	
Zip-A-Dee-Doo-Dah / Reelin' And Rockin'	

Songs on compilation albums:

"Bring It On Home To Me (Live) on **At The Cavern**	UK- Decca LK 4597 / 1963

Unreleased tracks:

The original **Cass & the Casanovas** backed **Johnny Gentle** on his demo *After The Laughter Came Tears*, which was recorded during a Scotland tour in 1960.

CILLA BLACK

Liverpool born **Priscilla White** started her singing career in the early Sixties when she appeared with various bands on stage at the 'Cavern', where she was working as a cloakroom girl.

She performed with **Rory Storm & the Hurricanes**, the **Big Three** as well as some others when **Brian Epstein** first became aware of her. He took over her management and led her along the same successful route that the **Beatles** had taken before - a recording contract with EMI with **George Martin** as producer.

Her first record was a **Paul McCartney** song *Love Of The Loved*, which had climbed up the charts to No. 35 by the end of 1963. The follow-up, *Anyone Who Had A Heart*, a **Dionne Warwick** original written by Bacharach/David, became her first chart topper in February 1964. This was the opener for a string of Top 10 positions by 1966 - *You're My World* (No.1), *It's For You* (No. 7), *You've Lost That Loving Feeling* (No.2), *Love's Just A Broken Heart* (No.5), *Alfie* (No.9) and *Don't Answer Me* (No.6). She also had two Top 20 hits with *I've Been Wrong Before* (No.17) and *A Fool Am I* (No.13).

Cilla Black also appeared in the **Gerry & the Pacemakers** film 'Ferry cross the Mersey', where she sang the song *Is It Love*. This was also featured on the UK release of the soundtrack album, as well as on the B-side of her chart success *You've Lost That Loving Feeling*. Though doubtless a big success, **Cilla Black** was never a real Beat singer, in the style of the great **Beryl Marsden**.

Cilla had quite a thin voice and her records were not very exciting, not even the Lennon/McCartney compositions. But her chart success continued until 1971, and included further Top 10 records like *Step Inside Love* (No.8 in 1968), probably her best record *Surround Yourself With Sorrow* (No.3 in 1969), *Conversations* (No.7 in 1969) and *Something Tells Me* (No.3 in 1971).

After the **Beatles** she was the most successful recording act out of **Brian Epstein**'s Liverpool stable. Because she was already more of a family entertainer in the Sixties, it is not too surprising that she later became a TV star with her own shows, which are still quite popular in England.

Discography

Love Of The Loved / Shy Of Love	**UK- Parlophone R 5065 / 1963**
Anyone Who Had A Heart / Just For You	**UK- Parlophone R 5101 / 1964**
You're My World / Suffer Now I Must	**UK- Parlophone R 5133 / 1964**
It's For You / He Won't Ask Me	**UK- Parlophone R 5162 / 1964**
You've Lost That Loving Feeling / Is It Love	**UK- Parlophone R 5225 / 1965**
I've Been Wrong Before / I Don't Want To Know	**UK- Parlophone R 5296 / 1965**
Love's Just A Broken Heart / Yesterday	**UK- Parlophone R 5395 / 1966**
Alfie / Night Time Is Here	**UK- Parlophone R 5427 / 1966**

Don't Answer Me / The Right One Is Left	UK- Parlophone R 5463 / 1966
A Fool Am I / For No One	UK- Parlophone R 5515 / 1966
What Good Am I / Over My Head	UK- Parlophone R 5608 / 1967
I Only Live To Love You / From Now On	UK- Parlophone R 5652 / 1967
Step Inside Love / I Couldn't Take My Eyes Off You	UK- Parlophone R 5674 / 1968
Where Is Tomorrow / Work Is A Four Letter Word	UK- Parlophone R 5706 / 1968
Surround Yourself With Sorrow / London Bridge	UK- Parlophone R 5759 / 1969
Conversation / Liverpool lullaby	UK- Parlophone R 5785 / 1969
If I Thought You'd Ever Change Your Mind / It Feels So Good	UK- Parlophone R 5820 / 1969
Child Of Me / That's Why I Love	UK- Parlophone R 5879 / 1970

EP discography:

ANYONE WHO HAD A HEART   UK- Parlophone GEP 8901 / 1964
- Anyone Who Had A Heart / Just For You / Love Of The Loved / Shy Of Love
IT'S FOR YOU   UK- Parlophone GEP 8916 / 1964
- It's For You / He Won't Ask Me / You're My World / Suffer Now I Must
CILLA'S HITS   UK- Parlophone GEP 8954 / 1966
- Don't Answer Me / The Right One Is Left / Alfie / Night time Is Here
TIME FOR CILLA   UK- Parlophone GEP 8967 / 1967
- Abyssinian Secret / Trees And Loneliness / There I Go / Time

Different French EP:
LOVE'S JUST A BROKEN HEART   F- Odeon MEO 114 / 1966
- Alfie / Love's Just A Broken Heart / Yesterday / Nighttime Is Here

LP discography:

CILLA   UK- Parlophone PMC 1243 / 1965
- Going Out Of My Head / Every Little Bit Hurts / Baby It's You / Dancing In The Street / Come To Me / Ole Man River / One Little Voice / I'm Not Alone Anymore / What'cha Gonna Do 'bout It / Love Letters / This Empty Place / You'd Be So Nice To Come Home To
CILLA SINGS A RAINBOW   UK- Parlophone PCS 7004 / 1966
- Love's Just A Broken Heart / Lover's Concerto / Make It Easy On Yourself / One Two Three / There's No Place To Hide / When I Fall In Love / Yesterday / Sing A Rainbow / Baby I'm Yours / The Real Thing / Everything I Touch Turns To Tears / In A Woman's Eyes / My Love Come Home
SHER-OO   UK- Parlophone PCS 7041 / 1968
- What The World Needs Now Is Love / Suddenly You Love Me / This Is The First Time / Follow The Path Of The Stars / Misty Roses / Take Me In Your Arms And Love Me / Yo Yo / Something's Gotten Hold Of My Heart / Step Inside Love / A Man And A Woman / I Couldn't Take My Eyes Off You / Follow Me
STEP INSIDE LOVE   UK- EMI (MFP) SPR 90019 / 1968
- same as 'Sher-oo'
BEST OF CILLA   UK- Parlophone PCS 7065 / 1968
- Love Of The Loved / Anyone Who Had A Heart / You're My World / You've Lost That Lovin' Feelin' / Love's Just A Broke Heart / Alfie / I Only Live To Love You / What Good Am I / Step Inside Love / Where Is Tomorrow / Sing A Rainbow / It's For You / Yesterday / Goin' Out Of My Head
SURROUND YOURSELF WITH CILLA   UK- Parlophone PCS 7079 / 1969
- Aquarius / Without Him / Only Forever Will Do / You'll Never Get To Heaven / Forget Him / It'll Never Happen Again / Think Of Me / I Am A Woman / Words / Red Rubber Ball / Liverpool Lullaby / Surround Yourself With Sorrow
YOU'RE MY WORLD (12 Big Hits)   UK- Regal Starline SRS 5044 / 1970
- You're My World / If I Thought You'd Ever Change Your Mind / Conversations / Liverpool Lullaby / Surround Yourself With Sorrow / Make It Easy On Yourself / What The World Needs Now Is Love / Don't Answer Me / When I Fall In Love / Every Little Bit Hurts / A Lover's Concerto / Take Me In Your Arms And Love Me

SWEET INSPIRATION   UK- Parlophone PCS 7103 / 1970
  - Sweet Inspiration / Put A Little Love in Your Heart / The April Fools (from film of same name) /
I Can't Go on Living Without You / From Both Sides Now / Across the Universe / Black Paper Roses
/ Mysterious People / Dear Madame / Oh Pleasure Man / Little Pleasure Acre / For Once in My Life
/ Rule Britannia

Different US album:
IS IT LOVE   US - Capitol   ST 2308 / 1966
  - Is It Love / I'm Not Alone Anymore / You've Lost That Lovin' Feelin' / Going Out Of My Head /
Watcha Gonna Do / You'd Be So Nice To Come Home / Love Letters / Ole Man River / Love Is Like A
Heatwave / This Empty Place / Anyone Who Had A Heart

Songs on compilation albums:
Is It Love on   'Ferry cross the Mersey'   UK- Columbia   SX 1693   / 1963

THE BLACK CATS

This band is sometimes named Liverpool's first Rock 'n' Roll group, and it was certainly one of the very important pioneering groups of the big Merseybeat era.

Formed in early 1955, the group played Skiffle music and appeared regularly at the 'Merryfield', at first as **The Black Cats Skiffle Group** and then as **Benny & the Black Cats**. With their electric lead and rhythm guitars, they were one of the first guitar-dominated bands on Merseyside. **The Black Cats** at that time consisted of:

Benny Page	(voc/bg)
Peter Rice	(lg)
Jimmy Lynch	(rg)
Dave Stead	(dr)

In 1957, still as a Skiffle group, they played the 'Cavern' for the first time, together with **Lonnie Donegan**. A little later their sound changed to Rock 'n' Roll and, with **Gerry Stewart,** added a sax player to the line-up.

The **Black Cats** appeared regularly at the legendary 'Jive Hive' in Crosby, and when they played the 'Cavern' for the second time in 1958, not only had their music changed but also their line-up, as **Dave Stead** had been replaced by **Mal Thory** on drums. They became the resident band at the 'Holy Oak Hall'. The **Black Cats** probably were the first Liverpool group to have a TV appearance, even if not playing a main role. They were shown performing in a film made by English Electric in July 1961.

A little later **Jimmy Lynch** left and was replaced by **Alan Stratton** and when shortly after that **Pete Rice** also left, **Jimmy Lynch** returned to the group as lead guitarist. But he left again very soon to join **The Dimensions** and **Dave Moore**, who had formerly played with the **Bobby Bell Rockers** and **Steve Bennett & the Syndicate**, joined.

Gerry Stewart also left to join **The Mastersounds**. He later played with **The Bluesville Bats**, the **Faces** and then with **Just Us**, a group which became very popular on Merseyside in the late Sixties. The new sax player with the **Black Cats** was **Peter Dobson**.

It seems that all these changes within a very short time led to the group splitting in 1962. **Benny Page** became a compere at a Skelmersdale venue before he joined the navy and later performed for the British Forces in Gibraltar with his **Gibraltar Delta Rhythm & Blues Band. Peter Dobson** joined **Alby & the Sorrals**, while **Mal Thory** became the new drummer with **Johnny Templer & the Hi-Cats.**

Alan Stratton joined the **Kansas City Five** who for a while also backed singer **Freddie Fowell**, who later became very famous under the name **Freddie Starr**. After that **Alan Stratton** played with **Johnny Marlowe & the Whip-Chords**, the **Fables** and the **Chesterfields**. In the Nineties he was a member of **Karl Terry & the Cruisers**.

In 1963, the **Black Cats** were re-formed by former members **Peter Rice** and **Dave Stead**, together with **Billy Morris** (voc), **Alan Ashton** (rg) and **Tony Riley** (bg).

This group continued quite successfully on the scene and it is interesting that the **Black**

Cats also played at **Gerry Marsden's** wedding, which shows how popular and appreciated the group was at that time.

Despite their success, the **Black Cats** disbanded totally in 1966 and **Peter Rice,** together with **Billy Morris,** formed the nationally popular Country band **The Saddlers,** while **Alan Ashton** and **Tony Riley** disappeared from the scene. **Dave Stead** joined **Just Us,** where he met up again with **Gerry Stewart**. When this group disbanded, **Gerry Stewart** emigrated to Canada where he still lives in Ontario and publishes the magazine 'Britannia'. **Dave Stead** moved to Scotland, while **Billy Morris** emigrated to Australia after the **Saddlers** split.

Peter Rice played in various local groups until 1982 and in 1989 became a member of the 'Mersey Cats' organisation and arranged that the **Black Cats** appeared one more time in the original line-up at a 'Mersey Cats' event at the 'Grafton Ballroom'. Later on, he occasionally appeared with the **Kansas City Five,** when he stood in for **Peter Cooke** at various 'Mersey Cats' concerts.

The Black Cats

THE BLACKHAWKS

This real Rock 'n' Roll group was formed in 1958 in the Seaforth area of Liverpool and accordingly has to be counted as one of the pioneer groups of the Merseybeat scene.

With one exception for all members it was their first group and the **Blackhawks**, as they were named right from the beginning consisted of the following musicians:

Cliff Webb	**(voc)**
Ken Shalliker	**(lg)**
George Watson	**(rg)**
Bernie Holloway	**(bg/voc)**
Ray Kavanagh	**(dr)**

George Watson was the only one with a bit of experience in the music business as he formerly had already played with the **Sinners** and the **Dominoes**, soon to become **King Size Taylor & the Dominoes**. Within a short time **The Blackhawks** locally became quite popular and played the usual dance circuits, for example Litherland Town Hall, St. Luke's Hall, the 'Iron Door' or Blair Hall. It was probably in late 1960 or early 1961 that the group went into the studio

of P.F. Phillips in Kensington and cut a complete album on acetate, which amongst others included songs like *Move It, I Don't Want No Other Baby But You, Wild Cat* and *Way Down Yonder In New Orleans.* An interesting piece of history but of course in those days it did not help along the **Blackhawks** career. Probably the first to be replaced was **Ray Kavanagh**, whose place was taken by **Rod Hughes** and when **Cliff Webb** left, the new singer became **Jeff Price**. It is not known if the new members had played or sung in other groups before.

At the end of 1961 **Ken Shalliker** left also and he became a member of **King Size Taylor & the Dominoes**, with whom he also went over to Hamburg. He did not stay too long with them and went on to play with **Deke Rivers & the Big Sound** from Manchester but later returned to the Liverpool scene and formed the Country group **The Foggy Mountain Ramblers**, with whom he recorded the Unicord single *Lovin' Lady's Man,* which by the way was written by **Ken Shalliker**. When he left the **Blackhawks**, the group continued on the scene for a while with **George Watson** taking over the lead guitar but disbanded totally in 1963. None of the members later appeared again from which could be concluded that they all quit the music business.

<u>Discography :</u>
Little Queenie / Move It / Whole Lotta Shakin' Goin' On / Johnny B. Goode / I Don't Want No Other Baby But You / Bad Boy / Wild Cat / Way Down Yonder In New Orleans

UK- Kensington acetate-album / 1961

<u>The Foggy Mountain Ramblers</u> (featuring <u>Ken Shalliker</u>) :

Lovin' Lady's Man / Tomorrow   **UK- Unicord   UP 664 / 1964**

THE BLACK KNIGHTS

This trio was formed in Liverpool in 1962 and were indistinguishable from most of the other groups, although they were musically good and had a rough sound that was admired at that time. They were a semi-professional group and well established on the scene because of their numerous appearances in Liverpool and its surrounding area.

In the early days, drummer **Cliff 'Taffy' Jones** was with the group, but he left to join **The Tempos** and after that nothing was heard of him again. In 1963 the line-up of the **Black Knights** consisted of:

Bill Kenny	**(voc/bg)**
Kenny Griffiths	**(g/voc)**
Alan Schroeder	**(dr/voc)**

Bill Kenny was a former member of the **Classics**, where also **Kenny Griffiths** had played for a short time, while drummer **Alan Schroeder** came from **Cliff Roberts' Rockers**, one of the important pioneer groups of the Liverpool scene.

In 1964, the **Black Knights** were paid the attention they deserved when they were chosen to appear in the film 'Ferry Cross The Mersey'. They were featured with their own composition *I Gotta Woman*, which can also be found on the US release of the soundtrack album. This song also came out as a single on the Columbia label, and it was coupled with another original track by the group - a really great number with a strong Rhythm & Blues influence called *Angel Of Love*.

In retrospect, this single makes it clear that the **Black Knights** were underrated all the time. This record was not a great success and so the band made no significant breakthrough, but in Summer 1965 they went over to Hamburg for a six week engagement at the 'Star Club'.

After their return **Alan Schroeder** left disillusioned. He was 22 and did not want to play for teenies anymore. But he continued in the music scene as a freelancing drummer for the agency of **Dave Forshaw** and at some point joined another band called **Admiral Street**, but only for a few months.

It is not known whether the **Black Knights** tried to continue with another drummer or broke up right away. What is certain is that they did not stay together for too long afterwards.

Bill Kenny and Kenny Griffiths obviously then quit show business and disappeared from the scene. Of **Bill Kenny** it is known that he later moved down to Swansea and there became a member of the internationally successful **Morriston Phoenix Choir. Kenny Griffiths** sadly died at the end of 2003 from cancer. **Alan Schroeder** returned to the group scene at the beginning of the Nineties via the 'Merseycats' organisation as a member of **Johnny Sandon & the Specials**. After **Johnny Sandon** had left they continued as the **Mersey Specials** but split up totally in 1995.

After that **Alan Schroeder** re-formed the **Black Knights** with other musicians, mainly Merseybeat veterans from the Sixties, who are still playing quite regularly but mainly for the 'Merseycats' or one of the related organisations.

Discography
I Gotta Woman / Angel Of Love   **UK - Columbia   DV 7443 / 1964**

Songs on compilation-albums:
I Gotta Woman   on 'Ferry Cross The Mersey'   **US-United Artists UAS 6387 / 1964**
I Gotta Woman   on 'Liverpool Hop'   **G - Columbia   SMC 83983 / 1964**

Unreleased tracks:
The **Black Knights** recorded one more original with the title '*That Feeling*' for the film Ferry Cross The Mersey, which sadly stayed unreleased.

THE BLACKWELLS

This band was formed in Liverpool in 1962. As a distinguishing mark, all the members dyed their hair blonde, earning them the nickname of the 'Blonde Bombshells'. Of course this little trick was good for publicity and won many female fans' hearts. Thus, they quickly became very popular on the scene and so the musicians were able to turn professional.

At that time the **Blackwells** consisted of the following musicians:

Alby Cook	**(voc/rg)**
Tex McDermott	**(lg/voc)**
Dave Trimnell	**(bg/voc)**
Roy Little	**(dr)**

Dave Trimnell, who was the only one with naturally blonde hair, and **Roy Little,** were former members of an amateur group named **The Ravens**, which may have had connections to **Faron's Flamingos** predecessor.

In 1964 the **Blackwells** were chosen to take part in the **Gerry & the Pacemakers** music film 'Ferry Cross The Mersey' which, of course, helped to increase their popularity. Their film song *Why Don't You Love Me* was a great Beat tune in the typical Mersey Sound and was featured on the US release of the soundtrack album. Columbia released this song on single, coupled with *All I Want Is Your Love*, which had the same quality as the A-side. Unfortunately, it had no great success and so it was their first and last recording at the same time.

In January 1965, **Alby Cook**, whose real name was **Alby Gornall**, left the group and disappeared from the scene. He was replaced by **Jimmy McManus**, a former member of **Bob Evans & the Five Shillings**, the **Vegas Five**, the **Undertakers** and the **Renegades** from Liverpool.

In May 1965 **Roy Little** is said to have joined the **Flower Pot Men**, but this is doubtful as at this time the **Ivy League** still existed and only later became the **Flower Pot Men.** Maybe there was another group with the same name around at that time that might have been a predecessor of the later group, led by **John Carter** and **Ken Lewis**. There was a drummer called Little in a later line-up of the **Flower Pot Men**, but this was **Carlo Little**, who hailed from the London scene.

However, the departure of **Roy Little** probably led to the **Blackwells** splitting up, as after that nothing more was heard of the group, nor of the individual musicians. The only exception was **Tex McDermott**, who later appeared again on the scene as a studio musician. What remains of the **Blackwells** is a good name and a very good and interesting record, worth seeking out.

Discography

Why Don't You Love Me / All I Want Is Your Love	**UK - Columbia**	**DB 7442** /
Songs on compilation albums:		
Why Don't You Love Me on 'Ferry Cross The Mersey'	**US-United Artists**	**UAS 6387 / 1964**
Why Don't You Love Me on 'Liverpool Hop'	**G - Columbia**	**SMC 83983 / 1964**

THE BLUE CHIPS

The story of this group starts in 1961, when **Adam & the Sinners** were formed in Ormskirk by **Bill Pye** (voc), **Jim Fox** (lg), **Phil Graham** (rg), **John Cheetham** (bg) and **Brian Anderton** (dr), who by the way is a cousin of **Paddy Chambers**.

Adam & the Sinners played a lot in their hometown and the local Liverpool area. In 1963 **Bill Worthington**, who owned some local restaurants and coffee bars, took over the management and invested quite a lot of money in the group.

At the end of 1963, **Phil Graham** and **Bill Pye** left the band and probably quit show business. When **John Cheetham** also left a little later, the group changed their name to **The Fortunes** and were made up of the remaining original members **Jim Fox** (lg/voc) and **Brian Anderton** (dr), as well as of **Arthur Hughes** (rg/voc), **Ken Renfry** (bg) and **Dennis Pickering** (voc). But the group could not keep the name as there was already a recording group with the same name - the fabulous **Fortunes** from Birmingham.

Bill Worthington suggested using the name **The Blue Chips** and the musicians agreed. Around that time, **Dennis Pickering** and **Ken Renfry** left and were replaced by **Lenny Chantry** (org) and the returning **John Cheetham**. So, the **Blue Chips** in 1964 appeared with the following line-up:

Jim Fox	(lg/voc)
Arthur Hughes	(rg/voc)
John Cheetham	(bg/voc)
Lenny Chantry	(org/voc)
Brian Anderton	(dr)

There was no real lead singer anymore and so all the members shared the vocals.

The **Blue Chips**, whose music was a sort of Beat influenced by Soul and Rhythm & Blues, mainly played at the legendary 'Orrel Park Ballroom' and the 'Macca Dancehalls', owned by the 'Top Rank' organisation. They also played a lot of venues in Leeds and Sheffield, but did not appear too often in the Beat metropolis Liverpool at that time.

In 1965, PYE became aware of the **Blue Chips** and signed them. The band went down to London for a recording session in 1965 and recorded between 15 and 20 of their own numbers. But this was without **Lenny Chantry** who had left again and was not replaced in the group. Maybe that **Lenny Chantry** is the same '**Silver**' **Chantry**, who later appeared in **The Shuffler's Sound**, but this is not certain.

However, in 1965 the first **Blue Chips** single was released with the songs *I'm On The Right Side / You're Good To Me*, but this record was not too successful and did not help the band make a bigger breakthrough. Despite this PYE decided to release some more of their songs, and in 1966 two more singles were released - *Some Kind Of Lovin'* and *Tell Her*. Like their debut, these good Beat records didn't achieve any bigger success. But the **Blue Chips** continued on the scene as the musicians were semi-professionals and the group was very busy on the club circuit until the end of 1967.

Then the good times for live bands came to an end and the **Blue Chips** disbanded. As far as it is known, **John Cheetham** later had a short spell with the **Nashville Teens**, while **Jim Fox** worked as a freelancing guitarist for a time. **Brian Anderton** moved up to Carlisle where he later became involved into the local Folk scene.

Jim Fox emigrated to Canada in 1970, but returned to Merseyside in 1976. He didn't join any group thereafter, and none of the former members of the **Blue Chips** appeared on the scene again.

Discography

I'm On The Right Side / You're Good To Me	**UK- PYE 7N 15970 / 1965**
Some Kind Of Lovin' / I Know A Boy	**UK- PYE 7N 17111 / 1966**
Tell Her / Good Lovin' Never Hurts	**UK- PYE 7N 17155 / 1966**

Unreleased tracks:

In early 1965 the **Blue Chips** recorded around 15 numbers for PYE, only six of which were released. The others, around 10 originals with unknown titles, are probably still in the PYE archives in London.

The Blue Chips

BILLY BUTLER & THE TUXEDOS

This group was originally formed in 1959 in Liverpool as a vocal/guitar trio under the name **Terry & the Tuxedos**, by **Les 'Terry' Williams**, **Alan Crowley** and **Johnny O'Brian**. A little later, **Dennis Swale** joined as bass guitarist, but the group disbanded again in the early Sixties.

Dennis Swale joined the **Groupiers** and later played with various Merseybeat groups, while **Alan Crowley** and singer **Billy Butler** formed a new group called **The Cherrypickers**. **Les Williams** and **Johnny O'Brian** later replaced leaving members of the group. As the original line-up of **Terry & the Tuxedos** was together again, the new group changed its name to **Billy Butler & the Tuxedos** and the line-up consisted of :

Billy Butler	**(voc)**
Les Williams	**(lg/voc)**
John O'Brian	**(rg)**
Alan Crowley	**(bg)**
Ronnie Myers	**(dr)**

Billy Butler had appeared sporadically as a guest vocalist with the **Merseybeats**, as well as with other Liverpool groups but never became a steady member in any of them.

In February 1963 **Billy Butler** recorded the single *I Reckon You*, with songstress **Polly Perkins** who sang the B-side alone, but this record did not sell too well. **The Tuxedos**, for unknown reasons, were not featured on this single.

Billy Butler & the Tuxedos never made a breakthrough but had a large following on Merseyside and did very well on the music scene until **Billy Butler** left in December 1964. He became a popular disc-jockey, at first at various Liverpool venues and then with 'Radio Merseyside'. After he left the **Tuxedos** they split up. **Les Williams** joined **Group One** for a short time and then became a member of the **Four Dimensions**, also named **Tiffany's Dimensions**, who later recorded as **The Dimensions**.

Until the early Nineties, he was with the cabaret trio **Pendulum**, a very busy act on the Liverpool circuit. These days he is a member of the re-formed **Mojos** who mainly play for the 'Merseycats'. Of the others, only **Alan Crowley** appeared again on the scene, but more as a songwriter than as musician. For example, he wrote *You Don't Have To Whisper,* the B-side of the **Dimensions** single *Tears On My Pillow* and with **Billy Kinsley** of the **Merseybeats** he co-wrote the songs *Is It Love* and *I Hope You're Happy*, both of which were

Terry & The Tuxedos

released on single by **The Merseys** in 1967 and 1968 respectively.

In 1970 the former **Cryin' Shames** vocalist **Charlie Crane** recorded the **Alan Crowley** number *Come Day, Go Day Man* on a single. His biggest success as songwriter was in 1989 when a complete album was released which, without exception, consisted of numbers written by **Alan Crowley** and **Frank O'Connor**, a member of the **Hideaways** and **Confucius** in the Sixties.

The album, titled 'The Class Of '64' on the Holly label, besides Alan and Frank, featured various well-known Merseybeat musicians like **Tony Crane** and **Billy Kinsley (Merseybeats)**, **Mike Pender (Searchers)**, **Kenny Parry (Liverpool Express)**, **Ozzie Yue (Hideaways)**, as well as **Johnny O'Brian** and **Billy Butler** again. Thus, three of the original group of **Billy Butler & the Tuxedos** recorded together for the first time.

It's an interesting album which clearly shows the song-writing talent of **Alan Crowley** and **Frank O'Connor**. From 1971 until 1974, **Alan Crowley** and **Frank O'Connor** teamed up in the cabaret duo **Two's Company**. In 1992, **Billy Butler & the Tuxedos** made one more appearance at a 'Merseycats' event, but this of course was an exception.

Discography:

'Billy Butler & Polly Perkins':
I Reckon You / The Girls Are At It Again   UK- Decca F.11583 / 1963

Billy Butler & the Tuxedos never released a record and nothing is known about demos or test recordings. **Billy Butler**, **Alan Crowley** and **Johnny O'Brian** recorded together for the first time in 1989 on the album 'Class Of '64'. Interestingly, **Billy Butler** released a single on the 'Radio Merseyside' label in 1975, on which he was backed by **Kenny Johnson & Northwind**. The songs *There Will Never Be Anyone Else But You* and *Little Helpers* were recorded at a live performance.

THEM CALDERSTONES

This group was formed as a four-piece in Liverpool in 1964 and accepted a **Bob Wooler** suggestion to call themselves **Them Calderstones**, after the well-known stone monument close to their home area.

Them Calderstones soon became a busy band in the Merseybeat scene, playing a sort of Beat and Rhythm & Blues. As soon as 1964, the drummer **Alan Moss** left to join the **Elektrons**, and a little later **Phil Inksip** quit the music business for unknown reasons.

In early 1965 **Them Calderstones** consisted of the following musicians:

Tom Evans	(voc/lg)
Jeffrey Edmondson	(org/voc)
Norman Bellis	(bg/voc)
Billy Gillaher	(dr)

Tom Evans and **Norman Bellis** were the remaining original founder members of the group, whereby **Norman Bellis** had played with **The Cordays** before and **Billy Gillaher** came from the **Modes**.

In 1965 the **Calderstones** recorded a Unicord acetate as a demo with the songs *Don't You Believe It* and *What'cha Gonna Do About It.* At the end of that year, **Charlie McBain**, who hired out sound equipment to bands and clubs (including the early 'Cavern'), took over the group's management. Thus, he had very good contacts with the scene's promoters, which of course was advantageous for the band.

In early 1966, **Johnny Hutchinson** of the **Big Three** replaced **Billy Gillaher** for a few months on drums but quit when the old drummer returned to the **Calderstones**.

With his connections to Decca, **Johnny Hutchinson** managed to get a recording session for the **Calderstones**. They recorded the song *Children And Flowers* as a demo, which was meant to be released on a compilation album, but sadly this did not happen in the end, although it was a nice melodic song and very well recorded. So, the **Calderstones** didn't achieve the national breakthrough they hoped for and this might have been one reason for the group disbanding in 1967.

Tom Evans then was a founder member of the **Iveys**, who later became **Badfinger**, and found international stardom with hit records like *Come And Get It, Day After Day* and *Baby Blue.* He sadly died very young in the Eighties.

Jeff Edmondson joined **Bernie & the Buzz Band**, led by **Bernie Wenton** and played a sort of **Temptations/Drifters** type of music. After that he disappeared from the scene. **Billy Gillaher** became a member of **Curiosity Shoppe** and **Norman Bellis** joined the **Seftons**, who changed their name to **The Perishers** and went down to London.

In 1969 **Norman Bellis** emigrated to the USA, where he played sessions with well-known artists such as **The Temptations**, **Jr. Walker & the All Stars** and the **Walker Brothers**. After nine months, he returned to London and re-formed **The Perishers** under the name of **Worth**, after he playing for a short time with the band **Rusty Harness**. **Worth** later changed their name to **Tiger** and became a real Hardrock band. When this group split, **Norman Bellis** returned to Liverpool and in the Seventies was a member of **Perfumed Garden**. After that he stayed in the music business as a producer and today he runs his own recording studio in Devonshire.

Discography

Don't You Believe Me / What'cha Gonna Do About It	**Unicord-acetate**	**/ 1965**
Children And Flowers / Children And Flowers	**Decca - demo (acetate)**	**/ 1966**

CAROL & THE MEMORIES

The beginning of this group's story is a little bit intricate, but it seems the **Five Aces** were formed in Aintree in about 1963/64. Although obviously a good group, they only played local gigs and that was it.

This unsatisfactory situation began to change when their Burnley based management offered the group the chance to play the US bases in France. Sometime at the end of 1964, the **Five Aces** travelled to the continent to entertain the American soldiers. They went down quite well and were invited to tour the US airbases in Germany, but only on the condition that they included a girl singer in their line-up. This most probably led to their original singer leaving in 1965, and the then unknown **Carol Whitfield** was introduced to them as new vocalist and accordingly, the group went to Germany in a line-up with:

Carol Whitfield	**(voc)**
Jimmy Chadwick	**(lg/voc)**
Steven Harvey	**(rg/voc)**
Kenny Harvey	**(bg/voc)**
Billy Bryden	**(dr)**

In Germany they played mainly in the Darmstadt and Aschaffenburg areas, close to Frankfurt. As the group went down well with their new girl singer, they stayed together after their return to Liverpool. Very soon, their Burnley management got CBS interested in signing the group, but the record company insisted on a name change because of an American group with the name **Four Aces**. CBS at first suggested **Margaret & the Memories**, but as **Carol Whitfield** insisted on her name being used, in the end the group became **Carol & the Memories**.

In 1966 they went to London and recorded the single *Tears On My Pillow* – a great song they did a good job on. The b-side, *Crying My Byes Out* was written by **Johnny Stewart**, part of the **Kingston Trio**.

CBS wanted publicity for the group and the record and tried to create a story about a love affair between Carol and **Scott Engel** of the **Walker Brothers.** They did in fact meet once at a dinner CBS arranged for the two in London, to which of course the press were also invited. The only problem was that the two main protagonists didn't like each other very much and so only one big article was published in a London newspaper and that was the end of that story.

Nothing is known about the sales figures of the record but it obviously didn't become a big seller and wasn't followed by any further releases. They returned to Liverpool where they then played the big clubs like the 'Cavern', the 'Iron Door' or the 'Mardi Gras'. They also appeared in the Manchester area.

In 1967 the management took **Carol Whitfield** out of the group as they wanted her to become a solo act on the cabaret circuit. The group continued as **The Memories** on the Merseyside scene but did not make the headlines anymore and one day simply faded away.

Unfortunately it is not known what happened to the individual members after that. **Carol Whitfield** tried to go solo after the separation but did not like it and very soon joined a Country & Western band from Ellesmere Port called **The Renos,** with whom she sang for two years. In 1969 she joined **The Image**, where she met her future husband **Jeff Loftus.** She formed the group **Carousel** with him in the mid-Seventies and finally, both became members of a group called **Miller's Bridge**.

Today she sometimes appears at 'Merseycats' events, where she proves she is still a great singer. With her husband she also got another group together, originally called **Smoky Joe Band** but occasionally they also appear as **Carol & the Memories**.

Discography

Tears On My Pillow / Crying My Eyes Out   CBS 202 086 / 1966

Carol presenting her single
to the Lord Mayor

THE CARROLLS

This is the story of a group that was obviously more a part of Liverpool's cabaret circuit than of the real Merseybeat scene, but there is a special reason for including them here. **Irene Carroll** started to sing in the early Sixties and it could have been her, when on 4th November 1960 a group with the name of **Irene & the Santa Fe's** had an appearance at the 'Cavern'.

After winning a contest, she became the resident singer at the 'Rialto Ballroom' for a time. There she was backed by a local group during her performances, which could have been the **Tall Boys**, as around that time there was a group appearing as **Irene & the Tall Boys**, who later continued with a certain **Jenny Ellison** as vocalist under the name of **Jenny & the Tall Boys**.

Up to here these connections with the groups are just suppositions, whereby it is known for a fact that **Irene Carroll** for some time appeared with the **Invaders**, better known on the scene as **Liam & the Invaders**.

In late 1964 or early 1965; **Irene Carroll** formed a duo with her younger brother **Michael Carroll**, who was most probably the musician of the same name who was a member of the **Stormers** until 1964, who had also backed girl singer **Jacki Martin** for a time. A little later the two other brothers joined forces with them and so the **Carrolls** were born with:

Irene Carroll	**(voc)**
Michael Carroll	**(voc/g)**
Ronnie Carroll	**(voc/g)**
Leslie Carroll	**(voc/g)**

As all four members obviously concentrated on singing, they of course needed a backing group for their live appearances. Nothing is definitely known about the group, but it is a possibility that **Len Wady** was on bass guitar, and he later had a big role in **Irene Carroll**'s life.

ELECTRECORD

Surprisingly, in 1966 a 10-inch album by the **Carrolls** was released in Romania on the Electrecord label. This eight-track album, which had standards like *Hey, Good Looking, Mister Postman* and *Sweet Talking Guy* also included the **Beatles** numbers *This Boy* and *Gonna Loose That Girl*. The backing group on that record was named as **The Guys** and so there could have been some connection to the Liverpool group **Gay & the Guys**, but this is not proven. It is this album that places the **Carrolls** close to the Merseybeat scene, although it clearly was one of the softer groups, with quite a harmless Beat.

Most probably, the **Carrolls** recorded the tracks in England for an independent producer, who secretly sold them to the Romanian label. The songs *Hey, Good Looking, Mr. Postman* and the two **Beatles** numbers featured the lead vocals of **Michael Carroll** and from his singing it can be concluded that his musical roots were in the Merseybeat. All the other tracks were sung by **Irene Carroll**, who proved that she was a good singer but did not have too much in common with Rock 'n' Roll. On 23rd July 1966 the **Carrolls** played the re-opening concert of the 'Cavern', which also shows that it could not have been a purecabaret band.

In 1967 the **Carrolls** had their first single out in England on the obscure BM label with the songs *Surrender Your Love* and *The Folk I Love*, which were also featured on the above mentioned album and really didn't call to mind the Merseybeat sound.

CBS signed the group in 1968 and in the same year the singles *So Gently Falls The Rain, Ever Since* and *A Lemon Balloon And A Blue Sky* were released. *Ever Since*, coupled with *Come On* seems to be the most interesting one, but in the end had no greater success than its predecessors or *We're In This Together* from 1969, which was the final release of the **Carrolls** that probably disbanded at that time.

Only **Irene Carroll** continued in professional showbusiness, when she became **Faith Brown** – a first-class impressionist and entertainer with her own TV shows, an actress and also one of the biggest comedy stars in England. In spite of this, she continued to sing and later appeared again with a group under the name of **Faith Brown & the Shades** in a line-up with:

Faith Brown	**(voc)**
Barry 'Baz' Davis	**(lg)**
Len Wady	**(bg)**
Pete Saunders	**(dr)**

Barry Davis, an excellent guitarist, came from the Beat scene as a former member of the **Wild Harks**, the **Connoisseurs**, **King Size Taylor's** new band and the German group **Mike Warner & his New Stars** from Bielefeld. The above mentioned line-up was often joined by the resident keyboarders of the clubs in which **Faith Brown & the Shades** performed. It is not known if **Faith Brown's** final CBS release *The Game Of Love* or *Anyway That You Want Me* on the Pen label (both from 1970) were recorded with the group or were just solo records with studio backing.In 1972 she switched to PYE, where she released four more singles until 1975, none of which became too successful.

In the meantime, **Faith Brown** had got married to **Len Wady**, who was then her husband, bass player and manager. In the end it can be said that none of the **Carrolls** or **Faith Brown & the Shades** recordings got any closer to the Merseybeat than the Romanian album, which is certainly a very interesting collector's item today.

Discography:

as **The Carrolls**:

Surrender Your Love / The Folk I Love	UK – BM	56081	/ 1967
So Gently Falls The Rain / Nice To See You Darling	UK – CBS	3414	/ 1968
Ever Since / Come On	UK – CBS	3750	/ 1968
A Lemon Balloon And A Blue Sky / Make Me Belong To You	UK – CBS	3875	/ 1968
We're In This Together / We Know Better	UK – CBS	4401	/ 1969

LP **THE CARROLLS**   ROM – Electrecord EDD 1150 / 1966
 - Surrender Your Love / Hey, Good Looking / No Regrets / Mr. Postman / Sweet Talking Guy / This Boy / Gonna Loose That Girl / The Folk I Love

Faith Brown – solo:

Lock Me In / The Game Of Love	UK- CBS	4724	/ 1970
Any Way That You Want Me / City Wine	UK- Pen	766	/ 1970

HOWIE CASEY & THE SENIORS

At first there were the **Hy-Tones**, sometimes spelt as **Huy-Tones** as they came from Huyton, where they were formed in 1958. The original line-up most probably consisted of **Billy Hughes** (bg/voc), **Jim O'Connor** (rg/voc), **Stan Johnson** (lg), **Stan Foster** (p) and **Derek Gill** (dr).

The Hy-Tones

The drummer left and was replaced by **Jeff Wallington** and a little later also **Jim O'Connor** was replaced by **Phil Whitehead** (bg/voc), while **Billy Hughes** switched to rhythm guitar. **Jim O'Connor**, by the way a step-brother of **Stan Foster**, quit showbiz for many years and only in 2001 was back on the scene, when he occasionally sang with various groups at 'Merseycats'-events. The group was also joined by singer **Jimmy 'Ginger' Geary** and a little later by sax player **Howie Casey**.

Stan Johnson also left the group, which was then joined by **Brian Griffiths**, and when the singer left again to become **Rip Van Winkle** of **Rip Van Winkle & The Rip-It-Ups**, he was replaced by coloured singer **Derry Wilkie** and the group's name was changed to **Derry & The Seniors** at the end of 1959.

The group soon became very popular on the Northern scene with their **Little Richard** and **Ray Charles** inspired Rock 'n' Roll. They also made repeated appearances at the famous '2 Is' coffee bar in London, where they met German promoter **Bruno Koschmieder**. So **Derry & The Seniors** became the first group from Liverpool to play in Hamburg at the legendary Kaiserkeller in summer 1960.

After their return to Liverpool, their equipment was destroyed when the 'Top Ten' club in Liverpool burned down. This fact probably led to **Billy Hughes**, **Jeff Wallington** and **Stan Foster** leaving. Seen in retrospect, this fire disaster led to the birth of a local super group of Liverpool's Sixties' scene, under the name **Howie Casey & the Seniors** in a line-up with:

Derry Wilkie	**(voc)**
Freddie Fowell	**(voc)**
Brian Griffiths	**(lg/voc)**
Howie Casey	**(sax)**
Phil Whitehead	**(bg)**
Frank Wibberley	**(dr)**

The group's name had been changed because with **Freddie Fowell**, a second lead singer was added to the group's line-up. As **'Freddie the Teddy'**, he had formerly been backed by various groups such as the **Five Stars**. **Frank Wibberley**, a fantastic drummer, had formerly played with the **Four Aces** and the **Rhythm Rockers**.

Howie Casey & the Seniors became the first recording group on Merseyside when the album 'Twist at the Top' was released on Fontana in 1962. From that album the single *True Fine Mama / Double Twist* was coupled out. Further singles were *I Ain't Mad At You* (1962) and **Brook Benton**'s *Boll Weevil Song* (1963).

In 1965 their album was reissued under the title 'Let's Twist' on the Wing label, and for this release the name was changed slightly, to **Wailin' Howie Casey & the Seniors**. The group did not actually exist anymore at that time. Short after recording the original album, **Phil Whitehead** had left to join the **Vigilantes** and then the **Aristocrats**. For a short time he was replaced by **Lu Walters**, who came from **Rory Storm & the Hurricanes** but then he returned to his old group.

In the meantime he had recorded the songs *Gone Gone Gone* and *Nashville Blues* with **Howie Casey & the Seniors**. But these songs, where he was featured as lead vocalist, were sadly never released. His replacement in **Howie Casey & the Seniors** was **Frank Bowen**, formerly of the **Teenbeats**, **Cliff Roberts' Rockers**, the **Blue Stars** from Glasgow and the **Lonely Ones**. But **Howie Casey & the Seniors** only continued together till the middle of 1962 and then disbanded totally.

Derry Wilkie & Freddie Starr

The coloured singer **Derry Wilkie**, whose real name was **Derek Davis,** at first appeared together with **Geoff Stacey & the Wanderers**, but then amalgamated with the **Pressmen** under the name of **Derry Wilkie & the Pressmen**. But this is another story in this book. After that, the tall show star archetype joined the **Others** - of course under the name of **Derry Wilkie & the Others** and after that he disappeared from the scene for years.

In 1980 he appeared again at the re-opening of the 'Star-Club' in Hamburg and can also be found on a corresponding live sampler. Besides this, he toured for a short time with **Screaming Lord Sutch** in Germany, but then returned to Liverpool and, it is said, looked for the right backing group, until he sadly died on 22nd December 2001.

Freddie Fowell teamed up with the **Kansas City Five** but then changed his name into **Freddie Starr** and appeared with groups like **Freddie Starr & the Ventures**, **Freddie Starr & the Midnighters**, **Freddie Starr & the Starr Boys** (the former **Pressmen**) and **Freddie Starr & the Delmonts**, before he started a very successful solo career as an actor and entertainer. He is still a popular TV star these days and sporadically releasing records.

Howie Casey first went to Hamburg as a session musician and played with **Tony Sheridan & the Beat Brothers** amongst others, before he became a member of **King Size Taylor & the Dominoes**.

After that he joined the **Pawns** for a short time and then played with the **Krewkats**. Back in Liverpool he had short spells with the **Big Three** and the **Griff Parry Five,** but then he re-formed the **Krew.** He was later a member of the **Roy Young Band** and **Rigor Mortis**.

These days, he is still a successful session and studio musician and has appeared on lots of records by well-known artists, for example **Paul McCartney** and the **Hollies**. He also still leads his own group – the **Howie Casey Band**.

Derry & The Seniors

Brian Griffiths, undoubtedly one of the most talented guitarists from Merseyside, became a member of the **Big Three** and after that he formed a trio under the name of **The Seniors**, together with **Johnny Gustafson**, a former member of **Cass & the Casanovas** and **The Big Three** which also included **Ian Broad**, the former drummer of **The Five Stars**, **Gus Travis & the Midnighters** and **Freddie Starr & the Midnighters**. But this band was short-lived and broke up again after a German tour.

Brian Griffiths was then one of the founder members of the **Griff Parry Five** before he joined **The Johnny Gus Set**. After that he disappeared from the scene and later emigrated to Canada. In 1973 he was a member of the newly-formed **Big Three** that recorded the album 'Resurrection', but after that he returned to Canada where he is still living.

Frank Bowen became the lead guitarist of **Lee Curtis & the All Stars**, then played with the **Pathfinders**, for a short time with **Rory Storm & the Hurricanes** and after that with **Mike & the Merseymen**, who changed their name into **The Trends** and went down to London. After a spell with the **Bootleggers** from London he returned to Liverpool in 1965 and became a member of **Earl Royce & the Olympics**. He died at a very young age in 1966.

Frank Wibberley joined the **Lee Eddie Five** and after that played with **Emile Ford & the Checkmates**.

Discography

Double Twist / True Fine Mama	**UK- Fontana H 364 / 1962**
I Ain't Mad At You / Twist At The Top	**UK- Fontana H 381 / 1962**
Boll Weevil Song / Bony Moronie	**UK- Fontana TF 403 / 1963**

LP TWIST AT THE TOP   **UK-Fontana TFL 5180 / 1962**
- **Double Twist / The Fly / Yes Indeed / Bony Moronie / Taki Blues / Hey, Hey, Hey, Hey / The Boll Weevil Song / Big Daddy / True Fine Mama / Bone Shakin' Annie / Say / Let's Twist Again**
   (this album was re-released in 1965 on the Wing label - WL 1022 - in England)

Unreleased tracks :
Howie Casey & the Seniors recorded the songs *Gone Gone Gone* and *Nashville Blues* with **Lu Walters** as lead vocalist in 1962, which were sadly never released.

CASS & THE CASANOVAS

They were one of the very first Rock 'n' Roll groups in Liverpool, if not the first one. Like lots of other very good groups in the first wave they had their big time prior to the boom and that is why there were no records released by **Cass & the Casanovas**.

In their early days they recorded the demo *After My Laughter Came Tears* with singer **Johnny Gentle** during a tour in Scotland. They only played the clubs and venues in Liverpool and its surrounding area, where their quality ensured they had a large following. In their original line-up, **Cass & the Casanovas** consisted of:

Brian 'Cass' Cassar	**(voc)**
Adrian Barber	**(lg)**
Johnny Gustafson	**(bg/voc)**
Johnny Hutchinson	**(dr)**

Brian 'Cass' Cassar left the group as early as 1962. From that moment on they were called **The Big Three** and became one of Liverpool's great Merseybeat legends, but the group's story can be followed under **The Big Three**.

Brian Cassar initially went down to London in search for international stardom as **Casey Jones**. There, he formed a new group under the name **Casey Jones & his Engineers**, which at first consisted of **Casey Jones** (voc), **Eric Clapton** (lg), **Tom McGuinness** (bg) and **Ray Stock** (dr). **Eric Clapton** and **Tom McGuinness** were former members of the **Roosters**.

Ray Stock then was replaced by **Cozy Powell**, who previously had played with **Pat Wayne & the Beachcombers** from Birmingham, amongst others. Seen in retrospect, this was something like an early super group, but disbanded again very soon for unknown reasons.

Eric Clapton became a member of the **Yardbirds** and later played with the **Greek Loone Band, John Mayall's Bluesbreakers, Cream, Blind Faith, Delany, Bonnie & Friends** and **Derek & the Dominoes** before he formed his own successful group and became an international superstar.

Tom McGuinness joined **Manfred Mann**, and after that he formed **McGuinness Flint** and then was a member of the **Blues Band**. Today he is back with the original **Manfred Mann** group who, for legal reasons, appear under the name of the **Manfreds**.

Cozy Powell later became a member of **Ace Kefford Stand** and after that played with **Big Bertha**, the **Jeff Beck Group, Cozy Powell's Hammer, Strange Brew, Ritchie Blackmore's Rainbow** and the **Michael Schenker Group**.

Casey Jones amalgamated with the **Midnights** from Bristol, who also adopted the name **Casey Jones & his Engineers** - in a line-up with:

Casey Jones	**(voc)**
Dave Coleman	**(lg/voc)**
Roger Hook	**(rg)**
Jim Redford	**(bg)**
Peter Richards	**(dr)**

In 1963 this group recorded the single *One Way Ticket* for the Columbia label, which sadly didn't have much success, although it was a really good driving Beat number. **Casey Jones & his Engineers** then emigrated to Germany where they settled in Hamburg for years and became a famous part of the 'Star-Club' scene. They were signed by Bellaphon and released the singles *Tall Girl* and *Don't Ha Ha,* which sold quite well. After these recordings, the band changed their name to **Casey Jones & the Governors** and were signed by 'Golden 12'.

Casey Jones & The Governors

With lots of hits like *Jack The Ripper*, their new release of *Don't Ha Ha*, an adaptation of **Screaming Lord Sutch's** *Don't you just know it, Yockomo, Little Girl* and *Come On And Dance*, the band continually stepped back into the limelight. The re-recorded *Don't Ha Ha* was their biggest success and became something of an evergreen of the Beat age in Germany. In the meantime, the band had been joined by sax-player **Phil Cantley**.

In 1967 **Casey Jones** left the group, which continued under the name of **The Gaslight Union** and released some more singles on the German Columbia and Cornet labels, for example *Silly Miss Lilly Pfefferkorn, Stupid Party* or *Do The Kasaboo* (the last one under the name of **Phil Cantley & the Gaslight Union**), none of which were too successful.

But the solo career of **Casey Jones** was also not as successful as he might have thought, and singles like his good version of **Solomon Burke's** *Down In The Valley* or *Mervyn Guy* and *Zebedy Zak* failed to make it.

He also recorded a wild version of *Keep A Knockin'* with a group by the name of **The Casey Jones Government**, but it seems this was only a studio session as this name did not appear again. **Casey Jones** is still gigging around in Germany and sometimes releases a record, but without much success. **Dave Coleman** became a well-known disc jockey with the WDR radio station after **The Gaslight Union** had disbanded at the end of the Sixties.

In the late Seventies **Jim Redford** appeared again on the scene as a member of **Rangers VSOP**, a follow-up group to the German Sixties recording band **Frederic & the Rangers**.

Of the other members of the **Governors** nothing was heard after that.

Discography
as **Cass & the Casanovas** they backed **Johnny Gentle** on his demo
After The Laughter Came Tears   **UK-demo unreleased   / 1960**

as **Casey Jones & his Engineers**:
One Way Ticket / I'm Gonna Love   **UK- Columbia DB 7083 / 1963**
Tall Girl / Blue Tears   **G- Bellaphon   BL 1006 / 1964**
Don't Ha Ha / Long Gone Train   **G- Bellaphon   BL 1013 / 1964**

as **Casey Jones & the Governors**:

Slow Down / Mickey's Monkey	G- Golden 12	G 12/01 / 1964	
Don't Ha Ha / Nashville Special	G- Golden 12	G 12/27 / 1965	
Candy Man / Tallahassee Lassie	G- Golden 12	G 12/32 / 1965	
Jack The Ripper / So Long Baby	G- Golden 12	G 12/35 / 1965	
Bumble Bee (in German) / Rootin' Tootin' Baby	G- Golden 12	G 12/37 / 1965	
Yockomo / Baby Why Did You Say Goodbye	G- Golden 12	G 12/40 / 1966	
Little Girl / A Legal Matter	G- Golden 12	G 12/44 / 1966	
Come On And Dance / It's Alright	G- Golden 12	G 12/49 / 1966	
Dream A Girl / Pretty, Pretty Girl	G- Golden 12	G 12/59 / 1966	
Dizzy Miss Lizzy / Casey's New Hand Jive	G- Golden 12	G 12/171 / 1973	

(***please note, *Don't Ha Ha* on the 'Golden 12' label was only credited to **The Governors**, but featured the lead vocals of **Casey Jones**. The single *Dizzy Miss Lizzy* was released at a time when the group was not in existence anymore. *Dizzy Miss Lizzy* was from the album 'Don't Ha Ha' and *Casey's New Hand Jive* from the album 'Casey Jones & the Governors'.

Casey Jones - solo:

Down In The Valley / It Seems I've Waited Too Long	G- Golden 12	G 12/56 / 1966
Mervyn Guy / Sands	G- Dt. Vogue	DV 14661 / 1967
Zebedy Zak / Casey's Blue Train	G- Dt. Vogue	DV 14872 / 1968

as **The Casey Jones Government**:

Keep On Knocking / Beechwood Park	G- Dt. Vogue	DV 14778 / 1968

The Gaslight Union:

Silly Miss Lilly Pfefferkorn / Groovin'	G- Columbia	C 23474 / 1967
Destiny Cryin' / Every Now And Then	G- Columbia	C 23551 / 1967
Stupid Party / You've Got To Find A New Love	G- Columbia	C 23705 / 1967

as **Phil Cantley & the Gaslight Union**:

Do The Kasaboo / I Wouldn't Want To Be An Officer	G- Cornet	5013 / 1968

Dave Coleman - solo:

Mister Gallilei / Alaska Quinn	G- Columbia	C 23755 / 1967
Mama Nicolina / Füllt man sich so'n Schatz wie dich in Flaschen	G- Columbia	C 23964 / 1968

EP by **Casey Jones & his Engineers**:

DON'T HA HA	G- Bellaphon BL 151 / 1965

- **Don't Ha Ha / Blue Tears / Tall Girl / Long Gone Train**

LPs by **Casey Jones & the Governors**:

DON'T HA HA	G-Golden 12 G12/LP 106/1965

- **Don't Ha Ha / Love Potion No.9 / Mickey's Monkey / Parchment Farm / Slow Down / Too Much Monkey-Business / Sounds Like Locomotion / Dizzy Miss Lizzy / Talking 'bout You / Do The Dog / Can't Judge A Book / So Long Baby / Jack The Ripper / Nashville Special**

CASEY JONES & THE GOVERNORS	G-Golden 12 G12/LP 108/1966

- **Yockomo / Casey's New Hand Jive / Smoking The Blues / My Babe / Lucille / All You Wanna Do / Hall Of The Mountain King / Come On Everybody / Baby Why Did You Say Goodbye / Doctor Feelgood / All My Sorrows / You Got What It Takes / Beautiful Delilah / Guitar Boogie**

Songs on compilation albums:

Love Potion No.9	on 'Best Of Beat'	G- Metronome HLP 10.050 / 1965
Mickey's Monkey	on 'Best Of Beat'	G- Metronome HLP 10.050 / 1965

Don't Ha hHa	on 'Beat Hits Vol.2'	**G- Bellaphon**	**BWS 305 / 1967**
Long Gone Train	on 'Beat Hits Vol.2'	**G- Bellaphon**	**BWS 305 / 1967**
Tall Girl	on 'Beat Hits Vol.2'	**G- Bellaphon**	**BWS 305 / 1967**
Blue Tears	on 'Beat Hits Vol.2'	**G- Bellaphon**	**BWS 305 / 1967**

LEE CASTLE & THE BARONS

This band was formed by **Frank Knight** in Liverpool in 1962 under the name of **Frank Knight & the Barons** and right from the start was one of the typical Merseybeat groups that soon became quite popular on Merseyside.

In the original line-up, the band consisted of **Frank Knight** (voc/rg), **Les Stuart** (lg), **Jimmy Bannon** (bg) and **Johnny Rocco** (dr).

Les Stuart was the former leader of the **Les Stuart Quartet** and **Johnny Rocco** the former leader of **Johnny Rocco & the Jets**, while **Jimmy Bannon** came from **Deke Wade & the Ambassadors** and before that had played with the **Phoenix Five**.

When **Johnny Rocco** left, he was replaced by **Bob O'Hanlon**, who had formerly played with **Ken Dallas & the Silhouettes**, the **Zephyrs** and the **Classics** from Liverpool. **Johnny Rocco**, whose real name is **Graham Hodgson**, later emigrated to Spain, where he is still playing guitar in clubs.

A little later **Les Stuart** left to join **The Ventures**, the new backing group for singer **Freddie Starr**. They later developed into **Danny Havoc & the Ventures**. After that he played with the **Kansas City Five**, before he changed his name to **Les Saints** and joined **The Long & The Short**. His place in the **Barons** was taken by **Lee Castle**, which certainly wasn't his real name.

Then **Frank Knight** left to form **Groups Inc.**, and was replaced by **Jimmy Martin**, the former leader of **Jimmy Martin & the Martinis**. The group had to change their name now and so **Frank Knight & the Barons** became **Lee Castle & the Barons**.

Jimmy Bannon left to join the **Mersey Bluebeats** and was replaced by **Tommy Bennett**, who was not the drummer of the same name, who amongst others played with the **Pressmen**.

Bob O'Hanlon re-joined the **Silhouettes**, who in the meantime had become the backing group for **Mark Peters**, and with him, the last member besides **Lee Castle** who played under the name of **Frank Knight & the Barons**, had left. That was not a good omen for the group, which then disbanded as there was no suitable drummer replacement to recruit.

The individual members joined other groups, with the exception of **Lee Castle** and **Tommy Bennett**, who re-formed **Lee Castle & the Barons** in October 1963 in the following line-up:

Lee Castle	**(voc/rg)**
Mike Liston	**(lg)**
Tommy Bennett	**(bg)**
Mel Preston	**(dr)**

Mel Preston (aka **Mel Gallagher**) had formerly played with the **Classics**, while **Mike Liston** was a former member of **Bobby Angelo & the Tuxedos**. But he left again very soon and joined **The Kansas City Five**. His replacement in **Lee Castle & the Barons** was **Johnny Fallon**, who came from the **Del Renas**.

With this line-up **Lee Castle & the Barons** were signed to Parlophone in 1964. In the same year they released the single *A Love She Can Count On*, which was coupled with *Fooling,* a song written by another Liverpool group - **The Wheels**, formerly known as **Lee**

Paul & the Boys, and who also wrote quite successfully for other artists, but never released a record in their own right.

A Love She Can Count On sadly only became a local success and so did not help **Lee Castle & the Barons** to a bigger breakthrough, which probably was the reason for the group disbanding in January 1965. All the individual members disappeared from the scene. Only **Tommy Bennett** might have been the musician of the same name who later played with the **Georgians**.

Discography

A Love She Can Count On / Fooling   **UK- Parlophone R 5151 / 1964**

LEE CASTLE AND THE BARONS

EDDIE CAVE & THE FYX

This is the continuation of the story of the **Terry Hines Sextet,** who, after the singer **Terry Hines** was replaced by **Jeff Workman** (org/voc), had continued on the scene as **The Sextet**, the name being only a temporary solution.

Towards the end of 1965 the **Sextet** recruited a new singer with **Eddie Cave**, who had formerly sung with the **Richmond Group**. The band then signed a management deal with

Eddie Cave & The Fix

Bob Wooler and, at his suggestion, was renamed **The Fix**. Their music was classic Afro-American Rhythm & Blues and within a short time the **Fix** had built a great name for themselves on the local scene. By early 1966 they were booked to play the 'Star-Club' in Hamburg.

In spite of that immediate success the sax player **Alby Donnelly**, a former member of the **Plainsmen** and the **Terry Hines Sextet**, left to join the **Clayton Squares**. After that he was also a member of the shortlived **T-Squares**, who consisted of ex-members of the **Clayton Squares** and **Karl Terry & the T.T.'s**. His replacement in the **Fix** was **Ray Rens**, who for a short time had also been a member of the **Terry Hines Sextet**.

The next to leave was band leader **Bob Hardy** (g/sax), who formerly had played with **T.L.'s Bluesicians** and the **Terry Hines Sextet**. By late 1969 he was back on the Liverpool scene, managing the very successful 'Wooky Hollow' theatre club.

When guitarist **Terry Kenna** (ex **St. Louis Checks** and **Terry Hines Sextet**) quit to become the manager of Crane's music shop, the group was joined by **Dennis Swale**, the group's former 'roadie', who had also played with the **Groupiers** and the **Dimensions** earlier in the 60's.

The Fix signed a contract with PYE and at the request of the record company the spelling of the name was changed to the **Fyx**. They went down to London in the following line-up:

Eddie Cave	**(voc)**
Dennis Swale	**(lg)**
Pete Newton	**(bg/voc)**
Jeff Workman	**(org/voc)**
Ray Rens	**(sax)**
Dave Irving	**(dr)**

Pete Newton, **Jeff Workman** and **Dave Irving** were now the sole remaining members of the **Terry Hines Sextet** or the **Sextet**, as they were named at last.

In 1966 the single *It's Almost Good* was released under the name of **Eddie Cave & the Fyx**. It was a straight pop record, produced by **Searchers** drummer **Chris Curtis** and featuring the backing vocals of **Madelaine Bell** and **Dusty Springfield**. This record did not sell well, although it was presented on 'Ready, Steady, Go'. Accordingly it was not followed by a second release from the group whocontinued to play all over England.

Eddie Cave was replaced by **Steve Aldo**, formerly with **Steve Aldo & the Challengers**, **King Size Taylor & the Dominoes**, the **Nocturns** and the **Griff Parry Five**.

Dennis Swale soon parted from the group, which had now gone back to being called **The Fyx** again. **Paul Pilnick** was the new guitarist in the line-up, which now included **Dick Hanson** on trumpet and **Alby Donnelly** on tenor-saxophone again. **The Fyx** were now a Soul band and became one of the busiest and most popular live groups on Merseyside in the late Sixties.

In spite of this success the personnel changes continued and **Ray Rens** and **Dick Hanson** left to be replaced by **Les Smith** (sax) from the **Clayton Squares** and **Steve Collins** (tr). **Fred Smith** from the **Bobby Patrick Big Six** took over the drums when **Dave Irving** left. Finally **Steve Aldo** left to form a group called **The In Crowd** and as new singer came **Colin Areety**, who amongst others formerly had sung with the **Almost Blues** and the **Escorts**.

The **Fyx**, did not survive for too much longer and finally disbanded in 1968 when **Pete Newton** and **Alby Donnelly** teamed up with **Dave Irving** and **Geoff Workman** again and together with **Paddy Chambers** and the great Liverpool songstress **Beryl Marsden** formed the group **Sinbad**. This quite short-lived group recorded a great demo with the ballad *Here We Go Again*, which sadly was never released.

It was in 1969 that **Bob Hardy** needed a resident group for the 'Wooky Hollow' and he recruited his old mates **Eddie Cave** (voc), **Dave Irving** (dr), **Alby Donnelly** (sax) and **Pete Newton** (bg). Together with the great guitarist **Lance Railton**, formerly with **Earl Preston & the T.T.'s** and **Bob Hardy** himself on organ they became the **Buzz Band**.

At some point **Lance Railton** was replaced by **Paddy Chambers** and when **Eddie Cave** left, **Bernie Wenton** became the new singer. Of course then it was **Bernie & the Buzz Band** again, although with the exception of the vocalist this new group did not have any connection to **Bernie Wenton**'s former recording group with the same name. When this group disbanded, **Dave Irving** went to London and joined **Sad Cafe**.

Alby Donnelly disappeared from the scene for a while before forming the group **Supercharge**, which was to become phenomenally successful and achived international fame.

Robert Hardy quit playing again until 1978, when **Terry Connor** persuaded him to join the recording line-up of **Karl Terry & the Cruisers**. This group separated from **Karl Terry** after a year and became **Gaz & the Groovers**, who also started to work in Liverpool as **Juke**.

In 1984 **Bob Hardy** did a deal with **Alby Donnelly** and **Juke** teamed up with him in Germany to form **Supercharge '84**, recording the 'Live At Tina Onassis Wedding' album in early 1985.

In the middle of that year **Juke** split with Alby and during the next ten years enjoyed a great deal of success – including a 'number-one' tour as **Ben E. King**'s band. **Pete Newton** also played with **Karl Terry & the Cruisers** for a while but later became a member of the great Country Rock group **Kenny Johnson & Northwind**. After that he appeared with the **Dions**, who had no connection to the Liverpool Sixties group **Roy & the Dions**. Today he is a member of **Nighttrain**.

Discography
It's Almost Good / Fresh Out Tears   **UK- PYE 7N 17161 / 1966**

THE CHANTS

The Chants didn't really fit into the Merseybeat scene optically or musically, but was a very good group and an important part of Liverpool's Beat scene.

Formed under the name of **The Shades** in the early Sixties, this group consisted entirely of black vocalists who did not play any instruments. They were the first group of their kind but soon there were many such groups in Liverpool, like for example **The Sobells**, the **Conquests** and **The Poppies**, all consisting only of black singers. But the **Chants** were not only the first, they were also the most successful. They found their own style, which always reminded one a bit of the sound of the American vocal groups of the Fifties. After their name change to **The Chants**, the group consisted of:

Eddie Amoo	**(lead voc)**
Joey Ankrah	**(voc)**
Edmond Ankrah	**(voc)**
Nat Smeeda	**(voc)**
Alan Harding	**(voc)**

Because the **Chants** depended on live appearances like all the other groups, the vocalists teamed up with the remaining members of **Vince & the Volcanoes**, who now changed the name into **The Harlems**, consisting of:

Vincent Ismael	**(lg)**
Robert Eccles	**(bg)**
Dave Preston	**(dr)**

Vincent Ismael was also known on the scene as **Vinnie Toe** and probably was the former leader of **Vince & the Volcanos**, who had disbanded a few months earlier.

Dave Preston, who in the meantime had played with **Sonny Webb & the Cascades**, did not stay too long and joined **The Secrets**. After that he played with the **Kinsleys**, before becoming a member of the hit group **The Creation**. His replacement in the **Harlems** was **John Bedson**, who formerly had played with the **Four Clefs**, the short-lived **Roadrunners** (II) and with the **Challengers**. **Bob Gilmore** came in as a additional guitarist, having previously also played with the **Challengers**.

The Harlems at the Cavern

As it seems Bob Gilmore did not stay too long with the **Harlems**, a little later they were joined by **Brendon McCormack**, a superb musician, who had formerly played with **Rikki & the Red Streaks** and the **Memphis Three**.

It was probably with this **Harlems** line-up that the **Chants** recorded their first single *I Don't Care* in 1963 for PYE, which was not too successful, just like the follow-up *I Could Write A Book* in 1964.

Their next single, *She's Mine*, sounded very much like a **Phil Spector** production, but in spite of good drive and a nice melody it did not become a chart success for the **Chants**, though it did sell quite well. *Sweet Was The Wine* (1965) had the same quality and also sold well, but as it too had no chart success, it was their last single on the PYE label.

The Chants switched to Fontana where they recorded a superb single with *Come Back And Get This Loving Baby* in 1966, and it is very hard to understand why this production was not a hit. It certainly was not the fault of the **Chants**, who did a great job on it.

In the same year the group also signed a contract with the American MGM label, but the only known release was the single *Respectable*, which obviously sold quite well in the United States, but was not released anywhere else. The follow-up in England was *Lover's Story* which came out on the Decca label. It was also released in Germany - as their only single over there.

In 1967, the **Chants** switched to Page One but it was clear from the beginning that their debut for the new label, *Ain't Nobody Home,* would not become a big success as it was not commercial enough for that time.

In 1968, RCA signed the **Chants** and in the same year released the singles *A Man Without A Face* and *I Got The Sweetest Feeling*. Neither helped the **Chants** achieve a breakthrough.

Despite the lack of success with their records, the **Chants**, and of course **The Harlems**, have to be counted as one of the leading Liverpool groups of the Sixties and, as they knew how to adapt their musical style to the changing fashion of the times, they existed until the mid-Seventies.

In 1974, they released *Love Is A Playground* on the little known Fresh Air label, and in 1976, the last single as **The Chants** was *Lucky Old Me* on Chipping Norton, but both records already had a more Disco sound.

At that time, **Chris Amoo** had joined the band, which a little later became a top European Disco act as **The Real Thing** and had a few really big hits, like *You To Me Are Everything* or *Can't Get By Without You*. **The Real Thing** were always one of the better Disco groups and are still going strong, even if the line-up has changed a few times in the meantime. It is only known for sure that **Chris Amoo** is still with them. **Joey Ankrah** became a solo singer and is playing the Liverpool clubs these days.

Regarding the **Harlems,** it should be pointed out that in December 1964 **Vinnie Ismael** and **Rob Eccles** together with drummer **Johnny Sze** of the **St. Louis Checks** became the backing group for the great Liverpool songstress **Beryl Marsden** for a Germany tour with appearances at the 'Star-Club'.

After that tour the connection broke up again and **Rob Eccles** returned to Liverpool and joined **Henry's Handful**. **Johnny Sze** went to Sweden, where he joined the **Cherry Stones** who later developed into the **Kinetic**, who for a long time were going very strong in France.

Vinnie Ismael stayed in Germany and became a member of the **Top-Ten All Stars**, the resident group at the famous 'Top-Ten' club in Hamburg. After that, he returned to Liverpool and at first was also a member of **Henry's Handful** but then joined the **Valentinos**, who tried to be like **The Chants** with the five singers. They were **Ramon 'Sugar' Dean, Tony Fayle,**

Lawrence Phylburne, **Lawrence Areety** and **Vinnie Ismael**, who was the only member who played guitar.

It is often stated that there have been records released by the **Valentinos**, but in a line-up, which also included **Tommy Brown** (of **The Almost Blues**), **Gene Latter** (of **The Shake Spears**) and **Ricky Yates** (of **The Detours**).

The Valentinos later changed their name into **Harlem** and recorded the single *It takes A Fool Like Me* on the DJM label, but this was long after the backing group for the **Chants** had disbanded.

In the Eighties, **Vinnie Ismael** was a member of **Karl Terry & the Cruisers** for quite a long time. Of **Brendon McCormack** it is known that he later appeared again on the scene as a classical guitarist.

Discography
I Don't Care / Come Go With Me	UK- PYE 7N 15557 / 1963
I Could Write A Book / A Thousand Stars	UK- PYE 7N 15591 / 1964
She's Mine / Then I'll Be Home	UK- PYE 7N 15643 / 1964
Sweet Was The Wine / One Star	UK- PYE 7N 15691 / 1965
Come Back And Get This Loving Baby / Lovelight	UK- Fontana TF 716 / 1966
Lover's Story / Wearing A Smile	UK- Decca F.12650 / 1967
Ain't Nobody Home / For You	UK-Page One POF 016/ 1967
A Man Without A Face / I Don't Need Your Love	UK- RCA 1754 / 1968
I Got The Sweetest Feeling / Candy	UK- RCA 1823 / 1968
Love Is A Playground / Sophisticated Junkyard	UK- Fresh Air 6121.109/1974
Lucky Old Me / I've Been Trying	UK- Chipping Norton CHIP 2 / 1976

Different US-releases :
Respectable / Kiss Me Goodbye	US- MGM K 13008 / 1966

Tracks on compilation-albums:
You Don't Know Like I Know	on 'Silver Soul' **Vol. 1**	UK- DJM Silverline DJML 010 / 1970
Progress	on 'Silver Soul' **Vol. 1**	UK- DJM Silverline DJML 010 / 1970

(both songs were recorded in 1969)

The Harlems - solo:
It Takes A Fool Like Me / There I Go	UK- DJM DJS 10748 / 1977

(This was not the backing-group of the **Chants** but the former **Valentinos**, who had adopted that name – see story)

The Chants

THE CLAYTON SQUARES

Without any doubt this was one of Liverpool's leading Rhythm & Blues groups of the Sixties and obviously the most popular one. The **Clayton Squares** were formed in February 1964 and their management was taken over by none other than **Bob Wooler**, who made it possible for the musicians to become professionals after a very short time. In their original line-up the **Clayton Squares** consisted of the following musicians:

Terry Hines	**(voc)**
Pete Dunn	**(lg/org)**
Arthur Megginson	**(bg)**
Mike Evans	**(sax/voc)**
Eddie Williams	**(sax/voc)**
Bob Scott	**(dr)**

Bob Scott was a former member of **Clay & the Classics** and **Pete Dunn** was the former leader of the **Flintstones** and after that he played with the **Fontanas**. **Arthur Megginson** left the group very soon and quit show business. He was replaced by **Geoff Jones**, who came from the **Georgians** and probably before that had played the bass guitar with **Joan & the Demons**.

In March 1964 **Eddie Williams** left the group to join the **Almost Blues**, where he became the lead singer under the name of **Jerkin' George Paul**. He was replaced in the **Clayton Squares** by sax player **Les Smith**.

In early 1965 **Terry Hines** left to form the **Terry Hines Sextet**, who were also quite successful on Liverpool's Rhythm & Blues scene, but this is another story in this book. He was replaced in the **Clayton Squares** by **Denny Alexander**, who had formerly played with the **Aarons**, the **Secrets** and the **Kinsleys**.

In this line-up **Bob Wooler** introduced the band to **Andrew 'Loog' Oldham**, who a little later produced their first single *Come And Get It* for the Decca label, also released in Germany, but sadly without much success, although it was a great record with an interesting and commercial Rhythm & Blues sound.

The Clayton Squares

The group at that time also recorded *I've Been Loving You Too Long* for Oldham, though it wasn't released. Instead, in 1966, the **Clayton Squares** released their second single with *There She Is*, but this one also failed.

The book 'Beat in Liverpool', which was written by the German **Jürgen Seuss** in 1966, deals mainly with the **Clayton Squares**, as well as with the **Hideaways**, another great Liverpool Rhythm & Blues band. It included an EP insertion which featured one group on either side, taken from live performances at the 'Cavern' and the 'Sink' respectively. Sadly, it is of such poor recording quality that the record is only interesting for collectors or people who have a deep interest in the Liverpool scene and its groups.

The **Clayton Squares** were featured with the songs *Watch Your Step, Hey Good Looking* and *Tell Me How Do You Feel,* recorded live at the 'Cavern'. Nothing is known of further recordings by the **Clayton Squares**, who existed in this line-up until the end of 1966.

When **Les Smith** left, he was replaced by **Alby Donnelly**, who had formerly played with the **Plainsmen**, the **Terry Hines Sextett** and the **Fyx. Les Smith**, who at the end of the Sixties was a member of the **Fyx**, died very young in 1970 in a motorbike accident, as far as it is known.

Pete Dunn also left and was replaced by **Lance Railton**, a great lead guitarist, who was a former member of **Johnny Tempest & the Tornadoes**, which became the **TTs** and backed singers like **'Faron'**, **Earl Preston**, **Cy Tucker**, **Vic Wright**, **Amos Bonny** and **Karl Terry**.

Barry Womersley was also a member of the **Clayton Squares** for a short time. He had formerly played with the **Diplomats** from Southport, the **Rhythm & Blues Inc.** and the **Big Three**. He later became a member of **Jasmin T** and **Inner Sleeve**.

The **Clayton Squares** gradually disbanded and **Lance Railton** and other remaining members amalgamated with **Karl Terry** (ex **Karl Terry & the Cruisers**, the **Delemeres** and **Karl Terry & the TTs**) and other remaining members of the **TTs** under the name of **The T-Squares**, who changed the name back to **The Clayton Squares** for a German tour.

The T Squares feat. Karl Terry

After this tour the group disbanded again, but was re-formed under the name of **The Clayton Squares** for a second tour in Germany with **Karl Terry** (voc/bg), **Lance Railton** (lg), **Alby Donnelly** (sax), **Pete Hallican** (sax), **Chris Hatfield** (org) and **Paul Hitchmough** (dr). It is known that **Paul Hitchmough** had previously played with the **Victims, Sounds Plus One** and the **Kruzads**.

After this tour the **Clayton Squares** split up completely. **Alby Donnelly** later formed **Supercharge**, a band that for years did extremely well in Germany. **Mike Evans** became a member of the poetry and comedy group **Liverpool Scene**, before he went down to London, where he is still living and looking after the interests of other musicians in a type of musicians union. In 1977 he was the co-producer of the radio series 'Merseybeat in Liverpool'.

Karl Terry became a member of **Rory Storm & the Hurricanes** but then formed a new group under the name **Karl Terry & the Cruisers** again, where **Lance Railton** and **Chris Hatfield** also played for a time. This band is still going strong in the Liverpool club scene. **Lance Railton** died in 1989. **Paul Hitchmough** joined **Curiosity Shoppe** and in 1990 toured Germany as a member of **Beryl Marsden's** backing group. He later returned as a member of **Karl Terry & the Cruisers**.

Discography

Come And Get It / And Tears Fell	**UK- Decca F.12250 / 1965**
There She Is / Imagination	**UK- Decca F.12456 / 1966**

Beside this the **Clayton Squares** were featured on an EP which was enclosed in the book 'Beat in Liverpool', written by **Jürgen Seuss** in 1966. On this EP the **Claytons Squares** can be found with *Watch Your Step, Hey Good Looking* and *Tell Me How Do You Feel* - all live-recordings from the 'Cavern'

G- Sonopress EVA 101 / 1966

Unreleased tracks:

In 1965 **Andrew Loog Oldham** produced *I've Been Loving You Too Long* with the **Clayton Squares**, which sadly was never released.

THE CONCORDS

This band was formed in the Anfield/Kensington area of Liverpool in 1962 as an instrumental group under the name of **The Four X's**.

In 1963 they changed their name to **The Concords**, following a suggestion by their manager's wife - before that the name was also used for the airplane. A little later they also changed their musical style, shared the vocals and played American, mainly Soul influenced material, which was not too well-known in England at that time. From the beginning, **The Concords** consisted of the following musicians:

Ritchie Bennett (voc/rg)
Jim Whitfield (lg/voc)
Ray Adams (bg/voc)
Kenny Meachin (dr)

In 1963 the **Concords** cut a demo of the **Bob Hilliard/Burt Bacharach** song *Any Day Now,* which became a favourite on Radio Caroline, but was never released on record. Of course, this helped the group to increase their popularity, but it took another year before they were signed by a recording company.

After a very successful tour in Belgium where they played in front of more than 2000 people at the 'White House' in Ostend, and in Germany, where they stayed for four weeks at a club in Remagen, EMI gave them a contract and in September 1964 they recorded *Ecstasy* and **Sam Cooke**'s *Bring It On Home To Me* for a single. But for mysterious reasons this record was never released. This sad fact might have been the reason for two changes in the line-up in 1965.

Ray Adams left the **Concords** to join the re-formed **Pilgrims**, while **Kenny Meachin** also left and disappeared from the scene. As new members, **Gordon L. Young** (bg) and **Billy Hewitt** (dr) joined. With this line-up the **Concords** continued quite successfully on the scene until 1968.

Although they never had great national success or any record releases, the **Concords** were very popular all over Lancashire and Cheshire and today are still remembered fondly. After the split all the members quit show business.

Discography
Ecstasy / Bring It On Home To Me   **UK- EMI (unreleased) / 1964**

Additionally, the **Concords** cut a demo with the song *Any Day Now* in 1963, which became a favourite on Radio Caroline, but was never released on record.

THE CONNOISSEURS

The roots of this Liverpool band go back to 1957, when **Mike Harkess** and **Barry 'Baz' Davis** formed the Skiffle group **The Wild Harks**, together with **Dave Owin** on guitar and a drummer named **'Tony'**.

In 1959 the **Wild Harks** changed their music style and became a Rock'n'Roll band. This lasted until 1962 and when **Mike Harkess** had to join the Army, the group disbanded. Back in Liverpool in 1963, **Mike Harkess** met up again with **Barry Davis** and they formed a new group under the name **The Connoisseurs**. This group also consisted of **Joey Bowers** (bg) and **Geoff Bamford (dr)**. **Joey Bowers** was a former member of the **"Four Jays"** and the **"Four Mosts"**, while **Geoff Bamford** came from the **Memphis Three**. But **Geoff Bamford** did not stay too long with the group and left again to join **Ian & the Zodiacs**, who had a long residence in Hamburg. His replacement in the **Connoisseurs** was **Kenny London**.

In 1964, the group almost disbanded when first **Barry Davis** left to join the new backing group of **King Size Taylor**, and a little later was followed by **Kenny London**, who disappeared from the scene.

Then **Mike Harkess** and **Joey Bowers** joined forces with a Liverpool trio called **The Mersey Gamblers**, and this new band continued under the name of **The Connoisseurs** in the following line-up:

Mike Harkess	**(voc)**
Colin Fabb	**(rg/voc)**
Dave Kent	**(lg/voc)**
Joey Bowers	**(bg/voc)**
Les Mason	**(dr)**

Before **Dave Kent** became a member of the **Mersey Gamblers**, he had played with the **Galaxies**. **Joey Bowers** and **Colin Fabb** swapped places on instruments and in this line-up the **Connoisseurs** won the 'Northern Beat Contest' in 1965 and came second in the 'All Britain Finals' in London in the same year. **George Martin** took the group to the 'Abbey Road' studios where they recorded the **Dave Kent** original *Make Up Your Mind* as a demo disc, which was not released on record.

At the end of 1965, the **Connoisseurs** were joined by **Vince Earl** as an additional vocalist, who had formerly led the groups **Vince Earl & the Zeros** and **Vince Earl & the Talismen**, and who had also been a member of **Rory Storm & the Hurricanes**

The original line-up of The Connoisseurs

before that. Then **Les Mason** left and disappeared from the scene, and his replacement was **Jimmy Tushingham**, a former member of the **Four Clefs** and **Rory Storm & the Hurricanes**. This line-up toured Germany in 1966 and appeared quite often at the well-known 'Star-Palast' in Kiel.

THE CONNOISSEURS

Back in England, the **Connoisseurs** recorded another **Dave Kent** song with the title *Do I Love You* and the standard *Once In A While* on acetate, but this of course did not help increase their popularity, especially as they were already a top act in Lancashire anyway. Up until 1967 they recorded some more songs on acetate, of which only the following ones are known: *In My Life, I Look Through You, I Do* and *Sailor Boy,* which were probably all originals, with the exception of the latter.

The recording line-up of The Connoisseurs

Joey Bowers left and at first became a member of the **Cheaters**, before he returned to the **Fourmost**, as his former group was spelt now. In the early Nineties, he was a member of the **Clouds**, who in some way had developed from the **Fourmost**. His replacement in the **Connoisseurs** was **Peter Wallace**, who came from the **Mike Cotton Sound**, but who originally was a member of **Ian & the Zodiacs**.

Colin Fabb left in 1967 to play Jazz and **Charly Flynn** replaced him, who also came from **Ian & the Zodiacs**. A year later **Dave Kent** left and his replacement was none other than **Ian Edwards** himself, who after **Ian & the Zodiacs** split had had a short stint with the **Fourmost**. But this line-up also didn't exist for too long and disbanded again probably in 1969. **Ian Edwards** became a member of **The Chesterfields** for a short time, but then retired until he re-formed **Ian & the Zodiacs** in 1999. Sadly, he died unexpectedly on 22 October 2007.

Vince Earl formed the **Vince Earl Attraction**, who still are quite successful on the local club scene and released two albums. In the later years he became quite a successful TV actor, while **Dave Kent** was still active in a group called **Sounds Sixties** in the Nineties. The **Vince Earl Attraction** are still active on the scene and **Charly Flynn** now plays with them. **The Connoisseurs** occasionally played together again for the 'Merseycats' in the Nineties, but it is not known who from the Sixties' line-ups beside **Dave Kent** and **Vince Earl** was with them.

In 2000 **Colin Fabb** was a member of the re-formed **Ian & the Zodiacs** and after the group had parted again from **Ian Edwards**, the remaining **Zodiacs** were also joined by original **Connoisseurs** member **Barry Davies** in 1965 had left **King Size Taylor** again to join **Mike Warner & his New Stars** from Bielefeld/Germany.

After that, he had played with the **Vince Earl Attraction** and internationally famous groups like **Jimmy James & the Vagabonds** and the **New Vaudeville Band** before he started a career as solo performer and also recorded in his own right. Today, like **Colin Fabb,** he still appears with the **Zodiacs** but is also a member of the **Undertakers**.

Discography

Make Up Your Mind / —	UK- Abbey Road demo-disc / 1965
Do I Love You / Once In A While	UK- Deroy acetate / 1965
In My Life, I Look Through You, Sailor Boy and I Do	UK- various acetates / 1966 /67

THE CORDES

At the beginning of the Sixties there was the group **Peter Lewis & the Raiders**, formed somewhere in the Childwall area of Liverpool.

In 1962, they were joined by bass player **Dave Dover**, who came from **Deke Wade & the Ambassadors**. The group then consisted of **Peter Lewis** (voc), **Steve Lister** (lg), **Derek Fulwood** (rg), **Dave Dover** (bg/harp) and **Johnny Brown** (dr).

By 1963, the musicians were tired of playing **Cliff Richard & the Shadows** tunes and decided to break away from **Peter Lewis**, who did not appear on the scene again after that.

The group members shared the vocals and probably at first continued as the **Raiders** and played more rough Rhythm & Blues music. They then changed the group's name to **The Cordes**. When **Johnny Brown** left and obviously quit show business, the **Cordes** continued in the following line-up :

Steve Lister	**(voc/lg)**
Derek Fullwood	**(rg/voc)**
Dave Dover	**(bg/harp/voc)**
Clive Smith	**(dr/voc)**

The new drummer, **Clive Smith**, was a former member of the recently disbanded **Mike Byrne & the Thunderbirds**.

In the same year, 1963, the **Cordes** recorded two acetates in the Lambda studios in Liverpool with the songs *Clarabella* and *The Evening*, which were just demos and never came out on record. They quickly achieved local popularity and played regularly at the many clubs in the city, for example the 'Cavern', 'Mardi Gras', 'Iron Door', 'Peppermint Lounge' and 'Victoriana'.

At 'Hope Hall' they met with the **Roadrunners** for the first time, became good friends and after that often appeared together at the same venues.

In September 1964, the **Cordes** recorded an acetate EP in the studios of the Alan Cheetham agency in Manchester, which also included the **Jodimars** song *Clarabella* again, which obviously was their favourite at that time, as well as the rocking *Betty, Betty, Betty*, the standard *You Are My Sunshine*, (the **Ray Charles** version), as well as **Leroy Carr**'s *When The Sun Goes Down*.

Around that time they recorded many of their rehearsals in the front room of Steve's house.

The Cordes

These tapes include standards like *Roll Over Beethoven, I Got My Mojo Working, Watch Your Step, It Hurts Me So* and *You've Really Got A Hold On Me*. Very interesting recordings which show the outstanding quality of the group and especially of guitarist **Steve Lister**. After the **Cordes** had played regularly at the 'Cavern' for a while, they were chosen to be the first recording group on the new 'Cavern Sound' label.

In March 1965, they went into the studio in a cellar in Matthew Street and recorded the songs *Give Her Time* and *She's Leaving,* most probably originals by the group. Although this record has a real order number, it seems it was never released or if so, only in a very limited edition as a demo disc.

In 1965 **Dave Dover** was sent down to London by his employers and was replaced in the group by **Mike Byrne** (voc/bg), the former leader of **Mike Byrne & the Thunderbirds**, who in the meantime had played with **Them Grimbles** and the **Roadrunners**. From that moment on **The Cordes** did more harmony material. This line-up was re-joined by the returning **Dave Dover**, while **Mike Byrne** put the bass guitar aside and stepped up front as singer. It was probably in late 1966 when **Steve Lister** left the group and quit the music business for many years. He was replaced by organist **Stan Broster** from the **Marescas**.

Clive Smith also left and the drums were taken over by **Terry McCusker**, who had formerly played with **Pete Demos & the Demons**, the **Four Dymonds**, **Rip Van Winkle & the Rip-It-Ups**, the **Valkyries** and the **Roadrunners**. This new line-up changed their name to **French Benefit** and mainly played Tamla Soul material.

Stan Broster left again and was replaced by **Rod Stanson** and besides this the group was joined by **Brian Farrell** from the **Georgians** as lead singer, he was the brother-in-law of **Mike Byrne**, who at that time switched to keyboards.

In early 1968 **French Benefit** became **Colonel Bagshot's Incredible Bucket Band** (…what a name!), when **Derek Fulwood** was replaced by **Mike Kontzle**, who also came from the **Roadrunners** and before that had played with the **Beatwoods** and **Chick Graham & the Coasters**. This group cut a version of **Edwin Hawkins'** *Oh Happy Day* on single for the French Vogue label and this record, coupled with the nice **Mike Kontzle** original *Gina* became a chart success in France and Belgium.

When **Mike Byrne**, **Rod Stanson** and **Mike Kontzle** left, the group was restricted to a quartet again as with **Kenny Parry** (key/g/voc), only one new member joined the remaining **Brian Farrell**, **Dave Dover** and **Terry McCusker**.

The group existed until the early Seventies and in that time released the album 'Oh! What A Lovely War' on the Cadet label, which was originally recorded for the Japanese market, where it was obviously also released.

With the exception of the **Kenny Parry** number *I've Seen The Light,* all album tracks were written by **Brian Farrell**. From that album the single *Smile* was released on Parlophone, a very nice folksy song, which in 1971 was followed by *Georgia Fireball* - again on Parlophone and again a great single. After that, little was heard of the group but two years later *She's My Sun* came out on the German Polydor label. This single was not as good as the preceding ones and accordingly failed to have any success. It was the final release by **Colonel Bagshot's Incredible Bucket Band** who disbanded a little later. **Dave Dover, Kenny Parry** and **Terry McCusker** continued at first as trio under the name **Nickelodeon**, and later became the group **Bunny**, together with girl singer **Linda Millington**.

After the split, **Kenny Parry** became a member of the new **Merseybeats** and then joined **Liverpool Express** and today, together with **Brian Farrell** plays in a Country band called **Hambone**. Sometimes they are joined by **Terry McCusker** on drums.

Mike Byrne later appeared again as a solo performer in the Liverpool pubs and beside this he was the manager of the 'Beatles Museum' in the Albert Dock in Liverpool for a few years. After that he played with various groups, such as **Persuader** and **Rocket 88**. Finally, he was a member of the **Juke Box Eddies**, which without exception consisted of well known Merseybeat veterans.

Dave Dover continued in the music business, at first as session musician and in the early Eighties as a member of **Supercharge.** From 1987 until 1994 he played in **Cy Tucker**'s band, which sometimes still appeared as **Cy Tucker & the Friars**. After that he joined the tribute band **Cocker Power** and finally he was with the rock band **Space Cadets** who are still in existence.

Of the other original **Cordes** members, **Steve Lister** only lately stepped back onto the music scene as a member of the **Lune Valley Vintage Jazz Band**, which is popular all over the Lancashire/Cumbria area. **Derek Fulwood** emigrated to Germany in the Seventies, where he sadly died in 2005 of a heart attack, while **Clive Smith** obviously stopped drumming in the Sixties and became a successful salesman.

Discography
The Cordes:

Give Her Time / She's Leaving	UK- Cavern Sound IMSTL 1 / 1965

Unreleased tracks:

Clarabella (one-sided demo)	UK- Lambda acetate / 1963
The Evening (one-sided demo)	UK- Lambda acetate / 1963

Colonel Bagshot's Incredible Bucket Band:

Oh Happy Day / Gina	F - Vogue INT. 80186 / 1969
Smile / Heading Home	UK - Parlophone R 5910 / 1971
Georgia Fireball / One Look In Her Eyes	UK - Parlophone R 5893 / 1971
She's My Sun / Meet Down The Middle	G - Polydor 2058.381 / 1973

LP **OH! WHAT A LOVELY WAR**	US - Cadet 9037-50010 / 1970

   - Six Day War / Lay It Down / Lord High Human Being / Headhunters / I've Seen The Light / Dirty Delilah Blues / Sometimes / That's What I Like To Know / Smile / Tightrope Tamer / Oh! What A Lovely War

Colonel Bagshot's Incredible Bucket Band

THE CROSSBEATS

This group might be the most obscure of Liverpool's Merseybeat scene. The **Crossbeats** were formed in 1961 in the youth section of the Anglican St. Leonard's church in Bootle. They were not really a part of the Merseybeat scene because they did not play the usual songs and the usual clubs in Liverpool but mainly appeared at various church events. They were something of a Gospel Beat group, and their exceptional self-composed songs all had religious themes, but their music was pure Merseybeat, even if not in the hard manner. From the beginning, **The Crossbeats** consisted of the following musicians:

Tony Mathias	(voc)
John Boyes	(lg/voc)
Eddie Boyes	(rg/voc)
John Millington	(bg/voc)
Eric Knowles	(dr)

It was quite surprising when, in early 1965, the first single by the **Crossbeats** was released. The songs *If Only* and *He Wants To Know* did not come out on one of the usual record labels, but on the 'Pilgrim' label, which was probably owned by the Anglican Church of England. This can be figured from the fact that the label and cover layout seemed quite religious. This release was followed by the **Tony Mathias** composition *I Know*, coupled with *He Waits*, a song by **Tony Mathias** and **John Boyes**. Again the same signs: good Merseybeat with religious themes and a religious cover on the Pilgrim label from London. As a result of this release, the **Crossbeats** made some TV appearances and also played a lot of universities, hospitals and prisons all over the country. But of course this single did not become a hit success, nor did the following one *Step Aside*.

At the beginning of 1966, **John Millington** left the group because he got married and **Eddie Boyes** switched to bass guitar, while with **Sam Pennington**, who had formerly played with the **Questers**, a new rhythm guitarist joined the **Crossbeats.** The new member also wrote the song *Busy Man* which was released as their next single in 1966.

In 1967 there was an album by the **Crossbeats** released called 'Crazy Mixed Up Generation' which, besides the songs from the last single, comprised eight band originals. On 24 March 1967 the group even played the 'Cavern' but as far as it is known it was their only appearance in this famous Beat cellar.

Apart from this, little was heard of the **Crossbeats** on the beat scene as the group mainly appeared in youth centres and other social clubs and never had any publicity. This is also the reason that it is not known how long the group existed on the scene and what happened to the individual musicians after they split.

Discography

If Only / He Wants To Know	UK- Pilgrim PSR 7001 / 1965
I Know / He Waits	UK- Pilgrim PSR 7002 / 1965
Step Aside / Forgive Me	UK- Pilgrim PSR 7003 / 1965
Busy Man / Change	UK- Pilgrim PSR 7004 / 1966

LP CRAZY, MIXED UP GENERATION   UK- Pilgrim KLP   12 / 1967
- **Busy Man / Do Not Disturb / Are yYou Afraid? / Back Where You Belong / Snow Covered Mountains / Change / Tears / Time / Crazy Mixed Up Generation / Do You Remember?**

THE CRYIN' SHAMES

This band was formed in 1962 in Liverpool's Norris Green suburb under the name of **The Bumblies**, who were initially just one of a few hundred groups of the Beat metropolis.

There was a record released in 1965 by a group with the name of **The Bumblies**, but this probably was not the Liverpool band because the lead guitarist on the single *I Gotta Tell* was Terry Ward, who never appeared in the line-up of **Bumblies** from Norris Green. But this release might have been the reason for the Merseybeat group changing its name to prevent confusion with the recording band.

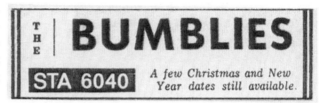

The new name of the group was **The Cryin' Shames**, and so was open to confusion with the US group with the name of **The Cryan' Shames**, but this group obviously was still not known in Europe at that time. However, before the name change to **Cryin' Shames**, the Liverpool group consisted of **Joe Kneen** (voc), **John Bennett** (lg), **Barry Davison** (rg/org), **Brian Norris** (bg) and **Charlie Gallagher** (dr).

Brian Norris left quite soon to join **Earl Preston's Realms** and after that also played with the **Dimensions**, who later became the trio **Pendulum**. He was replaced by **George Robinson**, and when a little later **Joe Kneen** also left, the group was joined by **Charlie Crane**, who formerly was the lead vocalist with the **Blue Angels**. But this was not the end of the personnel changes which continued when **John Bennett** left.

His replacement was **Ritchie Rutledge**, another great singer and guitarist, who came from the **Aztecs**. A little later **Barry Davison** also left the group and was replaced by **Phil Robert**. So, within a very short time, with the exception of the drummer, the whole line-up had changed and the **Cryin' Shames** now appeared with:

Charlie Crane	(voc)
Ritchie Rutledge	(lg/voc)
Phil Robert	(org)
George Robinson	(bg)
Charlie Gallagher	(dr)

A little later **Ritchie Rutledge** put the guitar aside and stepped in front as the second lead vocalist. **Mike Espie** joined as the new lead guitarist, and so the band had become a sextet. The popularity of the **Cryin' Shames** started to increase and Decca became interested and signed them in late 1965.

With their first single, a moody version of the **Drifters** number *Please Stay,* the **Cryin' Shames** had their first chart success when the record climbed up to No.26 in March 1966. Conspicuous on this release are the lisping vocals of **Charlie Crane**, but also noticeable is the very good arrangement with the full organ.

It was probably after this release when with **Charlie Gallagher**, the last original member, left the group and was replaced by **Paul Comerford**, the former drummer with the **Pulsators** and

Tiffany & the Thoughts. The follow-up *Nobody Waved Goodbye* was also a brilliant song with a good arrangement and it is quite hard to understand why this record did not make the charts, especially because it was in the same style as *Please Stay*: Maybe it was too similar? However, it still sold quite well and was not a real flop.

In 1966 the group's last single was released with *September In The Rain,* under the name of **Paul + Ritchie & the Cryin' Shames**. This may mean that **Charlie Crane** had left the group in the meantime, but this is not absolutely sure. **Phil Robert** left the group, and with **Pete Byrne** (key) the final line-up of the **Cryin' Shames** was completed. They probably disbanded in the middle of 1967 and left a really deep impression behind - because of their only hit *Please Stay*, which on the single was coupled with *What's New Pussycat,* probably the best recording by the **Cryin' Shames**, which was very different from the **Tom Jones'** hit song of the same name. **Paul Comerford** became a member of the **Escorts** after the split,

but when they also disbanded very soon he disappeared from the scene. In 1968 **Pete Byrne** was a member of the Liverpool group **Mumble**.

Ritchie Rutledge, who today is still quite popular in Liverpool, was a member of the **Hideaways** in 1968. They changed their name to **Confucius** a little later, and **Ritchie Rutledge** was featured on their only single. In 1972 he played for a short time with the **Swinging Blue Jeans** but after that did not appear with another band again.

In 1970 **Charlie Crane**

released a solo single with *Come Day, Go Day Man*, which was not too successful. Suddenly in 1973, the name **The Cryin' Shames** appeared again on the scene when the single *I'm Gonna Tell The World* with its flip-side *I Don't Believe It* was released on the York label. Both songs were co-written by **Charlie Crane**, together with a certain Marshal on the A-side, and a certain Mitchell on the B-side, who might have been members of the new **Cryin' Shames** at that time. The record was held in a commercial and modern sound for that time and *I'm Gonna Tell The World* reminded one a little bit of the **Cryin' Shames** sound of the Sixties, but mainly because of the vocals of **Charlie Crane**.

After that release nothing was heard again of the **Cryin' Shames**, who most probably disbanded again after the record. If not, only a recording session with **Charlie Crane** used this group name. None of the other members of the **Cryin' Shames** appeared again on the scene and probably quit show business.

Discography

Please Stay / What's New Pussycat	**UK- Decca F.12340 / 1966**
Nobody Waved Goodbye / You	**UK- Decca F.12425 / 1966**
September In The Rain / Come On Back	**UK- Decca F.12483 / 1966**
I'm Gonna Tell The World / I Don't Believe It	**UK- York YR 202 / 1973**

Charlie Crane - solo:
Come Day, Go Day Man / Face On The wWind   UK- Decca F.13089 / 1970
Terry Ward & the Bumblies:
Gotta Tell / When I Come Home   UK-Fontana TF 558 / 1965

(*** please note that it is doubtful that there was a connection between **Terry Ward & the Bumblies** and the predecessor group of the **Cryin' Shames**, but it cannot be absolutely ruled out and that is why the above single is listed in this discography - see story)

THE CURIOSITY SHOPPE

As can be seen from the group's name, they were something like the third generation of the Merseybeat wave. The story started when **Billy Hargreaves** left the **Aztecs** in 1966 and joined another Liverpool group with the name of **The Mistake**, where he met **Harry Shaw** and **Sam Rothwell**.

When the line-up of this group also started to crumble away in 1967, the above named three recruited other musicians and continued under the name **Curiosity Shoppe**, in a line-up with:

Harry Shaw	**(voc)**
Mick Rowley	**(lg/voc)**
Sam Rothwell	**(key/voc)**
Billy Hargreaves	**(bg)**
Bill Gillaher	**(dr)**

Bill Gillaher was a former member of the **Modes** and the **Calderstones** and **Mick Rowley**'s former group is sadly not known. The music of **Curiosity Shoppe** of course was not pure Merseybeat anymore but, in line with the fashion of that time, had a certain psychedelic touch.

The group very soon went down to London to play the club scene where they became quite popular. **Curiosity Shoppe** were signed to the Decca sub label Deram and in 1968, had their first single on the market with *Baby I Need You.* A very interesting record that was also released on the European continent but in the end it was not commercial enough to become a chart success.

They returned to Liverpool and when they had to go down to London again, **Bill Gillaher** left the group and disappeared from the scene. **Paul Hitchmough** came in as his replacement. He was a well known Merseybeat drummer who had already played in groups like the **Hangmen**, **Victims**, **Corals**, **Sounds plus One**, **Kruzads** and **Clayton Squares**.

The **Curiosity Shoppe** continued playing all over England for another two years and disbanded in 1971. **Billy Hargreaves** left show business as **Mick Rowley** probably did too.

Paul Hitchmough also disappeared at first but in the Nineties was back with the **Beryl**

Marsden Group and then joined **Karl Terry & the Cruisers** before he withdraw again from the music scene, although he kept on playing sporadically with different groups, not becoming a steady member of any.

Of **Sam Rothwell**, it is known that he joined **Confucius** and finally played with the re-formed **Merseybeats**. **Harry Shaw** also continued in showbiz and later played with groups like **Export** and **Garth Rockett & the Moonshiners**. In 2003 there was a reunion concert which, besides all the other original members, included **Paul Hitchmough** on drums again. But this was a one-off thing and not repeated – yet.

Discography

Baby I Need You / So Sad   **UK- Deram DM 220 / 1968**

LEE CURTIS & THE ALL STARS

Lee Curtis, whose real name is **Peter Flannery**, was an ideal Rock'n'Roll star. Because of his succinct voice, similar to **Elvis Presley**, he was also called the 'Elvis of Liverpool'. If one takes his good looks, his tall slim figure, his toothpaste smile, his pleasant aura and his great voice, it's not surprising that his success was almost pre-programmed. He started his career as a singer at the beginning of the Sixties with the Liverpool group **The Detours**.

As **Lee Curtis & the Detours** the group appeared regularly at Liverpool clubs until the end of 1962 but then the singer parted from the group, who continued as the **Detours**. But that is another story. The singer formed a new group under the name of **Lee Curtis & the All Stars**, the original line-up consisted of:

Lee Curtis	**(voc)**
Frank Bowen	**(lg)**
Tony Waddington	**(rg/voc)**
Wayne Bickerton	**(bg/voc)**
Bernie Rogers	**(dr)**

Bernie Rogers was a former member of the **Travellers**, and **Johnny Saint & the Travellers**, while **Wayne Bickerton** had formerly played with the **Bobby Bell Rockers** and **Steve Bennett & the Syndicate**.

Tony Waddington was a former member of the **Comets, Gene Day & the Jango-Beats** and **Steve Bennett & the Syndicate**, and **Frank Bowen** had already played with the **Teenbeats, Cliff Roberts' Rockers**, the **Blue Stars** and the **Lonely Ones**, as well as with **Howie Casey & the Seniors**. **Bernie Rogers** left in 1963 to join **Denny Seyton & the Sabres**, and his replacement in the **All Stars** was none other than **Pete Best**, the former drummer with the **Blackjacks** and the **Beatles**.

In this line-up **Lee Curtis & the All Stars** were featured on the Decca compilation 'Live At The Cavern' with the songs *Jezebel* and *Skinny Minnie*. This group also cut the singles *Let's Stomp* and *What About Me* on the Decca label, after **Lee Curtis** had already released the solo single *Little Girl*. They all failed to make the charts, although *What About Me* was an especially good record.

This **All Stars** also recorded the very interesting acetate *Hide And Seek* without Lee, that was coupled with the great instrumental *Czardas*, which made clear what an excellent

Lee Curtis
Chuck-Berry-Club

guitarist **Frank Bowen** was. For some unknown reason **Lee Curtis** left the group again, and they continued at first under the name of **The Original All Stars**, and then as **Pete Best & the All Stars**.

Frank Bowen left and became a member of the **Pathfinders** and after that he joined **Rory Storm & the Hurricanes.** Later he played with **Mike & the Merseymen,** who a little later changed their name to **The Trends** and went down to London. After a short spell with the **Bootleggers** in London, **Frank Bowen** returned to Liverpool and joined **Earl Royce & the Olympics**. He sadly died much too young in the Sixties. His replacement in the **Original All Stars** was **Tommy McGuirk,** a former member of the **Comets** and the **Aarons**. A little later the band's name was changed into **The Pete Best Four,** which later developed into the **Pete Best Combo,** but that is another story.

Lee Curtis formed a new group under the name of **Lee Curtis & the All Stars** again and for the first time toured Germany, where he became a top act at the 'Star-Club' in Hamburg. Besides **Lee Curtis,** this band consisted of **Paul Pilnick** (lg), **George Peckham** (rg), **Dave 'Mush' Cooper** (bg) and **Don Alcyd** (dr).

Don Alcyd was a former member of **Johnny Tempest & the Tornadoes** and **Faron & the Tempest Tornadoes,** as well as the Liverpool **Renegades,** from which **George Peckham** also came. **Dave Cooper** had played before with the **Topspots, Bob Evans & the Five Shillings** and **The Vegas Five,** which in some way all were predecessor groups of the **Undertakers,** but he also had a short spell with **Faron's Flamingos**. **Paul Pilnick** came from **Vince & the Volcanoes**. Despite their very successful German tour, the group disbanded again very soon. **George Peckham** and **Paul Pilnick** (under the name **Paul St. John**) at first joined **Groups Inc.,** before **George Peckham** met up with **Dave Cooper** again in the **Pawns,** while **Paul Pilnick** became a member of the **Big Three**.

Dave Cooper later played with the **Vauxhalls** and the **Fruit Eating Bears** and **Don Alcyd** at first went down to London as a session musician, but then returned to Liverpool and joined **The Delmonts**. **Lee Curtis** amalgamated with a Liverpool group called **The Casuals,** who were not the hit group of the same name. **Mike Cummins** (lg), **Simon Hind** (rg) and **Mike Banks** (bg) of the **Casuals** were joined by **Joe Walsh** as the new drummer, who had played before with the **Teenbeats** and the **TJ's**.

Under the name of **Lee Curtis & the All Stars** they went to Germany again, where they became as successful as the other line-up before. They regularly played the 'Star-Club', but in 1965 they disbanded again.

Lee Curtis and **Joe Walsh,** together with the returning **Paul Pilnick** formed a new group - once again under the name of **Lee Curtis & the All Stars,** and this line-up became the most successful and longest lasting of them all. The band then consisted of:

Lee Curtis	**(voc)**
Paul Pilnick	**(lg)**
Christopher P. Dannis	**(rg)**
Robert F. Garner	**(bg)**
David McShane	**(sax)**
Joe Walsh	**(dr)**

Robert Garner and **Dave McShane** both came from the recently disbanded **Ice Blues,** and before that **Robert Garner** was a member of the **Brokers, Tony Sheridan & the Beat**

Brothers, and had a short spell with **The Merseybeats**.

Lee Curtis & the All Stars recorded for the 'Star-Club' label and their legendary single *Extacy* was voted 'record of the week' on Radio Caroline, but it was a German release and Philips missed the great chance by delaying the British release. This misfortune was probably the reason that there was no big breakthrough for the group, who had also recorded another single with the not good title *Shame and Scandal In The Family*, as well as two albums with the titles 'Star-Club Show 3' and 'It's Lee'. The first one was a very good album, on which everything a real fan wanted from Rock'n'Roll via Beat to great Blues ballads can be found.

All these records were released on the German 'Star-Club' label and **Lee Curtis & the All Stars** were one of the really big stars of the so-called 'Star-Club scene', but because they had such a long residence in Germany, they sadly missed the boat in England. In 1966, this line-up of **Lee Curtis & the All Stars** disbanded again. **Robert Garner** became a member of **Mark Four**, which a little later developed into the hit group **The Creation** and had international chart success with the records *Painter Man* and *Tom Tom*.

Joe Walsh joined **Ian & the Zodiacs** and after that disappeared from the scene. However, in the Eighties, he was back with the newly formed **Undertakers** before he quit show business. **Paul Pilnick** appeared again as a member of the groups **Stealer's Wheel**, **Badger**, **Sinbad**, **Deaf School** and **Jake**.

Lee Curtis remained in Germany and formed a new backing group which, besides the Scot **Dave Watt** (lg) and the Germans **Edgar Köhler** (dr) and **Frank 'Piggy' Jarnach** (org/p), also included **Simon Hind** (bg) again. **Frank Jarnach** was the former leader of the Hamburg group **Piggy & the Jokers**, while 'Eddie' Köhler' had played before with the **Jaguars** from

Hereford, but he was replaced in the **All Stars** quite soon again by **Wolfgang Krüger**. But this band did not last too long and after that **Lee Curtis** went solo.

For a short time, the group continued under the name of **The All** and recorded the single *You Don't Have To Say* for the German Fontana label. **Lee**

LEE CURTIS & THE ALL STARS

Curtis recorded two more singles with a great version of **Del Shannon**'s *Kelly*, probably his best record ever, and *Come On Down To My Boat*. He then had a bad car accident, which was followed by complicated operations. He returned to Liverpool and quit show business for years, but when the 'Star-Club' was re-opened in 1980, he was back on the scene and since then he has toured Germany at regular intervals, most of the time backed by the **Bonds '81** and his former pianist **'Piggy' Jarnach** is always with him. **Lee Curtis** is still a great stage personality and has still got a great voice, but he is performing just for fun and hasn't seriously tried for a comeback yet. He still loves to sing in Germany, where he was a big star in the Sixties and where he is not forgotten today.

Discography

as **Lee Curtis & the All Stars**:

Let's Stomp / Poor Unlucky Me	UK- Decca F.11690 / 1963
What About Me / I've Got My Eyes On You	UK- Decca F.11830 / 1964
Extacy / A Shot Of Rhythm & Blues	UK- Philips BF 1385 / 1965

Different German releases:

Shame And Scandal In The Family / Nobody But You	G- Star-Club 148.542 / 1965
Kelly / Mohair Sam	G- Star-Club 148.553 / 1965

(*** please note that *Extacy / A shot of Rhythm & Blues* was originally recorded in Germany on 'Star-Club' 148.504 in 1965)

Lee Curtis - solo:

Little Girl / Just One More Dance	UK- Decca F.11622 / 1963

Different German release:

Come On Down To My Boat / Concerto For Her	G- Star-Club 148.590 / 1966

The All Stars (without Lee Curtis):

Hide And Seek / Czardas	UK- Demo on acetate / 1963

The All (last line-up of the "All-Stars" without Lee Curtis):

You Don't Have To Say / I Don't Go Back	G- Fontana 269.374 / 1967

LP discography:

as **Lee Curtis & the All Stars**:

'STAR-CLUB SHOW 3'	G- Star Club 158.002 / 1965

- Memphis Tennessee / Mess Of Blues / When I Get Paid / It's Only Make Believe / I've Got My Eyes On You / Boys / Boppin' The Blues / My Babe / Where Have All The Flowers Gone / Blue Suede Shoes / Let's Stomp / Hello Josephine / Can't Help Falling In Love

'IT'S LEE'	G- Star Club 158.017 / 1965

- Shame And Scandal In The Family / Um um um um um / Stand By Me / Little Egypt / Stupidity / Slow down / Jezebel / Wooly Bully / Irresistible You / It's No Good For Me / Mickey's Monkey / Sticks And Stones / One Night / Nobody But You

Tracks on compilation albums:

Skinny Minnie on **'At The Cavern'**		UK- Decca BLK 16294 / 1964
Jezebel	on **'At The Cavern'**	UK- Decca BLK 16294 / 1964
Extacy	on **'Star-Club Informationsplatte'**	G- Star-Club 111.371 / 1965
Um um um um um on **'Star-Club Scene '65'**		G- Star-Club 158.018 / 1965
Extacy	on **'Sweet Beat'**	G- Star-Club 158.022 / 1965
Extacy	on **'Beater's Hitparade'**	G- Philips 75283 P 13 / 1967

Unissued tracks:

As unissued tracks of **Lee Curtis** the songs *No Other Love* and *Lovesick Blues* are known, which were probably both recorded on acetate in 1963.

THE CYCLONES

After **Peter Fleming**, better known as **Mark Peters**, had disbanded his old group **Dean Fleming & the Flamingos**, he and his brother **Steve 'Tiger' Fleming** formed **Mark Peters & the Cyclones** in Liverpool in 1960. The band at that time consisted of **Mark Peters** (voc), **Vic Grace** (lg/voc), **Steve Fleming** (p/org), **Frank Dudley** (bg) and **Les Watkins** (dr).

Around a year later **Mark Peters & the Cyclones** were established among the leading Liverpool groups and in October 1961 were voted No.8 in the popularity poll of 'Mersey Beat'. But this line-up did not last too long and the first to leave was **Frank Dudley**, who was replaced by **Tony Webster**, the former bass guitarist of the **Metronomes** and **Tommy & the Metronomes** or **Tommy Lowe & the Metronomes** as they were also announced sometimes. About the same time, **Les Watkins** left to join **Lee Shondell & the Boys** and he was replaced on drums by **Roy Cresswell**, a former member of the **Travellers**, who sometimes also appeared as **Johnny Saint & the Travellers**. A little later the group nearly disbanded totally when **Vic Grace** left to form the **Hi-Cats**. After that he was a member of **Danny Havoc & the Ventures** who with him developed into the **Secrets**.

Mark Peters and his brother **Steve Fleming** teamed up with the **Silhouettes**, who had just separated from singer **Ken Dallas**, and this group then continued under the name of **Mark Peters & the Silhouettes**, but this is another story. **Roy Cresswell** and **Tony Webster** formed a new group and continued under the name of **The Cyclones** in the following line-up:

Freddie Ennis	(voc/bg)
Tony Webster	(lg/voc)
Bill Wesley	(sax)
Roy Cresswell	(dr)

Freddie Ennis was also a former member of **Johnny Saint & the Travellers** and in the meantime he had played with **Karl Terry & the Cruisers**. This new line-up of the **Cyclones** was signed by Oriole in 1963 and the same year the single *Nobody* was released. But this record wasn't successful and no further release followed.

After that, **Bill Wesley**, whose real name is **Billy Burton**, left to join the **Pete Best Combo** and later played with **The Denims** and **Karl Terry & the Cruisers**. The others remained as a trio and a little later changed their name to **The Few**, at first it had been planned to change it to **The Blues**. They were at this time quite successful and popular on the Merseybeat scene and played all the important venues along Merseyside, but sadly without any national success. It is a little confusing that **The Few** were often introduced as 'Oriole recording artists' until their split, although there was never a release under that name. The reason was probably the fact that the group recorded with Oriole under the name **The Cyclones**, but it might also be possible that **The Few** made some further recordings for Oriole which were not released.

The group existed only until late January 1964 and then disbanded totally.

Tony Webster later appeared again as a member of the **Runaways** which was the group that backed singer **Bill Kenwright** on his single *I Want To Go Back There Again* in 1967, but this is also another story in this book.

Of **Billy Burton**, it is known that he later emigrated to South Africa where he lived for many years. In the early Nineties he returned to Liverpool, played with **Karl Terry & the Cruisers** again and after that gigged around with various groups.

Discography

Nobody / Little Egypt   **UK- Oriole CB 1898 / 1964**

RICK E. DARNE & THE TOPLINS

Very little information was available about this group. It was formed under the name of **The Overlanders** in Chester in the early Sixties, but later changed its name into **Rick E. Darne & the Dee-Fenders**.

In 1965, the group entered the so-called 'Toplin Beat Contest', which was sponsored by the Rael Brook Company in Liverpool. The first prize was a recording contract, on condition that the winning group changed their name to **The Toplins**. **Rick E. Darne & the Dee-Fenders** were the winners and so became **Rick E. Darne & the Toplins** - with the following line-up:

Rick E. Darne (voc)
Vic Stamper
Dennis Collins
Dave Beatty
Tony Koziol

It seems that the promised recording contract was something of a false promise as nothing is known of a single released by **Rick E. Darne & the Toplins**. Nevertheless, the group became a local attraction in Liverpool and in July 1965 it was the bill topper at the Beat events on the 'Royal Iris', the legendary Beat ship on the River Mersey. But after that, little was heard of the band until December 1965.

At this time, a private single (or was that the promised record?) with the Christmas Beat songs *Sleigh Bells* and *Christmas Message* was released on the Unicord label. Both songs were composed by Liverpool songwriter **Ron Anderson**, but the record sadly did not cause a sensation on the market and it is doubtful anyway that it was ever distributed in the shops. **Rick E. Darne** probably left the group after that as **The Toplins** were then taken over as a quartet by 'Cavern Artists' management. What is left of **Rick E. Darne & the Toplins** is only a private Christmas single, which is a most admired collector's item today but, of course, it never had the chance to cause a sensation in 1966.

As the music press did not take too much notice of the group after this, it is not known when it disbanded and what happened to the musicians after that, none of them appeared on the scene again.

Discography
Sleigh Bells / Christmas Message   UK- Unicord UP 663 / 1965

STEVE DAY & THE KINSMEN

This story starts with the foundation of the Beat-group **The Masqueraders** in the beginning of the Sixties most probably in Wallasey on the Wirral, the Westside of the River Mersey.

The group originally consisted of **Ricky Dickinson** (voc/rg), **Adrian Flowerday** (lg/voc), **Alan Peers** (bg) and Tony Aldridge (dr). **Adrian Flowerday** was a former member of **Dave & the Rave-Ons**. When **Ricky Dickinson** left the group and disappeared from the scene, he was replaced by **Tom Earley** and a little later the group's name was changed to **The Kinsmen**.

When Tom Earley and Tony Aldridge left to join the newly formed **Pathfinders** from Birkenhead, the remaining two recruited new members and in May 1963 amalgamated with **Rod Pont**, who was known on the scene as **Steve Day** and had formerly led the groups **Wump & his Werbles**, **Steve Day & the Jets** (formerly the backing group for **Johnny Rocco** under the name of **Johnny Rocco & the Jets**), and its follow on band, the very popular **Steve Day & the Drifters**.

The Drifters, after **Steve Day** left, first continued as the backing group for **Gus Travis**, and later went solo under the name of **The Rainchecks**, but this is another story. **Steve Day & the Kinsmen**, as the group was called from that time on appeared in the line-up with:

Steve Day	**(voc)**
Adrian Flowerday	**(lg)**
Kingsley Foster	**(rg)**
Alan Peers	**(bg)**
Steve Skelly	**(dr)**

From which groups the new members came is sadly not known. **Steve Day & the Kinsmen** in the end were more successful than **Steve Day & the Drifters**, but for mysterious reasons their name did not impact on the scene like **Steve Day**'s former group.

In 1964 EMI became interested in **Steve Day & the Kinsmen** and recorded the songs *Last Bus Home* and *You Ask Me Why,* but only as a demo on acetate which was not followed by a record release. Both songs were written by the group and both were really nice Beat numbers.

After this, no more songs were recorded by the group, which is hard to understand because it was certainly one of the really good groups from Merseyside who existed quite successfully on the live scene for a long time and probably did not disband before the end of the Sixties.

Adrian Flowerday had already left the group in 1965 to join **The New Pressmen** but it is not known who was his repacement in **Steve Day & the Kinsmen**. **Steve Day** himself was active in the Liverpool pub and cabaret scene until the mid-Seventies and, after a break, he formed a new group under the name **Steve Day & the Kinsmen** at the beginning of the Eighties, but this lasted only a short time and it is not known if any of the old members were featured in it. After that **Steve Day** quit show business but stepped back onto the scene with the birth of the 'Merseycats' but more as a compere and disc jockey than as a singer.

There were no plans for forming a new group and plans to release a solo single under the direction of **Billy Kinsley** (a member of the **Merseybeats** and **Liverpool Express**) were discarded again very soon.

In 1995, **Steve Day** emigrated to Portugal, where he worked as disc jockey, but sadly died very soon after. What happened to the former members of the **Kinsmen** after they disbanded is sadly not known as none of them appeared on the scene again. So what is left from **Steve Day & the Kinsmen** is a nice demo, which provides the material for a late release.

Discography

Last Bus Home / You Ask Me Why   **UK- EMI - acetate / 1964**

THE DEFENDERS

This band was formed as an instrumental group in the style of the **Shadows** on the west side of the River Mersey, probably in Birkenhead or Wallasey in the early Sixties. Because instrumental music was outdated at this time, the group at first did not make any impact on the scene. **The Defenders**, in their original line-up, consisted of the following musicians:

Kenny Baker   (lg)
Graham Pugh   (rg)
Phil Howard   (bg)
Lesley Reynolds   (dr)

The group was handled by 'Dave Forshaw Enterprises' and most of the time appeared in the Wirral, where it became quite popular, but also had some appearances in the important venues on the other side of the River Mersey.

In March 1964, **Phil Howard** left the group and it is sadly not known who his replacement was, but a little later the **Defenders** were joined by singer **Amos Bonny**, whose real name is **Ronnie Cotton** and who had formerly sung with the very well-known **TT's** under the name of **Amos Bonny & the TT's**. This, of course, helped the group to increase their popularity and in 1964 some test recordings were made for the Decca label. But nothing was ever released, and it is sadly not known which songs were recorded at these sessions.

There is also nothing known about any later recordings by the **Defenders**, and because of the sad fact that the press did not take too much notice of the band, it is not clear when it finally split up, but this was most probably in the middle of 1966, after they had toured the US army bases in France.

During this tour, they were joined by **Tommy Limb** on drums, who was a former member of **Ricky Gleason & the Topspots,** but he then went on to join the **Mersey Monsters**. **Amos Bonny** later was a member of the **Easybeats** from Liverpool and after that sang with a group called **Mumble**, before he disappeared from the scene. Of the other members of the **Defenders**, only **Phil Howard** appeared again, when he became a member of the **Four Originals**, which in some way originated from the defunct **Dale Roberts & the Jaywalkers**. He was a member of that group until he sadly died in May 2005.

Discography

The Defenders in 1964 made some test recordings for Decca, already as a vocal group with **Amos Bonny**, but there was never anything released, and so it is not known which songs were recorded in these sessions.

THE DELMONT FOUR

This group was formed by brothers **Terry** and **Kevin Lappin** in Liverpool as a four-piece group in 1962, and there was no connection to another Liverpool group with the name **Rick & the Delmonts**, which featured **Rick Yates** as lead vocalist.

The **Delmont Four** had a very high musical standard and established themselves very soon on the Merseybeat scene. Their original line-up consisted of the following musicians:

Terry Lappin	**(voc/rg)**
Allan Davies	**(lg)**
Kevin Lappin	**(voc/bg)**
George	**(dr)**

The surname of the drummer sadly got lost with time, but he did not stay too long anyway and was replaced by **Don Alcyd**, who had formerly played with **Tommy & the Metronomes**, **Faron & the Tempest Tornadoes**, the **Renegades** from Liverpool and **Lee Curtis & the All Stars**.

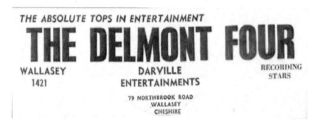

THE ABSOLUTE TOPS IN ENTERTAINMENT

THE DELMONT FOUR

WALLASEY 1421 · DARVILLE ENTERTAINMENTS · RECORDING STARS

79 NORTHBROOK ROAD
WALLASEY
CHESHIRE

This line-up of the **Delmont Four** recorded a private EP on the Unicord label a little later, with the songs *Reet Petite, Blue Moon, First Taste Of Love* and *Before You Accuse Me*. In 1964, the **Delmont Four** toured Germany as the backing group for Chester's songstress **'Jeannie'**, formerly with **Jeannie & the Big Guys**, but this connection did not last too long.

In early 1965, **Don Alcyd** left and was replaced by **Johnny Gee**, a former member of Liverpool's **Tokens** and the **Secrets**.

Still in 1965, the **Delmont Four** were called into a studio to record some songs for the compilation 'Liverpool Goes Country', on which the group was only featured with the song *Beyond The Shadow* - a nicely done number, but it seems this was their only step into Country music. With this song, plus their nice version of *Sea Of Heartbreak* they were featured on a split EP together with **Tom O'Connor** on the Rex label. For these recordings their name was shortened to **The Delmonts**, and they continued with that name from then on.

When popular singer **Freddie Starr** was looking for a new backing group, he became aware of them and they amalgamated as **Freddie Starr & the Delmonts**. The singer's real name is **Freddie Fowell**, and he had sung before with **Howie Casey & the Seniors**, the **Kansas City Five, Groups Inc., Freddie Starr & the Ventures, Freddie Starr & the Midnighters** and **Freddie Starr & the Flamingoes**. With the latter he recorded as **Freddie Starr & the Starr Boys**. **Freddie Starr & the Delmonts** toured Germany quite successfully in 1965 and, after their return, they continued for a long time together. But the group did not make any more records, and it is also not known if they cut acetates or made test recordings, which is quite hard to understand as it was a great group and very popular in the North. It was at the end of the Sixties when **Freddie Starr** left the **Delmonts**. He later started a very successful career as an entertainer and today is one of the best known TV stars in England. The **Delmonts** continued together as a group, although it is not known if there were any personnel changes in the line-up.

In 1971 the single *A Ra Chicera* was released on the Spiral label, but sadly it had no great success. That was the last anyone heard of the **Delmonts**, who probably split up in the early Seventies, and of the individual musicians later only **Johnny Gee** appeared again on the scene as a member of the **Pikkins**. In the end it can be said that neither the **Delmont Four** or **Delmonts** ever made the headlines, but they were one of the really good and interesting Liverpool bands, still remembered today.

Discography
A Ra Chicera /   **UK- Spiral**   **/ 1971**

Split EP with Tom O'Connor:
'Tom O'Connor Meets The Delmonts'   **UK- Rex**   **EPR   5003 / 1966**
The Delmonts : Sea Of Heartbreak and **Beyond The Shadow**
Tom O'Connor : Pretty Pictures and **I Can't Imagine, What Went Wrong**

Songs on compilation albums:
Beyond The Shadow   on **'Liverpool Goes Country' UK- Decca-Rex LPR 1002 / 1965**

Unreleased tracks:
Reet Petite, Blue Moon, First Taste Of Love, Before You Accuse Me
                                                    UK- Unicord acetate-ep   / 1963

Freddie Starr & the Delmonts

THE DEL RENAS

This group originated from the **Deltics**, a Skiffle trio which was formed in Liverpool in 1958 by **Brian Young** (g), **Brian James** (p) and **Brian Dean** (dr). A little later the singer **Ray Walker** joined and the band then called themselves **Ray & the Del Renas**. The name 'Del Rena' was adopted from a Liverpool shipping line.

In 1959, the group was joined by the two guitarists **Terry Fisher** (lg) and **Derek Green** (rg) and their music changed to Rock'n'Roll. They became very popular with **Ray Walker** singing in the style of **Roy Orbison** and **Del Shannon**. **Ray & the Del Renas** were probably the first Merseyside group to feature an electric organ, playing instrumentals like *Telstar* and *Red River Rock*.

In 1960, the female singer **Joan Molloy** came in as an additional member, but left again in 1961 and became the lead singer with **Joan & the Demons**. **Brian Young** also left in the same year and disappeared from the scene. He was replaced by **John Withy**. The band at that time quite often appeared at the big venues, such as the 'Cavern', 'Iron Door', 'Orrel Park Ballroom' and the 'Tower-Ballroom'. In 1962 **Ray Walker** left to join the **Escorts**, but after a short time with them he disappeared from the scene.

Brian Dean also left and the new drummer was **Eddie Edwards**, who came from the **Flames** but he did not stay too long and joined the **Nashpool Four**, who for some time also appeared as **The Nashpool**. After that he had a short spell (like all their drummers) with **Rory Storm & the Hurricanes** and then played with the **Beechwoods** before he also disappeared from the scene. **Ian Howe** became the new drummer with the **Del Renas**, as they were called now.

John Withy and **Brian James** teamed up to sing in harmony like the **Everly Brothers**, but the group a little later changed their musical style to Rhythm & Blues and Beat and all the members shared the vocals.

All these changes are quite hard to understand because the band was really successful and voted at No. 9 in the popularity poll of 'Mersey Beat' in October 1961, which was very successful if one considers how many groups were already around in Liverpool at that time.

However in March 1963 the band was offered an engagement at the 'Star-Club' in Hamburg, but not all members were able to accept the offer.

Brian Dean came back and took over his old place on drums, while **Terry Fisher** and **Derek Green** were replaced by **Johnny Fallon**. This group then went to Hamburg for a few months and when it returned to Liverpool it recorded for both volumes of 'This Is Merseybeat' - in a line-up with:

Brian James	**(p/voc)**
Johnny Fallon	**(g/voc)**
John Withy	**(bg/voc)**
Brian Dean	**(dr)**

The Del Renas were featured on the above mentioned Oriole compilations with very nice versions of *Sigh, Cry, Almost Die, Nashville Blues* and *When Will I Be Loved*.

At that time they again sounded like the **Everly Brothers,** but these were the only recordings

104

by the group that continued under the name of **The Del Renas** and was quite successful on the scene until it disbanded totally for unknown reasons in 1964.

Of the individual members only **Brian Dean** and **Johnny Fallon** appeared again on the scene, and while **Brian Dean** joined **The Coins**, **Johnny Fallon** became a member of **Lee Castle & the Barons**. It's hard to understand why there were not more records released by the **Del Renas** as their three songs on the compilation sounded great and proved that they were one of the better Liverpool groups.

The Motifs

When the earlier **Del Renas** members **Terry Fisher**, **Derek Green**, whose real name is **Derek Gretty**, and **Ian Howe** turned down the offer to go to Hamburg and were left behind in Liverpool, they formed a trio under the name of **The Motifs**. They were also quite successful on the local scene and appeared regularly at the big venues, but never recorded anything. This group existed until late 1966, and then disbanded totally and the individual members disappeared from the scene for years - until 1987, when **Terry Fisher** and **Derek Green** for a short time teamed up again as a cabaret duo under the name of the **Contraband**. These days, **Derek Green** is a member of the **Four Originals**, who also sometimes appeared as **Dale Roberts & the Jaywalkers** as is **Terry Fisher**.

When, in 1990, **Terry Fisher** became a member of the 'Merseycats' organisation, he tried for years and years to get the **Del Renas** together again and in the end succeeded, even if the group only appears occasionally for the 'Merseycats' events – in a line-up with **Terry Fisher** (lg/voc), **John Whity** (rg/voc), **Brian James** (p/org/voc), **Derek Green** (bg/voc) and **Ian Howe** (dr). With that the full 1963 line-up has come together again and the **Del Renas** are thus the only original Merseybeat group in Liverpool. What a fantastic thing!

Discography
Songs on compilation-albums:

Sigh, Cry, Almost Die	on **'This Is Merseybeat' Vol. I**	**UK- Oriole 40047 / 1963**
Nashville Blues	on **'This Is Merseybeat' Vol. II**	**UK- Oriole 40048 / 1963**
When Will I Be Loved	on **'This Is Merseybeat' Vol. II**	**UK- Oriole 40048 / 1963**

The Del Renas

THE DENNISONS

This Liverpool group was formed in 1962 and was very typical of the Merseybeat groups. While **The Dennisons** stayed more or less unknown on the European continent, they became one of the leading groups in Northern England at that time and they honestly deserved bigger international success as they were very good.

In their first year of existence they went into a studio and recorded the song *Tutti Frutti* on acetate, which was never released as an official record. Their national breakthrough came in 1963 when they were featured on the legendary Decca sampler 'Live At The Cavern' with the songs *Devoted To You* and *You Better Move On*. **The Dennisons** at that time consisted of:

Eddie Parry	**(voc/g)**
Ray Scraggs	**(lg/voc)**
Steve McLaren	**(rg/voc)**
Alan Willis	**(bg/voc)**
Clive Hornby	**(dr)**

All the members were very young and for all of them it was the first group they played with, which might also have been the reason for their very good cohesion. In spite of this, **Allan Willis** left the group quite early and was replaced by **Terry 'Tex' Carson**, but this was the only change in the line-up for years.

Decca signed the group and in 1963 their first single *(Come On) Be My Girl* was released, which was a great Beat record and climbed the charts to No. 46. This was without doubt a good start and great success for their debut on the record market, which was increased with its follow-up, their interesting version of **Rufus Thomas**' *Walking The Dog*, which reached No.36. But this was also the last chart success for the **Dennisons**, although the next single *Nobody Like My Baby* again was a very good Beat record. In 1964 the **Dennisons** also recorded the **Coasters** hit *Yakety Yak*, but this was never released.

The group continued as a very busy live act in Northern England and appeared regularly at the 'Cavern' and other important venues. In 1967 **Eddie Parry** left the group and probably quit show business. He was replaced by the great coloured singer **Colin Areety**, a former member of the **Conquests**, the **In Crowd** and the **Almost Blues**. Sometime at the end of the Sixties, the **Dennisons** disappeared from the scene and none of them appeared again in the music business, with exception of **Colin Areety**.

In 1992 **Terry Carson** died of multiple sclerosis and this sad occasion brought the **Dennisons** together again for one concert, but the group did not continue. **Eddie Parry** sadly also died in 1995 aged 49 and the cause of his death was most probably a heart attack. **Ray Scraggs** is also not with us anymore.

After the **Dennisons** had split, **Colin Areety** joined the **Michael Henri Group** and then continued as a very successful solo act in the Northern club scene and also recorded in his own right in the Seventies. He was a popular singer in Liverpool and the area of Blackpool until he died in 2007.

Clive Hornby, who became very popular as an actor through his roll as Jack Sugden in 'Emmerdale', died in July 2008.

Discography

Come On Be My Girl / Little Latin Lupe-Lu	**UK- Decca**	**F.11691 / 1963**
Walking The Dog / You Don't Know What Love Is	**UK- Decca**	**F.11880 / 1964**
Nobody Like My Baby / Lucy (You Sure Did It This Time)	**UK- Decca**	**F.11990 / 1964**

Songs on sampler-albums :

Devoted To You	on **'Live At The Cavern'**	**UK-Decca BLK 16294 / 1964**
You Better Move On	on **'Live At The Cavern'**	**UK-Decca BLK 16294 / 1964**

Unissued tracks :

In 1962 **The Dennisons** recorded the song *Tutti Frutti* on acetate and in 1964 the **Coasters** number *Yakety Yak* for Decca but, for unknown reasons, these were not released.

The Dennisons

THE DETOURS

This group originated from the **Farenheits**, which were formed in Liverpool in the very early Sixties. After singer **Alan Peters** (not identical to the member of the **Almost Blues**) had left and quit show business: and after some other changes in the line-up, the band changed their name to **The Detours** and probably at first continued as an instrumental group. This changed when, in 1962, the **Detours** became the backing group for singer **Lee Curtis** and from that time on appeared as **Lee Curtis & the Detours** on the scene. In the meantime, drummer **Jimmy Wade** had left and joined **Eddie Dean & the Onlookers**.

Lee Curtis & the Detours became a busy and successful live act in Liverpool's Merseybeat scene and appeared at all the important venues. But in 1962, the singer parted from the group and formed a new band under the name of **Lee Curtis & the All Stars**, but this is a story of its own. The **Detours** continued as a vocal / instrumental group in the line-up with:

Richard Quilliam	**(voc/lg)**
Pete Brown	**(rg)**
Charlie Robinson	**(bg)**
John Puddifer	**(dr)**

The group for a short time backed girl singer **Barbara Dee**, who actually was a disc-jockey and had made her first appearances as a singer with the **Mersey Monsters** as her backing group. **Barbara Dee & the Detours** became a successful live act in Liverpool, but then their way separated again.

In 1964 the **Detours** were engaged to appear at the 'Star-Club' in Hamburg, where they went down very well, which proves that they must have had been of a very good musical standard. That is why it is hard to understand why the group split after their return to Liverpool, after **Pete Brown** had already been replaced by **Billy Churchill**. **Richard Quilliam** and **Charlie Robinson** (aka **Charly King**) joined **The Tokens** from Liverpool, while all the others disappeared from the scene.

In October 1965 the **Detours** were reformed by founder member **Richard Quilliam** together with **Billy Churchill** - in the line-up with:

Ricky Yates	**(voc)**
Richard Quilliam	**(lg/voc)**
Billy Churchill	**(rg)**
James Carnaby	**(bg)**
Kenny Guy	**(dr)**

Ricky Yates was the former leader of **Rick & the Delmonts**, who had no connection to the backing group of **Freddie Starr** named **The Delmonts** or the **Delmont Four**, respectively. **Kenny Guy** had formerly played with the **Bonnevilles**, and it is interesting to know that **James Carnaby**'s real name is **Jimmy Connell**.

The Detours in this line-up moved down South, probably to London, where they came second in a big Beat contest, which of course increased their popularity down there. In spite of that success, there were some changes in the line-up when **Richard Quilliam**, **Billy Churchill** and **James Carnaby** left and returned to Liverpool.

New members were **Vinnie Ismael** (g) and **Tommy Husky** (sax) from Liverpool, as well as **Sid Gardner** (bg). **Vinnie Ismael** was a former member of the **Harlems** and the **Top-Ten All Stars**, while **Tommy Husky** had played with the **Deejays**, the **Nashpool** and **Earl Preston's Realms**. In this line-up the **Detours** were signed by CBS in 1967 and a little later had their first single released with *Run To Me Baby*. One year later the follow-up *Whole Lot Of Lovin'* came out, but also did not make any big impression on the scene, which might have been the reason for CBS dropping the band again.

The Detours then teamed up with singer **Gene Latter** from Cardiff's **Shake Spears** and released a third single, this time on the Spark label under the name of **Gene Latter & the Detours**. But when *My Life Ain't Easy* was released, there had already been some personnel changes again and a little later the **Detours** disbanded totally.

Gene Latter, **Vinnie Ismael** and **Ricky Yates** teamed up again in the **Valentinos**, who later changed their name into **The Harlems** and recorded one single as **Harlem** on the DJM-label. **Kenny Guy** went back to Liverpool and joined **Karl Terry & the Cruisers**, where he played quite a long time and then became a member of **Kenny Johnson & Northwind**. **Vinnie Ismael** was later also a member of **Karl Terry & the Cruisers** but after that quit show business. In the Seventies **Ricky Yates** was a member of **Capricorn** and then he also turned his back to the showbiz. He sadly died in 2005.

Gene Latter carried on as solo singer and released some quite successful singles, while **Tommy Husky** became a successful session musician as sax player and in the Nineties also released solo albums. Nothing more was heard of the other members of the **Detours** after that.

Discography
as **The Detours**:

Run To Me Baby / Hanging On	UK- CBS	3401 / 1967
Whole Lot Of Lovin' / Pieces Of You	UK- CBS	3712 / 1968

as **Gene Latter & the Detours**:

My Life Ain't Easy /	UK- Spark SRL. 1015 / 1968	

GERRY DE VILLE & THE CITY KINGS

This particular Beat group was formed in 1959 in Liverpool and during its existence had a large following on Merseyside, but its popularity only reached up as far as Blackpool and down to the Midlands. **Gerry De Ville & the City Kings**, whose name is a superb example of the musicians' imagination, in the early Sixties consisted of:

Gerry De Ville	(voc)
Dave Passy	(lg/voc)
Jimmy Carter	(rg/voc)
Ritchie Mitchell	(bg/voc)
Pete Rogers	(dr)

Gerry De Ville started his career under his real name of **Gerry Hale** in **The Mystery Five** in Liverpool and after that became **Gerry Bach** of **Gerry Bach & the Beathovens**, who continued as **The Crescendos** after he left. When he joined **The City Kings**, he called himself **Gerry Temple**, before he changed it to **Gerry De Ville**. **Ritchie Mitchell** and **Jimmy Carter** both were former members of the **Aarons**.

In 1964 Parlophone invited **Gerry De Ville & the City Kings** to London for test recordings, but nothing was released. This fact did not prevent the group from building up a good name on the Liverpool music scene, although tours through Scotland and England did not bring the success that was hoped for and which obviously was deserved.

Gerry De Ville & the City Kings were one of the interesting Liverpool bands, but information about them is very hard to find, because the press did not pay too much attention to the group. 'Mersey Beat' had a column written by **Gerry De Ville**, but for mysterious reasons he never wrote about his own group.

At the end of 1964 **Ritchie Mitchell** left to join **Phil Brady & the Ranchers** and was replaced by **Malcolm Shelbourne**, who was a former member of **Clay Ellis & the Raiders** and **Savva & the Democrats**. A little later **Peter Rogers** also left and was replaced by **Bill Robinson**, who came from the **Excerts** and before that had played with the **Heartbeats**. But he did not stay too long and then returned to the **Excerts**, that soon changed it's name into **Georgie's Germs**. After that he was a member of the **Kop**, the **Almost Blues** and the **George King Group**. His place on drums in **Gerry De Ville & the City Kings** was taken over by **Ritchie Galvin**, who had played with the **Galvanisers**, **Earl Preston & the TT's** and then with **Earl Preston's Realms**. There were probably some more changes over the years, but no further details are known.

In 1969 **Gerry De Ville & the City Kings** released the song *Alone In The Night,* their only single on the little known Virginia label. This record, which was only credited to **Gerry De Ville** and perhaps was even a private release, sadly had no success. The A-side as well as the B-side *You Never Tell Me* were both **Gerry Hale** originals.

The group existed until 1972, which in itself was a success. Of the former members, it is known that **Malcolm Shelbourne** joined the group **Purple Grass**, which a little later was re-named **Rainbow**. He played with this group until 1982 and then quit show business.

Ritchie Galvin later became a member of the Country & Western band **Western Union** and **Gerry De Ville** continued as solo performer on the club circuit until the end of the Eighties.

Discography

Alone In The Night / You Never Tell Me　　　　　　　　**UK- Virginia　V 101 / 1969**

Besides this, **Gerry De Ville & the City Kings** made some test recordings in 1964 for Parlophone of which nothing was ever released, and so it is sadly not known which songs were recorded in these sessions.

THE DIMENSIONS

This group was formed under the name **J.C. & the Strollers** in Liverpool in 1960, J.C. being the initials of **Jimmy Clarke**, the bandleader.

In 1963, the name was changed to **The Four Dimensions**, after the original drummer had left. The line-up then consisted of **Jimmy Clarke** (voc/bg), **Ray Jones** (lg), **Kenny McGunahan** (rg) and **Mike Easthope** (dr).

The Four Dimensions were very busy on the local scene and built up a good name for themselves, but they nearly disbanded when, in quick succession, both guitarists left and disappeared from the scene.

Jimmy Clarke and **Mike Easthope** then formed a new group under the old name and were joined by **Jimmy Lynch** (lg), who came from the **Black Cats** and **Grae Pugh** (rg).

A little later this group was joined by the girl singer **Irene Green**, better known as **'Tiffany'**, who was formerly in the original line-up of the **Liverbirds**, who became a very popular all girl vocal/instrumental group, especially in Germany. Under the name **Tiffany's Dimensions**, the band was booked for a Scotland tour and for that the musicians had to become professionals. **Jimmy Lynch** didn't agree and didn't want to leave Liverpool and was therefore replaced by **Tony Raynor**, who normally was a member of the **Blues Unlimited** and only stood in for this tour.

While in Scotland, the entire band's equipment was stolen, leading to the band splitting up. **Tony Raynor** probably returned to **Blues Unlimited** while **Grae Pugh** disappeared from the scene. **Jimmy Clarke** and **'Tiffany'** re-formed the group with **Karl Terry** (rg) and **Les Williams** (lg), as well as with another drummer, who was very soon replaced again by the returning **Mike Easthope**.

Karl Terry (the 'Sheik Of Shake') and **Les Williams** both came from **Group One**, and before that **Karl Terry** was the leader of **Karl Terry & the Cruisers**, while **Les Williams** originally was a member of **Terry & the Tuxedos** and **Billy Butler & the Tuxedos**.

Karl Terry then left again to join the **Delemeres** from Newcastle and later played in various Merseybeat groups, like **Rory Storm & the Hurricanes**, **Karl Terry & the TT's** and **The Clayton Squares**, before he re-formed **Karl Terry & the Cruisers**.

In 1965, **Tiffany & the Dimensions** were signed by Parlophone and it is said that **George Martin** was so enthusiastic about them that he wanted to build two acts. So **'Tiffany'** split from the group and started a solo career. She later was backed by the **Thoughts** under the name of **Tiffany & the Thoughts**, but this is a separate story.

The former **Four Dimensions** or **Tiffany's Dimensions** now continued under the name **The Dimensions** with the following line-up:

Jimmy Clarke	(voc/rg)
Les Williams	(lg/voc)
Dennis Swale	(bg)
Mike Easthope	(dr/voc)

Dennis Swale, the cousin of **Les Williams**, had played before with **Terry & the Tuxedos** and the **Groupiers**.

In 1965 the **Dimensions** recorded their great version of *Tears On My Pillow*, which is a Merseybeat classic and probably one of the most beautiful ballads that ever came out of Liverpool. It is a real masterpiece with excellent vocals, but sadly failed to become a chart success, although it must have sold very well.

Around the same time the group cut an acetate with the two ballads *I'll Take You Home Again Kathleen* and *I Wonder If I Care As Much*, as well as one standard rocker, *Hello Josephine*. *I'll Take You Home Again Kathleen* especially was a great song and the heights **Jimmy Clarke** reached with his voice are unbelievable. It is a shame that this song was never released!

In 1966 **Dennis Swale** left the group and first became a roadie with **Earl Preston's Realms**, but later played with **Eddie Cave & the Fyx**, the **Buzz Band** (not identical to **Bernie & the Buzz Band**) and the **St. Ive's Trio**, before he disappeared from the scene for years. In 1978 he was back on the scene as a member of **Karl Terry & the Cruisers**, then played with a group called **Honey** and after that became a member of **Faron's Flamingos**.

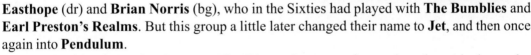

After he had left in 1966, the **Dimensions** continued as a trio and when in 1967 **Mike Easthope** also left to join **Shane Fenton & the Fentones**, the remaining **Jimmy Clarke** and **Les Williams** continued as a duo under the name of **The Two Dimensions** (what else?) on the cabaret scene, before they also separated. **Jimmy Clarke** is known to have moved to the north-east of England and continued as a solo performer.

In 1970 **Les Williams** re-formed the **Dimensions** as a trio together with **Mike Easthope** (dr) and **Brian Norris** (bg), who in the Sixties had played with **The Bumblies** and **Earl Preston's Realms**. But this group a little later changed their name to **Jet**, and then once again into **Pendulum**.

In 1978 this trio, under the name **The Dimensions**, was featured on the revival sampler 'Mersey Survivors' with the songs *Little Queenie, Something Else, Drift Away* and *Another Saturday Night*. After this record the group continued as **Pendulum** on the club and cabaret scene for many years.

Brian Norris was replaced in the meantime by **Ted Thompson**, who in the Sixties was a member of **Savva & the Democrats**. When this trio split, **Mike Easthope** quit show business, as did **Les Williams**, at first.

In 1989, there was a group with the name **The Dimensions** on the scene again, formed by **Dennis Swale**, but besides him, there was no connection to the **Dimensions** of the Sixties. **Les Williams** returned to the scene through the 'Merseycats' and today is a member of the newly-formed **Mojos** under the leadership of **Nicky Crouch**.

Discography

Tears On My Pillow / You Don't Have To Whisper   UK- Parlophone R 5294 / 1965

Tracks on compilation albums:

Another Saturday Night	on 'Mersey Survivor'	**UK- Raw**	**RWLP 104 / 1978**
Little Queenie	on 'Mersey Survivors'	**UK- Raw**	**RWLP 104 / 1978**
Something Else	on 'Mersey Survivors'	**UK- Raw**	**RWLP 104 / 1978**
Drift Away	on 'Mersey Survivors'	**UK- Raw**	**RWLP 104 / 1978**

Unreleased tracks:

I'll Take You Home Again Kathleen / I Wonder If I Care As Much / Hello Josephine

                                        UK- EMI (?) acetate   / 1966

THE DIONS

This is the story of an unlucky Merseybeat group and their manager, who ended up more successful than the band. It all started in Liverpool in early 1962 when the band **Roy & the Dions** was formed with **Roy Brooks** (voc/rg), **Mike Johnson** (lg), **Gerry Osborne** (bg) and a drummer, whose name sadly has been lost with the passing of time.

Roy & the Dions appeared regularly at all the important venues on Merseyside, including the 'Cavern' and so became quite popular on the scene. At the end of 1963 the group almost disbanded when **Roy Brooks** and the unknown drummer left. **Roy Brooks**, by the way, never appeared again on the scene. **Mike Johnson** and **Gerry Osborne** recruited other musicians and then continued under the name of **The Dions** in the following line-up:

Arthur Patterson (voc)
Mike Johnson   (lg/voc)
Stan Alexander (rg/voc)
Gerry Osborne   (bg/voc)
John Sticks   (dr)

Stan Alexander was a former member of the **Black Velvets** and **John Sticks'** real name is **John Foster**. He is the cousin of **Ringo Starr** and had formerly played with the **Escorts**. The management of this new group was taken over by **Darryl Philip Core**, a young man who also had musical ambitions, but more about him later in this story.

1964 should have been the big year for this really young group. At first the **Dions** were chosen from hundreds of other groups to be featured in the film 'Ferry Cross The Mersey', alongside **Gerry & the Pacemakers** and other well-known Liverpool groups. But when this film was almost finalized, it had to be restricted and one of the groups had to be dropped. This group, for mysterious reasons, was **The Dions**, who had needed the publicity of the film so badly. In an article in the music paper 'Combo' in connection with this, the group's name was written as the **Deans**, another group from the Liverpool scene, but this obviously was a confusion resulting from their similar names. The **Dions** and the **Deans** were two different bands. This negative development with the film could have been the reason for them disbanding shortly after that decision.

In the meantime, German promoters showed their interest in booking them for a tour, and so they were re-formed in the former line-up with the exception of **Mike Johnson**, whose replacement was **Robin Bruce** on lead guitar and **Andy O'Hagan** (harp) was added.

This German tour was quite successful and, amongst other places, the **Dions** appeared at the 'Star-Club' in Hamburg. In spite of all this, a bigger breakthrough did not happen for the band, who continued playing in Liverpool and its surrounding area.

In early 1966 **Stan Alexander** and **Andy O'Hagan** left to join **The Times**, who became the backing group for the Liverpool vocal trio **Signs**. After that, **Andy O'Hagan** was a member of **Bernie & the Buzz Band**. **The Dions** continued as a four-piece and in the middle of 1966 changed their name into **Dions Sole Band**. After a two-month tour of France the group disbanded totally in early 1967 and none of the members appeared again on the scene after that.

115

Darryl Philip Core in the meantime had given up management and concentrated on his singing career under the name of **David Garrick**. He was signed by PYE in 1965 and a little later had his first single out with *Go* on the Piccadilly label. This had no success, just like the

follow-up *One Little Smile.* On both records he was backed by a group called **The Iveys**, who included Liverpool musicians and later became very famous as **Badfinger**. They most probably also backed **David Garrick** on his next single, which earned a national breakthrough for him - his version of *Lady Jane* climbed up to No.28 in the charts in 1966, and the follow-up *Dear Mrs. Applebee* stopped at No.22 and became a monstrous hit in Germany. He then went to Germany for a long time with his own backing group named **Dandy**, which may have included some former **Dions** members. In Germany he had another big hit with *Please Mr. Movingman*, a catchy pop tune in the same style as the *Dear Mrs. Applebee* - with no connection to the Beat anymore.

Over there **David Garrick** had a long string of hits, like for example *Rainbow, A Little Bit Of This, A Certain Misunderstanding* and *Don't Go Out Into The Rain,* until the early Seventies, but after some flops he disappeared quietly from the scene, until the wave of the Sixties revivals brought him back into the limelight in the early Nineties, although there was no comparison with his success of the late Sixties.

Discography

The Dions:

This group sadly never released a record but they definitely recorded some songs for the film 'Ferry Cross The Mersey' in 1964, which sadly were not featured as the film had to be restricted and so one of the chosen groups had to be dropped - namely **The Dions**. That is why it is sadly not known which songs were recorded by the band.

David Garrick:

Go / When The World Was Our Own	UK- Piccadilly 7N 35231 / 1965
One Little Smile / We Must Be In Love	UK- Piccadilly 7N 35263 / 1965
Lady Jane / Let's Go Somewhere	UK- Piccadilly 7N 35317 / 1966
Dear Mrs. Applebee / You're What I'm Living For	UK- Piccadilly 7N 35335 / 1966
I Found A Love / A Broken Heart	UK- Piccadilly 7N 35371 / 1968
Ave Maria / Please Stay	UK- Piccadilly 7N 35398 / 1967
Rainbow / I'll Be Home	UK- PYE 7N 17509 / 1968
A Little Bit Of This / Flutterby Butterfly	UK- PYE 7N 17610 / 1968

Different German releases:

Please Mr. Movingman / A Broken Heart	G- Hit-Ton HT 300 082 / 1967
A Certain Misunderstanding / I'm Looking Straight At You	G- Hit-Ton HT 300 090 / 1967
Hey Mr. Möbelmann / Zeig Den Anderen Nicht Dein Herz	G- Hit-Ton HT 300 098 / 1967
Don't Go Out Into The Rain / Theme For A Wishing Heart	G- Hit-Ton HT 300 124 / 1968
Maypole Mews / I'd Like To Get To Know You Better	G- Dt. Vogue DV 14.840 / 1968
Poor Little Me / Molly With The Hair Like Silver	G- Dt. Vogue DV 14.935 / 1969
Ave Maria / Only A Rose	G- Dt. Vogue DV 14.967 / 1969
Rüdesheim Liegt Nicht An Der Themse / Lady Marmelade	G- Columbia 006-28777 / 1969
Lieber Dr. Eisenbart / Mein Herz Ist Doch Kein Bienenhaus	G- Columbia 006-29810 / 1969

Heya Mississippi-Girl / Piccadilly Lady　　　　　　**G- Columbia 006-29862 / 1970**
Bake Me A Woman / House In The Heart　　　　　　**G- Columbia 006-91313 / 1970**

EPs (French releases):
'DEAR MRS. APPLEBEE'　　　　　　　　　　**F- Vogue   PNV 24182 / 1967**
- Dear Mrs. Applebee / Lady Jane / You're What I'm Living For / Let's Go Somewhere
'I'VE FOUND A LOVE'　　　　　　　　　　　**F- Vogue   PNV 24187 / 1967**
- I've Found A Love / A Broken Heart / It's Not That Easy / I'm Looking Straight At You

LPs (English and German releases):
'A BOY CALLED DAVID'　　　　　　　　　　**UK-Marble Arch MAL 822/1967**
- So Much Love / I'm Looking Straight At You / A Groovy Kind Of Love / Dear Mrs. Applebee / Liza Brown / You Don't Know / Dandy / I've Been Loving You Too Long / Lady Jane / Ain't Gonna Lie / When The World Was Our Own / Master John / It's Not That Easy / The Man Who Took The Valise Off The Floor Of Grand Central Station At Noon
　　'DON'T GO OUT INTO THE RAIN'　　　　　　　**G-Hit-ton HTSLP 340042/ 1968**
- I Go The Feelin' / Somewhere / Don't Go Out Into The Rain (You're gonna melt, Sugar) / What Becomes Of The Broken Hearted / Theme For A Wishing Heart / Dancing In The Street / The Gentle People / Unchained Melody / Then You Can Tell Me Goodbye / That's How Love Goes / Please Stay / I've Found A Love

　as **David Garrick & Dandy**:
　'BLOW-UP LIVE !'　(live from the 'Blow-Up', Munich)　**G-Hit-ton HTSLP 340058/ 1968**
- See See Rider / Mr. Pleasant / Words / Simon Says / If I Were A Carpenter / Medley : Rainbow, Please Mr. Movingman, Lady Jane, Dear Mrs. Applebee / River Deep Mountain High / Dandy / Gimme Little Sign / Dedicated Follower Of Fashion / World / Bend Me, Shape Me

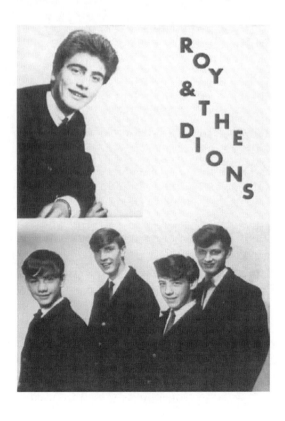

VINCE EARL & THE TALISMEN

This group was formed in the Liverpool area in 1963, probably on the west side of the Mersey, or 'over the water' as the Liverpudlians say. They very soon became one of the top local acts of the Merseybeat movement.

Vince Earl & the Talismen consisted of experienced musicians who had played in other Merseyside groups before. In 1964 they appeared in the following line-up:

Vince Earl	**(voc)**
Geoff Pollit	**(lg/voc)**
John Bethel	**(org/voc)**
Tony McDonough	**(bg/voc)**
Jake Acock	**(dr)**

Vince Earl had started his singing career with the **Teenage Rebels**, and after that he was the leader of the locally very popular **Vince Earl & the Zeros**. **Geoff Pollit** and **Jake Acock** had played together in the **Thunderbeats**. Which groups **Tony McDonough** and **John Bethel** were with before is sadly not known.

Vince Earl & The Zeros

After **Vince Earl & the Talismen** became more and more successful, they turned professional and very soon signed a recording contract with Oriole. But then they were put on ice and, as far as it is known, there was never a record released, maybe because of the takeover of Oriole by CBS, where the connection to Liverpool was not as close as with Oriole. However, **Vince Earl & the Talismen** had to survive on their live appearances and it seems they did not have a problem with that because they were really busy in Liverpool and it's greater area. But because of the recording contract flop, the group did not achieve national stardom, and nothing is known about the group touring the European continent. At the end of 1964 **Vince Earl** left to join the **Connoisseurs**, and later became a member of **Rory Storm & the Hurricanes**.

In 1965, **The Talismen** were joined by **Karl Terry** (voc/g) and **Gordon Evans** (aka **Gordon Loughlin**) (bg), who came from the recently disbanded **TT's**, but they only had a short spell with the **Talismen** and then went back to re-form the **TT's**, and soon both joined up with the rest of the just disbanding **Clayton Squares** under the name of **The T-Squares**. The **Talismen** continued as a four-piece and in 1966 recorded an acetate with the songs *Break My Heart* and *Wall.*

Around that time **Dave Keegan** joined the group, but it is not know if as additional guitarist or the replacement for **Geoff Pollit**. However, the band broke up very soon after and all the members disappeared from the scene - with the exception **Dave Keegan**, who joined the **Locations** who then continued under the name of the **Talismen**. For details about that, see the story of the **Victims**.

Vince Earl formed the **Vince Earl Attraction** in the late Sixties with former **Earl Royce & the Olympics** drummer **Jimmy Jordan**, **Graham Jones** (lg), **Ray Whitehead** (bg) and **Barry Triggs** (org/p). This was more a cabaret group, and, after **Jimmy Jordan** was replaced by **Billy Dunlop** in September 1973, the group released an album with the title 'First' on the Liverpool Sound-label (LS 1778).

After **Ray Whitehead** left, **Vince Earl** played the bass guitar again and in 1974 the **Vince Earl Attraction** released their second album 'Can't Get Enough on Amazon records (unnumbered).

In 1992 **Vince Earl** appeared again with the **Connoisseurs** for one more concert for the 'Mersey Cats' organisation. He is now quite a popular TV actor, but he has kept the **Vince Earl Attraction** going to this day and for a time, guitarist **'Baz' Davis** (ex **Connoiseurs**, **King Size Taylor**, a.s.o.) was a member, just like **Charly Flynn** (ex **Ian & the Zodiacs** and **Connoisseurs**), **Steve Fleming** (ex **Mark Peters & the Silhouettes**), and **Dave Lovelady** (ex **Fourmost**) who are all still with that group.

Discography

Vince Earl & the Talismen had signed a recording contract with Oriole, but there was never anything released.

The Talismen :
Break My Heart / Wall   **UK- Acetate   / 1966**

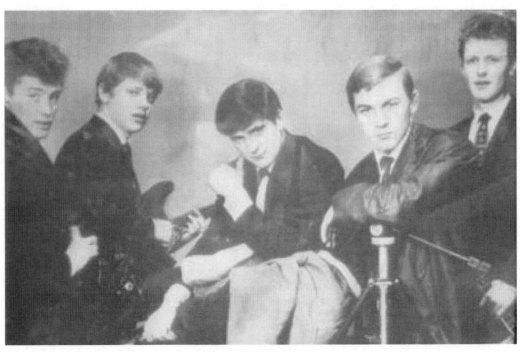

Vince Earl & The Talismen

119

THE EASYBEATS

At first it is important to point out that there was absolutely nothing in common between the Australian hit group **The Easybeats** and this Liverpool band, which was formed in 1961. But there is a connection between them and this connection is the Liverpool drummer **Gordon 'Snowy' Fleet**, who was with the **Mojos** in the early Sixties for a short time. He was an admirer of the Liverpool **Easybeats** and followed them around before he emigrated to Australia. Over there, he continued in the music business as a drummer and when his group were looking for the right name he remembered his time in Liverpool and suggested **The Easybeats**, which was accepted by the other musicians - the rest is history.

The Liverpool **Easybeats** were formed by **Frank Townsend** under the name **The Texans**, and from the beginning their manager was **Gerry Jackson**, the brother of **Searchers** vocalist **Tony Jackson**. It must have been some time in 1962 that lead guitarist **Frank McTigue** left to form the **Kruzads**. However, he did not stay away too long and returned to the **Easybeats**, while the original bass guitarist **Eddie Hill** joined the **Kruzads** as their new lead guitarist.

Accordingly, in 1963 the line-up of the **Easybeats** consisted of :

Frank Townsend (voc/rg)
Jim Doran   (lg/voc)
Frank McTigue (bg/voc)
Robert Ninnim   (dr)

Jim Doran was the new member who had taken over the lead guitar when **Frank McTigue** had left for the **Kruzads**, and after his return, **Frank McTigue** continued with the band as bass guitarist.

The **Easybeats** were the only known Liverpool group whose sound was influenced by American Surf music and the group very soon became one of the top club attractions in Liverpool and its surrounding areas. They signed a contract with Ponte & Oates agency in London and went down there for a long residence. For a short period, the group changed their name to **The Dealers** and during this time they cut the song *Girl From New York City* from a live performance at the famous 'Marquee' club. On the actual acetate the song was coupled with an interesting version of *Stagger Lee* and it should have come out as a single but the group fell out with their management and returned to Liverpool, to their former management and their own name **The Easybeats**. Of course, the planned single release was cancelled.

Robert Ninnim left the group and was later a member of a group called **Time & Motion**. His replacement was **Pete Orr**, a former member of the **Hi-Cats**, **Groups Inc.**, as well as of **Freddie Starr & the Ventures**, **Danny Havoc & the Ventures** and **Danny Havoc & the Secrets**, which were basically the same group under different names and with slightly changed line-ups.

Soon after this the group was booked for a big festival in South Wales and there a certain **Kit Lambert** came up to them with a song written by **Pete Townsend** of the as yet unknown group, called **The Who**. He wanted the **Easybeats** to record it and so the group left the festival, went straight into a studio and cut an acetate of *The Kids Are Alright*. When **Kit**

Lambert heard it he was enthusiastic about the arrangement and recording and wanted to release it on single and to sign the **Easybeats** to his management. Because of their experience with their former London agency, the **Easybeats** turned that offer down and so the song with the **Easybeats** arrangement idea was recorded a little later by **The Who**, and became a million seller.

Meanwhile **Pete Orr** had left the group who with **Frank Cork** recruited a new drummer from the London scene. Also in 1966, a publicity single for both Liverpool football teams 'Liverpool F.C.' and 'Everton F.C.' was released with the songs *Roarin' And Scorin'* and *The Toast Of Merseyside*. The artists of this single on the obscure 'Major Records' label were only named with a question mark, but without any doubt it was a Merseybeat group which played and sang in the Surf style, and it is rumoured that **Frank Townsend** was featured on the record. This of course is unproven, but provides more than enough reason for the supposition that the recording artists were the **Easybeats**, especially because it was always said the record was made by a famous Liverpool group.

In both its music and its melody, the song *Roarin' And Scorin'* is identical to the big **Beach Boys** hit *Barbara Ann,* only with different words. From the sound of the other side of this single, it was played by a Country group, whose featured musicians are also not known.

However, in the same year, 1966, **Frank Townsend** left the **Easybeats** and went back to London to join **Tony Rivers & the Castaways**, another great harmony group who a little later changed their name to **Harmony Grass**. While in London, **Frank Townsend** lived together with the **Fruit Eating Bears** from Liverpool who were down there as the backing group for the **Merseys**. Probably for that reason it was sometimes stated that **Frank Townsend** had joined them but that is definitely not true. When he returned to Liverpool, he became a member of the **Escorts**.

His replacement in the **Easybeats** in 1966 was **Pete Carter**, but he did not stay too long and was then replaced by **Adrain Lord**, whose real name is **Adrian Wilkinson**, and who was a former member of the **Missouri Drifters**, the **Nomads** (who became the **Mojos**), the **Mastersounds** and the **Bluesville Bats**, as well as Liverpool's **Faces**. But he also soon left to become a member of **Them Grimbles**, and after that disappeared from the scene. As the new singer in came **Ronnie Cotton**, better known as **Amos Bonny**, who had formerly sung with **Amos Bonny & the TT's** and the **Defenders**.

The **Easybeats** continued quite successfully in this line-up on the local scene until they broke up in 1968. **Amos Bonny** joined a group called **Mumble**, while **Frank McTigue** together with **Jim Doran** became a member of the **George King Group**, which, beside them consisted of former **Excerts**- and **Georgie's Germs**-members **John Hodgson** an **Barry Robinson**.

John Hodgson in that group then was replaced by **Frank Townshend** and when the **George King Group** broke up again, **Frank McTigue** had a short spell with the **Big Three** and the **Alan Price Set**, before he quit the music business for years. In the Seventies he was a member of a group called **Faith**.

Jim Doran teamed up again with **Frank Townsend** and together with **George Cassidy** (ex **Dingle Dices**, **Clay & the Classics**, the **Masterminds** and **Fruit Eating Bears**) formed the group **The Beechwoods**, again a great harmony group in the style of the **Easybeats**. In addition to those three the group consisted of **John Larkin** (lead-voc), **Billy Pimblet** (lg/voc) and **Eddie Edwards** (dr), a former member of the **Flames**, **Del Renas**, **Nashpool Four** and **Rory Storm & the Hurricanes**. At a later point also **Kevin Short**, the former bass guitarist of the **Notions** should have been with the group.

The **Beechwoods** continued quite successfully on the scene and are said to have recorded again, but there were no details about this available. In 1969, the band name was changed to **Taste Of Honey** and a little later an album was released on the little known Rediffusion label which without exception featured **Beach Boys** songs and was accordingly entitled 'Pay A Tribute To The Beach Boys. Besides this, there was meant to have been a single out called *Goody Goody Gumdrops,* but again no details were available.

The Beechwoods

Sometime in the early Seventies **Taste Of Honey** also split and, with the exception of **Frank Townsend**, probably all the members quit show business. A few years ago he teamed up again with **Jim Doran** and **Dave Morgan** from the **Clouds** in a harmony vocal / guitar trio, using the name of **The Easybeats** again. This group is still going on the scene.

Discography

as **The Dealers**:
Girl From New York City (live-version) / Stagger Lee   UK- acetate   / 1964

as **The Easybeats**:
The Kids Are Alright   UK- onesided acetate / 1965

The A-side of the following publicity single for the two Liverpool football teams probably was recorded by the **Easybeats**, although this is not proved (see story) :
Roarin' And Scorin' / The Toast Of Merseyside   UK- Major   MAJ 001 / 1966

Taste Of Honey:
LP 'PAY A TRIBUTE TO THE BEACH BOYS'   UK-Rediffusion RYM ZS22 / 1969

JASON EDDIE & THE CENTREMEN

This group was formed as **Vance Williams & the Rhythm Four** in Liverpool in 1962. In January 1963, the vocalist **Vance Williams** left and was replaced by the songstress **Beryl Ward**, and correspondingly the name was changed into **Beryl Ward & the Centremen**. But the vocalist problem was not resolved as **Beryl Ward** left again in the same year.

Her place then was taken by **Albert Wycherley**, the brother of Liverpool's Rock'n'Roll hero **Billy Fury**, whose real name was **Ronald Wycherley**. Like his brother, **Albert Wycherley** also changed his name - to **Al Trent**. From that moment on the band's name was changed to **The Centremen** and the line-up included the following musicians:

Al Trent	**(voc)**
Terry Barrett	**(lg)**
John Kirkpatrick	**(p/voc)**
Cy Redmond	**(bg)**
Bill Conroy	**(dr)**

John Kirkpatrick was a former member of the **Travellers, Karl Terry & the Cruisers** and **Lee Shondell & the Boys**. **Terry Barrett** left quite soon and was replaced by **John Peters**, who had formerly played with the **Arrows**.

In 1964 the **Centremen** were signed by Parlophone, but this was not followed by a record release, although it can be taken for granted that some test recordings were made. Despite the fact that at that time the group did not have national success, the musicians became professionals as they obviously had lots of engagements in the North.

In 1965 the name of the band was changed into **Jason Eddie & the Centremen**, and of course **Jason Eddie** was identical to **Al Trent** or **Albert Wycherley**, respectively. There were no personnel changes in the line-up.

In November 1965 the band had their first single released with *What'cha Gonna Do Baby*, which was not too successful, although seen in retrospect it was their best record. The follow-up came in 1966 with a strange version of **Guy Mitchell**'s classic *Singin' The Blues*, produced by **Joe Meek**.

Joe Meek is known to have produced some very bad records with various Beat groups of that time, but this was absolutely the worst of all and the record is not even worth listening to, although this certainly wasn't the fault of **Jason Eddie & the Centremen**. Not too much imagination is necessary to create various good arrangements for this song, but this version was really perverted with its nerve-wracking guitar which never stopped.

However, this was the last record by **Jason Eddie & the Centremen**, and the group disbanded at the end of the Sixties after they had recorded the song *Mr. Busdriver* in 1968, which is still unreleased. **John Kirkpatrick** later became a member of the **Albion Dance Band** and **Billy Conroy** appeared again on the scene in 1992 as a member of **Karl Terry & the Cruisers** before he quit show business again.

All the other former members of **Jason Eddie & the Centremen** did not appear on the scene again. **Albert Wycherley** appeared later as a singer, at one time also impersonating his brother **Billy Fury**.

Discography

as Jason Eddie & the Centremen:
What'cha Gonna Do Baby / Come On Baby   UK- Parlophone R 5388 / 1965
Singin' The Blues / True To You   UK- Parlophone R 5473 / 1966

Unreleased tracks:
Mr. Busdriver   UK- acetate   / 1968

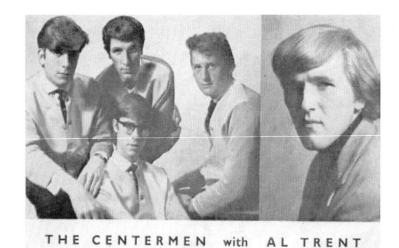

LEE EDDIE & THE CHEVRONS

The **Chevrons** were formed in Liverpool in 1962 and were one of the more popular groups in the British capital of Beat, but never had any outstanding success.

At the end of 1963 the group was joined by singer **Brian Lee**, also known as **Lee Eddie**, who had previously led the **Lee Eddie Five**, who had also been quite successful on the scene. Due to the popularity of the new singer, the band changed its name to **Lee Eddie & the Chevrons**. The line-up at that time consisted of:

Lee Eddie	**(voc)**
Alan Ryan	**(lg)**
Arthur Boughey	**(bg)**
Mike Logan	**(org)**
Andre Eustance	**(dr)**

In 1964 an acetate was recorded by **Lee Eddie & the Chevrons** with the **Roy Orbison** success *Running Scared* and the folk song *Born On The Wind*. Both were very nice, melodic numbers but with a weak sound quality. This demo was made for EMI, but sadly was not followed by a real record release.

At the end of 1964 **Mike Logan** left to join the **Denny Seyton Group**, which a little later, after **Denny Seyton** had left, for a short time should have continued as **The Lovin' Kind**, but then as **The Motowns** went to Italy for a long residence, where they recorded and became quite popular. His replacement in the **Chevrons** was a guitarist called **'Anton'**, whose surname sadly got lost with time. Because of the fact that, with the exception of **Lee Eddie**, all the members had an 'A' as the first letter of their first names, the group sometimes jokingly was announced as 'Four A's & one Lee' in the music papers.

The group probably disbanded in 1964 as singer **Lee Eddie** appeared on the scene with a new group under the name of **The Lee Eddie Show Group** around that time. But there is also the possibility that all this was only a change of the group's name as none of the musicians appeared in other bands after that.

Discography

Running Scared / Born On The Wind   **EMI acetate-demo / 1964**

THE LEE EDDIE FIVE

This was one of the pioneering groups of Liverpool's Fifties' music scene, formed as a Skiffle band under the name **The Lee Eddie Five** in 1957, they switched to Rock 'n' Roll and became a significant band on Merseyside - with the following line-up:

Lee Eddie	**(voc)**
Norman Scroggei	**(g/voc)**
Pete McFayden	**(g/voc)**
Jeff Nixon	**(bg/voc)**
John Nugent	**(dr)**

The real name of **Lee Eddie** was **Brian Lee** and he was probably the founder of the group, which sadly was never signed by a recording company, though the **Lee Eddie Five** did some recording sessions, but most probably on a private basis. Despite the fact that the group had a really good name and a large following in the North, it never achieved national importance or popularity and as far as it is known also never played outside England.

In 1962 **John Nugent** left the group and disappeared from the scene. He was replaced by **Frank Wibberley**, who had formerly played with the **Rhythm Rockers**, the **Four Aces**, **Derry & the Seniors** and **Howie Casey & the Seniors** respectively.

In 1963, before the big Beat boom, the **Lee Eddie Five** had already disbanded without having achieved any major success. **Lee Eddie** amalgamated with the Liverpool group **The Chevrons** under the name of **Lee Eddie & the Chevrons**. They later cut a nice acetate.

After that, **Lee Eddie** was the leader of the **Lee Eddie Show Group**, before he disappeared from the scene. **Jeff Nixon** and **Frank Wibberley** joined **Emile Ford & the Checkmates** and probably later were also members of the **Original Checkmates** after **Emile Ford** had left that group.

Norman Scroggei became a member of **Mark Peters & the Silhouettes** and after that was with **The Three Cheers**, who later changed their name to **Phase Three** and are said to have recorded for Polydor. Nothing was heard of **Pete McFayden** on the scene after that.

Discography
The **Lee Eddie Five** never released an official record but have had some private recording sessions. Sadly it is not known which songs were recorded and if there were any acetates produced.

CLAY ELLIS & THE RAIDERS

This group was formed in Wallasey in early 1962 on the west side of the River Mersey and was certainly one of the area's first and very important Beat bands, who, within a short time, also became very popular in the Beat metropolis of Liverpool. In the original line-up **Clay Ellis & the Raiders** consisted of the following musicians:

Clay Ellis	**(voc)**
John Edmunds	**(lg)**
Les Belamere	**(rg)**
Malcolm Shelbourne	**(bg)**
Kenny Cochran	**(dr)**

But this line-up did not last too long and when **John Edmunds** returned to London, where he hailed from, and **Les Belamere** also left, only one new guitarist, **Bobby Turner**, was added to the group. In 1963, **Clay Ellis & the Raiders** went into the studio and recorded an EP with the songs *Put The Blame On Me, I'm A Fool For You, Here's Hopin', Smile A Little Smile For Me* and *I'm A Hog For You*, which sadly was only released as a demo on acetate. It seems this very good group was never signed by a major recording company and so did not make a national breakthrough, but they existed very well on the scene because of lots of engagements in the Wirral and Liverpool and its greater area.

In late 1963 **Clay Ellis & the Raiders** disbanded for unknown reasons. **Clay Ellis** teamed up with the **Corsairs** from Liverpool under the name of **Clay Ellis & the Corsairs**, but this connection only lasted a short time and then **Clay Ellis** formed a new group under the name of **Mr. Lee & Co.**, which is a another story. **Malcolm Shelbourne** joined **Savva & the Democrats**, who also hailed from Wallasey, where he played until that group broke up in 1965. He then became a member of **Gerry De Ville & the City Kings**, where he played until 1972 and then joined **Purple Grass**, who a little later changed their name to **Rainbow**. When this group disbanded in 1982, **Malcolm Shelbourne** quit showbiz and went back to a normal job.

Kenny Cochran, after **Clay Ellis & the Raiders** had disbanded, joined the **Koobas**, that also hailed from the west side of the River Mersey and later became quite popular all over England and on the European continent. But **Kenny Cochran** did not stay too long with them and became a member of the backing group for the **Excelles**. When this group went down to London, **Kenny Cochran** left and, it seems, quit show business. **Bobby Turner** later appeared again as a member of the **Black Abbots**.

It is really sad that **Clay Ellis & the Raiders** never had a real record released which could have helped the group to make the breakthrough it doubtlessly deserved as it was one of the very good bands on the Merseybeat scene. **Clay Ellis** sadly died much too young in 1996.

Discography

EP (no title)   **UK- Eroica-acetate / 1963**
- Put The Blame On Me / I'm A Fool For You / Here's Hopin' / Smile A Little Smile For Me / I'm A Hog For You

THE ESCORTS

This was a typical Merseybeat group, and certainly one of the very best, even if they didn't have much international chart success.

Formed in Liverpool in 1962, the **Escorts** mainly consisted of very young musicians, and these teenagers of course at first had to obtain some musical experience. But the day was not too far away when the **Escorts** would show the outstanding musical quality they possessed. In their original line-up the group consisted of:

Ray Walker	**(voc)**
Terry Sylvester	**(lg/voc)**
John Kinrade	**(rg/voc)**
Mike Gregory	**(bg/voc)**
John Foster	**(dr)**

Ray Walker was the only one who had previously been in another group as he was the former leader of **Ray & the Del Renas**. But shortly after the foundation, he left the **Escorts** and disappeared from the scene.

John Foster was a cousin of **Ringo Starr** and probably through this connection the **Escorts** became the resident group at the famous 'Blue Angel' in Liverpool. **John Foster**, who had changed his name to **John Sticks**, also left the group quite soon to join the **Dions**, who were formerly known as **Roy & the Dions**. His replacement in the **Escorts** was **Pete Clarke**, the former drummer of **The Tiyms** and **Groups Inc.**. In this line-up the **Escorts** took part in a Beat contest sponsored by the 'Record Mirror' and won, followed by the **Merseybeats** and **Freddie Starr & the Midnighters** who came third.

THE ESCORTS

The prize was a recording contract with Fontana and in 1963 the first single by the **Escorts** was released. *Dizzy Miss Lizzy* was a No.1 hit in Texas, but had no great chart success in England or elsewhere, although it was a great driving version of the **Larry Williams** Rock 'n' Roll classic. With the follow-up *The One To Cry*, the **Escorts** were placed at No.49 in the British charts, while the third single *I Don't Want To Go On Without You* failed to enter the top 100. This song later became a really big hit for the **Moody Blues** from Birmingham. **Pete Clarke** left the **Escorts** again to join the **Krew** (also known as **The Crew**), and after that he became a member of **Them Grimbles**. He was replaced in the **Escorts** by **Kenny Goodlass**, a former member of the **Kirkbys**.

In 1965 with *C'mon Home Baby*, another great record came out, their only release that year. This song was also released on the German 'Star-Club' label as the reverse side of *Dizzy Miss Lizzy*. It also had no chart success but at least it helped the **Escorts** to achieve some popularity in Germany.

In 1966, the group had its last single out on the Fontana label with *Let It Be Me,* but this wonderful melodic **Gilbert Becaud** song again failed to get into the charts. The **Escorts** switched to Columbia and in 1966 released their final single with the great songs *From Head To Toe* and *Night Time,* which some people say was their best record. It is curious that this single was released in Germany on the Dt.Vogue label, which was something like the German connection for PYE records. However, even this interesting record did not enter the charts. In the meantime, there were some changes in the line-up of the **Escorts**. **Terry Syvester** had joined the **Swinging Blue Jeans**, and after that played with the **Hollies**. His replacement was **Frank Townsend**, who originated from Liverpool's **Easybeats** and in the meantime had played with **Tony Rivers & the Castaways** from London. He left again to form **The Beechwoods**. This group then became **Taste Of Honey**. Nowadays he is back with a re-formed trio of the **Easybeats**.

The Escorts with Paddy Chambers

He was replaced in the **Escorts** by **Paddy Chambers**, a former member of well-known groups like **Faron's Flamingos**, the **Big Three**, the **Eyes** and **Paddy, Klaus & Gibson**. This then was the recording line-up for their final single.

Pete Clarke came back to replace **Kenny Goodlass**, who had left to join the **Swinging Blue Jeans** for a short time and then played with the **Fruit Eating Bears**, who were the backing group for the **Merseys**. **Pete Clarke** then joined **Liverpool Scene** and was replaced by **Paul Comerford**, a former member of the **Pulsators** and the **Cryin' Shames**.

Later there was another change on drums when **Paul Comerford** left and was replaced by **Tommy Kelly**, who had formerly played with **Danny Royl & the Strollers**, the **Sensations**, **Young Ones**, **Rikki Janson & the Q-Kats** and **Earl Preston's Realms**.

For a short time **Bruce McCaskill** was also with the **Escorts** (on their last German tour), having formerly played with the **Bluegenes**, the **Kansas City Five** and with **Groups. Inc.**, but it is not known for sure if he was a member of the group or of the crew. In 1968 the **Escorts**, one of the most underrated Liverpool groups disbanded totally.

Mike Gregory had a short spell with the **Hollies** and then became a member of the **Swinging Blue Jeans**, where he played until 1972. After that he and **Paddy Chambers** were members of **Big John's Rock'n'Roll-Circus**. He later appeared again on the **Bay City Rollers** album 'Once Upon A Star. **Bruce McCaskill** later became the manager of the **Average White Band** and he sadly died at Christmas 1993 from a heart attack.

Kenny Goodlass was a member of the newly formed **Merseybeats** until 1980 and from 1993 until 1996 he has been the drummer with **Karl Terry & the Cruisers** but later returned to his re-formed original group **The Kirkbys**, where he is still playing today.

Paddy Chambers, after his membership in **Big John's Rock'n'Roll-Circus** together with Merseybeat songstress **Beryl Marsden**, was a member of the Liverpool Soul band **Sinbad** and later was the leader of **Paddy Chambers & the Java Jive**. He sadly died in the Nineties.

Terry Sylvester left the **Hollies** again in the middle of the Eighties and it was reported that he would form the **New Escorts**, but there was never anything heard about such a group, and **Terry Sylvester** continued to make solo records.

John Kinrade and **Tommy Kelly** obviously quit show business and went back to normal day jobs.

Discography

Dizzy Miss Lizzy / All I Want Is You	**UK- Fontana**	**TF 453 / 1964**
The One To Cry / Tell Me Baby	**UK- Fontana**	**TF 474 / 1964**
I Don't Want To Go On Without You /Don't Forget To Write	**UK- Fontana**	**TF 516 / 1964**
C'mon Home Baby / You'll Get No Lovin' That Way	**UK- Fontana**	**TF 570 / 1965**
Let It Be Me / Mad Mad World	**UK- Fontana**	**TF 651 / 1966**
From Head To Toe / Night Time	**UK- Columbia**	**DB 8061 / 1966**

Different German release:

Dizzy Miss Lizzy / C'mon Home Baby	**G- Star-Club**	**148.540 / 1966**

THE EXCELLES

This five-piece vocal group was formed in 1963 by twins **Maureen** and **Frank Collins** in Speke, South Liverpool.

Their music concentrated on the Motown sound, and so the **Excelles** were one of the outstanding groups on the Liverpool music scene. But this does not mean that they were a real Soul band, they just took the songs and the rhythm of the Motown scene and mixed it up with a real Beat. In the beginning **The Excelles** consisted of the following members:

> **Frank Collins**   (voc/g)
> **Maureen Collins** (voc)
> **Carrol Carter**   (voc)
> **Vicky Bird**   (voc)
> **Patrick McHugh** (voc)

For their first live appearances, the **Excelles** teamed up with various local groups before they formed their own backing group in 1964.

This band had no name and besides an organist, also included **Pete Williams** (bg) and **Kenny Cochran** (dr). **Pete Williams** and **Kenny Cochran** came from the **Kubas**, and **Kenny Cochran** before that had played with **Clay Ellis & the Raiders**.

The **Excelles** then appeared at all the important venues on Merseyside, including the 'Cavern', where they were recorded together with the **Hollies** for the programme 'Sunday Night At The Cavern' in 1964. They became very popular in the North, but for mysterious reasons did not sign a recording contract.

Vicky Bird was the first to leave and probably quit show business. She was not replaced in the **Excelles**. When **Maureen Collins** also left the group to get married, she was replaced by **Dyan Birch**. This change probably happened in 1966 and one year later the group decided to turn professional and moved down to London.

Their backing group split because **Kenny Cochran** and **Pete Williams** wanted to stay in Liverpool, but both did not appear on the scene again. The **Excelles** formed a new backing group and amalgamated with them under the name of **Arrival**, and the line-up was as follows:

> **Frank Collins**   (voc/g)
> **Carrol Carter**   (voc)
> **Dyan Birch**   (voc)
> **Paddy Hough**   (voc)
> **Don Hume**   (org/p)
> **Tony O'Malley**   (bg)
> **Lloyd Courtney** (dr)

Paddy Hough of course was identical to **Patrick McHugh**, who had changed his name for some reason, and **Don Hume** might have been the organist, having already played with the **Excelles** in Liverpool, but this is not certain.

With their new name, the group became very popular in the capital of England and soon was signed by Decca. In 1969 their first single *Friends* was released, and this great Soul-influenced record climbed up to No.8 in the British charts. **Arrival** were also quite successful on the European continent with their debut single.

Arrival

This release was followed by the album 'Arrival', which was a little bit disappointing after that superb single, which was also included on that LP. Other nice tracks were the Gospel influenced songs *Prove It, See The Lord* and *Take Me*, as well as the melodic *Not Right Now,* while their version of the **Doors** hit *Light My Fire* was not bad, but a little bit too jazzy. In May 1970 *I Will Survive,* another strong single was released, which stopped at No.16 in the charts. This new success was followed by some more television appearances and radio shows, also on the Continent, but surprisingly not by a follow-up single, which after that success is very hard to understand. Because of various personnel changes it took **Arrival** two years until they signed a new recording contract, this time with CBS where in 1972 the album 'Arrival' was released. At that time, **Carrol Carter** and **Don Hume** had left the group.

Arrival was joined by **Raphael Pereira** as additional guitarist and the place on piano was taken over by **Tony O'Malley**, while the new bass guitarist was **Philip Chen**, who was replaced through **Lee Sutherland** during that production. **Lloyd Courtney** had also left and become a member of the hit group **Casuals** who, in 1967, had a huge international hit with *Jesamine*. (By the way, they had no connection to the Liverpool group of the same name). His replacement was **Glen Lefleur**.

1973 saw another album release by the group, this time with the title 'Heartbreak Kid', from which the single *The Theme From 'The Heartbreak Kid'* was coupled out and became a real flop, although the B-side *Sweet Summer*, a Birch/Collins original was quite nice.

In Germany this record was followed by another single. The titles *Love Song* and *Out Of Desperation* came out on the German CBS label in 1973. Nothing is known of a corresponding release for the British market. This obviously was the final record by **Arrival**, who broke up quite soon after its release. **Frank Collins**, **Paddy McHugh** and **Dyan Birch** became members of the progressive group **Kokomo**.

In 1977, all three were featured on the **Brian Ferry** album 'In Your Mind'and in 1978 **Dyan Birch** and **Frank Collins** also appeared on an album by **Andy Desmond**. Both Decca singles by **Arrival** were re-released, *I Will Survive* in 1975 and *Friends* in 1978, but there was no chart entry for them in those days.

Discography:
The Excelles never released an official record under that name but in 1964 a live performance by them was recorded for the Radio programme 'Sunday Night At The Cavern'. Which songs were recorded from that concert is sadly not known.

as **Arrival**:

Friends / Don't Turn His Love Away	UK- Decca F.12986 / 1969	
I Will Survive / See The Lord	UK- Decca F.23026 / 1970	
The Theme From 'The Heartbreak Kid' / Sweet Summer	UK- CBS 1350 / 1973	

Different German release:

Love Song / Out Of Desperation	G - CBS 7035 / 1973	

LP Arrival   UK-Decca SKL 5055 / 1970

- Live / Light my fire / Friends / No good advice / Prove it / See the Lord / Sit down and float / Don't turn his love away / Take me / La Virra / Not right now / Hard road

LP Arrival   UK-CBS   64733 / 1972

- Glory Be / So it is written / Not gonna worry / You, love and me / Family tree / Part of my dream / Not preconceived / Have a drink on your father / Understanding / Weary sad, weary down

LP Heartbreak Kid   UK-CBS   70125 / 1973

-

THE EXCERTS

Here everything started in Speke, on the outskirts of Liverpool in the very early Sixties, when the group **The Abstracts** was formed by friends **John Hodgson** (lg/voc), **Barry Robinson** (rg/voc), **Bill Cole** (bg/voc) and **Ray Timmins** (dr).

They played the youth and church clubs in the immediate vicinity but broke up when **Barry Robinson** joined the already established **Billy & the Heartbeats** as drummer, who then consisted of **Billy Formby** (voc), **Arthur Roberts** (lg), **Glenn Smith** (rg/voc), **Harry Millington** (bg) and **Barry Robinson** (dr).

The Abstracts

This group at first played a lot of Cliff Richard and similar stuff but this changed when still in 1963 singer **Billy Formby** left as the other members did not want to play that 'soft music' anymore. **Glenn Smith** took over the lead vocals and the group continued as the **Heartbeats**. **Arthur Roberts** was replaced by **John Hodgson** and shortly after this **Glenn Smith** also parted from the group, which was then joined by **Alan Bradshaw** as new rhythm guitarist.

Now, that the changes had started, it was time for a new beginning and a new name – **The Excerts**. **Harry Millington** for some reason did not agree with this and left the group. **Alan Bradshaw** was also unhappy with the new direction and vacated his place for the returning **Arthur Roberts**. Accordingly the **Excerts** in early 1964 consisted of:

Brian McTigue	(voc/perc)
John Hodgson	(lg/voc)
Arthur Roberts	(rg)
Thomas Shire	(bg/voc)
Barry Robinson	(dr)

From which group **Thomas Shire** came is sadly not known and **Brian McTigue** obviously was a newcomer to the scene. He by the way was the brother of **Frank McTigue** of the **Easybeats**.

The **Excerts** became very popular locally and also started to play the clubs in the city centre of Liverpool. In the middle of 1964 the group took part in a Beat contest at the 'Cavern' and won, which, beside the price and a sensational parade through the city centre, of course meant further bookings at the most popular music club of that time. Their first full timeappearance at the 'Cavern' was in October 1964 and from then on they played the famous cellar quite regularly throughout 1965.

In late 1964 or early 1965, the **Excerts** went into a studio in Stockport and cut an interesting demo with the title *24 Manhattan Place,* which was written by

John Hodgson. On the flipside *Crawling Kingsnake,* a **John Lee Hooker** number, featured. This demo was not followed by an official record and so did not help the group to heighten its popularity.

Ray Timmins replaced **Barry 'Basher' Robinson,** who left for **Gerry De Ville & the City Kings.** After that he formed his own group under the name of **The Sect,** but after their first appearance at the 'Cavern' the name, following a **Bob Wooler** suggestion, was changed to **The Kop.**

Brian McTigue for unknown reasons left the **Excerts** in early 1966 and probably quit show business. The group continued as a four-piece and the vocals then were shared between the members. The group changed its name to **Georgie's Germs** and appeared for the first time again at the re-opening night of the 'Cavern' on 23 July 1966. Towards the end of that year **Barry Robinson** returned and took over his old place again, while nothing was ever heard of **Ray Trimmins** again.

They continued to play regularly at the club until they split up sometime in 1967. **John Hodgson** and **Barry Robinson** stayed together and formed the **George King Group** with the ex-**Easybeats** members **Frank McTigue** (voc/bg) and **Jimmy Doran** (voc/rg). This did not last too long as **John Hodgson** went on to play with the **Almost Blues** and was replaced by **Frank Townsend**, also formerly with the **Easybeats**, who meanwhile had played with some other groups.

The **George King Group** did not last too long after this and broke up when **Barry Robinson** also joined the **Almost Blues.** Later **John Hodgson** played with the great Country rock group **Kenny Johnson & Northwind**, where he met up with his old mate **Arthur Roberts** again. **Barry 'Basher' Robinson** later became a member of the group **Faith**, where he played for a real long time. **Thomas Shire** obviously quit show business after **Georgie's Germs** had disbanded and he sadly died of cancer, aged 32.

Discography:

24 Manhattan Place / Crawling Kingsnake   **UK- (Deroy ?) acetate / 1964**

TOMMY SHIRE   BRIAN McTIGUE   BARRY ROBINSON   JOHN HODGSON   ALBY BRADSHAW
BASS GUITAR   LEAD SINGER   DRUMS   LEAD GUITAR   RYTHM GUITAR

The Excerts

THE EXCHECKERS

This band was formed in Chester in the early Sixties and after a short time turned professional as they obviously did very well through lots of appearances in their hometown, the Beat metropolis Liverpool and the area of Manchester. In the original line-up the **Excheckers** consisted of the following musicians.

Peter Johnsson (voc/lg)
Phillip Blackwell (p/voc)
John Pickett   (bg)
George Roberts (dr)

George Roberts was a former member of **Jeannie & the Big Guys**, who were originally known as the **Pacemakers** (not to be confused with **Gerry & the Pacemakers**) and as **Four Hits & A Miss**.

In 1964 **The Excheckers** were signed to Decca, and a little later their first single *All The World Is Mine* was released. A nice Beat record, which sadly did not achieve the success that it deserved, and so did not help the group to increase its popularity.

After that the band went to Germany for a long period and there the **Excheckers** were

signed to Ariola. Their first single on the German label was *Buzz, Buzz, Buzz,* which in spite of its not too intelligent title was a great driving Beat record. It sold quite well, but did not get any chart honours, just like the follow-up *Mama Didn't Know,* which was a little bit too commercial.

Around the same time **The Excheckers** were signed by Dt. Vogue, another German label, where they recorded under the name of **The Liverpool Beats** for contractual reasons.

On this label they released the German versions of *Memphis Tennessee* and *Big Bad John* on a single in 1965. The latter song is more than similar to *Unhappy Girls* of the **Searchers** on their *Sugar & Spice* album. It did not sell too well, just like the follow-up *Boys,* which was also sung in German and coupled with a song of **Shorty Miller & the Raylads**.

Interesting is the fact that Dt. Vogue also released an album by the **Liverpool Beats** titled 'This Is Liverpool'. It was from a live performance, recorded at the famous 'Iron Door' club in Liverpool. In this connection, it is important to point out that these **Liverpool Beats** were not identical to the group of the same name that released the album 'The New Merseyside-Sound' on the American 'Rondo' label, because that group probably consisted of studio musicians who were identical with **Billy Pepper & the Pepperpots**. The German album of the Chester group is a very rare and a precious collector's item today, just like their singles in the German language.

Besides this the **Liverpool Beats** were featured on the two Swiss compilations 'Beat' and 'Yeah Yeah' in 1964 on the Elite Special label with the songs *Let's Get Together* and *Walking The Dog.*

The **Liverpool Beats** can also be found on the German compilation 'Original Beat aus England' from 1964 with the songs *Poison Ivy* and *Hello Josephine,* which were both taken from the live album. On this obscure compilation on the Pop label, altogether eight numbers were featured under the name **The Liverpool Beats**, but only the song *Don't Let Me Be Misunderstood* might also have been played by them, even if it does not seem too probable because the sound is totally different from their other recordings.

Of the other songs *Lucille, Tutti Frutti, Rip It Up* and *Mean Woman Blues* were played by **Freddie Starr & the Starr Boys**, and *I'll Never Find Another You* by an unknown group, which had no connection to the **Liverpool Beats** or **Exrheckers**, respectively. There is nothing known about other releases on the continental market and the group returned to England, but of course under the name of **The Exrheckers** again.

In the meantime **George Roberts** had left the group and become the roadie for the **Takers**, formerly known as **The Undertakers**. His replacement in the **Exrheckers** in early 1965 was **Aynsley Dunbar**, the former drummer with the **Merseysippi Jazz Band**, **Derry Wilkie & the Pressmen** and **Freddie Starr & the Starr Boys** (also known as **The Flamingoes**). But in March 1965 he left the **Exrheckers** to join the **Mojos**, and after that he played with **John Mayall's Bluesbreakers**, the **Aynsley Dunbar Retaliation**, **Journey**, **Jefferson Starship** and other famous groups. His replacement this time in the **Exrheckers** was **John Bell**, but the group very soon disbanded without having another record released. None of the individual members appeared on the scene again.

Discography
as **The Exrheckers**:

All The World Is Mine / It's All Over	UK- Decca F.11871 / 1964
different German releases:	
Buzz, Buzz, Buzz / You Are My New Love	G- Ariola 18.596 AT / 1964
Mama Didn't Know / Do The Bird	G- Ariola 18.598 AT / 1964
as **The Liverpool Beats**:	
Memphis Tennessee / Big Bad John	G-Dt.Vogue DV 14173 / 1964
Boys /B-side by **Shorty Miller & the Raylads** :	
Hey, Hey Shorty	G-Dt.Vogue DV 14201 / 1964
LP as '**The Liverpool Beats**':	
THIS IS LIVERPOOL	G-Dt. Vogue LDV 17005 / 1964

- I Wanna Be Your Man / Roll Over Beethoven / 24 Hours From Tulsa / My Prayer / My Baby Left Me / I'm Talking About You / Here's Hoping / Little Queenie / Poison Ivy / Memphis Tennessee / Thou Shalt Not Steal / Hello Josephine (recorded live at the 'Iron Door', Liverpool)

Tracks on compilation albums:
as '**The Liverpool Beats**':

Walking The Dog	on '**Beat**'	CH- Elite Special SOLP-S-33-250 / 1964
Let's Get Together	on '**Yeah Yeah**'	CH- Elite Special SOLP-S-33-251 / 1964
Poison Ivy	on '**Original Beat aus England**'	G- Pop Z 10006 / 1964
Hello Josephine	on '**Original Beat aus England**'	G- Pop Z 10006 / 1964
Don't Let Me Be Misunderstood	on '**Original Beat aus England**'	G- Pop Z 10006 / 1964

(***please note that it is not certain if the song **Don't Let Me Be Misunderstood** was really played by the **Liverpool Beats** as it was too different in sound. All the other songs which were included on the German compilation under the name of **The Liverpool Beats** were certainly not played by them. - see story for detailed information)

THE EXECUTIONERS

This group was formed in the early Sixties somewhere on the Wirral. **Alan Webster** (lg), **Rodney Lewis** (bg) and drummer **Alexander Carroll** went under the name of the **Threebeats** in 1961. A few months later they added a rhythm guitar to the line-up and changed the name to the **Executioners.** They became very popular locally and very soon also appeared at big venues like the 'Majestic' and the 'Cubik' in Birkenhead, as well as the Tower Ballroom in New Brighton. It was time to conquer the scene of Liverpool and on 22nd March 1963 the **Executioners** had their first appearance at the 'Cavern'.

When they had established themselves, guitarist and singer **Alan Webster**, a former member of the **Young Ones** from Birkenhead, left the group in 1963. He apparently emigrated to Australia later and it is rumoured that down there he continued in the music business. **The Executioners** continued in the following line-up:

Rod Lewis	**(voc/bg)**
Ray Milne	**(rg/voc)**
Graham Dixon	**(lg/voc)**
Alexander Carroll	**(dr)**

Alexander Carroll left quite soon and was replaced by **Frank McLaughlin** on drums, who came from the **Atomics**. This line-up of the **Executioners** became very popular in the centre of Liverpool and started to play regularly at the 'Cavern', as well as at many of the other more or less important venues but without making the headlines.

In 1964, they were chosen, along with other groups like the **Four Clefs** and the **Reds Inc.**, to be part of the new Merseybeat compilation 'Cavern Alive' and were recorded by **John Schroeder** for Oriole. This record, for mysterious reasons, was sadly not released in the end and therefore it is only known that **Chan Romero**'s *Hippy Hippy Shake* was amongst the songs that were recorded by the **Executioners**. This non-release could have been the reason for **Graham Dixon** leaving the group and he continued to play in various dance bands. His replacement was a certain **Richard Mumford**, whose former group is unknown.

It was probably this line-up that recorded a demo-disc with the **Alan Webster** original *Time Will Tell* for **Brian Epstein** in the Kensington studios of **P.F. Phillips**. A nice song that later was covered by other Merseybeat groups but it did not help the **Executioners** in those days. They continued to play on the Mersey scene, had a large following but nothing is known about further recordings or any outstanding success.

Towards the end of 1965 they disbanded and while **Rod Lewis** continued to play in a cabaret-duo, **Richard Mumford** later should have been a member of the **Pathfinders**, before he quit showbiz. **Ray Milne** became a fireman and sadly died a few years ago of cancer.

Frank McLaughlin, after the split with the **Executioners,** at first disappeared from the scene but then was back with a group called the **New Executioners**, which beside him consisted of **Terry Amos** (lg/voc), **Dave Ward** (rg/voc) and **Chris Kelly** (bg/voc). This band was not that successful anymore and did not survive too long. After that he played in a Country group by the name of **The Texas Reds**, with whom he also toured the American bases in Germany.

Discography:

Time Will Tell / I've Been There   **UK- Kensington   acetate / 1964**

Before that acetate was cut, **The Executioners** in 1964 were recorded by **John Schroeder** with three or four songs for the new Oriole Merseybeat compilation 'Cavern Alive', which in the end did not come out. Therefore it is only remembered that **Hippy Hippy Shake** was amongst the recorded songs.

THE EYES

This group was formed in Liverpool in 1964 and, like the **Liverbirds, Ian & the Zodiacs** and **Lee Curtis**, they had a long residence in Germany, where they became popular and successful in the so-called 'Star-Club' scene. In spite of this it was a real Merseybeat group consisting of the following musicians:

Paddy Chambers (lg/voc)
John Frankland (rg/voc)
Lew Collins (bg/voc)
Gibson Kemp (dr/voc)

All members were experienced musicians who had played in other well known groups before. **Paddy Chambers** was a former member of **Faron's Flamingos** and the **Big Three**, while **John Frankland** came from **King Size Taylor & the Dominoes**.

Lewis Collins had previously played with the **Renegades** from Liverpool, the **Kansas City Five** and **The Georgians** - in the first two groups as the drummer, before he switched to the bass guitar.

Gibson Kemp had started his career with the **Night People,** before he became a member of the **Memphis Three** and played with **Rory Storm & the Hurricanes** and **King Size Taylor & the Dominoes**. **Lewis Collins** left to return to Liverpool where he joined the **Mojos** and was replaced in the **Eyes** by the German **Klaus Voormann**.

In this line-up the single *She* was recorded, with the 'Star-Club' standard *Peanut Butter* on the reverse side. This record, in contrast to the musical quality of the group, was not very good and did not become a great success in Germany, where it was released exclusively.

Paddy, Klaus & Gibson

But the **Eyes** had already been in the studio before where the songs *Another Saturday Night, Love Is A Swinging Thing, Twenty Flight Rock* and *Baby Baby* were recorded. *Baby Baby*, by the way, was identical to the **Supremes** hit *Where Did Our Love Go*. These songs were released on the two Swiss compilations 'Beat' and 'Yeah Yeah' on the Elite Special label.

John Frankland was replaced for a short time by **Johnny Phillips** (sax), who came from the **Roadrunners** and joined the **Krew** (aka **The Crew**), when **John Frankland** returned to the **Eyes**. When he left to get married to a girl from Hamburg and quit show business in 1965, the others continued as a trio under the name of **Paddy, Klaus & Gibson**.

They were signed by PYE and in 1965 their first single was released with *I Wanna Know,* which was the English version of the French Eurovision Song Contest winning song *N'avoue Jamais* by **Guy Mardel**. Correspondingly, it was quite an unusual record for a group like

Paddy, Klaus & Gibson and there was no connection to the roots of Merseybeat in this release. It sounded more like the **Walker Brothers**, only the voices were not really comparable.

The following single *No Good Without You Baby* was better but also was not successful, just like the third and final release by the band, *Teresa,* although this was a very nice and melodic song, even if not hard Beat anymore. It seems that **Brian Epstein**, who had taken over the group's management, tried to make something like the new **Walker Brothers** out of **Paddy, Klaus & Gibson**, but this failed in the end.

The trio disbanded in 1966 and **Klaus Voormann**, who had also designed the cover of the **Beatles** album 'Revolver', became a member of **Manfred Mann**. After that he was sometimes regarded as a fifth member of the **Beatles** because he had played on some sessions with them, but of course without becoming a steady member.

Gibson Kemp joined **Lee Curtis & the All Stars** for a short time in one of their last line-ups, but then became a member of the 'Star-Club' band **The Giants** from Hamburg. Around this time he also had a solo single released on the German Polydor label. Later, he played in the backing group of the **Les Humphries Singers** before he became a studio musician and then a producer for Phonogram, at first in Hamburg and then in London, before he went to Australia. He later returned to Hamburg where he is still living today.

Paddy Chambers joined the **Escorts**, where he played until the group split up in 1967. He then became a member of **Big John's Rock'n'Roll-Circus** and after that played with **Sinbad** and then led **Paddy Chambers & the Java Jive** until he sadly died too young in 2000.

Lewis Collins later had a successful career as an actor (for example he was 'Bodie' of The Professionals), but in 1983 he started to record some solo singles again from time to time.

Discography

as **The Eyes**:

She / Peanut Butter	G - Star-Club	148.519 / 1965

Tracks on compilation albums:

Baby Baby (Where did our love go) on 'Beat'	CH- Elite Special SOLP-S-33-250 / 1964	
Another Saturday Night on 'Beat'	CH- Elite Special SOLP-S-33-250 / 1964	
Love Is A Swinging Thing on 'Yeah Yeah'	CH- Elite Special SOLP-S-33-251 / 1964	
Twenty flight Rock on 'Yeah Yeah'	CH- Elite Special SOLP-S-33-251 / 1964	

as **Paddy, Klaus & Gibson**:

I Wanna Know / I Tried	UK - PYE	7N 15906 / 1965
No Good Without You Baby / Rejected	UK - PYE	7N 17060 / 1966
Teresa / Quick Before They Catch Us	UK - PYE	7N 17112 / 1966

Gibson Kemp - solo:

Make Love Not War / My Magic Room	G - Polydor	52975 / 1967

(***please note that the A-side of **Gibson Kemp**'s solo single was an instrumental soundtrack number for the film of the same name, which was written by **Gibson Kemp**. The B-side is sung by **Gibson Kemp**, but was recorded together with the **Giants** from Hamburg and already released before - on the reverse side of their single *Even The Bad Times Are Good* in 1967 - Polydor 52963)

FARON'S FLAMINGOS

This group originated from the **Hi-Hats**, a Skiffle group formed in a Liverpool bicycle club at the end of the Fifties. **The Hi-Hats** then developed into the **Ravens**, a Beat group which at first appeared with **Mike McPhillips** as vocalist under the name **Robin & the Ravens**. He was then replaced by **Billy 'Faron' Ruffley**, who had sung before with the **Tempest Tornadoes** under the name of **Faron & the TTs**.

There were probably also some more changes in the line-up and, following a **Bob Wooler** suggestion, the name of the group very soon was changed from the **Ravens** into **Faron & the Flamingos**, and a little later became **Faron's Flamingos**. Within a very short time the group became one of the local attractions - in the following line-up:

Billy 'Faron' Ruffley	**(voc)**
Nicky Crouch	**(lg/voc)**
Billy Jones	**(rg/voc)**
Eric London	**(bg/voc)**
Trevor Morais	**(dr)**

Trevor Morais, a really great drummer, was a former member of the **Cadillacs**, while it seems likely that **Nicky Crouch**, **Eric London** and **Billy Jones** were the remaining members of the original group.

In January 1962, **Eric London** left to join **Group One** and his replacement in **Faron's Flamingos** was **Dave 'Mushy' Cooper**, a former member of the **Topspots**, not identical to the group of **Ricky Gleason**. After the **Topspots**, **Dave Cooper** had played with **Bob Evans & the Five Shillings** and **The Vegas Five**. All three groups in some way were predecessor bands of the **Undertakers**. **Pam Conelly** then joined **Faron's Flamingos** as an additional singer, but left a little later, as did **Billy Jones**. Both disappeared from the scene.

The new members were **Paddy Chambers** (rg/voc), who had formerly played with **Steve Bennett & the Syndicate**, and **Barbara Harrison** (voc), who had sung with the **Hi-Cats** and **Johnny Templer & the Hi-Cats** before.

When, in January 1963, **Dave Cooper** joined the **Pawns**, **Faron** himself took over the bass guitar, and the band continued as a quartet, **Barbara Harrison** also having left again to join **Danny Havoc & the Ventures**, who later became the **Secrets**. After that she sang with the **Kansas City Five**.

Shortly after that change **Faron's Flamingos** were signed by Oriole and featured on the legendary compilation albums 'This Is Merseybeat' Vol.1 and Vol.2 with the songs *Let's Stomp, Shake Sherry, Talkin' 'bout You* and *So Fine*. The first two of these songs were later released on a single, but sadly had no chart success, although it was great rough Beat, just like the follow-up *See If She Cares* with its superb B-side *Do You Love Me,* which became a big hit a little later for **Brian Poole & the Tremeloes**.

Faron's Flamingos disbanded in early 1964. **'Faron'**, also called 'The Panda Footed Prince Of Prance' and **Paddy Chambers** joined the **Big Three**. After that **'Faron'** emigrated to France, where he was a member of a group called **Blue Suede**.

Paddy Chambers later played with the **Eyes**, **Paddy, Klaus & Gibson**, the **Escorts**, **Big John's Rock'n'Roll-Circus**, **Sinbad** and finally appeared with a group under the name **Paddy Chambers & the Java Jive** – until he sadly died in 2000.

Nicky Crouch became a member of the **Mojos** or **Stu James & the Mojos** respectively, before he disappeared from the scene for years. Then he came back with a group called **Ace Of Clubs** and, in the early Nineties, played with the re-formed **Cliff Roberts' Rockers**, before he disappeared again for a while and then re-formed the **Mojos**, where besides him and other well-known Merseybeat musicians, **Eric London** is also still playing today.

Trevor Morais at first formed his own band under the name **Trevor Morais Combo**, who also backed Manchester songstress **Lorraine Gray** for a short time. After that he joined **Ian Crawford & the Boomerangs** from Manchester, but then returned to Liverpool and had a short spell with **Rory Storm & the Hurricanes**. He then went back to Manchester and became a member of the **Peddlers**, where he played until they split up in the Seventies. He appeared again in the backing group for **Elkie Brooks** and after that as a member of **Stealer's Wheel**.

Billy 'Faron' Ruffley returned to Liverpool in the mid-Seventies and formed the new **Faron's Flamingos**, who were also featured on the revival sampler 'Mersey Survivors' in 1978 (UK- Raw RWLP 104) with the songs *Some Other Guy* and *Let's Twist Again.* But this group had more of a session character and besides **'Faron'**, only **Chris Evens** was known. From that session a single was also released with a strong version of *Bring It On Home To Me*, coupled with a totally disappointing version of **Eddie Cochran**'s *Come On Everybody* (UK-Raw 27).

But after that **'Faron'** had a steady line-up again for his **Flamingos**, which also included **Brian Jones** (sax), who, in the Sixties, was a member of the **Undertakers**, and later played with the **Glitter Band**. But then he returned to **Gary Glitter** before joining the great Liverpool Soul band **Y-Kickamoocow**. Finally, he was a member of **Nighttrain** and besides this still appears with the re-formed **Kirkbys**.

In 1987, **Faron's Flamingos** toured Germany again under the wing of **Horst Fascher**, the former manager of the legendary 'Star-Club' in Hamburg. **'Faron'**, whose singing was still as good as in the Sixties, presented himself to the audience in a very good condition and did full credit to his name as the 'Panda Footed Prince Of Prance'. There was no doubt he was still a Rock 'n' Roller from top to toe, supported by a good group with the line-up of **Phil Melia** (lg/voc), **Graham Price** (bg), **Steven Robertson** (sax) and **Derek Smallridge** (dr). **Phil Melia** was a former member of **Mojo Filter**, **Graham Price** came from **Supercharge** and **Derek Smallridge** was also a pioneer of Liverpool's music scene.

But the line-up of the band kept steadily changing, and **Phil Melia** was replaced by **Steve Roberts**, the younger brother of **Cliff Roberts**, the leader of the pioneering Liverpool group **Cliff Roberts' Rockers**. **Graham Price** was replaced by **Dennis Swale**, who in the Sixties had been with groups like **Terry & the Tuxedos**, the **Groupiers**, the **Four Dimensions** and the **Fyx**. The preceding line-up had been great but this new one was excellent and exactly what is expected of a Rock 'n'Roll band.

But sadly, this only lasted until 1989 and then **Steven Robertson** joined **Geoff Nugent**'s **Undertakers**, **Steve Roberts** changed to the **Fourmost**, before he joined his brother's band **Cliff Robert's Rockers**, and **Dennis Swale** formed an agency, before forming a new band under the name of **The Dimensions**, and even **Derek Smallridge** left to join a circus orchestra.

But **'Faron'** got a good band together again under the name of **Faron's Flamingos**, which also included **Chris Evens** on guitar again, as well as **Bernie Rogers** on drums, who in the Sixties had played with **Lee Curtis & the All Stars** and **Denny Seyton & the Sabres**.

In 1992 he had a heart attack and was seriously ill but after that was back with his band again, playing the bass guitar and jumping around as he did before - until he had a second heart attack in 1996. After that, he never got a steady group together again and appears only from time to time at the 'Merseycats' events, where he sings with various groups.

Discography

See If She Cares / Do You Love Me	**UK- Oriole CB 1834 / 1963**
Shake Sherry / Give Me Time	**UK- Oriole CB 1867 / 1963**
Let's Stomp / Rory Storm & the Hurricanes: I Can Tell	**UK- Columbia 43018 / 1964**

Tracks on compilation albums:

Let's Stomp	on	**'This Is Merseybeat' Vol.1**	**UK- Oriole PS 40047 / 1963**
Talkin' 'bout You	on	**'This Is Merseybeat' Vol.1**	**UK- Oriole PS 40047 / 1963**
Shake Sherry	on	**'This Is Merseybeat' Vol.2**	**UK- Oriole PS 40048 / 1963**
So Fine	on	**'This Is Merseybeat' Vol.2**	**UK- Oriole PS 40048 / 1963**
Do You Love Me	on	**'Group-Beat '63'**	**UK- Realm RM 149 / 1963**
See If She Cares	on	**'Group-Beat '63'**	**UK- Realm RM 149 / 1963**
Let's Stomp	on	**EP "Take Six"**	**UK- Oriole EP 7080 / 1963**

FARONS FLAMINGOS

THE FOUR CLEFS

This was certainly one of the most important and popular groups on Liverpool's early Merseybeat scene. Although they never made a big breakthrough or had any outstanding success, the **Four Clefs** were always there where it happened and placed very highly in the monthly popularity poll run by the 'Mersey Beat'.

Formed in 1961 in the area of Crosby, this group, beside the normal standards concentrated mainly on **Buddy Holly** material and so were often named as *'Liverpool's own Crickets'*.

In their original line-up the **Four Clefs** consisted of:

Arthur Raynor	**(voc/g)**
Norman Trump	**(g)**
Frank Morris	**(bg)**
John Bedson	**(dr)**

John Bedson left very soon and first became a member of the short lived **Roadrunners**. When they broke up he joined the **Challengers**, at that time backed **Tommy Quickly** and after that amalgamated with coloured singer **Steve Aldo** of **Steve Aldo & the Challengers**, but this is another story in this book. His place on drums with the **Four Clefs** was taken by **Jimmy Tushingham**, who was obviously a newcomer on the scene.

In 1962 **Norman Trump** left the group on a temporary basis and for approximately three months was replaced by **Derek Watling**. But then he returned to the **Four Clefs** and took his old place again while **Derek Watling** disappeared from the scene.

Les Ackerley, owner of the famous 'Iron Door' took over the management of the group and the **Four Clefs** of course became regulars at his club, where they were recorded in late 1962 or early 1963. This was at around the same time as the **Searchers** also recorded there, who through that obtained a recording contract with PYE, while the **Four Clefs**, for some reason, were not signed to a recording company. The 'Iron Door' recordings most probably were cut on acetate but nobody knows what happened to it and it is therefore not known which songs were recorded at that session.

In 1964 the **Four Clefs** were recorded again, this time by **John Schroeder** for the planned Oriole sampler 'Live at the Cavern', but this never came out and so it is only known that *Memphis Tennessee* was amongst the four or five songs that were recorded by the **Four Clefs**.

A little later, the group was offered a tour on the continent but **Arthur Raynor** decided to leave the group and joined **Chick Graham & the Coasters**, where he took over the lead vocals when **Chick Graham** left the group. When the **Coasters** split in 1965, **Arthur Raynor** became a solo entertainer on the cabaret circuit and still today is a big name in that scene as **Tony Marsh**. After he had left, the **Four Clefs** disbanded totally and while **Frank Morris** and **Norman Trump** obviously quit the music business, **Jimmy Tushingham** went to join **Rory Storm & the Hurricanes**. After that he was a member of the **Connoisseurs** until that group finally disbanded in 1969.

<u>Discography</u>

Nothing was ever released by the **Four Clefs** but in 1963, they were recorded at the 'Iron Door' and of that session most probably an acetate was cut that went missing and so it is not known which songs were recorded.

In 1964 the **Four Clefs** were chosen to be featured on the Oriole sampler 'Live at the Cavern' and recorded four or five numbers under the wing of **John Schroeder**. But this record was not released in the end and so it is only known that *Memphis Tennessee* was amongst the recorded songs.

The Four Clefs.

THE FOUR JUST MEN

Although counted as a Manchester scene group, this actually was a real Liverpool outfit. In 1961, a certain **Demetrius Christopholus** took part at a singers' contest at the Grafton Ballroom in Liverpool and won.

Encouraged by this success, he asked some friends to form a group with him and a few months later **Dee Fenton & the Silhouettes** had their first appearances – in the line-up with vocalist **Dee Fenton** (alias **Demetrius Christopholus**), **Peter Turner** (g), **Harry Bear** (bg) and **Larry Arendes** (alias **Larry King**) on drums.

At the end of 1962 guitarist **John Kelman** joined the group, having formerly played with the **Dons** and the **Five Stars**. **Harry Bear** left and **Peter Turner** took over the bass guitar.

At that time **Dee Fenton & the Silhouettes** were quite popular in Liverpool and always placed under the first 20 groups in the popularity poll of 'Mersey Beat'. They became much more successful when 'Kennedy Street Enterprises' took over their management and made them change their name into **Four Just Men** and to settle down in Manchester in the following line-up:

Demetrius Christopholus	**(voc/rg)**
John Kelman	**(lg/voc)**
Peter Turner	**(bg)**
Larry King	**(dr)**

The singer's name leaves no doubt that he was of Greek origin, just like **Savva Hercules**, the singer of the Liverpool beat group **Savva & the Democrats**.

In 1963 **John Kelman** left to go back to Liverpool and joined **Freddie Starr & the Midnighters**, that almost without exception consisted of former members of the **Five Stars**. He was replaced by **Harold 'Lally' Stott** from Prescot who had formerly played with the **Phantoms**. But in 1964 **John Kelman** returned to the **Four Just Men** and took over his old

place again, while **Lally Stott** went to Liverpool to join the **Denny Seyton Group**. He later went to Italy with the **Motowns** and became a very successful songwriter, but this is a different story that can be followed under **Denny Seyton & the Sabres** in this book.

The **Four Just Men** recorded the original *Half Past Five* for Decca in 1964, but this was not released. They also wrote and played the theme music for TV's 'Friday Night' and maybe through that they landed at EMI where they were signed for the Parlophone label.

Their first single *That's My Baby* was a real classic Merseybeat record, coupled with the very nice *Things Will Never Be The Same*. In spite of this it sadly failed to make a deserved breakthrough. *That's*

My Baby somehow became quite popular in Germany, where it was covered by some German beat groups, although the record was never released over there. When the single was just freshly released another group claimed the name **Four Just Men** as their own. Accordingly the Liverpool outfit changed its name to **Just Four Men** and under that name *That's My Baby* was re-released still in 1964.

Peter Turner left and probably quit show business. His replacement in **Just Four Men** was **Keith Shepherd**, who came from Manchester's **Johnny Martin & the Tremors**. Probably with this line-up the next single *There's Not One Thing* was released – again a great song, coupled with a great B-side *Don't Come Any Closer*, but also again without any further success.

Keith Shepherd left again and was replaced by **Stuart Sirett**, something of a musical globetrotter who formerly had played with the Manchester groups **Bing Stanley & the Dominator Four**, the **Javalins, Deke Rivers & the Big Sound, Wayne Fontana & the Jets, Johnny Peters & the Crestas** and **Johnny Peters & the J.P.s**. It was not really surprising that he did not stay too long and then joined the **Black Cat Bones,** after that he played with **Wayne Fontana & the Opposition** and then in a cabaret duo called **Musicbox**.

The **Just Four Men** were joined by **Barry Ashall** and probably with this line-up the band was offered the **Burt Bacharach** song *Trains And Boats And Planes* for their next release. The group recorded it but in the end did not want it to be released. It was given to **Billy J. Kramer** and it became a huge hit. The originals *Tomorrow, Norman Needs A Man, I Just Can't Make Up My Mind, Thinkin' About Your Love* and *Shelter Of Your Arms* were probably recorded at these recording sessions too, but never released.

Just Four Men went on a 30-day tour through Britain with **Del Shannon** and the **Shangri-Las** and after that on a short tour with the **Rolling Stones**, which was followed by a six-week engagement together with **David Garrick** in Paris, but none of that brought the sought after breakthrough. When they came back from France they joined singer **Pete MacLaine** for a time under the name **Pete MacLaine & the Four Just Men**.

Pete MacLaine, of course, was popular on the Manchester scene, being the former singer with **Pete MacLaine & the Dakotas** and **Pete MacLaine & the Clan**. This new connection did not record and when the **Four Just Men** separated again from the singer, the group decided on a fresh approach with a new sound and a new name and so in 1966 the legendary freak-beat outfit **Wimple Winch** was born. The group was signed to Fontana and the first release under the new name was *What's Been Done*, coupled with *I Really Love You*.

Both songs were still Merseybeat at its best, but on the follow-up *Save My Soul* the psychedelic touch was already there. That single hit the top of the local charts and stayed there for ten weeks but was not matched by sales in the rest of the country, for whatever reasons. The unusual *Rumble On Mersey Square South* was their third release and is very often named as their best single, but the public at large obviously did not like it as it took them nowhere.

It was probably in early 1968 that **Wimple Winch** disbanded and the musicians went their separate ways. **John Kelman** joined **Terry Rowland & the Explosions** for a short time, but then it seems he went back to Liverpool and quit show business, as did **Barry Ashall**.

Dee Christopholus was later featured in the musical 'Hair' but then concentrated on writing songs and later also became a record producer for GTO.

Larry King joined a band called **Sponge**, who were also backing group for **Dave Berry** for a while. This group, still with **Larry King**, later changed their name to **Pacific Drift** and recorded one single, and 'Feelin' Free' an interesting progressive album for Deram in 1970.

When this group split, **Lawrence Arendes**, as his real name is, concentrated on photography but also kept playing – lastly with **Mr. Suit**, the residential group at 'The Hangout' in Liverpool.

Discography:

as **The Four Just Men**:
That's My Baby / Things Will Never Be The Same   UK- Parlophone R 5186 / 1964

as **Just Four Men**:
That's My Baby / Things Will Never Be The Same   UK- Parlophone R 5208 / 1964
There's Not One Thing / Don't Come Any Closer   UK- Parlophone R 5241 / 1965

Different US-release (as **The Four Just Men**):
There's Not One Thing / Freddie & the Dreamers :
Send A Letter To Me   US- Tower   163 / 1965

Tracks on compilation albums:
That's My Baby   on **'I'm Telling You Now'**   US- Tower   DT   5003 / 1965
Things Will Never Be The Same on **'I'm Telling You Now'** US- Tower   DT   5003 / 1965

as **Wimple Winch**:
What's Been Done / I Really Love You   UK- Fontana TF   703 / 1966
Save My Soul / Everybody's Worried About Tomorrow   UK- Fontana TF   718 / 1966
Rumble on Mersey Square South / Typical British Workmanship UK- Fontana TF   781 / 1966
(*** please note that some copies of the last single were mispressings and had the song *Atmospheres* as B-side)

Unreleased tracks:
as **Four Just Men** or **Just Four Men**:
Friday Night   TV-music theme recording / 1964
Half past Five   UK- Decca demo   / 1964
Nightmare / Working Day Blues   UK- ??? acetate   / 1964
Further unreleased tracks from Parlophone recording sessions are
Trains And Boats And Planes, Tomorrow, Norman Needs A Man, I Just Can't Make Up My Mind, Thinkin' About Your Love, Shelter Of Your Arms   -   probably all from **1965**

as **Wimple Winch**:
Atmospheres, Three Little Teddy-Bears, You're A Big Girl Now, Coloured Glass, Those Who Wait, Sagitarius and **The Last Hoory** probably all from the Fontana recording sessions in **1966 / 67 Marmalade Hair, Bluebell Wood, Lollipop Minds** and **Pumpkin pie** - all independent recordings from **1967**

THE FOURMOST

It all started with the duo **The Two Jays**, which was formed by **Brian O'Hara** and **Joey Bowers** in Liverpool in the late Fifties in the style of the **Everly Brothers**.

After that, both musicians had a short spell with one of **Gerry Marsden**'s Skiffle groups, before they formed a band under the name of **The Four Jays**. This name was changed in **The Four Mosts** a little later - following a suggestion by **Bob Wooler**.

When **Brian Epstein** took over their management in 1963, he shortened that name to **The Fourmost**. Shortly before the final name change **Joey Bowers** (g/voc) had left the group to join the **Connoiseurs** and after that he became a member of **The Cheaters**.

So, in 1963, **The Fourmost** consisted of the following musicians:

Brian O'Hara	**(voc/rg)**
Mike Millward	**(lg/voc)**
Billy Hatton	**(bg/voc)**
Brian Redman	**(dr)**

Mike Millward was the new member of the **Fourmost**, formerly playing with **Bob Evans' Five Shillings**. **Brian Redman** left again to join **King Size Taylor & the Dominoes**, and later played with **Sonny Webb & the Cascades** from which the internationally successful Country band **The Hillsiders** developed.

The new drummer with the **Fourmost** was **Dave Lovelady**, a former member of **Ian & the Zodiacs** and **King Size Taylor & the Dominoes**. With this line-up, the group was signed by Parlophone and the first single *Hello Little Girl* became a top 10 hit in 1963, when it climbed up to No. 9 in the charts.

This great debut success was followed by *I'm In Love* (No.17 in 1963), *A Little Lovin'* (No. 6 in 1964), *How Can I Tell Her* (No. 33 in 1964), their good version of the **Four Tops** success *Baby I Need Your Loving* (No. 24 in 1964) and the Leiber/Stoller composition *Girls, Girls, Girls* (No.33 in 1965), which was more comedy than Merseybeat.However, the **Fourmost** had six big chart hits from their first seven singles, which was an outstanding success. Only *Everything In The Garden* (1965) did not enter the charts, although it was one of their better recordings. In the meantime, the **Fourmost** were featured in the film 'Ferry Cross The Mersey' with the song *I Love You Too*, which was included in the British and German release of the corresponding soundtrack album.

The Four Mosts
FORMERLY THE FOUR JAYS

BRO 3454
WAT 4338

In November 1965, the **Fourmost** had their first album out with the title 'First and Fourmost', that showed them to be very varied in their music, which was not generally positive. There were real rockers like *The Girl Can't Help It* or *Heebie Jeebies*, Soul influenced material like *The In-crowd, Some Kind Of Wonderful* or *Something's Got A Hold On Me,* Country songs like *Sure To Fall*, really good Merseybeat like *Till You Say You'll Be Mine* and the great *My Block,* Swing like *Bound To Lose My Heart*, and there are songs featured like *Girls, Girls, Girls* and *Baby Sittin' Boogie*, which showed that the group's trend was more towards being a comedy band than a Beat group.

It can be said that the **Fourmost** were the first cabaret group on the Merseybeat scene, although in 1966 they released a nice Beat ballad with the Lennon/McCartney composition *Here, There And Everywhere.* But the follow-up to this, *Auntie Maggie's Remedy,* was a real comedy song again, and only from the B-side *Turn The Lights Down* could it be figured that this group originated from the Merseybeat.

In the meantime, **Mike Millward** became ill with leukaemia and for a short time was replaced by **Bill Parkinson**. But he returned to the **Fourmost** and **Bill Parkinson** later became a member of **Chris Lamb & the Universals** and after that played with the **Circles**, who also sometimes backed **Screaming Lord Sutch** under the name of **The Savages**. He then joined the backing group of **Tom Jones** (what a contrast...) and became a successful songwriter. He, for example, wrote *Mother Of Mine,* which was a big international hit for **Neil Reid**.

In December 1965, **Mike Millward** left the **Fourmost** again because of his illness and sadly died a little later, which was a big shock for the whole Liverpool music scene, as he was a really likeable guy. At first, he was replaced by **George Peckham**, a former member of Liverpool's **Renegades**, **Lee Curtis & the All Stars**, **Pawns**, **Groups Inc.**, **Kinsleys** and **Earl Royce & the Olympics**. When he left, **Ian Edwards**, who had just disbanded **Ian & the Zodiacs**, took over, but a little later he changed to the **Connoisseurs** and the original founder member **Joey Bowers** returned to the **Fourmost**.

In 1969, **Paul McCartney** produced the single *Rosetta* with the **Fourmost** on the CBS label, quite a poor production and the best on that record is the B-side *Just Like Before.* This record did not sell too well and had no chart success, nor did the far better *Apples, Peaches, Pumkin' Pie* one year before.

The next single was *Maxwell's Silver Hammer* that for mysterious reasons was released under the pseudonym **Format**. This, by the way, was the only single that was ever released by them in Germany but it did not become a big seller. The follow-up, *Easy Squeeze,* again did not make any progress on the record market and was the final one for CBS.

1972 saw the final single release by the **Fourmost** with the songs *Goodnight Sweet Dreams* and *Memphis* on the obscure Phoenix label.

In 1975, the **Fourmost** released a second album, entitled 'The Fourmost', which included studio versions of their live act, for example *Down At The Club, I've Got You Under My Skin, Save The Last Dance For Me, Without You, Rag Doll* and *Will You Still Love Me Tomorrow.* It was not too bad, but also no 'knockout'.

The end for the **Fourmost** came in 1979, when **Joey Bowers**, **Bill Hatton** and **Dave Lovelady** decided to form the cabaret band **Clouds**, which also included **Steve 'Tiger' Fleming** (org), who had formerly played with various Merseybeat groups like **Mark Peters & the Cyclones**, **Mark Peters & the Silhouettes**, and finally with the newly formed **Merseybeats**.

When **Clouds** split again, **Steve Fleming** and **Dave Lovelady** joined **Vince Earl & the Attractions**, where they are still playing today. **Brian O'Hara** amalgamated with another Liverpool group under the name of **The Fourmost**, but in 1982, he left that band and became a compere and solo entertainer in the cabaret scene until he committed suicide in 1999.

The other group continued under the name of **The Fourmost** with a line-up of **Billy Haisman** (voc/bg), **Ronnie Hughes** (lg/voc), **Bernie Crossley** (rg/voc) and **John Campbell** (dr/voc). But they were not a cabaret band anymore and their live programme included the old hit songs of the **Fourmost**, as well as stuff of the **Beach Boys** and **Four Seasons**, and so on.

The original **Fourmost** came together again a few times for the 'Mersey Cats' organisation, but these were only occasional performances.

Discography

Hello Little Girl / Just In Case	**UK- Parlophone R 5056 / 1963**
I'm In Love / Respectable	**UK- Parlophone R 5078 / 1963**
A Little Lovin' / Waiting For You	**UK- Parlophone R 5128 / 1964**
How Can I Tell Her / You Got That Way	**UK- Parlophone R 5157 / 1964**
Baby I Need Your Loving / That's Only What They Say	**UK- Parlophone R 5194 / 1964**
Everything In The Garden / He Could Never	**UK- Parlophone R 5304 / 1965**
Girls, Girls, Girls / Why Do Fools Fall In Love	**UK- Parlophone R 5379 / 1965**
Here, There And Everywhere / You've Changed	**UK- Parlophone R 5491 / 1966**
Auntie Maggie's Remedy / Turn The Lights Down	**UK- Parlophone R 5528 / 1966**
Apples, Peaches, Pumkin Pie / I Couldn't Spell	**UK- CBS 3814 / 1968**
Rosetta / Just Like Before	**UK- CBS 4041 / 1969**
Easy Squeeze / Do I Love You	**UK- CBS 4461 / 1970**
Goodnight Sweet Dreams / Memphis	**UK- Phoenix S NIX 126 / 1972**

EPs:

FOURMOST SOUNDS   **UK-Parlophone GEP 8892/ 1963**
- I'm In Love / Respectable / Hello Little Girl / Just In Case
HOW CAN I TELL HER   **UK-Parlophone GEP 8917/ 1964**
- How Can I Tell Her / You Got That Way / A Little Lovin' / Waiting For You

LP FIRST AND FOURMOST   **UK-Parlophone PMC 1259/ 1965**
- Till You Say You'll Be Mine / Yakety Yak / Girls, Girls, Girls / My Block / So Fine / Some Kind Of Wonderful / The Girl Can't Help It / Today I'm In Love / The In-crowd / Baby Sittin' Boogie / Heebie Jeebies / Sure To Fall (in love with you) / Bound To Lose My Heart / Something's Got A Hold On Me

LP THE FOURMOST   **UK- private release SOF 001 / 1975**
- Down At The Club / My Eyes Adored You / Zing Went The Strings Of My Heart / I've Got You Under My Skin / Save The Last Dance For Me / The Girl Can't Help It / Without You / Take Your Finger Out Of Your Mouth / Rag doll / Will You Still Love Me Tomorrow
(*** please note that this album was a private release by the band for selling at gigs only)

Tracks on compilation-albums:
I Love You Too   on '**Ferry Cross The Mersey**'   **UK-Columbia 33 SX 1676 / 1964**
as **Format**:
Maxwell's Silver Hammer / Music Man   **UK- CBS 4600 / 1969**
Unissued tracks:
Among the unissued tracks of the **Fourmost** are the songs **Little By Little** (1964),
If You Cry (1964), **Running Bear** (??) and **Love Of The Common People** (probably 1969).

GERRY & THE PACEMAKERS

This legendary Merseybeat group originated from the **Mars Bars**, a Skiffle group formed in Liverpool in the late Fifties that consisted of **Gerry Marsden** (voc/g), **Dixie Dean** (g), **Jimmy Tobin** (bg), **Tommy Ryan** (wb) and **Freddie Marsden** (dr).

When, a little later, **Arthur McMahon** (p) joined, the name of the group was changed to **The Gerry Marsden Skiffle Group**. **Arthur McMahon** by the way was the same person as **Arthur Roy**, the former leader of **Arthur Roy & the Rockers**.

This line-up was probably joined by the **Two Jays** for a short time, which were **Joey Bowers** and **Brian O'Hara,** who then formed **The Four Jays**, which later became the **Fourmost**.

When the brothers **Gerry** and **Freddie Marsden** together with **Arthur McMahon** continued as a trio under the name of **The Gerry Marsden Trio**, **Dixie Dean** joined the **Kruzads** and from 1972 until 1974 was a member of **McGuinness Flint**. **Jimmy Tobin** and **Tommy Ryan** disappeared from the scene.

When the members of the **Gerry Marsden Trio** decided to continue as a Beat group, they looked for a bass guitarist and at first wanted **Keith Draper**, but he then became a member of **Alby & the Sorrals**. So **Les Chadwick** was recruited and the group changed their name to **Gerry & the Pacemakers.** The next to leave was **Arthur McMahon** who joined the **Nocturns** and accordingly, the group now consisted of:

Gerry Marsden	**(voc/lg)**
Les Maguire	**(p/voc)**
Les Chadwick	**(bg/voc)**
Freddie Marsden	**(dr)**

The new member **Les Maguire** had formerly played saxophone with the very early **Undertakers**. In this line-up, **Gerry & the Pacemakers** recorded all their Sixties material, which was released on the Columbia label.

Some people like to say that this band grew up in the slipstream of **The Beatles** and was no more than a fare dodger, but this is nonsense because for some time **Gerry & the Pacemakers** were as successful and popular as **The Beatles** in Liverpool, and they had a different sound and their own hits, which had no connection to the Fab Four's. Amongst them was the first No.1 hit ever to come out of Liverpool.

Their most successful records were *How Do You Do It* (No. 1), *I Like It* (No. 1), *I'm The One* (No. 2), *You'll Never Walk Alone* (No. 1), *Don't Let The Sun Catch You Cryin'* (No. 6), *Ferry Cross The Mersey* (No. 8), *I'll Be There* (No. 15), *Walk Hand In Hand* (No.29) and *Girl On A Swing*.

You'll Never Walk Alone became the anthem for Liverpool Football Club and is played at all their matches. **Gerry Marsden** still loves to remember that more than 30,000 football fans sang him this song on his wedding day in 1965 in Liverpool's stadium, and that his wife Pauline could not hold back the tears. What in God's name has such popularity got to do with the **Beatles** slipstream?

Ferry Cross The Mersey, of course, was the title song of the motion picture, which featured, besides **Gerry & the Pacemakers** in the main role, the Liverpool artists **Earl Royce & the Olympics**, the **Black Knights**, the **Blackwells**, the **Koobas**, the **Fourmost** and **Cilla Black**. Even if this music film was not a bestseller, it is an important, very interesting and nice document of that unique Liverpool Beat era. The title song was later re-released by lots of other artists and so brought in quite a lot of money for the composer **Gerry Marsden**.

When, at the end of the Sixties, the Beat lost more and more ground, **Gerry Marsden** disbanded the **Pacemakers** and accepted a part in the musical 'Charlie Girl', from which a record of him together with **Derek Nimmo** was released, but *Liverpool/Charlie Girl* was quite a poor single and had no great success.

Freddie Marsden went back to a normal day job and never returned to show business. He sadly died in 2007. **Les Chadwick** emigrated to Australia, where he owned a music shop in Sidney and **Les Maguire** became a sailor but in 1999 he stepped back into the music business as a member of the re-formed **Ian & the Zodiacs**, who, after **Ian Edwards** left, still continue under the name **Zodiacs** today.

Gerry Marsden continued in the music business and recorded some nice solo singles like *Please Let Them Be* or the fantastic *My Home Town*, until he formed a new group under the name of **Gerry & the Pacemakers** in the mid-Seventies.

In 1977, this group toured Germany again, with the line-up of **Gerry Marsden** (voc/lg), **Mark Kirkpatrick** (bg), **Bob Haddrell** (org) and **Keith Hall** (dr).

Mark Kirkpatrick was a former member of **Vemon**, while **Keith Hall** had been a professional musician since the age of 12, and amongst others had played with **Picketywitch**.

Bob Haddrell came from a Jazz background and a little later was replaced by **Alan Greenwood** (p/org), who for Rock 'n 'Roll music was much better and, as a session musician, had formerly played with various groups.

In 1978 a TV film about **Gerry & the Pacemakers** was shown in England and Germany, which made very clear how popular the pleasant singer with the inimitable grin and his group still was at that time, even if very good singles like the second take of *You'll Never Walk Alone, Unchained Melody* and *Oh My Love* did not become chart hits.

In the mid-Eighties **Gerry Marsden** had a hit comeback, when he was the leader of the session **Crowd**, which also included **Frank Allen** of the **Searchers**, **Joe Fagin** (formerly **The Strangers**), **Paul McCartney**, as well as a lot of other popular musicians. They recorded the benefit record *You'll Never Walk Alone* for the victims of the fire disaster in Bradford's football stadium, and this record became a chart topper.

In 1989 **Gerry Marsden** was a member of another session, which also included **Paul McCartney**, **Holly Johnson** (of **Frankie Goes To Hollywood**) and the **Christians**. This session, which had no special name, recorded another benefit record for the victims of the terrible and unforgettable disaster in the Hillsborough football stadium in Sheffield, which happened during the match between 'Liverpool FC' and 'Nottingham Forest'.

This record, a re-arranged version of **Gerry Marsden**'s *Ferry Cross The Mersey*, became another top 5 hit. Some people may say **Gerry Marsden** only had his later successes because of these benefit records, but this would be unfair, as he is as good a musician today as he ever was, which is especially clear from various old and new albums by **Gerry & the Pacemakers**.

The only exception is the 'Lennon/McCartney Songbook' LP by **Gerry Marsden** alone, which was released by K-tel in 1985. From the point of view of a real Beat fan, it can only be described as extremely gruesome and boring with all that noise of synthesizers and drum machines and it is hard to understand how a pioneer of the Beat movement like **Gerry Marsden** could condescend to do something like this. But even this slip-up does not change the fact that the group **Gerry & the Pacemakers** truly deserves to be called a legend of that unique Merseybeat era.

Discography
How Do You Do It / Away From You	UK- Columbia DB 4987 / 1963
I Like It / It Happened To Me	UK- Columbia DB 7041 / 1963
You'll Never Walk Alone / It's Alright	UK- Columbia DB 7126 / 1963
I'm The One / You've Got What I Like	UK- Columbia DB 7189 / 1964
Don't Let The Sun Catch You Cryin'/ Show Me That You Care	UK- Columbia DB 7268 / 1964
It's Gonna Be Alright / It's Just Because	UK- Columbia DB 7353 / 1964
Ferry Cross The Mersey / You, You, You	UK- Columbia DB 7437 / 1964
I'll Be There / Baby, You're So Good To Me	UK- Columbia DB 7504 / 1965
Walk Hand In Hand / Dreams	UK- Columbia DB 7738 / 1965
La la la / Without You	UK- Columbia DB 7835 / 1966
Girl On A Swing / Fool To Myself	UK- Columbia DB 8044 / 1966

Different French release:
You'll Never Walk Alone / Jambalaya	F- Columbia 7 XCA 10.054 / 1964

Different German releases:
Pretend / Why Oh Why	G- Columbia C 22929 / 1965
Girl On A Swing / The Way You Look Tonight	G- Columbia C 23325 / 1966

Different US-releases:
It's Gonna Be Alright / Skinny Minnie	US- Laurie 3293 / 1965
I Like It / Jambalaya	US- Laurie 3271 / 1964
Give All Your Love To Me / You're The Reason	US- Laurie 3313 / 1965
Looking For My Life / Bright Green Pleasure Machine	US- Laurie 3370 / 1966

Gerry Marsden - solo:
Please Let Them Be / I'm Not Blue	UK- CBS 2784 / 1967
Gilbert Green / What Makes Me Love You	UK- CBS 2946 / 1967
In The Year Of April / Everyday	UK- Nems 3831 / 1968
Every Little Minute / In Days Of Old	UK- Nems 4229 / 1969
I've Got My Ukelele / What A Day	UK- Decca F. 13172 / 1971
Amo Credo / Come Break Bread	UK- Phoenix 129 / 1972

Gerry Marsden & Derek Nimmo:
Liverpool / Charlie Girl	UK- CBS 3575 / 1968

EPs:
HOW DO YOU DO IT   UK-Columbia SEG 8257/ 1963
- How Do You Do It / Away From You / I Like It / It Happened To Me

YOU'LL NEVER WALK ALONE   UK-Columbia SEG 8295/ 1963
- You'll Never Walk Alone / Jambalaya / Chills / A Shot Of Rhythm & Blues
I'M THE ONE   UK-Columbia SEG 8311/ 1964
- I'm The One / You've Got What I Like / You Can't Fool Me / Don't You Ever
DON'T LET THE SUN CATCH YOU CRYIN'   UK-Columbia SEG 8346/ 1964
- Don't Let The Sun Catch You Cryin' / Show Me That You Care / Summertime /
Where Have You Been
IT'S GONNA BE ALRIGHT   UK-Columbia SEG 8367/ 1964
- It's Gonna Be Alright / It's Just Because / Maybelline / You're The Reason
GERRY IN CALIFORNIA   UK-Columbia SEG 8388/ 1965
- Skinny Lizzie / My Babe / Away From You / What'd I Say
HITS FROM 'FERRY CROSS THE MERSEY'   UK-Columbia SEG 8397/ 1965
- It's Gonna Be Alright / I'll Wait For You / Ferry Cross The Mersey / Why Oh Why
RIP IT UP   UK-Columbia SEG 8426/ 1965
- Rip It Up / Reelin' And Rockin' / Whole Lotta Shakin' Goin' On / You Win Again

Different French releases :
YOU'LL NEVER WALK ALONE   F-Columbia ESRF 1446 / 1963
- You'll Never Walk Alone / Jambalaya / A Shot Of Rhythm & Blues / Where Have You Been
DON'T LET THE SUN CATCH YOU CRYIN' / I'M THE ONE   F-Columbia ESRF 1549 / 1964
- Don't Let The Sun Catch You Cryin' / Show Me That You Care / You've Got What I Like / I'm The One
FERRY CROSS THE MERSEY   F-Columbia ESRF 1637 / 1965
- Ferry Cross The Mersey / You, You, You / It's Gonna Be Alright / It's Just Because

LPs:
HOW DO YOU LIKE IT   UK-Columbia SX 1546 / 1963
- Shot of Rhythm & Blues / Jambalaya / Where Have You Been / Here's Hoping / Pretend /
Maybelline / You'll Never Walk Alone / Wrong Yo-yo / You're The Reason / Chills / You Can't Fool Me/
Don't You Ever / Summertime / Slow Down
FERRY CROSS THE MERSEY   UK-Columbia SX 1693 / 1965
- It's Gonna Be Alright / Why oh Why / Fall In Love / Think About Love / This Thing Called Love
/ Baby You're So Good To Me / I'll Wait For You / She's The Only Girl For Me / Ferry Cross The
Mersey / + The Fourmost : I Love You Too + George Martin Orchestra : All Quiet On The Mersey-
Front + Cilla Black : Is It Love
YOU'LL NEVER WALK ALONE   UK-Regal   SREG 1070 / 1967
- same songs as on 'How Do You Like It'-album

Different US-releases :
DON'T LET THE SUN CATCH YOU CRYIN'   US-Laurie   SLP 2024 / 1964
- Don't Let The Sun Catch You Cryin' / I'm The One / Away From You / Jambalaya / Mabellene /
You'll Never Walk Alone / How Do You Do It / You're The Reason / Don't You Ever / Summertime / Slow
Down / Show Me That You Care
SECOND ALBUM   US-Laurie   SLP 2027 / 1964
- I Like It / A Shot Of Rhythm & Blues / Where Have You Been / Here's Hoping / Pretend / The
Wrong Yo-Yo / Chills / You Can't Fool Me / It's Happened To Me / It's All Right / Slow Down /
Jambalaya
FERRY CROSS THE MERSEY   US-United Artists UAS 6387/ 1965
- songs of Gerry & the Pacemakers are the same as on UK-release
 + The Black Knights : I Gotta Woman
 + Earl Royce & the Olympics : Shake A Tail Feather
 + The Blackwells : Why Don't You Love Me

I'LL BE THERE US-Laurie SLP 2030 / 1965

- I'll Be There / What'd I Say / Rip It Up / You Win Again / You You You / Now I'm Alone / My Babe / Reelin' And Rockin' / I Count The Tears / Whole Lotta Shakin' Goin' On / It'll Be Me / Skinny Minnie

GREATEST HITS US-Laurie SLP 2031 / 1965

- Ferry Cross The Mersey / How Do You Do It / I'm The One / My Babe / Away From You / I'll Be There / It's Gonna Be Alright / Pretend / I Like It / Chills / It'll Be Me / Don't Let The Sun Catch You Crying

GIRL ON A SWING US-Laurie SLP 2037 / 1966

- Girl On A Swing / The Way You Look Tonight / Guantanamera / Pretty Flamingo / At The End Of The Rainbow / Looking For My Life / The Big Bright Green Pleasure Machine / See You In September / Who Can I Turn To / Without You / Strangers In The Night / La La La

Tracks on compilation-albums:

It's Gonna Be Alright	on 'Liverpool'	G- Columbia C 83777 / 1964
It's Just Because	on 'Liverpool'	G- Columbia C 83777 / 1964
Whole Lotta Shakin' Goin' On	on 'Liverpool '65'	G-Columbia SMC 83990 / 1965
Rip It Up	on 'Liverpool '65'	G-Columbia SMC 83990 / 1965
You Win Again	on 'Liverpool '65'	G-Columbia SMC 83990 / 1965
Pretend	on 'Liverpool Hop'	G-Columbia SMC 83983 / 1965
How Do You Do It	on 'The Best Of The Liverpool Sound'	F- Columbia FPX 272 / 1964

Unreleased tracks:

The only known unreleased tracks by **Gerry & the Pacemakers** are *Come Back To Me, When oh When* and *Hallelujah I Love Her So*, probably all from 1963/1964.

For collectors it might be interesting to know that all three songs were included in the 1984 album "The Very Best Of Gerry & the Pacemakers" (UK- MFP 41 5654 1)

Besides this **Gerry Marsden** cut the one-sided EMIDISC acetate *I Ain't Got Time,* probably in late Sixties / early Seventies.

RICKY GLEASON & THE TOPSPOTS

To clear up one thing in advance, this group did not have any connection to the **Topspots** from the Wirral, the predecessor group of the **Undertakers**.

This band was formed by **Derek Banks** (aka **Ricky Gleason**) under the name of **Denny & the Escorts** in Liverpool in 1962. They became quite successful on the local scene but they were never an outstanding success. In 1963, the name of the band was changed to **Ricky Gleason & the Topspots** and the line-up at this time consisted of the following musicians:

> **Ricky Gleason** (voc)
> **Len Burman** (g/voc)
> **Graham Little** (g)
> **Kalvin Harrison** (bg/voc)
> **Tommy Limb** (dr)

In 1963 the group was also signed to Oriole and according to **Ricky Gleason** it was featured on the third volume of the legendary samplers 'This Is Merseybeat' with the songs *I'm A Hog For You* and *Johnny B. Goode*. This volume three was apparently released in the United States only and in a very small edition. Generally there is nothing known about this release, but who can claim that it is not true?

The fact is that **Ricky Gleason & the Topspots,** in 1963, recorded two Kensington acetates and the first one amongst others also included *I'm A Hog For You*. While the first acetate was an EP, the second one was a single with the songs *Talk About You* and *You're No Longer Mine*, probably both originals by the group.

In 1963 **Ricky Gleason & the Topspots** were booked to play the 'Star-Club' in Hamburg, where they went down well. During their stay in Hamburg, the group is said to have been recorded by the German Polydor label, but again there is nothing known about a release, but this does not necessarily mean that nothing was released, because the German Polydor label was well-known for sometimes releasing records under wrong or different band names.

In 1964 **Len Burman** left the group and disappeared from the scene, while **Kalvin Harrison** joined **J.J. & the Hi-Lites**, which a little later became the **Mersey Monsters**. After that he was a member of the **Rebels**. They were replaced by **Keith Dodd** (g/voc) and **Kenny Rees** (bg/voc).

RICKY GLEASON & THE TOPSPOTS
Would like to wish all friends, fans, promoters etc
especially Dave Forshaw, Don Read and Bill and Virginia
of 'Mersey Beat'—ALL THE BEST FOR THE COMING
SEASON

MERSEYSIDE'S NEW No.1 GROUP—
RICKY GLEASON
AND THE
TOPSPOTS
(B.B.C. RECORDING ARTISTES)
Just back from the Star Club

Manager:
DAVID FORSHAW Enterprises
6 DALEY PLACE
BOOTLE 20
AINtree 9654

London Representative:
DON READ LTD.
1 WEIGHHOUSE STREET
LONDON W.1.
HYDE PARK 5164

Keith Dodd was a former member of the **Beathovens** and the **Principals**, while **Kenny Rees** had played before with the **Black Velvets**. A little later, **Ricky Gleason** also left the group, who continued under the name of the **Topspots** - probably with **Kenny Rees** on lead vocals.

Ricky Gleason first formed the group **Ricky Gleason & the Nighthawks** who existed

159

until 1966. After that he became a member of the **Rebels**, who were formerly known as **Ian & the Rebels** and now also sometimes appeared under the name of **Ricky Gleason & the Rebels**.

When this group also disbanded in the late Sixties, he became a member of the **St. Ive's Trio** and, until 1975, he sang in a cabaret duo together with **David May**, a former member of **Mark Peters & the Silhouettes** and **Rory Storm & the Hurricanes**. Then he quit show business and did not return.

Before the **Topspots** disbanded in 1965, they cut two more acetates on Deroy. The first one, recorded immediately after the departure of **Ricky Gleason**, included the songs *Jam, Nothin's Shakin', Chills* and *Little Latin Lupe-Lu*. The second one came in 1965 with *True Love, Milkcow Blues, What Is This Feeling* and *Welcome To My World*.

RICKY GLEASON is back again ! !
WITH THE
REBELS
Phone J. Cropper
Ormskirk 2317

When the **Topspots** split up, drummer **Tommy Limb** became a member of the **Mersey Monsters** and **Kenny Rees** joined the new group of **King Size Taylor** before he disappeared from the scene. All the other members probably quit showbiz.

In 1998 there was a revival concert by **Ricky Gleason & the Topspots** for the 'Merseycats' at the 'Aintree Institute' with **Ricky Gleason, Kalvin Harrison, Graham Little** and **Tommy Limb.** As, for unknown reasons, **Keith Dodd** did not show up at that event, **Geoff Nugent** of the **Undertakers** stood in for him. Such a revival of the group was sadly not repeated, but **Keith Dodd** these days sometimes appears in Sixties shows again where he plays as guitarist with different groups that mainly have a jam session character.

Ricky Gleason and THE TOP SPOTS

Discography

According to the statement by **Derek Banks, Ricky Gleason & the Topspots** could have been featured on the third volume of the Oriole samplers 'This Is Merseybeat' with the songs *I'm A Hog For You* and *Johnny B. Goode*. This album may have been released only in the USA and in a very small edition, what seems improbable but not impossible.

Besides this **Ricky Gleason & the Topspots** recorded in 1963 in Germany for the Polydor label, but there is nothing known about a release under the name of the band.

as **Ricky Gleason & the Topspots**:
Remember Me / I'm A Hog For You /	
Pistol Pickin' Mama / Now I Know	UK- Kensington acetate / 1963
Talk About You / You're No Longer Mine	UK- Kensington acetate / 1963

as **The Topspots**:
Jam / Nothin's Shakin' / Chills / Little Latin Lupe-Lu	UK- Deroy acetate	/ 1964
True Love / Milkcow Blues / What Is This Feeling /		
Welcome To My World	UK- Deroy acetate	/ 1964

160

CHICK GRAHAM & THE COASTERS

At first this group was called **The Sandstormers** and in 1962 as **The Phantoms,** they became the backing group for a singer named **Billy Forde,** whose real name was **William Howard Ashton** and who later as **Billy J. Kramer** had international stardom.

Billy Forde & the Phantoms were one of the hundreds of Liverpool amateur beat groups specialising in the imported U.S. Rock'n'Roll sound. **Ted Knibbs** took over their management and following his advice they changed their name to **Billy Kramer & the Coasters**.

BILLY KRAMER
WITH
THE COASTERS

Ted Knibbs' influence obviously worked well on the group that came third in the 'Mersey Beat' pop poll of 1963. At a following appearance at the 'Cavern', **Brian Epstein** became interested in taking over the management of **Billy Kramer & the Coasters** and recorded the demo *She's My Girl* with them. But, with the exception of **Billy Kramer,** none of the group members wanted to make the step forward into the professional music business.

So **Brian Epstein** only signed the singer and brought him together with the **Dakotas** from Manchester, the former backing group of **Pete MacLaine**. The name of this new group then was **Billy J. Kramer with the Dakotas** - the band in some way had to stay individual as they also recorded without Billy J. in their own right. But this is a completely different story.

The **Coasters** continued under the management of **Ted Knibbs** and he brought them together with the boyish singer **Graham Jennings**. Under the name **Chick Graham & the Coasters,** the group had a real impact on the scene and turned professional in 1963 - in the following line-up:

Chick Graham	**(voc)**
Arthur Ashton	**(lg/voc)**
Ray Dougherty	**(rg)**
George Braithwaite	**(bg)**
Tony Saunders	**(dr)**

Arthur Ashton, by the way, the cousin of **Billy J. Kramer,** had formerly played with the **Confederates** together with **Mike Pender** of the **Searchers. George Braithwaite** left and probably quit the music business and his replacement was **Arthur Raynor,** a former member of the **Four Clefs.** He took over the rhythm-guitar, while **Ray Dougherty** switched to bass.

In 1964, **Chick Graham & the Coasters** were signed to Decca and in the same year released two nice Beat singles with *Education* and *A Little You.* The latter had some minor success but did not enter the charts. *A Little You,* in 1965, became a big chart success

Chick Graham

161

for **Freddie & the Dreamers** from Manchester although their version was no better than the one by **Chick Graham & the Coasters**.

Recorded versions of *Ciao Ciao Bambino* and the **Shirelles** number *Will You Still Love Me Tomorrow* which were meant to be included on a Decca EP by the group for mysterious reasons were not released. In spite of that bad luck **Chick Graham & the Coasters** had a large following in the North and their popularity also reached down as far as London.

Still in 1964, for unknown reasons a series of changes started in the line-up. The first to leave was **Arthur Ashton** who joined **Mark Peters & the Silhouettes** and later played with **Ian & the Zodiacs**. He was replaced by **Mike Kontzle**, who came from the **Beatwoods**.

Tony Saunders followed **Arthur Ashton** to **Mark Peters & the Silhouettes** and later became a member of the **Squad,** which had developed from **Mark Peters & the Method** and **The Riot Squad**. The new drummer with the **Coasters** was **Jimmy Lacey**, a former member of the **Profiles** and **Johnny Templer & the Hi-Cats**. These changes obviously were too much for **Chick Graham**, who left the group and quit show business.

The new frontman then became **Arthur Raynor** and the group for a while continued as **The Coasters**. When they disbanded, **Arthur Raynor** changed his name into **Tony Marsh** and became a successful solo artist on the cabaret scene, where he is still going today.

Jimmy Lacey joined **The Three Cheers** who later should have developed into the Polydor recording group **Phase Three**. **Mike Kontzle** at first became a member of the **Roadrunners** and later appeared with **Colonel Bagshot & his Incredible Bucket Band**.

The other members of **Chick Graham & the Coasters** did not appear on the scene again. Only the group's name stayed on as a legend of Merseybeat.

Discography
as **Billy Kramer & the Coasters**:
She's My Girl   UK - Epstein-Demo / 1963

as **Chick Graham & the Coasters**:
Education / I Know   UK-Decca F.11859 / 1964
A Little You / Dance, Baby, Dance   UK-Decca F.11932 / 1964

Unissued tracks:
In 1964, **Chick Graham & the Coasters** recorded the songs *Will You Still Love Me Tomorrow* and *Ciao Ciao Bambina* at Decca for an EP which in the end was not released - for unknown reasons.

THE GRIFF PARRY FIVE

This group was formed in Liverpool in February 1964 by **Ron Parry**, the former drummer with **Joe Brown & the Bruvvers** and **Brian 'Griff' Griffiths**, who had formerly played with **Derry & the Seniors**, **Howie Casey & the Seniors** and the **Big Three**.

Right from the start the **Griff Parry Five** consisted of the following musicians:

Steve Aldo	**(voc)**
Brian Griffiths	**(lg/voc)**
Vinnie Parker	**(p/org)**
Frank Galloway	**(bg/sax)**
Ron Parry	**(dr/voc)**

Steve Aldo, whose real name is **Eddie Berisford**, had sung before with **Steve Aldo & the Challengers**, the **Nocturns** and with **King Size Taylor & the Dominoes**.

Frank Galloway was also a former member of **King Size Taylor & the Dominoes**, who had just disbanded. In this line-up, the **Griff Parry Five** also appeared as the backing group for **King Size Taylor** at some gigs in England.

The band then was signed to Decca and in 1964 recorded the songs *Don't Make My Baby Blue, Irresistible You* and the **Crests** success *Sixteen Candles* according to an announcement in 'Mersey Beat'. For some mysterious reason none of them were ever released.

Finally the first single came out with a very strong version of **Marvin Gaye**'s *Can I Get A Witness,* under the name of **Steve Aldo**. This single, which was coupled with **Jimmy Reed**'s *Baby What You Want Me To Do,* sadly had no chart success, and remained the only release by the group. **Howie Casey** was a member also, he had had a short spell with the **Big Three** but left to reform his old group the **Krew**.

It was probably in late 1964 that **Ron Parry, Brian Griffiths** and **Vinnie Parker** left to team up with **Johnny Gustafson** in the **Johnny Gus Set,** which is another story in this book.

Because the name giving musicians had left, the group could not continue under this name and the remaining **Steve Aldo** and **Frank Galloway** recruited **Spike Jones** (org) and **Brian Low** (dr) plus a guitarist, whose name sadly is lost and continued as the **Steve Aldo Quintet.**

The group disbanded when **Steve Aldo** left to follow former member **Howie Casey** to the **Krew.** When this band also split up, **Steve Aldo** joined the **Fyx** and then became a member of **The In-Crowd** before he was backed by the **Fairies** for a short time. In the meantime, he had released his second single *Everybody Has To Cry*, a good version of **Arthur Alexander**'s *Everyday I Have To Cry.* Later, **Steve Aldo** was a Jazz singer but then disappeared from the scene.

Frank Galloway formed a new group together with **Daryl Dougdale** (org) of the **Johnny Gus Set**, drummer **Pete Clarke** of the **Escorts** and a certain **Nick La Grec** (voc), but the name of the band sadly got lost over the years.

Discography
In 1964 the **Griff Parry Five** recorded for Decca the songs *Sixteen Candles, Irresistible You, Don't Make My Baby Blue* and probably two others, but there was never anything released.

The following records were released under the name of **Steve Aldo** although on the first one the whole line-up of the **Steve Aldo Quintet** (formerly the **Griff Parry Five**) was featured.

as **Steve Aldo**:
Can I Get A Witness / Baby What You Want Me To Do	**UK- Decca**	**F.12041 / 1964**
Everybody Has To Cry / You're Absolutely Right	**UK- Parlophone R 5432 / 1964**	

(please note that the second single was not recorded with the **Griff Parry Five** or the **Steve Aldo Quintet**, but as far as it is known it was a recording session which at least partially consisted of Liverpool musicians.)

GROUP ONE

This pure Liverpool group was formed in the beginning of 1962 by experienced musicians, who had already played before in other established groups on the Merseybeat scene.

They had left their former bands because they did not want, for whatever reasons, to become professionals in the music business. **Group One**, in their first line-up, consisted of:

>**Dave Williams** (voc/lg)
>**Eric London** (rg/voc)
>**Keith Stokes** (bg/voc)
>**Harry Prytherch** (dr)

Dave Williams was a former member of the **Firecrests** and **Dale Roberts & the Jaywalkers,** while **Eric London** had played before with the **Ravens** (or **Robin & the Ravens**) who became **Faron's Flamingos. Keith Stokes** and **Harry Prytherch** were former members of the **Remo Four,** or the **Remo Quartet** as this group was originally named.

In November 1962, **Eric London** left and quit show business and only lately appeared again as a member of the re-formed **Mojos**, where he is still playing. He was replaced in **Group One** by **Brian Hilton**, a former member of **Vince Earl & the Zeros**.

One month later **Group One** was placed at number 13 in the popularity poll of 'Mersey Beat' - really a big success if one considers that at this time there were hundreds of Beat groups around in Liverpool. This placement showed the great popularity of **Group One**, who a little later featured on various TV and radio programmes. Oriole was interested in signing them and probably did, although there was never a record released.

Dave Williams left the group and he later appeared again in the line-up of the **Four Originals** which was something of a successor group to his old band **Dale Roberts & the Jaywalkers,** where he is still playing. His replacement in **Group One** was **Karl Terry** (g/voc), the legendary 'Sheik of Shake', who had formerly led his own group **Karl Terry & the Cruisers.**

A little later, **Brian Hilton** also left to join **Sonny Webb & the Cascades,** who then became the **Hillsiders.** He was replaced by **Les Williams** who was a former member of **Terry & the Tuxedos** and **Billy Butler & the Tuxedos. Group One,** in addition to the **Searchers** and the **Undertakers** was one of the groups who regularly performed at the 'Iron Door'.

In 1964 the group disbanded totally without having had any national success, but they were very popular all over the North and, let's face it, that is a lot for an amateur band, isn't it?

Karl Terry joined Newcastle's **Delemeres** and then became a member of **Amos Bonny & the TT's,** who a little later were re-named **Karl Terry & the TT's**.

After that, he had a short spell with the **Talismen** but then re-formed the **TT's,** before the remaining members of this group and the remaining members of the **Clayton Squares** amalgamated as the **T-Squares.** He later re-formed **Karl Terry & the Cruisers** again and is still playing the Liverpool pub circuit.

Les Williams became a member of the **Four Dimensions,** later shortened to the **Dimensions,** before they changed to **Jet** and after that to **Pendulum**. Today he is also a member of the re-formed **Mojos**. **Harry Prytherch** quit show business in the Sixties, as did **Keith Stokes**.

In 1993, **Group One** was re-formed for the 'Merseycats' organisation in the original line-up of 1962 with **Dave Williams**, **Keith Stokes**, **Eric London** and **Harry Prytherch**, but the group only plays sporadically at 'Merseycats' benefit concerts.

Discography

Group One never released a record but probably recorded some songs for Oriole in 1963. Certainly there were also some sessions for various TV and radio shows recorded but the songs are sadly not known - with the exception of *Pretend*, which was recorded live for the BBC in October 1963.

Group One

GROUPS INC.

When **Freddie Starr** was still appearing with the **Kansas City Five** and a tour of France was offered to him at the end of 1962, he wanted the group to come with him. But as most of the musicians did not want to turn professional, only **Bruce McCaskill** and **Peter Cooke** of the **Kansas City Five** accepted the offer.

They found further members in **Sid Edwards** (bg), formerly with the **Flames**, **Nutrockers** and **Lee Shondell & the Capitols** and the drummer **Pete Orr** from the **Hi-Cats**.

This line-up then was joined by the girl singer **Wendy Harris**, as it was a presupposition for the tour to have a girl in the line-up. **Wendy Harris** had just returned from a tour of France with the **TT's**. This new line-up was named **Groups Inc.,** but broke up again after their return from France.

Sid Edwards and **Pete Orr** were founder members of the **Ventures**, who a little later became the backing group for **Freddie Starr** for a time, while **Wendy Harris** disappeared from the scene. **Bruce McCaskill** and **Peter Cooke** formed a new group under the name of **Groups Inc.** that consisted of:

Frank Knight	**(voc/g)**
Peter Cooke	**(lg/voc)**
Bruce Monroe	**(rg/voc)**
Pete Jones	**(bg)**
Pete Clarke	**(dr)**

Bruce Monroe of course was **Bruce McCaskill**, who originally was the founder of the **Bluegenes**, the predecessor group of the **Swinging Blue Jeans** and after that he was the founder and bandleader of the **Kansas City Five**.

Peter Cooke had started with the **Topspots**, (not **Ricky Gleason**'s group), and then played with **Dee & the Dynamites**, the short-lived **Roadrunners** (II) and the **Kansas City Five**. **Frank Knight** was the former leader of **Frank Knight & the Barons**, who after his departure became **Lee Castle & the Barons**.

Pete Jones came from Liverpool's recently disbanded **Renegades** and before that he had played with the **Crosbys**, while the former group of **Pete Clarke** were the **Tiyms**.

But this line-up of **Groups Inc.,** did not last too long because **Frank Knight** left again and was replaced by **George Peckham**, a former member of the **Skylarks**, the **Renegades** and **Lee Curtis & the All Stars**. **Peter Cook** joined **Earl Royce & the Olympics** and after that played with the **Trend** (without 's'). In the Seventies he was a member of the newly formed **Faron's Flamingos**.

Frank Knight

He was replaced in **Groups Inc.,** by **Paul St. John**, whose real name was **Paul Pilnick** and who had formerly played with **Vince & the Volcanoes** and **Lee Curtis & the All Stars**.

Besides this, **Pete Jones** left to join the **New Avengers** and was replaced by **Robert Allen**. With the exception of **Bruce McCaskill** (**Bruce Monroe** then) and **Pete Clarke**, the whole line-up had changed within a very short time and so **Groups Inc.,** now appeared in the following line-up:

> **George Peckham** (voc/g)
> **Paul St. John** (lg)
> **Bruce Monroe** (rg/voc)
> **Robert Allen** (bg)
> **Pete Clarke** (dr)

In spite of all the changes the band kept up a really good quality and was very popular along Merseyside and other areas in the North of England.

Groups Inc., became something like the resident group of the famous 'Iron Door' but also appeared quite often at the 'Cavern' and other Liverpool clubs. Because of the steadily changing line-up, the band never signed a recording contract and also never had the chance of a national breakthrough. It was still in 1964 when **Groups Inc.,** disbanded totally and the individual members joined other groups.

Pete Clarke became a member of the **Escorts** and later played with the **Krew** (better known as **The Crew**) and **Them Grimbles** before he re-joined the **Escorts**. In 1966, he was a member of the **Fruit Eating Bears** and later a founder member of **Liverpool Scene**, who musically did not really belong to the Merseybeat scene anymore.

Bruce McCaskill (**Monroe**) also became a member of the **Escorts** but probably of the road crew and not of the band. After that he was the road manager for **Eric Clapton** and then became the very successful manager of the **Average White Band**. He sadly died much too young in 1994. **George Peckham** joined the **Pawns** but then changed to the **Kinsleys** who very soon disbanded again. After that he appeared with **Earl Royce & the Olympics** and later became a member of the **Fourmost**. **Paul Pilnick** (**St.John**) at first played the **Big Three** but then re-joined **Lee Curtis & the All Stars**, before he played with various groups like for example **Stealer's Wheel**.

In 1978 the band name **Groups Inc.,** appeared again on the revival sampler 'Mersey Survivors' but only for this recording session and with the exception of **George Peckham** and **Pete Jones,** probably none of the former members were included.

On that interesting compilation **Groups Inc.,** made a good impression in performing **Arthur Alexander**'s classics *Where Have You Been* and *Soldier Of Love*. These, sadly, were the only releases of **Groups Inc.,** for certain one of the good and very interesting groups of the unique Merseybeat era.

<u>Discography</u>

There never was a record released by **Groups Inc.,** in the Sixties, and as far as it is known no acetates or demos were recorded. But, in 1978, the band name appeared again with **George Peckham** and **Pete Jones** of the Sixties line-up, when **Groups Inc.,** was featured on the following compilation:

Where Have You Been	on **'Mersey Survivors'**	**UK-Raw**	**RWLP 104 / 1978**
Soldier Of Love	on **'Mersey Survivors'**	**UK-Raw**	**RWLP 104 / 1978**

THE JOHNNY GUS SET

This group was formed by **Johnny 'Gus' Gustafson** in Liverpool in 1965, after he had formerly played with the groups **Cass & the Casanovas**, the **Big Three**, the **Seniors** and the **Merseybeats**. The original line-up of the **Johnny Gus Set** consisted of the following musicians:

Johnny Gustafson	**(voc/bg)**
Brian 'Griff' Griffiths	**(g/voc)**
Vinnie Parker	**(org)**
Ron Parry	**(dr)**

Brian 'Griff' Griffiths was a former member of **Derry & the Seniors** who became **Howie Casey & the Seniors**, the **Big Three,** the **Seniors** and the **Griff Parry Five**, while **Ron Parry** had formerly played with **Joe Brown & the Bruvvers** and the **Griff Parry Five**.

Vinnie Parker, who had also been in the **Griff Parry Five** before, left again quite soon and at first the **Johnny Gus Set** continued as a trio. They were signed by Polydor and in 1965 recorded the single *Just To Be With You*, that had little success, although it was also released in Germany on the black Polydor International label.

In May 1965 **Daryl Dougdale** (org) the former leader of the **Daryl Dougdale Trio** joined the group but left again in July to form a new group with **Frank Galloway** (bg/sax), **Pete Clarke** (dr) and **Nic LaGrec** (voc/g). The **Johnny Gus Set** once again remained as a trio and recorded a new single in December 1965. Their version of *Take Me For A Little While* was also released on Polydor, but this time it was only credited to **Johnny Gustafson**. As this single was no big success the group disbanded in early 1966.

Johnny Gustafson, together with **John Banks** of the just disbanded **Merseybeats**, formed the duo **Johnny & John** and for a time they were backed by the **Thoughts** from Liverpool, also on their only single *Bumper To Bumper,* which also failed to become a bigger success.

After that, both joined the **Quotations**, a London based group who released a great single with *Cool It / Mark Of Her Head,* where the B-side was written by **Johnny Gustafson**.

John Banks joined **Rupert's People** and stayed a little longer with the group who also recorded as **Johnny B. Great**. After that **Johnny Gustafson** appeared for a short time with **Episode Six** and later became a member of **Quartermass** and **Hard Stuff**. He also played on the **Roxy Music** album 'Stranded' and after that he sang the 'Simon Zealotes' in the musical '*Jesus Christ Superstar*', where he was featured on the original album. In 1973 he re-formed the **Big Three** together with former member **Brian Griffiths**, as well as with the drummer **Nigel Olson**, who had formerly played with **Plastic Penny**, the **Spencer Davis Group** and in **Elton John**'s backing group **Dodo**, but this band only recorded the album 'Resurrection' and then disbanded again.

While **Brian Griffiths** emigrated to Canada, **Johnny Gustafson** appeared again at the end of the Seventies with the **Ian Gillan Band** and in the Eighties he was a member of a London band, which appeared under the two names of **Rowdy** and **The Rock Band**.

Finally, **Johnny Gustafson** was a member of the **Pirates**, who had developed from **Johnny Kidd**'s former backing group of the same name. Nothing more was heard of the other members of the quite short-lived **Johnny Gus Set**.

<u>Single discography</u>

Just To Be With You / Sweet Day   UK- Polydor 56 022 / 1965

as **Johnny Gustafson**:
Take Me For A Little While / Make Me Your Number One   UK- Polydor 56 043 / 1965

Johnny (Gustafson) **& John** (Banks):
Bumper To Bumper / Scrape My Boot   UK- Polydor 56 087 / 1966

(*** please note, that the second single was only released under the name of **Johnny Gustafson** but was played in by the **Johnny Gus Set**. The duo **Johnny & John** was backed by the **Thoughts** from Liverpool on their only single.)

THE HIDEAWAYS

This pure Rhythm & Blues band was formed by three Liverpudlians, one American and a musician of Japanese descent in Liverpool at the end of 1963.

In spite of their multinational line-up, the **Hideaways** definitely belong to the Liverpool scene and became a quite important part of it. But because Rhythm & Blues was not as popular at that time as the more commercial Merseybeat, the group was not paid the attention that it deserved. Within one year, the **Hideaways** became one of the leading Rhythm & Blues bands in the North - in the line-up with:

Judd Lander	**(voc/harm)**
Frank O'Connor	**(voc/rg)**
Ozzi Yue	**(lg)**
John Shell	**(bg/voc)**
John Donaldson	**(dr)**

At the end of 1964 **John Shell** was called up by the US army for the Vietnam war, possibly because, in spite of his steady residence in England, he was still an American citizen. In 1967, he lost his life in this controversial war. His replacement in the **Hideaways** in 1964 was **Dave**

Collins, another Liverpudlian, who had formerly played with the **Hi-Cats** and their follow-on groups **Freddie Starr & the Ventures**, **Danny Havoc & the Ventures** and **The Secrets**.

The **Hideaways** regularly appeared at all important clubs in Liverpool and its surrounding area, but it took until 1966 for the **Hideaways** to be recorded for the first time. This was not an official record but contained live recordings from the 'Sink' club in Liverpool, which together with two numbers by the **Clayton Squares** were featured on an EP enclosed to the German book 'Beat in Liverpool', written by **Jürgen Seuss**.

On this record, the **Hideaways** can be heard with *Momma Keep Your Big Mouth Shut* and their version of **Arthur Alexander**'s *Black Night*. The sound quality of this record is pretty poor and so the EP is only interesting for collectors or other people who are interested in the Liverpool music scene of the Sixties.

It is a mystery why a regular record was never released by this very good group, who in addition to the **Clayton Squares** was paid quite good attention in the above mentioned book. Important and interesting is the fact that the **Hideaways** played the most of all the bands at the 'Cavern' - a total of 412(!) gigs. These appearances also include the final gig before the

'Cavern' was closed in February 1966, as well as the first night when it was re-opened in July 1966.

At the end of 1967 **Judd Lander** left the group and a little later joined the **Selofane** from Liverpool who, in the same year, cut two excellent singles for CBS, but that is another story. With this group, **Judd Lander** went down to London, where he later became a successful session and studio musician. Amongst others, he can be heard playing that great harmonica on the hit record *Karma Chameleon* by **Boy George**'s **Culture Club**.

The **Hideaways** were joined by **Ritchie Rutledge** as an additional singer, formerly with the **Aztecs** and the **Cryin' Shames**, who now shared the lead vocals with **Frank O'Connor**.

Dave Collins left and was replaced by **Chris Finley**, a former member of the **Kruzads**, **Masterminds** and the **Fruit Eating Bears** and a little later the **Hideaways** changed their name to **Confucius**. When **John Donaldson** also left, **Phil Chittick** joined the group as new drummer.

Probably with this line-up **Confucius** recorded the **Yardbirds** song *I Wish You Would,* **Sammy Davis'** *But Not For Me,* as well as *Life's A Drag, I Know What You're Thinking, The Times I Wish* and *Sally Go Round The Moon,* which were all band originals, most of them written by **Frank O'Connor** and **Chris Finley**. Sadly none of these songs were ever released.

In late 1968 **Confucius** recorded their only single with *The Brandenburg Concerto* for RCA, which was coupled with *The Message,* once again an original by **Frank O'Connor** and **Chris Finley**. This record sadly did not have any chart success and so the band did not achieve a greater and no doubt deserved, breakthrough. **Confucius** most probably disbanded in the very early Seventies.

Phil Chittick later appeared again with the new **Merseybeats** and after that played with **Cy Tucker & the Friars**. **Chris Finley** also joined the new **Merseybeats**, then became a member of **Herman's Hermits** and after that played with some other bands. **Ritchie Rutledge**, in 1972, was a member of the **Swinging Blue Jeans** for a short time and then disappeared from the scene although he continued in the music business.

Frank O'Connor at first teamed up with **Alan Crowley** (ex **Billy Butler & the Tuxedos**) in the cabaret duo **Two's Company**, before he started a solo career and released some nice solo singles, in particular *Liverpool - It All Came Tumbling Down* is a very good one. He wrote this song at the same time as his brother **Freddie O'Connor** wrote a book of the same title.

In 1989 **Frank O'Connor** and **Ozzi Yue** along with some other famous Liverpool musicians like **Mike Pender** of the **Searchers**, **Tony Crane** and **Billy Kinsley** of the **Merseybeats**, and then **Liverpool Express**, **Kenny Parry** (**Liverpool Express**) and **Alan Crowley**, **John O'Brian** and **Billy Butler** (all formerly **Billy Butler & the Tuxedos**) were part of the session **The Class Of '64** which recorded an album of own songs, written by **Frank O'Connor** and **Alan Crowley**. Even if it was more Country influenced, it was a really good album which also clearly showed the song writing talent of Frank and Alan.

The Class Of '64, in 1991, also recorded a memorial cassette with *Cavern Days,* which sadly was not released on record. Of course it was another line-up in the meantime but also included **Frank O'Connor** again.

Ozzi Yue later became an actor but still leads his own group **Yue Who**, which is quite successful on the Liverpool club scene.

The group never released an official record under the name of **The Hideaways** but can be found on a live EP together with the **Clayton Squares** which was enclosed in the German book 'Beat in Liverpool' by **Jürgen Seuss**.

On this EP, the **Hideaways** are featured with the tracks *Black Night* and *Momma Keep Your Big Mouth Shut* which were recorded at the 'Sink' club in Liverpool.

The book and also the EP were released in 1965/1966 by Bertelsmann (G-Sonopress EVA 101) but because of the bad sound quality is only interesting for collectors.

After the band had changed their name to **Confucius** in 1968, the following numbers were recorded but sadly never released: *I Wish You Would, But Not For Me, Life's A Drag, I Know What You're Thinking, The Times I Wish* and *Sally Go Round The Moon*.

as **Confucius**:

The Brandenburg Concerto / The Message   UK- RCA   ???   / 1968

THE TERRY HINES SEXTET

This real Rhythm & Blues group was formed in Liverpool by former members of the recently disbanded **T.L.'s Bluesicians** in early 1965 – namely **Bob Hardy** (g/sax), **Phil Perry** (p) and **Pete Newton** (bg).

They teamed up with the vocalist **Terry Hines**, who had just parted from the **Clayton Squares**, the sax-player **Ray Rens** and **Dave Irving** on drums. **Phil Perry** and **Ray Rens** left again quite soon and while **Phil Perry** stopped playing, **Ray Rens** later appeared again as a member of the **Fyx**. With the new members the **Terry Hines Sextet** now consisted of the following musicians :

Terry Hines	**(voc)**
Bob Hardy	**(g/tr/sax)**
Terry Kenna	**(lg)**
Pete Newton	**(bg)**
Alby Donnelly	**(sax)**
Dave Irving	**(dr)**

Terry Kenna was a former member of the **St. Louis Checks,** while **Dave Irving** had played in a Modern-Jazz trio before. **Alby Donnelly** for a very short time had also played with the **St. Louis Checks** and before that had been a member of the **Plainsmen**.

Bob Hardy

The **Terry Hines Sextet** within a short time became very popular on the scene and later in 1965 went into the CAM studio and recorded the songs *Caldonia* and *Back Door Blues.* Of these two, *Caldonia* especially is a real knockout.

In July 1965 the group also recorded at the famous 'Marquee' in London for a commercial radio station, but it is not known which songs were played in that gig. A little later the **Terry Hines Sextet** provided the music for the 'Jack Of Spades', a play featured in Liverpool's 'Commonwealth Arts Festival' at the 'Everyman' Theatre. **Terry Hines** discovered his love of the theatre here and left the group in October 1965 to concentrate on his new career. **Jeff Workman** (voc/org/p), formerly of the **Feelgoods** then joined the band, which changed its name for a short period to **The Sextet**, before recruiting a new vocalist / frontman with **Eddie Cave**, who formerly had sung with the **Poets** and then from that developed **Richmond Group**. This line-up, following a suggestion of **Bob Wooler**, who became the band's manager and agent, changed its name to the **Fix**. But this is another story in this book.

Discography

In 1965 the **Terry Hines Sextet** recorded the songs *Caldonia* and *Back Door Blues* at the CAM—studio in Moorfields on a reel-to-reel tape. These numbers sadly were never released on record, but were featured on the Mayfield-CD 'This Is Merseybeat Vol. 3' in 2002.

IAN & THE ZODIACS

Two groups were formed in the Crosby/Liverpool area in 1958, which were both predecessor groups to **Ian & the Zodiacs**. These groups were **The Deltones** and **The Zodiacs**.

The Deltones originally consisted of **Paul Dougherty** (voc), **Ian Edwards** (voc/g), **Geoff Bethel** (p/org), **George Hodges** (bg) and **Peter 'Mesh' Stephenson** (dr).

In 1960 **Geoff Bethel** joined **King Size Taylor & the Dominoes** and **Ian Edwards** became a member of the **Zodiacs**, while the remaining three musicians together with **Dave Edwards** (lg) continued as a band under the name **St. Paul & the Angels** but later changed the name back to **The Deltones.** They disbanded in 1963 and only **'Mesh' Stephenson** in the late Nineties appeared again - as a member of the re-formed **Dominoes**, that sometimes were joined by **King Size Taylor**.

The Zodiacs originally consisted of **John Kennedy** (voc/g), **Pete Griffiths** (bg), **Pete Pimlett** (g), **Jerry Garagan** (p), a sax-player with the name **Dave**, as well as **Dave Lovelady** on drums. When **Johnny Kennedy** left in 1960 to become a member of **King Size Taylor & the Dominoes**, the **Zodiacs** were joined by **Ian Edwards** of the **Deltones**, but the group nearly disbanded when **Pete Griffiths** died in a motorbike accident and at the same time **Jerry Garagan** and the sax-player **Dave** left.

The remaining **Ian Edwards, Pete Pimlett** and **Dave Lovelady** were then joined by **Peter Wallace** (bg) and changed their name to **Ian & the Zodiacs**. But this line-up only lasted for one year and then **Pete Pimlett** left and probably quit show business, while **Dave Lovelady** became a member of **King Size Taylor & the Dominoes**.

Ian Edwards and **Peter Wallace** were joined by **Charly Flynn** (g/voc), **Geoff Bethel** (p/org) and **Cliff Roberts** (dr), who all came from **King Size Taylor & the Dominoes**. **Charly Flynn** had played before that with the **Bobby Bell Rockers** and **Geoff Bethel** of course with the **Deltones**. With all these changes **Ian & the Zodiacs** in 1961 consisted of :

Ian Edwards	**(voc/g)**
Charly Flynn	**(g/voc)**
Peter Wallace	**(bg)**
Geoff Bethel	**(p/org)**
Cliff Roberts	**(dr)**

This line-up lasted longer and in 1963 was chosen to be featured on the Oriole compilations 'This Is Merseybeat' Vol.1 and Vol.2, with the songs *It Ain't Necessarily So, Let's Turkey Trot* and *Secret Love.*

A little later **Ian & the Zodiacs** released their first single on the same label with a great version of the **Marvelettes** number *Beechwood 4-5789*, but it was sadly unsuccessful.

A few weeks later, the album tracks *Let's Turkey Trot* and *It Ain't Necessarily So* were also released on single, but under the name of **Wellington Wade**.

Charly Flynn had used this name when he wrote the B-side of the first single and it is hard to explain why this name was chosen by Oriole for the second single, because it was clearly the **Ian & the Zodiacs** recordings from the compilation. However, this record also did not make it, although the magazine 'Reveille' saw a bright future for the *'new talented singer'* **Wellington Wade**.

Despite the two unsuccessful singles, 1963 became a good year for **Ian & the Zodiacs** as

they were booked to play the 'Star-Club' in Hamburg, where they went down very well.

Geoff Bethel had left the group before the trip to Hamburg and especially for that Germany tour was replaced by **Mike Partridge**, who had come out of Birmingham's 'Brumbeat' scene. After that tour he left again and **Ian & the Zodiacs** continued as a four-piece.

When **Cliff Roberts** joined the new **King Size Taylor** band in 1964, he was replaced by **Geoff Bamford**, the former drummer with **Rikki & the Red Streaks**, **The Connoisseurs** and the **Memphis Three**.

In 1965 the group released the single *Just The Little Things I Like* under the name **Ian Edwards & the Zodiacs** on Fontana, as well as the album 'Gear Again' on the Wing label, which featured cover versions of the big hits of that time.

In the meantime, **Ian & the Zodiacs** had been back in Germany where they had become big stars in the so-called 'Star-Club' scene. The group also became quite popular in the United States after the album 'Ian & the Zodiacs' was released over there. This was a great long player, which also came out in Germany as 'Star-Club Show 7' on the 'Star-Club' label, but for mysterious reasons was never issued in Great Britain.

For the German market, *Message To Martha* was coupled out as a single, followed by further great recordings like *So Much In Love, Bitte Komm Wieder,* the German version of *Message To Martha*, which did not come out at that time but was only released in 1999, the superb *Leave It To Me, No Money No Honey* and *Na-na-na-na-na* - all by 1966.

Beside this **Ian & the Zodiacs** had two more great albums out in Germany with the titles 'Just listen to ...' and 'Locomotive', while in England and USA only a few more singles were released.

It is very hard to understand that the English market did not pay more attention to that excellent group. It was one of the Liverpool groups that had a great influence on the German music and band scene and was regarded as one of the best beat groups that ever came out of England.

In 1966, one more double album was released on the English Fontana label, but this one under the pseudonym of **The Koppykats** and it featured exceptional cover versions of **Beatles** hits. It became the biggest selling success for **Ian & the Zodiacs** in England and was also released on the continental market - in Germany as two single albums with the titles 'The Beatles Best Done By The Koppykats' and 'More Beatles Best Done By The Koppykats', of which the songs *Help* and *Nowhere Man* were coupled out as single on the obscure 'Pop Ten' label. Without doubt, these records were played, sung and produced very well but were not half as interesting as the other albums by **Ian & the Zodiacs**.

Meanwhile there had been some more changes in the line-up. **Peter Wallace** had left in August 1966 and at first became a member of the London based group **The Mike Cotton Sound** but then returned to Liverpool where he joined the **Connoisseurs**.

He was replaced in **Ian & the Zodiacs** by **Tony Coates** from Liverpool, who formerly had played with the **Corsairs** and **Mark Peters & the Method**. **Geoff Bamford** had also returned to Liverpool, where he disappeared from the scene and his replacement was **Fred Smith**, a former member of the **Bobby Patrick Big Six** and **Tony Sheridan & the Big Six**, but he left again and later became a member of the **Kevin Ayers Band**. The new drummer with **Ian & the Zodiacs** in 1967 was **Joe Walsh**, who had played before with the **Teenbeats**, the **TJs** and finally with **Lee Curtis & the All Stars**.

In March 1967 **Charly Flynn** followed **Peter Wallace** to the **Connoisseurs** and he was replaced by **Arthur Ashton**, a former member of the **Confederates, Billy Forde & the Phantoms** and the follow-on groups **Billy Kramer & the Coasters** and **Chick Graham & the Coasters**, as well as of **"Mark Peters & the Silhouettes**. Beside this **Klaus Doldinger** occasionally appeared on the **Ian & the Zodiacs** records as organist. He had previously, under the name of **Paul Nero**, led his own group the **Blue Sounds Inc.**.

In July 1967 **Ian & the Zodiacs** disbanded totally when **Ian Edwards** returned to Liverpool, where he at first became a member of the **Fourmost** - but only for a short time, and then joined the **Connoisseurs**. After that he played with the **Chesterfields** before he quit show business.

Tony Coates was later a member of **Crane** and **Liverpool Express**, while **Arthur Ashton** emigrated to the USA and **Joe Walsh** became a member of the newly formed **Undertakers** before he also quit. It is very hard to understand that this fabulous group never had bigger international chart success and that they were added to the Liverpool legends simply did not do enough justice to their great quality and their reputation on the continental music scene of the Sixties. In the end it can be said that England missed out on one of their very best groups of that time.

In 1999 **Ian Edwards** stepped back onto the music scene and re-formed **Ian & the Zodiacs**, together with former **Gerry & the Pacemakers** member **Les Maguire** (p/org/voc), **Colin Fabb** (bg/voc), who in the Sixties was a member of the **Connoisseurs, Carl Hardin** (dr) plus **Malcolm Little** (lg).

The drummer **Carl Hardin** was a member of **Paul Dean & the Tuxedos** in the Sixties, a band of English soldiers based in Bielefeld / Germany and after that played with various beat groups in England. In this line-up **Ian & the Zodiacs** toured Germany in 2000 and at least their gig in Bielefeld went down a bomb.

In 2003 the group parted from **Ian Edwards** for unknown reasons and with the singer **Neil Lancaster** and **Barry 'Baz' Davis** as new lead guitarist continued as the **Zodiacs**.

Barry Davis was an original member of the **Connoisseurs** and after that had played with **King Size Taylor, Mike Warner & the New Stars** from Bielefeld, the **New Vaudeville Band** and **Jimmy James & the Vagabonds**. Today, besides playing with the **Zodiacs** he is also a member of the **Undertakers**.

Ian Edwards quit show business again but then tried a new comeback with different backing groups. He sadly died unexpectedly on 22nd October 2007, which was not only a shock for the Merseybeat scene, but also a tragic loss.

Single discography
Beechwood 4-5789 / Can You Think Again	UK- Oriole CB 1849 / 1963
No Money, No Honey / Where Were You	UK- Fontana TF 708 / 1966
Wade In The Water / Come Along Girl	UK- Fontana TF 753 / 1966

as **Wellington Wade**:
Let's Turkey Trot / It Ain't Necessarily So	UK- Oriole CB 1857 / 1963

as **Ian Edwards & the Zodiacs**:
Just The Little Things I Like / This Won't Happen To Me	UK- Fontana TF 548 / 1965

different US releases as **Ian & the Zodiacs**:
Livin' Lovin' Wreck / Crying Game	US-Philips	40244 / 1965
Good Morning Little Schoolgirl / Message To Martha	US-Philips	40277 / 1965
So Much In Love / This Empty Place	US-Philips	40291 / 1965
Leave It To Me / Why Can't It Be Me	US-Philips	40343 / 1966
No Money, No Honey / Where Were You	US-Philips	40369 / 1966

different German releases as **Ian & the Zodiacs**:
Message to Martha / Spartacus	G- Star-Club	148.514 / 1965
So Much In Love With You / All Of Me	G- Star-Club	148.535 / 1965
Bitte Komm Wieder / All Of Me	G- Fontana	269.325 / 1965
Leave It To Me / Why Can't It Be Me	G- Star-Club	148.543 / 1966
No Money, No Honey / Ride Your Pony	G- Star-Club	148.548 / 1966
Na-na-na-na-na / Any Day Now	G- Star-Club	148.572 / 1966

as **The Koppykats**:
Help / Nowhere Man	G- Pop Ten 6805.015 / 1966

LP discography
GEARAGAIN	UK- Wing WL 1074 / 1965

- Eight Days A Week / It's All Over Now / The Rise And Fall Of Flingel Bunt / We're Through / Tired Of Waiting For You / I Feel Fine / All Day And All Of The Night / Game Of Love / When You Walk In The Room / Um-um-um-um-um / A Hard Day's Night / Silhouettes

different German releases:

STAR-CLUB SHOW 7	G- Star-Club 158.007 / 1965

- Good Morning Little Schoolgirl / Rockin' Robin / The Crying Game / Message To Martha / Jump Back / This Empty Place / So Much In Love With You / Livin' Lovin' Wreck / Clarabella / Spartacus / Baby I Need Your Lovin' / It's Alright / A Hard Day's Night

JUST LISTEN TO IAN & THE ZODIACS   G- Star-Club 158.020 / 1966
- The 'In' Crowd / Make It Easy On Yourself / I Need You / Face In The Crowd / It's A Crying Shame / Nature Boy / Can't Stop Running Away / Headin' Back To You / Donna Donna / Believe Me / Strong Love / As You Used To Do / What Kind Of Fool / No, Not Another Night

LOCOMOTIVE   G- Star-Club 158.029 / 1966
- Ride Your Pony / Respect / See-Saw / Where Were You / Cool Jerk / This Won't Happen To Me / Come On Along Girl / Going To A Go-Go / Wade In The Water / Get Out Of My Life Woman / No Money, No Honey / Thinkin' About You Girl / Working In The Coal-Mine / Soulful Dress

as **The Koppykats**:
THE BEATLES BEST DONE BY THE KOPPYKATS   G-Fontana 700.153 WGY/1966
- You Can't Do That / Little Child / All My Lovin' / Eight Days A Week / I'll Follow The Sun / Long Tall Sally / I Feel Fine / A Hard Day's Night / The Things We Said Today / I'm A Loser / I Saw Her Standing There / Roll Over Beethoven

MORE BEATLES BEST DONE BY THE KOPPYKATS   G-Fontana 701.543 WPY/1966
- Nowhere Man / Norwegian Wood / We Can Work It Out / Yesterday / Day Tripper / I'm Looking Through You / Help / You've Got To Hide Your Love Away / Ticket To Ride / I'm Down / Dizzy Miss Lizzy / Please Mr. Postman

(*** please note, that these two LPs were released in England as double album on Fontana)

Different US releases:
IAN & THE ZODICAS   US-Philips PHS 600-176 / 1965
- same as the German 'Star-Club Show 7', only without *Livin' Lovin' Wreck*

Tracks on compilations:
Let's Turkey Trot	on 'This Is Merseybeat' Vol.1	UK - Oriole PS 40047 / 1963
Secret Love	on 'This Is Merseybeat' Vol.2	UK - Oriole PS 40048 / 1963
It Ain't Necessarily So	on 'This Is Merseybeat' Vol.2	UK - Oriole PS 40048 / 1963
That's Nice (live)	on 'Beat und Prosa live im Star-Club'	G-Philips (Twen) 843.933 / 1966
Ride Your Pony (live)	on 'Beat und Prosa ....'	G-Philips (Twen) 843.933 / 1966
No Money, No Honey (live)	on 'Beat und Prosa ....'	G-Philips (Twen) 843.933 / 1966
Intro Let's Go / No Money No Honey	on Beat-Club	G-Philips (Bild und Funk) 111.576 / 1967
Take A Message To Martha	on 'Beater's Hitparade'	G-Philips 75283 P.13 / 1967

THE INCAS

This band was formed by **Terry Broughton** and **Bob Martin** in St. Helens, not too far from Liverpool, in 1963. Before that both had played in a school band called **The Falcons**.

At first, the **Incas** played a lot of **Cliff Richard & the Shadows** numbers, as well as related material, but then developed more and more into a real Beat group. It did not take too long until they became popular on the local scene and appeared regularly at such well known venues as the 'Plaza' in St. Helens, the 'Orrel Park Ballroom', as well as at the 'Cavern' and the 'Peppermint Lounge' in Liverpool. At that time the **Incas** consisted of the following musicians:

Jed White	**(voc)**
Terry Broughton	**(g/voc)**
John Crogan	**(g/voc)**
Bob Martin	**(bg/voc)**
Alf Anslow	**(dr)**

Jed White, **John Crogan** and **Alf Anslow** were all newcomers to the music business and **Jed White** left very soon after. He most probably quit show business as he did not appear on the scene again. He was not replaced in the **Incas**, who continued as a four piece and all members shared the vocals.

It was in early 1966 that **Terry Broughton** and **John Crogan** also left the group, which then disbanded. **Terry Broughton** and **John Crogan** continued together under the name **The Morning Duo** until **John Crogan** emigrated to Canada in 1970 where he is still living. **Terry Broughton** quit the music business, but stepped back into it in 1990, when he joined a group with the name **Old Kids On The Rocks** (do you see any relation to **New Kids On The Block**?). But back to the **Incas**:

The remaining members **Bob Martin** and **Alf Anslow** formed a new group in early 1966 under the old name, which also included **Martin O'Brian** as lead singer. He was a former member of the popular **Federal Five** from St.Helens, who in the meantime had changed the name into the **Streamers**.

Sadly the guitarist or guitarists in that new line-up are not known, but it may have been **Phil Gason** or **'Shirt' Clayton**, if not both, who were also former members of the **Federal Five** and the **Streamers** respectively, who obviously had just disbanded at that time. Therefore it is possible that **Bob Martin** and **Alf Anslow** not only teamed up with **Martin O'Brian**, but also with other remaining members of his former group. But this is only a supposition.

Their manager became **Norman Thomas** and somehow he acquired a recording contract with Parlophone for the group, who in the same year released a great Beat record with the songs *One Night Stand* and *I'll Keep You Holding On*.

It sold well but in the end failed to make the charts, so it was not followed by another record, but around the same time a group with the name of the **Incas** was featured with one song on a flexi disc from Keele University (Lyntone LYN 765/5). This might have been the **Incas** from St. Helens, but this is not certain and the song, featured on that EP together with three other groups, is unknown.

However, after their Parlophone release little was heard of the **Incas** and they soon disappeared from the scene. What happened to the individual musicians after the split is sadly not known.

Discography

One Night Stand / I'll Keep Holding On   **UK- Parlophone R 5551 / 1066**

(Besides this, there was a flexi EP from the Keele University released in the Sixties (Keele Rag Record Lyntone LYN 765/6) on which, besides three other bands, one named **The Incas** was featured. This may have been the group from St. Helens, but it is quite improbable as Keele is quite far south of Liverpool)

TONY JACKSON & THE VIBRATIONS

This group was formed in 1964 by Liverpudlian **Tony Jackson**, who had started his career in the Fifties as a guitarist/vocalist with the Skiffle group **The Martinis** and was then a solo performer named **Clint Reno**. After that he became the lead vocalist and bass guitarist with the **Searchers**, who at first backed **Johnny Sandon** before starting a big hit career in their own right.

Tony's lead vocals can be heard on the worldwide hits *Sweets For My Sweet* and *Sugar And Spice*. After he parted from the **Searchers** for mysterious reasons, he formed his own group under the name of **Tony Jackson & the Vibrations**, which consisted of non Liverpool musicians. The reason why he left the Liverpool Merseybeat scene in such a way was probably only known by **Tony Jackson**, but it is possible it was an act of defiance stemming from his departure from the **Searchers**. However, **Tony Jackson & the Vibrations** were a very good group and in their original line-up were:

Tony Jackson	**(voc/bg)**
Ian Bruisel	**(g/voc)**
Martin Raymond	**(org/voc)**
Paul Francis	**(dr)**

Paul Francis hailed from Beckenham and was a former member of the **Rolf Harris Band** and **Bobby Christo & the Rebels** from the London scene. **Martin Raymond** was from Croydon and had played before with the **Westmister Five**, while **Ian Bruisel**, who sometimes changed his name to **Ian Leighton**, hailed from Streatham.

Tony Jackson and his new group were signed by PYE, where he had also been with the **Searchers**. The first single by **Tony Jackson & the Vibrations** was a very strong version of

Mary Wells' *Bye Bye Baby*, which climbed up to No. 25 in the British charts. This debut success was followed by another **Mary Wells** original, but *You Beat Me To The Punch* was not as successful as the predecessor.

Love Potion No.9 didn't make the charts either, but if it is compared to the **Searchers** version, it is easy to hear that **Tony Jackson & the Vibrations** played a much harder style. It was more Rock than the harmony styled **Searchers** sound.

In 1965 Tony and his band recorded a final single for PYE with *Stage Door,* a really great, melodic song which deserved to be successful but did not make it in the end. The band changed its name to **The Tony Jackson Group** in early 1966 and a few months later **Martin Raymond** left. His replacement was **Ian Green**, a former session musician who had just worked with the **Everly Brothers** on their album 'Two Yanks in London'. The **Tony Jackson Group** was signed by CBS and their first single for the new label was the strong *You're My Number One*, but it also failed to become a chart success. The follow-ups were *Never Leave Your Baby's Side, Follow Me* and *Anything Else You Want*, which were all released in 1966.

At the end of that year, the group was joined by **Chris Thompson** as bass guitarist, while **Tony Jackson** concentrated on the vocals. One more EP came on the CBS label, also released in France and which exclusively consisted of songs from the former singles.

The **Tony Jackson Group** became a quartet again when **Ian Green** left in early 1967. **Ian Bruisel**'s brother Jimmy had a girlfriend from Portugal whose father ran a recording studio and a radio station in Lisbon. The group went to Portugal on holidays in 1967 but also accepted some gigs in the sunny south. On this holiday tour the **Tony Jackson Group** was taken into the above mentioned studio where an EP was recorded on the studio-owned label 'Estudio' with the songs *Just Like Me, He Was A Friend Of Mine, Understanding* and *Shake*. This record is a desired collector's item these days, but in 1967 was unsuccessful, probably because this small private label had no real distribution system.

Quite soon after, the **Tony Jackson Group** returned to England and broke up. **Dennis Thompson** emigrated to the USA, while **Paul Francis** opened a recording studio. **Ian Bruisel** quit show business and in 1987 he died of a brain haemorrhage. **Tony Jackson** became the manager of a golf club near Liverpool. When **Mike Pender** separated from the **Searchers** in 1986 to form his own group under the name **Mike Pender's Searchers**, it was rumoured that **Tony Jackson** would join this new band, but it did not happen in the end.

In 1990 **Tony Jackson** and **Paul Francis** re-formed **Tony Jackson & the Vibrations** with new members **Colin Free** (lg), **Steve English** (bg) and **Chris Teeder** (key) but as they had no outstanding success and no record releases, they did not exist too long. **Tony Jackson** died in 2004.

Single discography

Bye Bye Baby / Watch Your Step	UK- PYE 7 N 15685 / 1964	
You Beat Me To The Punch / This Little Girl Of Mine	UK- PYE 7 N 15745 / 1964	
Love Potion No. 9 / Fortune Teller	UK- PYE 7 N 15766 / 1964	
Stage Door / That's What I Want	UK- PYE 7 N 15876 / 1965	

as **The Tony Jackson Group**:

You're My Number One / Let Me Know	UK- CBS	202.039	/ 1966
Never Leave Your Baby's Side / I'm The One She Really Thinks A Lot Of	UK- CBS	202.069	/ 1966
Follow Me / Walk That Walk	UK- CBS	202.297	/ 1966
Anything Else You Want / Come And Stop	UK- CBS	202.408	/ 1966

EP discography

THE TONY JACKSON GROUP	UK- CBS	5726	/ 1966

- You're My Number One / Let Me Know / I'm The One She Really Thinks A Lot Of / Never Leave Your Baby's Side

(*** please note that this EP was also released on French CBS under the same order number with the title 'You're My Number One')

Different Portuguese release:

TONY JACKSON GROUP	P - Estudio	/ 1967

- Just Like Me / Understanding / Shake / He Was A Friend Of Mine

JEANNIE & THE BIG GUYS

This band started in 1962 under the name of **The Pacemakers** in Chester, not too far from Liverpool. To prevent confusion with **Gerry & the Pacemakers**, the name was changed to **Four Hits & A Miss** in 1963, after the group was joined by songstress **Rita Hughes**, who performed under the name 'Jeannie'. But of course this new name was ambiguous and probably because of that it was changed again to **Jeannie & the Big Guys**. At that time the group consisted of the following musicians:

Jeannie	**(voc)**
David Jones	**(g/voc)**
Geoff Dawson	**(g/voc)**
Owen Roberts	**(bg/voc)**
Terry Lynch	**(dr)**

Owen Roberts was sometimes also named **Owen Rickets**, but it is not known if this was a misprint or a real name change, it was, however, one and the same musician.

In 1963 **Jeannie & the Big Guys** were signed by PYE and recorded the single *Don't Lie To Me*, which was coupled with the **Shirelles** classic *Boys*, a song often covered by Liverpool groups like the **Beatles** or **Lee Curtis & the All Stars**.

In January 1964 **Terry Lynch** left the group and was replaced by **George Roberts**, no relation to **Owen Roberts**. With this line-up, the second single by **Jeannie & the Big Guys** was released, but their cover version of *Sticks And Stones* did not succeed.

Shortly after this, **Jeannie** left to go solo while the group continued for a some time under the name **The Big Guys** but then disappeared from the scene.

George Roberts later joined the **Excheckers** from Chester and then became the roadie for Liverpool's **Takers**, who were formerly known as **The Undertakers**. **Owen Roberts** (or **Rickets**) later played in one of the early line-ups of the re-formed **Faron's Flamingos**.

Jeannie appeared for a short time with **Earl Royce & the Olympics** from Liverpool, but in 1964 toured Germany with the **Delmont Four**. In the same year, her first solo single *I Love Him* was also released under the name 'Jeannie'. After that she changed her name to **Cindy Cole** and from November 1964 on she was backed by the **Fugitives** from Chester, who were perhaps an offshoot of the former **Big Guys**.

In April 1965 the single *A Love Like Yours* was released under the name **Cindy Cole**, but like its predecessors it did not become a hit, nor did the follow-up *Just Being Your Baby (turns me on)*. Despite this lack of success she was one of the really good girl singers on the British Beat scene. She, and

Cor!

Gorgeous girl with the dark brown hair is Jeannie. Guys down in the South of England will have the benefit of Jeannie's looks from June onwards when she goes on a Southern tour.
Backing her on her public engagements is Earl Royce and the Olympics.

her new backing group, never made a breakthrough and at the end of the Sixties **Cindy Cole** and the **Fugitives** disappeared from the scene without much attention being paid to the fact.

Of **Rita Hughes**, who besides being a good singer was also very beautiful, it is known that in later years she had some prestige cabaret bookings. She died unexpected and far too early in April 1989 - at the age of 42.

Single discography

as **Jeannie & the Big Guys**:
Don't Lie To Me / Boys	UK- PYE	7 N 35147 / 1963
Sticks And Stones / I Want You	UK- PYE	7 N 35164 / 1964

'**Jeannie**' - solo:
I Love Him / With Any Other Girl	UK- Parlophone R 5343 / 1964

as **Cindy Cole**:
A Love Like Yours / He's Sure The Boy I Love	UK- Columbia	DB 7519 / 1965
Just Being Your Baby / Lonely City Blue Boy	UK- Columbia	DB 7973 / 1966

(*** please note that on the last two singles, **Cindy Cole** (aka **Jeannie**) was most probably backed by the **Fugitives** who at that time were her regular backing group.)

DAVID JOHN & THE MOOD

This band hailed from Preston, Lancashire and without a doubt was the number one group of its hometown.

It should have been formed in 1962 under the name of the **Mood Rhythms** by singer **David John Smith**, but this information seems a littledoubtful as **David John** had been in the **Bobcats** before and after that with the very shortlived **Questions** that beside him consisted of **Reg Welch** (g), who came from the **Rebels, John Brierley** (bg) from the **Thunderbeats** and **Gene Carberry** (dr), a former member of the **Crusaders**.

This group only made four gigs and the last one was at the 'Daily Herald Beat Festival' in Liverpool in 1963 at which the **Questions** backed **Ricky Valence. Reg Welch** and **John Brierley** went on to play with **Freddie Starr & the Midnighters** and **Gene Carberry** became a member of the **Thunderbeats** and then joined the **Prestons**, another story in this book.

Original lineup featuring
Robb Deka and Rick Greenwood

David John joined the **Falcons**, which, besides him, consisted of **Robb Deka** (p/voc), **Peter Illingworth** (g/voc), **Rick Greenwood** (bg) and **Freddie Isherwood** (dr).

Peter Illingworth was a former member of the **Bruff Boys** and the **Travellers**, formerly known as **Wendy & the Travellers**. Drummer **Freddie Isherwood** (sometimes named **Mal Isherwood**) came from the **Corries**, while **Robb Deka** and **Rick Greenwood** had been in the **Crusaders** before. This line-up of the **Falcons** changed the name into **David John & the Mood** in 1963.

Robb Deka, whose real name is **Robert Eccles** and who should have played in the backing group of **Julie Grant**, in 1963 left and went down to London for test recordings, on which he was backed by the trio, that a little later became the **Puppets**, which are also featured in this book. After that he joined the **Prestons. Rick Greenwood** also left and accordingly **David John & the Mood** in early 1964 consisted of:

David John	**(voc)**
Peter Atkinson	**(rg/voc)**
Peter Illingworth	**(lg/voc)**
John Brierley	**(bg/voc)**
Freddie (Mal) Isherwood	**(dr)**

David John & the Mood were signed by Decca for their new sub-label Vocalion, which was quite a surprise as the group had not yet had any outstanding success. In May of the same year, their first single *A Pretty Thing* was released, coupled with *To Catch That Man.* Both numbers were not really commercial but a very interesting mixture of Rhythm & Blues and Mod sound.

This record was not very successful, not least because both group and label were still unknown at that time and in 1964, the commercial Merseybeat still played a leading role in the music business. But it seems *A Pretty Thing* did not sell too badly, as the group's next single was planned for release on the Decca label.

Still in 1964 the song *It's So Exciting* was recorded and already announced in 'Mersey Beat', but it is uncertain whether it was really released as it was never mentioned in any discography and is also not found in the Decca catalogue.

However, the popularity of the group started to increase and the music press showed more and more interest in them. Suddenly **David John & the Mood** was quite a well known name, and not only in the North.

The group then was signed by Parlophone and produced by **Joe Meek**. Two more singles were released in 1965: *Bring It To Jerome* was a great one, again the typical mixture of Rhythm & Blues and Mod sound, as was the B-side *I Love To See You Strut*, but this record sadly also failed to make the charts. *Diggin' For Gold* was not as strong anymore and of course also failed to bring **David John & the Mood** headlines, let alone any chart success.

In the middle of 1966 **David John** disbanded the group and for a short time joined **Sound Five**, who later changed their name to **Barbed Wire Soup**. He also guested with an outfit called **Three-D**, which consisted of former **Puppets** members and with **David John** as lead vocalist developed into the recording group **Thundermother**.

Peter Illingworth joined **Purple Haze**, who later recorded as **Little Free Rock**.

Single discography

A Pretty Thing / To Catch That Man	UK- Vocalion	V 9220 / 1964
It's So Exciting /	UK- Decca	??? / 1964
Bring It To Jerome / I Love To See You Strut	UK- Parlophone	R 5255 / 1965
Diggin' For Gold / She's Fine	UK- Parlophone	R 5301 / 1965

(*** please note that it is not sure if *It's So Exciting* was really released after it was recorded for Decca. It was announced in the music press but is not found in the official Decca catalogue)

THE JYNX

Whether or not this band should be featured in this book may be open to debate, as it is not known where exactly they came from. They appeared on the scene suddenly in 1962 and insiders regard them as part of the Merseybeat scene of Liverpool. This is improbable as there was never anything written about them in the Liverpool music papers like 'Mersey Beat' or 'Combo' – their name did not even show up in the club's advertisements.

However, they were there and sounded very much like Merseybeat and were of an outstanding quality, judging by their only single. The **Jynx** consisted of the following musicians:

Keith Wells	**(voc)**
Brian Ashley	**(g/voc)**
Gordon Lincoln	**(g)**
George Hunt	**(bg/voc)**
C. John Curtis	**(dr)**

The group was signed to Columbia in 1964 and in June of the same year their first single was released with the songs *How* and *Do What They Don't Say*, which were great songs and excellent examples of Beat music at its best.

The song *How* was written by **Gordon Wingrove** and *Do What They Don't Say* by **Keith Street**, both unknown songwriters, but maybe were identical with **Gordon Lincoln** and **Keith Wells** of the band. This fantastic single was produced by **Norrie Paramor**.

The **Jynx** were also featured with both songs on the French sampler 'The Best Of The Liverpool Sound' and in spite of hard competition from groups like **Tony Rivers & the Castaways**, the **Dave Clark Five**, **Freddie & the Dreamers**, **Gerry & the Pacemakers**, **Mike Sheridan & the Nightriders**, **Chris Farlowe & the Thunderbirds** and others, they left behind the best impression on that record.

With regard to **The Jynx**, it seems that recording directors, producers, managers, promoters and the press all made the same mistake in not taking more notice of this group. They should have been pushed a little more and probably they would have become big stars of the Beat business, because they had the right quality and the right sound. At the end of the Beat boom the **Jynx** disappeared from the scene and no one really noticed. It was as though they had just been another 'one record band'. If it hadn't been for this one excellent record, probably one of the best of that era, it would have been as if they never existed.

Single discography

How / Do What They Don't Say	UK- Columbia DB 7304 / 1964

Tracks on compilations:

How on 'The Best Of The Liverpool Sound'	F- Columbia	FPX 272 / 1964
Do what they don't say" on 'The Best Of The Liverpool Sound'	F- Columbia	FPX 272 / 1964

THE KANSAS CITY FIVE

As can be concluded from their name, this group's music was initially oriented towards Rock-A-Billy, influenced by **Carl Perkins** but also **Jerry Lee Lewis**, which could be heard in the heavily featured piano. That is why their musical style became more Rock 'n' Roll with time.

The **Kansas City Five** were formed by ex-**Bluegenes** founder member **Bruce McCaskill** in Liverpool in 1962 and within a short time became very popular and successful on the local scene. The original line-up consisted of the following musicians:

Bruce McCaskill	**(voc/g)**
Peter Cook	**(voc/g)**
Tommy Hughes	**(p/voc)**
Alan Stratton	**(bg)**
Colin Middlebrough	**(dr)**

Peter Cook had previously played with the **Topspots**, **Dee & the Dynamites** and with the short-lived **Roadrunners**, who were not the Rhythm & Blues group who became well-known later. **Tommy Hughes** had started his career with the **Pinetop Skiffle Group** and then also was a member of the **Bluegenes**, who, of course, were the predecessors of the **Swinging Blue Jeans**. **Alan Stratton** was a former member of the **Black Cats**, one of the very early and important Liverpool groups, while **Colin Middlebrough** came from the **All Blacks Skiffle Group**.

From August until November 1962, the **Kansas City Five** were the regular backing group for singer **Freddie Fowell**, a former member of **Howie Casey & the Seniors**, who a little later changed his name to **Freddie Starr** and led groups like **Freddie Starr & the Ventures, Freddie Starr & the Midnighters, Freddie Starr & the Starr Boys** (aka as **Freddie Starr & the Flamingoes**) and **Freddie Starr & the Delmonts**. After **Freddie Starr**, who later became a well-known TV star, had separated from the **Kansas City Five**, the group was joined by **Robbie Hickson**, who had sung before with **Alfie Diamond & the Skiffle Kings**, the **Casuals** (not the hit group of the same name), the **Topspots** and he was the 'Dee' of **Dee & the Dynamites**. The last two groups were forerunner bands of the **Undertakers**. Although the band was a six piece now, it continued under the name of the **Kansas City Five**. They became the resident group at the famous 'Iron Door' and sometimes also backed great Liverpool songstress **Beryl Marsden** at her gigs.

At the end of 1962 **Bruce McCaskill** and **Peter Cook** left and formed a backing-group for **Freddie Starr** on his French tour, together with other musicians. This newly-formed band was the foundation for **Groups Inc**. After that, **Peter Cook** became a member of **Earl Royce & the Olympics**, where he also used the stage name **Pete Melody**. He later formed a new group under the name **The Trend** and in the Seventies was a member of the newly-formed **Faron's Flamingos** before he continued on the cabaret scene.

Bruce McCaskill, who sometimes also appeared as **Bruce Monroe**, joined the **Escorts**. But it is not certain if he was a member of the group or of the crew. He later became popular as manager of the **Average White Band**, after he had been the road manager for **Eric Clapton** for a time.

Back to the **Kansas City Five**, who were left as a four-piece but became a quintet again when they were joined by **Les Stuart** as a new guitarist in 1963. He was the former leader of the **Les Stuart Quartet** and after that had played with **Frank Knight & the Barons** and **Danny Havoc & the Ventures**.

When **Robbie Hickson** left and probably quit show business as early as 1963, he was not replaced and **Les Stuart** took over the lead vocals. At this time the **Kansas City Five** became the resident group at the 'Odd Spot', a popular Liverpool live club run by their manager **Jim Turner**. Around that time they were joined by songstress **Barbara Harrison**, who sometimes also used the stage name **'Deanne'** and who had sung before with the **Hi-Cats**, **Faron's Flamingos** and **Danny Havoc & the Ventures**. **Les Stuart** left to join the **Long & Short**, where he used the stage name **Les Saints**. His replacement in the **Kansas City Five** was **Mike Liston**, a former member of **Bobby Angelo & the Tuxedos** and of **Lee Castle & the Barons**.

The next to leave was **Colin Middlebrough**, who joined the **Four Originals**, that had developed from the very popular **Dale Roberts & the Jaywalkers**. He was replaced in the **Kansas City Five** by **Lewis Collins**, who came from Liverpool's **Renegades**.

Probably with this line-up the band toured France and Germany, where they are also likely to have appeared at the 'Star-Club' in Hamburg, although no record can be found of it. Despite the success the **Kansas City Five** had on Merseyside, they split totally in 1964 without having obtained any national stardom.

Mike Liston joined the **Classics** from Liverpool and later became a successful session musician and record producer in Nashville. **Lewis Collins** joined the **Georgians**, where he switched to the bass guitar. After that he was the bass guitarist with the **Eyes** and the **Mojos**. He later became a successful actor (do you remember 'Bodie' of the 'Professionals'?) and in 1983 started to record again, but without any great success.

Barbara Harrison continued as a solo singer. She was signed by Decca but as far as it is known there was never anything released. She then simply faded from the scene.

Alan Stratton became a member of **Johnny Marlowe & the Whip-Chords**, where he stayed until the group disbanded in 1966. He then joined the **Fables** and in the early Seventies was a member of **The Chesterfields**, where he obviously replaced **Ian Edwards**.

In the line-up with ex **Stereos** guitarist **Irvin Banks**, **Alan Stratton** (bg) and **Dave Smith** (voc) the **Chesterfields** recorded an EP on the 'Liverpool Sound' label in 1973 (LS 1740 EP) with the songs *Things, Girl From Ipanema, Matrimony* and *Wham Bang*. On this acetate also **Tommy Hughes** (p), **Ray Smith** (sax) and **Les Reynolds** (dr) were featured as guest musicians. In 1974 **Ray Smith** was replaced by **Malcolm Andrews** (voc/g), a former member of the **Mastersounds** and the **Kruzads**. After the **Chesterfields** record, **Tommy Hughes** quit show business but now is back with the re-formed **Mojos**.

In 1991 the **Kansas City Five** were re-formed for appearances at the 'Mersey Cats' events with the original members **Alan Stratton**, **Robbie Hickson**, **Peter Cook**, **Tommy Hughes** and **Colin Middlebrough**, who is these days still a steady member of the **Four Originals**. One time the **Kansas City Five** were also joined by founder **Bruce McCaskill**, who sadly died unexpected on 24th December 1993.

In 1994 **Alan Stratton** became a temporary member of **Karl Terry & the Cruisers**, where he played the double bass when this band toured in Germany and he was also featured in the line-up when **Karl Terry & the Cruisers** cut the great album 'Rock 'n' Roll - that's all' for the German 'Merseyside' label.

SONNY KAYE & THE REDS

Real Liverpudlians would say this was a group from 'over the water', as it was formed in the coffee bar 'El Cappucino' in Runcorn on the west side of the River Mersey by **Frank Keenan**, in 1962. The founder of course was the one who then used the stage name **Sonny Kaye**. The members wore red suits and one highlight in their live programme was a terrific version of *Moon River*. In the original line-up the group consisted of the following musicians:

Sonny Kaye	**(voc)**
Bill Mullan	**(g/voc)**
John Aston	**(bg)**
Terry Lewis	**(dr)**

Sonny Kaye & the Reds appeared regularly at the important Liverpool clubs like the 'Cavern' and the 'Iron Door' and so they became quite popular within a very short time and 'Darville Entertainments' took over their management. A little later the group was joined by **Paddy Mullan** on bass guitar while **John Aston** switched to rhythm.

In 1963, **Sonny Kaye & the Reds** recorded an acetate on 'Northampton Sounds' with the songs *Long Tall Sally* and *Jacky.* The latter one was a group original, written by **Sonny Kaye** and **Bill Mullan**, who of course was the brother of the new bass guitarist.

'Darville Entertainments' arranged a tour of Germany for the band, where it appeared at the 'Star-Palast' clubs in Kiel, Eckernförde, Rendsburg, Lüneburg, as well as at the 'Beat-Club' in Dortmund, which was also part of the 'Star-Palast' chain. At the end of this really successful tour they also played Mainz. Especially for that tour **Sonny Kaye & the Reds** had been joined by **Gary Lloyd** as additional guitarist.

Back in England, they took part in the Fontana competition 'Kings Of The Big Beat' and won, so they went down to London and did a recording test for the Fontana label, but sadly nothing was released on record.

John Aston was temporary replaced in the group by **Derek Gilbert**, who came from the **Paladins**, but this was only for a few gigs and then **John Aston** returned and **Derek Gilbert** probably went back to his old group.

In September 1964 **Sonny Kaye** left show business, for health reasons as it was rumoured. The group continued as a four-piece, changed their name to **We Few** and went to Germany for the second time. After their return, they were joined by a girl singer named **Rita** and so they became **We Few & Rita**. But this only lasted for a short time and then **Sonny Kaye** returned but did not stay too long with the group. When he left again, former tour member **Gary Lloyd** returned and the band was also joined by **Bobby Didsbury** as an additional singer. At the same time, the group's name was changed again, this time to **Reds Inc**. Under this name the group recorded the songs *Shake, Rattle And Roll* and the **Larry Williams** classic *Lawdy Miss Clawdy* for the Oriole sampler 'Cavern Alive', and probably some more, but no further details are known, because this record was not released in the end. Another acetate was made of the two named songs, also on Northampton Sounds.

It was probably in 1966 when **Sonny Kaye** returned again and the name of the band was changed back to **Sonny Kaye & the Reds**. In March 1968 the group had a television appearance but sadly did not make any further records.

The line-up now changed quite often and amongst others **Ronnie Quinn** (bg), **Tony Moffatt** (rg) and **Alan Cosgrove** (dr) joined and left again. But it is also known that the original drummer **Terry Lewis** in the end returned again to **Sonny Kaye & the Reds**, who in the meantime had been the resident drummer at the 'Linnets' pub in Runcorn. It was in the early Seventies that **Sonny Kaye & the Reds** finally disbanded.

In 1980 **Sonny Kaye & the Reds** played a reunion concert at 'Linnets' in Runcorn, as far as it is known with the 1964 line-up, but there was sadly no repetition later.

Bill Mullan and **John Aston** are still active in the music business and the temporary drummer **Alan Cosgrove** appeared again as a member of the **Merseybeats** in the Nineties. **Sonny Kaye,** who in the meantime had worked as a disc jockey, died unexpectedly and much too young in April 1994. At his funeral a Jazz band played *When The Saints Go Marching In.*

Discography

as **Sonny Kaye & the Reds**:
Jacky / Long Tall Sally   '**Northampton-Sounds' acetate / 1963**

as **The Reds Inc.**
Shake, Rattle & Roll / Lawdy Miss Clawdy   '**Northampton-Sounds' acetate / 1965**

Besides this **Sonny Kaye & the Reds** recorded for Fontana after the group had won the 'Kings Of The Big Beat' competition, but there was sadly never anything released.

It is also possible that beside *Shake, Rattle And Roll* and *Lawdy Miss Clawdy,* **Reds Inc.** recorded some more songs for Oriole sampler 'Cavern Alive' which in the end was not released.

SONNY KAYE & THE REDS
Sole Representation
DARVILLE ENTERTAINMENTS   WALLASEY CHESHIRE.

THE KINETIC

It all started with the occurrence that there was a backing group needed for **Beryl Marsden** to play at the 'Star-Club' in Hamburg in December 1964. The management hurriedly recruited **Vinnie Ismael** (lg/voc) and **Rob Eccles** (bg) from the **Harlems**, who both were former members of **Vince & the Volcanoes.**

The drummer was **Johnny Sze**, who came from the **St. Louis Checks** but before that had been a member of the **Satanists**. This line-up played a few shows with **Beryl Marsden** in Hamburg as the **Harlems**.

In early 1965 this connection split up again and while **Rob Eccles** returned to Liverpool and joined **Henry's Handful, Vinnie Ismael**, who is also known as **Vinnie Toe**, stayed in Hamburg and joined the **Top Ten Allstars**, the resident group at the famous 'Top Ten' club. He then also returned to Liverpool and joined **Henry's Handful**. After that he was a member of the **Valentinos**, who later recorded as **Harlem**. In the Eighties he played with **Karl Terry & the Cruisers**.

Drummer **Johnny Sze** went to Sweden and became a member of the **Cherry Stones**. This originally was a real Swedish group who, a few months before, had released an interesting single with *Muddy Hands /Go Away* (HMV X 8661), but for mysterious reasons had disbanded short after that.

The **Cherry Stones** now consisted of the Liverpudlians **Bob Weston (lg) and Johnny Sze** (dr/voc), **Andy Mowbray** (voc/harp) and the two Swede **Lennart Blomkvist** (rg) and **Leif**

jo may produktion
The Cherry Stones

Matses (bg), who probably were the remaining members of the Swedish recording line-up. After playing the clubs in and around Stockholm for some time, the **Cherry Stones** were engaged to support the **Kinks** on their Finland tour. The group went down very well but after a few gigs got sacked again – did they go down too well? Whatever, somehow it happened that the German **Jo May** took over their management and brought them to Germany. Very soon a great version of the **Timi Yuro** success *What's The Matter Baby* was released on the new manager's own label, but was not distributed too well and so did not become a bigger success.

Jo May got the group a gig, opening an Art Gallery in Munich. The French owner, Madame Renai, was enthusiastic about the **Cherry Stones** and asked them, if they were interested to play also in Paris. Of course they were – but with the exception of the two Suede, who returned home. The remaining three recruited other Liverpool (?) musicians and continued as the **Kinetic** in the line-up with:

Andy Mowbray	**(voc/harp)**
Bob Weston	**(lg)**
Mick Humphries	**(org/p)**
Geoff Capper	**(bg)**
Johnny Sze	**(dr)**

The new member Mick Humphries sometimes was also delivered as Michael Humby and therefore it is not known what his real name was. Whatever, the group went to Paris and the management was shared between **Jo May** and **Madame Renai.**

After the **Kinetic** successfully had supported some of the real big artists, like for example **Cat Stevens**, **Jimi Hendrix** or the **Spencer Davis Group**, they were signed to Disques Vogue, a major record company in France. In 1966 the first EP was released with 'Suddenly Tomorrow', all songs on that were originals by the **Kinetic**. This obviously sold quite well as in 1967 it was followed by another EP with 'Live Your Life' and when this also became a good seller, a complete album with own material of the group was released, also entitles 'Live your life'.

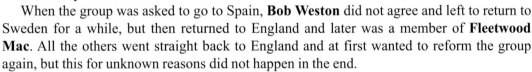

In between, the group toured in Germany again and also played the 'Star-Club' in Hamburg but it can be said that the **Kinetic** had settled down in Paris and mainly toured in France in those days. They became a very successful part of the French music scene and stayed there until the early Seventies.

When the group was asked to go to Spain, **Bob Weston** did not agree and left to return to Sweden for a while, but then returned to England and later was a member of **Fleetwood Mac**. All the others went straight back to England and at first wanted to reform the group again, but this for unknown reasons did not happen in the end.

As the **Kinetic** during the time of the big Beat boom had always played in Sweden, Germany or France, it was not paid too much attention in the Merseybeat scene. Judging by their records it can be said, that England missed out on another great group.

Discography :
EP **'Suddenly Tomorrow'**   **FR- Vogue EPL 8520 / 1966**
- **Suddenly Tomorrow / Letter To Rosetta / Time Of Season**

EP **'Live Your Life'**   **FR- Vogue EPL 8544 / 1967**
- **Live Your Life / Hall Of The Viking / Sunny Cloud / The Train**

LP **'Live Your Life'**   **FR- Vogue CLVLX 148 / 1967**
- **Live Your life / Hall Of The Viking / Letter To Rosetta / Child's Song / Sunny Cloud / Suddenly Tomorrow / Willy 'D' Fixer / Time Of Season / The Train / Jam Around**

as **The Cherry Stones:**
What's The Matter Baby / The Things She Says   **G- JMP 19 702 / 1966**

THE KINSLEYS

This band was formed by **Billy Kinsley** in Liverpool in April 1964 after he had formerly played with the **Pacifics**, the **Maverick** and of course the **Merseybeats**. As it seems, he and the other members of this new group had major problems choosing a name and at first names like the **Rivals** and the **Nameless Ones** were discussed and one of their first appearances was made under the latter name, before they decided to call the band **The Kinsleys**.

Of course the group profited from the popularity their leader gained through his membership in the **Merseybeats**, but this for sure was not the only reason for their great success locally.

The **Kinsleys** in fact were a really good group and in the original line-up consisted of:

> **Billy Kinsley**   (voc/bg)
> **Dave Percival**   (g/voc)
> **Denny Alexander** (g/voc)
> **Dave Preston**   (dr/voc)

All members were experienced musicians - **Denny Alexander** had played before with the **Aarons** and the **Secrets**, while **Dave Preston** was a former member of the **Harlems** and the **Secrets**.

Dave Percival came from the original trio line-up of the **Pawns** and before that had played with the **Climbers**. He possibly was the musician named **Dave Percy**, who also had played with the **Roadrunners**. But **Dave Percival** did not stay too long and then joined the newly formed **Epics** who in the end sadly never performed publicly together. His place in the **Kinsleys** was taken by **Tommy Murray**, who had formerly played with the **Memphis Rhythm & Blues Combo**. Probably with this line-up the group recorded the songs *Goodbye* and *Do Me A Favour,* both great Merseybeat songs, which were sadly never released. The reason for that might have been **Billy Kinsley** leaving, when, at the end of 1964, he rejoined the **Merseybeats**, where he stayed until that group disbanded in 1966.

After that he and **Tony Crane** of the **Merseybeats** formed the duo **The Merseys** and had a big hit with their version of *Sorrow*, as well as some other records that sold well. They then changed their name to the **Crackers** but only released one more single.

After that, **Billy Kinsley** had a short spell with the **Swinging Blue Jeans** and in 1970 he and **Jimmy Campbell** (ex **Kirkbys**) were members of **Rockin' Horse**, who amongst others released an absolutely great single with *The Biggest Gossip In Town*, which was pure Merseybeat at its best.

He then joined **Gerry & the Pacemakers** for a short time and after that formed **Paper Chase**, who developed into **Liverpool Express** in the early Seventies. This group had a string of hits before it disbanded again and **Billy Kinsley** joined the **Cheats**. Later he reformed **Liverpool Express** and since 1993, he has been back with the **Merseybeats**.

But back to the **Kinsleys** who did not disband when **Billy Kinsley** left. **Denny Alexander** also left and at first he wanted to form a new group together with **Tommy McGuirk**, with whom he had played in the **Aarons** and who in the meantime was a member of the **Pete Best Four**, but this did not happen and so **Denny Alexander** became a member of the **Clayton**

Squares in early 1965.

Dave Preston and **Tommy Murray** remained together with **Tim Dougdale** (voc/g) of the **Georgians** and at first continued as a trio under the name of **The Kinsleys**. Then they were joined by **George Peckham** (voc/bg), who had formerly played with the **Renegades** from Liverpool, the original **Pawns**, **Lee Curtis & the All Stars**, the re-formed **Pawns** and **Groups Inc**. In 1965, he left the **Kinsleys** again to join **Earl Royce & the Olympics** and later became a member of the **Fourmost**.

He was replaced in the **Kinsleys** by **Mike Hart**, who came from the **Richmond Group** in July 1965, after having played before with the **Roadrunners** and the **Krew**. At the end of the same year the **Kinsleys** disbanded totally without having recorded again.

Tommy Murray joined the **Krew**, better known as **The Crew,** and after that played with the group called **Mumble. Dave Preston** became a member of the **Mark Four** from Cheshunt who a little later had international hit success as **The Creation**.

Mike Hart formed **Henry's Handful** and after that appeared for a short time with another group called **Mike Hart & the Moondogs** before becoming a founder member of **Liverpool Scene**. After that he went solo, while **Tim Dougdale** disappeared from the scene.

Discography

There was no official record released by the **Kinsleys** but the group recorded two great songs with *Goodbye* and *Do Me A Favour* in 1964, probably for Fontana.

THE KIRKBYS

As this band's name suggests, they originated from the Liverpool suburb Kirkby, where it was formed in 1961 by **Jimmy Campbell** together with **John Lloyd**, **Kenny Goodlass** and the singer **Gerry Savage** under the name **The Tuxedos**. When **Gerry Savage** left, the group was joined by **Joey Marooth** and **Alby Power** and very soon changed their name to **The Panthers**.

In 1962 the **Panthers** cut a Kensington acetate with the songs *For You* and *Searchin',* but a little later changed their name to **The Kirkbys** and recorded an EMI acetate with five tracks, of which now only the song *Feel So Bad* is still known to have been included. When they decided to become professionals a little later, the **Kirkbys** consisted of the following musicians:

Joey Marooth   **(voc)**
Jimmy Campbell **(g/voc)**
John Lloyd   **(g/voc)**
Alby Power   **(bg/voc)**
Kenny Goodlass **(dr)**

They very soon became one of the leading groups on Merseyside and occasionally also backed boxing champion **John Conteh**, who also hailed from Kirkby and who in the meantime had started a singing career. The **Kirkbys** were signed to RCA and in 1965, their first demo *Cos' My Baby's Gone* was recorded, which was only released in Finland, where it was apparently quite successful.

However, it was a great song - an original by the group which was written by **Jimmy Campbell**, a very talented songwriter. Around the same time, the **Kirkbys** toured Germany quite successfully playing lots of gigs in the South. The follow up *It's A Crime* was released in England - again a very good Beat record but sadly it did not become a bigger success. Today

it is a highly desired and expensive collector's item.

After that record, **Kenny Goodlass** left to join the **Escorts** and later had a short spell with the **Swinging Blue Jeans**, before he became a member of the **Fruit Eating Bears**, who also backed the **Merseys** on their hit single *Sorrow*, in 1966.

He was replaced in the **Kirkbys** by **Mervyn Sharp**, who came from the **Pulsators** and this line-up cut the single *Don't You*

Want Me No More, which again was only released in Finland and seems to have been a minor hit over there.

Don't You Want Me No More and the B-side, *Bless You*, both **Jimmy Campbell** originals, were great songs in the **Byrds** style and normally would have been successful in England as well as on the continent so it's hard to understand why it didn't come out on record anywhere else. However, it seems that after that release the **Kirkbys** spent some time in Scandinavia but nothing is known of further recordings.

In 1967 **Mervyn Sharp** left the group again and disappeared from the scene. He was replaced by the returning **Kenny Goodlass** and a little later the group's name was changed to **23rd Turn-Off**, the name of the motorway turn off to Kirkby. The band was signed to Deram and in 1968 the single *Michelangelo* was released. When this record wasn't too successful, the group with the outstanding name **23rd Turn-Off** disbanded, probably in early 1969.

In 1969 **Jimmy Campbell** recorded one solo album and two singles and in 1970 he formed the group **Rockin' Horse** together with former **Merseybeats**, **Kinsleys** and **Merseys** member **Billy Kinsley**. This group also consisted of **Bobby Falloon** (g), **Stan Gorman** (dr) and **Mike Snow** (p/org).

Rockin' Horse cut an album with the title 'Yes It Is' in 1970, from which the great single *Biggest Gossip In Town* was coupled out. This song was great Merseybeat again and, although the LP was really interesting, the other album tracks didn't compare to it. Some more singles were released by **Rockin' Horse** but none in the class of *Biggest Gossip In Town* and none were very successful. When this group disbanded, **Jimmy Campbell** went solo and cut two more solo albums and a few singles, sadly not bringing him the success he deserved.

In 1979 **John Lloyd** appeared on the scene again in a duo with **Earl Preston** under the name of **The Raffles**, which existed until the early Eighties. He then disappeared from the scene, just like **Alby Power**. **Joey Marooth** emigrated to Australia but later returned to Liverpool, where he did not join another group.

Kenny Goodlass later played with the newly-formed **Merseybeats** and from 1992 until 1995 he was a member of **Karl Terry & the Cruisers**, who recorded the album 'Rock 'n' Roll – That's All' in Germany.

In the mid-Nineties the **Kirkbys** were re-formed by the original members **Joey Marooth**, **John Lloyd**, **Alby Power** and **Kenny Goodlass**. The top-class saxophonist **Brian Jones,** a member of the **Undertakers** in the Sixties, was added to this line-up, as well as **Dave Goldberg** on keyboards, who is also still playing with the **Merseybeats**.

Jimmy Campbell was too ill and joined his old group on stage only at some gigs. They were a very good and a very interesting group that didn't just play all the old standards over and over again. **Alby Power** had to leave for health reasons and his place in the **Kirkbys** was taken by **Alan Crooks**. **Alby Power** sadly died on 22 September 2004, aged 59, and **Jimmy Campbell** also left us on 12th February 2007, at the age of 63. **The Kirkbys** only appear occasionally these days, but their performance is always worth watching.

<u>Single discography</u>
<u>as **The Kirkbys**</u>:

It's A Crime / I've Never Been So Much In Love	UK- RCA	1542	/ 1965

<u>Different Finnish release:</u>

Cos' My Baby's Gone / She'll Get No Lovin' That Way	SF- RCA	FAS 942	/ 1965
Don't You Want Me No More / Bless You	SF- RCA	FAS 948	/ 1966

as **23rd Turn-Off**:
Michelangelo / Leave Me Here   UK- Deram   DM 150 / 1968

Jimmy Campbell - solo:
On A Monday / Dear Marge   UK- Fontana TF 1009 / 1969
Lyanna / Frankie Joe   UK- Fontana TF 1076 / 1970
Don't Leave Me Now / So Lonely Without You   UK- Fontana 6007025 / 1970

LPs:
SON OF ANASTASIA   UK- Fontana STL 5508 / 1969
 - When I Sit Down To Reason / Mother's Boy / Another Vincent Van Gogh / Penny In My Pocket /
Bright Side On The Hill / Dear Marge / Lyanna / They All Come Marching Home / On A Monday /
Lovely Elisa Cope Is Dead / You'll Break My Heart In Two / Tremendous Commercial Potential /
Adrian Henry's Party-Night / Another Springtime / Michelangelo / Painting A Sign
    HALF BAKED   UK-Vertigo 6360 010 / 1970
   - Green Eyed American Actress / Loving You Is All I Do / So Lonely Without You / In My Room
That's Right - That's Me / I Will Not Mind / Dulcie (It's December) / Forever Grateful / Half Baked/
Closing Down The Shop / Don't Leave Me Now

(*** please note that the songs *Green Eyed American Actress, So Lonely Without You* and *That's
right - That's Me* were recorded with **Rockin' Horse**)

Rockin' Horse:
Biggest Gossip In Town / You Say   UK- Philips 6006 156 / 1970
Julian The Hooligan / Stayed Out Late Last Night   UK- Philips 6006 200 / 1970
(*** please note that later releases by **Rockin' Horse** on the 'Randy' and 'Pyramid' labels were by
a different group)

LPs
YES IT IS   UK- Philips 6308 075 / 1970
  - Biggest Gossip In Town / Oh Carol I'm So Sad / You're Spending All My Money / Baby Walk Out
With Your Darlin' Man / Don't You Ever Think I Cry / Yes It Is / Stayed Out Late Last Night / Delicate
Situation / Son, Son / Golden Opportunity / I'm Trying To Forget You / Julian The Hooligan

Unissued tracks (acetates):
as **The Panthers**:
For You / Searchin'   UK - Kensington-acetate / 1962

as **The Kirkbys**:
Feel So Bad + four other tracks   UK - EMI - acetate   / 1963
beside this the following album without title was recorded on acetate :
**Dreaming / Friends And Relations / Penny In My Pocket / Flowers Are Flowering / I'll Be With You
/ Mother's Boy / I'll Be Round / Michael Angelo   UK - Emidisc acetate-album / 1966**

as **23rd Turn-Off**:
Michelangelo (alternative version) / **Dreaming**   UK - Deram - acetate   / 1967

THE KLUBS

This was a group from the second Merseybeat generation as it was only formed in 1964 in Birkenhead on the west side of the River Mersey. They started as a six-piece Rhythm & Blues group with an ever changing line-up. Before they became popular in the area of Liverpool they won a national Beat contest on the Isle of Man in August 1965 and were presented with a large silver cup by famous DJ **Jimmy Saville** and £250, which was an astronomical sum at that time. After bass guitarist **Tony Woods** had parted from the group, the **Klubs** consisted of the following musicians:

Paddy Breen	(voc)
Alan Walker	(voc/harp)
Trevor Griffiths	(lg/voc)
John Reid	(rg/voc)
Norris Easterbrook	(bg/voc)
Kenny Marshall	(dr)

Norris Easterbrook was a former member of the **Legends**.

The group now played a sort of Rhythm & Blues in the harder style of the **Rolling Stones** and **Pretty Things** and besides venues in Liverpool they also appeared quite regularly down in London, where they mainly played the 'Tiles' in Oxford Street and the famous 'Marquee Club'.

In early 1966, **Alan Walker** left the group which continued as a quintet and perfected such an explosive stage act that they were also nicknamed **The Wild Wild Klubs** - a name that was also used in some advertisements and announcements. In the meantime they had become really popular in their hometown and appeared at all the important venues along Merseyside.

At the end of 1966, 'Cavern Enterprises' took over the management of the **Klubs**. They then became regulars at the 'Cavern', where they often shared the bill with famous artists like **Chuck Berry**, **Chris Farlowe & the Thunderbirds**, **John's Children** or the American **Coasters**. They were probably one of the groups with the most appearances at the 'Cavern' in 1967.

The **Klubs** also went to France for a longer tour which obviously wasn't too successful, as in the end **Alf Geoghegan**, at that time owner of the 'Cavern', had to go over to France to bring them back. **Kenny Marshall** left the group and a little later died in a boating accident on the River Dee. His replacement was **Peter Sinclair-Tidy**, the former drummer with the **Crazy Chains**. It was probably with this line-up that the **Klubs** recorded the one-sided demo *Livin' Today* on Chart Records, which in some way was connected to the 'Cavern'.

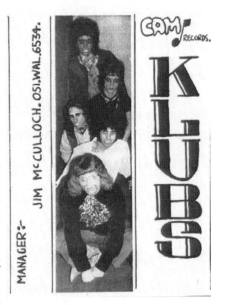

After that a Granada TV talent show presented them singing their original song *Only John Tring* and probably through that, in 1967, the **Klubs** were invited by EMI to the Abbey Road Studios for some test recordings. Under the wings of **David Paramor**, they recorded a new version of their *Livin' Today*, as well as the **Cream** success *NSU* and the **John's Children** number *Desdemona* but in the end, their wild sound was declared unrecordable and so nothing was released.

In 1968, the group went down to London again where they were discovered by producer **Don Arden**, who took them to the Decca studios. Two sessions produced recordings of the **Beatles** number *Drive My Car*, **Arthur Brown**'s smash hit *Fire* and the two originals *Midnight Love Cycle* and *Ever Needed Someone*. For the release, **Don Arden** wanted the band to change their name to **Revolution** which the musicians immediately refused to do and so again no record came out.

The **Klubs** were added to the BBC's **Pink Floyd** concerts as a support act in 1968 and after that returned to Liverpool. **Jim McCulloch**, a local nightclub owner, took over their management and recorded them for his own label 'CAM' records. Of the original numbers *Indian Dreams, Can't Ebenezer See My Friend, Oh Baby, I Found The Sun* and a new version of *Ever Needed Someone* the last two were chosen for a release on single.

So, in late 1968, the only single by the **Klubs** came out but 'CAM' did not have a real distribution system and accordingly the record only sold quite well on Merseyside.

It was a very interesting record with a nice ballad on the A-side and a solid beat on the flip side, both with a slightly psychedelic influence. Of course it was not the Merseybeat of the early Sixties anymore but the melodies of both songs were quite commercial and so was the musical arrangement.

In 1969 the **Klubs** started to fall apart after another engagement at the 'Marquee' in London. The first to leave was **Norris Easterbrook** in May 1969, followed by **Trevor Griffiths** in August of the same year. **Trevor Griffiths** became a solo artist in the cabaret scene at first, and then formed a duo with **Alan Greer**, a former member of **Me & Them**, that was also the backing group for **Chris Andrews** for a time. After that **Trevor Griffiths** became a member of **Strife**, the group that in the meantime had been formed by former **Klubs** member **John Reid.** They became quite successful in the European Heavy scene and recorded two or three albums. **Trevor Griffiths** did not stay too long with that group and in 1972 teamed up again with **Alan Greer** in the **Lettermen** who also consisted of **Ronnie Crampton** (bg/voc) and **Tony Mac** (dr/voc).

After Easterbrook and Griffiths had left, the **Klubs** continued as a trio and in 1969 recorded another demo with *The Stripper* and a new arrangement of *Can't Ebenezer See My Friend,* for DJM.

Norris Easterbrook returned to the group who, under its old name, had developed into a heavy metal band, and split up totally when **John Reid** formed **Strife** with **Paddy Breen**, who left after a short time and returned to Liverpool. There, he teamed up again with **Peter Sinclair-Tidy** and guitarist **Steve Wright** under the name of **Wardog**. When this group split, **Peter Sinclair-Tidy** joined **Shane Fenton & the Fentones** but in 1976 he teamed up again with **Paddy Breen** and guitarist **Steve Burkhill** in **Goldilox**, who later changed their name to **Skytrain**.

In 1979, **Norris Easterbrook** teamed up with **Trevor Griffiths** again in a group called **Night Moves.** They played the cabaret circuit until the early Eighties.

At Christmas 1991, there was a **Klubs** reunion for the 'Merseycats', after that they were banned from participating in any further concerts because they played 'too loud and too wild' - the **Wild Wild Klubs** eh! In 1999, an album by the **Klubs** with all the surviving material from the Sixties was released on the Tenth Planet label, which was declared as 'album of the year' by famous magazine 'Record Collector'.

This resulted in another reunion of the group in May 2000 at the 'Cavern' where they appeared in the original Sixties line-up, with the exception of **Trevor Griffiths**, who was ill at that time.

The **Klubs** continued as a four-piece on the scene until the end of that year. Their final appearance was in November 2000, at the 'International Guitar Festival'.

Norris Easterbrook and **Steve Burkhill** still play together in a three-piece Rock band, sometimes appearing under the name **The Klubs** at local Merseyside venues.

Discography
I Found The Sun / Ever Needed Someone   UK- CAM Records CAM 681 / 1968

Unissued tracks:
Livin' Today (one-sided demo)   UK- Chart Records   acetate / 1967
The Stripper / Can't Ebenezer See My Mind   UK- DJM Demo   1969

Besides this the **Klubs** recorded the following songs, which obviously got stuck in the archives:
Old John Tring   TV-Granada talent-show   / 1967
NSU, **Desdemona** and **Livin' Today**   Test-Recordings for EMI   / 1967
Drive My Car, **Fire**, **Midnight Love Cycle** and **Ever Needed Someone**
          Test-Recordings for Decca   / 1968
Indian Dreams (two versions), **Can't Ebenezer See My Mind** and **Oh Baby**
          CAM-Recording Session   / 1968

THE KOOBAS

Here everything started in 1961 on the Wirral with the group **Roy Montrose & the Midnights**, that beside the vocalist **Roy Montrose** also included the brothers **Roy Morris** (lg) and **John Morris** (dr), as well as **Pete Williams** (bg) and **Dave Austin** (rg).

In 1962 **Dave Austin** left and emigrated to Canada. He for a short time was replaced by

the singer's brother **Robert Montrose**, but then **Stu Leithwood** took over the rhythm-guitar. At that time the group changed it's name into **The Kubas**. A little later **Roy Montrose** left but was not replaced as **Stu Leithwood** took over the lead vocals. He continued with his brother Robert in a duo called **Take Two** and later he was performing on his own as singer/guitarist under the name of **Roy Malcolm**.

When **John Morris** decided to become the roadie for the group, the **Kubas** were joined by **Kenny Cochran**, who came from **Clay Ellis & the Raiders** and accordingly appeared in the following line-up:

Stu Leithwood	**(voc/rg)**
Roy Morris	**(lg/voc)**
Pete Williams	**(bg/voc)**
John Morris	**(dr)**

In 1963 the group was chosen to take part in the motion picture 'Ferry Cross The Mersey' with **Gerry & the Pacemakers** in the main role. For this film, the **Kubas** recorded the originals *Steady Girl* and *Oh Little Fool,* which were not too impressive and later not featured on one of the soundtrack albums.

In spite of this, the group was signed to Columbia and a little later their first single was released with an interesting version of *Magic Potion*, coupled with *I Love Her,* which was the song *Steady Girl* from the above-mentioned film. But this line-up did not last too long as

Kenny Cochran and **Pete Williams** left again to join the backing group of the **Excelles**, a newly-formed Liverpool vocal group who later became the hit group **Arrival**.

The new members of the **Kubas** were **Tony O'Reilly** (dr) and **Keith Ellis** (bg/voc), who both were former members of the **Pilgrims**. Due to legal reasons, the spelling of the group's name was changed to **Koobas** and under this name, a second single was released in 1965, this time on PYE.

Take Me For A Little While sold better than their debut release, but sadly also failed to make the charts. These two records, of course, helped to increase the band's popularity on Merseyside. Despite this positive development, it can be said that the **Koobas** were one of the unlucky Liverpool groups as their first German tour, with appearances at the famous 'Star-Club' in 1963, did not bring the expected breakthrough and when the big boom in Liverpool started, the band had a long residence in Spain, and accordingly, not too much notice was taken of them by producers, promoters and so on. But in 1965, they had the chance of a great breakthrough when they supported the **Beatles** on their UK tour. Once again, nothing happened to improve the fortunes of the band, perhaps with the exception of the fact that they were chosen to take part in the film 'Merry Go Round The Roses' from which an EP was recorded with them. But the bad luck stuck with them and this very interesting EP was never released.

The next single by the **Koobas** with the songs *You'd Better Make Up Your Mind* and *A Place I Know* was not as commercial as its predecessors and once again failed to become a success, which probably led to the end of their contract with PYE.

The **Koobas** switched back to Columbia and, in 1966, their best single ever was released with *Sweet Music*. Great, rough and truthful Beat, just like the B-side *Face*, but once again it was mysteriously ignored by the public at large. This record was also released in Germany, but

over there it also did not make too much progress, which is more than sad. It was simply too late for the **Koobas** to jump on the big success train, although they certainly were one of the good and very interesting Liverpool bands.

The follow-ups, *Sally* and *Gibsy Fred*, also were not too successful, while the next single, a great version of **Cat Stevens**' *First Cut Is The Deepest* was a highlight again, but once again failed to make the charts.

This was the final single by the **Koobas** for the British market and the band was almost forgotten when suddenly and surprisingly an album with the title 'The Koobas' was released in 1969, from which one more single was coupled out with 'Where Are The Friends', especially for the French market. This long player, of course, was not Beat anymore but more the Psychedelic sound, popular at the time. Accordingly, the album must have been a bit disappointing for the Beat freaks, perhaps with the exception of their bluesy version of **Erma Franklin**'s *A Little Piece Of My Heart,* which was perfect and in every respect the best number on that album.

An interesting addition to this story is the fact that the three guitarists' silhouettes on the record sleeves of the German Ariola label for their 'Star Club' series were the **Koobas**, although they never had a contract with, or any other connections, to Ariola.

Short after the release of the album, probably still in 1969, this highly underrated group disbanded totally and **Tony O'Reilly** joined **Bakerloo**, while **Keith Ellis** became a member of **Spooky Tooth** and later played with **Van der Graff Generator**. None of the other members appeared on the scene again.

Single discography

Magic Potion / I Love Her	UK- Columbia	DB 7451 / 1964
Take Me For A Little While / Somewhere In The Night	UK- PYE	7 N 17012 / 1965
You'd Better Make Up Your Mind / A Place I Know	UK- PYE	7 N 17087 / 1966
Sweet Music / Face	UK- Columbia	DB 7988 / 1966
Sally / Champagne And Caviar	UK- Columbia	DB 8103 / 1967
Gypsy Fred / City Girl	UK- Columbia	DB 8187 / 1967
First Cut Is The Deepest / Walking Out	UK- Columbia	DB 8419 / 1967

Where Are The Friends / Royston Rose   **F- Columbia CF   165 / 1969**
(*** please note that the first UK single was released under their original name - **The Kubas**)

LP discography
THE KOOBAS   **UK- Columbia SCX 6271 / 1969**
- Royston Rose / Where Are The Friends / Constantly Changing / Here's A Day / Fade Forever /
Barricades / A Little Piece Of My Heart / Gold Leaf Tree / Mr. Claire / Circus

Unreleased tracks:
When the **Koobas** took part in the motion picture 'Merry Go Round The Roses', an EP was recorded with them which sadly never saw the light of the record market. That is why it is not known which songs were recorded at that time.

BILLY J. KRAMER WITH THE DAKOTAS

In the beginning of the Sixties, the group **Billy Forde & the Phantoms** was formed in Liverpool and when **Ted Knibbs** took over their management, he changed their name to **Billy Kramer & the Coasters**. It was a real amateur outfit, but within a short time became very popular on the scene and in 1962 was placed at number 3 in the 'Mersey Beat' popularity poll. Probably because of that success **Brian Epstein** became interested in managing the up and coming group.

Billy Kramer & the Coasters recorded the demo *She's My Girl,* a song by Liverpool songwriter **Ralph Bowdler**. **Brian Epstein** took it to EMI and they became interested in signing the band. But with the exception of **Billy Kramer**, none of the musicians wanted to become professional, and so the singer separated from the group and signed a contract with **Brian Epstein**.

The Coasters continued together under the wing of **Ted Knibbs** and found a new singer in **Chick Graham** and in 1963 they also turned professional under the name of **Chick Graham & the Coasters**.

Brian Epstein changed his singer's name from **Billy Forde** to **Billy J. Kramer** and arranged a co-operation between him and the Manchester band **The Dakotas**, who formerly backed **Pete MacLaine**.

It should be pointed out here that the 'J' was added to his name because **Brian Epstein** thought it sounded more interesting and not because **Billy J. Kramer** was a big fan of **'J'ohn Lennon**, as it is often claimed by badly informed people.

However, the new amalgamation's full name was **Billy J. Kramer <u>with</u> the Dakotas**, because the **Dakotas** also recorded solo and had two chart hits with the instrumentals *Magic Carpet* and *The Cruel Sea* in 1963, while the 1964's follow-up *Oyeh* failed to make the hit parade.

Billy J. Kramer with the Dakotas were voted 'the best new group of the year' by the music paper 'Melody Maker' in 1963. This fact alone makes clear how popular the group was all over England. Their line-up at that time was:

> **Billy J. Kramer**   (voc)
> **Mike Maxfield**   (g)
> **Robin McDonald** (g)
> **Ray Jones**   (bg)
> **Tony Mansfield** (dr)

Mike Maxfield was a former member of **Don Curtis & the Coasters** and **Tony Mansfield**'s real name is **Tony Bookbinder** a brother of **Elkie Brooks** who was later very successful.

The first single released by the Liverpool/Manchester connection *Do You Want To Know A Secret* was written by **John Lennon** and **Paul McCartney** and went straight to number 2 in the British charts in 1963, and with the follow-up *Bad To Me*, **Billy J. Kramer with the Dakotas** had their first chart topper later in the same year.

This success was followed by *I'll Keep You Satisfied* (no. 4 in 1963), their biggest success

Little Children (no.1) and *From A Window* (no.10), both in 1964. The next single *It's Gotta Last Forever* did not chart, but the **Burt Bacharach** song *Trains And Boats And Planes* was another Top 20 hit for the group and reached No.12 in 1965. **Billy J. Kramer with the Dakotas** also charted in the USA with some of these records, where they were very popular at that time.

In England the group had a special tour programme under the name 'The Billy J. Kramer Pop Parade', but in the rest of Europe, they were mysteriously unsuccessful with their records.

In 1965, **Ray Jones** left and was replaced by **Ken Sherrat**, who came from Stoke's **Marauders**. **Mike Maxfield**, who still sporadicly played with **Don Curtis & the Coasters** also left and became the manager of the Manchester group **Ivan's Meads**. He was replaced by **Mick Green**, a former member of **Johnny Kidd & the Pirates**.

In 1966, **Tony Mansfield** temporarily replaced the then returning **Bobby Elliott** in the **Hollies**, before he had another short spell with **Dave Berry & the Cruisers**. He then obviously quit show business but in 1981 was back on the scene as a member of **New Music**. For a while, **Roy Dyke** of the **Remo Four** stood in for him with the **Dakotas**, but then **Frank Farley** took over that position, having formerly played with **Johnny Kidd & the Pirates**.

In the meantime further singles like *Neon City, We're Doing Fine* and the nice ballad *Take My Hand* were released, but all failed to make the charts. When **Ken Sherrat** left again to join the newly-formed **Tennesseans, Billy J. Kramer** also separated from the **Dakotas**, who found a new singer in **Lou Rich**, and released two more singles with *I'm An 'ardworking Barrow-man* and *Can't Break The News*.

Then **Mick Green**, the only remaining original member **Robin McDonald** and **Frank Farley** became the new **Rebel Rousers** for great singer **Cliff Bennett**. When they disbanded only **Mick Green** appeared again - as a member of the reformed **Pirates**.

But this is not the end of the **Dakotas** story as they were reformed by founder members **Tony Bookbinder** and **Mike Maxfield** together with **Eddie Mooney** (voc/bg) and **Pete MacDonald** (key). The group kept very busy on the scene, but a new co-operation with **Billy J. Kramer** never took place.

After he left the **Dakotas** in 1967, **Billy J. Kramer** went solo and for a while was backed by the **Remo Four** on live appearances. His records *Sorry, Town Of Tuxley* (both in 1967) *1941, A World Without Love* (both in 1968) as well as *Colour Of My Love* (1969) did not make the charts, although they were quite interesting.

He continued recording for different labels and in 1971 he released *And The Grass Won't Pay No Mind* on Polydor as the only record under his real name **William Howard Ashton**.

He later formed a new backing group that in England toured as the **B.J.K.-Band**, but also used the name of **Dakotas** sometimes. The line-up of this group changed permanently and in

1977 consisted of **Max Milligan** (g), **Chris Cole** (org/p), **Mike Clustin** (bg) and **John Dillon** (dr).

Max Milligan, **Mike Clustin** and **John Dillon** were former members of a band called **Breeze**, while **Chris Cole** was a former classical musician. In this line-up, they toured Germany as **Billy J. Kramer & the Dakotas** for the first time since the Sixties, but this tour unfortunately wasn't too successful and accordingly not repeated.

Around this time **Billy J. Kramer** also released some good singles like the melodic *Warm Summer Rain* (1977), the very interesting *Ships That Pass In The Night* and in 1982 the Merseybeatish *Dum Dum* as B-side of the not that good *Rock It.*

He later emigrated to the USA and there he released a new album with quite good second takes of his big Sixties hits on one side, as well as some interesting new songs on the other.

The title of that long player was 'Kramer v/s Kramer' (US-Attack ATA 007 / 1986).

Single discography
as <u>**Billy Kramer & the Coasters**</u>:
She's My Girl / (probably only one-sided)   UK- Epstein-demo (acetate) / 1963

as <u>**Billy J. Kramer with the Dakotas**</u>:

Do You Want To Know A Secret / I'll Be On My Way	UK-Parlophone R 5023 / 1963
Bad To Me / I Call Your Name	UK-Parlophone R 5049 / 1963
I'll Keep You Satisfied / I Know	UK-Parlophone R 5073 / 1963
Little Children / They Remind Me Of You	UK-Parlophone R 5105 / 1964
From A Window / Second To None	UK-Parlophone R 5156 / 1964
It's Gotta Last Forever / on't You Do It No More	UK-Parlophone R 5234 / 1965
Trains And Boats And Planes / That's The Way I Feel	UK-Parlophone R 5285 / 1965
Neon City / I'll Be Doggone	UK-Parlophone R 5362 / 1965
We're Doing Fine / Forgive Me	UK-Parlophone R 5408 / 1966
Take My Hand / You Make Me Feel Like Someone	UK-Parlophone R 5482 / 1966

different US release:

Twilight Time / Irrisistible You	**US- Imperial** 66115 / 1965

<u>**Billy J. Kramer**</u> - solo:

Sorry / Going, Going, Gone	**UK-Parlophone R 5552 / 1967**
Town Of Tuxley / Chinese Girl	**UK-Reaction** 591014 / 1967
1941 / His Love Is Just A lie	**UK-Nems** 56-3396 / 1968
A World Without Love / Going Through It	**UK-Nems** 56-3635 / 1968
Colour Of My Love / I'm Running Away	**UK-MGM** 1474 / 1969

As <u>**Wiiliam Howard Ashton**</u>:

And The Grass Won't Pay No Mind /	**UK-Polydor** / 1971

<u>**The Dakotas**</u> - solo:

The Cruel Sea / The Millionaire	UK-Parlophone R 5044 / 1963
Magic Carpet / Humdinger	UK-Parlophone R 5064 / 1963
Oyeh / My Girl Josephine	UK-Parlophone R 5203 / 1964
I'm An 'ardworking Barrow-man / 7 lbs Of Potatoes	**UK-Page One** 018 / 1967
Can't Break The News / The Spider And The Fly	**UK-Philips** 1645 / 1968

EP discography
as <u>**Billy J. Kramer with the Dakotas**</u>:

THE KRAMER HITS   UK-Parlophone GEP 8885 / 1963
- Do You Want To Know A Secret / I'll Be On My Way / Bad To Me / I Call Your Name

I'LL KEEP YOU SATISFIED   UK-Parlophone GEP 8895 / 1963
- I'll Keep You Satisfied / I Know / Dance With Me / It's Up To You

I'LL KEEP YOU SATISFIED No.2   UK-Parlophone GEP 8907 / 1964
- Little Children / They Remind Me Of You / Beautiful Dreamer / I Call Your Name

FROM A WINDOW   UK-Parlophone GEP 8921 / 1964
- From A Window / Second To None / Dance With Me / The Twelfth Of Never

BILLY J. PLAYS THE STATES   UK-Parlophone GEP 8928 / 1965
- Sugar Babe / Twilight Time / Irrisistible You / Tennessee Waltz (all live-recordings)

Different French release:
BILLY J. KRAMER / THE DAKOTAS   F- Odeon   SOE 3743 / 1964
- Bad To Me / Do You Want To Know A Secret / The Cruel Sea / The Millionaire

EP by **The Dakotas**:
THE DAKOTAS   UK-Parlophone GEP 8888 / 1963
- The Cruel Sea / The Millionaire / Magic Carpet / Humdinger

LP discography
as **Billy J. Kramer with the Dakotas**:

LISTEN   UK-Parlophone PMC 1209 / 1964
-Dance With Me / Pride / I Know / Yes / Twelfth Of Never / Sugar Babe / Da Doo Ron Ron / It's Up To You / Great Balls Of Fire / Tell Me Girl / Anything That's Part Of You / Beautiful Dreamer / Still Waters Run Deep / I Call Your Name

Different US releases:
LITTLE CHILDREN   US-Imperial   LP 12267 / 1964
- Little Children / Da Doo Ron Ron / Dance With Me / Pride / I Know / They Remind Me Of You / Do You Want To Know A Secret / Bad To Me / I'll Keep You Satisfied / Great Balls Of Fire / It's Up To You / Tell Me Girl

I'LL KEEP YOU SATISFIED / FROM A WINDOW   US-Imperial   LP 12273 / 1964
-I'll Keep You Satisfied / I Call Your Name / Beautiful Dreamer / The Twelfth Of Never / Sugar Babe / I'll Be On My Way / From A Window / Second To None / Anything That's Part Of You / Still Waters / Yes / The Cruel Surf ("Dakotas" Solo)

TRAINS AND BOATS AND PLANES   US-Imperial   LP 12291 / 1965
- Trains And Boats And Planes / Mad Mad World / Twilight Time / Under The Boardwalk / When You Walk In The Room / Sneaking Around / To Take Her Place / When You Ask About Love / I Live To Love You / Tennessee Waltz (Live) / Irrisistible You (Live)

Unreleased tracks
In 1963, **Billy J. Kramer with the Dakotas** recorded a great version of *I'm in love*, which then was released by **The Fourmost** and became a chart success for them. In 1964, the group recorded an alternative take of *When You Walk In The Room*, which was much more powerful as the later released take on the album. This song of course was released by the **Searchers** and became a chart success for them. Another **Paul McCartney** song was recorded with *One And One Is Two* in 1965, which then was released by a group called **The Strangers with Mike Shannon**, which was not the Liverpool one, but this time it did not become a hit.

THE KREW

This group originates from Birmingham, where it was formed by **Ray Thomas** and **Mike Pinder**, who formerly had played together in **El Riot & the Rebels**. Accordingly it was a real Brumbeat group and this could lead to the conclusion that they should not be included here, but their story will prove the contrary.

Their name was delivered in various spellings – from the Crew-Cuts, over the Krew-Cats up to the Krewkats, whereby the latter one most probably is the right one, judged by the records that came out. However, after some personal changes the **Krewkats** in 1962 consisted of the Birmingham musicians **John 'Brad' Bradley** (voc/bg), **Ted Tunnicliffe** (lg), **Rob Nicholls** (rg) and **Don Hawkins** (dr). They went to France and rapidly were signed by the Parisian record company 'Pathe Marconi'.

At first the group cut two EPs in their own right with 'Polaris' and 'Tonight' but still in 1963 also backed famous French Rock 'n' Roll singer **Dick Rivers** on three EPs and some album tracks.

Around that time **Don Hawkins** left and was replaced by Liverpudlian (?) **Eddie Sparrow**. The **Krewkats** toured Germany and amongst others played for a longer time at the 'New York City Club' in Duisburg. When they were finishing their engagement, the **Pawns** from Liverpool were due to take over. Sax player **Howie Casey**, who came there with the **Pawns** played a gig with the **Krewkats** and joined them. This five piece line-up returned to France and also worked with **Dick Rivers** again.

They were joined by **Mann Hoaurie** as additional sax player and accepted a month's offer to play a club in Itzehoe, North Germany. This club then burned down and most of the group's instruments were destroyed. **Peter Eckhorn** of the famous 'Top Ten' in Hamburg, helped out and offered them an engagement at his club. They were joined by **Johnny Phillips** (tr/sax), who formerly played with the **Roadrunners** and the **Eyes**.

As the **Top Ten Allstars** the group backed Scottish girl singer **Isabella Bond** on her records *Bread And Butter* and *Everything's Alright*, that came out on German Decca in 1964. Also they recorded a solo single as the **Top Ten Allstars** with *I Feel Fine*, no one, other than **Tony Sheridan** played the guitar to the lead vocals of **John Bradley**.

After that engagement ended, the **Krewkats** went to London, where the line-up changed again and again and the group finally broke up.

John Bradley followed **Howie Casey** back to Liverpool, where they both joined the **Big Three** for a short time. After that **Howie Casey** had a short spell with the **Griff Parry Five**, while **John Bradley** played with the **Jam Buttees**. Then both got together again with **Eddie Sparrow** and resurrected their former group under the shortened name of **The Krew,** together with **Mike Hart** (g/sax/voc), formerly with the **Tenabeats** and the **Roadrunners. John Bradley** again left quite soon and disappeared from the scene.

The **Krew** were joined by **Archie Leggett** as bass guitarist, who came from the **Bobby Patrick Big Six**. The new singer became **Steve Aldo**, who formerly had sung with **Steve Aldo & the Challengers**, the **Nocturns**, for a short time with **King Size Taylor & the Dominoes** and the **Griff Parry Five**.

He did not stay too long with the group and joined the **Fyx**, but later sang with the **In Crowd** and then was backed by the **Fairies** from Colchester for a short time before he quit showbiz.

Mike Hart had left a bit earlier and joined the **Richmond**. After that he played with the **Kinsleys** and then formed the new group **Henry's Handful**. He later appeared with **Mike Hart & the Moondogs** and **Liverpool Scene**, before he started a successful solo career.

The **Krew** under the leadership of **Howie Casey** in 1965 decided to go back to France in the line-up with:

Owen Gray	(voc)
Tommy Murray	(g)
Howie Casey	(sax)
Archie Leggett	(bg)
Alan Reeves	(org)
Eddie Sparrow	(dr)

Tommy Murray, a great guitarist had formerly played with the **Memphis Rhythm & Blues Combo** and with the **Kinsleys**. The former groups of **Owen Gray** and **Alan Reeves** are sadly not known, but both hailed from the Mersey scene.

The **Krew** used France as their base and from there toured all over Europe. It is said that around that time they also backed successful Fench girl singer **Sylvie Vartan** on various recordings but this could not be confirmed. At least the group was never named on any of the labels of her singles or EPs.

The big Barclay recording company signed the **Krew** for its Riviera label and in 1966 an EP was realeased with the songs *Everything's Alright, 63-45789, Somebody Stole My Girl* and *Sugar Pie*. This record showed the **Krew** to be a great group and obviously sold quite well but was not followed by further releases. The reason for that might have been the fact, that the changes in the line-up kept continuing.

Eddie Sparrow left and was replaced by **Pete Clarke**, who formerly had played with the **Tiyms, Groups Inc.** and the **Escorts**. He did not stay too long and joined **Them Grimbles**, before he returned to the **Escorts**. Later he was a member of **Liverpool Scene**. As his replacement **Chris Mutch** came from Liverpool.

Beside this the group was joined on saxes by **Ivan Roth** and the **French Gilbert D'Alanese**. When **Owen Gray** left, his replacement was **Ernie Garrett Jn.** and later the **Krew** was also joined by songstress **Barry St. John**, who formerly had various solo singles released on Decca and Columbia, of that the most popular one was her great version of *Bread And Butter*.

It was probably in 1968 that the group disbanded totally, when **Tommy Murray** joined a group called **Mumble** and after that became a member of the **Swinging Blue Jeans**, who at that time recorded as **Music Motor**. **Archie Leggett** appeared again on the scene as a member of the **Kevin Ayers Band**, where he met up again with **Owen Gray**. **Chris Mutch** also joined the **Swinging Blue Jeans** and after that disappeared from the scene.

Howie Casey got married to **Barry St. John**, who from 1968 on kept recording in her own right, while **Howie Casey**, who in the meantime had a short spell with the **Big Three**, continued in groups like the **Roy Young Band** and **Rigor Mortis**. Beside this he became a very successful studio musician and as such appeared on lots of records of well known artists, like for example **Paul McCartney** and the **Hollies**. Today he is married to **Sheila McKinley** of the **McKinleys** recording duo and still leads his own group, the **Howie Casey Band**.

The group name **Krew** did exist on the scene until the early Seventies, but it is not known, who were the members of the steadily changing line-ups.

The Krew with Beryl Marsden

Discography:
The Krew:
EP **Everything's Alright** / 63-45789 / **Somebody Stole My Girl** / **Sugar Pie**
                                               F – Riviera 231 214 / 1966

The Top Ten Allstars:
I feel fine / **Sha-la-la**   G – Decca D 19651 / 1964
Isabella Bond & the Top Ten Allstars:
Bread And Butter / **Downtown**   (both titles sung in English) G – Decca D 19650 / 1964
Bread And Butter / **Downtown**   (both titles sung in German) G – Decca D 19657 / 1964
Everything's Alright / **Thanks**   G – Decca D 19668 / 1964

Tracks on compilation-albums:
Bread And Butter   on   **'Beat Party'**   G – Decca ND 106 / 1965
Hurt   on   **'Beat Party'**   G – Decca ND 106 / 1965

The Krewkats:
EP **Tonight** / **Tuxedo Twist** / **You Are My Sunshine** / **Diggedle Boing**
                                               F - Pathe Marconi   / 1963
EP **Polaris** / **The Ice Cream Man** / **Bleak House** / **For My Good Fortune**
                                               F – Pathe Marconi   / 1963
As backing-group for **Dick Rivers**:
   EP **A Séville** / **Pour Une Fille** (Why Little Girl) / **J'ai Choisi L'amour** (For My Good Fortune) / **Virginie** (please note that the **Krewkats** were only featured on the 2nd and 3rd title)
                                               F – Pathe EG 630   / 1963
   EP **Bien Trop Court** (Life's Too Short) / **La Fille Qu'on A Tant Aimée** / **Au Cœur De La Nuit** (A Picture Of You) / **Je Suis Bien**   F – Pathe EG 639   / 1963
   EP **L'effet Que Tu Mes Fais** (How Do You Do It) / **Je Ne Peux Pas T'oublier** (Can't Get Used To Losing You) / **Sarah Jane** (The Folk Singer) / **T'as Seize Ans Demain** (Sweet Little Sixteen)
                                               F – Pathe EG 650   / 1963
   Album tracks:
T'as Seize Ans Demain (Sweet Little Sixteen)on **'100 % Rock'**   F - MF 5602   / 196?
Tobacco Road   on **'100 % Rock'**   F – MFP   5602   / 196?
Whole Lotta Shakin' Goin' On   on **'100 % Rock'**   F – MFP   5602   / 196?

(Please note that all the French recordings as the **Krewkats** obviously were without participation of Liverpool musicians)

215

THE KRUZADS

This group was formed in Liverpool in 1962 by **Frank McTigue**, who formerly had played with the **Texans,** together with **Ken 'Dixie' Dean**, a former member of **Gerry Marsden's Skiffle Group**, formerly known as the **Mars Bars**. Shortly after their formation **Frank McTigue** returned to his old group, which now were called **The Easybeats** and for him **Eddie Hill** came from the **Easybeats**.

The **Kruzads** very soon established themselves as one of the local attractions and in 1963 accepted an offer to tour the army bases in France and Germany with the following line-up:

'Dixie' Dean	(voc/g)
Billy Roberts	(g)
Eddie Hill	(bg/voc)
Danny Bell	(dr)

Billy Roberts and **Danny Bell** both were former members of the **Citybeats**.

While the **Kruzads** were in Germany, they were apparently signed by the German Polydor label and **Dixie Dean** claims they recorded the songs *Tell Me* and **Arthur Alexander**'s *You Better Move On* as a single, but nothing is known about such a release. Maybe it was released under another name, but this is only a possibility and not absolutely certain, although German Polydor was known for confusing or simply changing the names of their artists.

Back in Liverpool, their manager **Gordon Brown** built up a big name for the **Kruzads**, who were then trumpeted as Liverpool's answer to the **Rolling Stones**, and obviously there were similarities in their sounds. The **Kruzads** were one of the hard Beat and Rhythm & Blues bands from the River Mersey, as well as being one of the very good groups from the Beat metropolis. In spite of this they never achieved nationwide popularity but had a large following in the North.

In late 1964, **Eddie Hill** left the band was replaced by **Mal Jefferson**, whose real name is **Malcolm Andrews** and who had played before with **Buddy Dean & the Teachers** and the **Mastersounds**. He, by the way, is the brother of **Don Andrews** of the **Remo Four**.

This line-up then was joined by **Chris Finley** as additional guitarist. A little later **Dixie Dean** left the group and went down to London where he became a session musician. From 1972 until 1974, he appeared as a member of **McGuinness Flint**, who had a big hit with the great *When I'm Dead And Gone*.

Mal Jefferson had become the lead singer of the **Kruzads**, who were joined by **Paul Eker** (bg) from the **Profiles**. But he was soon replaced again by **Jimmy Ikomidis**, the former bass guitarist of the **Mafia**.

Mal Jefferson and **Chris Finley** left, and while **Mal Jefferson** later was a member of the **Chesterfields** (see story of the **Kansas City Five**), **Chris Finley** joined the **Masterminds**. He later appeared again with **Confucius**, who had developed from the **Hideaways** and after that played with the new **Merseybeats** and **Herman's Hermits**. **Chris Finley** was not replaced in the **Kruzads** but as new singer came **Steve Barton**.

The next to leave was **Danny Bell** and the new drummer was **Paul Hitchmough**, who came from **Sounds Plus One** and before that had played with the **Hangmen**, **Victims** and the **Corals**.

Besides this, the group was joined by **John Thompson** as additional singer, who also came from **Sounds Plus One** and in this line-up the **Kruzads** cut a great acetate with the **Kinks**-number *Stop Your Sobbing,* which sadly was not followed by a record release.

They toured France again very successfully, where they also had some TV appearances, but in spite of this success the group split in 1966, and **Paul Hitchmough** joined the **Clayton Squares**, who a little later also disbanded, but then with a different line-up (including **Paul Hitchmough**) continued as **The T-Squares** and toured Germany as the **Clayton Squares** again. After that **Paul Hitchmough** joined **Curiousity Shoppe** and then disappeared from the scene like all the other former members of the **Kruzads**.

In 1990, however, he toured Germany again as a member of **Beryl Marsden**'s backing group and after that joined **Karl Terry & the Cruisers**, before he withdraw again.

Discography

Tell Me / You Better Move On	**G- Polydor**	**???**	**/ 1964**

(*** please note, that it is not certain if this record was really released, but it is possible that it was released under another name (perhaps on a sampler album), because the German Polydor was known for things like that. However, Dixie Dean claims that it was released - any doubts?)

Stop Your Sobbing /	**UK- acetate**	**/ 1966**

MR. LEE & CO.

This band came together in Birkenhead on the west side of the River Mersey in March 1964. Their sound was based on Rock 'n' Roll and the group became very popular on Merseyside within a short time. They probably came too late to have any notable national or international success, in spite of having quality. **Mr. Lee & Co.**, right from the beginning, consisted of the following musicians:

Mr. Lee	**(voc)**
Paul Wise	**(g/voc)**
Alan Chesters	**(bg/voc)**
Mike Grannon	**(sax)**
Nigel Whinyates	**(dr)**

The mysterious **Mr. Lee** was none other than **William Carruthers**, who formerly had been very popular under the name **Clay Ellis** when he led the groups **Clay Ellis & the Raiders** and **Clay Ellis & the Corsairs**. Sadly, nothing is known about the musical past of the other members, if the group already existed before it teamed up with **William Carruthers**

(if so, than most probably under another name), or if it was formed for or by him. Of **Mike Grannon** it is only known that he had formerly played with a Tradjazz band.

F.G. Scanes became their manager. He was also the owner of the 'Witch's Cauldron' club in Birkenhead and so it was not surprising, that **Mr. Lee & Co.** became the resident band there, but the group also played all the other clubs - up to the 'Iron Door' and the 'Cavern' in Liverpool.

In May 1964, **Mr. Lee & Co.** cut the first demo record with their original *Cry A Little,* written by **William Carruthers**. Sadly, this was never released as an official record and so did not help the group too much. Neither did their other demos, including songs like *Peter Gunn* and *All Night Worker.*

The band then went down to London to live and to work, probably with the hope of being signed by one of the major recording companies, but sadly this did not happen, for whatever reasons, and so they returned to Liverpool a few months later, at the end of 1965. **Mr. Lee & Co.** did not survive for long after that and disbanded totally in 1966.

Mr. Lee then used the name **Clay Ellis** again and became a solo entertainer in the club and cabaret circuit. He then retired and went back to a normal day job, as the other members of his group had done before. He sadly died much too young sometime in the Nineties.

In the end can be said with a clear conscience that **Mr. Lee & Co.** was one of the very good Merseyside groups and that it made only one mistake - it simply came too late!

Discography
Mr. Lee & Co. never released an official record but in 1964/65 cut a couple of demo records which included songs like *Cry A Little, Peter Gunn* and *All Night Worker.*

THE LIVERBIRDS

This band was certainly not the first all female vocal and instrumental group in Liverpool when they came together in 1962, but with the slogan 'what men can do, we can do all the time', they were the first female group that made real impact on the male dominated scene - something of an early act of emancipation.

The **Liverbirds** were named after the mythological birds of Liverpool's Atlantic coast that also became the emblem of the harbour city and still can be seen as an iron monument on the top of the Liver Building. Within a quite short time the **Liverbirds** rocked themselves into the hearts of the Beat fans on Merseyside. The original line-up consisted of:

Irene Green	**(voc)**
Sheila McGlory	**(g/voc)**
Valerie Gell	**(g/voc)**
Mary McGlory	**(bg/voc)**
Sylvia Saunders	**(dr)**

Mary McGlory had played with **The Bikinis** (what a nice name) and **The Squaws** before she teamed up with her sister **Sheila McGlory**, **Valerie Gell** and **Sylvia Sounders** in a group called **The Debutones**. A little later this band was joined by **Irene Green** and then the name was changed to **The Liverbirds**. **Irene Green** left quite soon again and started a successful solo career under the name of **'Tiffany'**.

At first she was backed by the **Four Dimensions** (as **Tiffany's Dimensions**) and later by the **Thoughts** (as **Tiffany & the Thoughts**).

With the latter group she recorded the nice single *Find Out What's Happening,* but before that she had already released a solo single with the great *Am I Dreaming*. But that is a different story which can be followed under **Tiffany & the Thoughts** in this book. She was not replaced in the **Liverbirds** and when the group received an offer to play the 'Star-Club' in Hamburg, **Sheila McGlory** left because she wanted to stay in Liverpool, where she then joined **The Demoiselles**. The **Liverbirds** were joined by **Pamela Birch** (voc/g), a very impressive stage personality.

With this line-up, the group went to Hamburg for a long residence, where it became a steady and significant part of the so-called 'Star-Club' scene. Over time, the **Liverbirds** achieved popularity all over Germany, but because they only seldom returned to Liverpool, they lost a lot of importance in the Beat scene of their hometown.

Thus, they never released a record in England but were quite successful in Germany with their singles *Diddley Daddy* (No. 1 in the musicbox hit parade in 1965), *Shop Around, Peanut Butter and Loop Di Loop,* all were released on the 'Star-Club' label.

Beside this the **Liverbirds** cut two albums for the same label with 'Star-Club Show 4' and 'More Of The Liverbirds'. Both were quite interesting, and ballads like *Love Hurts, Leave All Your Old Loves In The Past, He Hardly Ever Calls Me 'Honey' Anymore* and *Why Do You Hang Around Me* left an especially good impression, as did the rocking numbers like *It's So Exciting, He's About A Mover* and so on.

The statement that the **Liverbirds** had no outstanding musical quality is probably true but they had a good driving sound at the right time and so their success in Germany was not undeserved.

In 1967 **Sylvia Saunders** got married to **John Wiggins**, the former organist of the **Big Six** and with him she returned to England. She was replaced by German girl drummer **Dixie Wassermeyer**, who came from the **Rag Dolls** from Duisburg. Assuming there had been no other changes; the **Liverbirds** toured Japan with this line-up, where they were quite successful. They may have recorded again in Japan, but there is nothing known about any releases in the Far East different to the ones that had already been out in Germany.

Shortly after their return to Germany, the group disbanded totally. **Valerie Gell** got married in Munich, while **Mary McGlory** got married to **Frank Dostal**, a German musician from the 'Star-Club' scene who had played with the **Tornados**, the **Faces**, the **Rattles** and **Wonderland**.

Dixie Wassermeyer returned to Duisburg and sadly died at a very young age. **Pamela Birch**, who also worked sporadicly as a songwriter, stayed to live in Hamburg and occasionally appeared again at different sessions. In 1977 she featured at a revival concert together with other former musicians of the legendary 'Star-Club' scene at the Markthalle in Hamburg.

At this concert, the group **Rock Circus** was formed where she became one of the members. But this group had more a session character and a steadily changing line-up.

After that, **Pamela Birch** was a member of the very short-lived group **Full O'Juice** and then disappeared again from the scene.

Single discography

Shop Around / It's Got To Be You	G- Star-Club	148508 / 1965
Diddley Daddy / Leave All Your Old Loves In The Past	G- Star-Club	148526 / 1965
Peanut Butter / Why Do You Hang Around Me	G- Star-Club	148528 / 1965
Loop Di Loop / Bo Diddley Is A Lover	G- Star-Club	148554 / 1966

Different US release:
Why Do You Hang Around Me / Diddley Daddy	US- Philips	40288 / 1965

LP discography
STAR-CLUB SHOW 4   G- Star-Club   158003 / 1965
- Johnny B. Goode / Can't Judge A Book By Looking At The Cover / Love Hurts / Talking About You / Mona / Money / Too Much Monkey-Business / Roadrunner / Diddley Daddy / Hands Off / Before You Accuse Me / Leave All Your Old Loves In The Past / Got My Mojo-workin'

MORE OF THE LIVERBIRDS   G- Star-Club   158021 / 1965
- Peanut Butter / It's So Exciting / He Hardly Ever Calls Me 'Honey' Anymore / For Your Love / Oh No, Not My Baby / Around And Around / Down Home Girl / He's Something Else / Heatwave / Why Do You Hang Around Me / He's About A Mover / Long Tall Shorty

Tracks on compilation albums:
Diddley Daddy	on 'Star-Club Parade'	G- Philips	6558 / 1965
It's So Exciting	on 'Beater's Hit parade'	G- Philips	75-283 / 1967
He Hardly Ever Calls Me 'Honey' Anymore	on 'Beater's Hit parade'		
		G- Philips	75-283 / 1967

Some people state that there is a connection between the **Liverbirds** and another girl group called **Gilded Cage**, who may have included at least some of the former **Liverbirds**. This is not proven but highly improbable as **Gilded Cage** consisted of musicians from different countries, including the United States and Scandinavia. But this of course does not necessarily mean that it is impossible that one of the former **Liverbirds** was also included and therefore here are the records by **Gilded Cage**, which, by the way, were quite good, especially the first one:

Long Long Road / Baby Grumbling	**G- Philips**	**384596 / 1968**
My Bonnie / Hair	**G- Philips**	**388381 / 1969**

THE LONG & THE SHORT

This group with the quite unusual name was formed in Liverpool in the late Fifties as a Skiffle band under the name **The L'Ringos**.

When the big Beat boom came the group jumped on this train, they changed their music and their name - to **The Long & the Short**. The band at this time consisted of the following musicians:

Bob McKinnley	**(voc)**
Les Saints	**(g/voc)**
Alan Grindley	**(g/voc)**
Bob Taylor	**(bg/voc)**
Gerry Watt	**(dr)**

The individual members had not appeared on the scene before, with the exception of **Les Saints** whose real name is **Les Stuart** and who was the former leader of the **Les Stuart Quartet**. He had also played with **Frank Knight & the Barons**, **Danny Havoc & the Ventures** and the **Kansas City Five**.

In 1964 the **Long & Short** were featured in the music picture 'Gonks Go Beat' and can be found on the corresponding soundtrack album with the song *Take This Train*, which probably was an original by the group. They were signed to Decca in the same year and a little later their first single *The Letter* was released and climbed up to No.30 in the British charts.

The mysterious thing about this was that no one really took notice of this undoubtedly surprising success, not even the Liverpool music papers like 'Mersey Beat' or 'Combo'. Maybe Liverpool was too spoilt by the success of lots of other local groups, but that should not have been reason enough to justify this ignorance, especially as it was unfair to **The Long & the Short**. But much more mysterious is the fact that this group and their records was also ignored in discographies of Liverpool's Merseybeat groups printed later. They were for sure a Liverpool outfit and had another top-50 hit with their second single *Choc Ice*, which climbed up to No.49, also in 1964.

After this release, the lead vocalist **Bob McKinnley** left the group to join the newly formed **Epics** who partially consisted of former members of the **Mojos**. This group was paid more attention by the press than **The Long & the Short**, although the **Epics** never performed together in public and, in the end, broke up again. What happened to **Bob McKinnley** afterward is sadly unknown. His departure from the **Long & Short** was probably the reason for the group disbanding, which is very hard to understand as there were more potential vocalists in the group which, all in all, was very successful with their two hit singles. It should not have been too difficult for them to solve the vocalist problem, so there must have been another reason for the split, but no detailed information was obtainable.

However, it seems that even Decca did not care too much for that really good group, and so **The Long & the Short** disappeared as if they had never existed, and none of the members appeared again on the scene. What is left is just two really good singles, worth seeking out!

Discography

The Letter / Love Is A Funny Thing	**UK- Decca F.11959 / 1964**
Choc Ice / Here Comes The Fool	**UK- Decca F.12043 / 1964**

Tracks on compilation-albums:

Take This Train	on **'Gonks Go Beat'**	**UK- Decca LK 4673 / 1964**

THE MARACCAS

It was already 1964 when this band came together in Liverpool, and so the **Maraccas**, as they were named right from the beginning, were a group from the second Merseybeat generation. By that stage, the Liverpool sound had achieved worldwide success.

This was a real advantage for young groups like the **Maraccas** as the star bands of the scene had engagements all over the world (mostly on the European continent) and so had left room on the local scene and in the programmes of the important clubs, which they could use - and the **Maraccas** knew how to do it. Their members, all between 16 and 17 years of age, were:

Dave Rhodes	**(voc)**
Frank Baker	**(g/voc)**
Tommy Cunningham	**(g/voc)**
Fred Seddon	**(bg/voc)**
Brian Donovan	**(dr)**

Tommy Cunningham might have been the same musician who had played with the **Demonstrators** before, while all the other members were obviously newcomers on the scene. The **Maraccas** established themselves within a very short time and played all the famous and important venues along Merseyside.

They found their own musical style, which made a difference to the other groups. They were one of the very first bands that mixed poetry and Beat in reading their own poems against the background of their own compositions and called this mixture 'Bluestempo Music'. But their program was not restricted to this kind of sound, but also included the normal Beat songs, and one of the highlights of their live appearances was the **Bob Dylan** composition *Blowin' In The Wind,* which became a big hit for various artists.

In early 1965 the band went into the 'Cavern-Sound' studio in Matthew Street and recorded a private single under the wings of the famous Birmingham singer **Jimmy Powell.** Sadly, no more details are known. Their producer **Jimmy Powell** was of course the former leader of **Jimmy Powell & the Five Dimensions**, who had a giant hit with *Sugar Babe* in the early Sixties. It can be taken for granted that the **Maraccas** recorded some of their own compositions, but even this is not definitely certain.

A little later, the band went down to London and did a recording test for PYE, but in the end nothing was released, and again it is not known which songs were recorded. However, the **Maraccas** probably came too late anyway to make a big breakthrough, even if there records had been released. Because the band wasn't paid too much attention on the national scene, it is sadly not known when it disbanded and what happened to the individual members after that.

<u>Discography</u>

The **Maraccas** never released an official record, but in 1965 recorded a private single in the 'Cavern-Sound' studio in Liverpool under the wing of hit singer **Jimmy Powell**. Also in 1965, the group made some test recordings for PYE in London but as before there are no details known about the songs recorded.

THE MARKFOUR

This is the story of another very interesting Liverpool group. Now every insider will know that the **Mark Four** later became the hit group **The Creation**, but this was a totally different band. Considering that the **Creation** guitarist **Bob Garner** was a former member of **Lee Curtis & the All Stars** and the **Merseybeats**, and that the **Creation** drummer **Dave Preston** also hailed from Liverpool where he had played with groups like the **Harlems** and the **Secrets**, it is only natural to assume that the **Creation** came from Liverpool, but that (sorry) is an error that has confused lots of people in the past. The **Creation** and so the **Mark Four** (written as two words) hailed from Cheshunt in the south-east of England and there were absolutely no connections between them and the **Markfour** (written as one word), that hailed from the Prescot area of the Liverpool.

To prevent more confusion it should be pointed out that there were also no connections to the **Mark Five**, as that was a totally different group which hailed from Scotland and only had a longer residence in Liverpool.

Now that all the confusion has been removed, we can concentrate on the Merseybeat group **The Markfour**, formed as **The Sapphires** in the early Sixties and at first was based at the 'B.I.C.C. Social Club'.

When they joined the Musicians' Union they were instructed to change the name, because another **Sapphires** existed. So they decided on the name **The Markfour**, and from the beginning the group consisted of the following musicians:

Bill Rawlinson	**(voc/g)**
Derek Shaw	**(g/voc)**
Bev Brown	**(bg/voc)**
Gordon Harrison	**(dr)**

The group was managed by a certain **Ray Charles** (of course, <u>not</u> the Soul singer) and became quite popular on Merseyside, where it often played at the 'Cavern' and other important clubs and venues.

In early 1964 the **Markfour** were recorded by CBC (Canadian Broadcast Corporation) for the TV show 'Live At The Cavern', together with the **Merseybeats** and the German **Rattles**. A little later, the group was signed to Decca and recorded the **Everly Brothers** song *Walk Right Back* and the group's original *Karen* for a single release. But shortly after the recording sessions, **Derek Shaw** decided to leave the group and go to college, so the **Markfour** broke up before the single was released.

Of **Gordon Harrison** it is known that he later joined a group named **The Colts**, who probably had no connection to **Johnny Ringo**'s group with the same name. **Bill Rawlinson** and **Bev Brown** stayed together as a duo and named themselves **Mark & John**.

Despite the split, Decca released the single in December 1964, but decided to name the artists **Mark & John**, though it was recorded by **Markfour**. This was probably to prepare for follow-ups if this record became a hit. But it did not, although it was a well-produced commercial record and showed the **Markfour** to be a really good group, especially on B-side *Karen,* which was clearly the better song.

Mark & John continued as a duo, but they did not get any further recording chances from Decca. So they gigged around the local clubs as a duo, nothing being known of a backing group. **Bill Rawlinson (Mark)** and **Bev Brown (John)** later simply disappeared from the scene.

Suddenly, in 1972, the name **Mark & John** appeared again when the record *This One's For You* was released on the UK label in Germany, where it was distributed by the Decca group (DL 25 551). This **Ken Howard** / **Alan Blaikley** song of course wasn't Merseybeat anymore, but a catchy
pop tune with orchestral backing. This was really the last time that the name **Mark & John** appeared again and it is not known for certain if it really was **Bill Rawlinson** and **Bev Brown** behind this pseudonym this time.

Discography

as **Mark & John**:
Walk Right Back / Karen   UK- Decca F.12044 / 1964

(*** please note that this single was recorded by the complete line-up of the **Markfour**, but because of their split it was released under the duo's name **Mark & John**, who continued on the scene.)

BERYL MARSDEN

Born **Beryl Hogg**, she started her singing career at a very young age and doubtless was the best female singer of the male dominated Merseybeat scene. She had her first live appearance in 1961 at 'Picton Road Town Hall' when she sang *Boys* and was backed by **Karl Terry & the Cruisers**.

Beryl Marsden, as she was named then, started to sing regularly with the **Undertakers**, but also had appearances with the **Renegades** (from Liverpool), the **Kansas City Five** and probably also some other groups, but without becoming a steady member of these bands. When **Joe Flannery** took over her management, she appeared mostly with Joe's brother **Lee Curtis** and his band, the **All Stars**.

Joe Flannery acquired a recording contract with Decca for her and soon after this **Beryl Marsden** was featured on the legendary live compilation 'At the Cavern' with the song *Everybody Loves A Lover*, and she did a really great job on it. This impressive debut was followed by the great single *I Know*, also in 1963, but sadly this record was not paid the attention it deserved and so failed to become a chart success, although these days it is something of an evergreen of the unique Liverpool Beat decade.

The **Supremes** number *When The Lovelight Starts Shining Through His Eyes* was her next single in 1964. This was also well done but again failed to make the charts and did not help that great singer gain a bigger breakthrough. **Beryl Marsden** was a real Beat singer and terribly underrated at that time, although she was already a star on the Liverpool scene.

In 1965 she was booked to have her first appearance at the 'Star-Club' in Hamburg and because she was only aged 17 then, her manager **Joe Flannery** became her 'legal guardian' for that time, as otherwise she would not have got the required special license. She did not have a long residence in Hamburg, but appeared regularly at that famous club, where she went down a bomb, mainly backed by the **All Stars**. **Beryl Marsden** became a big name in the so-called 'Star-Club' era.

In Liverpool she appeared with the **Griff Parry Five**, as well as later with the **Krew**, and also occasionally as a guest singer with **Johnny Kidd & the Pirates** on the national circuit. Probably around that time she recorded **Little Eva**'s *He Is The Boy, I've Got To Find A Way, You're A User* and her version of *This Empty Place*, which was her final recording for Decca and was sadly not released.

She signed with Columbia and her first single for that new label was the great *Who You Gonna Hurt*, which was coupled with another potential A-side *Gonna Make Him My Baby*.

The following single *Music Talk* was coupled with a great version of the **Jackie DeShannon** composition *Break-a-Way*, which had been a hit for black singer **Irma Thomas** and became an international success again for **Tracy Ullman** in 1983. It could have become a hit also for **Beryl Marsden**, as her version was, at least, as good as the others, if it had not been banned to the B-side. However, in 1966 she recorded her final single for Columbia with *What's She Got (what I ain't got)*, which sadly also failed to make any progress.

At the end of the Sixties, **Beryl Marsden** went down to London and after a short spell with **She Trinity** she joined **Shotgun Express**, a group that also included **Rod Stewart**, **Peter Green** and **Mick Fleetwood**.

This was probably the time of **Beryl Marsden**'s biggest international success when their single *I Feel The Whole World Turn Around* entered the lower regions of the British charts. When **Shotgun Express** broke up again, she returned to Liverpool where she became a member of the group **Sinbad**, a really great local band, which beside **Paddy Chambers** (g), also included **Pete Newton** (bg), **Bob Hardy** (sax), **Geoff Workman** (p/org) **and Dave Irving** (dr) – all former members of the **Terry Hines Sextett** and then from that evolved **Eddie Cave & the Fyx**.

She did some recordings with this band, of which the Soul influenced ballad *Here We Go Again*, sung by **Beryl Marsden** and **Paddy Chambers**, was a potential hit song, but sadly never was released on record, just like all the other recorded **Sinbad** material. This group sometimes also went out as **The Beryl Marsden Group**, but it was only shortlived.

Beryl Marsden later recorded solo again - as **Beryl Marsden**, but also under the name **Lynn Jackson**. In 1980, she returned to Hamburg for the re-opening of the 'Star-Club' and was featured on a corresponding live sampler with **Arthur Alexander**'s *Shot Of Rhythm & Blues*, and in 1990 she toured Germany again with her own band and it can be confirmed that she is still great looking and a great singer with a fantastic stage presentation. If you ever get the chance to see her live, don't miss it!

Discography

I Know / I Only Care About You	UK- Decca	F. 11707 / 1963
When The Lovelight Starts Shining Through His Eyes /		
Love Is Going To Happen To Me	UK- Decca	F. 11819 / 1964
Who You Gonna Hurt / Gonna Make Him My Baby	UK- Columbia DB 7718 / 1965	
Music Talk / Break-a-way	UK- Columbia DB 7797 / 1965	
What's She Got (that I ain't got) / Let's Go Somewhere	UK- Columbia DB 7888 / 1966	

Tracks on compilation albums:

Everybody Loves A Lover	on **At The Cavern**	UK- Decca	LK 4597 / 1963

Unissued tracks:

The known unissued tracks are *This Empty Place, You're A User, He Is The Boy* and *I've Got To Find A Way*, which were probably all recorded in the years 1965 and 1966. Of the first one it is known that it was recorded for Decca, as it should have been the third single for Beryl Marsden. All the others came out as acetates.

Beside this Beryl Marsden also recorded with the group **Sinbad** in 1968, but nothing was released on record. Of the various recordings only the great ballad *Here We Go Again* is known, which was a potential hit-record.

She Trinity (with **Beryl Marsden** ? ?):
He Fought The Law / Union Station Blues   UK- Columbia DB 7874 / 1966
Have I Sinned / Wild Flower   UK- Columbia DB 7943 / 1966
Wild Flower / The Man Who Took The Valise Off The Floor   UK- Columbia DB 7959 / 1966
Yellow Submarine / Promise You'll Never Cry   UK- Columbia DB 7992 / 1966

Shotgun Express (with **Beryl Marsden**):
I Could Feel The Whole World Turn Round / Curtains   UK- Columbia DB 8025 / 1966
Funny 'Cos Neither Could I / Indian Thing   UK- Columbia DB 8178 / 1967

EP
   I COULD FEEL THE WHOLE WORLD TURN ROUND   FR- Columbia ESRF 1864 / 1966
  - **I Could Feel The Whole World Turn Round / Funny Cos Neither Could I /Curtains / Indian Thing**

Shotgun Express

JACKI MARTIN

Of course, this should be the story of **Jacki Martin & the Dominators**, but because of a lack of information about the **Dominators**, it concentrates on the girl singer **Jacki Martin**.

She was born **Patricia Macken** in July 1947 in the Liverpool area of Clubmoor and started her singing career in 1963 with a group called **The Stormers**, who consisted of **David Rimmer**, **Michael Gavin**, **Michael Carroll** and **Roman Bomba**.

Michael Carroll most probably was the younger brother of singer **Irene Carroll**, who in the mid-Sixties teamed up with her three brothers in the **Carrolls**, but this is another story that can be found in this book. **Jacki Martin** also appeared with some other local rhythm groups until she teamed up with the **Dominators**. Sadly, none of the members are known. There may have been a connection with the **Four Dominators**, who came from Kirkby and later became the **Verbs**, but this is just a possibility.

In 1964 **Jacki Martin & the Dominators** under the management of **Dr. Bernard Hart** became quite a popular club act and in July of that year played the 'Cavern' for the first time, albeit in a lunchtime session. They went down to London and did lots of shows, and it was probably at one of these gigs when someone from Fontana became aware of the seventeen year old girl singer and signed her – but as it seems without the group.

In July 1964, her first and only single was released with *Will You* on the A-side, backed by *Till He Tells Me*. After that, **Jacki Martin** was announced as Liverpool's 'Little Miss Five-Foot Nothing' and Fontana organised good publicity for the release, including TV appearances. But all attempts to build up an image for the girl singer failed and the record did not make the charts, although it shows her to be a good singer with a delightful soprano voice.

After the record, very little was heard of **Jacki Martin**, but it is known that she continued with the **Dominators** as her backing group on the club-circuit of the Northwest.

Discography
Will You / Till He Tells Me   **UK- Fontana TF 487 / 1964**

THE MASTERMINDS

The group had its origins in the foundation of a school band at the 'Dingle Vale Secondary Modern School' in Liverpool by **Dougie Meakin** and **George Cassidy**, and some other schoolmates, under the name **The Dingle Dices**, in 1961.

In 1962 **George Cassidy** left the school and also left the group to become a merchant seaman. He was replaced by **Tommy Meakin**, a cousin of **Dougie Meakin**. A little later, the **Dingle Dices** changed their name to **Clay & the Classics.**

In 1963 **George Cassidy** returned to the group, but they very soon disbanded because the singer **Clay**, whose real name was **Frank Campbell,** left the group, as did as the rhythm guitarist **Harry**.

Drummer **Bob Scott** joined the **Clayton Squares**, while **Dougie Meakin** and **George Cassidy** formed the **Mindbenders**. The name of the new group was very soon changed to prevent any confusion with Manchester hit group **Wayne Fontana & the Mindbenders**.

So, the Liverpool **Mindbenders** became the **Masterminds** - with the following line-up:

> **Dougie Meakin** (voc/g)
> **Brian Slater** (g)
> **George Cassidy** (bg/voc)
> **Jay Rathbone** (dr)

They featured in the German TV documentary 'In den Kellern von Liverpool', which showed them to be a real beat group playing at the 'Blue Angel'. **Brian Slater** left in October 1964 and was replaced by **Joey Molland**, who had formerly played with the **Assasins** and the **Profiles**.

In this line-up, the **Masterminds** established themselves on the Mersey scene within a very short time, and in August 1965, they had their first recording session in the Unicord studios, where they recorded the song *She's About A Mover,* which sadly was not released on record.

It was **Bob Wooler** who then drew the attention of producer **Andrew 'Loog' Oldham** to the group and later in 1965 he produced the single *She Belongs To Me* with the **Masterminds** for the new 'Immediate' label. The B-side *Taken My Love* was written by **Andrew Oldham** himself.

So the **Masterminds** were the first Liverpool group to record a **Bob Dylan** song and so sounded more American than the other Merseybeat groups. The record was performed and produced well and had that slightly West Coast touch, which was very popular at that time.

Shortly after that single release, which sadly did not make the charts, the

Masterminds were joined by **Chis Finley** on organ as an additional member, who had previously been with the **Runaways** and the **Kruzads**. The group existed in this line-up until 1966 but did not have any more records released.

The split came when **Dougie Meakin** took over the **Denny Seyton Group**, that had just separated from their vocalist **Denny Seyton**, who left show business. This group then gigged around in Liverpool for a short time under the name of **The Lovin' Kind** but then emigrated to Italy as **The Motowns**, where they became very popular and released a string of great records. **Dougie Meakin** still lives down there.

John 'Jay' Rathbone (born **Jaskett**) joined the **Almost Blues** and was later a member of the newly-formed **Faron's Flamingos**. In the late Eighties and early Nineties he was the drummer with **Karl Terry & the Cruisers** and after that joined the new **Dimensions** before he disappeared from the scene.

The three remaining members **George Cassidy**, **Joey Molland** and **Chris Finley** joined the **Fruit Eating Bears**, the backing group of the **Merseys**. But that is a different story that can be found under **The Merseybeats** in this book. After that, **Joey Molland** had a short spell with the **Cryin' Shames** in 1967, before he went down to London and joined **Gary Walker & Rain**.

In 1969 he became a member of the very successful hit group **Badfinger** that had developed from the **Iveys** and who also included Liverpudlian **Tom Evans** (bg), formerly of the **Calderstones**, as well as **Pete Ham** (voc/g) and **Mike Gibbins** (dr), both from Wales.

Chris Finley later appeared in the line-ups of various groups from the Mersey, such as **Confucius** (the former **Hideaways**) and the newly-formed **Merseybeats**, as well as **Herman's Hermits** from Manchester. **George Cassidy** teamed up with former **Easybeats** members in the **Beechwoods**, that later recorded as **Taste Of Honey**. After that he most probably quit show business.

Discography
She Belongs To Me / Taken My Love   UK- Immediate IM 005 / 1965

Unissued tracks:
In August 1965, the **Masterminds** recorded the song *She's About A Mover* in a private session in the Unicord studios, but it was sadly never released on record.

THE MASTERSOUNDS

This group was formed in Liverpool in early 1963 and at first, not too much attention was paid to the **Mastersounds**, as they were named right from the start. The original line-up of that really good band consisted of the following musicians:

Tony Kane	**(g/voc)**
Mal Jefferson	**(bg/voc)**
Frank Hopley	**(bg/voc)**
Mike Price	**(dr)**

Tony Kane's real name is **Anthony Cockayne**, while **Mike Price** was **Mike Neilson**'s pseudonym.

Mal Jefferson real name is **Malcolm Andrews** and he was a former member of **Buddy Dean & the Teachers** and is, by the way, a brother of **Don Andrews** of the **Remo Four**.

Frank Hopley left again quite soon and was replaced by **Gerry Stewart**, who had played before with the **Black Cats**, one of Liverpool's very early Rock 'n' Roll groups.

Tony Ashton (voc/org) was also added to the line-up. He had formerly played with the **College Boys** from Eton, the **Executives** from Liverpool (Preston?), the **Tony Ashton Trio**, the backing group for **Jimmy Justice** and with the **John Barry Seven**. Then he left to join the **Remo Four** and after that was a member of the internationally very successful trio **Ashton, Gardner & Dyke**.

His replacement in the **Mastersounds** in April 1964 was **Peter Cook** (org), a former member of Birmingham's **Gerry Levene & the Avengers**. But he didn't stay too long and then probably returned to Birmingham.

The **Mastersounds** were joined by **Adrian Lord**, whose real name is **Adrian Wilkinson**. This singer and guitarist was a former member of the **Missouri Drifters**, the **Nomads**, as well as of their successors, the **Mojos**.

In this line-up the **Mastersounds** were signed to RCA and amongst others recorded the

songs *Don't Leave Me* and *What Went Wrong* in 1964, on which the background vocals are said to have been sung by **Marvin Gaye** and **Dusty Springfield**. But all the songs, probably **Adrian Lord** originals, were never released on record, although the songwriter maintained that there were singles released in the USA under the name **Adrian Lord & the Mastersounds**. This is not proven but of course this doesn't mean it is absolutely impossible.

Also in 1964 the group, which was managed by **Gordon Brown**, changed their name to the **Bluesville Bats**, but disbanded soon after that. **Adrian Lord** and **Gerry Stewart**, together with other musicians, formed the **Faces**. This group was not very successful and very soon disappeared again from the scene. **Adrian Lord** was later a member of Liverpool's **Easybeats** and after that joined **Them Grimbles**.

Gerry Stewart played with **Just Us**, who were quite successful in the Northern music scene for a while. He later emigrated to Canada, where he is still living today. **Mal Jefferson** became a member of the **Kruzads** and played with the **Chesterfields** in the Seventies. Today he owns the 'Mastersound Studios' in Southport. **Tony Kane** later emigrated to the USA, where he left the music business.

Mick Price (aka **Mike Neilson**) went to Germany, where he continued to play but it is sadly not known what happened to him over there, if he's still living there or if he returned to England after a while.

Discography

It is not certain if the assertion of **Adrian Lord** that some singles by the group were released in the USA under the name **Adrian Lord & the Mastersounds** is true, because there is really no information about these records.

But the **Mastersounds** recorded some songs for RCA in 1964 - for example the **Adrian Lord** originals *Don't Leave Me* and *What Went Wrong*, which must have been released on acetate, at least.

The Mastersounds feat.Adrain Lord (left)

THE MERSEYBEATS

Although this band never had big hits like the **Beatles**, **Searchers** and **Gerry & the Pacemakers,** it was one of the most important and popular groups of the Liverpool scene, and therefore became a legend in the music business.

The story of the group goes back into the late Fifties, when **Tony Crane** and **Billy Kinsley** formed a band under the name of the **Mavericks**, who later changed their name to **The Pacifics** but then, following a suggestion by the famous 'Cavern' DJ **Bob Wooler,** called themselves **The Merseybeats**.

In the very early days **Billy Butler** also appeared with the group as guest vocalist but he was never a steady member and later amalgamated with the **Tuxedos**.

In 1962 drummer **Frank Sloane** left the **Merseybeats** to join the newly-formed **Nocturns** and a little later was followed to that group by the original bass guitarist **Dave Elias**, who in the meantime had had a short spell with the **Four Musketeers**. **Billy Kinsley** switched to the bass guitar and the most popular line-up of the **Merseybeats** had come together with:

Tony Crane	(voc/g)
Billy Kinsley	(voc/bg)
Aaron Williams	(g/voc)
John Banks	(dr)

Aaron Williams and **John Banks** were obviously newcomers to the scene, at least their names had not appeared with other groups prior to that.

In this line-up, the **Merseybeats** were featured on the Oriole compilation 'This Is Merseybeat' Vol.1 with a version of the **Ruby & the Romantics** success *Our Day Will Come,* which was their first recording ever.

The group was immediately signed to Fontana and their first single *It's Love That Really Counts,* a great tune, brought the first chart success for the **Merseybeats** in 1963 when it climbed to No.23.

The follow-up became their biggest success, when *I Think Of You* went to No.5 in the British charts in 1964. *Don't Turn Around* and *Wishin' And Hopin'* both stopped at no. 13 in 1964, while records like *Last Night* (Top 30), *Don't Let It Happen To Us, I Love You, Yes I Do* (Top 20) and *I Stand Accused* (all in 1965) were not that successful and some only reached the lower regions of the charts, which still means that they sold quite well. All of their singles were nice and catchy Beat ballads and are still very interesting within the colourful picture of Merseybeat.

As early as spring 1964 **Billy Kinsley** had left the group to form his own band under the name **The Kinsleys**. His replacement in the **Merseybeats** was **Terry Sylvester**, who came from the **Escorts** but he very soon left again to join the **Swinging Blue Jeans**. He later became a member of the **Hollies**.

The **Merseybeats** were joined by **Bob Garner**, who formerly had played with the **Brokers**. But he also didn't stay too long and then became a member of the **Ice Blues** before he went to Hamburg where he played with **Tony Sheridan & the Beat Brothers** before joining **Lee**

Curtis & the All Stars. Following this, he was a member of the hit group **Creation**.

His place in the **Merseybeats** was taken by **Johnny Gustafson**, who was very popular on the scene as a former member of groups like **Cass & the Casanovas**, the **Big Three** and the **Seniors**. This means that **Johnny Gustafson** was featured on most of the above mentioned singles from 1964, as well as on the album 'The Merseybeats' and the great rocking EP 'The Merseybeats On Stage'.

At the end of 1964, **Billy Kinsley** returned to the **Merseybeats** and stayed until they disbanded in 1965. After the **Merseybeats** had split up, **John Banks** together with **Johnny Gustafson**, who in the meantime had led the **Johnny Gus Set**, formed a duo under the name **Johnny & John**, which were backed by the **Thoughts** from Liverpool and released a quite unsuccessful single with *Bumper To Bumper*. After that, both went down to London where they joined the **Quotations**, with whom they recorded the great single *Cool It* in 1968.

John Banks became a member of **Rupert's People** but then emigrated to Israel. He returned to Liverpool in the Eighties and sadly died much too young in 1988.

Johnny Gustafson later played in groups like **Episode Six**, **Quartermass**, **Hard Stuff**, **Roxy Music**, the re-formed **Big Three** and finally with the internationally successful **Pirates**, who are in some way the former backing group with **Johnny Kidd**.

Aaron Williams left show business, while **Tony Crane** and **Billy Kinsley** continued as a duo under the name of **The Merseys** and had a No. 4 hit with their first single *Sorrow* in early 1966.

On the initial recording the **Merseys** were backed by a group that included **Jimmy Page** (g), **John Paul Jones** (g), **Jack Bruce** (bg) and **Clem Cattini** (dr), but this original version sadly was never released, while on the released record, they were backed by the **Fruit Eating Bears** who also appeared with them 'live'. The **Fruit Eating Bears**, in spite of this connection, were an independent group that consisted of:

Joey Molland	**(g)**	- ex **Profiles** and **Masterminds**
George Cassidy	**(g)**	- ex **Masterminds**
Chris Finley	**(bg)**	- ex **Kruzads** and **Masterminds**
Kenny Munda	**(dr)**	- ex **Santones**
Kenny Goodlass	**(dr)**	- ex **Kirkbys**, **Escorts** and **Swinging Blue Jeans**

Kenny Goodlass was replaced by **Terry McCusker** in 1967, and around the same time **Dave 'Mushy' Cooper** took the place of **George Cassidy**, who joined the **Beechwoods**, who later recorded as **Taste Of Honey**. After that **George Cassidy** disappeared from the scene.

In the Seventies, **Kenny Goodlass** appeared again as a member of the newly-formed **Merseybeats** and in the Nineties was the drummer with the legendary **Karl Terry & the Cruisers**, before he joined his re-formed original group **The Kirkbys**, where he is still playing today.

Terry McCusker was a former member of **Pete Demos & the Demons**, the **Four Dymonds**, **Rip**

Van Winkle & the Rip-It-Ups, the **Valkyries** and the **Roadrunners**, while **Dave Cooper** had formerly played with the **Topspots**, **Vegas Five**, **Faron's Flamingos** and the **Pawns**.

Joey Molland later became a member of the hit group **Badfinger**, while **Chris Finley** joined **Confucius** and in 1974 played with **Herman's Hermits**. **Terry McCusker** joined the **Cordes**, another story that can be followed in this book.

The singles released by the **Merseys** after that powerful debut, like the fantastic *So Sad About Us* and *Rhythm Of Love* (both in 1966), as well as their version of *The Cat*, coupled with the great *Change Of Heart* and the weak *Penny In My Pocket* (both from 1967) did not bring anymore chart honours for them. On their final single *Lovely Loretta*, which became a big hit in Holland in 1968, the **Merseys** were backed by the **Funky Bottom Congregation**, whoever that was. After that the duo released one more single as **The Crackers**, but *Honey Do* didn't make it either.

Billy Kinsley joined the **Jackie Lomax Band** and then had a short spell with the **Swinging Blue Jeans** and **Gerry & the Pacemakers**. Later, he and **Jimmy Campbell** (formerly with the **Kirkbys**) formed the group **Rockin' Horse**, who released a real great Merseybeat tune with *The Biggest Gossip In Town*, but this story can be followed under **The Kirkbys**.

After that, **Billy Kinsley** played with **Paper Chase**, who under his leadership developed into the hit group **Liverpool Express**.

From this band, **Roger Craig** (key), **Tony Coates** (bg) and **Derek Cashin** (dr) teamed up with **Tony Crane** under the name of **Crane** at the end of 1974 and recorded the singles *American Dream /Julie* (UK-Buk BU 3003) and *I Just Ain't Good Enough For You* (Uk-Buk BU 3015) .

It was probably at exactly this time, the end of 1974, when **Billy Kinsley** was a member of the **Cheats**. He then joined the **New Merseybeats**, which most probably was the line-up for the **Crane** singles.

Later they became **Liverpool Express** again - with the exception of **Tony Crane**, who had already formed a line-up of the **New Merseybeats** in 1970 and re-formed it now with other musicians and a little later dropped the 'New' from the name. Since then **Bobby Packham** (bg) has been a member of the **Merseybeats**, having played with the **Galvanisers** in the Sixties. **Kenny Goodlass** and **Chris Finley** were included again in the **Merseybeats** until 1980, as well as **Billy Kinsley**, **Kenny Barry** (key), **Steve Fleming** (org) and other musicians in a steadily changing line-up.

Steve 'Tiger' Fleming, a brother of **Mark Peters**, had played with bands like **Mark Peters & the Cyclones**, **Mark Peters & the Silhouettes** and **Mark Peters & the Method** in the Sixties.

After his time with the 'new' **Merseybeats** in the Eighties, he became a member of **Clouds**, a cabaret band which had developed from the **Fourmost** and now is with the **Vince Earl Attraction**.

The Mersey Beats

238

The **Merseybeats** released an album with the title 'Greatest Hits' in 1977, mainly including second takes of their big Sixties hits, as well as the new recordings *I'll Be Home* and a great version of *American Dream*, which seems to be one of **Tony Crane**'s favourites. Besides this, a single with the title *This Is Merseybeat* was released, which was a medley of big Merseybeat hits with new arrangements.

In August 1978, **Tony Crane** recorded a live album as a tribute to **Elvis Presley** entitled 'Tony Crane sings Elvis Presley'. On this record he was backed by **Kenny Parry**, **Phil Chittick** (later the drummer with **Cy Tucker**), **Bobby Packham**, **Kenny Berry** and **Sammy Rothwell**, who were the complete **Merseybeats** at that time, as well as by **Billy Kinsley** and **Tony Coates** of **Liverpool Express**. This album on 'Downing Records' most probably was a private production of **Tony Crane**.

When **John Banks** died in 1988, the **Merseybeats** in their successful Sixties' line-up with **Tony Crane**, **Billy Kinsley** and **Aaron Williams**, came together for a memorial concert. The place on drums was taken by none other than the former **Beatles** drummer **Pete Best**. This concert led to the founding of the 'Mersey Cats' organisation.

The **Merseybeats** continued successfully on the British club scene and in 1992 **Billy Kinsley** also returned to the group, which then consisted of **Tony Crane** (voc/g), **Billy Kinsley** (voc/g), **Bobby Packham** (bg/voc), **Dave Goldberg** (key) and **Alan Cosgrove** (dr), who was a member of **Sonny Kaye & the Reds** in the Sixties.

In 1993, they recorded a modern version of the **Beatles** song *I'll Get You* as a single on vinyl and CD, but it flopped. **Alan Cosgrove** was later replaced by **Lou Rosenthal**.

The **Merseybeats** are still a very successful and busy live act in England these days and **Tony Crane** proudly confirms that there are now as many bookings as there were during their heyday in the Sixties, which is easy to believe, as it is still a fantastic group.

Single discography

as **The Merseybeats**:

It's Love That Really Counts / Fortune Teller	**UK- Fontana TF 412 / 1963**
I Think Of You / Mr. Moonlight	**UK- Fontana TF 431 / 1964**
Don't Turn Around / Really Mystified	**UK- Fontana TF 459 / 1964**
Wishin' And Hopin' / Milkman	**UK- Fontana TF 482 / 1964**
Last Night / See Me Back	**UK- Fontana TF 504 / 1965**
Don't Let It Happen To Us / It'll Take A Long Time	**UK- Fontana TF 568 / 1965**
I Love You, Yes I Do / Good Good Lovin'	**UK- Fontana TF 607 / 1965**
I Stand Accused / All My Life	**UK- Fontana TF 645 / 1965**

Different German release:

Nur Unsere Liebe zählt / Nur Du Allein	**G- Fontana 269310 / 1964**

(the German versions of *It's Love That Really Counts* and *I Think Of You*)

as **The Merseys**: (Tony Crane & Billy Kinsley)

Sorrow / Some Other Day	**UK- Fontana TF 694 / 1966**
So Sad About Us / Love Will Continue	**UK- Fontana TF 732 / 1966**
Rhythm Of Love / Is It Love	**UK- Fontana TF 776 / 1966**
The Cat / Change Of Heart	**UK- Fontana TF 845 / 1967**
Penny In My Pocket / I Hope You're Happy	**UK- Fontana TF 916 / 1967**
Lovely Loretta / Dreaming	**UK- Fontana TF 955 / 1968**

as **The Crackers**: (Tony Crane & Billy Kinsley)
Honey Do / It Happens All The Time   UK- Fontana TF 995 / 1969

as **Johnny & John**: (Johnny Gustafson & John Banks)
Bumper To Bumper / Scrape My Boot   UK-Polydor BM 56087/ 1966
(on this record **Johnny Gustafson & John Banks** were backed by the **Thoughts** from Liverpool)

EP discography
as **The Merseybeats**:
MERSEYBEATS ON STAGE   UK-Fontana TE 17422/ 1964
- Long Tall Sally / You Can't Judge A Book By It's Cover / I'm Gonna Sit Right Down And Cry /
Shame

I THINK OF YOU   UK-Fontana TE 17423/ 1964
- I Think Of You / Mr. Moonlight / Fortune Teller / It's Love That Really Counts

WISHING AND HOPING   UK-Fontana TE 17432/ 1964
- Wishin' And Hopin' / Milkman / Jumping Jonah / Hello Young Lovers

Different French release:
as **The Merseys**:
RHYTHM OF LOVE   F- Fontana   465356 / 1966
- Rhythm Of Love / Is It Love / So Sad About Us / Sorrow

LP discography:
as **The Merseybeats**:
THE MERSEYBEATS   UK-Fontana TL 5210/ 1964
- Milkman / Hello Young Lovers / He Will Break Your Heart / Funny Face / Really Mystified / The
**Girl That I Marry / Fools Like Me / My Heart And I / Bring It On Home To Me / Lavender Blue /
Jumping Jonah / Don't Turn Around**

Different German release:
THE MERSEYBEATS   G-Fontana 832 259-1/ 1964
- Wishin' And Hopin' / Milkman / Hello Young Lovers / Fortune Teller / He Will Break Your Heart
/ Funny Face / Really Mystified / Nur Unsere Liebe Zählt / Mr. Moonlight / Fools Like Me / My Heart
And I / Bring It On Home To Me / Jumping Jonah / Don't Turn Around / Nur Du Allein

Releases on compilation albums:
Our Day Will Come   on 'This Is Merseybeat' Vol.1   UK- Oriole   PS 40047 / 1963
I Think Of You   on 'Liverpool Beat'   G- Fontana 681 557 TL / 1964
It's Love That Really Counts   on 'Liverpool Beat'   G- Fontana 681 557 TL / 1964

Unreleased tracks:

Unissued tracks by the **Merseybeats** are *Things I Want To Hear* (1962), *Soldier Of Love* and *Cry Me
A River*, probably from 1964, as well as the original version of *Sorrow* and *Nothing Can Change This
Love* by the **Merseys,** and *Charly Noone* from 1966. The latter was recorded together with **Kiki Dee**.

THE MERSEY FIVE

There is an interesting story on the development of this group, formed in Liverpool by **Pete Campbell** and **Robert James Peter Montgomery** in 1964.

Pete Campbell was a former member of the **Mersey Four**, **Karl Terry & the Cruisers** and the **Fontanas**, while **Robert Montgomery** had played with **Derry Wilkie & the Others**.

They both teamed up with **Tony Nelson** (voc/g) and **Carl Riche** (dr) in the backing group of Oldham singer **Tony Prince** under the name the **Tony Prince Combo**, who had a successful residence down in Bristol. **Tony Nelson** was a former member of the **Mersey Four** and of **Sonny Webb & the Cascades**, while **Carl Riche** had also played with the **Mersey Four**.

When the **Tony Prince Combo** split up, obviously without having released a record, **Tony Prince** became a very popular radio DJ in London.

Pete Campbell and **Bob Montgomery** formed the **Mersey Five**, which despite their name was a four-piece band, but because **Pete Campbell** liked the name of his first group so much and the **Mersey Four** still existed, they looked for a solution of approaching the original name. So they decided to take an inflatable rubber puppet as the 'fifth member' and called themselves **The Mersey Five** - in the following line-up:

Pete Campbell	(voc/g)
Gerard Anthony Gilbertson	(g/voc)
Robert J.P. Montgomery	(bg/voc)
Charles Richard Evans	(dr)

It is more than probable that **Gerard Anthony Gilbertson** and **Charles Richard Evans** were the other two former members of the **Tony Prince Combo** and just changed their names - (Gerard) **Anthony Gilbertson** to **Tony Nelson** and **Charles Richard** (Evans) to **Carl Riche**. This, of course, is only a supposition, but a justified one as there were lots of parallels - not only in their names, but having three original members of the **Mersey Four**, they would have been more than entitled to call themselves the **Mersey Five**.

However, shortly after their foundation (or name change), the group made the headlines in the Northern music papers for the first time when they went to tour Germany, together with **King Size Taylor**, who shortly before had parted from his old group the **Dominoes**. It is not clear if the **Mersey Five** really backed **King Size Taylor** on that tour or if they only went to Germany at the same time.

Over in Germany, the **Mersey Five** made every effort to obtain an image as 'the dirtiest beat group in the world' for themselves. These efforts were successful - so successful that at one time they were not allowed into a recording studio in Hamburg because of their (artificially made) untidy looks. When they were finally let in after their German record company exerted some pressure, the producer refused to work with such 'down-at-heel' types, until he was knocked out by the musical quality of the four Liverpool boys.

So in the end the **Mersey Five** recorded two singles for the German 'Storz' label with a great version of **Larry Williams**' *Slow Down* (very unusually without piano) and the original *What's It All About*. Both records had that naturally unaffected Beat sound typical of all singles on that more than interesting 'Storz' label at that time. In spite of this, the records were not too successful in those days but now are highly desired and expensive collector's items. *Slow Down* was coupled with a no less interesting version of *Ecstasy*, while their version of **Chuck Berry**'s *Sweet Lil' Rock 'n' Roller* on the reverse side of *What's It All About* is not worth powder and shot.

The **Mersey Five** were really one of the hard and uncompromising beat groups out of Liverpool. Like their stage show, their image was quite wild, with their long hair brushed into their faces. In Germany they had all the markings of a beat band and made appropriate headlines in the papers. Over there they were nicknamed 'the artistic beat machines' and that was an accurate description.

As the group spent most of its active time in Germany, it missed the boat in England where they did not become very popular and never released a record. At the end of 1965, the **Mersey Five** disbanded totally and all the members returned to Liverpool.

Carl Riche joined **Rory Storm & the Hurricanes**, while **Tony Nelson** and **Bob Montgomery** disappeared from the scene. **Pete Campbell** became a member of the **Secrets**, but then he went back to Germany where he joined **John O'Hara & the Playboys**, a group of Scottish origin, who had a longer residence in Germany.

Discography
Slow Down / Ecstasy	G- Storz SRI 45205 / 1964
What's It All About / Sweet Lil' Rock 'n' Roller	G- Storz SRI 45206 / 1964

The Mersey Five with German producer Erich Storz

THE MERSEY FOUR

This group was formed in Southport in the early Sixties and for a long time was one of the local attractions and appeared regularly at all the important clubs and halls along the Merseyside.

During the big Beat boom, various record companies and producers were interested in signing the **Mersey Four** and they probably had some recording sessions, but for mysterious reasons no record was released - at least not at that time. The original line-up of the **Mersey Four** consisted of the following musicians:

Tony Nelson	**(voc/g)**
Pete Campbell	**(g/voc)**
Ray Marshall	**(bg/voc)**
Carl Riche	**(dr)**

Ray Marshall was a former member of **Little Gene & the Outlaws**, while all the others were probably newcomers to the music business.

In 1963 **Tony Nelson** left the group to join **Sonny Webb & the Cascades** and his replacement was **Tony Carlton**, the former singer with the **Citadels** from Litherland. A little later, **Pete Campbell** also left to join **Karl Terry & the Cruisers** and after that he played with the **Fontanas**.

Both former members of the **Mersey Four** met up again in the **Tony Prince Combo** in 1964, and this newly-formed backing group for Oldham singer **Tony Prince** was also joined by **Carl Riche**. This band then later became the **Mersey Five**, but this is another story which can be found in this book.

The **Mersey Four** were joined by **Russell Perat** (lg), **Eric Wright** (rg) and **Alex Paton** (dr) and as there were now five, they changed their name to **Tony Carlton & the Mersey Four**. It was probably this line-up that toured the south of Germany in 1964, where they appeared in such well-known clubs like the 'K 52' in Frankfurt and the 'Habana Bar' in Munich, amongst others. When they returned from Germany, the only remaining original member, **Ray Marshall**, left to join the **Big Three**. He was replaced by **Billy Abbott** and a little later the group changed their name to **Tony Carlton & the Merseyboys**, which then was shortened to **The Merseyboys**.

At that time the band was signed to Decca and in the same year recorded an album with **Beatles** covers for the sub-label 'Ace Of Clubs' with the title '15 Great Songs Composed By John, Paul, George'. This is a really good album and got some very good reviews, selling quite well in the Sixties, but sadly did not bring anything bigger for the **Merseyboys**. As is clear on the album, the **Merseyboys** were one of the better Merseybeat bands, but their own creations were badly missed. Sadly, after that long player, no more records were released by the group.

It was probably in late 1965 / early 1966 that the **Merseyboys** disbanded totally and it is sadly not known what has happened to the individual members. It is only known that **Ray Marshall** obviously stayed in show business and did become the leader of **Ray Marshall & the All Stars**.

Discography

The **Mersey Four** never released a record in their original line-up. With this name but in a totally different line-up they cut the following album which was later released under the name **The Merseyboys**:

'15 GREAT SONGS COMPOSED BY JOHN, PAUL, GEORGE'
UK-DECCA (ACE OF CLUBS) ACL1169 / 1964
- From Me To You / All My Loving / Please Please Me / It Won't Be Long / Misery / She Loves You / I'll Get You / I Wanna Be Your Man / Don't Bother Me / Hold Me Tight / Thank You Girl / All I've Got To Do / Ask Me Why / Do You Want To Know A Secret / I Want To Hold Your Hand

THE MERSEY MONSTERS

This is a case of two stories in one, and could also have been entitled **J.J. & the Hi-Lites** as that group was the starting point when it was formed by the singing twin brothers **Alan** and **Brian Grundy**, most probably in January 1963 in Bootle. The initials J.J. stood for the two brothers. There isn't too much information available about their early days but it seems they were one of the softer groups that played in a line-up with:

Alan Grundy	**(voc)**
Brian Grundy	**(voc)**
John Tarpey	**(lg)**
Gregg Murphy	**(rg)**
Ron Smith	**(bg)**
Geoff Lloyd	**(dr)**

Only **Geoff Lloyd** had appeared on the scene before, when he was a member of **Vic & the Spidermen** and after that with **Ken Dallas & the Silhouettes**, who shortly before his departure had become **Mark Peters & the Silhouettes**.

J.J. & the Hi-Lites became part of the 'Dave Forshaw Enterprises' stable which ensured them lots of gigs at all Merseyside venues. But there was no real outstanding success for them and for some reason **Brian Grundy** left

J J & The HI-LITES

and disappeared from the scene, while his brother then kept the 'J.J.' for him alone.

The group hit the headlines of the music papers only once, when they cut a demo disc for Parlophone towards the end of 1963. But in the end nothing was released and so it is unknown which songs were recorded at that time, but it is highly probable that one of the group's own compositions called *Saturday Morning* was included.

Gregg Murphy was the next to leave and he became a member of the **Jaguars** from Birkenhead in 1963. He was not replaced and the group continued as a four-piece.

For unknown reasons, **J.J. & the Hi-Lites** parted from **Dave Forshaw** and their management was taken over by a certain **Tony Reuben**. Like **Brian Epstein**, he was also Jewish and owned record shops where he mainly dealt with so-called 'ex jukebox' records. He had big plans for the group who were obviously the only one under his management at that time.

Following the example of **Screaming Lord Sutch**, he wanted something like a monster group and so in early 1964, **J.J. & the Hi-Lites** became the **Mersey Monsters**. It seems that the start was a bit difficult because they didn't just have to change their name but also their music, programme and stage presentation.

Ron Smith, who also used the stage name **Chuck Vincent**, obviously did not think too much of it and left the group to join **Johnny Templer & the Hi-Cats**. He was replaced in the **Mersey Monsters** by **Kalvin Harrison**, who came from **Ricky Gleason & the Topspots**.

It was in May 1964 when the **Mersey Monsters** appeared on Merseyside for the first time, in the following line-up:

Alan Grundy	**(voc)**
John Tarpey	**(g)**
Kalvin Harrison	**(bg)**
Geoff Lloyd	**(dr)**

They played at the 'Majestic Ballroom' and also backed the resident DJ **Barbara Dee** at that gig. She temporarily appeared with the **Detours** after that.

This debut did not make headlines for the **Mersey Monsters** and this didn't suit **Tony Reuben**'s plans, who also took **Paul Ryan & the Streaks** from Newcastle under his wings around the same time. With regard to the **Mersey Monsters**, he decided to let them play outside Liverpool at first, so that the group could develop an exciting stage act.

In June 1964 he sent them down to London for two weeks and from July until November 1964 the group played at the 'Casino Ballroom' in Blackpool every Friday night.

Meanwhile, **Tony Reuben** generated clever publicity for the musicians, who always wore special make-up or masks that made them look like monsters and whose names were kept a secret, as the members were nicknamed as *'Igor'*, *'Morfo'*, *'Krom'* and *'Orlak'*. Do not ask, who was who!!

A myth developed around the group, who still did not play Liverpool at that time. Advertisements and articles in the newspapers made sure that the audience's attention was steadily drawn to them by imaginative stories such as the **Mersey Monsters** had emerged from the depths of the river Mersey or had climbed from the graves behind the Anglican cathedral. It must have been around that time that the group cut their first Deroy acetate.

That EP included the **Johnny Ray** classic *Yes Tonight Josephine* and the three **Don Gibson** songs *Don't Tell Me Your Troubles, Love Has Come My Way* and *Just One Time*. They were rough and interesting recordings, but too Country to be acceptable for a monster group.

The following single on acetate featured the two **Coasters**- numbers *Wait A Minute* and *Wake Me, Shake Me* and was a step in the direction expected by their management and, of course, their audience. As the group always played away from its hometown, the musicians needed to become professionals, but **Geoff Lloyd** did not want to and so left the group. His replacement was **Tommy Limb**, who came from the recently disbanded **Topspots**.

The **Mersey Monsters** now had gigs mainly down in Gloucestershire while their management kept the fire burning in Liverpool. **Tony Reuben** had good contacts with the Radio Luxembourg DJ **Pat Campbell**, who in turn had good connections to the RCA Victor record company. He sent some of his own song material for the **Mersey Monsters** to record and as it seems RCA really became interested in signing the group.

An ABC television team from the United States also filmed a clip about the group, a very mythological one, which was shown on American television.

After a Scotland tour with tremendous success it was time for the 'monsters' to return to Merseyside, where their first appearance was at the 'Floral Hall' in Southport.

That big place was absolutely packed and the **Mersey Monsters** went down a bomb with their new heavy Rock 'n' Roll sound, their frightening outfits and their wild stage act.

Now they appeared regularly on Merseyside, the question was, how to keep a variation and freshness in their live act. This must have been a continuous strain, involving a lot of work.

It was **Alan Grundy** who came up with the answer. He was a good looking guy, really admired by girls in the past and he didn't want to continue disguised as a monster. **Tony Reuben**, on the other hand, only wanted a monster-group, and so the **Mersey Monsters** broke up not too long after their impressive and powerful return to Merseyside and before a contract with RCA was signed.

Alan Grundy and **Kalvin Harrison** joined the **Rebels**, who had just parted from **Ricky Gleason**. After that **Alan Grundy** got married and emigrated to Australia, where he is still living.

Kalvin Harrison emigrated to Canada, where he possibly stayed in the music business. After a few years, he returned to England, where he lived in Leeds.

Tommy Limb quit show business at first but then returned to the scene as a freelancing drummer in the Liverpool clubs and pubs, but he never joined a group again.

In 1998, **Kalvin Harrison** and **Tommy Limb** teamed up again at a revival concert of their former group **Ricky Gleason & the Topspots** at the Orrel Park Ballroom.

John Tarpey, a great guitarist by the way, became the sales manager for British Leyland and had an impressive career in the British motor industry.

Discography:
Yes Tonight Josephine / Don't Tell Me Your Troubles
Love Has Come My Way / Just One Time   UK- Deroy acetate EP / 1964

Wait A Minute / Wake Me, Shake Me   UK- Deroy acetate   / 1964

Unissued tracks:
At the end of 1963, **J.J. & the Hi-Lites** recorded a demo-disc for Parlophone, most probably with the group's own composition *Saturday Morning*. The other songs are sadly not known. In late 1964 / early 1965 the **Mersey Monsters** recorded some songs for RCA-Victor, but disbanded before a contract was signed and so there are no details known about these recordings.

THE MOJOS

This group originated from a trio formed by **Keith Karlsson** (voc/g), **Roy Wood** (g) and **John Runt** (dr) in Liverpool in 1960.

Roy Wood left in 1962 to join **Johnny Templer & the Hi-Cats** and after that became the lead guitarist of **Sonny Webb & the Cascades**. He was replaced by **Adrian Wilkinson** (voc/g), who also used the stage name **Adrian Lord** and who had formerly played with the **Missouri Drifters**.

The Nomads

John Runt was replaced by **Bob Conrads** a little later and this line-up was then joined by the pianist **Stuart Slater**, who had formerly played with **Dave Bell & the Bell Boys**. He changed his name to **Stu James**.

In this line-up the musicians called themselves **The Nomads** and in 1963 they were featured under this name on the Oriole compilation 'This Is Merseybeat' Vol.2 with the song *My Whole Life Through*. Because there was also a London group named **The Nomads**, the Liverpool band changed its name to **The Mojos**.

When **Terry O'Toole** (aka **Tim Stavely**), the former band roadie joined as pianist, resulting in **Stu James** taking over the lead vocals and lead guitar, **Adrian Lord** was so angry that he left the group to join the **Mastersounds**, who later changed their name to **The Bluesville Bats**. After that he formed the **Faces** and was later a member of Liverpool's **Easybeats** and of **Them Grimbles**.

His place in the **Mojos** was taken by **Nicky Crouch**, a former member of **Robin & the Ravens** and the just disbanded **Faron's Flamingos**. He became the new lead guitarist, while **Stu James** switched to rhythm. The longest lasting line-up of the **Mojos** thus consisted of:

Stu James	**(voc/g/harp)**
Nicky Crouch	**(g/voc)**
Terry O'Toole	**(p/voc)**
Keith Karlsson	**(bg/voc)**
Bob Conrads	**(dr)**

In 1963 the **Mojos** were signed to Decca and a little later had their first single released with *Forever,* which was not hugely successful.

In 1964 their second single *Everything's Alright,* an original of the group, went straight up to no.9 in the British charts and helped the **Mojos** to establish themselves on the national Beat scene. *Why Not Tonight* reached no.25 and their version of *Seven Golden Daffodils* stopped at no.30, and so the **Mojos** had three top-30 hits in a row in 1964.

Seven Golden Daffodils could have been more successful, but at the same time Columbia had released the same song by the **Cherokees** from Leeds, and this record climbed to no. 33. If the **Mojos** version had been the only one out at that time it would certainly have become another Top 10 hit for the group. However, these three singles were the only chart hits for the

Mojos, although their only EP 'The Mojos' still sold quite well.

The **Mojos** almost disbanded at the end of 1964 when **Keith Karlsson**, **Tim Stavely** (aka **Terry O'Toole**) and **Bob Conrads** left to form the **Epics**, who in the end never made a public appearance. **Keith Karlsson** emigrated to the USA but in 1989 returned to Liverpool and joined **Faron's Flamingos**. **Tim Stavely** joined a Jazz band and **Bob Conrads** later appeared again with a group called **Nasty Pop**.

The remaining **Mojos** members **Stu James** and **Nicky Crouch** formed a new band under the old name with **Lewis Collins** (bg/voc) and **Aynsley Dunbar** (dr).

Lewis Collins had formerly played the drums for the **Renegades** from Liverpool and with the **Kansas City Five**, before he had switched to bass guitar and played with the **Georgians** and the **Eyes**.

Aynsley Dunbar was a former member of the **Merseysippi Jazz Band**, **Derry Wilkie & the Pressmen**, the **Flamingoes**, **Freddie Starr & the Starr Boys** and the **Excheckers**. But he left again in 1965 to join **John Mayall's Bluesbreakers**. Later he formed his own group under the name **Aynsley Dunbar Retaliation** and then played with groups like **Journey** and **Jefferson Airplane**. His replacement in the **Mojos** was **Stan Bennett**, who came from the **Denims**. It was probably in this line-up that the singles *Comin' On To Cry* and *Wait A Minute* (the latter released as **Stu James & the Mojos**) were recorded. Both records sold quite well but did not get near the charts.

Around that time the **Mojos** became the backing group for **Paul & Barry Ryan**, but they also continued to play in their own right. **Stu James** and **Nicky Crouch** also worked as a composer duo together and amongst others, wrote the single *I Come Smiling Through* for the **Le Roys.**

Stan Bennett left again and was replaced by **'Snowy' Fleet**, who then emigrated to Australia, where he was a founder member of **The Easybeats** (*Friday On My Mind, Hello How Are You*, etc.) who later became famous internationally. He was replaced in the **Mojos** by **'Deakin' Vernon**, while **Lewis Collins** had also left and was replaced by **Steve Snake**. **Lewis Collins** started quite a successful career as an actor and in 1983 recorded a solo single.

The final Decca single *Goodbye Dolly Grey* was probably released with this line-up in 1967. The **Mojos** then switched to Liberty, where they released one more single with *Until My Baby Gets Home* in 1968. Both records failed to make the charts and after that the **Mojos** disbanded totally.

Stu James started a solo career, but this was obviously not too successful and all that is known is that he released two solo singles with the titles *I Only Wish I Had The Time* and *I'm In The Mood* on the Bradleys label in 1974 and 1976 respectively. Neither record sold any better than the last **Mojos** singles.

Stan Bennett was later a member of **Poacher**, while of the other former members of the **Mojos** or **Stu James & the Mojos**, only **Keith Karlsson** appeared again when he started a new, short-lived group under the name **Mojos** in the Nineties.

Nicky Crouch quit the music business, but in the early Nineties was back on the scene with the newly-formed **Cliff Roberts' Rockers**. After that he appeared on a quite regular basis at the 'Merseycats' events, where he played with various groups.

In 2005 he re-formed the **Mojos** with fellow Merseybeat musicians from the Sixties. This line-up consisted of **Les Williams** (rg/voc) of the **Dimensions**, Eric London (bg/voc) of **Group One**, **Tommy Hughes** (p/voc) of the **Kansas City Five** and **Brian Johnson** (dr) of the **Strangers**.

<u>Single Discography</u>

Forever / They Say	**UK- Decca F.11732 / 1963**
Everything's Alright / Give Your Lovin' To Me	**UK- Decca F.11853 / 1964**
Why Not Tonight / Don't Do It Anymore	**UK- Decca F.11918 / 1964**
Seven Daffodils / Nothing At All	**UK- Decca F.11959 / 1964**
Comin' On To Cry / That's The Way It Goes	**UK- Decca F.12127 / 1965**
Wait A Minute / Wonder If She Knows	**UK- Decca F.12231 / 1965**
Goodbye Dolly Grey / I Just Can't Let Her Go	**UK- Decca F.12557 / 1967**
Until My Baby Gets Home / Seven Park Avenue	**UK- Liberty 15097 / 1968**

(please note that *Wait A Minute* was released as **Stu James & the Mojos**)

EP **THE MOJOS**   **UK-Decca DFE 8591 / 1964**
- Everything's Alright / I've Got My Mojo Working / The One Who Really Loves You / Nobody But Me

as **The Nomads**:
My Whole Life Through   on **'This Is Merseybeat' Vol.2**   **UK-Oriole PS 40048 / 1963**

<u>Unreleased tracks:</u>

As unissued tracks by the **Mojos,** the songs *Spoonful* and *Drive It Home* are known, which were recorded for Decca, as well as *Call My Name* and *To Know Her Is To Love Her,* which were recorded for PYE.

For collectors, it might be of interest that in 1982 there was an album released on the Edsel label (ED 110) with the title 'The Mojos Working', on which all single titles and songs can be found on the EP that the **Mojos** recorded for Decca between 1963 and 1965.

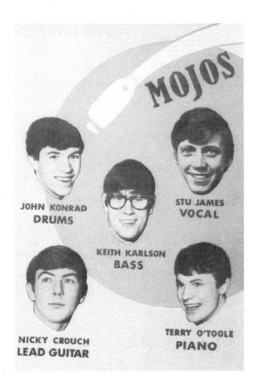

THE NASHPOOL FOUR

This group was formed in Liverpool in 1963 and very soon became one of the local attractions in the Beat city. They appeared regularly at the important clubs and venues, but in spite of their local success, they never obtained popularity nationwide. The original **Nashpool Four** line-up consisted of:

Jan Ferguson	**(voc/g)**
Eric Savage	**(g/voc)**
Sid Edwards	**(bg/harp/voc)**
Eddie Edwards	**(dr)**

Sid Edwards was a former member of the **Flames**, the **Nutrockers** and had also played with **Lee Shondell & the Capitols**, **Danny Havoc & the Ventures** and **Groups Inc.**, while his brother **Eddie Edwards** came from the **Del Renas**, but before that he had also been a member of the **Flames**. **Jan Ferguson** left the group again quite soon and disappeared from the scene. He was replaced by the sax player **Tommy Husky**, who came from the **Deejays**.

Eric Savage took over the lead vocals but then he also left to join the **St. Louis Checks**. **Sid Edwards** took over the lead guitar and shared the lead vocals with the new bass guitarist **Harry Scully**, who was a former member of **Lee Shondell & the Boys**.

The group then became a five piece when **Rob Deka** (org) joined as an additional member, having formerly played with the **Prestons**. They shortened their name to **The Nashpool** and around that time **Joe Meek** became aware of this Liverpool outfit and produced the songs *Shakin With Linda* and *Sweet Mary* with them for EMI in 1964, but for mysterious reasons these recording sessions were not followed by a release. A little later, the **Nashpool** were engaged to play the 'Star-Club' Hamburg for a long residence, which helped the group to increase its popularity.

Harry Scully left to join the **Trends** and he was replaced by **Reg Welch**, who had formerly played with **Freddie Starr & the Midnighters**. When **Tommy Husky** left shortly after that to join **Earl Preston's Realms** and later to play with the **Almost Blues** and the **Detours**, he was not replaced and the group, then changed the name back to **The Nashpool Four**. **Reg Welch** left again and became a member of the **Suspects** and his replacement was **Alan Burton**, who came from the **Valkyries**. But very soon the **Nashpool Four** disbanded totally, when the brothers **Sid** and **Eddie Edwards** were the only remaining members of the original line-up. **Eddie Edwards** joined **Rory Storm & the Hurricanes** and after that played with the **Beechwoods** while none of the other members appeared on the scene again. **Harry**

Scully, who had left the group earlier, later became a member of the **Bootleggers**, formed by **Brian Auger** in London.

Discography

There were no records released by the **Nashpool Four**, but in May 1964, when the group was a five-piece under the name of **The Nashpool** the well known producer **Joe Meek** recorded *Shakin With Linda* and *Sweet Mary* with them for EMI, which sadly were never released.

As the Nashpool

THE NEW AVENGERS

When in early 1964 the **Travellers** from Birkenhead (not identical with the group of **Johnny Saint**) disbanded, their two guitarists **Mike Rudd** (real name Rudzinski) and **Billy Knaggs** formed the **Avengers**, together with **Dave Pritchard** (bg) and **Robert Dennis** (dr). The new bass-guitarist was **Denny Jeffcoate** from the local **Young Ones**, who did not have any connections to the recording group of the same name. Besides this **Pete Smith** joined as lead vocalist and made the group a quintet, but he also did not stay and soon left again. When **Robert Dennis** joined **The Night Walkers** still in 1964, the **Avengers** consisted of:

Jim Byers	**(voc)**
Billy Knaggs	**(lg)**
Mike Rudd	**(rg/voc)**
Denny Jeffcoate	**(bg)**
Les Hall	**(dr)**

The Liverpool singer/songwriter **Ron Anderson** offered the group one of his songs, and so it was probably in late 1964 that the **Avengers** together with **Ron Anderson** went into the studio and cut an acetate of *Any Day Now* on the Unicord label. This was a great bluesy number, which was sung by **Ron Anderson** himself, coupled with an interesting version of **Johnny Kidd**'s success *Shakin' All Over* (sung by **Jim Byers**).

Record producer **Cyril Stapelton** got hold of this acetate and wanted to record the **Avengers** with *Any Day Now* for PYE, but this of course meant that the musicians had to become professionals, which the majority did not want. The disagreements led to **Jim Byers** and **Les Hall** leaving and they were replaced by **Derek Peckham** on drums and a singer, called **'Mitch'**, whose surname sadly is lost.

At that time the group's name was changed into the **New Avengers**. Despite the fact that the group continued to be successful on the scene, playing a sort of heavy Rhythm & Blues, **Les Hall** left and a new drummer called **George Peckham** came. When **Denny Jeffcoate** also left, **Mike Rudd** took over the bass guitar. Beside this **Billy Knaggs** was temporarily replaced with **Pete Jones**.

When the singer **'Mitch'** and **George Peckham** left again, the **New Avengers** continued as a trio with **Billy Knaggs**, **Mike Rudd** and **Derek Cashin** (dr). **Mike Rudd**

was sharing the vocals with the new drummer. But this also did not last for too long and in 1965 the group broke up, when **Mike Rudd** was offered the place as bass guitarist in **Johnny Kidd & the Pirates** and went down to London to join this legendary, international successful group. **Billy Knaggs** disappeared from the scene and **Derek Cashin** later joined **Billy Kinsley** in **Paper Chase** and from that developed **Liverpool Express**. He was also a member of the recording group **Crane**.

After **Johnny Kidd** had disbanded his **Pirates** and tried to go solo, **Mike Rudd** returned to Liverpool and re-formed the **Avengers**, together with his old mates **Billy Knaggs** and **Les Hall**.

This trio again played all the main venues in and around Liverpool, as well as in North Wales, where they became quite popular. When one day **Mike Rudd** received a telephone call from **Johnny Kidd**, who was seeking a group again, Mike suggested the **Avengers**. **Johnny Kidd** came up to Wallasey, rehearsed with the trio in the garage of Mike's father and still in 1965 the **Avengers** became **Johnny Kidd & the Pirates**.

For almost a year the group toured all over England, had an appearance at the 'Star-Club' in Hamburg and also recorded in a studio in Baker Street in London. Of that session the songs *The Fool, Let's Talk About Us* and an alternative version of *Please Don't Touch* are known. None of these recordings were ever released.

With **Johnny Kidd** still living in London it became quite exhausting for the Wallasey group and so in 1966 they parted again from the singer. The **Avengers** continued playing the local circuit, but still kept in touch with **Johnny Kidd**, until he died in a car crash soon after the split. **Mike Rudd** was so upset about his death that he decided to pack in playing and sold his guitar and amplifier. That was the definite end of the **Avengers** in 1966.

It is not known what happened to **Billy Knaggs** and **Les Hall** after that but **Mike Rudd** returned to the scene in the Seventies as a member of the **Dees**, and today he plays the bass with **Karl Terry & the Cruisers**.

Discography
The Avengers:
Any Day Now / Shakin' All Over   **UK- Unicord acetate / 1964**

Unreleased tracks as **Johnny Kidd & the Pirates** :
The Fool, Let's Talk About Us and **Please Don't Touch** and probably some more – all from late 1965

THE NEWTOWNS

This interesting group was formed in late 1962 by the guitarists **Glyn Harris** and **Jim Jones** in the Liverpool suburb of Kirkby. As Kirkby was a new built town, they decided on the name of the **Newtowns** and engaged local vocalist **Denis Donafee** to front the group. They then recruited **Dave Pickstock** on bass guitar and the drummer **Eric Lee** to complete this melodic Beat group, who were sometimes advertised as **Denis & the Newtowns**.

Ian Comish, at that time also the manager of the **Fontanas**, another Kirkby based outfit, took the group under his wing and the **Newtowns** soon became a popular live act. **Dave Pickstock** and **Eric Lee** left again and both obviously quit showbiz in 1963. The **Newtowns** from that moment on appeared in the following line-up:

Denis Donafee	**(voc)**
Glyn Harris	**(g/voc)**
Jimmy Jones	**(g/bg/voc)**
Bob Frazer	**(bg/org/voc)**
Bob Williams	**(dr/voc)**

Bob Williams was a former member of **Dino & the Wild Fires**, who went down to London and continued as the **Wackers**, but this is another story in this book.

The original lineup

The **Newtowns** appeared at the 'Cavern' but apart from this they seldom actually played in the Liverpool 'Beat centre'. They never obtained national popularity but were very busy in the North and especially in South Lancashire.

According to the May issue of the 'Combo' music paper they were *'mobbed and chased by hordes of screaming girls'*, when they appeared for the *'Freedom From Hunger Campaign'* in 1964.

It was in early 1966 that the **Newtowns** recorded two acetates in the Unicord studios in Moorfields with the songs *Somewhere Over The Rainbow,* the little known **Georgie Fame** number *Something,* the orginal *Tomorrow* and an interesting version of *Please Stay,* which in a very similar arrangement became a big hit for the **Cryin' Shames** in the same year. Sadly these recordings were not followed by an official release and so did not help the **Newtowns** in those days.

The group continued to play the normal Merseyside gigs until 1966 and disbanded when **Denis Donafee** and **Bob Frazer** left. **Denis Donafee** later was a member of a group called **Sandlewood**. The remaining three teamed up with **Brian Jones** and **Geoff Nugent** to re-form the **Undertakers**, but when they wanted to turn professional, **Glyn Harris** left again and was replaced by the returning **Bob Frazer**.

Harris decided for a solo career as singer and comedian. Sometimes he also teamed up again with **Bob Williams** in a trio called **Northern Lights**. **Bob Williams** is still active in the music scene, these days as drummer of the **Prime Suspects**.

Discography

Somewhere Over The Rainbow / Something	**UK- Unicord acetate / 1966**
Please Stay / Tomorrow	**UK- Unicord acetate / 1966**

(Please note that *Somewhere Over The rainbow, Tomorrow* and *Please Stay* were released recently

THE NOCTURNS

This typical Merseybeat group was formed in 1963 in Liverpool and as all the members were experienced musicians who had played in other well-known groups before, the **Nocturns** established themselves on the scene and became professionals within a very short time. The group from the beginning consisted of:

Barry Elmsley	**(voc/p)**
Keith Draper	**(g/voc)**
Brian Cox	**(g)**
Dave Foley	**(bg)**
Frank Sloane	**(dr)**

Keith Draper, **Brian Cox** and **Dave Foley** were former members of the **Cadillacs** and the follow-on group **Sorrals** or **Alby & the Sorrals**, respectively.

Drummer **Frank Sloane** came from the **Merseybeats** and had already been with their forerunner groups **The Mavericks** and **The Pacifics**. **Barry Elmsley** did not want to become a professional and left quite soon again. He was replaced by **Steve Aldo**, who had formerly sung with **Steve Aldo & the Challengers** and for a short time with **King Size Taylor & the Dominoes**. But he did not stay too long and then joined the **Griff Parry Five**, with whom he recorded under his name for Parlophone. After that he became a member of the **Krew** (better known as **The Crew**), the **Fyx** and the **In Crowd**, before he was backed by the **Fairies**.

His place in the **Nocturns** was taken by **Dave Wilcox**, whose real name is **David Christie** and who had formerly sung with **Danny Royl & the Strollers**, the **Sensations**, the **Young Ones** and **Rikki Jansen & the Q-Kats**, who, despite all the different names were only one group.

Brian Cox left and was replaced by **Arthur McMahon**, who was also known as **Arthur Roy** and had formerly played with **Arthur Roy & the Rockers**, the **Gerry Marsden Skiffle Group**, the **Gerry Marsden Trio** and **Gerry & the Pacemakers**. But he did not stay too long and then disappeared from the scene. His replacement was **Dave Elias**, who also was a former member of the **Merseybeats** and in the meantime had played with the **Four Musketeers**.

In this line-up the **Nocturns** had a part in the **Lionel Bart** musical 'Maggie May' and a little later their first single *Carrying On* was released, which was their song from the musical. This single, which was coupled with *Three Cool Cats*, climbed up to no.61 in the British charts. So it was no surprise that soon after that a second single was planned to be released on the Decca label, but the songs

On stage at the musical 'Maggie May'

Too Much Monkey Business and *I'm Hurt* were only recorded and announced in 'Mersey Beat', but obviously never released. At least there is no mention of it in the Decca catalogue.

At this time the **Nocturns** appeared regular the well-known 'Blue Angel' club in Liverpool. The group released no more records in their own name, but in 1964 backed the female vocal group **The Charmers** on their single *Are You Sure,* although the **Nocturns** were not named on the label.

After that little was heard of the **Nocturns**, who shouldn't be confused with the **Nocturnes** who probably came from Manchester and later released records on the Columbia label.

In 1965, the Liverpool **Nocturns** disbanded totally and it is known only that **Keith Draper** and **Dave Elias** continued in the music business, when they first joined the **Beat-Chicks** (from London?) and after that played in various groups, before they ended up as a cabaret duo under the name **Jade Brothers**. None of the other members appeared on the scene again after that.

Single discography
Carrying On / Three Cool Cats   **UK- Decca F.12002 / 1964**

Besides this the **Nocturns** were featured on the EP 'Carryin' on with more songs from 'Maggie May' (UK-Decca DFE 8602) in 1964, but most probably only with the songs from their first single.

as backing group for **The Charmers**:
Are You Sure / My Heart Has A Mind Of Its Own   **UK- Decca   ???   / 1964**

Unreleased tracks:
In 1964 the **Nocturns** recorded the songs *Too Much Monkey Business* and *I'm Hurt* for Decca as follow-up single to their debut, but for mysterious reasons this record was not released.

THE NOTIONS

When this real Beat group was formed in Liverpool in 1961, it appeared at first under the name **The Phantoms**, but because there were already other groups around with the same name, this band changed it to the **Notions** very soon after its foundation. The original line-up of the group included the following musicians:

David Delany   (voc/g)
Dave McCarthy (g/voc)
Joe Short   (bg/voc)
Dave Armstrong (dr)

The Notions, once established on the scene, became something like a resident group at the famous 'Cavern' club and, together with the **Hideaways**, they probably had the most appearances there of all the Liverpool groups.

This certainly was an outstanding success and should be honoured as such, but it also had the disadvantage that the steady engagement meant they very seldom played outside of Liverpool and so did not obtain a bigger popularity in the Northern music scene.

In 1964, it looked like they would make a national breakthrough, when they recorded no less than fourteen (!!) songs at the 'Cavern' for the mobile recording studio of Oriole, but surprisingly none of these songs was ever released and so a big chance for the **Notions** had passed. Maybe this was the reason for **Joe Short** leaving the group in 1964 and quitting the music business. He was replaced by his brother **Kevin Short**, who came from the **Jokers**.

A little later the group had another chance when it recorded the original *Another Time* in the new 'Cavern Sound' studio in Matthew Street, but once again this was not followed by a record release. In this regard the **Notions** were not just the luckiest group!

In spite of that misfortune, the group survived very well on the scene, even if the musicians never became professionals. **Dave McCarthy** later was replaced by **Keith Balcomb** and beside this the group for a short time was joined by **Steve Aldo** as lead-vocalist, who amongst others had sung with groups like the **Challengers** and **Griff Parry Five**. It was probably in 1968 when **Notions** disbanded totally. **Kevin Short** after that should have been a member of the **Beechwoods**, who in 1969 recorded as **Taste Of Honey**. It is sadly not known if he was still with the group at that point. None of the other members appeared on the scene again.

Discography

In 1964 the **Notions** recorded 14 songs for Oriole but sadly none of them were ever released and that is why it is not known which songs were recorded at these sessions at the 'Cavern'.

Also 1964, the group recorded the original *Another Time* for the 'Cavern Sound' label, but this song was also not released.

THE PATHFINDERS

This is another group from Birkenhead on the west side of the River Mersey, where it was most probably formed in 1963. So they were already a little bit too late to swim with the first and most successful Merseybeat wave that hit the world. But in spite of this, the **Pathfinders** established themselves within a short time on the Beat scene of the North - in a line-up with:

Billy May	**(voc/g)**
Tom Earley	**(g/voc)**
Roy Brocklehurst	**(bg/voc)**
Tony Aldridge	**(dr)**

Tom Earley and **Tony Aldridge** were former members of the **Masqueraders** and the **Kinsmen**, that continued as **Steve Day & the Kinsmen** on the scene, but this is another story. Whether or not **Billy May** was a member of the original line-up is uncertain as he had formerly played with the **Valkyries**, who also hailed from Birkenhead.

However, in 1964 the group was signed to Decca and recorded the originals *It's Time* and *I Can't Wait*, which were not released, unfortunately. A little later Decca called the group into the studio again and this time the sessions were followed by a release. *I Love You Caroline* and *Something I Can Always Do* were written by **Billy May** and **Tom Earley**. It should be pointed out here that the B-side *Something I Can Always Do* was the far better Beat number, although the A-side chosen by Decca was also quite interesting.

These numbers were good enough for two singles, but sadly this record failed to make the charts and so did not contribute to a breakthrough for the group, even though *I Love You Caroline* was a regularly played favourite on Radio Caroline.

If it had been successful in the charts it would most probably have meant a bright future for the **Pathfinders** as they were a really good group who had very talented songwriters.

They were popular in the greater Liverpool area and appeared regularly at all the important venues in and outside the city centre. Even without achieving the national popularity they deserved, they existed very well in the professional music business.

Around 1964 **Frank Bowen** was also a member of the **Pathfinders** for a while. He had previously played with such well-known groups as **Cliff Roberts' Rockers, Howie Casey & the Seniors, Lee Curtis & the All Stars** and some others. But he left again to join **Rory Storm & the Hurricanes** and later played with the **Trends** and the **Bootleggers** in London before he returned to Liverpool where he joined **Earl Royce & the Olympics**.

Tony Aldridge temporarily left the group and was replaced by **Tommy Bennett**, who came from the **Pressmen** and before that he had played with the **Topspots**, a forerunner group to the **Undertakers**. When **Tony Aldridge** returned, **Tommy Bennett** formed the **New Pressmen** and in the Nineties he was the chairman of the 'New Brighton Rock' organisation and was still active as drummer of the **Dees**.

In 1965, another single was released by a group with the name **The Pathfinders**, this time on Parlophone with *Don't You Believe It* and *Castle Of Love,* but this time it was definitely not the Birkenhead group.

It was probably in 1966 when the **Pathfinders** disbanded totally and **Billy May** and **Roy Brocklehurst** quit the show business. **Tony Aldridge** joined **The Trend** (without 's'), a group formed by **Peter Cook**, who had formerly played with various wellknown groups, for example with the **Kansas City Five** and **Earl Royce & the Olympics**. All the others disappeared from the scene for years.

In the middle of the Nineties there was a group named the **Pathfinders** on the scene again. Their line-up consisted of the original band members **Tom Earley** (voc) and **Tony Aldrige** (dr), plus **Ian Hunter** (lg) and **Allan Burton** (bg) who had both been with the **Valkyries**, as well as pianist **Tommy Hughes**, who in the Sixties had played with the **Bluegenes** and the **Kansas City Five**.

This band existed for quite some time on the scene and was occasionally joined by the original member **Billy May**, who nowadays plays in the clubs as a solo performer, as well as by sax player **Brian Jones** of the **Undertakers** fame.

Single discography
I Love You Caroline / Something I Can Always Do   **UK- Decca**   **F.12038 / 1964**

Unreleased tracks:
The **Pathfinders** first recorded the originals *It's Time* and *I Can't Wait* for Decca in 1964, which were never released. After their single release, they recorded the **Billy May** original *I'm Ashamed Of You Baby,* as well as *Love, Love, Love, In My Lonely Room, Can I Get A Witness* and *A Certain Girl* – all in 1964 / 65. None of the songs were ever released.

THE PAWNS

Originally, this Rhythm & Blues group was formed as a trio in Liverpool in 1963 and had no real success at first. It was just one of three or four hundred groups that were around at that time, but because the **Pawns**, as they were named from the beginning, had a lot of bookings on both sides of the River Mersey, they became more and more popular, not at least because of their good musical quality. The original line-up of the **Pawns** consisted of:

Dave Percival	(voc/g)
Derek France	(bg/voc)
Sid Knapper	(dr)

Dave Percival and **Sid Knapper** were former members of the just disbanded **Climbers** and it is possible but not certain that **Dave Percival** was **Dave Percy**, who had also played with the **Roadrunners** for a time.

But this line-up of the **Pawns** only lasted until spring 1964 and then **Dave Percival** left to join the **Kinsleys**. He then became a member of the **Epics** who mainly consisted of former members of the **Mojos**, but who never had a public performance together - a so-called 'still born child'. **Dave Percival** then disappeared from the scene. He was replaced in the **Pawns** by **Dave Myers**, who formerly had played with **Cliff Roberts' Rockers**, the **Climbers** and the **Renegades** from Liverpool.

When **Derek France** also left shortly after that and disappeared from the scene, the **Pawns** became a quartet when they were joined by **George Peckham** (voc/g) and **Dave 'Mushy' Cooper** (bg/voc).

THE IRON DOOR CLUB

THURSDAY. 4 JUNE
The Pawns
SONNY KAY & THE REDS
FRIDAY, 5 JUNE
Liquorice Lockings Allsorts
THE EXCHECKERS
RICKY GLEASON & THE TOP SPOTS
SATURDAY, 6 JUNE
Freddy Starr and The Flamingoes
THE ST. LOUIS CHECKS
THE PILGRIMS
SUNDAY, 7 JUNE
The Pawns
MARK PETERS & THE SILHOUETTES
THE PATHFINDERS
SUNDAY AFTERNOON SESSION
THE RIOT SQUAD
THE PRINCIPALS
TUESDAY, 9 JUNE
Earl Royce & The Olympics
THE DELEMERES

TEMPLE ST., L'POOL

George Peckham was also a former member of Liverpool's **Renegades** and in the meantime had been with **Lee Curtis & the All Stars**, together with **'Mushy' Cooper**, who before that had played with **The Topspots**, **Bob Evans' Five Shillings**, the **Vegas Five** and **Faron's Flamingos**.

It was probably this line-up that toured Germany at the end of 1964, where they amongst others also appeared at the 'Star Club' in Bielefeld, where they left a real impression behind. They recorded the songs *Casting My Spell* and *Who* for Decca, which sadly were not released in the end.

For a short time, the **Pawns** were joined by sax player **Howie Casey**, formerly with **Derry & the Seniors**, **Howie Casey & the Seniors** and with **King Size Taylor & the Dominoes**. But he very soon joined the **Krewkats** and after that played with the **Big Three** for a short time, and briefly with the **Griff Parry Five** before re-forming the **Krew**. Later he was a member of the **Roy Young Band** and with **Rigor Mortis**.

In late1964 **George Peckham** left the group to join **Groups Inc.**, who very soon disbanded. He then was a member of the **Kinsleys** and after that played with **Earl Royce & the Olympics** and the **Fourmost**. It is unknown if the **Pawns** continued as a group or if they then broke up. Whatever happened, nothing was heard of them again in 1965.

In 1978 the band name **The Pawns** appeared again on the revival sampler 'Mersey Survivors', on which the **Pawns** were featured with the songs *Let's Dance* and *Tallahassee Lassie*. But this was more a session that only came together to record these songs and **George Peckham** was probably the only featured member of the Sixties' line-up.

There will always be question marks about the **The Pawns** as they weren't paid the attention they had honestly deserved in the Sixties.

In the Nineties, **Dave Myers** suddenly appeared again on the scene, playing sessions with musicians of the 'New Brighton Rock' organisation. When the group **Johnny Sandon & the Specials** developed from these sessions, he became a member and after singer **Johnny Sandon** had left, the band continued as **The Mersey Specials** for some time.

Dave Myers after that was a member of **Persuader** who later changed their name to **Rocket 88**. Nowadays, he plays in the group **Tempest.**

Discography

In 1964, the **Pawns** (probably in the four-piece line-up) recorded the songs *Casting my spell* and *Who* for Decca, but as far as it is known there was never anything released on record.

Tracks on compilation-albums:
Tallahassee Lassie	on '**Mersey Survivors**'	**UK-Raw RWLP 104 / 1978**
Let's Dance	on '**Mersey Survivors**'	**UK-Raw RWLP 104 / 1978**

(Please note that the songs on the above named compilation were most probably recorded during a session that only included **George Peckham** as a member from the Sixties' line-up of the **Pawns**)

At the Star Club, Bielefeld

MARK PETERS & THE SILHOUETTES

Peter Fleming (aka **Mark Peters**) started his singing career in the late Fifties with the group **Dean Fleming & the Flamingos** and after that he had a short spell with the **Teen Tones** and the **Hi-Spots** in Liverpool. When he had changed his stage name to **Mark Peters**, he became the leader of **Mark Peters & the Cyclones**, quite a popular and important group on the Merseybeat scene.

In 1962 he left the **Cyclones** who continued as a group on the scene and later recorded for Oriole. **Mark Peters** amalgamated with the **Silhouettes**, who, until that time, had been the backing group for singer **Ken Dallas**. Under the name of **Mark Peters & the Silhouettes**, this new connection appeared in the following line-up:

Mark Peters	(voc)
Rod McClelland	(g/voc)
Malcolm Aston	(g/voc)
David May	(bg/voc)
Steve Fleming	(org)
Geoff Lloyd	(dr)

Steve Fleming, a brother of **Mark Peters**, was also a former member of **Mark Peters & the Cyclones**. **Geoff Lloyd**, who was also quite new in this line-up, had played before with **Vic & the Spidermen**. In January 1963 he left again to join **J.J. & the Hi-Lites**.

The original drummer **Bob O'Hanlon** returned to the **Silhouettes** after having played with Liverpool's **Zephyrs**, who then changed their name to **The Classics**, as well as with **Frank Knight & the Barons** and the follow-on band **Lee Castle & the Barons**.

In this line-up **Mark Peters & the Silhouettes** were featured on the Oriole sampler 'This Is Merseybeat' Vol.1 with a good version of *Someday (When I'm Dead And Gone)*.

Because of their convincing debut, the group was signed to Oriole and, still in 1963, a nice single with the original *Fragile* was released by **Mark Peters & the Silhouettes** and this song was also featured on the sampler 'Group Beat '63'. But *Fragile* wasn't a big hit and so did not help that real good group achieve a bigger breakthrough.

Bob O'Hanlon left and was replaced by **Tony Sounders**, formerly with **Chick Graham & the Coasters**. Probably in this line-up the single *Cindy's Gonna Cry* was recorded for Oriole, which was only credited to **Mark Peters**. Once again it wasn't successful and that might have been why **Rod McClelland** left and quit the music business.

He was replaced by **Arthur Ashton**, who also came from **Chick Graham & the Coasters**

MARK PETERS
ORIOLE RECORDING ARTIST

and before that had played with the **Confederates**. But he only stayed for a short time and then joined **Ian & the Zodiacs**. His replacement in **Mark Peters & the Silhouettes** was **Norman Scroggei**, who came from the recently disbanded **Lee Eddie Five**.

Tony Sounders left again to replace **Alan Newman** in the **Squad**, who were formerly known as **The Riot Squad**. They, by the way, had nothing in common with the PYE recording group which hailed from London. He was replaced by **Brian Johnson**, a former member of the **Strangers** and **Rory Storm & the Hurricanes**.

The band accepted an engagement at the 'Star-Club' in Hamburg, where it went down really well and probably would have been re-booked. However, after it looked like the line-up had become stable, **Mark Peters** left. At first he recorded the solo single *Don't Cry For Me,* which came out on the Piccadilly label. This again was a nice song but also failed to become any great success.

After that release, **Mark Peters** amalgamated with the **Squad** under the name **Mark Peters & the Method**. Besides him, this group consisted of **Tony Coates** (g), **Pete Ritson** (bg) and of course **Tony Sounders** (dr) after founder and band leader **Bill Ennis** had left and quit show business shortly before. He, by the way, is the brother of **Ray Ennis**, the leader of the **Swinging Blue Jeans**.

Tony Coates was a former member of the **Corsairs** and had replaced the original guitarist **Bob Reece**, while **Pete Ritson** was the only remaining member of the original **Riot Squad**. A little later **Steve Fleming** followed his brother also to this group, which continued until 1965 and then was disbanded by **Mark Peters**. **Tony Coates** appeared again in the Seventies as a member of the internationally successful hit group **Liverpool Express**.

Mark Peters teamed up with the **Rats** from Wigan, who shortly before had released their two singles with *Parchment Farm* on Oriole and *Sack Of Woe* on CBS. But **Mark Peters & the Rats**, as they were called then, did not record together, just like **Mark Peters & the Method** before them. **Mark Peters** quit show business and emigrated to Sri Lanka, where he is still living.

But back to the **Silhouettes**, who, after **Mark Peters** and **Steve Fleming** left, continued under their old name in a line-up with **Norman Scroggei** (voc/g), **Malcolm Aston** (g), **David May** (bg/voc) and **Brian Johnson** (dr). As far as it is known, this group toured Germany again, but did not record anymore. **David May** left to join **Rory Storm & the Hurricanes**, and it is sadly not known by whom he was replaced in the **Silhouettes**, who continued until 1965.

After the split, **Norman Scroggei** teamed up again with **David May** and, together with the drummer **Jimmy Lacey**

THE SILHOUETTES
Mickey Hayes. 17. Poulton Rd. Bebington. Wirral. Ches
Phone 051-Bro 1925

(formerly with the **Profiles**, **Johnny Templer & the Hi-Cats** and **Chick Graham & the Coasters**), formed a group under the name **The Three Cheers** who later became **Phase Three** and are said to have recorded for Polydor, although there is nothing known about such records.

David May later formed a duo together with **Ricky Gleason**, who formerly had led the groups **Denny & the Escorts**, **Ricky Gleason & the Topspots**, **Ricky Gleason & the Nighthawks** and the **Rebels**. After that, **David May** was a member of the cabaret band **The Maddisons**.

Malcolm Aston left show business after the **Silhouettes** had disbanded and **Brian Johnson** became a member of the **Tabs** and then also quit the music business for years. In the Nineties, he appeared again on the scene when he joined the newly formed **Cliff Roberts Rockers**, and today is a member of the newly formed **Mojos.**

In the Eighties, **Steve Fleming** was a member of the **Merseybeats** but then joined the **Clouds**, a cabaret band that mainly consisted of former **Fourmost** members. Today he is with **Vince Earl & the Attraction**.

THE THREE CHEERS

In the end, it can be said that although they were only short-lived and not too successful on the national scene, **Mark Peters & the Silhouettes** were one of the good and most interesting groups of the first Merseybeat wave and that it is a shame that more records were not released by them.

Single discography
as **Mark Peters & the Silhouettes**:

Fragile (Handle with care) / Janie	UK- Oriole	CB 1836 / 1963

as **Mark Peters**:

Cindy's Gonna Cry / Show Her	UK- Oriole	CB 1909 / 1964
Don't Cry For Me / I Told You So	UK- Piccadilly 7N 35207 / 1964

(Please note that *Cindy's Gonna Cry* was most probably recorded together with the Silhouettes, although the group was not named on the label, while the second one clearly was a solo release by Mark Peters.)

Tracks on compilation albums:
as **Mark Peters & the Silhouettes**:

Someday (when I'm dead and gone) on 'This Is Merseybeat' Vol.1		
	UK- Oriole	PS 40047 / 1963
Fragile (handle with care) on 'Group Beat '63'	UK- Realm	RM 149 / 1963

Unissued tracks:

Only the song *It Wasn't Meant To Be* is known, having come from the Oriole session for *Cindy's Gonna Cry* in 1963, which might have been a solo recording by **Mark Peters**, but most probably the **Silhouettes** were also featured.

Mark Peters & The Silhouettes at the Star Club

THE PREMIERS

This band originated from the Skiffle group **Tony Goldby & the Goldminers**, formed by **Tony Lane** in Liverpool in the late Fifties. The members at that time were **Tony Lane** (voc/g), **Dennis Conroy** (g/voc), **Alan Walton** (bass) and **Arthur Gilbert** (dr).

In the early Sixties, the group changed the musical style, and of course the name - and the result was a Rhythm & Blues band called **The Premiers**. Changes in the line-up followed, and when **Dave Forshaw** took over their management, the **Premiers** consisted of the following musicians:

Tony Lane	**(voc/g)**
Dennis Conroy	**(g/voc)**
Paul Lofthouse	**(bg)**
Ronnie Barker	**(dr)**

The former bass guitarist **Alan Walton** had become a member of the **Soul Seekers**, while **Arthur Gilbert** probably had quit show business.

Within a short time, the **Premiers** became popular on the local scene and they were something of a resident group at 'St. Johns' in Bootle, where the **Beatles** also appeared a few times.

In 1964 the above **Premiers** line-up recorded an EP on acetate with the songs *Beautiful Deliliah* and *Skinny Minnie,* as well as their own compositions *I'm Blue* and *Honest I Do,* the latter being a very nice and melodic Beat number, which would have been great on record. But of course, an acetate would never increase their popularity and so it did not contribute to a breakthrough for the **Premiers**.

In 1965 **Tony Lane** left and became a member of the **Inbeats**, who later became the **Phoenix Sound**. **Paul Lofthouse** and **Ronnie Barker** also left and most probably quit show business. The remaining lead guitarist **Dennis Conroy**, re-formed the group with former member **Alan Walton** (bg), who returned from the recently disbanded **Soul Seekers**.

The other new members were **Peter Wheelen** on drums and a singer and rhythm guitarist with the name **Gary**, whose second name sadly got lost with the years. But it is known that he formerly was also with the **Soul Seekers**.

This new line-up only continued for a short time as the **Premiers** and then followed the stupid fashion to name a group after TV dolls popular at that time. So the **Premiers** became the **Gonks**, but when the musicians found out that there was already a group of the same name in the South, the Liverpool outfit changed their name in **The Mersey Gonks**. But of course this new name did not help achieve a bigger breakthrough and, under the leadership of **Dennis Conroy,** the **Mersey Gonks** only existed until the end of 1966.

The group did not record anymore and nothing is known about any other outstanding success they may have had, but obviously there were some more personnel changes in the group, as for a short time, an organ and a saxophone was added to the line-up. The names of the musicians are sadly not known.

After the split up, all members disappeared from the scene. Former leader **Tony Lane** later was with **Barney Rubble's Boosband**, a seven-piece group that had some appearances on BBC Radio One.

<u>Discography</u>

The **Premiers** or **Mersey Gonks** never had an official record release but in 1964 - still as **The Premiers** – they recorded the following EP on acetate :

Beautiful Delilah / Skinny Minnie/ I'm Blue / Honest I Do   **UK- Deroy acetate / 1964**

EARL PRESTON'S REALMS

This band was formed by **George Spruce** (aka **Earl Preston**) in Liverpool in 1964, after he had sung before with **Gene Day & the Jango Beats**, the **Comets** and the **TT's**, at that time under the name **Earl Preston & the TT's**.

He had outstanding success on the scene and these days counts as one of the real Merseybeat legends. **Earl Preston's Realms,** in their original line-up, consisted of the following musicians:

Earl Preston	**(voc)**
Tony Priestly	**(lg/voc)**
John Caulfield	**(bg/voc)**
Dave Tynan	**(org)**
Tommy Husky	**(sax)**
Tommy Kelly	**(dr)**

Tony Priestly was a former member of **Mike & the Merseymen** and the **Beatcombers**, while **Tommy Kelly** had played before with **Danny Royl & the Strollers**, the **Sensations**, the **Young Ones** and **Rikki Janson & the Q-Kats**, which, in the end, was the one group under different names. **Tommy Husky** had formerly played with **John Paul & the Deejays** and the **Nashpool**.

In 1964 **Earl Preston's Realms** were signed to Fontana and in the same year their first single was released with an interesting version of the **Dee Clark** classic *Raindrops*. In spite of its quality, this record was not successful, but it is a desired collector's item today.

John Caulfield left to join the new band of the former **Roadrunners** member **Mike Hart**, which probably was **Henry's Handful** at that time. He was replaced by **Brian Norris** from the **Bumblies**, the predecessors of the **Cryin' Shames**.

After the recordings *I'll Be Doggone, Blue Monday, Missing You, Nobody But You* and *Daddy Rolling Stone* for the live compilation 'Liverpool Today', which was released on Ember in 1965, **Brian Norris** left again and later became a member of the **Dimensions**, who at that time were a trio, and then continued first as **Jet** and after that as **Pendulum**. His replacement in **Earl Preston's Realms** was **Charlie Smullan** who came from **Cy Tucker & the Friars**.

In August 1965 the band had a recording test with Decca, where the song *Memory Of Our Love* was recorded, but sadly never released. But then the group was signed to CBS and with *Hard Time Loving You,* another great single was released in 1966 - but under the changed name of **The Realm**. This record was not very successful and so did not help the band achieve a significant breakthrough.

After that, **Tommy Kelly** left to join the **Escorts** and he at first was replaced by **Ritchie Galvin**, a former member of the **Galvanisers** and **Earl Preston & the TT's**, but he soon left again to join **Gerry De Ville & the City Kings** and was replaced in **The Realm** by **Tommy Hart**, another

269

former member of **Cy Tucker & the Friars**. There were probably some more changes in the line-up before the group disbanded in 1968.

Even if **Earl Preston's Realms** or **The Realm**, as they were named later, had no international stardom, they were one of the very good and important Liverpool groups, which are still remembered today.

Tony Priestly later emigrated to Canada and **Tommy Husky** joined the **Detours**, before he became a successful session musician in the British Rockabilly scene of the Nineties and also recorded solo albums. **Earl Preston** joined the quite popular **Reflections**, where he sang until 1979.

After that he, together with **John Lloyd**, a former member of the **Kirkbys**, formed a cabaret duo under the name **The Raffels**, before **Earl Preston** quit show business for years and went back to a normal day job. Since 1987, he has been back on the scene, playing the Liverpool clubs as a solo act under the name **Joey Preston** and he still proves that he is an excellent vocalist.

FIRST EVER FABULOUSLY EXCITING

ALL NITE BEAT BOAT

Starring these Top Groups

★ THE CLAYTON SQUARES ★ EARL PRESTON'S REALMS
★ THE HIDEAWAYS ★ ST. LOUIS CHECKS
★ THE ROAD RUNNERS ★ AMOS BONNEY & THE TTs

and Special Guest Stars

THE SENSATIONAL MEASLES

MIDNIGHT EASTER SUNDAY, 18th APRIL, 1965
<u>IMPORTANT!</u> SEE OVERLEAF   Nº 1648

Discography
as <u>**Earl Preston's Realms**</u>:

Raindrops / That's For Sure	**UK-Fontana TF 481 / 1964**	

as <u>**The Realm**</u>:

Hard Time Loving You / A Certain Kind Of Girl	**UK- CBS 202044 / 1966**	

tracks on compilation albums:
as <u>**Earl Preston's Realms**</u>:

I'll Be Doggone	on **'Liverpool Today'**	**UK- Ember 5028 / 1965**
Blue Monday	on **'Liverpool Today'**	**UK- Ember 5028 / 1965**
Missing You	on **'Liverpool Today'**	**UK- Ember 5028 / 1965**
Nobody But You	on **'Liverpool Today'**	**UK- Ember 5028 / 1965**
Daddy Rolling Stone	on **'Liverpool Today'**	**UK- Ember 5028 / 1965**

Unreleased tracks:
In 1965, **Earl Preston's Realms** had a recording test with Decca but the song *Memory Of Our Love* sadly was never released.

EARL PRESTON & THE T.T.s

In the beginning there were **Johnny Tempest & the Tornadoes**, formed in Liverpool in 1958, in a line-up with **Johnny Tempest** (voc), **Lance Railton** (lg), **Dave Gore** (rg), **Wally Sheppard** (bg) and **Rod Cameron** (dr). It was one of the early Liverpool Rock 'n' Roll groups that became very popular within a short time.

Johnny Tempest & The Tornadoes

Because of illness, **Johnny Tempest** had to leave at the beginning of the Sixties and a little later he sadly died at a very young age. His place in the group was taken by **Billy 'Faron' Ruffley** and the band continued as **Faron & the Tempest Tornadoes**, but then shortened their name to **Faron & the T.T.s**. **Rod Cameron** left to join **Karl Terry & the Cruisers** and was replaced by **Don Alcyd**, who came from **Tommy & the Metronomes**. When **'Faron'** joined the newly formed **Flamingos**, this group changed their name to **Faron's Flamingos** and later wrote Merseybeat history.

The new singer with the **T.T.s** was **George Spruce**, who had formerly led the groups **Gene Day & the Jango-Beats** and the **Comets**. **George Spruce**, who was formerly known as **Gene Day**, changed his stage name to **Earl Preston** and the band continued under the name of **Earl Preston & the T.T.s**.

Around this time, drummer **Don Alcyd** left to join the **Renegades** from Liverpool and later, amongst others, also played with **Lee Curtis & the All Stars** and the **Delmont Four** for a time. He was replaced by **Richard Hughes**, who had chosen the stage name **Ritchie Galvin**, as he was a former member of the **Galvanisers**.

In 1961, the group was joined by **Cy Tucker** as an additional member, who played guitar and was the second lead singer. **Cy Tucker**, whose real name is **Thomas Thornton**, was the former leader of the **Cimarrons**. As a result of all these changes **Earl Preston & the T.T.s** in 1962 appeared in the following line-up:

Earl Preston	**(voc)**
Cy Tucker	**(voc/g)**
Lance Railton	**(lg)**
Dave Gore	**(rg)**
Wally Sheppard	**(bg)**
Ritchie Galvin	**(dr)**

In June 1963 **Dave Gore** left the group and quit show business, and one month later **Earl Preston & the T.T.s** were featured on the Oriole compilations 'This Is Merseybeat' Vol.1 and Vol.2 with the songs *Thumbin' A Ride* (sung by **Earl Preston**), as well as with *Hurt* and

All Around The World, which were both sung by **Cy Tucker**.

Because these songs had such quality, the group was immediately signed to Fontana and a few weeks later the first single was released, but *I Know Something,* a group's original, did not make it although it was a good song, coupled with a great version of *Watch Your Step.* Both songs featured the lead vocals of **Earl Preston**.

In September 1963, the band backed **Eden Kane** on his single *Like I Love You,* which was not too successful, but when the **T.T.s** backed the same singer four months later on *Boys Cry,* it became a Top 10 hit. Sadly, the group was not given any credit on the label and so this success did not help the band in any way. **Earl Preston & the T.T.s** then cut a great version of *Beautiful Delilah* for Fontana, but for mysterious reasons this was not released. The next single came out under the name of **Cy Tucker with Earl Preston's T.T.s,** but the great ballad *My Prayer* also failed to make the charts.

In 1964 **Earl Preston** left the group to form **Earl Preston's Realms,** who after their first single release changed their name to **The Realm,** which is another story in this book.

Eden Kane

The **T.T.s** continued under the name **Cy Tucker & the T.T.s** but did not make any more records. **Cy Tucker** also left very soon to form **Cy Tucker & the Friars,** who mainly consisted of former members of the **Cimarrons**. He was replaced in the **T.T.s** by **Vic Wright,** who had formerly led the groups **Pete Picasso & the Rock-Sculptors** and **Vic & the Spidermen,** the latter being very popular on the Liverpool music scene.

Vic & The T.T.s then recorded the originals *Miss You Baby, If You Would* and *Somewhere, Somehow, Sometime,* for Decca. The latter one was written by **Earl Preston** and **Lance Railton,** while the other two were solo compositions by **Lance Railton**. For unknown reasons these songs were never released.

Vic Wright left again, probably still in 1964, to form the group **Vic Takes Four.** They were most likely **The Take Four** prior to that and had their 'Cavern' debut in January 1964. **Vic Takes Four** became quite popular on the local scene for a short time, but then obviously split up again. In October 1965, he was a member of **The Script** and then disappeared from the scene. He later emigrated to Australia where he is still living.

The new singer with the **T.T.s** was a newcomer on the scene. His real name was **Ronnie Cotton,** but he adopted the stage name **Amos Bonny** and so the group continued as **Amos Bonny & the T.T.s**. But this also did not last too long and no records were released, which is very hard to understand because it was a really good group with a talented songwriter in **Lance Railton**.

Anyway, **Amos Bonny** left the group to join the **Defenders,** after that he sang with the Liverpool **Easybeats,** and in 1968 with a group called **Mumble**. Around the same time **Wally Sheppard** also left and quit show business.

FROM SUN., AUG. 9th, 1964
A SENSATIONAL NEW GROUP WILL BE APPEARING FOR THE FIRST TIME ON THE *MERSEY SCENE!*

NAME...........................?

VIC TAKES *FOUR*

ANCHOR PROMOTIONS
INVITE ENQUIRIES FROM PROMOTERS FOR DATES FROM AUGUST 9th ONWARDS.
ANDREW HARRIS, Widnes 2825 (OFFICE HOURS)
WILL BE ONLY TOO PLEASED TO DISCUSS WITH ANYONE FURTHER DETAILS CONCERNING THIS NEW GROUP
Appearing at the Cavern Club, Sun. Aug 9

The new members were the 'Sheik of Shake' **Karl Terry** (voc/g) and **Gordon Evans** (bg), whose real name is **Gordon Loughlin**. **Karl Terry** was a former member of the **Gamblers Skiffle Group, Terry Connor & the Teen Aces, Karl Terry & the Cruisers, Group One** and the **Delemeres**. **Karl Terry & the T.T.s**, as the group was named now, continued until 1966 and broke up when **Lance Railton** joined the **Clayton Squares**.

Initially it was planned to add **Neil Ford** as a new guitarist to the line-up, who at that time was a member of the **Vaaveros**, but he then joined **Johnny Ringo & the Colts**. **Karl Terry** and **Gordon Evans** joined the **Talismen**, who had just parted from **Vince Earl**. But then the two

Amos Bonny & the TT's

re-formed the **T.T.s** again as a trio together with **Ritchie Galvin**.

This only lasted a very short time and then **Karl Terry** and **Gordon Evans** followed **Lance Railton** to the **Clayton Squares**, but this group, who then sometimes appeared as the **T-Squares** and sometimes as the **Clayton Squares**, did not exist too long and after some personnel changes and two Germany tours in 1967 and 1968, faded away.

Karl Terry became a member of **Rory Storm & the Hurricanes**, played with a group called **Capricorn** and then re-formed **Karl Terry & the Cruisers** who are still going strong on the scene. **Gordon Evans** (aka **Gordon Loughlin**) disappeared from the scene for years but in 1990 he was a member of **Johnny Guitar & his Hurricanes**.

Lance Railton, who in the meantime was also a member of **Karl Terry & the Cruisers**, died on Christmas eve 1989 at the very young age of 46.

Ritchie Galvin appeared again when he at first joined **Earl Preston's Realms** and then became a member of **Gerry De Ville & the City Kings**. After that he joined Liverpool's Country scene and played with groups like the **Kentuckians, Phil Brady & the Ranchers** and at last with a Country & Western band called **Western Union**.

When **Lance Railton** died, **Earl Preston & the T.T.s** came together again for a charity concert in a line-up with **Earl Preston, Karl Terry, Dave Gore, Wally Sheppard** and **Ritchie Galvin**. They later did one or two concerts for the 'Mersey Cats' but then split up again.

But the formerly retired **Wally Sheppard** and **Dave Gore** remained in the music business and after they had played for a short time with **Karl Terry & the Cruisers**, both joined the newly formed **Cliff Roberts' Rockers**, who did not last for too long, and occasionally played for the 'Mersey Cats'.

After that, both musicians formed the group **Persuader** who later became **Rocket 88**, but then **Dave Gore** left and became the roadie for **Cy Tucker**. **Wally Sheppard** today plays with a group called **Tempest**. **Earl Preston** is also active again and under the name of **Joey Preston** sings to backing tapes in the Liverpool clubs. **Ritchie Galvin** died in 2001.

In spite of the fact that **Earl Preston & the T.T.s** never had any chart success in their own right or any notable national success, it is one of the Merseybeat legends that will certainly never be forgotten.

Single discography

as **Earl Preston & the T.T.s**:
I Know Something / Watch Your Step   UK- Fontana TF 406 / 1963

as **Cy Tucker with Earl Preston's T.T.s**:
My Prayer / High School Dance   UK- Fontana TF 424 / 1963

as backing-group for **Eden Kane**:
Like I Love You / Come Back   UK- Fontana TF 413 / 1963
Boys Cry / Don't Come Crying To Me   UK- Fontana TF 438 / 1964

Tracks on compilation albums: (all as **Earl Preston & the T.T.s**)
Thumbin' A Ride   on 'This Is Merseybeat' Vol.1   UK- Oriole PS 40047 / 1963
Hurt   on 'This Is Merseybeat' Vol.1   UK- Oriole PS 40047 / 1963
All Around The World   on 'This Is Merseybeat' Vol.2 UK- Oriole PS 40048 / 1963

Unissued tracks:

As unreleased tracks, the following **Earl Preston & the T.T.s** songs are known: *Too Much Monkey-Business, Betty Jean, Please Believe Me, Why Did It Have To Be You, Back Again To Me* and *Beautiful Delilah;*
by **Cy Tucker & the T.T.s** the songs *Bonie Moronie* (great version !!!) and *I Apologize;*
by **Eden Kane with the T.T.s** the tunes *Gonna Make A Comeback* and *Do You Love Me.*
All the above mentioned songs were recorded for Fontana in the years 1963 and 1964.
Besides this **Vic Wright & the T.T.s** recorded the songs *Miss You Baby, If You Would* and *Somewhere, Somehow, Sometime* for Decca in 1964.

Earl Preston & the TT's

THE PRESTONS

This group remained relatively unknown on the national music scene during its lifetime, but on Merseyside and especially in its hometown, Preston, it was a top act, even if only briefly.

The history tells that they originated from the **Downbeats**, that were formed in 1962 and some people say, that it was that group who backed **Eden Kane** on *I Won't Believe Them*, the B-side of his 1963 single *Tomorrow Night*. This is highly improbable as the **Downbeats** that backed Eden Kane, also released two singles in their own right in France and one of them is with the French versions of the two **Merseybeats** hits *I Think Of You* and *Don't Turn Around*. The latter one only came out in 1964 by the **Merseybeats**, but the **Downbeats** from Preston had already changed their name into the **Prestons** in 1963. At this time the group consisted of the following musicians:

Robb Deka	**(voc/p)**
Roger James	**(g/voc)**
Andy Leigh	**(bg)**
Gene Richie	**(dr)**

Robb Deka, whose real name is **Robert Eccles**, had already played with the Preston groups the **Crusaders**, the **Strangers**, the **Falcons** and with **David John & the Mood**. After that he had made a recording test for **Joe Meek** in London, on which he was backed by the **Puppets**, who also hailed from Preston. It is known that all the recorded songs were originals of **Robb Deka**, but there was never anything released.

Roger James formerly was a member of the resident band at the 'Top Rank Ballroom' in Preston, which might have already been the **Downbeats**.

Andy Leigh was a former member of the **Corries**, while **Gene Richie**, whose real name is **Gene Carberry**, formerly played with the **Crusaders**, the **Questions**, the **Thunderbeats** and toured Poland with the **Atoms**.

The **Prestons** were very active songwriters and in 1964, they already had 70 of their own compositions. That could have been why **Joe Meek** became interested and obtained a contract with Columbia for them and recorded the songs; *I Love You, That's What We're Going To Do, I'll Get Over You* and *Good To You*. In the music paper 'Combo' in April 1964 there was a notice that their first single was to be released very soon, but this was not followed by a release - at least not from the **Prestons** in their own right.

In 1964, however, there was the single *Hear You Talking* released on the Parlophone label by **Beverly Jones & the Prestons** and it is almost certain that these were the **Prestons** from Preston. This record is the only known release by the group who for unknown reasons disbanded again still in 1964.

Robb Deka went to Liverpool and became a member of the **Nashpool Four**, who then shortened their name to **The Nashpool**. From there he went down to London and joined **Flip & the Dateliners**, that with his lead vocals after a Germany tour continued as the **Dateliners**.

He remained in the business as vocalist and 1976 changed his name to **Robb Shenton** and in 1980 he recorded the Meek tribute *Lonely Joe*, co-produced by **Clem Cattini**, who also played drums on it. **Roger James** also went to Liverpool and joined **Freddie Starr & the Midnighters** as a pianist.

He is most probably the same musician who later led the **Roger James Four**, who cut two great Beat singles for Columbia with *Letter From Kathy* (with its terrific B-side *Leave Me Alone*) and *Better Than Here*. Sadly, there are no more details known about this group.

Gene Richie joined the **Executives** of *March Of The Mods*-fame and after that played with the **Wheels** from Belfast, with whom he recorded some great records in 1965 and 1966.

Andy Leigh became a member of **Matthews Southern Comfort**, with whom he appeared at the legendary Woodstock Festival.

Discography

As far as it is known, there was never a record release credited to the **Prestons** only, although there was an advance notice in 'Combo' in April 1964 suggesting an upcoming release.

In 1964, there was a single released by **Beverly Jones & the Prestons** and it can be taken for granted that this was the Merseybeat group from Preston.

The group recorded *I Love You, That's What We're Going To Do, I'll Get Over You* and *Good To You* for Columbia in 1964 but these songs were never released.

as **<u>Beverly Jones & the Prestons</u>**:
Hear You Talking / Heat Wave   UK- Parlophone   R 5189 / 1964

<u>The Roger James Four</u>:
Letter From Kathy / Leave Me Alone   UK- Columbia   DB 7556 / 1965
Better Than Here / You're Gonna Come Home Cryin'   UK- Columbia   DB 7813 / 1966

THE PROFILES

This typical Merseybeat group was formed by **Peter Feldman** in Liverpool in August 1963. At the beginning of 1964, the **Profiles** had established themselves as one of the leading and busiest groups on the local scene, although **Peter Feldman** had to struggle with changes in the line-up from the start. This might have been the main reason that they did not make a bigger breakthrough. The original line-up of the **Profiles** consisted of:

Peter Feldman	**(voc)**
Dave Williams	**(g/voc)**
Carl Stevenson	**(g)**
Paul Eker	**(bg)**
Jimmy Lacey	**(dr)**

Dave Williams was a former member of a group called the **Pacifics**, who may have been identical with, or somehow connected to the forerunners of the **Merseybeats** with the same name. This is not known for certain, but it is certain that **Dave Williams** was not the guitarist of the same name who played with **Dale Roberts & the Jaywalkers**, **Group One** and later with the **Four Originals**. It was probably with this line-up that the **Profiles** recorded their first acetate with the songs *My Heart Is Broken, If You Love Me, I Can't Tell* and *Sensation*, all obviously written by **Peter Feldman**.

In August 1964 **Jimmy Lacey** left to join **Johnny Templer & the Hi-Cats** and after that he played with **Chick Graham & the Coasters** and the **Three Cheers**, who later changed their name to **Phase Three**. His replacement in the **Profiles** was **Pete Wiggins**, who came from **The Mafia**.

Dave Williams also left and was replaced by **Eddie Gaye**, and when **Paul Eker** left a little later, the **Profiles** were joined by **John Owen**.

Then **Carl Stevenson**, the last remaining original member besides **Peter Feldman** left in 1964 and was not replaced. **Peter Feldman** took over the guitar and the group continued as a quartet under the name **The Profiles Four**. **Eddie Gaye** left and the guitarists **Joey Molland** and **Alan Stock** arrived as new members. **Joey Molland** had formerly played with the **Assasins**. The name was changed again - this time into **Peter & the Profiles**. With this, **Peter Feldman** obviously wanted to point out that in spite of all the changes in the line-up, he was still with the group.

In October 1964, **Joey Molland** left to join the **Masterminds** and later became a member of the **Fruit Eating Bears**, had a short spell with the **Cryin' Shames** and in 1967 went down to London where he joined **Gary Walker & Rain**. 1969 saw him a member of the hit group **Badfinger**, who still appears sporadically on the scene under his leadership, mainly in the USA. For him, **Carl Stevenson** returned to the **Profiles**, as they were named again from then on.

It is probable that this line-up recorded the demos *My Baby Kissed Me* and *You Know She's Mine*, both written by **Peter Feldman** once again. He was obviously a talented songwriter and so it is hard to understand that the group never was signed to a recording company.

Sometime in the mid-Sixties the **Profiles** disbanded totally and it is not known what happened to the individual members after that. It can be assumed that there had been some more personnel changes in the meantime and that **Peter Feldman** continued with his efforts to find a constant line-up for his group.

That the name of the **Profiles** is still well remembered these days is doubtless credit to **Peter Feldman** and to him alone.

Discography

The Profiles never released a record but recorded the following demos on acetate that exceptional featured original numbers by **Peter Feldman** :

My Heart Is Broken / If You Love Me / I Can't Tell / Sensation	**UK- Eroica - acetate / 1963**
My Baby Kissed Me / You Know She's Mine	**UK- Eroica - acetate / 1964**

THE PUPPETS

In the end it can be stated that this group in some way originated from **Bob Johnson & the Bobcats**, a local group in Preston, Lancashire that disbanded in late 1962.

Their drummer **Des O'Reilly**, who formerly had played with the **Rebels**, had a short stint with **Rory Storm & the Hurricanes**. He then met up again with his former guitarist from the **Bobcats** and together with the bassist from the **Thunderbeats** they reformed the **Bobcats** as a trio, which quickly was recruited by local singer **Robb Deka** to back him at test recordings for **Joe Meek**. The legendary producer was impressed with the trio, took it in his management and christened it the **Puppets** – in the line-up with:

Dave Millen	**(g/voc)**
Jim Whittle	**(bg/voc)**
Des O'Reilly	**(voc/dr)**

After some recording sessions which included *Little Bitty Pretty One, Zip-A-Dee-Doo-Da, Roll Over Beethoven* and *Money*, in September 1963 the first single of the **Puppets** came out on PYE with the original *Everybody's Talking* and a good version of *Poison Ivy*. The record sadly did not make it but PYE kept the contract and their next single, another original with the title *Three Boys Lookin' For Love* was recorded, but withdrawn for unknown reasons. In its place *Baby Don't Cry* was released in May 1964 but again did not make the charts. Maybe that was the reason for PYE to drop the **Puppets**, but they kept busy on the scene and built up a good name for themselves.

In 1965 they were joined by **Don Parfitt** (org/p/voc) from the **Keys** as additional member. The **Puppets**, beside having their own career, backed lots of well known singing stars, like the Liverpudlians **Billy Fury** and **Michael Cox**, plus American top acts like **Brenda Lee**, the **Ronettes** and **Gene Vincent** on their England tours. Still in 1965 they went on tour with **Gene Vincent** in Scotland and Germany, where they mainly played the 'Star-Club' circuit.

The original trio line up of the Puppets

1966 became another good year for the **Puppets** as they became the backing group for **Crispian St. Peters**, who had just had a big hit with *You Were On My Mind*. With him they toured all over England, where amongst others they also played the 'Cavern' in Liverpool, and probably also on the European continent. As well as touring, they recorded with him the titles *You Were On My Mind, Peggy Sue Got Married, Darlin', That's The Way I Feel* and

Lonely for the BBC radio show 'Saturday Club', as well as their solo numbers *My Name Is Mud* and a great version of *My Girl*.

The **Puppets** disbanded in 1967 and **Des O'Reilly** and **Dave Millen**, together with **Dave 'Daz' Smith** formed another trio under the name of **Three-D**, they were sometimes joined by **David John** as additional singer.

Des O'Reilly left and went solo on the cabaret circuit and in 1979 he emigrated to Australia, where he is still living and active in the showbusiness.

Three-D with **Fred Kelly** as new drummer and together with **David John** later developed into the recording group **Thundermother**. **Dave Millen** later went to London and there amongst others played with a group called the **Hi-Guys**. **Don Parfitt** later was a member of groups like **Stax Of Soul** and the **Soul Review** and of **Jim Whittle** it is told that in the Seventies he was a member of the **Four Just Men** but then retired from playing.

Discography

Everybody's Talking / Poison Ivy	UK - PYE 7N 15558 / 1963
Baby Don't Cry / Shake With Me	UK - PYE 7N 15634 / 1964

(beside this the single *Three Boys Lookin' For Love / Shake With Me* (PYE 7N 15625) was recorded but withdrawn in 1964)

Unreleased tracks:

From the **Joe Meek** recording sessions the following numbers are known: *Zip-A-Dee-Doo-Da, Roll Over Beethoven, Money* and *Little Bitty Pretty One* - all from 1963

In 1966 the **Puppets** recorded the numbers *My Name Is Mud* and *My Girl* for the popular BBC radio show 'Saturday Club' and beside this for the same show they backed **Crispian St. Peters** on *You Were On My Mind, Peggy Sue Got Married, Darlin', That's The Way I Feel* and *Lonely*.

The details of their very first recordings with **Robb Deka** are not known with the exception that they all were originals of the singer.

The Puppets

THE RAINCHECKS

To describe the complete development of this interesting band it is necessary to start with the stories of two other groups, as there were some very important connections and crossings.

The first one is **Wump & his Werbles**, formed in Liverpool in the late Fifties and consisting of **Rod 'Wump' Pont** (voc), **Dave Georgeson** (g), **Neville Humphries** (g), **Jim Mellor** (bg) and **John Cochran** (dr). **John Cochran** was a former member of **Gus & the Thundercaps** and **Gus Travis & the Midnighters.**

Wump & his Werbles were not too successful and so disbanded again very early. **Neville Humphries** and **Jim Mellor** quit show business, while **Dave Georgeson** and **John Cochran**, together with **Ian McQuair**, also a former member of **Gus & the Thundercaps** and **Gus Travis & the Midnighters**, formed a new group under the name **The Lil' Three**, that later became **The Chuckles**. **Rod Pont** became a popular Merseybeat singer under the name **Steve Day**.

The second group is **Johnny Rocco & the Jets** from Wallasey, one of the pioneering groups of the Merseybeat scene. They consisted of **Johnny Rocco** (voc/g), whose real name is **Graham Hodgson**, **Mike Nicholson** (g), **Spike Jones** (g), **Derek Bond** (bg) and **Phil Duggan** (dr).

Because **Johnny Rocco** had a bad throat he had to stop singing and left the group to join **Frank Knight & the Barons** as the drummer. Later he was active for a long time as a guitarist in the clubs of Tenerife/Spain. His place

The Rainchecks

in the **Jets** was taken by **Rod Pont** and the band continued under the name **Steve Day & the Jets** in the very early Sixties, but then changed to **Steve Day & the Drifters**.

Mike Nicholson left and was replaced by **Barry Ezzra**, who came from **Vince Earl & the Zeros** and before that was a member of the **Firecrests**. **Steve Day & the Drifters** became very popular on the scene until **Steve Day** left the band in May 1963 to join the **Black Jays** from London. Back in Liverpool, he formed **Steve Day & the Kinsmen**, but this is another story in this book.

The remaining **Drifters** then became the backing group for **Gus Travis**, the former singer with **Gus & the Thundercaps** and **Gus Travis & the Midnighters**. But he then also left the group who in the meantime had changed its name to **The Rainchecks**.

Around the same time, **Spike Jones** and **Derek Bond** also left the band and **Spike Jones** is most probably the musician of the same name who later played the organ with the **Griff Parry Five** or the **Steve Aldo Quintett**, respectively. **Derek Bond** became the new bass guitarist with **Derry Wilkie & the Others**. The **Rainchecks** continued in their own right with the following line-up:

281

Barry Ezzra	(voc/g)
Graham Nugent	(g/voc)
Colin Briscoe	(bg/voc)
Phil Duggan	(dr)

Colin Briscoe and **Graham Nugent** came from Liverpool's **Scorpions**, whereby **Graham Nugent** should have been a member of the **Pilgrims** before, which is possible but not absolutely certain. This new line-up very soon earned a good name in the Northern music scene and was signed to the new record label 'Solar'.

Their first single was released towards the end of 1964 with *Something About You*, coupled with the nice Beat ballad *My Angel*. Both numbers were **Barry Ezzra** compositions. This was a very good Beat record which was praised by a lot of critics and sold very well on the local scene - not least because there was a very good publicity surrounding it. But Solar was not able to publicize the record on the international market, probably because the distribution system of the new label had not matured enough yet. Also at the recording session a version of **Chris Kenner**'s *Something You Got* should have been played in, but this was never released.

So *Something About You* did not become a hit, but the **Rainchecks** toured the European continent shortly after its release. They were successful mainly in Germany, where they played the 'Star-Palast' in Kiel, the 'Savoy' in Hannover and a big club in Braunschweig, amongst others.

They were one of the hopeful 'new' groups in Liverpool, but obviously a little bit too late to make a bigger breakthrough because the Merseybeat had already started to lose ground on the international music scene. Later little was heard of the **Rainchecks** that had established themselves among the leading groups on Merseyside, where they regularly appeared at all the important venues.

If the **Rainchecks** had come together earlier in this line-up and if they had had a good manager, they probably would have had more success, perhaps even internationally because it was one of the really good groups from the River Mersey. But they had missed the boat and no further records were released, as Solar very soon faded from the scene again and there was no contract signed with another record company.

Keep the Liverpool light burning by sending your latest Recording Group up the Charts!!

THE DYNAMIC
RAINCHECKS
"Something About You"
Available from your local Record Shop on Solar Records S.R.P.104
Management: Darville Entertainments
WALLASEY 1421 & 2484

It was probably still in 1965 when the **Rainchecks** disbanded and apart from **Graham Nugent**, who joined the re-formed **Pilgrims**, none of the individual members appeared on the scene again until a type of revival took place in the early Nineties, when the **Rainchecks** appeared again at the 'Mersey Cats' and the 'New Brighton Rock' organisations' concerts.

The **Rainchecks**, who only appeared occasionally, always included **Phil Duggan** and **Graham Nugent** and sometimes **Barry Ezzra** and **Colin Briscoe**.

Single discography
Something About You / My Angel   **UK- Solar SRP 104 / 1964**
Unreleased tracks :
It is said that at the session for the above single **The Rainchecks** also recorded a version of **Chris Kenner**'s *Something You Got* which was never released, maybe due to the failure of 'Solar' records.

(Please note that the single *How Are You Boy* which was released on the 'R&B' label by a group called **The Rainchecks** in 1965, was definitely not by this Liverpool/Wallasey outfit)

THE RATS

This real Rhythm & Blues group hailed from Wigan near Liverpool, where it was formed in 1963. With **Jimmy Jenkins,** they had a manager from the Beat capital and so the group became a steady part of Liverpool's Merseybeat scene, where it first appeared in the following line-up:

Allan Parkinson (voc/harp)
Malcolm Grundy (g/voc)
Gerry Kenny   (bg)
Bill Geldard   (dr)

In a way, this group was something of an offshoot of the legendary Wigan group **The Beat Boys**, as **Allan Parkinson** and **Malcolm Grundy** came directly from them and **Gerry Kenny** was also a short-term member of that band in 1962. Beside this **Allan Parkinson** and **Gerry Kenny** were former members of the **Martinis**, probably prior their membership in the **Beat Boys**. What **Gerry Kenny** had done in the meantime and in which group **Bill Geldard** had played before, is sadly not known. **The Rats** became very popular within a short time, especially in Liverpool and soon were signed to Oriole, who at that time helped a lot of the Merseybeat groups with their first steps into the recording business.

Still in 1964, their first single was released with their version of *Parchment Farm*, a song that since the late Fifties had become something of a Rhythm & Blues classic and because of that there were already too many versions on the market and so the **Rats'** single didn't become a bestseller, though it really was done very well.

Around that time, Oriole was taken over by CBS and the **Rats** released their second single on that label. *Sack Of Woe* again was a pure Rhythm & Blues number and a great recording which showed the outstanding quality of the group. It got some very good critical acclaim, but in the end was not a big success.

There were the two singles *Gotta See My Baby* and *Spoonful* released by a group called the **Rats** on the Columbia label in 1965, but this definitely was not the group from Wigan.

After that release, **Allan Parkinson**, who in the meantime had adopted the stage name **Dave Allen**, left the **Rats** and formed a new group under the name of **Dave Allen & the Exotics** who had a longer residence in Italy, but this is another story in this book.

For a while, little was heard of the **Rats**, but they stepped back into the limelight when, still in 1965, they became the backing group for the very popular Liverpool singer **Mark Peters**, whose real name was **Peter Fleming** and who had sung before with the groups **Dean Fleming & the Flamingos**, the **Teen Tones**, the **Hi-Spots**, **Mark Peters & the Cyclones**, **Mark Peters & the Silhouettes** and **Mark Peters & the Method**. **Mark Peters & the Rats**, as they were called now, became quite successful on the scene but did not release any records.

In 1965 **Mark Peters** separated from the group and later emigrated to Sri Lanka, where he is still living.

The **Rats** disbanded totally in 1966 and only of **Malcolm Grundy** is known, that he in 1967 went down to Italy to join **The Bigs**, which was the new name for the **Exotics** after **Dave Allen** had left to start a solo career and recorded as **Al Torino** and later continued as **Guy Challenger**.

Single discography

Parchment Farm / Every Day I Have The Blues	**UK- Oriole CB 1967 / 1964**
Sack Of Woe / Gimme That Wine	**UK- CBS 201 740 / 1965**

(Please note that the two singles by the **Rats** on the Columbia label were certainly not by this Wigan band)

★ **THE RATS**   C B S RECORDING ARTISTS   ★   RACHEL ENTERPRISES Sefton Park 7202

THE REMO FOUR

This story could, of course, have been featured in this book under the name **Johnny Sandon & the Remo Four** or **Tommy Quickly & the Remo Four**. As one name had to be selected, the **Remo Four** is probably the best solution as it also includes the various singers that were backed by them for a certain time, while the **Remo Four** also played and recorded in their own right.

But let's start at the beginning, when the group was formed in the late Fifties by **Colin Manley** in Liverpool under the name the **Remo Quartet**, but soon changed their name to **The Remo Four**. The original line-up consisted of **Colin Manley** (g/voc), **Don Andrews** (g), **Keith Stokes** (bg) and **Harry Prytherch** (dr).

ROCK! ROCK! ROCK!
This Saturday and Sunday to
• DUKE DUVAL'S ROCKERS
• REMO QUARTET
• DERRY AND THE SENIORS
AT • METRONOMES
HOLYOAKE JIVE HALL
(Smithdown Road—Near Penny Lane) 7-30

They very soon became one of the most popular groups on Merseyside, but in 1962 **Keith Stokes** and **Harry Prytherch** left to form **Group One**, which is another story in this book.

The new members of the **Remo Four** were **Phil Rodgers** (bg) and **Billy Buck** (dr), who both came from the recently disbanded **Dale Roberts & the Jaywalkers**.

When, in 1963, the **Searchers** separated from their singer **Johnny Sandon**, he joined forces with the **Remo Four** under the name **Johnny Sandon & the Remo Four**. This development meant the musicians had to become professionals, which was the reason for **Billy Buck** leaving and joining a Liverpool dance band, but before he left, he suggested his successor be the young **Roy Dyke**, who at that time was a member of **Karl Terry & the Cruisers**. He agreed to join and from then on **Johnny Sandon & the Remo Four** appeared in the following line-up:

Johnny Sandon	(voc)
Colin Manley	(g/voc)
Don Andrews	(g)
Phil Rodgers	(bg)
Roy Dyke	(dr)

In the same year the group was signed to PYE and the singles *Lies* and *Yes* were released, gaining only local success. The first one was an original and written by lead guitarist **Colin Manley**. After these two singles failed to make it, **Johnny Sandon** separated from the group again to go solo. He recorded three further singles with *Sixteen Tons*, *Donna Means Heartbreak* and *The Blizzard*. The last of these came out initially as the B-side of *Sixteen Tons* and then again as an A-side, coupled with *I'd Be A Legend In My Time*.

These singles showed **Johnny Sandon** more as Country singer than as a Beat vocalist. After these releases, none of which were very successful, little was heard of **Johnny Sandon**, who then disappeared from the scene for years. In the early Nineties he was back and performed for the 'Mersey Cats' with his new backing group under the name **Johnny Sandon & the**

Specials. But when he quit again, the group continued on the scene as the **Mersey Specials** for some time. **Johnny Sandon** committed suicide at Christmas 1997.

When **Johnny Sandon** left, the **Remo Four** first backed **Gene Pitney** and **Gene Chandler** on their UK tours, but then they got together with singer **Tommy Quickly**. He and his sister **Pat Quigley** (the correct spelling of the surname) had formerly sung with the **Challengers**. **Tommy Quickly**, who had already released the solo single *Tip Of My Tongue* on Piccadilly, was managed by **Brian Epstein**, who was responsible for his co-operation with the **Remo Four**.

Tommy Quickly

The individual members of the **Remo Four,** as well as playing in their own group, also had some sessions, short spells and stand-ins with other Merseyside groups. **Colin Manley** stood in for **Nicky Crouch** with the **Mojos** at one time, and **Roy Dyke** for **Tony Mansfield** with **Billy J. Kramer & the Dakotas** at another time, which proved their musical abilities.

Tommy Quickly & the Remo Four kept the contract with Piccadilly and in 1964 released a string of good Beat records, like *Kiss Me Now, Prove It, You Might As Well Forget Him* and the great *Wild Side Of Life*, as well as the quite weak *Humpty Dumpty*, which had a good flip-side with *I Go Crazy*.

From these singles only *Wild Side Of Life* became successful when it climbed up to no. 33 in the British charts in 1964. But all the other records also sold quite well - perhaps with the exception of *Humpty Dumpty,* which was a (deserved) flop.

Tommy Quickly and the group separated again in 1964, after the **Remo Four** had recorded the singles *I Wish I Could Shimmy Like My Sister Kate,* which was coupled with an incredible version of the instrumental *Peter Gun,* and *Sally Go Round The Roses* without **Tommy Quickly**. Sadly, neither record had any success, but that terrific version of *Peter Gun* was a milestone in the story of Liverpool's Merseybeat. It was later apparently re-recorded by the **Remo Four** as an A-side for the German 'Star-Club' label in 1966, but that was not half as rough as the 1964 recording.

As well as this, the **Remo Four** also backed singer **Gregory Phillips** on his single *Everybody Knows* in 1964, while they were still backing **Tommy Quickly**. **Gregory Phillips**, who was not from Liverpool, had previously had a nice single released with *Angie* in 1963. It is also more than probable that the **Remo Four** backed him on his next single, a version of the **George Harrison** composition *Don't Bother Me*.

Although they were not named on the label the backing sound is identical to *Everybody Knows* and one member of the **Remo Four** once stated that they had backed **Gregory Phillips** on two singles. After that, **Gregory Phillips** recorded one more single with his version of the **Joe South** composition *Down In The Boondocks* for Immediate in 1965, which became a big hit for **Billy Joe Royal** in the same year.

In the meantime, **Don Andrews** had left the **Remo Four** to join the **Blue Mountain Showband**, an offshoot of the recording Liverpool Country band **The Blue Mountain Boys**, which were also quite popular at that time. The **Blue Mountain Showband** later changed their name to **The Quintones**. He was replaced in the **Remo Four** by **Tony Ashton** (voc/ org), who had formerly played with the **College Boys** (from Eton), the **Executives**, the **Tony Ashton Trio**, the backing group of **Jimmy Justice**, the **John Barry Seven**, the **Mastersounds** and **Mike Hurst & the Method**.

In 1965 the **Remo Four** went to Hamburg, where they became a very successful part of the 'Star-Club' scene, but they also appeared at other important clubs in Germany, for example the 'Top Ten' in Hamburg. Because of their many appearances on the very popular German TV music show 'Beat-Club', they became well-known all over the country, and so did their re-recording of *Peter Gun,* which was a little bit harmless in comparison to their Piccadilly record. In spite of this, and probably because the Germans did not know the other version, the German release became something like a hymn of the legendary 'Star-Club' era, but the following single, *Live Like A Lady*, with a superb version of *Sing Hallelujah* on its reverse side, was not that successful, although it was another masterpiece.

At this time the sound of the **Remo Four** was already totally different compared to that of other groups. In retrospect, it can be said that in their music they were far ahead of their time and maybe this was the reason that they did not have any great commercial success with their recordings. This is also valid for their only album 'Smile', on which the influences of Soul, Blues and Jazz can be found. The full organ and 'rusty' voice of **Tony Ashton** gave their sound a distinctive tone but it was simply not commercial enough for that time. The attention they deserved was only paid to the **Remo Four** after they had disbanded in 1967.

Phil Rodgers went to London where he joined a Country band. **Tony Ashton** and **Roy Dyke**, together with **Kim Gardner** (ex **Birds** and **Creation**), formed the trio **Ashton, Gardner & Dyke** who had a big international hit with *Resurrection Shuffle* and were very successful in the European music scene for years.

In 1972, that trio disbanded again and **Tony Ashton** joined **Family**, while **Roy Dyke** and **Kim Gardner** formed the band **Badger**, together with **Brian Parrish** (ex **Londoners**), **Paul Pilnick** (ex **Lee Curtis & the All Stars**, **Big Three**, etc.) and **Jackie Lomax** (ex **Undertakers**).

After that **Roy Dyke** appeared again on the German scene, where he played a lot of sessions in Hamburg and was also a member of the trio **Bauer, Garn & Dyke**, who played a sort of modern Rock 'n' Roll and sang in German. He is still living in Hamburg these days and was lastly a member of the **Shamrocks**.

Colin Manley, certainly one of the best guitarists to come out of England, first played in the backing groups for **Clodagh Rodgers** and **Freddie Starr** after the **Remo Four** had split.

He then joined the **Swinging Blue Jeans** in the mid-Seventies, where he played until he sadly died in 1999. **Tony Ashton** died in 2001.

Single discography
as **Johnny Sandon & the Remo Four**:

Lies / On The Horizon	UK- PYE	7N 15542 / 1963
Yes / Magic Potion	UK- PYE	7N 15559 / 1963

as **Tommy Quickly & the Remo Four**:

Kiss Me Now / No Other Love	UK-Piccadilly	7N 35151 / 1964
Prove It / Haven't You Noticed	UK-Piccadilly	7N 35167 / 1964
You Might As Well Forget Him / It's As Simple As That	UK-Piccadilly	7N 35183 / 1964
Wild Side Of Life / Forget The Other Guy	UK- PYE	7N 15708 / 1964
Humpty Dumpty / I Go Crazy	UK- PYE	7N 15748 / 1964

Unissued tracks:
Tommy Quickly & the Remo Four recorded the **Beatles** song *No Reply* for PYE in 1964, which sadly was not released.

as **Gregory Phillips & the Remo Four**:
Everybody Knows / Closer To Me   UK- PYE   7N 15593 / 1964

as **The Remo Four**:
I Wish I Could Shimmy Like My Sister Kate / Peter Gun   UK-Piccadilly 7N 35175 / 1964
Sally Go Round The Roses / I Know A Girl   UK-Piccadilly 7N 35186 / 1964

Different German releases:
Peter Gun / Mickey's Monkey   G- Star-Club 14855 STF / 1966
Live Like A Lady / Sing Hallelujah   G- Star-Club 14857 STF / 1967
Unissued tracks:
The Remo Four recorded the song *The Honeymoon Song* in their own right for PYE in 1964, but it was not released in the end.

Johnny Sandon - solo:
Sixteen Tons / The Blizzard   UK- PYE   7N 15602 / 1964
Donna Means Heartbreak / Some Kinda Wonderful   UK- PYE   7N 15665 / 1964
The Blizzard / I'd Be A Legend In My Time   UK- PYE   7N 15717 / 1964

(Please note that the songs *Donna Means Heartbreak* and *I'd Be A Legend In My Time* were most probably recorded with the **Remo Four** as these songs can also be found on two acetates that were coupled with the songs *Magic Potion* and *On The Horizon* that were both released as the B-sides of the two singles of **Johnny Sandon & the Remo Four**)

Tommy Quickly - solo:
Tip Of My Tongue / Heaven Only Knows   UK-Piccadilly 7N 35137 / 1963

Gregory Phillips - solo:
Angie / Please Believe Me   UK- PYE   7N 15546 / 1963
Don't Bother Me / Make Sure That You're Mine   UK- PYE   7N 15633 / 1964
Down In The Boondocks / That's The One   UK- Immediate IM 004 / 1965

(Please note that the single *Don't Bother Me* was most probably recorded together with the **Remo Four**, as it was stated that the **Remo Four** recorded two singles with **Gregory Phillips** and the sound on the record is absolutely identical with the single by **Gregory Phillips & the Remo Four**)

LP discography (as **The Remo Four**)
SMILE   G-Star-Club 158.034 STY/ 1967
- Peter Gunn / Mickey's Monkey / Heart Beat / The Skate / No Money Down / Rock Candy / The Seventh Son / Roadrunner / Brother Where Are You / Jive Samba / Nothing's Too Good For My Baby / Live Like A Lady / Sing Hallelujah

THE RENEGADES

This group was formed by drummer **Bob Evans** in the Wallasey/Birkenhead area on the west side of the river Mersey in early 1962, after leading both **Bob Evans & the Five Shillings** and the **Vegas Five**, who then became the **Undertakers**.

The Renegades, who should not be confused with the 'Cadillac' hit group from Birmingham, were a real Rock 'n' Roll group and very soon developed a good name and a large following on the Liverpool scene. In their original line-up, the group consisted of:

George Peckham	(voc/g)
Dave Myers	(g)
Derek Peckham	(bg)
Bob Evans	(dr)

George Peckham was a former member of the **Skylarks** and **Dave Myers** came from the recently disbanded **Climbers** and before that had played with **Cliff Roberts' Rockers**. In the same year, **Bob Evans** left and later played with **Dixie & the Dare Devils** and **Combo Six.** His replacement was **Lewis Collins**, a newcomer on the scene who did not stay too long. He joined the **Kansas City Five** and later played the bass guitar with the **Georgians**, the **Eyes** and the **Mojos**. His replacement in the **Renegades** was **Don Alcyd**, who had formerly played with **Tommy & the Metronomes** and **Faron & the T.T.s**.

Jimmy McManus joined the **Renegades** as an additional vocalist. He had formerly sung with **Bob Evans' Five Shillings** and the **Vegas Five**.

When **Derek Peckham** left and disappeared from the scene, his replacement was **Dave 'Mush' Cooper**, who had played with the **Vegas Five**, the **Undertakers** and **Faron's Flamingos**. **Dave Myers** left for the **Pawns** and was replaced by **Pete Jones**, who came from the **Crosbys**.

Sax player **Jack Curtis** joined the **Renegades** as an additional member. So, **George Peckham** was the only remaining member of the original line-up, and because all these changes happened within a very short time, it was not possible for the **Renegades** to make a breakthrough. In spite of this, they were chosen to be featured on the planned Oriole sampler 'Cavern Alive' and were recorded by **John Schroeder**. Sadly this record did not come out and so it is unknown which songs were recorded by the **Renegades**.

A little later, they split off totally when **George Peckham**, **Dave Cooper** and **Don Alcyd** left to form the new backing group for **Lee Curtis** under the name **Lee Curtis & the All Stars**. This group disbanded again after a successful tour of Germany and while **Dave Cooper** joined the **Pawns**, **George Peckham** first became a member of **Groups Inc.** before he also teamed up with the **Pawns**. **Dave Cooper** then played with the **Vauxhalls** and the **Fruit Eating Bears**, while **George Peckham** was later a member of the **Kinsleys**, **Earl Royce & the Olympics** and the **Fourmost**.

After a short spell on the London scene, **Don Alcyd** appeared again in Liverpool as a member of the **Delmont Four**, while **Pete Jones** joined **Groups Inc.** and after that played with the **New Avengers**. Vocalist **Jimmy McManus** firstly disappeared from the scene but in 1965 was back as a member of the **Blackwells**, while **Jack Curtis** joined the **Secrets**.

That was the Sixties' story of the **Renegades**, but in 1978 their name appeared again - on the revival compilation 'Mersey Survivors', where they were featured with the songs *Hippy Hippy Shake* and *My Babe*. In the end this was more a recording session than a real band and of the **Renegades** from the Sixties obviously only **George Peckham** and **Pete Jones** were featured. However, at least there were two recordings made under the name of the **Renegades**, sadly their only ones.

Despite the changes in the line-up and the short time that the **Renegades** were on the scene in the Sixties it was a really impressive group and has left behind a good name that still is remembered very well.

Discography

Nothing was ever released by the **Renegades** in the Sixties but it is known that they were recorded in early 1964 (?) by **John Schroeder** for the planned 'Oriole' sampler 'Cavern Alive', which in the end did not come out and accordingly, it is unknown which songs were recorded.

Tracks on compilations
Hippy Hippy Shake	on '**Mersey Survivors**'	**UK- Raw RWLP 104 / 1978**
My Babe	on '**Mersey Survivors**'	**UK- Raw RWLP 104 / 1978**

The RENEGADES

THE RHYTHM & BLUES INC.

It all started when a Beat group was formed by some pupils at the Catholic school in Southport in the early Sixties. Amongst them were **Pete Kelly** as vocalist, **John McCaffrey** on bass and the drummer **Pete 'Ollie' Halsall**. This band of course did not last too long and while **Pete Halsall** later switched to guitar and went on to play with such famous recording groups as **Timebox** and **Patto**, the other two formed a new group in 1963 under the name of **Rhythm & Blues Incorporated**. But the first line-up did not stay together and the original guitarist **Mike Foden** and the drummer **Barry Tweedale** were very soon replaced again. After these changes, the group consisted of:

Pete Kelly	(voc)
George Eccles	(lg)
Mike McKay	(rg)
John McCaffrey	(bg)
Alan Menzies	(dr)

George Eccles and **Alan Menzies** came from the **Gems**, formerly known as **Chris & the Quiet Ones**, a group already established on the local scene. Prior to that, **Alan Menzies** had been a member of the Liverpool school band **The Kestrels**, as well as of **Jan & the Vendettas** from Southport. **George Eccles** left again and was replaced by **Barry Womersley** (lg/voc), who came from the **Diplomats**, who were very popular on the local scene.

The **Rhythm & Blues Inc.** very soon became the No.1 group in Southport and at the same time became a steady and important part of Liverpool's Merseybeat scene.

Fontana signed the group in 1964 and in the same year their first single was released with a great version of the **Kingsmen** hit *Louie, Louie*, which was a real knockout!

It was coupled with an interesting version of the **Carl Perkins**' standard *Honey Don't*. This record deserved to become a big hit, but unfortunately it failed to make the charts. This may have been because the group's music, and thus the record, was not as catchy as the fans at large liked it. However, *Louie, Louie* really had everything needed to make a good Beat record and therefore it is very hard to understand why it was ignored that way.

In 1965, there were some more changes in the line-up and the first to leave was **Barry Womersley**, who joined the **Big Three** and after that played with the **Clayton Squares**. He was replaced by **Bill Lovelady**.

Next to leave was **Alan Menzies**, who became a member of the **Tabs** and later played with the **Expressions** from Liverpool. His replacement in the **Rhythm & Blues Inc.** was **Ian Magee**, who came from **Mike Dee & the Detours**. Besides this, the group was joined by **John Surguy** (sax) and **Colin Ashton** (tr) as additional members.

For mysterious reasons, the **Rhythm & Blues Inc.** did not get a second chance to record and it was probably in 1966 when the group changed its name to **Pete Kelly's Solution** and continued successfully on the scene.

They were signed to Decca and in 1968 released a great single with the **Grass Roots** song *Midnight Confessions*, which was coupled with the group's original *If Your Love Don't*

Swing. The record sold quite well but again failed to make the charts. Despite this, it was re-released towards the end of the year, this time coupled with *The House That Jack Built*, which was played by **Bernie & the Buzz Band** from Liverpool.

At this point we have to come back to the former **Rhythm & Blues Inc.** members **Barry Womersley**, **George Eccles** and **Alan Menzies**, who in 1967 had teamed up again in a group called **Wall Street Diversion**, together with **Brent Pickthall** (bg) and a Scot named **'Tam'** as sax player.

In 1968, this group broke up again and **Barry Womersley**, together with **John McCaffrey** and **John Surguy** from **Pete Kelly's Solution** plus original **Rhythm & Blues Inc.** drummer **Barry Tweedale** and **Alan Solomon** (key/sax) formed the group **Jasmin-T**.

A little later **Barry Tweedale** was replaced again by **Alan Menzies**, while **Brent Pickthall** took over the bass guitar in the **Pete Kelly's Solution**, who most probably broke up in the very early Seventies. **Ian Magee** appeared again on the scene in the Eighties as a drummer with the **Swinging Blue Jeans** and **Pete Kelly** obviously went solo in the cabaret circuit.

In 1969, **Jasmin-T** cut a single with a musically up-dated version of *Some Other Guy,* which was coupled with the bluesy **Barry Womersley** original *Evening.* This interesting record was also released on the Metronome label in Germany, and sold quite well over there but failed to become a chart success.

In June 1969 the group played the famous 'Top Ten' in Hamburg for one month and from there went on tour in Denmark, where **Barry Womersley**, for some reason became unnerved, sold his guitar and returned to Southport. The others kept playing in Denmark but in 1970 they also returned to Southport where they disbanded.

In 1975, **Barry Womersley** and **John Surguy** were members of the group **Inner Sleeve**, which probably also included **John McCaffrey** again. This group released a single for EMI with the **John Surguy** original *Here We Go* and then disappeared again from the scene.

Barry Womersley went solo after that and cut the single *Standing On The Corner* in 1977, produced by none other than **Bruce Welch** of the **Shadows**. After that, **Barry Womersley** disappeared from the scene for several years and only in 1983 was back with another solo single, but *You're My Wife* also did not make it. **Alan Menzies**, together with **George Eccles** and **Brent Pickthall**, formed a trio in 1970.

For a while they played without a name at the 'Westend Club' in Southport, but then carried on as **Jasmin-T**. At the instigation of **Lally Stott** and together with the girl singer **Sharon Day**, they went down to Italy, where they were meant to appear as a replacement for **Middle Of The Road** in the **Lally Stott** productions. Somehow, this did not work out and **Sharon Day** returned to England, while the group had a longer residence in the sunny South, was signed by RCA Italiano and in 1972 released the single *Sands Of Sahara*.

In 1974, **George Eccles** left the group and was replaced by **Terry Walters**. In this line-up, **Jasmin-T** cut the album 'Direct from Liverpool', which was most probably a private release, sold at gigs. The lead guitarist now changed quite often and after one more single, *Wait A Minute* for the Danish CBS label in 1979, **Jasmin-T** became a **Beatles** tribute band under the name of **The Bootles**.

They were still with **Brent Pickthall** and **Alan Menzies**, and in the beginning of the

Eighties cut a nice album with **Beatles** numbers on the Bulgarian 'Balkanton' label. This group has settled down in Denmark and is still going strong all over Scandinavia, with band leader **Alan Menzies** being the only surviving original member.

In November 1994 the **Rhythm & Blues Inc.** gave a very successful revival concert in Southport but all that is known about the line-up is that **Barry Womersley** and **Pete Kelly** were part of it.

<u>Single discography</u>
Louie Louie / Honey Don't   UK- Fontana TF 524 / 1964

<u>as **Pete Kelly's Solution**</u>:
Midnight Confessions / If Your Love Don't Swing   UK- Decca F.12755 / 1968
Midnight confessions / <u>Bernie & the Buzz Band</u>: The House That Jack Built
                                                                                    UK- Decca F.22829 / 1968
<u>release of **Jasmin-T**</u>:
Some Other Guy / Evening   G- Metronome 25158 / 1969

(for further releases of **Jasmin-T**, **Inner Sleeve**, **Barry Womersley** and **The Bootles** – please see story)

THE RICHMOND GROUP

This group was formed in Liverpool under the name **The Poets** in 1964, much too late for an international breakthrough as the Merseybeat already started to lose its leading role in the worldwide music business. As there already was a recording group from Glasgow with the same name, the Liverpool band became **The Richmond Group**, following a suggestion by **Bob Wooler**. Around the same time the second vocalist **Arthur Alcock** left the group and was replaced by **Dave Kerrigan**, who came from **Ricardo & the Toreadors**.

Accordingly the **Richmond** (the 'Group' was later dropped from the name) consisted of the following musicians:

Eddie Cave	**(voc)**
Dave Kerrigan	**(voc)**
Barry David	**(g/voc)**
Barry Wheldon	**(g)**
Howie Jones	**(bg)**
Peter Taylor	**(dr)**

It was quite unusual at this time to have two vocalists in the line-up of a Beat group, and the **Richmond** didn't just have two, they had two great ones.

In 1965, the **Richmond** were chosen to be featured on the Ember live compilation 'Liverpool Today', which was recorded at the 'Cavern'.

Besides **Earl Preston's Realms** and the **Michael Allen Group**, the **Richmond** were featured with the songs *That's All Right, I Shall Not Be Moved, Cops And Robbers, I'm Alright* and the great folksy *I Won't Let You Down*, which was a group's original.

Their music was a bit of a mixture of Folk and Rhythm & Blues, which was interesting and attractive. The **Richmond** on that album were deemed to be 'one of the youngest and most exciting new groups from Liverpool' by **Bob Wooler,** which was a justified comment, based on the record. Although the group left a good impression behind on this compilation, this was not followed by a contract with a record company and this could have been the reason for **Eddie Cave** to leave.

He teamed up with the **Sextet**, that recently had parted from their singer **Terry Hines** and this new group then continued as **Eddie Cave & the Fix** - another story in this book.

A little later **Mike Hart** (voc/g/sax) joined the **Richmond** after having played before with the **Roadrunners**, **Henry's Handful**, the **Kinsleys** and the **Krew**.

Bob Wooler arranged a meeting for the group with the well known record producer **Andrew 'Loog' Oldham** and, also in 1965, he recorded some songs with the **Richmond** for the new Immediate label, but nothing was released anymore as the **Richmond** disbanded again at Christmas 1965.

There is a rumour that **Howie Jones** shortly before the split-off was replaced by **Dennis Swale**, who formerly amongst others had played with the **Dimensions** and the **Groupiers**, but this is not absolutely sure.

However, **Howie Jones**, **Barry David**, **Barry Wheldon** and **Peter Taylor** disappeared from the scene while **Mike Hart** first teamed up with a new group under the name **Mike Hart & the Moon Dogs** and then became a member of **Liverpool Scene**, who also included poet **Adrian Henry**.

Mike Hart then started a solo career and released three albums and on one of those, the artists were named as **Mike Hart & the Comrads**, although this was certainly not a steady band. **Dave Kerrigan** formed a vocal trio under the name **The Signs**, consisting of **Dave Kerrigan**, **Tony Burns** and **Pete O'Connell**. They were always backed by the **Times** and recorded for Decca, but this is another story that can be followed in this book.

Discography

Tracks on compilations:

That's All Right	on '**Liverpool Today - Live At the Cavern**'	**UK-Ember NR 5028 / 1965**
I Shall Not Be Moved	on '**Liverpool Today - Live At the Cavern**'	**UK-Ember NR 5028 / 1965**
Cops 'n' Robbers	on '**Liverpool Today - Live At the Cavern**'	**UK-Ember NR 5028 / 1965**
I'm Alright	on '**Liverpool Today - Live At the Cavern**'	**UK-Ember NR 5028 / 1965**
I Won't Let You Down	on '**Liverpool Today - Live At the Cavern**'	**UK-Ember NR 5028 / 1965**

The **Richmond Group** was signed for the Immediate label in 1965, and **Andrew 'Loog' Oldham** produced some songs with them that sadly were not released as the group broke up shortly after these recordings. So it is sadly unknown which songs were recorded.

JOHNNY RINGO & THE COLTS

From this group's name it may be concluded that this was a Country & Western outfit but, on the contrary, it was a real Beat group formed in Liverpool by **Fred Fargher** (aka **Johnny Ringo**) and **Les Holt** in the very early Sixties.

It was undoubtedly one of the first Beat groups on Merseyside, but also one of the unlucky ones who never made a breakthrough on the national scene. **Johnny Ringo & the Colts**, as they were named right from the beginning, originally consisted of:

Johnny Ringo	**(voc/g)**
Les Holt	**(g)**
John Smith	**(bg)**
Derek Kay	**(dr)**

Derek Kay was replaced by **John Weathers** for a very short time. He then left again after some gigs because **Derek Kay** returned. **John Weathers** moved to South Wales, where he later played with the **Raiders** and **Peter Shane & the Vikings**.

Johnny Ringo & the Colts were without a manager for a long time and maybe this was the reason that the group did not have any great success and did not obtain a recording contract. But they had a lot of engagements in the leading clubs on Merseyside they must have had really good musical quality.

In 1963, **Johnny Ringo & the Colts** recorded an EMI acetate with the songs *Mean Woman* and *Baby You Make Me Cry*, but this was sadly never followed by a real record.

296

It was probably in 1964 that **Gerry Jackson**, the brother of **Searchers** vocalist **Tony Jackson**, took over the management and things started to go better for the group.

Les Holt had to leave for business reasons and he was replaced by **Neil Ford** (voc/g/harp), who came from the **Vaaveros** and who around that time was also asked to join the **T.T.s**. But after a couple of months, **Les Holt** returned to the group and took up his old place again while **Neil Ford** went down to London, where he became a professional musician. When he returned to Liverpool he joined **Bernie & the Buzz Band** in 1968.

It was sadly too late for **Johnny Ringo & the Colts** to join the Merseybeat boat of national or international stardom and, as far as it is known, there was nothing more recorded by the group. So after their split in 1966, only a good name, and of course that interesting acetate remained. All the members disappeared from the scene and probably quit show business. **Johnny Ringo** sadly died much too young in 1982.

Discography

Johnny Ringo & the Colts never released a record, but recorded the following acetate of which the A-side was an original by the group:

Mean Woman / Baby You Make Me Cry   **UK- EMI   acetate / 1963**

THE ROADRUNNERS

Formed in Liverpool in 1963, it did not take too long until the **Roadrunners** had established themselves as one of the leading Rhythm & Blues groups of the Beat city and had also obtained nationwide popularity. In an interview, **George Harrison** of the **Beatles** once described the **Rolling Stones** as being almost as good as the **Roadrunners**. This certainly overshot the mark a bit, but it also shows what kind of importance and acceptance the **Roadrunners** had in Liverpool at that time. In their original line-up, the group consisted of the following musicians:

Mike Hart	(voc/g/sax)
Dave Percy	(g/voc)
Pete MacKay	(bg)
John Peacock	(p)
Dave Boyce	(dr)

Pete MacKay was a former member of the **Tremeloes** (not to be confused with **Brian Poole**'s group) and he had also played with the **Tenabeats**, where he had met up with **Mike Hart**.

The **Roadrunners** very soon went to Hamburg where they had a long residence at the famous 'Star-Club'. They became a steady part of the so-called 'Star-Club' scene and, with one exception; all their records were recorded 'live' at the European 'Mecca of Beat' and originally released in Germany.

In 1964, **Dave Percy** left. He was perhaps the same musician, **Dave Percival,** who played in groups like the **Climbers**, **Pawns**, the **Kinsleys** and the **Epics**.

Mike Hart took over the lead guitar and new members joined in the shape of **NickCarver** (sax/fl) and the American **John Phillips** (sax), who formerly apparently played with **Danny & the Juniors**. It couldhave been this line-up that **John Schroeder** recorded for the planned Oriole compilation 'Cavern Alive', which sadly was not released in the end.

In 1965, the only studio recording of the **Roadrunners** was released with the EP 'In Pantomania', which was recorded by 'Cavern Sound' as a special edition for the Liverpool University, but the only typical **Roadrunners** song on this EP is the title *Cry, Cry, Cry,* while the instrumental *Fun At Twenty-one,* as well as the jokey rewrite of *Leaving Of Liverpool* seem to have been more studio games, from which the real quality of the **Roadrunners** can not be recognised. Of course, the whole record was more a joke than a serious one and the fourth title on that EP *If You Want To Know The Time* is a spoken sketch by students **Chris Edwards** and **Clive Wood**.

5,000 copies of the EP were pressed, and 10 of them were special copies that featured a sketch about the Royal Family with the title *My Husband And I*, but this of course was banned by Lord Chamberlain. This EP is a very expensive item these days.

The **Roadrunners** released one album on the German Ariola label with 'Twist Time im Star-Club Hamburg - Nr. 4', which, amongst others, featured Rhythm & Blues standards like *You Can Make It If You Try, Hoochie Koochie Man*, **Arthur Alexander**'s *You'd Better Move On* and a great version of *Slow Down* - all live recordings, of course. From this album the songs *Little Ruby/Beautiful Delilah* and *Slow Down/Roadrunner* were coupled out on single.

The **Roadrunners** also shared one album with Newcastle's **Shorty & Them** on the 'Star-Club' label. This was also a live recording from the 'Star-Club' with the title 'Star-Club Show 2' and featured songs like *Mary Ann, Have You Ever Had The Blues, My Baby Left Me, Cry, Cry, Cry* and *Got My Mojo Working*. It is interesting that, probably in 1965, a single was released in France with *Mary Ann* from this Philips album and *You Can Make It If You Try* from the Ariola long player.

In March 1965, **Bob Harrison** (tr) joined the **Roadrunners**, who slowly started to disband. In August of the same year, **Mike Hart** became a member of the **Kinsleys** and later played with **Henry's Handful**, the **Krew** (aka the **Crew**), the **Richmond Group**, **Mike Hart & the Moon Dogs** and **Liverpool Scene** before he recorded some solo albums. He was replaced in the **Roadrunners** by **Mike Byrne** (voc), a former member of **Mike Byrne & the Thunderbirds** and **Them Grimbles**, while the lead guitar was taken over by **Mike Kontzle** who came from the **Chick Graham & the Coasters** and before that had already played with the **Beatwoods**.

In September 1965, **John Phillips**, **Dave Boyce** and **Nick Carver** left, and while **John Phillips** became a member of the **Crew**, the others disappeared from the scene.

Drummer **Terry McCusker** from the **Valkyries** then joined the **Roadrunners**. Besides this, sax player **Dennis Overton**, who had formerly played with **John O'Hara & the Playboys,** may have been a member, but this information is very doubtful.

At the end of 1965, the **Roadrunners** disbanded totally after **Pete MacKay** and **John Peacock** were the only remaining original members. **Mike Byrne** got married and quit show business but rejoined in 1966 as a member of the **Cordes**, who later became **French Benefit** and **Colonel Bagshot's Incredible Bucket Band**, who also included **Terry McCusker** and **Mike Kontzle** again.

After that **Mike Byrne** became a solo performer on the cabaret scene but in 1995 he joined a group called **Persuader** who also included **Wally Sheppard** (bg) and **Dave Gore** (rg) from the Sixties line-up of **Earl Preston & the TTs**, **Nick Arnott** (dr) from **the Pressmen**, as well as **Dave Myers** (lg), who had played with a lot of Merseybeat groups, like **Cliff Roberts' Rockers** and **The Pawns**. This group later changed its name to **Rocket 88**, but then broke up. **Mike Byrne** joined the **Juke Box Eddies**.

To avoid confusion, it should be pointed out that in 1962 there was a short-lived Beat group with the name **The Roadrunners** in Liverpool, but this was a completely different band and had no connection with the recording group. Those **Roadruners** consisted of:

Brian ???	**(voc)**	- ex **Carribeans**
Pete Cook	**(g/voc)**	ex **Topspots** and **Dee & the Dynamites**
Ken Colly	**(bg)**	- ex **Columbians**
John Bedson (dr)		- ex **Four Clefs**

This group never recorded and, because it was so short-lived, they never had any outstanding success and the only members that appeared again on the scene were **John Bedson**, who became a member of the **Challengers** and then played with the **Harlems**, and **Peter Cook**, who later played with the **Kansas City Five**, **Groups Inc.**, **Earl Royce & the Olympics**, the **Trend**, as well as with the new formed **Faron's Flamingos** in the Seventies.

Single discography
Little Ruby / Beautiful Delilah (Live)   G- Ariola 10794 AT / 1964
Roadrunner / Slow Down   G- Ariola 18078 AT / 1964

Different French release:
You Can Make It If You Try / Mary Ann (Live)   F- Byg   529.705 / 1965

EP discography
IN PANTOMANIA   UK- Pantomania (Cavern Sounds) 2.BSN.L7 / 1965
- Cry, Cry, Cry / Fun At Twenty-one / If You Want To Know The Time / The Leaving Of Liverpool
(Please note that only *Cry, Cry, Cry* and the jokey rewriting of *The Leaving Of Liverpool* were played by the **Roadunners**, while *Fun At Twenty-one* was an instrumental (by the **Roadrunners**?) and the other track was a sketch by **Chris Edwards** and **Clive Wood**)

LP discography
STAR-CLUB SHOW 2   G- Star-Club 158.001 / 1964
- Mary Ann / Have You Ever Had The Blues / My Baby Left Me / Hitchhike / Cry, Cry, Cry / Got My Mojo Working
———— plus 5 tracks by **Shorty & Them** from Newcastle

TWIST-TIME IM 'STAR-CLUB' HAMBURG - 4   G- Ariola   71224 IT / 1965
- Rip It Up / You Can Make It If You Try / Little Ruby / Baby You Don't Have To Go / Slow Down / That's All Right / Beautiful Delilah / Long Tall Sally / Hoochie Koochie Man / You'd Better Move On / Roadrunner

Tracks on compilations
Have You Ever Had The Blues on **'Star-Club Informationsplatte'** G- Star-Club 111.371 / 1964
Beautiful Delilah   on **'Rock and Beat im Star-Club'** G- Ariola   70982 IT / 1965
(Please note that all German and French releases were live recordings from the 'Star-Club', Hamburg)

Unreleased tracks:
The Roadrunners in 1964 recorded under the wings of John Schroder for the Oriole sampler 'Cavern Alive', which was not released and therefore it is not known which songs were recorded

THE ROADRUNNERS

CLIFF ROBERTS' ROCKERS

Well, this was one of the real pioneering groups on the Liverpool music scene, which was formed by singer/guitarist **Cliff Roberts** on the west side of the River Mersey in the late Fifties. Before this, he was a member of the **Sinners**.

Beside lots of US Rock 'n' Roll numbers, the band mainly played **Cliff Richard** material and within a short time became very popular along Merseyside. In their original line-up, the group consisted of the following musicians:

Cliff Roberts	**(voc)**
Frank Bowen	**(g)**
Dave Myers	**(g)**
Malcolm Linnell	**(bg)**
Alan Schroeder	**(dr)**

It is known that lead guitarist **Frank Bowen** had formerly played with a group called **The Teenbeats**, while the other members were probably newcomers to the scene.

Cliff Roberts' Rockers played all the important venues of that time and were the main attraction at many concerts, while other groups who later became well known were still the supporting acts, for example the **Beatles**. Sadly, this really good group became less important when the Beat became more and more popular and so **Cliff Roberts Rockers** broke up again in the early Sixties, without having released a record. Nothing was heard of **Malcolm Linnell** after that and he probably quit the music business, as **Cliff Roberts** did, when he disbanded his group.

Frank Bowen, one of the most talented guitarists on the Merseybeat scene, first joined the **Blue Stars**, a Glaswegian group, who had obviously settled in the Liverpool area at that time.

After that he played with the **Lonely Ones** and then became a member of **Howie Casey & the Seniors**. When that band split, he joined **Lee Curtis & the All Stars** and was still a member when this group developed into **Pete Best & the Original All Stars**. He then joined the **Pathfinders**, had a short spell with **Rory Storm & the Hurricanes** and then became a member of **Mike & the Merseymen**, who changed their name to **The Trends** and went down to London.

When the **Trends** broke up, **Frank Bowen** stayed in London and became a member of the **Bootleggers**, led by **Brian Auger**. Then he returned to Liverpool where he joined **Earl Royce & the Olympics**. He sadly died much too young still in the Sixties.

Dave Myers at first played with the **Climbers** and then became a founder member of the **Renegades** from Liverpool. In 1963 he joined **The Pawns** with whom he toured Germany and where he stayed until this group disbanded. After that **Dave Myers** disappeared from the scene, but in the early Nineties was back as a member of the newly formed **Johnny Sandon & the Specials**.

After **Johnny Sandon** left, this band continued under the name **The Mersey Specials** on the club circuit in Liverpool. He is still active today as a member of a group called **Tempest**. **Alan Schroeder** joined the **Black Knights**, a trio that was also featured in the motion picture 'Ferry Cross The Mersey' in 1964. After the band released a single, **Alan Schroeder** left and became a freelance drummer on the scene. In the early Nineties he was a member of **Johnny Sandon & the Specials** and also played with the follow-on band the **Mersey Specials**. In addition to him and **Dave Myers**, they included **Mike Swift** (voc/rg) and **Colin Roberts** (a brother of **Cliff Roberts**) on bass guitar. Then **Alan Schroeder** reformed the **Black Knights** who are still around these days.

At the beginning of the Nineties, **Cliff Roberts** stepped back into show business and formed a new group under the name **Cliff Roberts' Rockers**, sometimes introduced as the **Cliff Roberts Band**. Besides him, this group initially consisted of the following well-known musicians:

> **Nicky Crouch (lg)-** who in the Sixties was with **Faron's Flamingos** and the **Mojos**
> **Dave Gore (rg)-** ex **Johnny Tempest & the Tornadoes** and **Earl Preston & the T.T.s**
> **Wally Shepard (bg)-** ex **Johnny Tempest & theTornadoes, Earl Preston & the T.T.s,**
> **Cy Tucker & the T.T.s, Vic Wright & the T.T.s** and **Amos Bonny & the T.T.s**
> **Sam Hardie (p/voc)-** the legendary pianist of **King Size Taylor & the Dominoes**
> **Brian Johnson (dr)-** who in the Sixties played with groups like **The Strangers, Rory Storm and the Hurricanes, Mark Peters & the Silhouettes** and **The Tabs**.

Later, **Nicky Crouch** was replaced by **Steve Roberts**, the younger brother of band leader **Cliff Roberts**, a really good guitarist who had formerly been a member of the re-formed **Faron's Flamingos**.

This group played the Rock 'n' Roll songs of the Fifties again as well as **Cliff Richard** material, which suited the voice of **Cliff Roberts** just like in the 'good old days'. But the group almost exclusively played benefit concerts for the 'Mersey Cats' or 'New Brighton Rock' until it disbanded again.

Cliff Roberts quit show business, while **Dave Gore** and **Wally Shepard** joined **Persuader**, who later changed their name to **Rocket 88** and then broke up again.

Sam Hardie reformed the original **Dominoes** who occasionally also appear again with their old singer as **King Size Taylor & the Dominoes**, while **Brian Johnson** recently joined the reformed **Mojos** under the leadership of **Nicky Crouch**.

DALE ROBERTS & THE JAYWALKERS

Insiders predicted a bright future for this band, formed in Ellesmere Port on the Wirral (on the west side of the River Mersey) in the late Fifties and, in fact, **Dale Roberts & the Jaywalkers** had a large following in the Liverpool area in the early Sixties. Rock 'n' Roll and a driving Beat was the mark of the band consisting of:

Dale Roberts	**(voc)**
Dave Williams	**(g/voc)**
Phil Rodgers	**(g)**
Ian Boyle	**(bg)**
Billy Buck	**(dr)**

All the musicians were the founding members of the group from their Skiffle days, whereby **Dave Williams** before that was a member of the **Firecrests**. It is important to point out that **Dale Roberts & the Jaywalkers** had nothing in common with **Peter Jay & the Jaywalkers**.

In spite of the fact that they were amateurs, they had regular appearances at the 'Cavern', as well as at all the other important clubs along Merseyside.

When **Ian Boyle** left the group, **Phil Rodgers** switched to bass guitar, while in **Terry Willet**, a new rhythm guitarist joined **Dale Roberts & the Jaywalkers**, but he did not stay too long and when he left again, **Dale Roberts** himself took over on rhythm guitar. No other member joined the band.

In January 1962, the group was voted No. 20 in the popularity poll of 'Mersey Beat', which was a big success as it has to be taken into account that there were already a few hundred groups on the scene at that time. Because of that placing, a recording contract was offered to **Dale Roberts & the Jaywalkers**. However, before it was signed the group disbanded in April 1962, because leader **Dale Roberts** wanted to get married in May and so quit show business.

Ian Boyle and **Terry Willet** disappeared from the scene, while **Phil Rodgers** and **Billy Buck** joined the **Remo Four**. **Billy Buck** left that group quite soon again and joined a Liverpool dance band. When the **Remo Four** split in the late Sixties, **Phil Rodgers** went down to London, where he joined a Country band. **Dave Williams** initially became a member of **Group One** and then was a founder member of the **Four Originals**. A little later, **Dale Roberts** joined them, returning to the music business only a few months after having left it.

Besides **Dale Roberts** and **Dave Williams**, they included **Phil Howard** (bg) who had played with the **Defenders**, and **Colin Middlebrough** (dr), who was a former member of the **Kansas City Five**. This band, sometimes appearing as **Dale Roberts & the Jaywalkers** (especially at 'Mersey Cats' concerts) in the Nineties, was joined by **Derek Green** as rhythm guitarist and as an additional singer. In the Sixties, he had been a member of the **Del Renas** and the **Motifs**.

When **Phil Howard** died in May 2005, **Terry Fisher** took his place. He had also played with the **Del Renas** and the **Motifs** in the Sixties. The group was also joined by **Phil Howard**'s daughter **Catherine Howard**, as an additional singer.

In January 2007 **George Roberts**, as his real name was, died unexpectedly, but the **Four Originals** did not add a new member to the line-up and are still playing on the scene.

EARL ROYCE & THE OLYMPICS

The forerunner of this group was most probably the band **Tommy & the Olympics**, formed in Liverpool in 1961. Who this mysterious **Tommy** was is sadly not known but he may have been the leader of the group **Tommy & the Satellites** later.

This is a supposition, but it is known for a fact that in early 1963, **Billy Kelly** (aka **Earl Royce**) was a member of the **Olympics**, who then changed their name to **Earl Royce & the Olympics** and appeared in the following line-up:

Earl Royce	**(voc)**
Peter Cook	**(g/voc)**
Derek Nodwell	**(g)**
Stu Hazzard	**(bg/voc)**
Jimmy Jordan	**(dr)**

Peter Cook had also just joined and was a former member of the **Topspots**, **Dee & the Dynamites**, the short-lived **Roadrunners** (II), the **Kansas City Five** and **Groups Inc**. For a time he changed his name to **Pete Melody**, while **Jimmy Jordan** sometimes called himself **Jimmy Young**.

Stu Hazzard, in the same tradition, was also named **Kenny Lazzard** occasionally and so it is more than probable that he was identical with the former bass guitarist with the **Five Stars**, the forerunners to the **Midnighters**, who backed **Gus Travis** and **Freddie Starr**.

Derek Nodwell soon left the group and was replaced by **Brian Myers**, who used the stage name **Brian Dee** and was identical with (the second) 'Dee' of **Dee & the Dynamites**, one of the groups who preceded the legendary **Undertakers**.

Earl Royce & the Olympics quickly became a top act in the North and toured Germany quite often, where they mainly appeared in the various 'Star-Clubs' and went down very well.

In 1964, the group was chosen to take part in the motion picture 'Ferry Cross The Mersey', where they are featured with an up-tempo version of *Shake A Tail Feather*, which is included on the US release of the corresponding soundtrack.

This was probably their first recording ever and it was followed by their first single, a nice, catchy version of **Doris Day**'s *Que Sera Sera,* which for sure was one of the outstanding records of that time and later became a real Merseybeat classic. Of course, this record helped the group a lot to increase its popularity but for incomprehensible reasons, it failed to make the charts. The second single *Guess Things Happen That Way* once again showed the musical ability of the group and was an interesting Merseybeat record, but all in all was not as strong as its predecessor and so it was no real surprise that it also did not make it.

During 1964 **Earl Royce & the Olympics** sometimes backed girl singer **Rita Hughes**, better known on the scene as **'Jeannie'** and who had already had two singles released with her old group **Jeannie & the Big Guys**, but this is a story on its own which also can be followed in this book.

In 1965 **Brian Dee** put aside his guitar and stepped in front as the group's second singer. When **Peter Cook** left a little later to form a new group under the name **The Trend** (without the 's'), he was replaced by **George Peckham**, who had formerly played with groups like the **Skylarks**, the **Renegades** from Liverpool, **Lee Curtis & the All Stars**, **Groups Inc.**, the **Pawns** and the **Kinsleys**. In the Seventies, **Peter Cook** was a member of the newly formed **Faron's Flamingos**.

George Peckham only stayed until December 1965 and then joined the **Fourmost**. He was replaced in **Earl Royce & the Olympics** by **Frank Bowen**, an excellent guitarist, who was a former member of various groups such as **Cliff Roberts' Rockers**, **Howie Casey & the Seniors**, **Lee Curtis & the All Stars**, the **Pathfinders**, **Rory Storm & the Hurricanes**, the **Trends**, as well as some others. He sadly died much too young shortly after he had joined the group in 1966. It is not known who replaced him in **Earl Royce & the Olympics**, who continued until 1967.

Billy Kelly, alias **Earl Royce**, left show business and went back to a normal day job, and **Jimmy Jordan** became a member of the **Vince Earl Attraction** until he also quit the music business in 1973. All the other members of **Earl Royce & the Olympics** disappeared from the scene.

So what's left of this great group who were popular in North and Middle England and also mainly in Scotland, where they were one of the most successful live acts for a long time, is a good name that is still remembered these days - and of course some records, worth looking out for.

<u>Single discography</u>
Que Sera Sera / I Really Do   UK- Columbia   DB 7433 / 1964
Guess Things Happen That Way / Sure To Fall   UK- Parlophone R 5261 / 1965

<u>Tracks on compilations:</u>
Shake A Tail Feather   on **'Ferry Cross The Mersey'** US-United Artists UAS 6387/ 1964

(Please note that this compilation is the US release of the original soundtrack album from the legendary film)

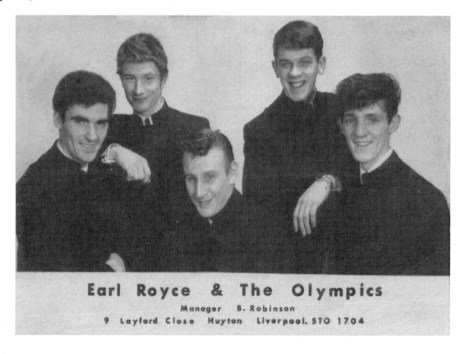

Earl Royce & The Olympics
Manager B. Robinson
9 Layford Close Huyton Liverpool. STO 1704

THE RUNAWAYS

This group was formed in the area of Wavertree by **Dave Potter** (voc/rg) and **Chris Finley** (org/g/voc), most probably in the middle of 1963.

As the Liverpool music press did not pay too much attention to the group, it was very difficult to recreate this story, but it is known that **Chris Finley** left the **Runaways** as early as 1964 to become a member of the **Kruzads**. After that he played with the **Masterminds** and then joined the **Fruit Eating Bears**. He later appeared again as a member of **Confucius**, who had developed from the **Hideaways** and after that he played with the reformed **Merseybeats** and **Herman's Hermits**. After he had left in 1964, the line-up of the **Runaways** consisted of:

Dave Potter	**(voc/rg)**
Tony Webster	**(lg/voc)**
Marion Hill	**(org/voc)**
David Cato	**(bg)**
Roy Smith	**(dr)**

The female keyboarder **Marion Hill** was the direct replacement for **Chris Finley** and before that she had played with the **Memphis Rhythm & Blues Combo**.

Tony Webster had only just joined the **Runaways** at that time as he had formerly played with **Tommy & the Metronomes, Mark Peters & the Cyclones**, the **Cyclones** and from that developed the trio **The Few**, who had only disbanded in 1964. The orginal guitarist with the group most probably was **Dave Davis**.

David Cato and **Roy Smith** were obviously the other remaining original members of the **Runaways** who went into the studio in late 1964, or early 1965 to cut an acetate with the songs *Back Again* and *I Remember So Well,* which were both originals by the group. This interesting acetate sadly did not lead to a record contract and so did not help for a bigger breakthrough of the **Runaways,** who continued to play the usual Merseyside gigs without making any headlines.

It was probably in early 1966 that the group was joined by **Bill Kenwright** as additional lead vocalist. Liverpool-born **Bill Kenwright** had started his music career in the early Sixties as a member of the **Chevrolets**, who did not achieve any major importance on the scene. As well as his main profession as an actor, he obviously also continued as a singer on the local music scene and in 1964, he recorded an acetate with the songs *I'll Find A Way* and *Karen*, though it is not known whether he was still backed by the **Chevrolets** on that.

The disc-jockey **Carl Gresham** took over their management and somehow obtained a recording contract with Columbia for **Bill Kenwright & the Runaways**.

In 1967, the single *I Want To Go Back There Again* was released – a nice medium-paced Beat song with a dominating organ, played in the typical commercial way of

307

that time. This record did not make the charts and as it seems, **Bill Kenwright** very soon separated from the **Runaways**, who continued as a group until the end of the Sixties, whereby **Tony Webster** later obviously was replaced by **Bob Wolem** on lead guitar.

After the **Runaways** had disbanded, all the members disappeared from the scene with the exception of **Dave Potter,** who later became the vocalist with the **B-Jays** from Widnes.

Bill Kenwright stayed on the music scene and in 1968 was signed to MGM and had his second single out with the nice ballad *Love's Black And White.* On this record, which he also produced himself, he was accompanied by the orchestra of **Lew Warbeton**.

This record had nothing in common with Beat anymore but sounded much more American with the full orchestral arrangement. It did not become a success although it was also introduced in 'Coronation Street'. After that, only one more record by **Bill Kenwright** was released – *Tiggy* in 1969, which had the same orchestral backing as the preceding one and it was equally unsuccessful. **Bill Kenwright** concentrated on acting again and later founded a production company. Today he is by far the biggest producer of musicals in England and besides this he is the chairman of the internationally successful Everton F.C. football club - what a career . . .

Discography:
Bill Kenwright & the Runaways:
I Want To Go Back There Again / A Walk Through Dreams   **UK- Columbia DB 8239 / 1967**
Bill Kenwright – solo**:**
Love's Black And White / Giving Up   **UK - MGM MGM 1430 / 1968**
Tiggy / House That Fell On Its Face   **UK - MGM MGM 1463 / 1969**
Unreleased tracks:
The Runaways:
Back Again / I Remember So Well   **UK- Emidisc-acetate   / 1965**
Bill Kenwright - solo:
I'll Find A Way / Karen   **UK - acetate   / 1964**

PHIL RYAN & THE CRESCENTS

This group did not come from Liverpool but from the little town of Crewe, where **Phil Ryan & the Crescents**, as they were named right from the beginning, were formed in 1962. They have to be added to the Mersey scene, as Crewe is not too far from Liverpool and the group played a lot more in the Beat centre than in their hometown. The original line-up of **Phil Ryan & the Crescents** consisted of:

Phil Ryan	**(voc)**
Bernard Hibbert	**(g/voc)**
Roger Keay	**(bg)**
Dave Birkenhead	**(dr)**

There may be some doubts that 'Birkenhead' was the drummer's real surname, but this is not too important. The group was semi-professionals at first, as at least two of the members worked for British Rail. Within a very short time they established themselves amongst the busiest groups on the Liverpool club scene, so they most probably became professional musicians very soon.

At the beginning of 1964 **Phil Ryan & the Crescents** went to Germany for two months, where they appeared mainly in the Frankfurt area. When they returned, they were signed to Columbia and in the same year a really great Merseybeat single was released with *Mary Don't You Weep* (arranged by **Phil Ryan**) and *Yes I Will* on the flip-side, which was written by **Bernard Hibbert** and **David Birkenhead**. Both tracks were catchy numbers and good enough to hit the charts, but in the end the record only sold quite well on the local scene.

It took until May 1965 before **Phil Ryan & the Crescents** went into the studio again, where the **Curtis Mayfield** number *Gypsy Woman* was recorded and a little later released as their second single. Again, it was a very interesting record, coupled with the good *Be Honest To Yourself*, but once again wasn't hugely successful, which is quite incomprehensible. The reason for that failure was certainly not the quality of the records or the musical ability of the band. It may have had something to do with the sad fact that the publicity by Columbia was a bit poor.

However, in spite of this unlucky fact, the group did not have to worry about its existence as **Phil Ryan & the Crescents**, in their music similar to the sound of the **Merseybeats**, were a really busy live act in the areas of Liverpool and Manchester.

Because the music press did not pay too much attention to this group after the second single, it is not known whether there were more recording sessions, line-up changes or, indeed, when exactly **Phil Ryan & the Crescents** disbanded, though this was probably in 1966/67.

Nothing was heard about the individual musicians after that.

Single discography:
Mary don't you weep / Yes I will	**UK- Columbia DB 7406 / 1964**
Gypsy woman / Be honest with yourself	**UK- Columbia DB 7574 / 1965**

CHRIS SANDFORD & THE CORONETS

The first group of Wallasey born **Chris Sandford** was named the **Tennessee Disciples,** but he quit the music business to become an actor. After some minor roles he had his breakthrough when he became the aspiring pop singer 'Walter Potts' in the successful TV saga 'Coronation Street'. The song he performed was *Not Too Little, Not To Much* which became very popular with the audience. Decca brought this out as a single in 1963 and it is almost certain that, on the record, **Chris Sandford** was already backed by the musicians with whom he later continued as **Chris Sandford & the Coronets** - in the line up were:

> **Chris Sandford** (voc)
> **Tony Cartwright** (p/voc)
> **Norman Hale** (g/voc)
> **Jim Kent** (bg)
> **Mitch Mitchell** (dr)

Not Too Little, Not Too Much, a catchy up-tempo song climbed to No.17 in the British charts and stayed in the hit parade for nine weeks. It also climbed to No. 27 in the charts of the national music paper 'New Musical Express'. This record was only credited to **Chris Sandford** as probably in the beginning his backing group did not have a name. However, it was a real Beat group that mainly consisted of Liverpool musicians.

In 1964 the second single was released with *You're Gonna Be My Girl* and this time it was credited to **Chris Sandford & the Coronets,** but it was not as successful as the debut, although it was more interesting in its arrangement. The record sold quite well but did not enter the charts.

Shortly after that release the group disbanded when **Chris Sandford** left. He released one more solo single in 1965, with the strange but interesting *I Wish They Wouldn't Always Say I Sound Like The Guy From USA*, which had quite a nice B-side with the folksy *Little Man, Nobody Cares*. This record was not successful and **Chris Sandford** quit the music business to concentrate on his acting.

In 1972, he sang again with a new group under the name **Chris Sandford's Friendship**, who released the single *Listen To The Music* on Decca. He didn't have much success with this and nothing was heard of him or his group again in the music business.

But now back to the **Coronets**, because their story was not finished when **Chris Sandford** left in late 1964. **Mitch Mitchell** became a member of the London recording group **The Riot Squad**, not to be confused with the Liverpool group of the same name, which did not record. At the end of 1965 he was a member of **Georgie Fame & the Blue Flames** and then he joined the **Jimi Hendrix Experience**. The rest is history.

The three Liverpool musicians **Tony Cartwright**, **Norman Hale** and **Jim Kent** stayed in London and formed the **Lively Set** in 1965, together with drummer **Eric Billon** from Swindon, and a lead guitarist from Southampton whose name is sadly not known.

Tony Cartwright took over the lead vocals in the new band, who were signed to PYE in 1965 and in July of that year released the single *Don't Call My Name*, probably a group's original, but sadly was not successful.

The 1966 single *Let The Trumpets Sound,* by a group called **The Lively Set** on Capitol was definitely not from the group that had developed from **Chris Sandford & the Coronets.**

It seems that the **Lively Set**, with mainly Liverpool musicians, were quite successful on the London scene until they disbanded sometime at the end of the Sixties.

Single discography:

Chris Sandford & the Coronets:
Not Too Little, Not Too Much / I'm Looking   UK- Decca F.11778 / 1963
You're Gonna Be My Girl / Don't Leave Me Now   UK- Decca F.11842 / 1964
 (Please note that the first single was only credited to **Chris Sandford**, although it was obviously recorded with the **Coronets**)

Chris Sandford - solo:
I Wish They Wouldn't Always Say I Sound Like The Guy From USA / Little Man, Nobody Cares
                                                                                UK-Fontana TF 633 / 1965

Chris Sandford's Friendship:
Listen To The Music / The Man Who Lost His Smile   UK- Decca F.13348 / 1972

The Lively Set:
Don't Call My Name / What Kind Of Love   UK- PYE 7N 15880 / 1965
 (Please note that the single *Let The Trumpets Sound* by the **Lively Set** on the Capitol label was not by the Liverpool group)

Chris Sandford

THE SEARCHERS

Three separate Liverpool Skiffle groups formed in 1957/1958. There were the **Wreckers** from Kirkdale, with guitarist **Mike Pendergast**, who a little later moved to the **Confederates** who played more Rock 'n' Roll orientated music.

Then there were the **Martinis** from the Sefton Park area, who, in addition to **Bernie Devey** (wb) and **Jimmy Moran** (g) also included the singer and guitarist **Tony Jackson** and drummer **Norman McGarry.**

And last but not least there was a Skiffle group from Kirkdale (probably without a name) which was led by guitarist **John McNally** and besides him included a singer called **'Big Ron'**, **Brian Dolan** (g), **Joe West** (bass) and **Joe Kennedy** (dr).

John McNally and **Mike Pendergast** knew each other from school and in 1959 they decided to form a guitar/vocal duo in style of the **Everly Brothers**. Around the same time the **Martinis** broke up and their singer **Tony Jackson** continued as solo performer in the Liverpool clubs, singing and playing Rock 'n' Roll songs under the name of **Clint Reno**.

One night he met up with **John McNally** and **Mike Pendergast** who had come to one of his performances. They had a chat about music and decided to form a group. Of course, they were in need of a drummer. **Tony Jackson** remembered **Norman McGarry**, his friend from the **Martinis**, and these four then formed the first line-up of the

Johnny Sandon & The Searchers

Searchers at the beginning of 1960. The group's name was adopted from a **John Wayne** western.

Norman McGarry had to leave again as he got a job in a bakery, where he also had to work a night shift. Later he was a member of the **Sassenachs,** who cut a nice single with *That Don't Worry Me* for Fontana.

John McNally and **Mike Pender**, as he now called himself, contacted an old friend from school - **Chris Crummey**, who then joined as their drummer under the name of **Chris Curtis**. Through his parents, **John McNally** knew **Billy Beck**, who at that time was singing Country songs in the clubs, where he was backed by John's father on accordion.

John McNally offered **Billy Beck** the job as lead singer in the new group, as **Tony Jackson** at that time was concentrating on learning the bass guitar. **Billy Beck** agreed and changed his name to **Johnny Sandon**.

So the group was called **Johnny Sandon & the Searchers** and within a very short time became highly popular on the scene. In December 1961 they were placed fifth in the 'Mersey Beat' popularity poll. In spite of that success **Johnny Sandon** and the group separated in 1962. At first the **Remo Four** backed him before he became a solo performer again.

The **Searchers** continued as a quartet in the following line-up:

Tony Jackson	**(voc/bg)**
Mike Pender	**(g/voc)**
John McNally	**(g/voc)**
Chris Curtis	**(dr/voc)**

Les Ackerley, the owner of the famous 'Iron Door' club, became their manager and it was probably in 1962 when he arranged an acetate LP of one of their live appearances at that club to be cut. This included a version of *Sweets For My Sweet*.

In 1963 the **Searchers** were signed to PYE and produced by **Tony Hatch**. Their debut single *Sweets For My Sweet* didn't sell too well at first.

When the **Searchers** returned from the 'Star-Club' in Hamburg, where they had played for a long time, this single had become a giant hit, holding the 'pole position' in the British charts for some weeks and from there it became a hit almost all over the world. The follow-up *Sugar And Spice* was not as successful as their debut but climbed to No. 2 in the charts and became another international best seller.

The Philips recording company wanted in on the action and the next single released in England was a live version of *Sweet Nothings*, taken from the recently released German album 'Sweets For My Sweet' (Live at the 'Star-Club'), just like it's flip-side *What'd I Say*. This single did not make it. The following PYE release *Needles And Pins* became the biggest hit for the **Searchers** when it climbed to No.1 in 1964 in all the important charts.

This outstanding success placed the **Searchers** next to the **Beatles** on the international scene. On this record the lead vocals came from **Mike Pender** for the first time, **Tony Jackson** having sung the other two. The follow-up, *Don't Throw Your Love Away,* another No.1 hit, was also sung by **Mike Pender.**

He then became the band's lead singer, which must have been frustrating and disappointing for **Tony Jackson** and might have been the reason for him leaving the **Searchers** in 1964. He then formed his own group under the name of **Tony Jackson & the Vibrations**, who later became **The Tony Jackson Group**, but this is another story which can be followed in this book. His replacement in the **Searchers** was **Francis McNiece**, who came from London and used the stage name **Frank Allen**. Originally, he had led his own group under the name **Frank Allen & the Skyways** but then was a member of **Cliff Bennett & the Rebel Rousers**.

The **Searchers** had met him during their stay in Hamburg, when **Cliff Bennett & the Rebel Rousers** also played at the 'Star-Club'. He was a good singer and bass guitarist and suited the rest of the group very well. They had continued chart success with records like Someday *We're Gonna Love Again*, the great *When You Walk In The Room* and a superb *What Have They Done To The Rain* in 1964, as well as the tremendous *Goodbye My Love*. Their own composition *When I Get Home*, another superb *Take Me For What I'm Worth* and a relatively unsuccessful *Take It Or Leave It* were released in 1965.

In the same year **The Searchers** also topped the US Billboard with their version of *Love Potion No.9*, which was belatedly coupled out from their first album.

In Germany, a great version of **Fats Domino**'s *I'm Ready* was released on single, and in the Netherlands *Where Have All The Flowers Gone*, together with the 1964 release *What Have They Done To The Rain* confirmed the **Searchers** as the first folk rock group with international stardom. They were later followed by groups like the **Byrds**, **Turtles** or **Leaves**, all with their own individual musical styles, but all influenced by the Liverpool quartet.

Chris Curtis, who in the meantime had also produced groups like **Eddie Cave & the Fyx** and the **Five A.M. Event** (formerly **The Crescendoes**) for PYE, left the group in early 1966 when the Beat boom was slowly coming to an end. He firstly recorded the solo single *Aggravation* with the nice flip-side *Have I Done Something Wrong* and after that formed the group **Roundabout**, where he was the drummer and lead vocalist.

This band, which included musicians like **Jon Lord** (org) and **Ritchie Blackmore** (g) later developed into the super group **Deep Purple**, but at that time **Chris Curtis** had already quit show business - too early as it seems. **Chris Curtis** sadly died in April 2005.

John Blunt then was his successor in the **Searchers**. He had formerly played with **The Tree** and his big idol was **Keith Moon** of **The Who**. He also looked a little bit like him. In this line-up the **Searchers** had their last chart entry with *Have You Ever Loved Somebody* in 1966.

Further PYE releases were the nice *Popcorn Double Feature*, a great version of *Western Union* with the nice flip-side *I'll Cry Tomorrow*. There was also the slightly boring *Second Hand Dealer* and the up-tempo *Everybody Come And Clap Your Hands*, which in its arrangement was a little bit outdated in 1967, not really surprising as this song was taken from the EP 'Four By Four' from 1965.

The **Searchers** switched to Liberty, where they had a great debut with *Umbrella Man,* which at least brought them back on to the TV music shows in England and Germany and which was followed by a good version of the **Andy Kim** song *Shoot 'Em Up Baby*.

But in spite of their quality both records failed to make the charts again, as did the follow-up *Kinky Kathy Abernathy*, which was not as good as the other two, and which was the last release for Liberty in 1969. Interestingly, in 1968, *Somebody Shot The Lollipop-man* was another single released by the **Searchers** on Liberty, but under the name of **Pasha**. This record was a real flop, and it deserved to be as it was a real awful record - the A-side as well as the B-side *Pussy Willow Dragon*.

In 1970 **John Blunt** left to join **Orange Seaweed** and later became a member of the **Love Affair** before he joined the revival band **The Reflections**. He was replaced in the **Searchers** by the Scottish **Billy**

The Searchers with John Blunt

Adamson, who hailed from Glasgow and had formerly played in the backing groups of **Emile Ford**, **Jet Harris**, **P.P. Arnold** and **Screaming Lord Sutch**. This new line-up was signed to RCA and with their first release *Desdemona,* the **Searchers** had a minor hit in the USA. It is worth mentioning the flip-side, the great *The World Is Waiting For Tomorrow*, which would have been good enough to be another A-side.

However, chart success remained an exception although in 1973, a well-arranged version of the **Bee Gees** classic *Spicks And Specks* was released. This was coupled with an even better version of **Neil Sedaka**'s *Solitaire,* which showed clearly the high quality of lead singer **Mike Pender**.

The following album 'Second Take' which also was released in 1973 was not that good and mainly included the second takes of the big **Searchers** hits, but the arrangements were thin and unimaginative. The only exceptions were their single success *Desdemona* and the song *Come On Back To Me*, which became the B-side of the next single *Sing Singer Sing*. That record had a popular Reggae influenced sound and turned out very well, but was also unsuccessful.

The follow-up *Love Is Everywhere* was also a great tune, while the final single for RCA *Vahevala* lost out again a little bit in comparison to its predecessor. In spite of this the **Searchers** had no problems existing as professionals in show business, mainly in Germany where they became a very popular live act.

In 1979 the **Searchers** (still in the same line-up) seriously tried a comeback for the first time when the album 'Searchers' was released on the Sire label. This had some very good reviews and was honestly a great album, which included some outstanding songs like *Hearts In Her Eyes* (in the very best **Searchers** sound) and *Too Late*. A correct decision was made to couple both songs out as singles and they sold quite well.

The following longplayer 'Love's Melodies' again was a good one, but outstanding songs were hardly missing. It is interesting to note that this album was initially intended to be released under the title 'Play For Today' but that only came out as promo copies. On that record, *Love's Melodies*, which became the **Searchers** next single, was not featured but instead of that a terrific version of *Sick And Tired*. This was a real knockout missing on the official release and alone for this song it is worth looking for a promo-copy of 'Play For Today. The **Searchers** were suddenly a group of topical interest again and very close to a real comeback, which for incomprehensible reasons did not happen.

It should be added here that on the first Sire album **Bob Jackson** was featured as keyboard player, but he was never a steady member of the group, while on the second one **Mick Weaver** played the keyboards.

In 1986, the group was close to disbanding when lead vocalist **Mike Pender** left to form his own group under the name of **Mike Pender's Searchers**. At first it was rumoured that the former original member **Tony Jackson** would be included in the line-up, but for unknown reasons it did not happen in the end. Maybe because he re-formed **Tony Jackson & the Vibrations** around that time. **Tony Jackson** died in 2004.

Besides **Mike Pender**, his group then included **Chris Black** (g), **Barry Howell** (bg) and **Steve Carlyle** (dr) and at the beginning of the Nineties released a CD, of course with the old **Searchers** hits again.

Before that, **Mike Pender** had released the solo single *It's Over* in 1986, which had a modern sound but was no great success and was honestly not very exciting.

The other **Searchers**, which these days only include one original member with **John McNally**, (if **Frank Allen** is not considered as such), were joined by **Spencer James** as guitarist and new lead singer, formerly a member of **First Class**, **Nightfly** and **Heyday**.

On the German bootleg album 'Live In Germany' it can be heard that he is a very good singer, but it is also a fact that the voice of **Mike Pender** was too characteristic for the **Searchers**-sound and couldn't just be replaced by another good singer. **Billy Adamson** also left the group, probably after that bootleg.

Single discography

Sweets For My Sweet / It's All Been A Dream	UK- PYE 7N 15533 / 1963
Sugar And Spice / Saints And Searchers	UK- PYE 7N 15566 / 1963
Sweet Nothin's / What'd I Say	UK-Philips BF 1274 / 1963
Needles And Pins / Saturday Night Out	UK- PYE 7N 15594 / 1964
Don't Throw Your Love Away / I Pretend I'm With You	UK- PYE 7N 15630 / 1964
Someday We're Gonna Love Again / Noone Else Could Love You	UK- PYE 7N 15670 / 1964
When You Walk In The Room / I'll Be Missing You	UK- PYE 7N 15694 / 1964
What Have They Done To The Rain / This Feeling Inside	UK- PYE 7N 15739 / 1964
Goodbye My Love / Till I Met You	UK- PYE 7N 15794 / 1965
He's Got No Love / So Far Away	UK- PYE 7N 15878 / 1965
When I Get Home / I'm Never Coming Back	UK- PYE 7N 15950 / 1965
Take Me For What I'm Worth / Too Many Miles	UK- PYE 7N 15992 / 1965
Take It Or Leave It / Don't Hide It Away	UK- PYE 7N 17094 / 1965
Have You Ever Loved Somebody / It's Just The Way	UK- PYE 7N 17170 / 1966
Popcorn Double Feature / Lovers	UK- PYE 7N 17225 / 1967
Western Union / I'll Cry Tomorrow	UK- PYE 7N 17308 / 1967
Second Hand Dealer / Crazy Dreams	UK- PYE 7N 17424 / 1967
Umbrella Man / Over The Weekend	UK- Liberty LBF 15159 / 1968
Shoot 'em Up Baby / Suzanna	UK- Liberty LBF 15202 / 1968
Kinky Kathy Abernathy / Suzanna	UK- Liberty LBF 15240 / 1969

as **Pasha**:

Somebody Shot The Lollipop-man / Pussy Willow Dragon	UK-Liberty LBF 15199 / 1968

Chris Curtis - solo:

Aggravation / Have I Done Something Wrong	UK- PYE 7N 17132 / 1966

The Sassenachs (with **Norman McGarry** on drums):

That Don't Worry Me / All Over You	UK-Fontana TF 518 / 1964

Different German releases:

Sweets For My Sweet / Listen To Me (Live)	G- Philips 345.606 / 1963
Sick And Tired / Led In The Game (Live)	G- Philips 345.621 / 1963
Money / Hungry For Love	G- Dt.Vogue DV 14111 / 1963
Süß ist sie / Liebe	G- Dt.Vogue DV 14116 / 1963
Tausend Nadelstiche / Farmer John	G- Dt.Vogue DV 14130 / 1964
I Sure Know A Lot About Love / Don't You Know	G-Star-Club 158500 STF / 1964
Someday We're Gonna Love Again / Alright	G- Dt.Vogue DV 14176 / 1964
Love Potion No.9 / What Have They Done To The Rain	G- Dt.Vogue DV 14277 / 1964
Verzeih' My Love / Wenn ich Dich seh	G- Dt.Vogue DV 14338 / 1965
Farmer John / Tricky Dicky	G- Dt.Vogue DV 14365 / 1965
I'm Ready / Don't You Know Why	G- Dt.Vogue DV 14458 / 1965
Bumble Bee / If I Could Find Someone	G- Dt.Vogue DV 15206 / 1965

(Please note that all other singles released in Germany by the group were identical with the British releases. *Süß ist sie* was the German version of *Sweets For My Sweet, Liebe* the German version of *Money, Tausend Nadelstiche* was *Needles And Pins* in German and *Farmer John* was also sung in German. *Verzeih My Love*, of course, was *Goodbye My Love* and *Wenn ich Dich seh* was the German version of *When You Walk In The Room*.)

Different Dutch releases:
Twist And Shout / Farmer John   NL- PYE 7N H 102 / 1963
Bumble Bee / Let The Good Times Roll   NL - PYE 7N H 108 / 1965
I Don't Want To Go On Without You / A Tear Fell NL - PYE 7N H 109 / 1965
Where Have All The Flowers Gone / Money   NL - PYE 7N H 113 / 1965

Different Danish releases:
Sugar And Spice / Sweets For My Sweet   DK - PYE 7N 15566 / 1963
Everybody Come And Clap Your Hands/Till You Say You'll Be Mine

                                                     DK - PYE 7N 312 / 1967

EP discography:
AIN'T GONNA KISS YA   UK-PYE NEP 24177 / 1963
- Ain't Gonna Kiss Ya / Farmer John / Alright / Love Potion No.9
SWEETS FOR MY SWEET   UK-PYE NEP 24183 / 1963
- Sweets For My Sweet / It's All Been A Dream / Since You Broke My Heart / Money
HUNGRY FOR LOVE   UK-PYE NEP 24184 / 1964
- Hungry For Love / Don't Cha Know / Saturday Night Out / Saints and Searchers
PLAY THE SYSTEM   UK-PYE NEP 24201 / 1964
- The System / This Empty Place / Sea Of Heartbreak / Can't Help Forgiving You
WHEN YOU WALK IN THE ROOM   UK-PYE NEP 24204 / 1964
- When You Walk In The Room / I'll Be Missing You / Someday We're Gonna Love Again / Noone
Else Could Love You
  BUMBLE BEE   UK-PYE NEP 24218 / 1965
- Bumble Bee / Everything You Do / Magic Potion / If I Could Find Someone
SEARCHERS '65   UK-PYE NEP 24222 / 1965
- What Have They Done To The Rain / This Feeling Inside / Goodbye My Love / Till I Met You
FOUR BY FOUR   UK-PYE NEP 24228 / 1965
- Till You Say You'll Be Mine / I Don't Want To Go On Without You / Everybody Come And Clap
Your Hands / You Wanna Make Her Happy
  TAKE ME FOR WHAT I'M WORTH   UK-PYE NEP 24263 / 1966
- Take Me For What I'm Worth / Too Many Miles / Take It Or Leave It / Don't Hide It Away

Different German releases:
HULLY GULLY   G-Philips PE 423469 / 1963
- Hully Gully / Listen To Me / Sweets For My Sweet / Sweet Nothin's
SUGAR AND SPICE   G- Dt.Vogue PNV 24112 / 1964
- Sugar And Spice / Saints And Searchers / Unhappy Girls /
  Ain't That Just Like Me
SOME OTHER GUY   G- Dt.Vogue PNV 24114 / 1964
- Some Other Guy / Since You Broke My Heart / Don't You
  Know / Hungry For Love
NEEDLES AND PINS   G- Dt.Vogue PNV 24116 / 1964
- Needles And Pins / One Of These Days / Saturday Night Out /
  Ain't Gonna Kiss Ya

Different French releases:
SWEETS FOR MY SWEET   F- Vogue PNV 24108 / 1963
- Sweets For My Sweet / Alright / Tricky Dickie / Farmer John
DON'T THROW YOUR LOVE AWAY   F- Vogue PNV 24120 / 1964
- Don't Throw Your Love Away / I Pretend I'm With You / It's All Been A Dream / Love Potion No.9
C'EST ARRIVE COMME CA   F- Vogue PNV 24121 / 1964
- C'est Arrivé Comme Ca / C'est De Notre Age / Mais C'était Un Réve / Ils La Chantaient Il y a
Longtemps
(these are the French versions of *Don't Throw Your Love Away, Sugar And Spice, It's All Been A
Dream* and *Saints And Searchers*)

BUMBLE BEE   F- Vogue PNV 24137 / 1965
- Bumble Bee / Till I Met You / Goodbye My Love / If I Could Find Someone

<u>LP discography</u>
MEET THE SEARCHERS   UK- PYE NPL 18086 / 1963
- Sweets For My Sweet / Alright / Love Potion No.9 / Farmer John / Stand By Me / Money / Da-Doo-
Ron-Ron / Ain't Gonna Kiss Ya / Since You Broke My Heart / Tricky Dicky / Where Have All The
Flowers Gone / Twist And Shout
SUGAR & SPICE   UK- PYE NPL 18089 / 1963
- Sugar And Spice / Don't You Know / Some Other Guy / One Of These Days / Listen To Me /
Unhappy Girls / Ain't That Just Like Me / Oh My Lover / Saints And Searchers / Cherry Stones / All
My Sorrows / Hungry For Love
IT'S THE SEARCHERS   UK- PYE NPL 18092 / 1964
- It's In Her Kiss/Glad All Over/Sea Of Heartbreak /Livin' Lovin' Wreck Where Have You Been/
Shimmy Shimmy /Needles And Pins /This Empty Place/Gonna Send You Back To Georgia/I Count The
Tears/Hi-Heel Sneakers/Can't Help Forgiving You/Sure Know A Lot About Love/Don't Throw Your Love Away
SOUNDS LIKE SEARCHERS   UK- PYE NPL 18111 / 1965
- Everybody Come And Clap Your Hands / If I Could Find Someone / Magic Potion / I Don't Want To
Go On Without You / Bumble Bee / Something You Got / Let The Good Times Roll / A Tear Fell / Till
You Say You'll Be Mine / You Wanna Make Her Happy / Everything You Do / Goodnight Baby
TAKE ME FOR WHAT I'M WORTH   UK- PYE NPL 18120 / 1965
- I'm Ready / I'll Be Doggone / Does She Really Care For Me / It's Time / Too Many Miles / You
Can't Lie To A Liar / Don't You Know Why / I'm Your Loving Man / Each Time / Be My Baby / Four
Strong Winds / Take Me For What I'm Worth

THE SEARCHERS' SMASH HITS Vol.1   UK-Marble Arch 673 / 1966
THE SEARCHERS' SMASH HITS Vol.2   UK-Marble Arch 689 / 1967
THE SEARCHERS' SMASH HITS Vol.3   UK-Marble Arch 704 / 1968
(All three above-named Marble Arch albums were compiled from the former albums and so were not originals)

<u>Different German releases:</u>
SWEETS FOR MY SWEET (Live At The Star-Club)   G- Philips P 48052 / 1963
- Sweets For My Sweet / Ain't That Just Like Me / Listen To Me / I Can Tell / Sick And Tired /
Mashed Potatoes / I Sure Know A Lot About Love / Rosalie / Led In The Game / Hey Joe / Always It's You
/ Hully Gully / What 'D I Say
NEEDLES AND PINS   G- Dt.Vogue LDV 17004 / 1964
- Needles And Pins / I Want To Hold Your Hand / Sweets For My Sweet / She Loves You / Sugar And
Spice / Roll Over Beethoven / Hungry For Love / Please Please Me / Saturday Night Out / Twist And
Shout / Farmer John / From Me To You

(It is often said that the **Beatles** cover versions included on the above album were not recorded by
the **Searchers** but by **Ian & the Zodiacs**. But fact is that the recordings were neither by the **Searchers,**
nor by **Ian & the Zodiacs**. These numbers were taken from an album on the German Tempo-label, called
'Beatlemania'. This label was a so called cheapo, which worked closely with 'Top Six' in England, who
at the same time also provided Dt. Vogue with cover versions for their 'Original Beat aus England'-series
on the sub-label 'Pop'. So the artists of that songs most probably were the **Beat Kings**, which cannot
be said for sure as it seems that 'Top Six' used various imagitive names for mainly one and the same
groups or various recording sessions.

<u>Tracks on compilations:</u>
Beautiful Dreamer	on '**Twist im Star-Club**'	**G- Philips**	**P 48036 / 1963**
Sweet Nothin's	on '**Twist im Star-Club**'	**G- Philips**	**P 48036 / 1963**
Shakin' All Over	on '**Twist im Star-Club**'	**G- Philips**	**P 48036 / 1963**

(These three live tracks from the 'Star-Club' were the very first recordings of the **Searchers**, a little later also released on the British Philips label - BL 7578 / 1963)

<u>Unissued tracks:</u>

From the **Searchers** the following Sixties' unissued tracks are known:

Bye Bye Johnny (sung by **John McNally** !), *Goodbye So Long* - probably both from 1963, *Somewhere In The Night* (written and released by **Jacki Trent**), *I Who Have Nothing, Shame, Shame, Shame* - all from 1964, *Once Upon A Time* from 1965, as well as various live tracks that were recorded for the BBC 'Saturday Club', for example *I'll Be Loving You* (a group's original), *See See Rider / Jenny Take A Ride, I Don't Believe, Goodbye So Long, Blowin' In The Wind* and *Sweet Little Sixteen*.

For the independent producer **Bill Landies** they recorded the song *The Great Train Robbery* in 1968, as well as *For What It's Worth* and *Don't Shut Me Out* for Liberty in 1969.

THE SECRETS

This group originated from the **Hi-Cats**, one of the first Beat groups in Liverpool, formed by **Vic Grace** after he had left **Mark Peters & the Cyclones** in the very early Sixties.

Danny Havoc (voc) and **Dave Collins** (bg/voc) of the **Hi-Cats** formed the **Ventures** in early 1963, together with **Les Stuart** (g), who had formerly played with the **Les Stuart Quartett** and **Frank Knight & the Barons**.

This trio was joined by drummer **Pete Orr**, also a former member of the **Hi-Cats** who had then played with **Groups Inc.** in France. **Sid Edwards** (g/voc), who had also played with **Groups Inc.** in France, joined with him. He had previously played with the **Flames**, **Nutrockers** and **Lee Shondell & the Capitols**.

The **Ventures** soon became the backing group for **Freddie Starr** (aka **Freddie Fowell**), formerly of **Howie Casey & the Seniors**, the **Kansas City Five** and **Groups Inc.** - on the above-mentioned French tour. But **Freddie Starr & the Ventures** only existed until the middle of 1963 and then the singer left to lead **Freddie Starr & the Midnighters** and later **Freddie Starr & the Starr Boys** (sometimes also appearing as **Freddie Starr & the Flamingoes** and **Freddie Starr & the Delmonts**).The **Ventures** continued as a group and were joined by songstress **Barbara Harrison**, also a former member of the **Hi-Cats** who in the meantime had sung with **Faron's Flamingos**. The group then changed their name to **Danny Havoc & the Ventures** and when **Vic Grace** replaced **Les Stuart** a little later, the **Hi-Cats** line-up was almost complete again. **Les Stuart** became a member of the **Kansas City Five** and after that played with **The Long & The Short**. When **Barbara Harrison** left again after a short time and also joined the **Kansas City Five**, the band name was changed again, this time to **Danny Havoc & the Secrets** and the group at that time consisted of the following musicians:

Danny Havoc	(voc)
Vic Grace	(g/voc)
Sid Edwards	(g/voc)
Dave Collins	(bg/voc)
Pete Orr	(dr)

But the changes in the line-up did not end there and the next to leave was **Danny Havoc**, who disappeared from the scene and was not replaced in the group, who continued as the **Secrets**. **Sid Edwards** left to join the **Nashpool Four**, who later became **The Nashpool**. **Pete Orr** also decided to leave the group and joined the **Easybeats** from Liverpool. The latest changes probably meant the best known and most successful line-up of the **Secrets** came together in late 1963 with:

Vic Grace	(voc/g)
Denny Alexander	(g/voc)
Dave Collins	(bg/voc)
Dave Preston	(dr)

Denny Alexander was a former member of the **Aarons**, while **Dave Preston** came from the **Harlems**, the backing group for the Liverpool vocal group **The Chants,** but before that he had already been a member of **Vince & the Volcanoes**.

It was most probably this line-up which was signed to Oriole, but it seems there was never a record released by the **Secrets**. The reason may have been the fact that Oriole was very soon taken over by CBS, but the reason for not releasing a record at that time may also have been due to the continually changing line-up.

However, **Dave Preston** joined the newly formed **Kinsleys** in April 1964 and a little later was followed by **Denny Alexander**. After that, **Dave Preston** became a member of the hit group **Creation**, who had developed from the **Mark Four** (not the Liverpool group), while **Denny Alexander** joined the **Clayton Squares**.

The new members of the **Secrets** were **Austin Brown** (g) and **Peter Hall** (dr). **Austin Brown** was a former member of **Johnny Templer & the Hi-Cats**, a successor group of the already named original **Hi-Cats**. **Peter Hall** only stayed for a few weeks and then joined **The Memphis Rhythm & Blues Combo**. He was replaced by **Johnny Gee**, from Liverpool's **Tokens**, and the **Secrets** were also joined by sax player **Jack Curtis** as an additional member, who had formerly played with the **Renegades** from Liverpool. Probably in this line-up the song *Mojo* was recorded, meant to be featured on the live album 'Cavern Alive', but in the end the compilation was cancelled for unknown reasons. **Dave Collins** left the group to join the **Hideaways** and was replaced in the **Secrets** by **Harold Williams**, who came from **The Mafia**.

At the beginning of 1965, **Johnny Gee** joined the **Delmonts** and was later a member of the **Pikkins**. **Jack Curtis** also left and disappeared from the scene. The **Secrets** were joined only by **Colin Woodruff** from the **Fontanas** as their new drummer and continued as a four-piece.

When **Austin Brown** left in April 1965, he was replaced by **Pete Campbell**, a former member of the **Mersey Four**, **Karl Terry & the Cruisers**, the **Fontanas**, the **Tony Prince**

Vic Grace & The Secrets

Combo and the **Mersey Five**. This line-up of the **Secrets** lasted until September 1965 and when **Pete Campbell** left again to join **John O'Hara & his Playboys**, the remaining **Vic Grace**, **Harold Williams** and **Colin Woodruff** continued together until 1967. Then **Colin Woodruff** became a member of the **Times**, who backed the Liverpool vocal trio **Signs** for a while and as new drummer **Roy Hesketh** was recruited.

As **Vic Grace & the Secrets** the group went to play Italy and down there met up with the two sax-players **Alan Gaskell** and **John Chisholm** and organist **Iain**

Bradshaw, who had just departed from the **Valkyries**, who had already been in the South for a few months. **Vic Grace & the Secrets** toured quite successful in Italy and then joined forces with the black Jamaican singer **Nevil Cameron** to become **Nevil Cameron & the Groove**.

Under that name the group signed a recording contract and it was probably in 1968 that the Italian 50's-star **Marino Marini** produced the single *L'ultima Partite* from the Western movie 'Sentenza di Morte' with them for the Tiffany label. It did not become a big hit and **Nevil Cameron & the Groove** continued touring in Italy for two more years and during this time **Alan Gaskell** was featured on the original version of *Chirpy Chirpy Cheep Cheep*, which was recorded by the composer **Lally Stott**, a former member of the **Denny Seyton Group** and the **Motowns**, who had settled down in Rome.

It was in the very early Seventies that **Nevil Cameron & the Groove** disbanded and the individual members mainly disappeared from the scene. **Alan Gaskell** kept playing with various Liverpool groups and in the late Seventies formed **Gaz & the Groovers** who became really successful and today still is a popular act on the Merseyside scene. **Vic Grace** also stayed in the music business and is still active today. It is said he is a real virtuoso on guitar.

In retrospect, it can be said that the **Secrets** were one of the really good and very interesting groups on Liverpool's music scene. This is in spite of the countless personnel changes, which in the end were the reason for the sad fact that this legendary and fondly remembered group never made a real breakthrough.

Discography

A lot has been written about connections between the **Secrets** and Oriole and for this label the group recorded the song *Mojo* in 1964, meant to be for the sampler 'Cavern Alive', but in the end the record was not released.

On the CBS label a group with the name of **The Secrets** released some singles, but that was not the Liverpool group.

as **Nevil Cameron & the Groove**:
L' ultima Partite (The Last Game) / Preghiera Negra   **IT- Tiffany   / 1968**

Nevil Cameron & The Groove

322

THE SEFTONS

This group was formed in Liverpool in 1966 and because one of their members came from Sefton Park, the musicians decided on the name **The Seftons**.

At first the band was influenced by the music of the **Beatles**, but as it was already a little bit late for pure Beat, the **Seftons** later also played a sort of Rhythm & Blues. From the beginning, the group consisted of the following musicians:

David Stephenson	**(voc/org/sax)**
Yanny Tsamplacos	**(g/voc)**
David Edwards	**(bg/voc)**
Michael Barron	**(dr/voc)**

All the musicians were newcomers on the scene and the **Seftons** was the first group for all of them. **Yanny Tsamplacos** was of Greek origin, just like **Dee Christopholus** of the **Four Just Men** or **Savva Hercules** of **Savva & the Democrats**.

Within a short time, the **Seftons** became popular along Merseyside and had appearances in well known venues such as the 'Mardi Gras', the 'Downbeat' (then known as the 'Victoriana') and of course, the 'Cavern'. But one of their most important appearances was one night at the 'Blue Angel', where they met **Alan Williams**, who was enthusiastic about the group and its music. It was probably him who organised a gig at the 'Cavern' for the group and arranged some clever publicity for it when he managed (in some way) to have a lot of girls present, as well as some magazine reporters.

He introduced the **Seftons** as 'Merseyside's new No.1 band', and exactly those words were written on the front page of a magazine a little later. Because of that, CBS became aware of the **Seftons** and signed them.

The group went down to London in 1967 and recorded the single *I Can See Through You*, which was produced by **Des Champ**, while the A+R man was none other than **Arthur Greenslade**. The single sold quite well but didn't climb the charts.

The **Seftons** became more and more influenced by the upcoming Tamla Motown sound from the USA, but did not remove the Beat from their programme, and so had an interesting mixture in their music. They continued to be very busy on the club scene of the North, but then decided to move down to London, which was why **David Edwards** left. He decided to continue on in college and did not want to become a professional musician. He was replaced by **Norman Bellis**, who had formerly played the bass guitar with the **Calderstones**.

In 1968 the **Seftons** changed their name to **The Perishers** and in July of that year, the group cut its first single under the new name. Fontana released the great *How Does It Feel,* which was coupled with *Bye Bye Baby,* but this record did not get into the charts.

In December 1968 the **Perishers** recorded the group's original *Living In The Land Of The Broken Hearted,* but this was sadly not released. In spite of this, they were kept very busy on the live scene in London and had no problems making a living.

In July 1969, **Norman Bellis** left for the USA, where he stayed for nine months, playing sessions with such well-known artists as **Jr. Walker & the All Stars**, the **Four Tops** and the **Walker Brothers**.

After he had left, the **Perishers** disbanded totally, but all the musicians stayed on London's music scene. When **Norman Bellis** returned to England, he played at first in the group **Rusty Harness**, who had a big hit in Scandinavia with the song *Ain't Gonna Get Married* at that time. (Ember EMB-S 283).

Norman Bellis then met up with his old friends from the **Perishers** again and they decided to re-form the group, this time under the name of **Worth**. It did not take too long before **Worth** was signed to CBS and in 1970 a nice version of the **Andy Kim** number *Shoot 'em Up Baby* was released. This single did not become a chart success but sold quite well and so it was followed by four more singles by **Worth**, none of which sadly brought any chart honours for the group. But all their singles, some of which were also released on the European continent, sold quite well.

In 1975 **Worth** broke up but **Yanny Tsamplacos**, **Norman Bellis** and **Mike Barron** continued together as a Hardrock band under the name **Tiger** and in the same year released one more single with the song *Heavy Animal* before they also disbanded.

As far as it is known, **Yanny Tsamplacos** stayed in the music business and **Norman Bellis**, who in the Seventies returned to Liverpool and joined **Perfumed Garden,** today owns a recording studio in Devonshire. What has happened to the other former members of the **Seftons**, **Perishers**, **Worth** or **Tiger** is sadly not known.

Single discography
as **The Seftons**:

I Can See Through You / Here Today	**UK - CBS**	**202491 / 1967**

as **The Perishers**:

How Does It Feel / Bye Bye Baby	**UK- Fontana TF 965 / 1968**	
Living In The Land Of The Broken-Hearted (unreleased)	**UK- Fontana acetate / 1968**	

as **The Worth**:

Shoot em Up Baby / Take The World In Your Hands	**UK- CBS**	**5309 / 1970**
Let's Go Back To Yesterday / Let Me Be	**UK- CBS**	**7460 / 1971**
Don't Say You Don't / Polecat Alley	**UK- CBS**	**7728 / 1972**
I Ain't Backing Down / I'm Not Fooling	**UK- CBS**	**1589 / 1973**
Keep It In The Family / Hey Mr. Lonely	**UK- Epic EPC S 1009 / 1973**	

as **Tiger**:

Heavy Animal /	**UK- Epic EP S 35848 / 1975**	

THE SELOFANE

This was one of the late Liverpool groups, only coming together at the end of 1967 or the beginning of 1968. It might also be debated whether the music of **The Selofane** was still Merseybeat or not, but who can really judge that. The simple fact is the members of the group hailed from the Merseyside scene and from the Beat days and their music was in the fashion of the time, but still with a Beat.

In the beginning there was the **Washington Soul Band** who had been playing the Liverpool clubs since the mid-Sixties without any outstanding success. It was at the end of 1967 when some musicians, whose names sadly got lost with time, left the group and some new ones were recruited. This new line-up then was called **The Selofane**, and after the original lead guitarist named 'Ray' had also left in early 1968, the group consisted of the following musicians:

John Gobin	(voc)	
Judd Lander	(g/harp)	
Les Martin	(bg/voc)	
Alex Galvin	(org/voc)	
Arnie Arnold	(sax)	
Richard 'Spider' Cuthell		(tr)
Geoff Hulme	(dr)	

Judd Lander was the new guitarist who came from the **Hideaways**, while **Les Martin** and **Alex Galvin** were also new members and both had formerly played with the **Expressions**.

Before that, **Les Martin** had been a member of the **Tabs**, quite popular on the Liverpool scene for a while. **John Gobin**, **Arnie Arnold**, **Richard Cuthell** and **Geoff Hulme** were probably the remaining members of the **Washington Soul Band**. The **Selofane** did not play too much on the Liverpool circuit but quite soon moved down to London in search for international fame. Down there, things went well for the group and soon the 'emigrated Liverpudlians' were signed to CBS.

A little later, their first single was released with the superb *Girl Called Fantasy*, written by **Tony Waddington** (see **Pete Best Four**), **Judd Lander** and a certain Marchant. This record, meant to be the theme music for the 'Musica '68' pop festival in Palma/Spain, was produced by the American **Albert Hammond**, later of *It Never Rains In Southern California* fame, who together with **Lee Hazlewood** also wrote the B-side *Happiness Is Love*. *Girl Called Fantasy* in its music, melody and arrangement was similar to the big hit success *From The Underworld* by **The Herd**.

It was a huge disappointment for the musicians, the producer and the record company when the 'Musica '68' festival was cancelled, as it could have been the big breakthrough for the **Selofane** and their first record. But the cancellation of the pop festival in no way affected the amount of plugging the record got, and the group was not only featured on almost every radio show, but also appeared a few times on the British television, for example in the 'Tony Blackburn Show'.

The single was also released on the European continent and did especially well in Spain, as well as in Germany and Holland. *Girl Called Fantasy* did not make the charts but what it did do was get **The Selofane** truly established on the scene. This played a big part in CBS releasing a second single by the group, also in 1968. *Shingle I-A-O* was also written by Hammond/Hazlewood and was again produced by **Albert Hammond**. It was a nice commercial song with a great musical arrangement but in the end didn't compare to their debut single and so also failed to become a chart success.

After that release, **Judd Lander** left the group and became a very successful session musician in London. Amongst others, his harmonica can be heard on the *Karma Chameleon* hit success by **Boy George**.

The **Selofane** were joined by **Ray Hall** as their new lead guitarist but though lots of insiders on the music scene saw a bright future for the group in 1969, it disbanded quite soon. The musicians returned to their hometown Liverpool, where they disappeared from the scene.

What was left of the short lived but very impressive career of the **Selofane** are two great singles, worth looking out for.

Discography

Girl Called Fantasy / Happiness Is Love	**UK - CBS 3413 / 1968**
Shingle I-A-O / Chase The Face	**UK - CBS 3700 / 1968**

DENNY SEYTON & THE SABRES

Brian Tarr (aka **Denny Seyton**) formed this very interesting group in 1961 in Liverpool and until the end of 1962 they toured as a relatively popular band on the Northern scene. Then they took part in the nationwide 'Frankie Vaughan Beatgroup Contest' - and won. Because of this success **Denny Seyton & the Sabres** were taken over by **Frankie Vaughan**'s manager and immediately signed to Mercury.

In 1963 with *Tricky Dicky*, their first single was released and sold very well, but did not become a chart hit. *Tricky Dicky* later became the most popular number for the group and was also covered by the **Searchers** and **Wayne Fontana & the Mindbenders** although it was not the most successful record by **Denny Seyton & the Sabres**, who in the meantime had become professionals. In the original line-up the group consisted of:

Denny Seyton	**(voc)**
Dave Maher	**(g/voc)**
John Francis	**(g/voc)**
John Boyle	**(bg/voc)**
Tommy Walker	**(dr)**

At the time the record was released, **Tommy Walker** had already left the group and quit show business. He was replaced by **Bernie Rogers**, who had formerly played with the **Travellers**, that sometimes also appeared as **Johnny Saint & the Travellers**, and with **Lee Curtis & the All Stars**.

Short Fat Fanny, the second single by **Denny Seyton & the Sabres** also became very popular and sold quite well but once again was only 'almost' a chart success. 'All good things come in threes' was an old truism and so it was in the case of **Denny Seyton & the Sabres**. Their third release, a moody ballad with the title *The Way You Look Tonight* brought their first chart success in 1964, when this record climbed up to No. 48 in the British charts.

This became the group's best selling record in England, but for mysterious reasons this song did not make as strong an impression over the years as did *Tricky Dicky,* although *The Way You Look Tonight* was also covered by **Gerry & the Pacemakers**.

Denny Seyton & the Sabres had engagements all over the country and especially in Scotland, where they were a top attraction. They went to Germany where they built up a big name and at that time were one of the Liverpool groups with the most TV appearances.

In 1964, an album was released by **Denny Seyton & the Sabres**, with the title 'It's The Gear' and exclusively featured cover versions of the big Beat hits of that time but sadly no original material. This album, which did not sell too badly, was the final record by the group under the name **Denny Seyton & the Sabres**. A little later, with the exception of leader **Denny Seyton**, all the group members were replaced, one after another.

John Francis emigrated to Vancouver, Canada and was replaced by **Eddie Murphy**, who had formerly played with **Dean Stacey & the Detonators**.

John Boyle was replaced by **Danny Dring**, who was a former member of the **Cimarrons** and **John Paul & the Deejays**, and when **Bernie Rogers** also left, the place on drums was taken by **Dave Saxon**, who came from the **Eden Kane Group**.

In 1989, **Bernie Rogers** appeared again with **Johnny Guitar & his Hurricanes** but in 1992 joined **Faron's Flamingos**. Organist **Mike Logan**, a former member of **Lee Eddie & the Chevrons** replaced **Dave Maher**, who quit show business.

Eddie Murphy had left the group again and his replacement **Harold 'Lally' Stott** from Prescot. Originally a member of the **Phantoms** he in the meantime had played with the **Four Just Men**. The band's name was changed to **The Denny Seyton Group** and a little later the group went to Germany again - most probably in the following line-up:

Denny Seyton	**(voc)**
Lally Stott	**(g/voc)**
Danny Dring	**(bg)**
Mike Logan	**(org/voc)**
Dave Saxon	**(dr)**

In Germany, the **Denny Seyton Group** was signed to Decca and in 1965 the singles *Do The Jerk, Hushabye* and *It's Alright* with its German flip-side *Du Bist Meine Wahre Liebe* were released.

Of these records, the German version of *Hushabye*, a real masterpiece and one of the loveliest Merseybeat ballads ever, released under the name the **Denny Seyton's Showgroup,** became their most successful single and entered the German hit parade.

In the meantime there were some more changes in the line-up. **Danny Dring** had left and firstly joined the **Dodos**. After that he played with **Mister X & the Masks** and then with **Cy Tucker & the Friars**, where he met up with the former members of the **Cimarrons** again and where he stayed until 1988, before he teamed up with his brother in a duo. He was replaced by **Rob Little**, and when **Dave Saxon** also left to form a new group with former member **Eddie Murphy**, he was replaced by **Tony Crawley**. **Dave Saxon** continued in the music business and today is still active as drummer on Merseyside.

George Martin took this new line-up under his wing and produced an album with them for Parlophone, which is said to have exclusively featured originals written by **Lally Stott**. But in the end only the single *Just A Kiss* with its flip-side *In The Flowers By The Trees* was

Denny Seyton Group

released, which sadly had no success in the charts and so all the other recorded songs stayed unissued. Maybe because of the permanent changes **Denny Seyton** decided to leave and quit show business in 1968.

The group was joined by **Dougie Meakin**, who came from the **Masterminds** and it is said that this line-up gigged around Liverpool for a short time under the name of **The Lovin' Kind**, but this is doubtful. It is a fact that the group changed its name to **The Motowns** and went down to Italy in the line-up with:

Dougie Meakin	**(voc/rg)**
Lally Stott	**(lg/voc)**
Rob Little	**(bg)**
Mike Logan	**(org/voc)**
Tony Crawley	**(dr)**

The **Motowns** became very popular in Italy within a very short time and were signed to RCA Italiana in 1966.

In the same year their first single, *Prendi La Chitarra E Vai* was released, which was the Italian version of the **David & Jonathan** success *Lovers Of The World Unite*.

This was very successful and the **Motowns** had released two more singles by 1967, which included the Italian versions of *Iko Iko* and *New York Mining Disaster 1941*. An album entitled 'Si, Proprio I Motowns' was released, which amongst others included the Italian versions of *See See Rider* and *Summer In The City*. Probably around that time the Italian **Piero Pintucci** replaced **Rob Little**.

The group had really settled down in Italy, signed a new recording contract with Durium and by 1970 had cut six more singles, which included the Italian versions of **Arthur Brown**'s *Fire*, the **Lemon Pipers** success *Blueberry Blue* and the **Steam** bestseller *Na Na Hey Hey, Kiss Him Goodbye*. Most of them entered the Italian hit parade and the **Motowns** had developed into a real top act.

The final single by the group was *Lassu*, which was released on the Carosello label in 1970 but by that time there had obviously been more changes in the line-up, although it can be taken for granted that **Dougie Meakin** and **Lally Stott** were still with them.

When the **Motowns** split in the early Seventies, **Dougie Meakin** continued successfully in the Italian music business, as did **Lally Stott**, who at first recorded the solo singles *Jacaranda* and *Sweet Meeny*.

He also continued as songwriter and amongst others wrote the big hit *Chirpy Chirpy Cheep Cheep* for **Middle Of The Road**, which he himself also released as a single. In 1971, a solo album was released under the title 'Chirpy, Chirpy, Cheep, Cheep' which consisted exclusively of his own compositions.

After that he formed the **Lovebirds**, with whom he was very successful on the Italian music scene and who also included his wife **Cathy Stott**. He later continued recording in a duo with her. On the day of the Queen's silver jubilee **Lally Stott** was killed in a motorbike accident. What happened to **Mike Logan** and **Tony Crawley** is not known, but probably they returned to England.

But back to **Denny Seyton**, who later returned to show business, but under his real name of **Brian Tarr**. Together with his former group member **John Boyle**, as well as with **Ron Burns**, he formed a cabaret trio under the name of the **Ron Hamilton Group**, which lasted until 1988 and then split again. After that **Brian Tarr** and **John Boyle** formed the duo **Old Gold**, which kept going for some years and sometimes was joined by **Paul Stewart**, who was normally the drummer with **Julian Lennon**'s group.

On the 2nd December 1990, at a 'Mersey Cats' concert at the 'New Montrose' club in Liverpool, **Denny Seyton & the Sabres** stepped back into the limelight with a really great performance. Besides **Denny Seyton**, this line-up featured **Dave Maher** and **John Boyle** again, as well as Denny's son on drums.

They did a few gigs for the 'Mersey Cats' and then broke up again, but this of course may not be forever as the musicians proved at those gigs their still great musical quality - so let's wait, hope and see ....

Single discography

as **Denny Seyton & the Sabres**:

Tricky Dicky / Baby What You Want Me To Do	UK- Mercury MF 800 / 1963
Short Fat Fanny / Give Me Back Your Heart	UK- Mercury MF 814 / 1964
The Way You Look Tonight / Hands Off	UK- Mercury MF 824 / 1964

as **The Denny Seyton Group**:

Just A Kiss / In The Flowers By The Trees	UK-Parlophone R 5363 / 1965

as **Denny Seyton's Showgroup**:

Do The Jerk / Along Came Jones	G- Decca D 19674 / 1965
Hushabye / Mir Geht Es Wieder Besser	G- Decca D 19681 / 1965
It's Alright / Du Bis Meine Wahre Liebe	G- Decca D 19682 / 1965

as **The Motowns**:

Prendi La Chitarra E Vai / Per Quanto Io Ci Provi	IT- RCA PM 45-3374 / 1966
Una come lei / Prendi la chitarra e vai	IT- RCA PM 45-3414 / 1967
Sagamafina / Mister Jones	IT- RCA PM 45-3420 / 1967
Dentro La Fontana / In Un Villaggio	IT- Durium LDA 7585 / 1968
Fuoco / In The Morning	IT- Durium LDA 7594 / 1968
Dai vVieni Giu' / (B-side by Los Marcellos Ferial)	IT- Durium LDA 7616 / 1969
Sogno, Sogno, Sogno / Hello To Mary	IT- Durium LDA 7629 / 1969
Na-na-hey-hey Kiss Him Goodbye (in Italian) /In The Morning	
	IT- Durium LDA 7667 / 1970
Lassu / Sai Forse T'amero	IT- Carosello CI 20254/ 1970

<u>LP discography</u>
as **Denny Seyton & the Sabres**:

IT'S THE GEAR   **UK- Wing WL 1032 / 1964**
  **- Hippy Hippy Shake / Needles And Pins / Candy Man / All My Loving / Good Golly Miss Molly /
Little Children / I Want To Hold Your Hand / Bits And Pieces / I Think Of You / Can't Buy Me Love /
Just One Look / Not Fade Away / I'm The One / Glad All Over**

as **The Motowns**:
SI, PROPRIO I MOTOWNS   **IT- RCA   S 14 / 1967**
  - Si Silvana (See See Rider**) / Una verita** (Summer In The City) **/ . . .**

<u>Tracks on compilation-albums:</u>
as **Denny Seyton's Showgroup**:
Along Came Jones   on **'Beat Party'**   **G- Telefunken ND 106 / 1965**
Hush-A-Bye   on **'Beat Party'**   **G- Telefunken ND 106 / 1965**
Mir Geht es Wieder Besser on **'16 Teen Tops'**   **G-Telefunken SHZT 525 / 1965**
Along Came Jones   on **'16 Teen Tops'**   **G-Telefunken SHZT 525 / 1965**

<u>Unissued tracks:</u>
  The known unissued tracks by **Denny Seyton & the Sabres** are the songs *House of Bamboo, That's
What Love Will Do, Hello Josephine* (on acetate) and *I'm Gonna Love You Too* - all of 1963 /64.
  The **Denny Seyton Group** recorded a complete album for Parlophone in 1965, under the wing of
George Martin. In the end, only the single *Just A Kiss* and its flip-side was released.

SIGNS (& TIMES)

This was probably the first Liverpool group which had no 'The' in its name; something that only later became popular with band names. Of course, this is not important but is unusual.

The second unusual thing about the **Signs** is it was a purely vocal trio, formed at the beginning of 1966 and consisting of:

Dave Kerrigan   **(voc)**
Pete O'Connell   **(voc)**
Tony Burns   **(voc)**

All members were experienced musicians from the Merseybeat scene.

Dave Kerrigan had sung with the **Toreardors** and the **Richmond Group** before, while **Pete O'Connell** was a former member of **September** and **Tony Burns** came from the **Kwans**.

Of course, (and thank God) at that time playback was unknown in the music clubs and because the **Signs** did not want to work with continually changing bands, they had a steady backing group with **The Times**. These two names suited each other - **Signs & Times** – and so did the musicians and that is why it became a quite successful co-operation.

The **Times** also consisted of experienced musicians from the scene and their line-up was as follows:

Stan Alexander   **(g)**
Andy O'Hagan   **(sax/harp)**
Dave O'Hagan   **(sax)**
Derek Marl   **(sax)**
Paul Eick   **(bg)**
Paul Comerford   **(dr)**

Stan Alexander had formerly played with the **Black Velvets** and the **Dions**, while **Dave O'Hagan** was also was a former member of the **Dions**, originally known as **Roy & the Dions**.

Paul Comerford probably was not the original drummer, as he had already played with the **Pulsators**, **Tiffany & the Thoughts**, the **Cryin' Shames** and the **Escorts**. Of **Derek Marl** it is known, that he at least occasionally appeared with the **Secrets** but most probably was not a steady member. **Andy O'Hagan** and **Paul Eick** had also played in other groups before, but the names of that have been lost.

The **Signs** appeared often at the 'Cavern' together with the **Times** of course, and became very popular. The famous songwriter **Les Reed** wrote a number especially for the **Signs** which was recorded for Decca. This song was *There's A Kind Of Hush* which for incomprehensible reasons was not released, but a little later became a million seller for **Herman's Hermits** on Columbia.

SIGNS at The Cavern
During a colour film session for N.B.C. Television — America

Dave
Pete   Tony

This must have been hugely annoying for the **Signs** as a release of their record would most probably have meant an international breakthrough for them. Once again Decca had missed the boat and they tried to patch up things with another release.

The **Murray/Callander** song *Ain't You Got A Heart* was released on single in 1966 with the **Leiber/ Stoller** composition *My Baby Comes To Me* on the flip-side. *Ain't You Got A Heart* had **Tony Burns** as lead singer, while *My Baby Comes To Me* featured the lead vocals of **Dave Kerrigan**.

Both songs, in no way comparable to *There's A Kind Of Hush*, had a full orchestra backing and it is not known if the **Times** were included in this **Ivor Raymonde** production or not. It was one of the typical pop records of that time, common in melody and arrangement and it showed the **Signs** to be really good singers. This record, also released on the continent, didn't make the charts.

Maybe in the end the frustration and disillusionment caused by the missed chance with *There's A Kind Of Hush* led to the **Signs** splitting in late 1967 or early 1968. All three singers disappeared from the scene.

The **Times**, who in the meantime had also appeared on their own, continued as a group on the Merseyside scene, but had changes in the line-up. **Dave O'Hagan** had left and was replaced by **Allen 'Gaz' Gaskell** in 1966, a great sax-player, who already had played with the **Young Ones** from Birkenhead, that may not be confused with the Decca recording group, the **Tiyms**, the **K-Ds** and **Combo Six**.

The next to leave was **Andy O'Hagan**, who followed his brother to **Bernie & the Buzz Band** and **Derek Marl** also parted from the **Times** and joined the **Almost Blues**. In the Seventies he was a member of the successful recording group **Champagne**.

In 1967 **Alan Gaskell** joined the **Robby Gray Soul Band**, before he became a member of the **Valkyries**, with whom he went down to Italy. In Rome he teamed up with **Vic Grace & the Secrets**, who had a long residence down there and with the Jamaican singer **Nevil Cameron** appeared and recorded as **Nevil Cameron & the Groove**.

In 1978 he was a member of **Karl Terry & the Cruisers**, from which then developed the first line-up of the legendary **Gaz & the Groovers**, that also appeared as **Juke** and in 1984 even as **Supercharge**. When Paul Comerford left, the new drummer was **Colin Woodruff**, having formerly played with the **Fontanas** and the **Secrets**.

It is not clear how long the **Times** continued on the scene, but of **Stan Alexander** it is known, that he later was a member of the Rock 'n' Roll band **Darts** who had some international hits in the Seventies.

Dave Kerrigan appeared again on the scene in the Nineties, but only as a committee member of the 'Mersey Cats" and not as singer of a band - yet!

Single discography
Ain't You Got A Heart / My Baby Comes To Me   UK- Decca F.12522 / 1966
Beside this, the **Signs** recorded the original of *There's A Kind Of Hush* for Decca in 1966, but this version was never released. One year later it became a million seller for Manchester's **Herman's Hermits**.

SOME PEOPLE

This Chester based group originated from **The Musketeers**, a college band formed by **Keith Muscott** and **Terry Ord** in 1961.

When this band split in the middle of 1962, the two friends decided to stay together in the music business and to form a new group - **Some People**. This new combo featured the following musicians:

Terry Ord	**(voc)**
Keith Muscott	**(g/voc)**
Nick Cowap	**(g)**
Dave Meredith	**(bg)**
Colin Harris	**(dr)**

Some People played a sort of Beat and Rhythm & Blues music and **Dennis Critchley** took over the management of the new group. He was the owner of the 'Royalty Theatre' in Chester and also managed the **Black Abbots**, who later became very famous in the English cabaret scene.

Under the wing of Mr. Critchley, **Some People** were soon on the way up. They, of course, played a lot at the 'Royalty Theatre', but also at the 'Quantways', the other important live venue in Chester. Because Chester is not far from Liverpool, **Some People** also had regular appearances in the Beat metropolis, where they played gigs at 'St.George's Hall', as well as at the well known clubs like the 'Cavern' and the 'Iron Door'. They became a popular act on the so-called Merseyside scene.

In 1964 **Some People** went down to London, where a recording session was held for Oriole. At that time they were joined by **Nick Bennett** as an additional guitarist. He had formerly played with **Clay Ellis & the Corsairs**. But he only came into the group for the recording sessions and after that disappeared from the scene.

The band recorded four songs and as well as the **Terry Ord** original *This Is The Night*, these were *Sure Know A Lot About Love, Jeremia Peabody* and *Just One More Dance*.

Sure Know A Lot About Love, also recorded by the **Searchers?** and *This Is The Night* were meant to be released on single, but for unknown reasons this did not come out in the end. This unlucky development, added to the fact that **Dennis Critchley** resigned as manager of the group to concentrate on the career of the **Black Abbots**, as well as the fact that a planned tour on the European continent did not happen, probably were the reasons for **Some People** to split up again in late 1964.

Keith Muscott and **Colin Harris** later played in various dance combos before they also quit show business, as the others had done before.

Discography
Some People never released a record but recorded the following songs for Oriole:
This Is The Might / Jeremia Peabody / Just One More Dance / Sure Know A Lot About Love

UK- Oriole demo- EP / 1964

SOUNDS PLUS ONE

It was somewhat of an adventure obtaining any information about this group, formed in the Tuebrook area of Liverpool, most probably sometime in 1964. It was a four-piece group, at least at some time, which included the following musicians:

John Thompson (voc)
Len Bowers (lg/voc)
Alan McDonald (bg)
Paul Hitchmough(dr)

For vocalist **John Thompson** it was his first group, while **Len Bowers** had probably already played before, but the name of his former group is unfortunately not known.

Paul Hitchmough was not the original drummer but before he joined the **Sounds Plus One**, towards the end of 1964 or the beginning of 1965, he had played with the **Hangmen**, the **Victims** and the **Corals**.

Sounds Plus One played the normal club circuit along Merseyside where they had a large following, especially in the area of West Derby, but they never really made the headlines.

It was most probably in early 1965 when they cut an interesting acetate on Unicord. The group's original *Girl Of My Dreams* is a very nice Merseybeat ballad, coupled with a re-arranged and slowed down version of the **Jessie Hill** success *Ooh-Poo-Pah-Doo.*

In spite of its quality, the acetate was sadly not followed by a record release and so did not help the group to increase its popularity, which might have been the reason for **Sounds Plus One** disbanding again in 1965.

Of **Len Bowers** it is known that he then joined Liverpool's successful Country scene and at a certain time he is said to have been a member of the **Kentuckians**. **Alan McDonald** also joined the Country scene but it is not known with which group.

John Thompson and **Paul Hitchmough** joined the **Kruzads** where they were featured on the acetate release of *Stop Your Sobbing.* After that **John Thompson** quit the music business and never returned to it, while **Paul Hitchmough** kept playing the drums and later was a member of popular groups like the **Clayton Squares** and **Curiousity Shoppe**. In the Nineties he appeared again as a member of **Beryl Marsden**'s group and after that he played with **Karl Terry & the Cruisers**.

What is left of the short career of the **Sounds Plus One** is a great acetate, worth seeking out.

<u>Discography</u>
Girl Of My Dreams / Ooh-Poo-Pah-Doo   **UK- Unicord   acetate / 1965**

THE SPORTSMEN

Around 1958 the two guitarists/singers **George Chamberlain** and **Ian Watts** formed a duo at Wigan Grammar School under the name of the **Rocking Vampires**.

Through the addition of **Maurice Myers** (t-bass) and **Roy Ellison** (dr) the **Rocking Vampires** became a real Rockabilly group, whereby **Roy Ellison** was replaced quite soon by **Dave Rylance**. **Ian Watts** left due to problems with his father and **Keith Wright** took over the lead guitar.

This line-up then changed their name into **Danny Lee & the Stalkers** and started to play outside Wigan – mainly gigs in Liverpool and Southport, as well as a little later in Manchester.

The group received an offer to play four nights a week at the 'Domino'-club in Manchester and this meant for the musicians to become professionals but only **George Chamberlain** was prepared for that step, so the group disbanded. **George Chamberlain** recruited **Jimmy Martin** (g) and **Keith Battersby** (bg) from the **Avalons**, as well as drummer **John Boffey** from the Wigan based **Dominoes**. This new line-up of **Danny & the Stalkers** accepted the offer but this adventure was shortlived.

After that **George Chamberlain** at first continued in the Manchester scene, where he had brief spells with **Pete & the Rebels** and the **Boydells**, while **Jimmy Martin** together with **Dave Rylance** and others formed the **Martinis**, sometimes appearing as **Jimmy Martin & the Martinis**.

When **George Chamberlain** returned to Wigan, he was contacted by his old comrad **Maurice Myers**, who meanwhile was playing with the resident band at the new 'Sportsman'-club in Wigan. They wanted to extend the group and **George Chamberlain** was asked to join, which he did. A little later the **Sportsmen** were born in the line-up were:

George Chamberlain	(voc)
Derek Taylor	(voc/perc)
Keith Wright	(lg)
Reg Parker	(rg)
George Twist	(org/p)
Maurice Myers	(bg)
Dave Rylance	(dr)

Accordingly the basis of that new group consisted of the complete first line-up of the former **Danny Lee & the Stalkers**. **George Twist** was a former member of the **Blues Set**, a name that the **Beat Boys** used for some time. The **Sportsmen** recorded some demos at

Alan Cheetham's studio in Stockport and sent them off to various record companies.

In the end it was a **George Chamberlain** number with the title *And It Shows*, that arouse the interest of **Ted Taylor**, the former leader of the **Ted Taylor Four**, who now was working as producer for CBS. The **Sportsmen** were invited and went down to London for test recordings – and in the end were signed.

It was in 1966 that the single with the **Buddy Buie** song *I Miss You (When I Kiss You)* was released by the **Sportsmen**, coupled with *If It's Love*. Both numbers were not Beat, but nice ballads, zapped up with a full orchestral backing by **Les Reed**. In its type and sound the record reminded one a little bit of the style of the **Fortunes**, which means that great vocals were also featured on it. The record got just into the Top-50 and it seems that this was not satisfactory for CBS as they did not extend the contract with the **Sportsmen**, but were interested in keeping **George Chamberlain** as a solo artist. This was not well received by the musicians and after several rows the group broke up still 1966. **George Chamberlain** signed with CBS, adopted the name of **Paul Craig** and still in the same year had his first solo single out with *Midnight Girl*. This record became quite popular around London and **Paul Craig** had some radio and TV appearances but in the end did not sell enough to make the charts.

Paul Craig

The singer had formed another band to promote the record, which was going under the name of **Paul Craig & the Theme** and besides him included **Keith Wright** and **George Twist** again, as well as **Ken Fillingham** (g) and **Johnny Hutchinson** (dr).

Kenny Fillingham was a former member of the **Beat Boys** and **Johnny Hutchinson** of course came from Liverpool's **Big Three**.

This group was shortlived and the former **Sportsmen** members **Paul Craig** (aka **George Chamberlain**), **Keith Wright** and **George Twist** formed a new group called **The New City Showband** with **Ronnie Carr** (bg), formerly with the **Beat Boys, John Kelly** (dr) and a brass section of **Steve McMahon** (trombone), **Tony Morgan** (trumpet) and **'Roz' Rosbottom** (saxophone). This group specifically played the cabaret-circuit, which had become a big business at this time.

The **New City Showband** became very successful on the scene and played all the big venues for a couple of years. When they split off **Paul Craig** together with **Ronnie Carr** went on to form a group called **Major Minor**, which also included **Barry Ascroft** (key), **Dave Brown** (lg) and another former **Beat Boys** member with **Eric Eastham** on drums.

After that **Paul Craig**, alias **George Chamberlain** retired from the showbiz, as probably all the others did as nothing was heard of them again .

Discography
I Miss You (When I Kiss You) / If It's Love	UK- CBS 202043 / 1966
<u>**George Chamberlain** solo as **Paul Craig**</u>:	
Midnight Girl / Autumn	UK-CBS 202406 / 1966

Unreleased tracks:
The **Sportsmen** recorded a number of tracks as demos to send out to the record companies in 1965, of that only the **George Chamberlain** original *And It Shows* is known.

THE ST. LOUIS CHECKS

This real Rhythm & Blues band was formed by **Eric Savage** in Liverpool in 1964, after he had previously sung with **The Nashpool Four**.

In addition to the **Roadrunners, Clayton Squares, Hideaways** and **Almost Blues,** the **St. Louis Checks** very soon were considered to be one of the leading bands of that sound in Liverpool. In their original line-up, the group consisted of the following musicians:

Eric Savage	(voc/harp)
Terry Kenna	(g/voc)
Lawrence Swerdlow	(org/p)
Alan Collins	(bg/voc)
Johnny Sze	(dr)

Johnny Sze, who came from the **Satanists**, left very soon after, to join the new backing group for **Beryl Marsden**, that went to Germany and played at the 'Star-Club' as the **Blueboys**.

After that he became a member of the **Cherry Stones** in Stockholm, from that later the **Kinetic** evolved, who settled down in Paris and released a string of records over there, but that is another story.

The new drummer with the **St. Louis Checks** was **Roy 'Triff' David.** It is unknown where he had played before that, but it might have been with the **Smokestack Blues Band**.

In the middle of 1964, after a really promising start, **Lawrence Swerdlow** and **Alan Collins** left the group. **Alan Collins** became a member of the **Memphis Rhythm & Blues Combo**, while **Lawrence Swerdlow** disappeared from the scene.

The **St. Louis Checks** were joined by **Julius David** (bg), who most probably was the brother of the new drummer, as well as by **Dave Carr** (p/sax), who both came from the

Smokestack Blues Band, who had obviously just disbanded.

This line-up lasted until the end of the year and the **St. Louis Checks** disbanded totally before they were signed to a recording company and, as far as it is known, there was never anything recorded by this really good group.

In spite of the fact that the **St. Louis Checks** were quite short lived and had steady changes in their line-up, they left behind a lasting impression on the Liverpool music scene of the Sixties. Of the individual members, **Terry Kenna** later appeared again when he was a member of the **Terry Hines Sextett** and the **Blues System**. It is known that **Roy David** joined the **Rebels**, formerly known as **Ian & the Rebels**, who after singer **Ian Gregson** left, had become the backing group for **Ricky Gleason** for some time. Then **Roy David** joined the **Richmond**, where already his brother **Barry David** was playing. What happened to the other musicians is sadly not known.

FREDDIE STARR & THE MIDNIGHTERS

The story of this group from the Wirral leads back to the Skiffle days and starts with the foundation of the **Five Stars**, most probably by the great guitarist **John Kelman**, who formerly had played with the **Dons**. One of the original members was **Kenny Lazzard** (t-bass), probably identical to the musician with the name **Stu Hazard**, who later played the bass guitar with **Earl Royce & the Olympics**.

In the early Sixties, **John Kelman** left to join **Dee Fenton & the Silhouettes** and was replaced in the **Five Stars** by **Dave Carden**, who came from **Gus & the Thundercaps**, one of the very first Rock 'n' Roll groups on the Wirral.

When **Gus & the Thundercaps** disbanded, singer **Gus Travis**, together with **Alan Watts** (p), **Ian McQuair** (g) and **John Cochran** (dr), teamed up with their old mates **Dave Carden** and **Brian Woods** (voc/bg) of the **Five Stars**, under the name of **Gus Travis & the Midnighters** in October 1962.

John Cochran left very soon to join **Wump & the Werbles** and was replaced by former **Five Stars** drummer **Ian Broad**. This line-up then lasted until **Gus Travis** separated from the group in May 1963. The story of this singer and the various groups which backed him can be followed in a story of its own.

He was not replaced in the **Midnighters** who continued with **Brian Woods** as lead vocalist. Then **Ian McQuair** left to form a new group with former member **John Cochran**, as well as with **Dave Georgeson** (bg) of **Wump & the Werbles** under the name of **The Lil' Three**, who later became the **The Chuckles**. His leaving was followed by the immediate departure of **Alan Watts** from the **Midnighters**, who were now left as a three-piece, but very soon joined by the returning **John Kelman**.

They then amalgamated with **Freddie Fowell**, who had already been backed by the **Five Stars** on some occasions in the Fifties, when he still appeared as **Freddy the Teddy**.

Meanwhile he had changed his name to **Freddie Starr** and sung with **Howie Casey & the Seniors**, the **Kansas City Five**, with **Groups Inc.** and **Freddie Starr & the Ventures**.

Freddie Starr & the Midnighters were born and accordingly consisted of:

Freddie Starr	**(voc)**
John Kelman	**(g/voc)**
Dave Carden	**(g)**
Brian Woods	**(bg/voc)**
Ian Broad	**(dr)**

Joe Meek became aware of this band and took it under his wing as the first group from Liverpool. In 1963 he produced the single *Who Told You* with **Freddie Starr & the Midnighters** for the Decca label, which was coupled with the interesting *Peter Gunn Locomotion,* but was sadly unsuccessful. The group was joined by **Roger James** on piano, who formerly had played the guitar with the **Prestons**.

Shortly after the first single, **John Kelman** left again to rejoin **Dee Fenton & the Silhouettes,** who in the meantime had settled down in Manchester under the name of **The Four Just Men**. After that he played with **Terry Rowland & The Explosions, Wimple Winch, Wayne Fontana & the Opposition** and the cabaret band **Strictly For Cash.**

His replacement in **Freddie Starr & The Midnighters** was **Reg Welch**, a great guitarist from Preston, where he formerly had played with the **Rebels** and the **Questions.**

At the same time **Brian Woods** left and joined **Heinz & the Wild Boys** but later returned to Liverpool and was a founder member of the group **Just Us**, who were quite popular on the scene for a while. He was replaced by **John Brierley** who also came from the **Questions.**

Their second single, *Baby Blue,* was a very nice ballad but was too harmless to cause a sensation or to become a chart success. Both records are desired collectors' items today and accordingly very expensive.

Ian Broad also left to join the **Seniors,** who had no connection with the former **Howie Casey & the Seniors.** He later played with **Heinz & the Wild Boys, Rory Storm & the Hurricanes** and finally with **Dave Allen & the Exotics.**

Freddie Starr & the Midnighters were joined by **Keef Hartley,** the former drummer with the **Thunderbeats** from Preston. Maybe because of all these changes, **Freddie Starr** separated from the group in 1964. He, at first, had a role in the Lional Bart musical 'Maggie May' and then teamed up with the **Flamingoes** (formerly **The Pressman**) under the name of **Freddie Starr & the Starry Boys**, which is another story.

After that he was backed by the **Delmont Four** under the name of **Freddie Starr & the Delmonts.** He later started a solo career on the cabaret scene and today is one of the most popular TV stars in England and is still recording from time to time.His leaving led to the **Midnighters** splitting up in 1964. **Dave Carden** joined the **Pressman** who a little later changed their name to the **Flamingoes** and then teamed up with **Freddie Starr** under the name of **Freddie Star & the Starr Boys.** After that he disappeared from the scene.

John Brierley returned to Preston, where he joined **David John & the Mood** and **Reg Welch** became a member of the **Nashpool** (formerly the **Nashpool Four**) and then went back to Preston and joined the **Suspects.**

Keef Hartley and **Roger James**, together with **Bob Garner** from the **Merseybeats** and another Liverpool guitarist formed **The Ice Blues**.

This group was only shortlived and after that **Keef Hartley** became a member of **Rory Storm & the Hurricanes** and later played with the **Artwoods** from London and **John Mayall's Bluesbreakers**, before he formed his own group under the name of **The Keef Hartley Band**. In the mid-Seventies, he played with the **Michael Chapman Group** and today he is still regarded as one of the best drummers in England.

Roger James formed the **Roger James Four** who cut two nice Beat singles for Columbia and later he led a Country & Western band.

Discography
Who Told You / Peter Gunn Locomotion	**UK- Decca F.11663 / 1963**
Baby Blue / It's Shaking Time	**UK- Decca F.11786 / 1963**

Nb: for further records by **Freddie Starr** see the story of **Freddie Starr & the Starr Boys**

FREDDIE STARR & THE STARR BOYS

This group originated from the **Pressmen**, formed in Wallasey in 1961.

The **Pressmen** were at first an independent band but then became the backing group for coloured singer **Derry Wilkie**, who had formerly sung with **Derry & the Seniors** and **Howie Casey & the Seniors**, and was backed by **Geoff Stacey & the Wanderers** for a short while.

When **Derry Wilkie** separated again to form **Derry Wilkie & the Others**, the **Pressmen** were joined by **Dave Carden** (g/voc), a former member of the **Five Stars**, **Gus Travis & the Midnighters** and **Freddie Starr & the Midnighters**, who replaced the original guitarist **Ritchie Prescott**.

After **Faron's Falmingos** had disbanded in 1964 and there was an offer for them to tour Germany, the **Pressmen** adopted the name **The Flamingoes** and toured Germany, where they went down well and recorded a single for the Dt. Vogue label with the songs *Mein Beatle Baby*, the German version of *Roll over Beethoven* and *Glücklich Wie Noch Nie,* the German version of *I'll Get You,* which sadly was not very successful, although it was a really good Beat record and today it is a most desired and expensive collectors' item.

The Flamingoes

During the stay in Hamburg, the group, under the name of **The Liverpool Triumphs**, also backed coloured singer **Tony Cavanaugh** on his poorly produced album 'Rock'n' Twist, Slop, Hully Gully' on the Somerset label.

Tony Cavanaugh was the former drummer with **Tony Sheridan**'s band and it should be pointed out very clearly that the poor production was certainly not the fault of the **Flamingoes** or **Liverpool Triumphs**.

The group kept the name **Flamingoes** until it teamed up with singer **Freddie Starr** as **Freddie Starr & the Starr Boys** - also in 1964. **Freddie Starr**, whose real name is **Freddie Fowell**, had sung before with the Liverpool groups **Howie Casey & the Seniors**, the **Kansas City Five**, **Groups Inc.**, **Freddie Starr & the Ventures** and **Freddie Starr & the Midnighters**. This new group sometimes also appeared as **Freddie Starr & the Flamingoes** in the following line-up:

Freddie Starr	**(voc)**
Dave Carden	**(g/voc)**
Bob Pears	**(bg)**
Dave Roberts	**(sax)**
Aynsley Dunbar	**(dr)**

With the exception of **Dave Carden** and **Freddie Starr**, all musicians were former members of the **Pressmen**.

Freddie Starr & the Starr Boys were signed to Decca and in September 1964, released the single *Never Cry (On Someone's Shoulder),* which was not too successful and so remained the only single by the group. But because of the connection the **Flamingoes** had to Dt.Vogue, an album was released in the same year by **Freddie Starr & the Starr-Boys** on that label in Germany with the title 'This Is Liverpool Beat'. This great live recording from the 'Iron Door' club in Liverpool kept the real excitement of the music of that time and today is one of the most desired collector's items around.

As early as 1965 **Freddie Starr** left the group and at first was backed by the **Delmont Four** under the name of **Freddie Starr & the Delmonts.** He later started a solo career as one of the most popular TV stars in England, but also kept on recording. In the Seventies, he had his biggest record success when his single *It's You* climbed up to No. 9 in the British charts in 1974, and the follow-up *White Christmas* in 1975 stopped at No. 41.

But back to the **Starr Boys**, who in 1965 changed their name back to **The Flamingoes** and for a short time were very successful on the Merseybeat scene but then disbanded without having released anymore records.

It seems that at this time **Aynsley Dunbar** had already left the group because in 1965, he was a member of the **Excheckers** from Chester. After that he played with such well known groups as **John Mayall's Bluesbreakers**, **Journey**, the **Aynsley Dunbar Retaliation, Aynsley Dunbar & Blue Whale, Frank Zappa's Mothers Of Invention** and **Jefferson Starship**. He is based in Los Angeles today and is still a world class drummer.

Dave Anthony Three

Bob Pears became a member of the **Chuckles** and in the Seventies teamed up with original **Pressmen** drummer **Nick Arnott** in a cabaret duo that appeared under various names. **Nick Arnott** later played with the groups **Persuader** and **Rocket 88** before he met up again with **Ritchie Precott** in the **Juke Box Eddies**.

What happened to **Dave Carden** after the **Flamingoes** broke up, is sadly not known, but it can be taken for granted that he remained in the music business.

Dave Roberts formed the **Dave Anthony Three** together with **Tony Crofts** (dr) and **Robin Thomas** (key). In this band **Dave Roberts** played bass guitar again, the instrument that he originally started with in the **Pressmen**. **Tony Crofts** later was replaced by **Pete James** and **Robin Thomas** by **Dave Saltrese**.

In this line-up the **Dave Anthony Three** were featured on the EP 'Four For You' by a duo called **Dual Control**, which consisted of the original **Pressmen** lead guitarist **Ritchie Prescott** and a certain **Gary Nicholls** (UK-Riga HP 49 / 1976). When the **Dave Anthony Three** finally split up in 1978, **Dave Roberts** left show business.

Single discography
as **Freddie Starr & the Starr Boys**:
Never Cry (On Someone's Shoulder) / Just Keep On Dreaming   UK- Decca   **F. 12009 / 1964**

as **The Flamingoes** - without Freddie Starr:
Glücklich Wie Noch Nie / Mein Beatle Baby   G- Dt.Vogue DV 14158 / 1964

LP discography
as **Freddie Starr & the Starr Boys**:
THIS IS LIVERPOOL BEAT   G-Dt.Vogue LDV 17006 / 1964
- **Tutti Frutti / Lucille / Peter Gunn / One Mint Julep / Rip It Up / Mean Woman Blues / Skinny Minny / You Are My Sunshine / Shop Around / Another Saturday Night / Oh Baby / Will You Love Me Tomorrow**
(This album is said be a live recording from the famous 'Iron Door' club in Liverpool)

as **Tony Cavanaugh & die Liverpool Triumphs**:
ROCK'N TWIST, SLOP, HULLY GULLY   G- Somerset   583 / 1964
- **My Babe / Mashed Potatoes / I'm Talking About You / What Did I Say / Hummel-Twist / Money / Jezebel / Hully Gully / We Are Slopping / Twiullyop / Tell Me Baby**
(This album, recorded with **Tony Sheridan**'s former drummer as singer, was released before the group teamed up with **Freddie Starr**)

Tracks on compilation - albums:
Lucille	on 'Original Beat aus England'	**G- Pop**	**Z 10006 / 1965**
Tutti Frutti	on 'Original Beat aus England'	**G- Pop**	**Z 10006 / 1965**
Rip It Up	on 'Original Beat aus England'	**G- Pop**	**Z 10006 / 1965**
Mean Woman Blues	on 'Original Beat aus England'	**G- Pop**	**Z 10006 / 1965**

(Please note that the songs on the above compilation were released under the name of **The Liverpool Beats**, but they are definitely by **Freddie Starr & the Starr Boys** as they were taken from their live album)

343

STEVE & THE SYNDICATE

This group was doubtlessly one of the important pioneering bands of the Liverpool Merseybeat scene, formed under the name of **The Syndicates** in 1961. Within quite a short time they had a large following in their hometown.

After a name change to **Steve Bennett & the Syndicate** or **Steve & the Syndicate** respectively, the group appeared in the following line-up at all the important venues along Merseyside:

Steve Bennett	(voc)
Charlie Mac	(g)
Wayne Bickerton	(g/voc)
Owen Clayton	(bg)
Charlie Mitchell	(dr)

Steve Bennett, whose real name is **Gordon Cummings**, **Wayne Bickerton** and **Owen Clayton** were former members of the **Bobby Bell Rockers**, while **Owen Clayton** before that had played with the **Gerry Owen Four** and the **Creoles**.

In January 1962 **Steve & the Syndicate** were voted No.17 in the popularity poll by the readers of the music paper 'Mersey Beat'. This was undoubtedly a big success if it is taken into account that there were already hundreds of groups around in Liverpool at this time. But in spite of that success, personnel changes started very soon in the line-up.

Charlie Mac was the first to leave and he disappeared from the scene. His replacement was **Paddy Chambers**, who had formerly played with the **Creoles**. **Charlie Mitchell** also left and disappeared and his place was taken by **Brian McNally**.

In this new line-up, **Steve & the Syndicate** were the first Liverpool group to go down to London in search of national stardom. But this turned out to be a poor move and the band's cohesion started to crumble.

Owen Clayton left in 1962 and became a member of the **Sundowners**, who had no connection with the recording group of the same name later. Then he disappeared from the scene for years but returned in the mid-Eighties as a member of **Karl Terry & the Cruisers**, where he played until 1987. He then formed a group called **The Blues Syndicate**, but this flopped and **Owen Clayton** returned to **Karl Terry & the Cruisers**, where he played the stand-up bass. Finally, he was with the **Juke Box Eddies**.

In 1962 **Steve Bennett** took over the bass guitar and the group continued as a quartet. When **Paddy Chambers** left to join **Faron's Flamingos**, he was replaced by **Tony Waddington**, a former member of the **Comets** and **Gene Day & the Jango-Beats**.

Paddy Chambers later became a member of the **Big Three**, the **Eyes**, who then developed into the trio **Paddy, Klaus & Gibson**, the **Escorts**, **Big John's Rock 'n' Roll Circus**, **Sinbad**, and was finally the leader of **Paddy Chambers & the Java Jive**.

In 1963, **Steve & the Syndicate** disbanded without having had the national success they deserved. **Tony Waddington** and **Wayne Bickerton** joined **Lee Curtis & the All Stars** and after that played with the follow-on bands **Pete Best Four** and **Pete Best Combo** - until

1965. They later became a very successful song-writing and production team for bands like the **Rubettes** and **Flirtations**, as well as for **World Of OZ**, of which **Wayne Bickerton** also was a group member. What happened to **Steve Bennett** and **Brian McNally** later is sadly not known, but they probably continued in the music business as members of other groups - perhaps down in London?

RORY STORM & THE HURRICANES

This legendary group developed from the **Alan Caldwell Skifflegroup**, which was formed in Liverpool in the mid-Fifties and consisted of **Alan Caldwell** (voc), **John Byrne** (g/voc), **Paul Murphy** (g/voc), **Jeff Truman** (t-bass) and **Reg Hales** (wb).

In 1958, **Jeff Truman** was replaced by **Spud Ward**, who came from the **Bluegenes**, the forerunner group of the **Swinging Blue Jeans,** who at that time still played a sort of Tradjazz.

Before that change, **John Byrne** and **Paul Murphy** had recorded the private metal single *She's Got It/Butterfly* at Kensington studio in Liverpool in 1957.

In 1959 the **Alan Caldwell Skiffle Group** split and **Paul Murphy** later played with the **Galvanisers**, the **Banshees** and **Eddie Dean & the Onlookers** before he became a quite successful producer for Polydor in Germany.

All the other musicians disappeared from the scene - with exception of **Alan Caldwell** and **John Byrne**, who formed the group **The Raving Texans**, that a little later changed their name to **Al Storm & the Hurricanes**, and then to **Rory Storm & the Hurricanes**. At this time, the group consisted of the following musicians:

Rory Storm	**(voc)**
Johnny Guitar	**(g/voc)**
Ty Brian	**(g)**
Lu Walters	**(bg/voc)**
Ringo Starr	**(dr)**

With the exception of **Lu Walters**, all the other musicians used stage names, and so **Rory Storm** of course was **Alan Caldwell** and **Johnny Guitar** was **John Byrne**. **Ty Brian**'s real name was **Tony O'Brian** and **Ringo Starr**'s real name of course is **Richard Starkey**. **Richard Starkey** formerly had played with the **Eddie Clayton Group** and the **Darktown Skiffle Group**.

Within a short time **Rory Storm & the Hurricanes** became one of the top groups on Merseyside and then a top attraction in the whole North and the Midlands. They were also one of the very first Liverpool groups that went to Hamburg, where they appeared regularly at the 'Kaiserkeller'.

It is interesting that in 1960 **Lu Walters** recorded in Hamburg with the **Beatles** as backing group, who already had **Ringo Starr** on drums, having stood in for **Pete Best**. In this private session the songs, *Fever, Summertime* and *September Song* were recorded with the lead vocals of **Lu Walters**, but they were sadly never released although 'Mersey Beat' announced they would be.

Rory Storm was certainly one of the most interesting and impressive personalities of the whole Merseybeat movement. He normally had a speech impediment but this, in a wondrous way, faded when he sang. He had a very good sense for publicity, coupled with a good sense of humour, and with lots of little escapades he knew how to draw the public's attention to himself and his group. One night at a gig at the 'Majestic Ballroom' he presented himself to the fans on the balcony and then jumped down to the stage, where his band was already playing -

and broke his leg. The press photographer, whom **Rory Storm** specially ordered to take a photograph of his jump, laughed so much that he forgot to press the shutter release. Another day a porter at Bootle Station caught a young guy writing 'I love Rory' on the walls, and this young guy was Rory himself.

He also directed a real show when he and his **Hurricanes** were engaged to play the legendary music ship 'Royal Iris'. He stayed at the pier head and combed his blonde hair with a giant comb until the ship cast off and his fans were afraid that he would miss it, but then he made a big jump and caught a rope hanging

The Hurricanes at the Kaiserkeller, Hamburg

from the ship and pulled himself on board, hand over hand. It seemed like a clip from an adventure movie, but of course this rope was not hanging down by chance, everything having been organised in advance by **Rory Storm**.

It would be worth writing a book on him, his life and his group, which certainly would be a very interesting read. **Rory Storm** was 'Mr. Showmanship' of the British Beat scene and lots of other stars of that time paled in comparison to him.

In 1962 **Ringo Starr** left to join the **Beatles** after there were rumours that he would become a member of **Howie Casey & the Seniors**. His place on drums with **Rory Storm & the Hurricanes** was taken by **Gibson Kemp**, a very talented drummer who formerly had played with the **Night People** and the **Memphis Three**.

Then **Lu Walters** left to join **Howie Casey & the Seniors**, where he sang the lead vocals on the recordings *Gone, Gone, Gone* and *Nashville Blues,* which once again were not released, probably because this group broke up shortly after these recordings for Fontana.

His replacement in the **Hurricanes** was **Bobby Thompson**, who came from **King Size Taylor & the Dominoes** and who was also a great singer. In 1962 he returned to his old group and **Lu Walters** returned to **Rory Storm & the Hurricanes**.

A little later, **Gibson Kemp** also joined **King Size Taylor & the Dominoes** and he was replaced by **Brian Johnson**, a former member of the **Strangers** and the backing group of French Rock 'n' Roll star **Dick Rivers**.

In this line-up, **Rory Storm & the Hurricanes** were featured on the Oriole compilations 'This Is Merseybeat' Vol.1 and Vol. 2 with the songs *Beautiful Dreamer* (sung by **Lu Walters**), *Dr. Feelgood* and *I Can Tell*. The latter two were also released as the first single by the group. Before that, songs like *Green Onions* and *Lend Me Your Comb* were recorded in private sessions - perhaps with **Ringo Starr** still on drums - but never released.

In 1963, the song *Peepin' And Hidin'* was recorded live and was meant to be featured on a Decca live sampler from the 'Cavern', but once again nothing was released in the end. **Brian Johnson** left to join **Mark Peters & the Silhouettes**. His replacement was **Trevor Morais**, the former drummer with the **Cadillacs**, **Ravens**, **Faron's Flamingos**, the shortlived **Trevor Morais Combo** who backed Manchester songstress **Lorraine Gray**, as well as the Manchester group **Ian Crawford & the Boomerangs**. But he then went back to Manchester where he joined the **Peddlers**, a kind of Jazz/Blues group, who later had nationwide success, for example with their single *Let The Sun Shine In.*

The new drummer with **Rory Storm & the Hurricanes** was **Ian Broad**, who had formerly played with the **Five Stars**, **Gus Travis & the Midnighters**, **Freddie Starr & the Midnighters**, **Heinz & the Wild Boys** and with the **Seniors**, who were not connected to the group of **Howie Casey**.

It was probably this line-up that cut the second single of **Rory Storm & the Hurricanes**, a version of *America* from 'West Side Story' for the Parlophone label, produced by none other than **Brian Epstein** - as the only record ever.

America was coupled with an interesting version of the **Everly Brothers** ballad *Since You Broke My Heart,* sung by **Lu Walters** and **Johnny Guitar**. The record had no great success which was not too surprising as it was a poor idea to record the song *America* because it was not timely and absolutely untypical of the music of **Rory Storm & the Hurricanes**. It did not help the group to a bigger career, though they were very popular in most parts of England and also on the European continent, especially in Germany, at that time.

Brian Epstein also produced the songs *I'll Be There* and *Ubangi Stomp* with **Rory Storm & the Hurricanes**, which in the end, for incomprehensible reasons again, were not released.

When **Lu Walters** left and this time obviously quit show business, he was replaced by **David May**, a former member of **Mark Peters & the Silhouettes**. The drummer carousel also kept on turning and after **Ian Broad** had joined **Dave Allen & the Exotics**, he was replaced by **Keef Hartley**, who had played with the **Thunderbeats** and **Freddie Starr & the Midnighters** before, But he also didn't stay too long and then became a member of the **Artwoods** from London and **John Mayall's Bluesbreakers**, before he formed his own group, the **Keef Hartley Band**. In the mid-Seventies, he was a member of the **Michael Chapman Group**.

The new drummer with **Rory Storm & the Hurricanes** became **Eddie Edwards**, who had formerly played with the **Flames**, **Del Renas** and the **Nashpool Four**, who sometimes also called themselves **The Nashpool**. But he left again to join the **Beechwoods** and was replaced by **Jimmy Tushingham**, a former member of the **Four Clefs**. **David May** left to return to the **Silhouettes** and then became a member of the **Three Cheers**, who later changed their name to **Phase Three**.

The new bass guitarist was **Vince Earl**, the former leader of **Vince Earl & the Zeros** and **Vince Earl & the Talismen**. He was also a good singer but did not stay too long and then joined the **Connoisseurs** and a little later **Jimmy Tushingham** followed him to this band, which is a separate story in this book.

New members of **Rory Storm & the Hurricanes** were **Carl Riche** as drummer and the legendary 'Sheik Of Shake' **Karl Terry** as bass guitarist. **Carl Riche**, who was sometimes also known as **Carl Bruce**, was a former member of the **Mersey Four**, the **Tony Prince Combo** and the **Mersey Five**. **Karl Terry** had led the **Gamblers Skifflegroup**, **Terry Connor & the Teen Aces** and **Karl Terry & the Cruisers** before and in the meantime had played with the **Delemeres**, **Group One**, **Karl Terry & the T.T.s**, the **Talismen** and the **Clayton Squares**.

When **Ty Brian** died in early 1967, the group almost disbanded, but was then was re-formed by **Rory Storm**, **Johnny Guitar** and **Carl Riche** together with **Adrian Lord** (voc/g), a former member of the **Nomads**, **Mojos**, **Mastersounds**, **Bluesville Bats**, the Liverpool **Faces**, the **Easybeats** from Liverpool and **Them Grimbles**, as well as with **Keith Karlsson** (bg), who formerly had played with the **Nomads**, **Mojos** and with the **Epics**. But this line-up only lasted for a very short time and then **Rory Storm & the Hurricanes** split forever. **Rory Storm** himself continued in show business as a disc-jockey and as such had a long residence in the Netherlands. On 28 September 1972 he died of an overdose of sleeping pills. Some people say that it was an accident and some others talk about suicide, but Rory took this secret with him to his grave. Because of this tragedy his old mate **Johnny 'Guitar' Byrne** decided to hang up his guitar. He went back to a normal day job and became an ambulance driver.

Rory Storm & the Hurricanes always were, still are and will always be a legend of this great and unique Merseybeat era, although they never had great success with their records. That is why they will always have their steady part in every good Merseybeat biography.

At the end of the Eighties and the beginning of the Nineties two plays about **Rory Storm & the Hurricanes** with the titles 'Need For A Hero' and 'King Of Liverpool' toured quite successfully in England and because of the intervention of the 'Mersey Cats' organisation, **Johnny Guitar** formed a new group in memory of **Rory Storm & the Hurricanes**.

This group was named **Johnny Guitar & his Hurricanes** and mainly played the old **Rory Storm** songs. Besides **Johnny Guitar**, the band in 1990 consisted of **Dave Blackstone** (g/voc), **Gordon Loughlin** (bg) and **Bernie Rogers** (dr) - all experienced musicians of the Sixties.

Dave Blackstone was a former member of the **Tabs**, while **Gordon Loughlin** once was with **Karl Terry & the T.T.s** and the **Clayton Squares** and **Bernie Rogers** played in a string of groups in the Sixties, for example with **Lee Curtis & the All Stars** and **Denny**

Seyton & the Sabres. **Dave Blackstone** later was replaced by **Billy Wright**, who came from the group **Y-Kickamoocow**.

Johnny Guitar & his Hurricanes were still a real Rock 'n' Roll band - with that individual Mersey touch - simply the best way to remember an important Merseybeat group with a really great showman as leader - **Rory Storm & the Hurricanes! Johnny Guitar** died on 18th August 1999 and with his tragic death the last chapter of this group was closed for eternity.

<u>Single discography</u>

Dr. Feelgood / I Can Tell	**UK- Oriole 45-CB 1858 / 1963**
I Can Tell / <u>Faron's Flamingos</u>: Let's Stomp	**UK- Columbia 43018 / 1964**
America / Since You Broke My Heart	**UK-Parlophone R 5197 / 1964**
<u>Johnny Guitar & Paul Murphy</u>:	
She's Got It / Butterfly	**UK-Kensington (private) / 1957**

<u>Tracks on compilation albums:</u>

Dr. Feelgood on **'This Is Merseybeat' Vol.1**	**UK- Oriole PS 40047 / 1963**
Beautiful dreamer on **'This Is Merseybeat' Vol.1**	**UK- Oriole PS 40047 / 1963**
I Can Tell on **'This Is Merseybeat' Vol.2**	**UK- Oriole PS 40048 / 1963**

<u>Unissued tracks:</u>

The unissued tracks by **Rory Storm & the Hurricanes** are *Green Onions* and *Lend Me Your Comb* (both from 1962), *Peepin' And Hidin'* (live) from 1963 and *I'll Be There* and *Ubangi Stomp* from 1964. The latter two were produced by **Brian Epstein** for Parlophone.

Lu Walters recorded the following songs which stayed unissued: *Fever, Summertime* and *September Song* in 1961 - backed by the **Beatles**; *Gone, Gone, Gone* and *Nashville Blues* in 1962 - backed by **Howie Casey & the Seniors**.

THE STRANGERS

This was not only one of the first but also one of the most important Beat groups in Liverpool, where it was originally formed as **Jet & the Tornados** at the end of the Fifties.

The **Strangers** are a legend of Liverpool's early beat days, who will never be forgotten at least on Merseyside, although they never had a big name on the international scene. The fact that in October 1961 they were voted at No.5 in the popularity poll of 'Mersey Beat' proves how popular they already were at this time. The original line-up of the **Strangers** consisted of the following musicians:

Joe Feegan   (voc/g)
Harry Hutchings   (g/voc)
George Harper   (bg/voc)
Brian Johnson   (dr)

The group played at all the important venues in its hometown and built up a really large following. Besides this, the **Strangers** were also one of the first Liverpool groups that played at the 'Star-Club' in Hamburg, where they became very successful and because of that stayed over there for a long time. The **Strangers** never recorded in their own right and in 1963, while in Germany, they disbanded for unknown reasons.

Harry Hutchings returned to Liverpool and disappeared from the scene, while **Joe Feegan**, **George Harper** and **Brian Johnson** went to France, where they became the backing group for famous French Rock 'n' Roll-singer **Dick Rivers**. Amongst others, they recorded with him his (French?) version of *Bo Diddley*, which became quite big over there. Sadly there are no records of all the recordings **The Strangers** made with him.

The Strangers at the Star-Club with Adrain Barber.

After that, **George Harper** and **Brian Johnson** also returned to Liverpool, where **George Harper** most probably quit show business, while **Brian Johnson** became a member of **Rory Storm & the Hurricanes, Mark Peters & the Silhouettes** and finally of the **Tabs**, before he also went back to a normal day job. In the early Nineties he returned to the music scene when he became a member of the newly formed **Cliff Roberts' Rockers**. Today he is the drummer with the newly formed **Mojos,** under the leadership of **Nicky Crouch**.

Joe Feegan stayed in France and became a member of the legendary rockers **Vince Taylor & The Playboys**. After **Vince Taylor** separated from the group, **Les Play-Boys** continued solo, but also backed **Johnny Hallyday** for a time and recorded with him. In the early Eighties, he went solo under the name of **Joe Fagin** and released some brilliant singles, like *Why Don't We Spend The Night*, had chart success in England with *That's Living Alright* and released four great albums which brought him international stardom. His smoky voice suited his handmade Blues influenced rock music, but in spite of all his success he sadly is still one of the most underrated musicians these days.

Les Playboys featuring Joe Feegan.

Discography

The **Strangers** never recorded in their own right, but three of them backed the French Rock 'n' Roll singer **Dick Rivers** on his hit version of *Bo Diddley* in 1964, as well as on some other recordings, of which sadly no details are known.

The Strangers

THE SWINGING BLUE JEANS

Ray Ennis and **Norman Kuhlke** had played together since 1956 in various Skiffle groups in Liverpool before they joined a Skiffle/Tradjazz band which was formed by **Bruce McCaskill** in 1957 under the name the **Bluegenes** and who also included **Tommy Hughes** (bj), a former member of the **Pinetop Skifflegroup**, as well as **Spud Ward** (t-bass).

The **Bluegenes** became something of a resident band at the 'Cavern', where over time they introduced lots of other Liverpool groups on their so-called 'guest night' - amongst them the very young **Beatles**.

Bandleader **Bruce McCaskill** split from the group and was replaced by **Ralph Ellis** (g) and **Johnny Carter** (voc), who had formerly led **Johnny Carter & the Hi-Cats**.

Probably in this line-up the **Bluegenes** made their first recordings with the songs *I'm Shy Mary Allen, I'm Shy, Yes Sir That's My Baby, Bonaparte's Retreat* and a nice and interesting version of *Isle Of Capri*, but these numbers were only released on acetate.

Tommy Hughes had to join the Army and his replacement was **Paul Moss**, who not only took the place of **Tommy Hughes** but also his banjo.

Bruce McCaskill and **Tommy Hughes** later formed the **Kansas City Five** and after that **Bruce McCaskill** joined **Groups Inc.** before he appeared again with the **Escorts**. In later years he managed the **Average White Band** and was the road manager of **Eric Clapton**. He sadly died on 24th December 1993.

When **Spud Ward** joined the **Raving Texans**, the forerunner group of **Rory Storm & the Hurricanes**, he was replaced by **Les Braid**, who also came from **Johnny Carter & the Hi-Cats** and before that had played with the **Gamblers Skiffle Group**, the first band of the 'Sheik Of Shake' **Karl Terry**. **Johnny Carter** emigrated to Canada, where he formed a Beat group whose name is sadly not known.

At the beginning of the Sixties, the **Bluegenes** went to play the 'Star-Club' in Hamburg where they flopped as they were totally out of date with their sound over there. After their return to Liverpool, **Paul Moss** became the bass guitarist with **Johnny Goode & the Kinfolk**.

The **Bluegenes** changed their sound to Rock 'n' Roll and their name into **Swinging Bluegenes**, which a little later became **The Swinging Blue Jeans**. Their second trip to Hamburg was much more successful because they had become a real Beat group now - in a line-up with:

Ray Ennis	(voc/g)
Ralph Ellis	(g/voc/g)
Les Braid	(bg/voc)
Norman Kuhlke	(dr/voc)

The **Swinging Blue Jeans** were signed to EMI and their first single in 1963 was the original *It's Too Late Now*, a nice but not very exciting Beat record which was no great success, just like the follow-up *Do You Know*.

Their third release, a wild version of **Chan Romero**'s *Hippy Hippy Shake* had the required excitement and climbed to No.2 in the British charts in 1963 and from there started to become an international hit success. The next single, also a wild version of *Good Golly Miss Molly* climbed to No.11, while the follow-up *You're No Good* hit the top 10 again when it stopped at No.3.

The **Swinging Blue Jeans** suddenly seemed to be potential hit makers, but no further chart success followed, although singles like *Promise You'll Tell Her, It Isn't There, Crazy 'bout My Baby, Sandy, Tremblin* and *Don't Go Out In The Rain* at least sold quite well, but only their great version of *Don't Make Me Over* became a minor hit.

In the beginning of 1968, **Ralph Ellis** and **Norman Kuhlke** left the group and obviously quit show business. They were replaced by **Terry Sylvester** (g/voc) and **Kenny Goodlass** (dr), who both came from the **Escorts. Kenny Goodlass** before that had played with the **Panthers** and the **Kirkbys**, as well as with the **Fruit Eating Bears** and with **23rd Turn-Off**.

For the next single *What Have They Done To Hazel*, the group's name was changed to **Ray Ennis & the Blue Jeans**, and the follow-up *Sandfly* came out as **The Blue Jeans** - both on the Columbia label.

In 1968 **Terry Sylvester** had left to join the **Hollies**, where he played until the Eighties and then went solo. At one time it was rumoured that he formed a new group under the name the **New Escorts**, but nothing was heard of it. So probably it was no more than a rumour.

The **Swinging Blue Jeans** were joined by **Mike Gregory** as new singer, also a former member of the **Escorts** who in the meantime had had a short spell with the **Hollies**. Beside this **Tommy Murray** (g/voc) was added to the line-up, who came from the **Krew** and before

that had already played with the **Memphis Rhythm & Blues Combo** and the **Kinsleys**.

In 1970, the group was signed to Deram and as **Music Motor** released one more single with the songs *Happy* and *Where Am I Going*, which sadly also had no success. The group went back to its old name **The Swinging Blue Jeans**.

In the meantime, **Kenny Goodlass** had left again and only appeared at the end of the Seventies as a member of the newly formed **Merseybeats**, where he played until the early Eighties. In 1992, he became a member of **Karl Terry & the Cruisers**, who at that time often toured in Germany, where they recorded a great Rock 'n' Roll album in 1994. His replacement in the **Swinging Blue Jeans** was **Chris Mutch**, a former member of the **Krew. Tommy Murray** also left and only later appeared again as a member of a group called **Mumble**.

Mike Gregory became a member of **Big John's Rock 'n' Roll-Circus** and for a short time **Billy Kinsley** joined the **Swinging Blue Jeans**, having played with the **Merseybeats**, **Kinsleys** and the **Merseys**. He then formed **Liverpool Express** and also became a member of the **Merseybeats** again. His replacement in the **Swinging Blue Jeans** was the Canadian

Mike Pynn, and around the same time **John Lawrence** joined the group in place of **Chris Mutch**. This line-up recorded the single *Ring Ring*, which again became a minor hit for the group in the early Seventies. They also released two albums.

In the meantime, **John Lawrence** was replaced by **Ian Magee**, who in the Sixties had played with **Mike Dee & the Detours** and the **Rhythm & Blues Inc.** from Southport.

In 1975, **Mike Pynn** left and was replaced by **Garth Elliott** (g), who very soon left again to join **Herman's Hermits**. His replacement was none other than **Colin Manley**, who in the Sixties was the lead guitarist with the legendary **Remo Four** and in the meantime had played in the backing groups of **Clodagh Rodgers** and **Freddie Starr**. This line-up released some more records and still toured Germany and Scandinavia.

In 1984, **Ian Magee** got married in Sweden and so left the group. He was replaced by **Phil Thompson**. The group continued releasing records on a sporadic basis. Some still had that typical driving Merseybeat sound, while others were more Pop, which was not really the characteristic music of the **Swinging Blue Jeans**, who did not become one of the typical cabaret bands. After **Colin Manley** sadly died in 2005 and **Les Braid** followed him in 2007 it looked like that was the end of the **Swinging Blue Jeans**, but **Ray Ennis** found other members with whom he still continues today.

Single discography
as **The Swinging Blue Jeans**:

It's Too Late Now / Think Of Me	UK- HMV POP 1170 / 1963
Do You Know / Angie	UK- HMV POP 1206 / 1963
Hippy Hippy Shake / Now I Must Go	UK- HMV POP 1242 / 1963
Good Golly Miss Molly / Shaking Feeling	UK- HMV POP 1273 / 1964
You're No Good / Don't You Worry About Me	UK- HMV POP 1304 / 1964
Promise You'll Tell Her / It's So Right	UK- HMV POP 1327 / 1964
It Isn't There / One Of These Days	UK- HMV POP 1375 / 1964
Make Me Know You're Mine / I've Got A Girl	UK- HMV POP 1409 / 1965
Crazy 'Bout My Baby / Good Lovin'	UK- HMV POP 1477 / 1965
Don't Make Me Over / What Can I Do Today	UK- HMV POP 1501 / 1966
Sandy / I'm Gonna Have You	UK- HMV POP 1533 / 1966
Rumors, Gossips, Words Untrue / Now The Summer's Gone	UK- HMV POP 1564 / 1966
Tremblin' / Something Coming Along	UK- HMV POP 1596 / 1967
Don't Go Out Into The Rain / One Woman Man	UK- HMV POP 1605 / 1967

as **Ray Ennis & the Blue Jeans**:

What Have They Done To Hazel / Now That You've Got Me	UK-Columbia DB 8431/ 1968

as **The Blue Jeans**:

Sandfly / Hey Mrs Housewife	UK-Columbia DB 8555/ 1969

as **The Music Motor**:

Happy I Am / Where Going	UK- Deram DM 282 / 1970

Different German releases
as **The Swinging Blue Jeans**:

Das ist prima / Good Golly Miss Molly (sung in German)	G - Elektrola 22734 / 1964
Tutti Frutti (in German) / **Das Ist Vorbei**	G - Elektrola 22870 / 1964
Hippy Hippy Shake / Lawdy Miss Clawdy	G - Elektrola 23607 / 1968

(*Das Ist Prima* is the German version of *Shaking Feeling* and *Das Ist Vorbei* the German version of *You're No Good*)

SHAKE   UK- HMV   EG 8850 / 1963
- Hippy Hippy Shake / Shaking All Over / Shake, Rattle And Roll / Shaking Feeling
YOU'RE NO GOOD MISS MOLLY   UK- HMV   EG 8868 / 1964
- You're No Good / Don't You Worry About Me / Good Golly Miss Molly / Angie

Different French releases:
HIPPY HIPPY SHAKE   F- HMV   EGF 707 / 1963
- Hippy Hippy Shake / Do You Know / Too Late Now / Now I Must Go
GOOD GOLLY MISS MOLLY   F- HMV   EGF 736 / 1964
- Good Golly Miss Molly / Don't You Worry About Me / You're No Good / Shaking Feeling
IT'S SO RIGHT   F- HMV   EGF 782 / 1964
- It's So Right / It Isn't There / Promise You'll Tell Her / Shake, Rattle and Roll
RUMORS, GOSSIP, WORDS UNTRUE   F- HMV   EGF 950 / 1966
- Rumors, Gossip, Words Untrue / Now The Summer's Gone / Don't Make Me Over / I'm Gonna Have You

LP discography
BLUE JEANS A' SWINGING   UK - HMV   CLP 1802 / 1964
- Ol' Man Mose / Save The Last Dance For Me / That's The Way It Goes / Around And Around / It's All Over Now / Long Tall Sally / Lawdy Miss Clawdy / Some Sweet Day / It's So Right / Don't It Make You Feel Good / All I Want Is You / Tutti Frutti

Different US - release:
THE SWINGING BLUE JEANS   US-Imperial LP 9261 / 1964
- Good Golly Miss Molly / Angie / It's Too Late Now / Think Of Me / Do You Know / Hippy Hippy Shake / Shaking Feeling / Shake, Rattle and Roll / Shakin' All Over / Now I Must Go / Wasting Time / Save The Last Dance For Me

Different German releases:
SHAKING TIME   G- Elektrola E 83716 / 1964
- Hippy Hippy Shake / Now I Must Go / Shaking Feeling / You're No Good / Good Golly Miss Molly / Don't You Worry About Me / Shake, Rattle And Roll / Too Late Now / Think Of Me / Shaking All Over / Do You Know / Angie
HEY HEY HEY HEY (Live aus dem 'Cascade-Club', Köln)   G-Elektrola SME 83927 / 1965
- Kansas City / Johnny B. Goode / Tutti Frutti / Eight Days A Week / Chug-A-Lug / I've Got A Girl / King Of The Road / Long Tall Sally / Good Golly Miss Molly (in German) / In The Mood / Das Ist prima

Tracks on compilation-albums:
It's So Right	on 'Liverpool'	**G-Columbia C 83777 / 1964**
Promise You'll Tell Her	on 'Liverpool'	**G-Columbia C 83777 / 1964**
One Of These Days	on 'Liverpool '65'	**G-Columbia SMC 83980 / 1965**
It's So Right	on 'Liverpool '65'	**G-Columbia SMC 83980 / 1965**

Unreleased tracks:

The group as Skiffle/Tradjazz band under the name of the **Bluegenes** recorded the songs *I'm Shy Mary Allen I'm Shy, Yes Sir That's My Baby, Bonaparte's Retreat* and *Isle Of Capri* on acetate in 1957 or 1958. Unissued tracks by the **Swinging Blue Jeans** are *Dizzy Chimes, Keep Me Warm 'til The Sun Shines, We're Here Again, Reddy Teddy* and *You Got Love* from various years.

THE TABS

This group was formed in Liverpool in 1964, which was obviously too late to make an international breakthrough. In spite of this the **Tabs** became one of the hopes of a new generation of bands on Merseyside within a very short time. There were various Beat contests in which they became quite successful, but this more or less happened only on the local scene. The original line-up of the **Tabs** consisted of:

Dave Crosby	**(voc/p)**
David Blackstone	**(g/voc)**
Les Martin	**(bg/voc)**
Ray Aubrey	**(dr)**

Dave Crosby was the former leader of **Dave & the Rave-Ons**, which was one of Liverpool's early groups. None of the other members had appeared on the scene before that.

In 1964, the **Tabs** recorded a private EP which was handed out to fans at their concerts and so, of course, is very rare these days. The record included the songs *Fever, I Still Remember, Caroline Caroline* and *Hurt,* the middle two most probably being originals by the band.

At the beginning of 1965 the first change in the line-up occurred when **Brian Johnson** replaced **Ray Aubrey** on drums, who disappeared from the scene.

Brian Johnson was a well known drummer on the scene as he had played before with such popular groups as the **The Strangers**, **Rory Storm & the Hurricanes** and **Mark Peters & the Silhouettes**.

The **Tabs** were also joined by **Steve McGhee** (sax) and **Terry Sterling** (tr) and so their music became more influenced by Rhythm & Blues and Soul, what can be clearly heard on their Unicord acetate with the songs *Finger Poppin'* and *Don't You Hear Me Calling.*

NORTHERN BEAT CONTEST WINNERS
DAVE: NEW 1898   THE TABS   RAY: GAT 2406
TABULOUS————————FANTASTIC
————ROCK 'N' SOUL MUSIC————

In August 1965, the **Tabs** won the big 'Northern Sounds '65' contest and a little later were signed to PYE. This recording contract may have been the prize for the winners of this contest but that is not certain.

The band went down to London and recorded the **John D. Laudermilk** classic *Tobacco Road*, and probably some other songs, but nothing was released in the end.

When these recording sessions were not followed by a release, **Brian Johnson** left the **Tabs** and quit show business for years. At the beginning of the Nineties he was back on the scene as a member of the newly formed **Cliff Roberts' Rockers** and today he is with the re-formed **Mojos**. He was replaced in the **Tabs** in 1965 by **Alan Menzies**, the former drummer with the **Rhythm & Blues Inc**. They were also joined by a new trumpet player, **Terry Hedley**.

The **Tabs** sadly did not get a second chance to record and so they disbanded, probably in early 1967, without having released a regular record. **Alan Menzies** later appeared again with the **Expressions**, **Jasmin-T** and then was a member of the **Bootles**, where he still plays today.

Dave Crosby, who today runs a record shop in West Kirby, later produced records with local artists on his own Rox label, including the only single by **Karl Terry & the Cruisers**. **Les Martin** joined **The Expressions**, but at the end of 1967 he became a member of **The Selofane**, who cut two great singles for CBS in 1968.

In the Nineties, **Dave Blackstone** was at first a member of **Johnny Guitar & his Hurricanes** and then joined **Karl Terry & the Cruisers** for some time, before he formed his own group under the name of **Mayday** who still play for the 'Merseycats'.

Discography
Fever / I Still Remember / Caroline Caroline / Hurt	UK - private EP	/ 1964
Finger Poppin' / Don't You Hear Me Calling	UK - Unicord acetate /	1964

Unreleased tracks:
After the **Tabs** won the big 'Northern Sounds '65' contest in August 1965, they were signed by PYE and went down to London for a recording session, where the song *Tobacco Road* was recorded, as well as some others, but in the end nothing was released.

KING SIZE TAYLOR & THE DOMINOS

This band story is probably one of the most complicated, but also one of the most interesting ones in the world of Merseybeat.

The best way to start might be with the very first line-up that ever appeared under the name of **King Size Taylor & the Dominoes**, whose forerunner groups were the **James Boys** and the **Dominoes**, which both were formed in Liverpool in the mid-Fifties. In 1960 **King Size Taylor & the Dominoes** in the first line-up under that name consisted of:

Ted 'King Size' Taylor (voc/g) - a former member of the **James Boys** and the **Dominoes**
Charly Flynn (g/voc) - formerly with the **Bobby Bell Rockers** and the **Dominoes**
John Kennedy (voc/g) - a former member of the **Zodiacs** and the **Dominoes**
Bobby Thompson (bg/voc) - ex **James Boys** and **Dominoes**
Geoff Bethel (org) - who had played with the **Deltones** and the **Dominoes** before
Sam Hardie (p) - who was the founder of the **Dominoes**, as well as
Cliff Roberts (dr) - who formerly only had played with the **Dominoes**.

In 1961 **Charly Flynn**, **Geoff Bethel** and **Cliff Roberts**, who shouldn't be confused with the leader of **Cliff Roberts' Rockers**, left together to join **Ian & the Zodiacs**, while **Johnny Kennedy** teamed up with **Carl Vincent & the Counts**. **King Size Taylor & the Dominoes** were only joined by two new musicians and accordingly consisted of:

King Size Taylor (voc/g)
Bobby Thompson (bg/voc)
John Frankland (g)
Sam Hardie (p/voc)
Dave Lovelady (dr)

Dave Lovelady was a former member of the **Zodiacs** and **Ian & the Zodiacs**, while **John Frankland** had not appeared on the scene before.

Dave Lovelady left very soon again to join the **Four Mosts**, who a little later became **The Fourmost**. **Brian Redman**, the drummer with the **Four Mosts**, formerly known as the **Four Jays**, then joined **King Size Taylor & the Dominoes**, and this was probably the line-up that went to Hamburg for the first time. It was a real Rock 'n' Roll group and doubtless one of the best that ever came out of Liverpool, if not England.

King Size Taylor & The Dominoes

So it was no surprise that **King Size Taylor & the Dominoes** went down a bomb in Germany and especially in Hamburg.

In 1962 **Bobby Thompson** played for a short time with **Rory Storm & the Hurricanes** and during that time at first was replaced by **Ken Shalliker,** formerly of the **Blackhawks,** who then went on to join **Deke Rivers & the Big Sound** from Manchester and after that played with the Liverpool Country group **The Foggy Mountain Ramblers**. His replacement was **Frank Galloway** (bg), but he also left when **Bobby Thompson** returned. **Frank Galloway** was later a member of the **Griff Parry Five**.

In the meantime, **King Size Taylor & the Dominoes** were joined by sax player **Howie Casey** as an additional member. He had just disbanded **Howie Casey & the Seniors**, who under the name of **Derry & the Seniors** was the first Liverpool band to go to Hamburg.

This was the line-up of **King Size Taylor & the Dominoes** that backed German girl singer **Audrey Arno** on her single *Bitte Bleib Doch Bei Mir*, which was released as **Audrey Arno & die Tony Taylor Band**. **Brian Redman** returned to Liverpool where he became a member of **Sonny Webb & the Cascades**.

His replacement was **Gibson Kemp**, a terrific drummer, who had formerly played with the **Night People**, the **Memphis Three** and **Rory Storm & the Hurricanes**.

In 1963 **King Size Taylor & the Dominoes** recorded the great album 'Let's Do The Slop, Twist, Maddison, Hully Gully' for the German Polydor label under the name of **The Shakers**.

From that, the singles *Hippy Hippy Shake, Whole Lotta Lovin'* and *Memphis Tennessee* were coupled out for the German market, as well as *Dr. Feelgood* for the English market. Around the same time the group recorded the single *Fortune Teller* with the tremendous B-side *Never In A Hundred Years* as **King Size Taylor & the Dominoes** for Philips. After that they switched to Ariola, where, in 1964, they recorded one album and two halves, the other sides featuring the **Bobby Patrick Big Six** from Scotland. From these really great albums, recorded live at the 'Star-Club' in Hamburg, a string of singles were coupled out for the German market, of which *Stupidity* was also released on Decca in England.

Despite fantastic records by **King Size Taylor & the Dominoes**, they never made the charts, although all the singles, EPs and albums sold quite well in Germany, where **King Size Taylor & the Dominoes** were really one of the absolute top groups on the whole Beat scene.

In 1964 **Steve Aldo** joined the group as additional singer, who had been with the **Challengers** before. The former Liverpudlian musician **Paul Murphy** (ex **Alan Caldwell Skiffle Group, Galvanisers,** etc.) recorded this line-up for German Polydor - under the pseudonym of **Boots Wellington & his Rubber Band**. They recorded songs for a complete album, but in the end only some of these songs were released on different German compilation albums – mainly featuring the lead vocals of **Steve Aldo**.

It is also interesting that the first album by Scottish **Alex Harvey** (also on Polydor) featured **King Size Taylor** (g), **Bobby Thompson** (bg) and **Gibson Kemp** (dr) of the **Dominoes** as backing musicians, although this album was credited to **Alex Harvey & his Soul Band**.

In 1964 **Sam Hardie** left to join **Tony Sheridan & the Beat Brothers** and after that became a member of the Hamburg group **The Tramps**, who recorded an interesting Beat single with *Eene-Meene-Ming-Mang-Mo* on the German Telefunken label. He was replaced by **Dave Woods**, another sax player, who is said to have previously played with the **Sons Of The Piltdown Men**.

Paddy Chambers, formerly of the **Creoles, Steve & the Syndicate, Faron's Flamingos** and the **Big Three** joined the group as an additional guitarist.

A little later, still in 1964, **King Size Taylor & the Dominoes**, one of the everlasting legends of Liverpool's Merseybeat and the German 'Star-Club' scene disbanded totally.

Bobby Thompson joined **Cliff Bennett & the Rebel Rousers** and was later a member of the **Rockin' Berries** from Birmingham. **Steve Aldo** became a member of the **Griff Parry Five**, where he met up with **Frank Galloway** again.

Howie Casey played with the **Pawns**, the **Krewkats** After short spells with the **Big Three** and the **Griff Parry Five**, he re-formed the **Krew** and later played with the **Roy Young Band** and **Rigor Mortis**, while **Steve Aldo** sang with groups like the **Krew**, the **Fyx**, the **In Crowd** and lastly was backed by the **Fairies** from Colchester.

John Frankland, **Paddy Chambers** and **Gibson Kemp** stayed in Hamburg, where they together with **Lewis Collins** (bg) formed the **Eyes**. **Lewis Collins** also came from Liverpool and was a former member of the **Renegades**, the **Kansas City Five** and the **Georgians**. **John Frankland** then left the **Eyes** to get married to a German girl, while **Lewis Collins** went back to Liverpool, where he joined the **Mojos**.

Klaus Voormann from Hamburg replaced them, and the recording trio **Paddy, Klaus & Gibson** was born, More Information about that is featured in the story of the **Eyes**.

Paddy Chambers later joined the **Escorts**, while **Gibson Kemp** stayed in Hamburg, where he played with the 'Star-Club' band **The Giants** and later in the backing group for the **Les Humphries Singers**.

King Size Taylor, who had disbanded the group, also returned to Liverpool, where he formed a new backing group with no special name, that featured **Barry 'Baz' Davies** (g), who came from the **Connoisseurs**, **Kenny Rees** (bg), a former member of the **Black Velvets** and the **Topspots**, as well as **Cliff Roberts** from the original **King Size Taylor & the Dominoes** line-up on drums again. Whether or not this group backed **King Size Taylor** on his Decca single *Somebody's Always Trying* is not certain, but very possible. **Kenny Rees** left and was replaced by another former 'Domino'- **Frank Galloway** of the **Griff Parry Five**.

In this line-up, **King Size Tayor & his Band** existed until 1965, toured Germany with the two additional sax players **Rolf Roger Reich**, formerly of the **Black Devils** from Brunswick,

King Size Taylor Band

and **Mahmoud Haari**, a French musician of Moroccan origin. In early 1965, this group split again and **Barry Davis** joined **Mike Warner & the New Stars** from Bielefeld.

On another Germany tour, **King Size Taylor** was backed by the **Tramps**, and at gigs in England by the **Griff Parry Five**. Around this time also the single *Let Me Love You* was released by **King Size Taylor** on the British Polydor label - his final record. **King Size Taylor** then quit show business and in spite of countless attempts by musicians and promoters, he did not return to the stage for many years.

In October 1990 on a memorial night for **Rory Storm**, planned by **Bob Wooler** and organised by the 'Mersey Cats', the **Dominoes** were also on the bill - sadly without **Ted Taylor**, who had taken over his parents' butcher shop in Southport in the Sixties.

The **Dominoes** appeared in a line-up with **Charly Flynn** (g/voc), **Bobby Thompson** (bg/voc), **Sam Hardie** (p/voc), **John Kennedy** (g/voc), **Howie Casey** (sax) and **Dave Lovelady** (dr) and in an impressive manner made clear that they were still great musicians. **Sam Hardie** joined the re-formed **Cliff Roberts Rockers**, where he played until the mid-Nineties.

When **King Size Taylor** started to appear again at the 'Merseycats' events in 2002, he was occasionally backed by the **Dominoes** again.

At first the line-up included **Sam Hardie**, **John Frankland**, **Barry Davis** and **Mesh Stephenson** as drummer, who in the Sixties had played with the **Deltones** and **St. Paul & the Angels**, who were both connected to **Ian & the Zodiacs.**

Later, for various gigs in Hamburg the group appeared in the full line-up of the Sixties again – with **King Size Taylor** (voc/g), **Bobby Thompson** (voc/bg), **John Frankland** (g/voc), **Sam Hardie** (p/voc), **Howie Casey** (sax) and **Gibson Kemp** on drums.

In 2006 **King Size Taylor** moved to live in Hamburg and occasionally appears on the scene again, where he is backed by various musicians, but from time to time by the original **Dominoes**, who meanwhile also go in their own right without their former bandleader.

<u>Single discography</u>
as **Audrey Arno & die Tony Taylor Band**:
Bitte Bleib Doch Bei Mir / Limbo Italiano   G- Polydor NH 52-098 / 1962
(the A-side is the German version of *Please Stay With Me*)
as **The Shakers**:
Hippy Hippy Shake / Money   G- Polydor NH 52-158 / 1963
Whole Lotta Lovin' / I Can Tell   G- Polydor NH 52-272 / 1963
Memphis Tennessee / Dizzy Miss Lizzy   G- Polydor NH 52-928 / 1964
Memphis Tennessee / Money   UK-Polydor NH 66-990 / 1964
Dr. Feelgood / Hippy Hippy Shake   UK-Polydor NH 66-991 / 1964
as <u>King Size Taylor & the Dominoes</u>:
The Fortune Teller / Never In A Hundred Years   G- Philips   345.618 PF / 1963
Hello Josephine / Stupidity   G- Ariola   10.578 AT / 1964
I'm Late / I've Been Watching You   G- Ariola   10.728 AT / 1964
Skyeboat Song / Down In The Valley   G- Ariola   10.730 AT / 1964
Lipstick, Powder And Paint / Heebie Jeebies   G- Ariola   18.074 AT / 1964
Stupidity / Bad Boy   UK- Decca   F.11874 / 1964

<u>King Size Taylor</u> – solo:
Somebody's Always Trying / Looking For My Baby   UK- Decca   F.11935 / 1965
Let Me Love You / Thinkin'   UK- Polydor N 56152 / 1966
<u>EP discography</u>
as **The Shakers:**
TWIST & SHAKE   G- Polydor   21628 / 1963
- **Mashed Potatoes And Hot Pastrami / Green Onions / Hello Josephine / Long Tall Sally**
(this EP was re-released as 'King Size Taylor & the Dominoes' in 1964 on the red Polydor label with the same catalogue number)

<u>Different French release</u>:
LES SHAKERS   F- Polydor   50035 / 1963
- **Memphis Tennessee / Money / Twist And Shout / Mashed Potatoes And Hot Pastrami**
as <u>King Size Taylor & the Dominoes</u>:
KING SIZE TAYLOR & THE DOMINOES - (TEENBEAT 2)   G- Ariola   41168 CT / 1964
- **I've Been Watching You / Shake, Shake, Shake / Clarabella / I'm Late**
TEENBEAT 2   UK- Decca DFE 8569 / 1964

- All Around The World / Slippin' And Slidin' / You Can't Sit Down / Hello Josephine

Different Spansh release:

SHOW EN STAR-CLUB   **E – Vergara   117 – XC / 1964**
- Unchain My Heart / Hello Josephine / Stupidity / All Around The World
LP discography
as **The Shakers**:
LET'S DO THE SLOP, TWIST, MADDISON, HULLY GULLY G- Polydor   46639 / 1963
   **- Twist And Shout / Hippy Hippy Shake / Money / Hello Josephine / Memphis Tennessee / Whole
Lot Of Lovin' / Domino Twist / I Can Tell / Mashed Potatoes / Ruby Ann / Long Tall Sally / Dr. Feelgood
/ Sweet Little Sixteen / Country Music / Dizzy Miss Lizzy / Green Onions**

   (Please note that this album was re-released in Germany in 1964 with the title 'Shaker's Twist Club
with King Size Taylor & the Dominoes' (G-Polydor 46639). It also came out in England with the title 'The
Shakers' in 1964 (UK-Polydor LPHM 46639) and in the USA as 'Real Gonk Man' (US-Midnight HLP
2101). On the US release the songs *Whole Lot Of Lovin', Domino Twist, Mashed Potatoes* and *Country
Music* were missing.)

   as **King Size Taylor & the Dominoes**:
TWIST-TIME IM STAR-CLUB HAMBURG - Folge 2   G- Ariola   70952 IT / 1964
   **- All Around The World / Stupidity / Slippin' And Slidin' / Unchain My Heart / Bad Boy / Short On
Love / Hello Josephine / You Can't Sit Down**
   - - - the other side of this album featured the **Bobby Patrick Big Six**   - - -
STAR-CLUB TIME MIT KING SIZE TAYLOR & THE DOMINOES G- Ariola   71430 IT / 1964
   **- I've Been Watching You / All Around The World / Down In The Valley / She Said Yeah / You Make
Me Happy / Sherry Baby / Shake, Shake, Shake / Skye Boat Song / Golly Golly What / Bad Boy /
Clarabella**
   KING SIZE TAYLOR & THE DOMINOES / BOBBY PATRICK BIG SIX
                                                                    G- Ariola   71764 IT / 1964
   - Heebie Jeebies / Oo Papa Doo / Wa-Watussi / Let's Dance / Broken Arrow / Lipstick, Powder And Paint
   - - -   the other side of this album featured the **Bobby Patrick Big Six** - - -

Tracks on compilation albums:
as **King Size Taylor & the Dominoes**:

Slow Down	on 'Liverpool Beat'	**G- Fontana 681557 TL / 1964**
Fortune Teller	on 'Liverpool Beat'	**G- Fontana 681557 TL / 1964**
Fortune Teller	on '11 Stars At The Star-Club'	**G- Star Club 148005 STL / 1964**

as **Boots Wellington & his Rubber Band**:
What 'd I Say on '16 Beatgroups from the Hamburg-Scene' G Polydor LPHM 46.439 / 1964

What 'd I Say	on 'Beat City'	**G-Polydor SLPHM 237.660 / 1965**
Summertime	on 'Beat City'	**G-Polydor SLPHM 237.660 / 1965**
Baby Face	on 'Beat City'	**G-Polydor SLPHM 237.660 / 1965**
Unchain My Heart	on 'Go, Go, Go'	**G-Polydor Intern. 623.001 / 1965**
Feel So Bad	on 'Go, Go, Go'	**G-Polydor Intern. 623.001 / 1965**

Unreleased tracks:
   In 1957/58, **The Dominoes** (feat. **King Size Taylor**) recorded the songs *Shortnin' Bread, Matchbox,*
and *Roll Over Beethoven* in private sessions which were probably the first Merseybeat recordings ever.
   Further songs by the group that were recorded and at least partially featured on acetates are *Whole
Lotta Shakin' Goin' On, Baby, Great Balls Of Fire, Guitar Boogie, So Long, I Want You To Know, Mean
Woman Blues, Autumn Leaves, Lend Me Your Comb, Good Golly Miss Molly, Hey, Hey, Hey, Hey, Your
True Love, Sad And Blue, My Soul, Saw My Baby With Another Boy*, as well as some instrumentals.

JOHNNY TEMPLER & THE HI-CATS

The **Hi-Cats** originally were formed by **Vic Grace** in Liverpool in 1961, after he previously had played with **Mark Peters & the Cyclones**.

Under the name of **Vic & the Hi-Cats**, the group in its original line-up consisted of **Vic Grace** (g/voc), **Austin 'Aussie' Brown** (g/voc), **Tony Gaskell** (bg) and **Brian Cochen** (dr). Except **Vic Grace** all the musicians adopted stage names and so **Austin Brown** became **Johnny Sanchez**, while **Tony Gaskell** called himself **Tony Tarson** and **Brian Cochen**'s name then was **Chick Broderick**.

Johnny Templer
Lead Singer

Vic & the Hi-Cats in the beginning mainly played instrumentals in the style of the **Shadows**, but realised that they needed a real lead vocalist. They found one in **Wally Staines**, who adopted the name of **Danny Havoc** and the group continued as **Danny Havoc & the Hi-Cats**, now mainly playing the topical hits and **Cliff Richard** stuff, from which can be concluded that it was not one of the harder Beat groups.

Between **Danny Havoc** and the other members some personal problems arose and during that time **Tony Tarson** temporarily was replaced by **Dave Collins** on the bass guitar. **Danny Havoc** and **Dave Collins** then left the group to form the **Ventures**, who later became the **Secrets**, but that is another story in this book.

Again the **Hi-Cats** were looking for a lead singer and recruited **John Dempsey** from the just disbanded **G-Men**, who then became **Johnny Templer** and the group accordingly **Johnny Templer & the Hi-Cats**.

When **Chick Broderick** left and quit showbiz he was replaced by **Pete Orr**, who left quite soon to join **Groups Inc.** and then also became a member of the **Ventures**. According all these changes **Johnny Templer & the Hi-Cats** then appeared in the following line-up:

Johnny Templer	**(voc)**
Vic Grace	**(lg/voc)**
Tony Gaskell	**(rg)**
Austin Brown	**(bg)**
Mal Thory	**(dr)**

Tony Gaskell had returned and the new drummer **Mal Thory** was a former member of the **Black Cats**.

Johnny Templer & the Hi-Cats quickly became popular on the scene and were recorded for the BBC radio show 'Here We Go'. They played two songs, of that only the **Tommy Roe** number *Sheila* is known. A little later the group recorded an acetate, not in one of Liverpool's studios but in a church hall somewhere on Rose Lane in Allerton. Beside the **Johnny Templer** original *Tonight Will Be The Night* they recorded three more cover versions, probably all **Cliff Richard** related stuff. As only **Vic Grace** kept his copy, and he died a few years ago in London, nobody can remember the other songs. **Johnny Templer** thinks that it was all **Cliff Richard** numbers, but could not recall the titles.

Because of disagreements about the musical direction, founder **Vic Grace** left to join **Danny Havoc & the Ventures**, who a little later, under his leadership became the **Secrets**, but that is another story in this book. The groups music from then on was more influenced by the American Rock 'n'Roll.

The new lead guitarist with **Johnny Templer & the Hi-Cats** was **Roy Wood**, who had formerly played with the **Nomads**, who a little later developed into the **Mojos**. He did not stay too long and went on to join **Sonny Webb & the Cascades**. A few months later he sadly committed suicide.

The young **Stan Smith** was selected as new guitarist, he was a newcomer on the scene and also the group was joined by girl singer **Barbara Harrison**, who had toured with **Faron's Flamingos** in France before.

In November 1962 **Johnny Templer & the Hi-Cats** were voted No.20 in the popularity poll of 'Mersey Beat' but in spite of that success **Barbara Harrison** soon went on to join **Danny Havoc & the Ventures** and a little later was followed by **Austin Brown** to this group, that were the **Secrets** now. **Johnny Templer & the Hi-Cats** were joined by **Ron Smith** as new bass guitarist, he had formerly played with **J.J. & the Hi-Lites** and **Mersey Monsters**.

The next to leave was **Mal Thory** and his replacement was **Jimmy Lacey**, who came from the **Profiles**. These continuing changes in the line-up led **Johnny Templer & the Hi-Cats** to disband in 1964.

Johnny Templer, together with his brother **Mike Dempsey** and drummer **Frank Stewart** formed the **Borderliners**, who were joined by **Tony Gaskell** as fourth member.

Tony Gaskell after that played with **Screaming Lord Sutch & the Savages** and then joined a group called **Hartford West**, where he met up again with **Austin Brown**. **Jimmy Lacey** appeared again on the scene as a member of **Chick Graham & the Coasters** and the **Three Cheers**, who had developed from **Mark Peters & the Method** and later changed the name into **Phase Three**.

Stan Smith joined the **Country Five** and later various Merseybeat groups. He sadly died earlier this year. **Tony Gaskell** is still active in the music business and today plays in the Country & Rock trio **Bojangles**.

Discography

Johnny Templer & the Hi-Cats never released an official record but were recorded for BBC's 'Here We Go Show" in 1962 with two songs of them only the **Tommy Roe** number *Sheila* is known.

Beside this the group in the same year recorded an acetate EP, which sadly has not survived the years and therefore it is only known that the **Johnny Templer** original *Tonight Will Be The Night* was amongst it.

Johnny Templer and the Hi Cats

KARL TERRY & THE CRUISERS

This began with the **Gamblers Skiffle Group**, formed in Liverpool by **Terry Connor** (voc/g) in 1956, together with brothers **Les Braid** (bass) and **Gordon Braid** (g).

Les Braid became a member of **Johnny Carter & the Hi-Cats** in 1957 and then joined the **Bluegenes**, who later became the **Swinging Blue Jeans**.

Gordon Braid obviously quit the music business, while **Terry Connor** formed **Terry Connor & the Teen-Aces**, who were more Rock 'n' Roll orientated. This group existed

The Gamblers Skiffle Group feat. Karl Terry

until the early Sixties and then disbanded without having had more than local popularity.

Terry Connor changed his stage name to **Karl Terry** and formed **Karl Terry & the Cruisers**, that in the original line-up consisted of:

Karl Terry	**(voc/g)**
David Hamilton	**(g/voc)**
Gerry Clayton	**(g/voc)**
Don McCormack	**(bg)**
Gordon Templeton	**(dr)**

This was a real Rock 'n' Roll group and the line-up was joined by **Larry Clarke** as an additional member, who a little later took over the lead guitar, when **David Hamilton** left the group. **Larry Clarke** was the former leader of **Jet & the Centerbeats**.

Karl Terry, who had put his guitar aside in the meantime, was given the epithet 'Lover Boy' by his fans, but a little later was christened the 'Sheik Of Shake' by famous Cavern DJ **Bob Wooler**.

Karl Terry's original Cruisers

In October 1961, **Karl Terry & the Cruisers** were voted No.7 in the 'Mersey Beat' popularity poll, clearly showing how popular this band had become within a very short time.

In 1962, **Gordon Templeton** left the group and was replaced by **Roy Dyke**, who did not stay too long and then joined the **Remo Four**. **Gordon Templeton** returned to **Karl Terry & the Cruisers**, who very soon disbanded as not all the musicians wanted to become professionals. **Larry 'Jet' Clarke** was most probably the leader of the Liverpool group **Jet & the Valiants** after that.

367

'The Sheik Of Shake' **Karl Terry** and **Gordon Templeton** then re-formed the band under the old name, together with **Freddie Ennis** (bg/voc) and **John Kirkpatrick** (g), who both came from **Johnny Saint & the Travellers**. The group was also joined by songstress **Nicolette Moran**.

But already in 1963, **Karl Terry & the Cruisers** split up again when **Karl Terry** first joined **Group One** and then became a member of the **Delemeres**, a Newcastle group that had settled down in Liverpool. **Freddie Ennis** joined **Mark Peters & the Cyclones**, who later developed into **The Few**, while **John Kirkpatrick** played with **Lee Shondell & the**

The Delemeres with Karl Terry live at the Cavern

Boys before he became a member of **Jason Eddie & the Centremen**. The drummer **Gordon Templeton** joined the **Valkyries** from Birkenhead.

When the **Delemeres** moved back to Newcastle, **Karl Terry** became a member of **Amos Bonny & the T.T.s**. They continued as **Karl Terry & the T.T.s** after their singer left.

Later there was an amalgamation between the remaining members of this group and the remaining members of the **Clayton Squares**, under the name of **The T-Squares**, who also included **Karl Terry** again, after he had played for a short time with the **Talismen**, who had separated from **Vince Earl**. The **T-Squares** toured Germany twice with different line-ups under the name of the **Clayton Squares** before they broke up again. **Karl Terry** then became a member of **Rory Storm & the Hurricanes** for a short time, and after that played with **Capricorn** but then he re-formed **Karl Terry & the Cruisers** in around 1967/68.

Since that time, **Karl Terry & the Cruisers** have been an original Rock 'n' Roll band, and in 1978 they were featured on the revival sampler 'Mersey Survivors' with their version of *I'm Gonna Be A Wheel Someday,* which was the first record ever to be released by 'The Sheik Of Shake' **Karl Terry**. It was not a very good one as it was played much too fast, but this was obviously a decision by the producer.

There was also a rumour that an album was released by the group with the title 'Cruisin'', including songs from the 'Mersey Survivors' recording session, but this has never been seen. Even **Karl Terry** is not sure if it really was released or not. Nobody can really swear that it does not exist, although this is most improbable.

A little later their first single *Haunted House* was released on **Dave Crosby**'s 'Rox' label, and this time it sounded like **Karl Terry & the Cruisers**, which is not really a surprise as the group at that time had a great line-up that consisted of **Bob Hardy** (lg), **Allen 'Gaz' Gaskell** (sax), **Mike Kearns** (sax), **Dennis Swale** (bg) and **Tommy McGuire** (dr).

Dennis Swale then got married and was replaced by **Tony Dunmore**, but shortly after this the complete group parted from **Karl Terry** and became the original **Gaz & the Groovers**, a legend of its own that had a longer residence in Germany under the name of **Juke** and at one point together with **Alby Donnelly** also appeared as **Supercharge**.

The permanently changing line-ups of **Karl Terry & the Cruisers** over the years involved lots of well known Merseybeat musicians from the Sixties scene.

They included, for example, **Vinnie Ismael** (g), who in the good old days was a member of the **Harlems** and **Valentinos**, **Chris Wilson** (g), a former member of the **Galvanisers**, **John Rathbone** (dr), who had played with the **Masterminds** and the **Almost Blues**, **Billy Conroy** (dr), who was once a member of **Jason Eddie & the Centremen** and **Lance Railton** (g), **Wally Shepard** (bg) and **Dave Gore** (g), all of the legendary **Earl Preston &**

Karl Terry & The Cruisers

the T.T.s, as well as **Brian Jones** (sax) of the **Undertakers**.

These are just a few of the names as it would take a complete book about **Karl Terry & the Cruisers** if all the different line-ups were considered. In 1993 the 'Sheik Of Shake' found a quite steady line-up for his group that included:

Kenny Goodlass   (dr) - who had formerly played with the **Kirkbys**, **Fruit Eating Bears**, **Escorts**, **Swinging Blue Jeans** and **Merseybeats**
Ritchie Prescott   (g) - who in the Sixties played with **Derry Wilkie & the Pressmen**
Alan Stratton   (bass) - a former member of the **Black Cats** and **Kansas City Five**
Andy Bourne   (sax) - a former member of **Faron's Flamingos**.

In this line-up, in the summer of 1994 **Karl Terry & the Cruisers** recorded the great album 'Rock 'n' Roll - That's All' on the small German collectors label 'Merseyside Records'.

This record was played live at the studio and accordingly captured the real sound of **Karl Terry & the Cruisers**, especially songs like *Sea Cruise, Twenty Flight Rock, Queen Of The Hop, Shake Rattle & Roll, Mess Of Blues,* the fantastic rocking *High School Confidential* or the **Karl Terry** original *What's Wrong With Me.*

After that, the line-up changed again numerous times but **Karl Terry** is still going strong on the scene and of course his music is still good old Rock'n'Roll.

Discography
It is hard to understand that there was no record released by this first class Rock 'n' Roll band in the Sixties, although it was one of Liverpool's pioneering groups.

But in 1978, the band had its first release on the revival sampler **'Mersey Survivors'** (**UK-Raw RWLP 104**) with the song *I'm Gonna Be A Wheel Someday.* From the same recording session an album by **Karl Terry & the Cruisers** may have been released with the title *Cruisin',* but this information is very doubtful as nobody has seen this long player yet, not even one of the involved musicians. Shortly after this, **Karl Terry & the Cruisers** released the following single:

Haunted house / Stick It In Your Pipe And Smoke It   **UK- Rox 008 / 1978**

LP **'Rock 'n' Roll – That's all'**   **G- Merseyside ME 00.102 / 1994**
   - Sea Cruise / Mess Of Blues / Blueberry Hill / What's Wrong With Me / High Shool Confidential / Ain't That A Shame / Twenty Flight Rock / My Blue Heaven / Queen Of The Hop / Will You Still Love Me Tomorrow / Pretend / Shake, Rattle & Roll / They Say
   The Delemeres (feat. Karl Terry):
See You On Saturday Night/Summertime   **UK-Eroica - acetate / 1963**

TIFFANY & THE THOUGHTS

This group appeared for the first time on the Liverpool scene under the name of the **Thoughts** in 1964 and was managed by **Geoff Leack**, who also was the manager of the **Four Dimensions**, and so already had the girl singer **Irene Green** (aka '**Tiffany**') under his wing.

Irene Green was originally a founder member of the **Liverbirds** and later appeared with the **Dimensions** for a while under the name of **Tiffany & the Dimensions**.

After she had separated from the **Dimensions**, she cut the really good solo single *Am I Dreaming*, under the name of '**Tiffany**', a little known but nice **Jackie DeShannon** number. Then **Geoff Leack** brought her together with the **Thoughts** and the group from that moment on appeared as **Tiffany & the Thoughts** in the following line-up:

Tiffany	**(voc)**
Phil Boardman	**(g/voc)**
Pete Beckett	**(g/voc)**
Alan Hornby	**(bg)**
Paul Comerford	**(dr/voc)**

Pete Beckett came from the **Modes**, while **Paul Comerford** was a former member of the **Pulsators**. The drummer left again to join the **Cryin' Shames** and later played with the **Escorts** and the **Times**. He was replaced by **Dave Croft**, who had formerly played with the **City Beats**, the **Cliftons**, **Blues System** and the **Aztecs**.

This line-up then was signed to EMI and released the nice single *Find Out What's Happening* in early 1965, which was coupled with a very good version of the **Irma Thomas** number *Baby Don't Look Down*. The record, which was also released in Germany, had an interesting arrangement and featured good vocals by '**Tiffany**', but sadly did not become a hit.

Probably still in 1965, '**Tiffany**' and the **Thoughts** separated again, when '**Tiffany**' quit show business and later got married to her manager **Geoff Leack**. The **Thoughts** carried on and also toured Germany, where they mainly appeared in the Frankfurt area.

In 1966, **Dave Croft** played with the **Fruit Eating Bears** for a short time, but then returned to the **Thoughts**, who

Tiffany

teamed up with the duo **Johnny & John**, consisting of the former **Merseybeats** members **Johnny Gustafson** and **John Banks**.

With this duo, the **Thoughts** recorded some songs for Polydor, of which *Bumper To Bumper*, coupled with *Scrape My Boot* were released on single in 1966. This was only credited to **Johnny & John**.

Also in 1966, the **Thoughts** recorded a single in their own right with the **Ray Davies** number *All Night Stand* for the Philips' sub label Planet, coupled with the group's original *Memory Of Your Love*.

Dave Croft left the group again for another three weeks and during this time played with the Australian **Easybeats**, who had just recorded the follow-up single to their big international hit *Friday On My Mind* with the title *Heaven And Hell,* on which **Dave Croft** was featured on drums. But then he returned to the **Thoughts**, who had settled down in London and most probably split in 1967. **Pete Beckett** emigrated to the USA and played with a group called **Paladine**, while **Phil Boardman** joined the Army. **Alan Hornby** worked for an insurance company in Formby and **Dave Croft** became a pub owner in Liverpool.

It should be mentioned that according a notice in 'Mersey Beat', the female organist **Marion Hill** was a member of the **Thoughts** in 1964, after she had played with the **Memphis Rhythm & Blues Combo** before, but in the end it is only known that she joined **The Runaways**.

It is also important to know that the above mentioned **Thoughts** had no connection to the recording group **Paul Dean & the Thoughts**, who hailed from London.

Discography
'Tiffany' - solo:
Am I Dreaming / I Know   UK- Parlophone R 5311 / 1964

as **Tiffany & the Thoughts**:
Find Out What's Happening / Baby Don't Look Down   UK- Parlophone R 5439 / 1965

Johnny & John (backed by the **Thoughts**):
Bumper To Bumper / Scrape My Boot   UK- Polydor BM 56087 / 1966

The Thoughts - solo:
All Night Stand / Memory Of Your Love   UK- Planet   PLF   118 / 1966

The Thoughts

T.L.'s BLUESICIANS

A real Blues group (as the name suggests), **T.L.'s Groundhogs** were formed in the Old Swan area of Liverpool during the Autumn of 1963.

When the quintet was booked to play the 'Cavern' for the first time in April 1964, they were on the same bill as the American Blues legend **John Lee Hooker**, who that night was backed by a London group also named **The Groundhogs**. **Bob Wooler**, resident DJ and also programme manager of the 'Cavern', insisted that the Liverpool group must change their name if they wanted the gig, which is how **T.L.'s Bluesicians** were born.

However, as this unexpected name change was requested at such short notice, the boys found themselves advertised in the Liverpool Echo to appear on the 'Peppermint Lounge' before midnight as **T.L.'s Groundhogs**, and after midnight on the 'Cavern All-Night Session' as **T.L.'s Bluesicians**. From that moment on they continued with that name in the line-up with

Tony Leeuwangh	**(voc/harp)**
Bob Hardy	**(lg/voc)**
Chris Lawson	**(rg)**
Pete Newton	**(bg/voc)**
Phil Perry	**(p)**
Vic Brunskill	**(dr)**

The group played material by artists such as **Sonny Boy Williamson**, **T-Bone Walker** and **Chuck Berry** and soon became popular on the local scene.

Still in 1964, **T.L.'s Bluesicians** went into the CAM studio in Moorfields and recorded **T-Bone Walker**'s *The Hustle Is On (T-Bone Blues)*, as well as the **Chuck Berry** version of the **Amos Milburn** hit *Down The Road A Piece*, which were kept on acetate.

This great and very interesting recordings only in 2002 were released on the compilation CD 'This Is Merseybeat Vol. 3', which was put out by BBC radio presenter **Mike Brocken**.

In 1965 some of the group wanted to turn professional and some did not – with the result that **Tony Leeuwangh**, **Chris Lawson** and **Vic Brunskill** quit playing. At least there is no record of them having joined any other bands after that.

Bob Hardy then organized **Phil Perry**, **Pete Newton**, former **Clayton Squares** frontman **Terry Hines** and two other Liverpool musicians into the **Terry Hines Sextet**, but that is another story that can be followed in this book.

Discography

Down The Road A Piece / The Hustle Is On (T-Bone Blues)   **UK- CAM acetate**   / **1964**
(The above mentioned two songs were released on the Mayfield CD **'This Is Merseybeat Vol 3'** in 2002).

THE TRAVELLERS

This group was formed under the name of **Johnny Saint & the Travellers** by **Johnny Laffin** in Liverpool in 1960 and accordingly was one of the pioneering groups of the Merseybeat scene. In 1962, the group's name was shortened to **The Travellers**, but later it was sometimes still announced under the original name and **Johnny Saint** of course was none other than founder **Johnny Laffin**. Right from the beginning, the group consisted of the following musicians:

Johnny Saint	**(voc/g)**
John Kirkpatrick	**(g/p/voc)**
Freddie Ennis	**(bg/voc)**
Roy Cresswell	**(dr)**

    John Kirkpatrick's name sometimes was shortened to **John Kirk**.

    In April 1962, the **Travellers** went down to London to make test recordings for PYE and, amongst others, the songs *Let's Twist Again* and *Dream Baby* were recorded, but sadly nothing was ever released on record.

    Roy Cresswell left the group a little later to join **Mark Peters & the Cyclones**, who after a while developed into **The Few**. The **Travellers** were joined by **Bernie Rogers** as their new drummer. But this line-up only existed until October 1962 and then the **Travellers** disbanded totally, which is quite hard to understand as the group counted as one of the most popular ones on the Merseybeat scene. However, **John Kirkpatrick** and **Freddie Ennis** became members of **Karl Terry & the Cruisers**, and after that **Freddie Ennis** also joined the **Cyclones**, where he met up with **Roy Cresswell** again.

    John Kirkpatrick became a member of **Lee Shondell & the Boys** and after that played with **Jason Eddie & the Centremen**. In the Seventies he was a member of the very successful **Albion Dance Band**. **Bernie Rogers** joined **Lee Curtis & the All Stars** and after that was a member of **Denny Seyton & the Sabres**. Later he appeared as freelancing drummer on the scene again. In the early Nineties, he played with **Johnny Guitar & his Hurricanes** and after that joined **Faron's Flamingos**. What happened to **Johnny Saint** is not known exactly, but in 1964 a group with the name the **Travellers** appeared again on the Liverpool scene.

    As it is impossible that the old band was re-formed in its original line-up, it might have been the case that the new **Travellers** were led by **Johnny Saint** again and included some new musicians. But this is not proven at all and only one of many possibilities. However, these new **Travellers** had no great success on the scene and disappeared again a little later.

Discography

Neither under the name of **Johnny Saint & the Travellers**, nor as the **Travellers** was a regular record released, but in 1962, the **Travellers** recorded the songs *Let's Twist Again* and *Dream Baby* for PYE and these are probably still sleeping in the archives of the record company – if they were actually kept at all.

GUS TRAVIS & (various groups)

It was most probably the music of **Gene Vincent**, that encouraged the young **Graham Bull** from Heswall on the Wirral to get into singing Rock 'n' Roll.

He changed his name into **Gus Travis** and in the late Fifties formed his first group under the name of **Gus & the Thundercaps** after the model used by **Gene Vincent & his Blue Caps**. From the beginning, their music was a sort of Country and Rock 'n' Roll in a line-up with:

Gus Travis	**(voc)**
Dave Carden	**(g)**
Ian McQuair	**(g)**
Alan Watts	**(p)**
Billy Bingham	**(bg)**
Ian Douglas	**(dr)**

Gus and the Thundercaps

Gus & the Thundercaps were definitely one of the very first Rock 'n' Roll groups on Merseyside and within a short time became very popular on the local scene. Because of his stage show, the singer was nicknamed **Gus *'Crazy Legs'* Travis**, an epithet that stayed with him over the years.

Dave Carden left to join the **Five Stars**, who were just changing from a Skiffle group to a Rock 'n' Roll band, where he replaced **John Kelman** (g), a former member of the **Dons**, who went on to join **Dee Fenton & the Silhouettes**. Besides **Dave Carden**, this group then consisted of **Brian Woods** (voc/bg), **Kenny Lazzard** (t-bass) and **Ian Broad** (dr). **Kenny Lazzard**, most probably identical to the musician **Stu Hazzard**, left to become a member of **Earl Royce & the Olympics**. **Dave Carden** was not replaced in **Gus & the Thundercaps**, while **Ian Malcolm** was replaced by **John Cochran**. The next to leave was **Billy Bingham**, who became a member of the **Four Sounds**. That was obviously too many changes for **Gus Travis**, who disbanded the **Thundercaps**. He and the remaining members teamed up with **Dave Carden** (g) and **Brian Woods** (bg) from the recently disbanded **Five Stars**.

This new group had the name of **Gus Travis & the Midnighters** and after **John Cochran** left to join **Wump & his Werbles**, the line-up consisted of:

Gus Travis	**(voc)**
Dave Carden	**(g)**
Ian McQuair	**(g)**
Brian Woods	**(bg)**
Ian Broad	**(dr)**

Ian Broad, of course, was also a former member of the **Five Stars**. This line-up lasted until May 1963 and **Gus Travis & the Midnighters** were counted among the leading groups of the Merseybeat scene.

That is why it is so hard to understand that the singer then separated from the group that continued as the **Midnighters**, where **Brian Woods** took over the lead vocals. A little later they teamed up with **Freddie Fowell**, who on some occasions already was backed by the **Five Stars** when he still appeared under the name of *'Freddy the Teddy'*. Meanwhile, he had changed his name into **Freddie Starr** and so the group became **Freddie Starr & the Midnighters** in 1963, but this is another story in this book.

The Four Sounds

Gus Travis teamed up with the new group of his old bass guitarist, who adopted the name of **Gus Travis & the Midnighers** for their appearances with **Gus Travis**, but besides this carried on in their own right as **The Four Sounds** in a line-up with **Dave Keighly** (voc/lg), **John Hinton** (p), **Billy Bingham** (bg/voc) and **Alan Denton** (dr). This cooperation was only temporary and the **Four Sounds** continued solo until 1964.

Dave Keighly and **Alan Denton**, who in the meantime had played with the **Exiles**, in 1965 re-formed the **Pilgrims**, while **John Hinton** became a successful professional musician in London and **Billy Bingham** later worked as a radio producer. **Gus Travis** himself amalgamated with the **Four Dymonds** from Birkenhead – of course under the name of **Gus Travis & the Dymonds** in a line-up with:

Gus Travis	**(voc)**
Geoff Brown	**(g)**
Jim Percival	**(g)**
John Holford	**(bg)**
Terry McCusker	**(dr)**

The Four Dymonds

Of **Terry McCusker** it is known that he was a former member of **Pete Demos & the Demons**, who also hailed from Birkenhead. Again, **Gus Travis & the Dymonds** became popular on the scene, but as with all the other groups before, **Gus Travis** also did not stay too long with them. In 1964 he left the group, that obviously disbanded at that time.

Of the individual members only **Terry McCusker** appeared again on the scene as a member of **Rip Van Winkle & the Rip-It-Ups**.

After that he played with the successful **Valkyries** and the legendary **Roadrunners**, before he joined **French Benefit**, who very soon changed their name to **Colonel Bagshot & the Incredible Bucket Band**.

The new backing group for **Gus Travis** became the **Drifters**, who originated from **Johnny Rocco & the Jets** and in the meantime were known as **Steve Day & the Drifters**. This new cooperation then continued under the name of **Gus Travis & the Rainchecks**.

It was a really great group that again had lots of success on the local scene but as with previous bands, the amalgamation with **Gus Travis** did not last too long. The reason for this was most probably the fact that the singer never wanted to leave Merseyside and accordingly always refused to turn professional.

The **Rainchecks** continued without him and not only remained one of the top acts on the scene, but also recorded a single in their own right - a different story again that is featured in this book.

The Rainchecks

Gus Travis continued as a singer on the scene in the period following this, but as far as it is known, he did not have a steady group anymore.

All through the years, his name was very popular, first on the Rock 'n' Roll scene and after that on the cabaret circuit of Liverpool and its surroundings.

In 1992, at a memorial concert for **Rory Storm** (an idea of **Bob Wooler** and realised by the 'Merseycats') the name **Gus Travis & the Midnighters** appeared again when they were on the bill. This line-up included the original members **John Cochran** and **Ian McQuair**, as well as **Gus Travis**.

After that gig the group sporadically appeared on the scene again, where it was joined by **Pete Watson** on lead guitar, who in the Sixties had played with the **Morockans**.

But this never became a steady group and **Gus Travis**, who is still a great stage personality, continued as solo singer in the Liverpool pubs and clubs.

Gus Travis

Discography:

Throughout his long career, **Gus Travis** never made a record, although he appeared with a few really good groups. Only an early Seventies concert was professionally recorded, which was solid Rock 'n' Roll with *Crazy Legs* and *Love Me* as outstanding numbers. At that concert he was not backed by one of the above named groups and as far as it is known, not even one of the musicians who played with him in his various groups of the Sixties was included.

THE TRENDS

At the beginning of the Sixties **The Beatcombers** were formed in Liverpool, and in 1963 changed their name to **Mike & the Merseymen**. They toured Germany the same year and, amongst other venues, appeared at the famous 'Star-Club' in Hamburg. Back in England, the band mainly worked in London, where their name was changed again, this time to **The Trends**.

This might have been a little confusing as in Liverpool there was a group with the name **The Trents**, and the only difference in the name was one letter, but they were two totally different groups that had no connections to each other. However, the **Trends** of this story consisted of:

Mike Kelly	**(voc/bg)**
Frank Bowen	**(g/voc)**
John Hayes	**(g/voc)**
Freddie Self	**(dr/voc)**

Until 1963, before their name was changed from **Mike & the Merseymen** into **The Trends**, **Tony Priestly** (g/voc) was a member of the group, but he then joined **Earl Preston's Realms** and was replaced by **Frank Bowen**, who had played with the **Teenbeats, Cliff Roberts' Rockers, Howie Casey & the Seniors** and **Lee Curtis & the All Stars**. It seems he was something of a Beat globetrotter.

In 1964 **Mike Kelly** left the group and returned to Liverpool, where he disappeared from the scene. He was replaced in the **Trends** by **Harry Scully** from Liverpool, where he had previously played with the **Nashpool Four**. The lead vocals were then most probably taken over by **Freddie Self**. This line-up was signed to PYE and very soon their first single was released on the Piccadilly label - a cover-version of the **Beatles** song *All My Loving*. This single wasn't successful in the charts but it sold quite well.

The follow up *You're A Wonderful One* was released on the PYE label and was a great record, with an interesting version of *The Way You Do The Things You Do* on the flip-side, but once again it was not a great success. On the next release, also in 1964, the **Trends** backed girl singer **Tammy St. John** on her PYE single *Hey, Hey, Hey, Hey*, an up-tempo number, which was coupled with the **Shirelles** classic *Boys*. The group most probably also backed **Tammy St.John** in her live appearances for a time, but in 1964 disbanded totally.

Frank Bowen and **Harry Scully** stayed in London and became members of the **Bootleggers**, led by **Brian Auger**. After that, **Harry Scully** disappeared from the

The Trends with Tammy St.John

scene, while **Frank Bowen** returned to Liverpool, where he joined **Earl Royce & the Olympics**. He died in 1966 at a very young age. **John Hayes** also disappeared but **Freddie**

Self started a solo career as singer, and in 1964 the single *Don't Cry* came out on Mercury under his name. After that release he continued recording as **Freddie Ryder**.

In 1965, he had three singles out with *To Get Your Love Back, Some Kind Of Wonderful* and *Man Of The Moment,* which showed him to be a really good singer, but in spite of this he did not make a breakthrough. Then he disappeared from the scene, but in 1968 **Freddie Ryder** was back with a new recording contract, when he cut the singles *Shadows (I Can't See You)* and *The Worst That Could Happen* for the Columbia label. Sadly, none of his records could make the charts and nothing was heard of him again, which could mean that he quit show business and went back to his hometown of Liverpool. This at least was rumoured but it is not certain.

Single discography
as **The Trends**:

All My Loving / Sweet Little Miss Love	UK- Piccadilly	7N 35171 / 1963
You're A Wonderful One / The Way You Do The Things You Do	UK- PYE	7N 15644 / 1964

as backing-group for **Tammy St. John**:

Hey, Hey, Hey, Hey / Boys	UK- PYE	7N 15682 / 1964

Freddie Self – solo:

Don't Cry / Why Should I	UK- Mercury	MF 839 / 1964

Freddie Self as **Freddie Ryder** - solo:

To Get Your Love Back / A Little Thing Called Love	UK- Mercury	MF 864 / 1965
Some Kind Of Wonderful / Slow Down	UK- Mercury	MF 879 / 1965
Man Of The Moment / My Block	UK- Mercury	MF 935 / 1965
Shadows / Airport	UK- Columbia	DB 8335 / 1968
The Worst That Could Happen / World Of My Own	UK- Columbia	DB 8427 / 1968

CY TUCKER & THE FRIARS

This group originated from **Wayne Calvert & the Cimarrons**, formed in Liverpool in 1960 and consisting of **Wayne Calvert** (voc), **Paul Doyle** (g), **Chris Prescott** (g), **Danny Dring** (bg) and **Les Cave** (dr). **Thomas Thornton** (voc/g) replaced **Wayne Calvert** in the group that continued as **The Cimarrons**.

But **Thomas Thornton**, who in the meantime had changed his name to **Cy Tucker** left the group in 1961 to become a member of **Earl Preston & the T.T.s**, and he was replaced in the **Cimarrons** by **Tony O'Brian**, who was not the guitarist of the same name, who as **Ty Brian** played with **Rory Storm & the Hurricanes**.

Cy Tucker, who had joined **Earl Preston & the T.T.s** as an additional guitarist, became a second singer in that group and his lead vocals could also be heard on the songs *All Around The World* and *Hurt*, which were featured on the Oriole compilations 'This Is Merseybeat' Vol. 1 and Vol. 2. He also recorded the single *Highschool Dance* for Fontana under the name **Cy Tucker with Earl Preston's T.T.s** in 1963.

After **Earl Preston** left he was the lead singer and the group changed its name to **Cy Tucker & the T.T.s**. In 1964 he left the **T.T.s** again and formed his own band together with former **Cimarrons** guitarist **Paul Doyle** under the name of **Cy Tucker & the Friars**, that at first consisted of:

Cy Tucker	**(voc/g)**
Paul Doyle	**(g/voc)**
Charly Smullan	**(bg/voc)**
Tommy Hart	**(dr)**

In the same year, this new group released the first single on Fontana with *Let Me Call You Sweetheart,* which was coupled with *I Apologize.* It was a really good and very interesting record but sadly didn't achieve any bigger success, probably because it was not commercial enough for that time. Short after that, **Cy Tucker** released a solo single with the song *My Friend* and on the flip-side was a re-recorded version of *Hurt*, but this record also failed to become a success.

In 1965 **Charly Smullan** left to join **Earl Preston's Realms** and was replaced by former **Cimarrons** member **Danny Dring**, who in the meantime had played with **John Paul & the Deejays**, the **Denny Seyton Group** and **Mister X & the Masks**.

A little later, **Tommy Hart** also joined **Earl Preston's Realms** and his replacement was **Les**

CY TUCKER & THE FRIARS

Cave, also a former **Cimarrons** member who in the meantime had played with **Steampacket**. So, with the exception of guitarist **Chris Prescott**, who had disappeared from the scene, the old **Cimarrons** line-up was complete again, but this time under the name of **Cy Tucker & the Friars**. The group existed until 1969 in this line-up, but did not release anymore records. **Les Cave** then left and was replaced by **Len Brady**, who had formerly played with the **Top-C-Three**.

In 1975, **Paul Doyle** left and at first was replaced by **Terry Barrat**, who came from the **Silver Set**. Between 1975 and 1978, this line-up recorded the songs *Once In a While, Sweet City Woman* and *Funny Face* for an album with comedian **Al Dean** (Stag-Music SG 1009 / 1975), a single with a cover version of the **Status Quo** hit *Rockin' All Over The World*, as well as four nice EPs with the songs *Something About You Baby I Like, Don't Play That Song, Sweet City Woman* (Amazon Records AR7 001S / 1975); *Leaving On Your Mind, Gifts, Long Tall Sally and Funny Face* (Amazon Records AR 70012 S / 1976); *Pearl's A Singer, My Prayer, Southern Nights* and *Hurt* (Amazon Records AR 70016S / 1977); *If We're Not Back In Love On Monday, Higher And Higher, It's So Easy* and *I Don't Wanna Talk About It* (Jungle-Records JR 7029S / 1978), which were only sold at gigs and are really worth looking out for.

In 1980 **Terry Barrat** left again and was replaced by **Alan Trear**. In the same year, **Len Brady** left and **Cy Tucker & the Friars** were joined by **Vince Cadmore**, who stayed until 1982 and then was replaced by the returning **Les Cave**. **Alan Trear** was then replaced by **Arthur Caravan** as the new lead guitarist, having formerly played with **Staxx** and a group called **Pepperbox**. With this line-up, still with three former **Cimarrons** members, **Cy Tucker & the Friars** existed until 1988 and were very successful in the Liverpool club scene.

In 1988 **Danny Dring** left and a little later he teamed up with his brother in a cabaret duo. He was replaced by **Dave Dover**, who in the Sixties amongst others had been a member of the **Cordes** and later had played with **Colonel Bagshot & his Incredible Bucket Band**. A little later, **Les Cave** also left and joined **Geoff Nugent**'s **Undertakers**, and so **Cy Tucker** was the only remaining member of the original group. **Cy Tucker** is still going strong on Merseyside but today only in a duo together with **Arthur Caravan**.

Single discography
as **Cy Tucker with Earl Preston's T.T.s**:
My Prayer / Highschool Dance   UK- Fontana TF 424 / 1963

as **Cy Tucker & the Friars**:
Let Me Call You Sweetheart / I Apologize   UK- Fontana TF 470 / 1964

Cy Tucker - solo:
My Friend / Hurt   UK- Fontana TF 534 / 1965

Please note that the group also recorded under the name of **Cy Tucker & the Friars** on different labels in the Seventies. For detailed information please see the story.

TYME & MOTION

This was another Liverpool harmony group in the style of the **Everly Brothers** and the **Beach Boys**, which had its origin in the foundation of **Rita & the Rebs** in the area of Crosby in 1963/64.

The group consisted of the two vocalists **Rita Jacobson** and **Roy Ennis**, guitarist and singer **Ray Bright**, singing bass guitarist **John Ross** and **Ritchie Conner** on drums. They played the usual local gigs but did not make the headlines and when **Rita Jacobson** left in early 1966 the group almost broke up but then continued as **Tyme & Motion** in the line-up with:

Roy Ennis	(voc)
Ray Bright	(voc)
Tony Petches	(lg)
Alan Lucket	(rg)
John Ross	(bg/voc)
Robert Ninnim	(dr)

Robert Ninnim came from the great Liverpool harmony group **The Easybeats** while the former groups of **Tony Petches** and **Alan Lucket** are not known. When **Robert Ninnim** sadly died in early 1967, his place was taken over by **Robert Milne** who came from the **Admins**.

Still in the same year **Tyme & Motion** cut a interesting acetate with the song *September In The Rain*, which had been released as a single shortly before by the **Cryin' Shames**. This song, as well as the B-side, a version of **Del Shannon**'s *Kelly*, showed the great singing ability of the group, but this acetate sadly did not help to obtain a deal with a record company.

Tony Petches left and **Alan Lucket** took over the lead guitar, while **Ray Bright** for a short time played guitar again. With the arrival of **Eric Woolley** as new rhythm guitarist, **Ray Bright** stepped in front again as second singer, but soon decided to leave. From this moment on the lead vocals were shared by **Roy Ennis** and **John Ross**, who at that time were the only remaining members of **Rita & the Rebs**.

In this line-up **Tyme & Motion** went down to London and did some test recordings for an agency that was looking for groups to tour on the Continent. The group did not go abroad but from these recordings another acetate was cut with the **Drifters** song *I'll Take You Where The Music's Playing* and the **Ronettes** classic *Be My Baby*.

Tyme & Motion returned to Liverpool and kept on playing the normal club circuit but split up totally in early 1969. **Robert Milne** and **Eric Woolley** joined the **Almost Young**, who later toured in Germany for some time. All the other members disapeared from the scene for years, until **Ray Bright** re-formed **Tyme & Motion** in the middle of the Eighties, together with his old comrades **Alan Lucket** and **John Ross**. New members were **Dave Smith** on lead guitar and the drummer **Chris Mutch**, who in the Sixties had played with the **Krew** and after that had been a member of the **Swinging Blue Jeans**. They played the cabaret circuit but the revival of **Tyme & Motion** did not last too long and later none of the members appeared again on the scene.

Discography :

September In The Rain / Kelly   **UK - Deroy (?) – acetate / 1967**
I'll Take You Where The Music's Playing/ Be My Baby   **UK - private acetate   / 1968**

Tyme & Motion - from left to right: Roy Ennis, Robert Ninnim and Ray Bright

THE UNDERTAKERS

It was very difficult to find out how this legendary Liverpool group developed, and thus quite complicated to write it down. It is not easy to follow, but here is the real story:

In the late Fifties there was a Birkenhead based group called **Bob Evans & the Five Shillings** consisting of **Bob Evans** (voc), **Geoff Nugent** (g/voc), **Mike Millward** (g/voc), a certain **Ike** (bg) and **Billy Evans** (dr).

At live appearances this group sometimes mixed with the musicians of another Birkenhead/Wallasey group - the **Topspots**, consisting of **Robbie Hickson** (voc), **Peter Cook** (g/voc), **Jimmy Sloan** (g), **Dave Cooper** (bg) and **Tommy Bennett** (dr). So, **Bob Evans & the Five Shillings** sometimes became a sort of 'Bob Evans & the Nine Shillings', which was disliked by some musicians who left the group because of this. They were, for example **Geoff Nugent**, **Billy Evans**, the band leader's brother, and **Mike Millward**, who later became a member of the **Fourmost**. **Bob Evans & the Five Shillings** were then joined by **Chris Huston** as new guitarist, while **Bob Evans** himself took over the drums.

The Topspots

When the line-up had stabilized again as a five piece, **Bob Evans & the Five Shillings** changed their name to **The Vegas Five** and consisted of **Jimmy McManus** (voc) the returning **Geoff Nugent** (g/voc), **Chris Huston** (g/voc), former **Topspots** member **Dave 'Mush' Cooper** (bg) and **Bob Evans** (dr).

The other group, the **Topspots**, in the meantime had changed its name to **Dee & the Dynamites** and after the original *'Dee'* **Robbie Hickson** had left to join the **Kansas City Five** and drummer **Tommy Bennett** became a member of the **Pressmen**, **Dee & the Dynamites** consisted of **Brian Myers**, who adopted the name *'Dee'* and called himself **Brian Dee** (voc/g), **Peter Cook** (g/voc), **Jimmy Sloan** (g), **Jackie Lomax** (bg/voc) and **Bugs Pemberton** (dr).

The **Vegas Five** in the above line-up then changed its name again - to **The Undertakers**. They became a six piece when sax-player **Les Maguire** joined. Due to illness, **Bob Evans** was replaced by **Bugs Pemberton** from **Dee & the Dynamites**.

Dave Cooper left to join **Faron's Flamingos** and after that played with groups like the **Renegades, Lee Curtis & the All Stars**, the **Pawns** and the **Fruit Eating Bears**. The new bass guitarist with the **Undertakers** was **Jackie Lomax** from **Dee & the Dynamites**, who obviously had split up at that time.

Jimmy Sloan from **Dee & the Dynamites** disappeared from the scene, while **Peter Cook** and **Brian Dee** later teamed up again in **Earl Royce & the Olympics**, after **Peter Cook** had in the meantime played with the **Kansas City Five** and **Groups Inc.** and **Brian Dee** was with the **Dawnbreakers**, where he had met **Bob Evans** again.

Les Maguire left the **Undertakers** to become the pianist with **Gerry & the Pacemakers** and he was replaced by **Brian Jones** as new sax player. Then **Jimmy McManus** left to join the **Renegades**, who were still led by **Bob Evans** and where he met up again with former bass guitarist **Dave Cooper**. **Bob Evans** later became a member of **Dixie & the Dare Devils** and **Combo Six**. **Jimmy McManus** was not replaced in the **Undertakers**, who continued as a five-piece with:

Jackie Lomax   (voc/bg)
Geoff Nugent   (g/voc)
Chris Huston   (g/voc)
Brian Jones   (sax)
Bugs Pemberton (dr)

The story that led to the name change from the **Vegas Five** to the **Undertakers** is also interesting: When the group had to play a gig at the 'Litherland Town Hall', there was a misprint in the newspaper and the **Vegas Five** were listed in the deaths column instead of under the concerts. **Bob Wooler**, then resident disc-jockey at 'Litherland Town Hall', made the best out of that mistake and that evening played the *Death March* and introduced the band as **The Undertakers**, which was a tremendous success. The musicians liked it and adopted the name and so the legendary **Undertakers** were born.

The Undertakers - Live

In 1963 the group was signed to PYE and in July of the same year released the single *Everybody Loves A Lover* (sung by **Geoff Nugent**), which was coupled with *Mashed Potatoes,* sung by **Jackie Lomax**. This record did not make it, although *Mashed Potatoes* became a standard for lots of bands after that, most probably because of the **Undertakers** release, which was a really great recording. The follow-up, a good version of the **Coasters** number *What About Us*, coupled with a great version of *Money*, also failed to become a chart success for incomprehensible reasons.

The **Undertakers** had their first chart hit in 1964 with the fantastic *Just A Little Bit*, climbing to No.38, although it was really good enough for the top 10.

This was sadly also the last chart entry for the **Undertakers**, who, in spite of that misfortune with their records, were one of the most important Liverpool groups and also influenced a lot of other European bands with their music - especially in Hamburg, where they played quite often at the 'Star-Club'.

In 1964 the **Undertakers** decided to change their image and so changed their outfit and also shortened their name to **The Takers**. But this did not bring them anymore luck or success and the first record under their new name, the great rocking *If You Don't Come Back* was probably the least successful of their singles.

At the beginning of 1965 the group split, when first **Chris Huston** and a little later **Geoff Nugent** left. But in the same year **Jackie Lomax**, **Brian Jones** and **Bugs Pemberton** went to USA on a tour as a three-piece, where they met up again with **Chris Huston**, who had emigrated earlier.

In the United States the attention of independent producer **Bob Gallo** was drawn to the group and he recorded the songs *If I Fell In Love* and *Throw Your Love Away* with them as a single, and probably more songs for a whole album, but in the end none of it was released.

Historically it is said that the group then changed their name twice, first to **The Lost Souls** and then to **The Mersey Lads**, but this is not right and the connection here is as follows: When **Brian Jones** had to return to Liverpool in late 1965 because of an illness, the group broke up and **Chris Huston** quit showbusiness, stayed in the U.S.A. and later became a Sheriff. **Bugs Pemberton** joined the **Mersey Lads**, which was a sort of a Beatle band, and after that teamed up together with **Jackie Lomax** a Rhythm & Blues group, called the **Lost Souls**. But this was only for a very short time and then both together with **Tom Gacetta** (bg) and **John Cannon** (lg) from that group formed the **Lomax Alliance,** that were signed to CBS and did some recording sessions.

When the group returned to England **John Cannon** did not go with them so the **Lomax Alliance** in Europe continued as a trio, whereby **Jackie Lomax** had switched to guitar in the meantime. This group also played the 'Star-Club' in Hamburg again, but over there did not become as popular as the **Undertakers** had been before.

In 1967 this group recorded two good singles for CBS in England with *Try As You May* and *Genuine Imitation Life,* of which only the first one was released as **The Lomax Alliance**, while the second one was only credited to **Jackie Lomax**, although it was recorded by the whole group. Neither record sold very well, and the **Lomax Alliance** returned to the U.S.A., where they were joined again by **John Cannon**. A little later Jackie Lomax went back to England split up again, while the others continued together. They released  one more single with the songs *Hey Taxi* and *Enter Into My World* of that at least the first named was still from the initial recording session with CBS and as Jackie Lomax was not with them anymore, the record was credited to **The One.**

After that release the group broke up and **Bugs Pemberton** stayed in the U.S.A. and later was a member of **Aim Of Blue Thumb**. **Jackie Lomax** started a solo career, was managed by **Brian Epstein** and recorded for the Apple label. He released three solo albums and four singles, before he became a member of **Badger**. Then he joined the Birmingham group **Balls** and after that went solo again and emigrated to the USA.

But back to the **Undertakers**. Their story continued when the group was re-formed under their old name by **Geoff Nugent** and the returning **Brian Jones** in Liverpool in 1966, together with **Bob Frazer** (org), **Jimmy Jones** (bg) and **Bobby Williams** (dr), who all came from the just disbanded **Newtowns**, before that **Bobby Williams** had played with **Dino & the Wild Fires** who had developed into the **Wackers** in the meantime.

This line-up played together until 1968 when **Geoff Nugent** quit showbusiness for years. Later he returned to the scene as a solo artist on the cabaret circuit under the name of **Vern Gordon**. He was replaced in the new **Undertakers** by **Dennis Barton**, but the group did not survive too long.

Brian Jones became a session musician and amongst others was featured on the B-side of the **Beatles** hit single *Let It Be*. In 1975 he appeared on the 'Sold Out' album by the **Scaffold** and shortly after that became a member of **Karl Terry & the Cruisers**. He then joined the **Glitter Band**, but in the Eighties played with the newly formed **Faron's Flamingos**, before he returned to the **Glitter Band**. After that he was a member of the great Liverpool Soul group **Y-Kickamoocow**, which also included former **Undertakers** vocalist **Dennis Barton** again.

In the early Eighties, **Geoff Nugent** formed a new band under the name the **Undertakers**, but he was the only member who had played before under that legendary name.

In 1987, this **Undertakers** recorded a nice EP with the songs *Just A Little Bit, Will You Still Love Me Tomorrow, Barefootin'* and *Ferry Across The Mersey* (SYNC 001), most probably a private record, produced to sell at gigs. It is already a collector's item. Because of quarrels with the musicians, **Geoff Nugent** left the group in 1988 and formed another band which also included **Les Cave**, the former drummer with **Cy Tucker & the Friars** and **Billy Good** (bg), who in the Sixties was a member of **The Shufflers Sound** and **Lee Curtis & the All Stars**.

This new band appeared under the name of **Geoff Nugent's Undertakers** for some time because the former band kept the name **The Undertakers** and was also still performing, but more as a kind of dance band, while **Geoff Nugent's Undertakers** was a really good rough band again.

In the meantime, they have gone back to the original name of **The Undertakers** and the line-up has also changed again. Besides **Geoff Nugent** and **Billy Good**, the group now also included drummer **Jimmy O'Brien**, who came from the **New Image** and **Barry 'Baz' Davis** as a replacement for lead guitarist **Chris Evens**, who had to leave due to health reasons.

In the Sixties **Barry Davis** had played with the **Connoisseurs**, the band of **King Size Taylor** and the German group **Mike Warner & his New Stars**. After that he had been a member of such well known groups as the **New Vaudeville Band** and **Jimmy James & the Vagabonds**. On special occasions this line-up of the **Undertakers** is also joined by original sax player **Brian Jones**, who nowadays plays with the **Kirkbys** and a soul band called **Nighttrain**.

Single discography
as **The Undertakers**:

Everybody Loves A Lover / Mashed Potatoes	UK- PYE 7N 15543 / 1963
What About Us / Money	UK- PYE 7N 15562 / 1963
Just A Little Bit / Stupidity	UK- PYE 7N 15607 / 1964

as **The Takers**:

If You Don't Come Back / Think	UK- PYE 7N 15690 / 1964

The Lomax Alliance:

Try As You May / See The People	UK- CBS 2729 / 1967

386

Jackie Lomax - solo:

Genuine Imitation Life / One Minute Woman	**UK- CBS**	**2554 / 1967**
Sour Milk Sea / The Eagle Laughs At You	**UK-Apple APPLE 3 /**	**1968**
New Day / Fall Inside Your Eyes	**UK-Apple APPLE 11/**	**1969**
How The Web Was Woven / ThumbIn' A Ride	**UK-Apple APPLE 23/**	**1970**

(Please note that the single *Genuine Imitation Life* for CBS was recorded by the **Lomax Alliance** although it was only credited to **Jackie Lomax**)

LP **IS THIS WHAT YOU WANT**   **UK-Apple ST 3354 / 1969**

- Speak To Me / Is This What You Want / New Day / Sunset / Sour Milk Sea / Fall Inside Your Eyes / Little Yellow Pills / Take My Word / The Eagle Laughs At You / Baby You're A Lover / You've Got Me Thinking / I Just Don't Know

as **The One** (see story) :

Hey Taxi / Enter Into My World   **US- CBS   / 1967**

Tracks on compilation albums:
as **The Undertakers**:

Mashed potatoes on 'Package Tour'   **US-Golden Guinea GGL 0268 / 1964**

Unissued tracks:

It is known that the **Undertakers** recorded the songs *Peaches And Cream, Tricky Dicky, Nothing Can Stop Me, Watch Your Step, What's So Good About Goodbye* and *Hey, Hey, Hey, Hey* – all great numbers that sadly stayed unreleased.

The group under the name of **The Takers** recorded the songs *If I Fell In Love* and *Throw Your Love Away Girl* for the independent US producer **Bob Gallo**, which were never released. It is also rumoured that they recorded songs for a complete album in the United States, but this is not absolutely certain.

THE VALKYRIES

This group came together in Birkenhead, on the west side of the River Mersey, in the year 1962. Within a short time they had established themselves amongst the popular groups on the Liverpool scene.

In the summer of 1963, the **Valkyries** were booked to appear at the 'Star-Club' in Hamburg and of course the musicians had to become professionals to do that. They went down well in Hamburg and a little later the group toured France, where they were also quite successful and obtained a certain popularity. The **Valkyries** at that time consisted of the following musicians:

Ian Hunter	(voc/g)
Billy May	(g/voc)
Allan Burton	(bg/voc)
Tony Conway	(sax)
John Adams	(dr)

When they returned from France, the **Valkyries** were signed to Parlophone and in 1964 the single *Rip It Up* was released, with *What's Your Name*, a group's original, on the flip-side.

Although it was a really interesting and good Beat record, it wasn't too successful and so the first record by the **Valkyries** was also their last one. The group was featured on the German compilation 'Great Beat From Great Britain' with both songs, but of course this was not sufficient to make a bigger breakthrough.

Billy May left to join the **Pathfinders** from Birkenhead and was not replaced in the **Valkyries**, who continued as a quartet. When **John Adams** also left, the group found a new drummer in **Gordon Templeton**, who came from **Karl Terry & the Cruisers**, but he did not stay very long and was replaced by **Terry McCusker**, a former member of **Pete Demos & the Demons**, the **Four Dymonds**, **Gus Travis & the Dymonds** and **Rip Van Winkle & the Rip-It-Ups**. As the big time for the **Valkyries** did not come the group split in 1965.

Allan Burton became a member of the **Nashpool Four**, while **Terry McCusker** joined the **Roadrunners** and later played with **French Benefit** and **Colonel Bagshot's Incredible Bucket Band**.

In 1967 the **Valkyries** were reformed by **Ian Hunter**, **Allan Burton** and **Tony Conway** together with **Tony Williams** as new drummer. When the group got an offer to tour Spain, **Tony Conway** was not interested and left the group, that recruited the two sax players **John Chisholm** from the **In Crowd** and **Allen 'Gaz' Gaskell**, who came from the **Times**, that backed the vocal trio **Signs** at that time. Before that **Allen Gaskell** had already played with the **Young Ones** from Birkenhead, the **Tiyms**, the **K-Ds** and **Combo Six**. They were joined by **Iain Bradshaw** on organ as additional member, who came from a group called **Speed**.

This line-up in April 1967 went down to Madrid, but the destination was changed mid-journey to Rome. After being down in the South for three month with continuing problems with the manager and promoter, **Iain Bradshaw**, **John Chisholm** and **Allen Gaskell** both left and joined another trio – the remaining members of **Vic Grace & the Secrets**, who were also in Italy for a longer residence at that time. But that is another story featured under **The Secrets**.

The remaining **Valkyries**, namely **Ian Hunter**, **Allan Burton** and **Tony Conway** returned to Liverpool and obviously recruited other musicians as they a little later went on a tour in Japan, but that was also the last that was heard of them in the Sixties.

In the mid-Nineties, **Ian Hunter** and **Allan Burton** played with the re-formed **Pathfinders** who were occasionally joined by **Billy May**, who is a solo performer these days. The group only played at 'New Brighton Rock' events, an off-shoot of the 'Merseycats'.

After that, **Ian Hunter** continued in the music business and today he is a member of the great soul-group **Nighttrain**, that also includes other well known Merseybeat musicians like **Brian Jones** of the **Undertakers**, **Pete Newton** of the **Eddie Cave & the Fix** and **Nick Arnott** of the **Pressmen**.

Discography
Rip It Up / What's Your Name   UK- Parlophone R 5123 / 1964

Tracks on compilation albums:
Rip It Up on **'Great Beat From Great Britain'**   G- Odeon   **O 83680 / 1965**
What's Your Name on **'Great Beat From Great Britain'** G- Odeon   **O 83680 / 1965**

VIC & THE SPIDERMEN

This real Merseybeat group was formed as **The Spidermen** in Liverpool in early 1962. When their singer **Norman Dunn** left in the same year, he was replaced by **Vic Wright**, who was formerly known as **Pete Picasso** and had led the group **Pete Picasso & the Rock Sculptors**. Because of that change, the group changed its name to **Vic & the Spidermen** and soon became very popular on the Liverpool scene.

In December 1963, they were voted No.11 in the 'popularity poll' by the readers of 'Mersey Beat'. This means that not only had they established themselves amongst the leading Liverpool groups, but they were also more popular than lots of them. **Vic & the Spidermen** in their original line-up consisted of:

Vic Wright	**(voc)**
Pete Molly	**(g/voc)**
Phil Roberts	**(bg/voc)**
Ray Binnion	**(dr)**

The group was also joined by guitarist **Glynn Jones** as a fifth member, in 1962.

In June of that year, **Geoff Lloyd** replaced **Ray Binnion**, who had to go to London on business matters for a month. But he returned to **Vic & the Spidermen** and **Geoff Lloyd** became a member of **Ken Dallas & the Silhouettes**, who a little later became **Mark Peters & the Silhouettes**. After that he played with **J.J. & the Hi-Lites** and the **Mersey Monsters** who developed from that group.

In 1963, **Glynn Jones** left again and most probably formed his own group, whose name is sadly not known, but it should be clearly pointed out that he was not the recording vocalist **Glyn Johns**. He was not replaced in **Vic & the Spidermen**, who in the same year went into the studio to record the originals *Cruel To You, Helpless One, Teenage Love* and *Don't Set Me Free*. But these were only test recordings, not followed by a recording contract, let alone a record release.

Vic Wright left the **Spidermen** in 1964 to take the place of **Cy Tucker** as lead vocalist with the **T.T.s**, who from that moment on of course appeared as **Vic & the T.T.s**.

For unknown reasons, he did not stay too long with them and teamed up with the **Take Four** under the quite unusual name **Vic Takes Four**, the members of which are sadly not known. The group was quite successful on the scene for a short time but then disappeared again. In 1965, **Vic Wright** was the singer of a group called **The Script** but after that nothing was heard of him again with the exception that he later emigrated to Australia.

But back to the **Spidermen**, who at first continued as a trio, and when **Ray Binnion** left and quit show business in August 1965, he was replaced by none other than **Johnny Hutchinson**, who came from the recently disbanded **Big Three**, but he only stayed for one month and then re-formed the **Big Three**.

This fact led to the **Spidermen** splitting up in September 1965 and all the members disappeared from the scene and most probably concentrated on their normal day jobs that they had kept all the time, never becoming professionals.

Discography

A real record was never released by the group, but in July 1963, **Vic & the Spidermen** recorded the originals *Cruel To You, Helpless One, Teenage Love* and *Don't Set Me Free* as test recordings, that might have been on acetate.

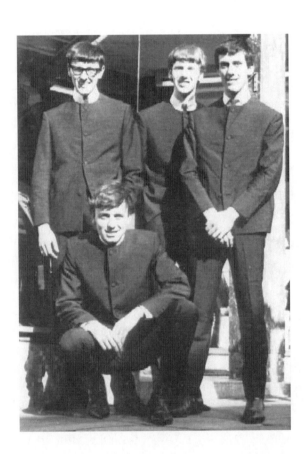

THE VICTIMS

This trio was formed in the Wavertree area of Liverpool in late 1962, inspired by the American Rock 'n' Roll sound. Very soon they became quite popular and started to play the usual Merseyside gigs in a line-up with:

Edward Gale	**(voc/bg)**
Peter Francis Barton	**(g/voc)**
Paul Hitchmough	**(dr)**

Eddie Gale and **Paul Hitchmough** were both former members of the **Hangmen**, whereby **Eddie Gale** before that had already played with the **Saints** from Liverpool. **Pete Barton** obviously was a newcomer on the group scene.

The **Victims**, as they were named right from the beginning in spite of the fact that they only were a three-piece group, had a very tight sound. They never made the headlines, didn't have any outstanding success and most probably did not even play outside Merseyside.

Therefore, it is quite surprising that in 1963 they went to the studio of **P.F. Phillips** and cut a Kensington acetate with the **Carl Perkins** classic *Blue Suede Shoes,* sung by **Eddie Gale**, and the nice Merseybeat ballad *I'd Never Find Another You*, an original of the group, sung by **Pete Barton**. This interesting acetate sadly did not help the group to obtain a recording contract

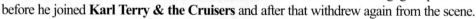

and so the **Victims** disbanded as early as the middle of 1964.

Paul Hitchmough became a member of the **Corals** and then joined a group called **Sounds Plus One** and with them he recorded a nice Unicord acetate, before he went on to join the **Kruzads**. After that he was a member of the **Clayton Squares**, who also toured Germany under the name of the **T-Squares**. After a spell with the Deram recording group **Curiosity Shoppe**, he disappeared for years but returned as a member of **Beryl Marsden**'s backing group in the Nineties, before he joined **Karl Terry & the Cruisers** and after that withdrew again from the scene.

What happened to **Eddie Gale** is sadly not known, but after the **Victims** split up, **Pete Barton** formed a new group under the name of **The Locations**, who in addition to him consisted of **'Dosi' Jones** (voc), **Billy Fidler** (bg) and **Tommy Longman** (dr). They were then joined by **Dave Keegan** as an additional guitarist, who apparently came from the final line-up of the recently disbanded **Talismen**, formerly known as **Vince Earl & the Talismen**. At his instigation, the **Locations** adopted the name of the **Talismen** and as such existed very well on the scene and even toured Germany and France. When they split up all the musicians disappeared from the scene, though it is known that **Pete Barton** carried on playing until he seriously injured his left hand in an accident in 1989.

Discography
Blue Suede Shoes / I'd Never Find Another You   UK- Kensington acetate / 1963

THE WACKERS

This group originated from the Liverpool band **Dino & the Wild Fires**, formed in 1961 in the Beat metropolis. After the group had played the clubs for around two years, most of the members wanted to become professionals. That was the time when their original drummer **Bobby Williams** left because he wanted to keep his job, as the future of a professional musician was too uncertain for him. He joined the **Newtowns** and in 1966 he was a member of the newly formed **Undertakers**, where he played until 1968 and then returned to the **Newtowns.** Today he is still active as a drummer on the scene.

Dino Grant, (whose real name is **Gwylim Philips**), **Bernard Lee** and **Julian Johnson** went down to London and became professionals when they formed **The Wackers** together with two London musicians, who then appeared in the following line-up:

Terry Anton	**(voc)**
Dino Grant	**(voc/g)**
Bernard Lee	**(g)**
Julian Johnson	**(bg)**
John Foster	**(dr)**

John Foster shouldn't be confused with the drummer of the same name who played in Liverpool with the **Dions** and the **Escorts** and used the stage name **John Sticks**.

The **Wackers** did not take part in the Liverpool scene further and only had a few gigs in their hometown, but they established themselves as a typical Mersey-styled Beat group on the London scene, where they became quite successful.

In early 1964, the group was signed to Oriole and a little later recorded their first single *I Wonder Why,* which was not the **Dion & the Belmonts** number but a composition by **Bernard Lee** and a really nice Beat record, which sadly did not achieve the success it deserved.

In the same year the **Wackers** were featured in the music film 'Swinging U.K.', which was followed by a recording contract with PYE. For their first single they recorded *Love Or Money*, the song which in the above film was announced as Merseybeat. The song really had the typical marks of Merseybeat, but sadly failed to enter the charts, although it sold quite well. This record and their collaboration in 'Swinging U.K.' of course helped the group to increase its popularity all over England.

In 1965 another single was released on the Piccadilly label, and *The Girl Who Wanted Fame* was undoubtedly the best record by the **Wackers**. A very nice Folk orientated Beat song with good arrangement and excellent vocals, but again it was not successful in the charts. After that release little was heard of the group that probably disbanded totally in 1965.

Terry Anton started a solo career after the split and in the same year released the single *Leave A Little Love* on the PYE label, but then disappeared from the scene just like **Dino Grant**, **Bernard Lee**, **Julian Johnson** and **John Foster** before him. They had probably all quit the professional music business.

In the end, it can be said that the **Wackers** were a really good group and perhaps they would have had more success on the scene if they had stayed in Liverpool, because at that time the Mersey scene still was paid more attention than the London scene. This of course is only speculation, but who knows?

Single discography

I Wonder Why / Why Can It Happen To Me   UK- Oriole   CB 1902 / 1964
Love Or Money / Hooka Tooka   UK- Piccadilly 7N 35195 / 1964
The Girl Who Wanted Fame / You're Forgetting Me   UK- Piccadilly 7N 35210 / 1965

Terry Anton - solo:
Leave A Little Love / Don't Say Goodbye   UK- PYE   7N 15871 / 1965

THE WASHINGTON D.C.s

Writing about this group in this book may mean that a non Liverpool group is being featured, but the quality of the band, their partly fantastic records and their interesting story justify that risk.

It was really hard to get information about the **Washington D.C.s**, who at least on their German tours claimed to be from Liverpool and most probably some of their members were Merseysiders. Supporting this assumption is the fact that the group played the 'Cavern' at an evening session together with other Liverpool outfits **Group One**, the **Beatcombers** and the **Easybeats** on 5th October 1963.

Of course this fact alone does not prove anything but according to **Bob Wooler**, non Liverpool groups mostly played an evening session and the next day a lunchtime session, but the **Washington D.C.s** did not play the next day's lunchtime session!

However, it seems that the band left the Liverpool area quite soon to try their luck elsewhere, most probably down in London and maybe that fact caused some personnel changes in the line-up and only two or three remaining members teamed up with musicians from another area as, for example, the **Wackers** did. In 1964 the **Washington D.C.s** consisted of the following musicians:

Barry Fitzgerald	**(voc)**
Roger Saunders	**(g/voc)**
Gary Lee Illingworth	**(org/voc)**
Bernie Trott	**(bg)**
Glen Duke	**(dr)**

Around this time, the group was signed to Ember and as their debut almost a complete album was released. On this LP the **Washington D.C.s** were featured with eight songs, while the other group on that long player, the **Dave Clark Five** only contributed two songs.

In spite of this only a photo of the **Dave Clark Five** was featured on the front cover and their name was written in big letters, while the **Washington D.C.s** almost faded compared to this. A clear case of sales politics! The back of the cover did not give any information about the artists, songwriters or the record itself.

With Merseybeatish songs like *Where Did You Go, Little One, Is It Me, Have You Seen My Baby* and a great version of the **Coasters** classic *Yakety Yak*, the **Washington D.C.s** left behind a great impression, while the other cover versions featured, *Shimmy Shimmy, Sweet Little Rock'n'Roller* and *Carol* also were not too bad. This album did not become a big seller and is accordingly a desired collectors' item these days but that of course did not help the **Washington D.C.s** to increase their popularity at that time.

Still in 1964 with a great version of *Kisses Sweeter Than Wine*, the group's first single was released on Ember in England and even on the obscure Flip label in the United States. In spite of the fact that this release had everything that a good Beat record needed at that time, it did not sell too well.

In France, a nice EP with *Kisses Sweeter Than Wine* plus the three album tracks *Where*

Did You Go, Shimmy Shimmy and *Yakety Yak* was released. The next single was also coupled out from the above mentioned album and featured the songs *Have You Seen My Baby* and *Is It Me*. This record was again released on Flip in the U.S.A. and of course on Ember in England and once again did not contribute to a bigger breakthrough for the group.

After that, the **Washington D.C.s** regularly appeared in Germany where they became quite popular and also backed singer **Paul Jones** of **Manfred Mann** fame. With him, they were also featured on the very successful German TV series "Beat-Club".

In 1966, an excellent single was released with *32nd Floor* on CBS in England, France, Germany and Denmark, as well as on 'Date' in the U.S.A. This was really a potential hit record with a great instrumental arrangement and it also showed the impressive vocal ability of the group which, judging by the picture on the German and Danish sleeve at that time, was still a five-piece.

32nd Floor, as well as the flip-side *A Whole Lot More* were written by Whittingham/ Bradley and obviously were original recordings. It is absolutely incomprehensible that this record did not make the charts as it was one of the best singles of that particular year.

In 1967 the follow-up, *Seek And Find* was again a great single, written and produced by none other than **Paul Samwell-Smith** (co-written by **Barry Mason**). Again it failed to become successful although it was released in England and Germany at least.

After that it became quiet for the **Washington D.C.s** for a time. They had obviously left CBS in those days. The reason for this might have been the personnel changes that took place at that time. **Bernie Trott** and **Glen Duke** left the group and disappeared from the scene. They were replaced by **Walt Monaghan** (bg) and **Brian Hillman** (dr.). Furthermore **Gary Lee Illingworth** also left the group who continued as a four-piece now.

In 1969 the **Washington D.C.s** were back with a new single, released on Hit-Ton in Germany and on the obscure Domain label in England. *Anytime,* as well as the flip-side *I've Done It All Wrong* was written by Fitzgerald, Hillman, Monaghan and Saunders, but in all honesty was weak compared to the previous records, especially *32nd Floor.* This time it was no surprise that it was not successful for the **Washington D.C.s**, who then disappeared totally from the scene and most probably broke up still in 1969.

Roger Saunders joined the group **Freedom** and after that became a member of **Medicine Head**, who had a big international hit with *One And One Is One* - and, by the way also hailed from Liverpool. In the Seventies, **Roger Saunders** appeared again in **Gary Glitter**'s band. Nothing was heard of the other former members of the **Washington D.C.s** after that.

Discography:

Kisses Sweeter Than Wine / Where Did You Go	UK- Ember EMB S 190 / 1964
Have You Seen My Baby / Is It Me?	UK- Ember EMB S / 1964
32nd Floor / A Whole Lot More	UK- CBS 202226 / 1966
Seek And Find / I Love Gerald Chevin The Great	UK- CBS 202464 / 1967
Anytime / I've Done It All Wrong	UK- Domain DOM 9 / 1969

EPs:

TEEN SCENE '64   UK-Ember EMB EP 4540 / 1964

 - The Washington D.C.s : Where Did You Go

 - compilation EP plus 2 songs by **Dave Clark Five** and one **by Ray Singer**

Kisses Sweeter Than Wine / Where Did You Go / Shimmy Shimmy / Yakety Yak

                                                                                            FR- Pathé   EGF 761 / 1964

LP DAVE CLARK FIVE and the WASHINGTON D.C.s   UK- Ember   FA 2003 / 1964

Songs by the **Washington D.C.'s**:

- Where Did You Go / Shimmy Shimmy / Sweet Little Rock 'n' Roller / Yakety Yak / Little One / Is It Me / Where Have You Been / Carole

Songs by the **Dave Clark Five**:

- Chaquita / In Your Heart

Tracks on compilation-albums:

Yakety Yak	on 'Live At The Pink Flamingo'	FR- Albatros 2001 / 1965
Where Did You Go	on 'Live At The Pink Flamingo'	FR- Albatros 2001 / 1965
Kisses Sweeter Than Wine	on 'Live At The Pink Flamingo'	FR- Albatros 2001 / 1965

(These were obviously really live-recordings from the 'Pink Flamingo' in London. Other artists featured on this interesting album were **Paul's Troubles**, the **Clockwork Oranges**, **Russ Hamilton**, **Ray Singer** and **Bobby Johnson & the Atoms**.)

To prevent any confusion, it should be pointed out that there was absolutely no connection between the **Washington D.C.s** of this story and **Tony Washington & his D.C.s**, who in 1964/65 cut four singles for the British 'Sue', 'Fontana' and 'Black Swan' labels. This was obviously an American group.

SONNY WEBB & THE CASCADES

The roots of this group, belonging to the 'pre-Beatles era', lead back to the beginning of 1960, when **Kenny Johnson** and **Joe Butler** formed the band **Kenny Johnson & the Country Four** in Liverpool.

This Country band consisted of **Kenny Johnson** (voc/g), **Joe Butler** (g/voc), **Tony Evans** (p), **Dave Stevens** (bg), who came from the **Vigilantes**, and **Freddie Cain** (dr). When **Kenny Johnson** had to leave Liverpool for professional reasons, he was replaced by **Brian Newman**, a former member of **Ron McKay's Skiffle-Group**. Because of that, the band changed its name to **The Country Four & Brian Newman**.

When **Joe Butler** also left the group, this was followed by two more name changes - first to **The Topics**, and later to **The Kentuckians**. Under the latter name the group released some singles, an EP and an album in the late Sixties, but in the meantime the line-up had changed again - of course.

In 1962, **Kenny Johnson** returned to Liverpool and joined **Mike Savage & the Wild Cats**, taking the place of **Mike Savage**, who had left the group together with rhythm guitarist **Jerry Gilbertson**. The group continued with **Kenny Johnson** as **The Wild Cats** and when the bass guitarist **Bill Duncan** also left, he was replaced by **Kenny Johnson**'s former partner **Joe Butler**. Very soon the group's name was changed from **The Wild Cats** to **Sonny Webb & the Cascades**.

Sonny Webb, of course, was none other than **Kenny Johnson**, who had chosen this name because he was a fan of the Country singers <u>Sonny</u> Curtis and <u>Webb</u> Pierce. Guitarist **John State**, who was a former member of the **Connoughts**, and drummer **Roger Wilcox**, who had formerly played with the **Gerry Owen Four**, both left the group. **Roger Wilcox**, by the way, became a member of the **Topics** and later played with the **Blue Mountain Showband**, while **John State** joined **Phil Brady & the Ranchers**.

The new members of **Sonny Webb & the Cascades** were **Roy Wood** (g), who had formerly played with the **Nomads** and **Johnny Templer & the Hi-Cats** and **Dave Preston** (dr) from **Vince & the Volcanos**. But both left again after a short time and while **Dave Preston** joined the **Harlems** and later played with groups like the **Secrets**, **Kinsleys** and **Creation**. **Roy Wood** left and a few months later committed suicide. **Sonny Webb** and **Joe Butler** very soon found new members for their group and then appeared with the following line-up:

Sonny Webb	**(voc/g)**
Frankie Wan	**(g)**
Joe Butler	**(bg/voc)**
Brian Redman	**(dr)**

The new drummer **Brian Redman** was a former member of the **Four Jays**, the **Four Mosts** and of **King Size Taylor & the Dominoes**. It was probably him who brought the Beat drive into the group's music, which had a strong Rockabilly influence. **Frankie Wan** had formerly played with **Gene Day & the Jango Beats**.

In this line-up, **Sonny Webb & the Cascades** were featured on the Oriole albums 'This Is

Merseybeat' Vol.1 and Vol.2 with *You've Got Everything, Border Of The Blues, Excuse Me* and *Who Shot Sam*. Their music was a very attractive mixture of Beat and Nashville sound, which was accepted on both scenes.

The songs *You've Got Everything* and *Border Of The Blues* were also released on single, sadly without any chart success, but in spite of this **Sonny Webb & the Cascades** were very successful all over the North.

In 1964 **Brian Hilton** (g/harp/perc) joined the group as an additional member, having formerly played with **Vince Earl & the Zeros** and with **Group One**.

Sonny Webb & the Cascades then changed their name to **The Hillsiders** and it is a very interesting fact that this line-up released an album in Germany with 'Western Songs', but still under the old and better sounding name of **Sonny Webb & the Cascades**.

The **Hillsiders** developed into a real Country & Western group and became one of the most popular, if not the leading band of this sound in England, for many, many years. They were also the first English Country band ever to appear at the 'Grand Ole' Opry' in Nashville, which is success in its own right.

For Beat fans, the first two singles released as **The Hillsiders** are also very interesting. They were the **Everly Brothers** song *I Wonder If I Care As Much* and the really great *Please Be My Love*, both released on Decca in 1964 and 1965, respectively.

In this line-up, the **Hillsiders** existed until the late Sixties and in that time cut two albums with the titles 'The Hillsiders Play Their Country Hits' (Decca-Rex) and 'Leaving Of Liverpool' (RCA), as well as some more singles and they were featured on the legendary 'Liverpool Goes Country' sampler.

Frankie Wan left the group and later was a member of the **Everglades**. His replacement in 1969 was **Ron Bennett**, who played the pedal steel guitar. This line-up cut the albums 'The Hillsiders' (1970) and 'Our Country' (UK-Polydor 2460-203 /1973), of which the latter is very nice and with one exception only included compositions of **Kenny Johnson** and **Joe Butler**.

In the meantime, the **Hillsiders** had recorded the album 'Heritage' (RCA) together with US Country star **George Hamilton IV** in 1971, and also backed this singer on his England and Europe tour, where amongst other places they appeared in the 'Royal Albert Hall' in London and the 'Wembley Stadium'. The following album, 'To Please You' (Stile-Records 2001 /1975) was a little boring as it was missing the necessary outstanding songs.

Also in 1975, **Kenny Johnson** left to form his own group under the name the **Kenny Johnson & Northwind**, but more about this later in the story. He was replaced in the **Hillsiders** by **Kevin McGarry** and with this line-up the album 'A Day In The Country' (LP-Records SRTX/LP004 / 1979) was released.

After that, **Ronnie Bennett** left and disappeared from the scene and he was replaced by **Dave Rowlands**. Two further albums were released with 'Hillsiders' (LP-Records LP 005 / 1980) and 'Only One You' (Suitbag-Records HS 36001 /1984).

The **Hillsiders** remained one of the most popular and successful Country bands in England, alongside **Kenny Johnson & Northwind, Phil Brady & the Ranchers** from Liverpool and the **Raymond Froggatt Band** from Birmingham until they split in 1994 when **Joe Butler** left and quit show business.

The new group of **Kenny Johnson**, appearing as **Kenny Johnson & Northwind** first consisted of **Kenny Johnson** (voc/g), **John Ferrington** (bg/voc), **Bobby Peters** (dr) and **John Hodgson** (g), who in the Sixties was a member of the **Heartbeats**, and from that developed **Excerts, Georgie's Germs** and the **George King Group**. In between he had had a short stint with the **Almost Blues**.

In 1976 the group cut an excellent album with 'Lakeside Highway' (North West Gramophone 76103). The following albums 'Let Me Love You Once' (OBM-Records OBM 1001 /1980) and 'A Tree In The Meadow' (OBM-Records OBM 1002/1981) were only released under the name of **Kenny Johnson**, although they were obviously recorded by the whole group, though it is sadly unknown with which line-up they played at that time.

In 1990, the group consisted of **Kenny Johnson** (voc/g), **Bobby Arnold** (g), who in the Sixties was a member of the **Kentuckians**, **Pete Newton** (bg), a former member of the Sixties bands **T.L.'s Bluesicians**, **Terry Hines Sextet**, **Eddie Cave & the Fyx** and **Karl Terry & the Cruisers**, as well as **Kenny Guy** (dr), who had played with the **Detours** and **Karl Terry & the Cruisers** before. This fantastic and musically brilliant line-up from time to time also appeared as **Sonny Webb & the Cascades** again and was going strong on the scene until the great guitarist **Bobby Arnold** sadly died a few years ago, which led to the split-up. **Kenny Johnson**, who is working as DJ at Radio Merseyside is still going out as a solo singer.

Single discography:
as **Sonny Webb & the Cascades**:
You've Got Everything / Border Of The Blues   UK- Oriole 45-CB 1873 / 1963

as **The Hillsiders**:

I Wonder If I Care As Much / Cotton Fields	UK- Decca	F.12026	1964
Please Be My Love / The Children's Song	UK- Decca	F.12161	1965
Almost Persuaded / Wastin' My Time	UK- Strike	JH 322	1966
Kentucky woman / Days	UK- RCA	RCA 1804	1969

LP discography
as **Sonny Webb & the Cascades**:

WESTERN SONGS / HILLBILLY JAMBOREE   G- Dt.Vogue Pop ZS 10124 P / 1964
- I'll Take A Chance On Loving You / Is It Wrong / Love's Gonna Live Here / I'm Tired / I'll Never Have To Be Alone / I've Got My Fingers Crossed / The Picture At St.Helene / High As The Mountain / Riders In The Sky / 500 Miles / Raining On The Mountain / There's More Pretty Girls Than One / I Ain't Never / Faded Bible / One Is A Lonely Number / I've Got Some

as **The Hillsiders**:
THE HILLSIDERS PLAY THEIR COUNTRY HITS   UK- Rex (Decca) LPR 1003 / 1965
- Act Naturally / You're The Reason / Release Me / Cotton Fields / Every Minute, Every Hour, Every Day / Just One Time / Please Be My Love / Hello Trouble / Abilene / Diggy Liggy Lo / I Wonder If I Care As Much / What Am I Gonna Do / Hillsliding / The Window Up Above

THE LEAVING OF LIVERPOOL   UK- RCA-Victor   SF 8002 / 1968
- The Leaving Of Liverpool / One Time And One Time Only / I Will Miss You When You Go / One Mile More / Someday, Someone, Somewhere / Don't Waste Your Time / (I'm A) Travelling Man / Doesn't Anybody Know My Name / Coming Home / If You Really Want Me To, I'll Go / The Road / Old Memories Never Die

THE HILLSIDERS   UK- Lucky   LUS 3002 / 1970
- Dear Heart / Tiger Woman / It Takes A Lot Of Money / You Just Can't Quit / Black Cloud / He's A Jolly Good Fellow / Sincere Best Wishes / Take Me / Big Job / We Don't Know / I Don't Love You Anymore / Isn't It About Time

Tracks on compilation albums:

as **Sonny Webb & the Cascades**:

You've Got Everything	on **'This Is Merseybeat' Vol.1**	**UK- Oriole PS 40047 / 1963**
Border Of The Blues	on **'This Is Merseybeat' Vol.2**	**UK- Oriole PS 40048 / 1963**
Who Shot Sam	on **'This Is Merseybeat' Vol.2**	**UK- Oriole PS 40048 / 1963**
Excuse Me	on **'This Is Merseybeat' Vol.2**	**UK- Oriole PS 40048 / 1963**

as **The Hillsiders**:

Hello Trouble	on **'Liverpool Goes Country'**	**UK- Rex LPR 1002 / 1965**
Above And Beyond	on **'Liverpool Goes Country'**	**UK- Rex LPR 1002 / 1965**
Release Me	on **'Liverpool Goes Country'**	**UK- Rex LPR 1002 / 1965**
Please Be My Love	on **'Liverpool Goes Country'**	**UK- Rex LPR 1002 / 1965**
You're The Reason	on **'Liverpool Goes Country'**	**UK- Rex LPR 1002 / 1965**
Diggy Liggy Lo	on **'Liverpool Goes Country'**	**UK- Rex LPR 1002 / 1965**
Abilene	on **'Liverpool Goes Country'**	**UK- Rex LPR 1002 / 1965**

The Hillsiders as backing group for **Tom O'Connor**:

For The Life Of Me	on **'Liverpool Goes Country'**	**UK- Rex LPR 1002 / 1965**
Pretty Pictures	on **'Liverpool Goes Country'**	**UK- Rex LPR 1002 / 1965**

Sonny Webb and the Cascades.
Royal 1795. Liverpool.

DERRY WILKIE & THE OTHERS

This group was formed in Liverpool in late 1963 or early 1964, as far as it is known by **Derry Wilkie** and **Phil Kenzie**, after both had left **The Pressmen**.

Derry Wilkie had started his career as singer with **Derry & the Seniors**, the first Liverpool group to play in Hamburg and who then developed into **Howie Casey & the Seniors**, also featuring **Derry Wilkie** and **Freddie Starr** as lead vocalists.

After that, **Derry Wilkie** was backed for a short time by **Geoff Stacey & the Wanderers** and then teamed up with the **Pressmen** as **Derry Wilkie & the Pressmen**, but that is another story. **Derry Wilkie & the Others** consisted of the following musicians:

Derry Wilkie	(voc)
Ernie Hayes	(g)
Bob Montgomery	(bg)
Phil Kenzie	(sax)
Mike Holmes	(dr)

Bob Montgomery very soon left the group to join the **Tony Prince Combo**, and after that he played with the **Mersey Five**.

Derek Bond took his place in **Derry Wilkie & the Others**, who was a former member of **Johnny Rocco & the Jets**, **Steve Day & the Jets**, **Steve Day & the Drifters** and the **Rainchecks**, who were one group under different names with different lead singers and slightly different line-ups. In this line-up, **Derry Wilkie & the Others** became really popular in Liverpool and also toured Germany quite successfully, the popularity of the coloured singer from his trips with **Derry & the Seniors** over there certainly being very helpful. After their return to England, **Mike Jeffries** from Newcastle took over the management, he was also the manager of the **Animals**.

A little later, **Derry Wilkie & the Others** recorded the song *Sweet Tasting Wine* for a single on Fontana. This was apparently coupled with *Can You Think Of Another,* a composition by **Ernie Hayes** and **Phil Kenzie** which was also recorded, but for mysterious reasons none of them were ever released. As far as it is known, this was not followed by any further recordings, although there was occasionally mention of recording sessions by the group in 'Mersey Beat'.

In 1966 **Derry Wilkie & the Others** disbanded again and it is not known what happened to the individual musicians after that. Only **Derry Wilkie** appeared again on the scene when the 'Star-Club' in Hamburg was re-opened in 1980, and on a corresponding live sampler he was featured with the songs *Halleluja, I love Her So* and *I Am Going Home*. After that he toured with **'Screaming Lord Sutch'** for a short time in Germany, but as the 'victim' of the Lord and not as singer. After that, it is said, he kept on looking for the right backing group – until he died on 22nd December 2001.

Discography

In May 1965, **Derry Wilkie & the Others** recorded the songs *Sweet Tasting Wine* and *Can You Think Of Another* for Fontana, but the planned single was never released.

It is not certain if there were further recordings made around that time, which in the end were also not issued, but fact is, there was never an official record released by **Derry Wilkie & the Others**.

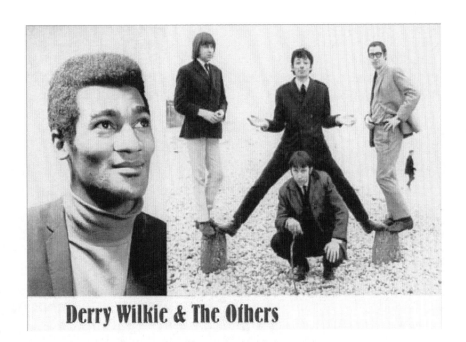

403

DERRY WILKIE & THE PRESSMEN

The **Pressmen** were originally formed as an instrumental/vocal group in the New Brighton area on the west side of the River Mersey in 1959 by **Dave Anthony Roberts** (voc/g), **Ritchie Prescott** (g), **Bob Pears** (bg) and **Nick Arnott** (dr).

Shortly after its foundation, the group disbanded again, but was immediately re-formed by the original members **Dave Roberts**, who now played saxophone, **Ritchie Prescott** and **Bob Pears** together with **Tommy Bennett** as their new drummer, who had formerly played together with **Dave Roberts** in the **Casuals** and after that was a member of the **Topspots**, as well as the follow-on band **Dee & the Dynamites**. A little later a second saxophonist was added to that line-up with **Phil Kenzie**.

Girl singer **'Mickey' Rooney** of the **Vernon's Girls** also sometimes appeared with the **Pressmen**, but she was never a steady member of the group.

In 1962, the black singer **Derek Davis**, who had adopted the stage name **Derry Wilkie**, teamed up with the band, who then changed its name to **Derry Wilkie & the Pressmen**.

Derry Wilkie had sung before with **Derry & the Seniors** and the follow-on group **Howie Casey & the Seniors** and after that for a short time was backed by **Geoff Stacey & the Wanderers**. In 1963 **Derry Wilkie & the Pressmen** appeared in the following line-up:

Derry Wilkie	**(voc)**
Ritchie Prescott	**(g)**
Bob Pears	**(bg)**
Dave Roberts	**(sax)**
Phil Kenzie	**(sax)**
Tommy Bennett	**(dr)**

With the two sax players, the group of course could make a different sound to most of the other Merseybeat bands. This can be clearly heard in the song *Halleluja, I Love Her So*, with which **Derry Wilkie & the Pressmen** were featured on the Oriole sampler 'This Is Merseybeat' Vol. 1 in 1963. This Soul influenced song was one of the outstanding tracks on that legendary **John Schroeder** produced album, but it did not help the group to obtain a recording contract.

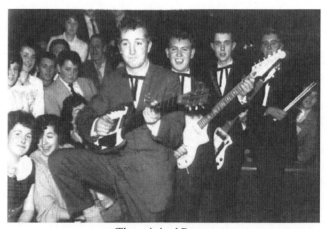

The original Pressmen

In December 1963, **Derry Wilkie & the Pressmen** were voted No.20 in the popularity poll of the music paper 'Mersey Beat' – undoubtedly a big success. Besides this, the group won a big Beat contest in the same year and the prize was a recording contract with Decca.

Derry Wilkie & the Pressmen went down to London and made some test recordings. Amongst others, the **Isley Brothers** classic *Twist And Shout* was recorded, which a little later became an international success for **Brian Poole & the Tremeloes** (on Decca!!!), while the version by **Derry Wilkie & the Pressmen** stayed unreleased.

Tommy Bennett left the group in early 1964 to join the **Pathfinders** and his replacement was none other than **Aynsley Dunbar**, who came from the **Allan De Aldo Quintet** and before that had played with the **Merseysippi Jazz Band**.

Because no record was released and a planned Germany tour was cancelled, **Derry Wilkie** and **Phil Kenzie** split from the group and formed **Derry Wilkie & the Others** – another story in this book. **Ritchie Prescott** also left the **Pressmen**, who were only joined by **Dave Carden** (voc/g) as a new member, having formerly played with **Gus & the Thundercaps**, the **Five Stars**, **Gus Travis & the Midnighters** and **Freddie Starr & the Midnighters**.

When **Faron's Flamingos** were offered a Germany tour shortly after their split, the offer was passed on to the **Pressmen**, who adopted the name **The Flamingoes** and went to the continent. In Germany, they were signed to Dt. Vogue and recorded the single *Glücklich Wie Noch Nie*, which was the German version of the **Beatles** song *I'll Get You*. Although this **Flamingoes** single is a desired collectors' item nowadays, it flopped in the Sixties.

The group then recorded a very poorly produced album with black singer **Tony Cavanaugh** for the German 'Somerset' label under the name **Tony Cavanaugh & the Liverpool Triumphs** before they returned to Liverpool, where they amalgamated with singer **Freddie Starr** under the name of **Freddie Starr & the Starr Boys**, but sometimes also appeared as **Freddie Starr & the Flamingoes**. For a continuation of this story, please see the story of **Freddie Starr & the Starr Boys**. But this was not the end of the **Pressmen** story, because the former drummer **Tommy Bennett** separated from the **Pathfinders** again in the end of 1964 and formed the **New Pressmen** together with **Howard Morris** (g), **Willie van Geffen** (voc/g) and **Adrian Flowerday** (bg).

Howard Morris was a former member of **Rip Van Winkle & the Rip-It-Ups**, while **Willie van Geffen** had formerly played with the **Alley Cats**, the **Rhythm Amalgamated** and the **Outcasts**. **Adrian Flowerday** had played with **Dave & the Rave-Ons** before, and with **Steve Day & the Kinsmen**. For a short time, the **New Pressmen** were quite successful on the scene but then disappeared again without having a record released. **Howard Morris** joined the **Chuckles** and **Tommy Bennett** became a member of the **Three Dees**.

In the early Nineties, **Tommy Bennett** and founder member **Ritchie Prescott** re-formed the **Pressmen**, but this band only played at 'Mersey Cats' events and broke up again quite soon afterwards.

Tommy Bennett then formed the **Dees** together with bass guitarist **Mike Rudzinsky**, who in the Sixties had played with the **Avengers** and **Johnny Kidd & the Pirates** amongst others. **Ritchie Prescott** became a member of **Karl Terry & the Cruisers**, with whom he also toured Germany again and in 1994 recorded a great Rock 'n' Roll album over there. After that, he joined the **Juke Box Eddies**, where he met up again with original **Pressmen** drummer **Nick Arnott**, who today plays with a Soul group called **Nighttrain**.

Ritchie Prescott is now back with **Karl Terry & the Cruisers**.

Bob Pears sadly died in 1995.

Discography
Hallelujah, I Love Her So on **'This Is Merseybeat' Vol.1**   **UK- Oriole PS 40047 / 1963**

   Derry Wilkie & the Pressmen also won a recording contract with Decca in 1963 and recorded some songs for that label, of which only *Twist And Shout* is known, but none of them was ever released.
   Here it should be pointed out that the **Pressmen** did not back **'Screaming Lord Sutch'** on his 1966 single *Purple People Eater* as is stated so often.

   For more record releases by the group please see the story of **Freddie Starr & the Starr Boys**.

THE YOUNG ONES

This group was formed in Liverpool under the name of **Danny Royl & the Strollers** in 1961. One year later, the band changed their name to **The Sensations**, and then again to **The Young Ones**. In the original line-up, this group consisted of the following musicians:

Dave Wilcox	**(voc)**
Wilma York	**(voc)**
Ricky Coburn	**(g)**
Alan Moorfield	**(g)**
George Varcas	**(bg)**
Tommy Kelly	**(dr)**

Dave Wilcox, whose real name is **David Christie**, was, in fact, **Danny Royl** from the original group name. Also in 1962, the **Young Ones** won a Beat contest at Liverpool's 'Broadway' club, followed by **Faron's Flamingos**, who came second.

The prize for the winners was a record release and a TV appearance and so in 1963, the **Young Ones** released their first single with *Baby That's It* on the Decca label.

Baby That's It was a classic Merseybeat number with a catchy melody, a really good drive and great vocals by **Dave Wilcox**, while the B-side *How Do I Tell You* was a sentimental ballad about the permanent problem of how to say Goodbye. This was sung by **Wilma York**, who proved that she also was a good singer. It was one of the better Merseybeat records with two totally different and very interesting sides, but it was unsuccessful, although it really had everything that was needed.

It is also interesting that the group in the meantime had changed its name again to **Rikki Janson & the Q-Kats** and sometimes also appeared as **The Q-Kats with Wilma**, but had then changed it back to **The Young Ones**, when the record was released.

This single was the first and only release by the **Young Ones** and the group disbanded totally as early as the end of 1963. **Wilma York** went solo and became one of the city's leading girl singers, but in spite of this did not release any more records.

In 1964, **Tommy Kelly** joined **Earl Preston's Realms** and after that was a member of the **Escorts**, with whom he also toured in Germany. **Ricky Coburn** appeared again on the scene, playing with the **Coins** in 1965, while **Dave Wilcox** became a member of the newly formed **Nocturns**, who were quite successful on the scene for a time, and had a part in the **Lionel Bart** musical 'Maggie May' and also recorded for Decca. After the group disbanded again, he disappeared from the scene, just as **George Varcas** and **Alan Moorfield** had done before. So, what is left of that really good group with the name **The Young Ones** is a great Beat single, worth looking out for!

Single discography
Baby That's It / How Do I Tell You
UK- Decca F.11705 / 1963

SOME OTHER MERSEYSIDE GROUPS

Almost at the end of this book, here are nearly 100 more Merseyside groups with their complete line-ups, not mentioned in this book before. To save space, only one line-up of every group has been listed and replacements were not considered.

A

THE ALPHAS
from Liverpool (1964)
Paul McLean (lg/voc)
Robert Baillie (rg/voc)
Brian Eccles (bg)
Derek Burnham (sax)
David Wamp (dr)

THE AMBASSADORS
from Liverpool (1962)
Deke Wade (voc)
Dave Dover (lg)
Dave Dickinson (rg)
Gene McCulloch (bg)
Stan Booth (dr)

B

THE BLACK JACKS
from Liverpool (1960)
Ken Brown (voc/g)
Bill Barlow (g)
Chas Newby (bg)
Peter Best (dr)

THE BLACK VELVETS
from Liverpool (1962)
Kenny Rees (voc/bg)
Leo Edwards (voc/rg)
Maurice Loughlin (lg)
Gerry Winstanly (dr)

THE BOBBY BELL ROCKERS
from Liverpool (1958)
Bobby Crawford (voc)
Dave Moore (lg)
Wayne Bickerton (rg/voc)
Steve Bennett (bg/voc)
Charlie Mitchell (dr)

BOBBY & THE BACHELORS
from Kirkby (1964)
Bobby Dalton (voc)
Mike Godwin
Mike Barrie
Ian Gordon
Pete Davies

PHIL BRADY & THE RANCHERS
(Country) from Liverpool (1964)
Phil Brady (voc/g)
Ray Owen (g)
Frank Peters (steel-g)
Tommy Bowness (bg)
Eddy Waff (dr)

MIKE BYRNE & THE THUNDERBIRDS
from Liverpool (1960)
Mike Byrne (voc/bg)
Rod McDonald (lg)
Dennis Aspinall (rg)
Clive Smith (dr)

C

THE CAVE DWELLERS
from Liverpool (1964)
Peter Anyon
Brian Atkinson
Peter G. Penter
Ray Hudson
John D. ProcteR

THE CAVERNERS
from Bromborough (1964)
Ken Smith (g)
Mark Farrell (g)
Steven Roberts (bg)
Colin Roberts (dr)

THE CHECKERS
from Liverpool (1964)
Harry Emmett (g)
Tony Kendall (g)
Doug Wollie (bg)
Pete Hodge (dr)

THE CHESSMEN
from Litherland (1963)
Tony Christian (voc)
Roy Backhouse (g)
Graham Dooley (bg)
Bob Ramsey (dr)

THE CITADELS
from Litherland (1964)
Ricky O'Neill (voc/g)
Tony Sefton (g)
John Jenkins (bg)
John Swift (dr)

THE CITROENS
from Liverpool (1964)
Willy Tomlinson (voc)
Bob Simpson
Charles Gorton
Arthur Torres
George Guile

COMBO SIX
from Birkenhead (1964)
Kenny Smith (voc/lg)
Billy Burrows (bg/voc)
Allen 'Gaz' Gaskell (sax)
Allan Halliday (sax)
Bob Evans (dr)

410

THE COMMANCHEROS
from Speke (1963)
Billy Quirk (lg)
Patrick Horne (rg)
John Morley (bg)
Kenny Williams (dr)

THE CORDAYS
from Huyton (1964)
G.A. Downes (voc/g)
Peter Glasby (g)
Norman Bellis (bg)
James Hughes (sax)
Richard Sillitoe (dr)

THE CORSAIRS
from Birkenhead (1964)
Tony Coates (voc/g)
Ray Dale (g/voc)
Pete Bowden (bg/voc)
Colin Sayers (dr)

THE CRACKSMEN
from Bootle (1964)
Steve Abernethy
Jimmy Coleman
Andy Harris
Terry Garvin

LEE CROMBIE & THE SUNDOWNERS
from Liverpool (1962)
Lee Crombie (voc)
Pete Goodall (g)
Gary Hughes (g)
Dave Calvely (bg)
Dave Crombie (dr)

D

DAVE & THE RAVE-ONS
from Wallasey (1963)
Harold Dickinson (g/voc)
Adrian Flowerday (bg/voc)
Dave Crosby (voc/dr)

EDDIE DEAN & THE ONLOOKERS
from Liverpool (1962)
Eddie Dean (voc)
Tony Randall (g)
Johnny Stephens (g)
Paul Murphy (bg)
William Brooks (dr)

MIKE DEE & THE DETOURS
from Southport (1963)
Mike Pierce (voc)
Dave Mason (g)
Ray Borsey (g)
Gary Barton (bg)
Ian Magee (dr)

THE DELEMERES
from Newcastle / Liverpool (1964)
Mac McGibbon (voc/bg)
Dave Shipley (g)
Karl Terry (g/voc)
Gordon Railton (org/p)
Mike Wakefield (dr)

THE DELEMERES

THE DEMOISELLES
from Liverpool (1964)
Sheila McGlory (voc/g)
Sheila Lewis (g/voc)
Susan Henderson (bg/voc)
Linda Turner (dr)

THE DEMONSTRATORS
from Litherland (1963)
John Almond
Alan Jones
Tony Cunningham
Brendon Jones

THE DETONATORS
from Liverpool (1963)
Dean Stacey (voc)
Eddie Murphy (g)
Doug Eaton (g/p)
Roger Eaton (bg)
John Morris (dr)

THE DIPLOMATS
from Southport (1962)
Barry Womersley (lg/voc)
Quentin Haggerty (rg)
Dave Tollins (bg)
Kelvin Finlayson (dr)

E

DAVE EAGER & THE BEAVERS
from Wrexham (1962)
Dave Eager (voc)
Roy McMahon (g)
Ron Nicholson (g)
Noddy Crewe (bg)
Jim Nobel (dr)

THE ELEKTRONS
from Huyton (1964)
Colin Bellingham (g/voc)
Syd Rimmer (bg/voc)
Alan Moss (dr/voc)

THE ELEMENTS
from Maghull (1964)
David E. Russel
Roger Asplin
Brian Clarke
William Wilson

F

THE FEDERAL FIVE
from St. Helens (1963)
Martin O'Brian (voc)
Phil Gason (g)
Shirt Clayton (g)
Mike O'Brian (bg)
John Gwilliam (dr)

THE FONTANAS
from Kirkby (1963)
Pete Campbell (voc/g)
Les Coates (g)
Pete Dunn (bg/voc)
Colin Woodruff (dr)

G

THE G MEN
from Liverpool (1962)
John Dempsey (voc/rg)
Dave Watson (lg)
John Davis (bg)
Bob Newport (dr)

The G Men

THE GALAXIES
from Liverpool (1963)
Doreen Savage (voc)
Dave Walker (voc/g)
Dave Kent (g)
Jim Stead (p)
Bob Hewlett (bg)
Robert Allin (dr)

THE GALVANISERS
from Liverpool (1962)
Roy Morton (g)
Chris Wilson (g)
Robert Packham (bg)
Derek Cumberledge (dr)

THE GEORGIANS
from Liverpool (1962)
Tim Dougdale (voc/g)
Lawrence Ashley (g)
Geoff Jones (bg/voc)
Roger Lewis (sax)
Mike Sloan (dr)

THE GHOSTRIDERS
from Liverpool (1964)
Howard Blackburn (lg/voc)
Pat Hughes (voc/rg)
Robert O'Hare (bg)
Brian McGarry (dr)

THEM GRIMBLES
from Liverpool (1963)
Mike Byrne (voc)
Ernie Hankin (lg)
Chris Stanton (org)
Robert Burns (bg)
Pete Clarke (dr)

THE GROUPIERS
from Liverpool (1963)
Arthur Hurst (voc)
Vincent Thomas (g/voc)
Dennis Swale (g/voc)
Geoff Barrow (bg)
Bobby Roberts (dr)

H

THE HAWKS
from Liverpool (1964)
David S. Masters
Ken Roberts
Jim Woodcock
Rick Malmsteen

HENRY'S HANDFUL
from Liverpool (1965)
Mike Hart (voc)
Peter Taylor (g)
Vinnie Ismael (g)
Rob Eccles (bg)
Chris Hatfield (dr)

THE HUSTLERS
from Liverpool (1964)
John Yeatrohmo
Austin O'Dowd
Frank Norton
Ron Payne

I

IAN & THE REBELS
From Liverpool (1963)
Ian Gregson (voc)
Keith Hubbard (lg)
Roy Smith (rg)
Derek Brough (bg)
Chris Kenny (dr)

THE INTERNS
from Wallasey (1964)
Charles Wood
Victor Rose
Andrew Wylie
Richard Bainbridge

THE INVADERS
from Liverpool (1963)
Dave Fowler (voc)
Kevin O'Brian (g)
John Kirwin (g)
Ronnie Woods (bg)
Mike Campbell (dr)

J

THE JAGUARS
from Birkenhead (1963)
Dave Scarratt (voc/bg)
Greg Murphy (g)
Alan Swindles (g)
Ken Hughes (dr)

JENNY & THE TALL BOYS
from Liverpool (1963)
Jenny Ellison (voc)
John Ellison (g)
Ray Hughes (g)
Pete Byrom (bg)
Keith Murray (dr)

JOAN & THE DEMONS
from Chester (1964)
Joan Molloy (voc)
Geoffrey Jones (g)
Dave Rushton (g)
Michael Daly (bg)
Paul Liddy (dr)

JUST US
from Liverpool (1965)
Little Jimmy (voc)
Brian Woods (g/voc)
George Dickinson (bg/voc)
Gerry Stewart (sax)
Dave Stead (dr)

K

THE K-Ds
From Birkenhead (1963)
Allen 'Gaz' Gaskell (lg/voc)
Harry Thomas (bg/voc)
Norman Smith (dr)

THE KOP
from Liverpool (1966)
Eddie Kennedy (voc)
Joey Youds (voc/harp)
Terry Cummins (lg)
Tommy   (org/p)
John Brothers (bg)
Barry Robinson (dr)

L

THE LAVELLS
from Aintree (1964)
Mauro Meadows (voc)
Roy Jenkinson (lg)
Robert Tracey (rg)
Tommy Pauline (bg)
John Allen (dr)

M

THE MAFIA
from Liverpool (1964)
Norby Del Rosa (voc)
Arthur Owen (g)
Jimmy Ikomidis (g)
Harold Williams (bg)
Pete Wiggins (dr)

JOHNNY MARLOWE & THE WHIP-CHORDS
from Liverpool (1963)
Johnny Marlowe (voc)
Chris Scutt (g)
Bob Caddock (g)
Colin Owen (bg)
Mike Donald (dr)

The Memphis Three.

THE MEMPHIS THREE
from Liverpool (1963)
Brendon McCormack (g/voc)
John Bancroft (bg)
Gibson Kemp (dr)

THE MINITS
from Wallasey (1964)
Trevor Thomas (voc)
Ian Heath (g)
John Duggan (g)
Barry Henry (bg)
Philip Dyer (dr)

THE MOROCKANS
From The Wirral (1963)
Frank Burns (voc)
Pete Watson (lg)
Robin Cartwright (bg)
Derek Cooper (dr)

N

THE NIGHTGUYS
from Liverpool (1964)
Tony Deller
Terence Maguire
Derek Devine
Brian Dodson

THE NIGHT WALKERS
from Wallasey (1964)
R.W. Dennis
D. Jones
W.H. Burrows
J. Piggot

O

THE ORIGINAL BLACKJACKS
from Liverpool (1964)
K.M. Burns
Andy McClaghlin
Peter Norman
Eric McDonald

THE OUTCASTS
from Birkenhead (1963)
Paul Christo (voc)
Willie van Geffen (g)
John Loy (g)
William Clare (bg)
John Clare (dr

P

THE PILGRIMS
From the Wirral (1965)
Dave Keighley (g/voc)
Graham Nugent (g/voc)
Ray Adams (bg)
Alan Denton (dr)

THE PRINCIPLES
from Liverpool (1963)
Brent Pickford (voc)
Trevor Wilkinson (g)
Maurice Wattbridge (g)
Malcolm Peart (bg)
Pete Cockhill (dr)

R

RICK & THE DELMONTS
from Liverpool (1963)
Ricky Yates (voc)
John Hare (g)
Peter Howe (g)
Frank Howard (bg)
Barry Coonbe (dr)

RIKKI & THE RED STREAKS
From The Wirral (1961)
'Rikki' Clusky (voc)
Brendan McCormack (lg/voc)
Billy Loane (rg/voc)
Dave O'Neill (bg)
Bob Evans (dr)

THE RIOT SQUAD
From Liverpool (1964)
Bill Ennis (lg)
Bob Reece (rg)
Pete Ritson (bg/voc)
Allan Newman (dr)

RORY & THE GLENEAGLES
from Wrexham (1963)
John 'Rory' Marubbi (voc)
David Johnston (g/voc)
Derick Pawis (g/voc)
Allan Bramwell (bg)
Fred Baker (dr)

S

THE SANTONES
from Liverpool (1964)
Eddie Lane (voc/g)
Johnny Wild (g)
Chris Ellis (bg)
Kenny Munda (dr)

THE SATANISTS
from Liverpool (1963)
Bill Rooney (voc/rg)
Garth Hennie (lg)
Alan Collins (bg)
Johnny Sze (dr)

SAVVA & THE DEMOCRATS
from Wallasey (1962)
Savva Hercules (voc)
Ted Thompson (g/voc)
Roger Parrott (p)
Malcolm Shelbourne (bg)
Billy Robinson (dr)

SAVVA WITH THE DEMOCRATS

PETE
GOODALL

ROC
6279

THE SCHATZ
from Kirkby (1965)
Kevin McCormack (lg/voc)
Jack Gordon (rg)
John Cushion (bg)
Pete Ward (dr)
(until '64 as the **"Warriors"**)

422

THE SET UP
from London /Liverpool (1963)
Stan Ferguson (voc/g)
Robbie Crawford (voc/bg)
Ron Southall (g)
Steve Davis (dr)

Lee Shondell

LEE SHONDELL & THE BOYS
from Liverpool (1963)
Lee Shondell (voc)
John Kirkpatrick (g)
Edward Houlihan (g)
Harry Scully (bg)
Les Watkinson (dr)

LEE SHONDELL & THE CAPITOLS
from Liverpool (1962)
Lee Shondell (voc)
Leonhard Kehoe (g)
John McGregor (g)
Jack Hughes (bg)
Martin Duncan (dr)

THE SINNERS
from Liverpool (1957)
Malcolm Smith (voc/perc)
George Watson (voc/g)
Cliff Roberts (g)
Brian Hall (g)
Eddie Rowlands (t-bass)

THE SKELETONS
from Liverpool (1964)
John Brownrigg
Peter Hornby
David Worthington
Jeffrey McCormick
Dennis McNeely

THE STEREOS
from Liverpool (1961)
Frank Evers (voc/g)
Irvin Banks (g/voc)
Kenny Harper (g/voc)
Mike Needham (dr)

THE STORMERS
from Liverpool (1964)
David Rimmer
Michael Gavis
Michael Carroll (g/voc)
Roman Bomba

THE STRETTONS
from Liverpool (1964)
Billy Pinto (voc)
Colin Lomas (g)
Freddie Hulse (g)
Eric Anderson (bg)
Jack Clarke (dr)
(formerly known as **"The Everests"**)

THE SUBTERRANES
from Birkenhead (1964)
Bill Fernley (voc)
Chris Blades (g)
Ron Bird (g)
John Kenney (bg)
Nicki Huggins (dr)

T

THE TIYMS
From Wallasey (1963)
Mike Cooper (voc)
Allen 'Gaz' Gaskell (lg/voc)
Stan Ellison (rg)
Mike White (bg)
Pete Clarke (dr)

THE TOKENS
from Liverpool (1964)
Terry McAdam (voc/g)
Richard Quilliam (g)
Stan Davis (g)
Charlie King (bg)
Derek Aveton (dr)

THE TRAVELLERS
From Wallasey/Birkenhead (1962)
Bill Knaggs (lg)
Mike Rudzinsky (rg)
Tony McDonough (bg)
Ron Smith (dr)

THE TRIUMPHS
from Liverpool (1964)
Raymond Wilson (voc)
Edward Ankrah (voc)
Bernie Wenton (voc)
Kenneth Davies
Raymond Pratt
Haydn Kirkwood
Ronald Wilson

THE TROLLS
from Liverpool (1963)
John Wishart (g/voc)
Paul Cronin (g)
Steve Watson (bg)
Jimmy Lunt (dr)

V

THE VAAVEROS
from Liverpool (1964)
David Tubb
Mike Espie
Neil Ford
David Ray Stinger

THE VABERS
from Liverpool (1964)
Jim McNaught (voc)
Steve Carey (g)
Bob Rowland (g)
Jim Carr (bg)
Stuart Henderson (dr)

THE VAMPIRES
from Liverpool (1963)
Mark Clifton (voc)
Chris Williams (g)
Terry Hughes (g)
Tony Kenny (bg)
Mike Cooper (dr)

THE VAQUEROS
from Liverpool (1964)
Eric Holding
Steve Lennett
James Atherton
Norman Downs

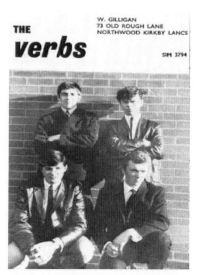

THE **verbs**

W. GILLIGAN
73 OLD ROUGH LANE
NORTHWOOD KIRKBY LANCS

SIM 3794

THE VERBS
from Kirkby (1965)
Bill Dunn (voc/g)
Tommy Perks (g)
Ron Duffy (bg)
Barney Curry (dr)
('til the end of '64 as "The
Four Dominators")

VIC TAKES FOUR
from Liverpool (1964)
Vic Wright (voc)
Ray Faulkner (lg)
Bill Faulkner (rg)
John Aston (bg)
Frank Houghton (dr)

THE VIGILANTES
(Country) from Liverpool (1962)
Ray Shaw (voc)
Arthur Quinn (g)
Mike Whitehead (g)
Alan Whitehead (bg)
Mike Donald (dr)
(from 1963 as **The Aristocrats**)

W

THE WHIRLWINDS
from St. Helens (1964)
Glyn Hourihan
Morris Scott
Ray Stockton
John Roberts

RIP VAN WINKLE & THE RIP-IT-UPS
from Birkenhead (1964)
Jimmy 'Ginger' Geary (voc)
Keith Nixon (g)
Geoff Brown (g)
Howard Morris (bg)
Terry McCusker (dr)

Y

DEE YOUNG & THE PONTIACS
from Liverpool (1961)
Dee Young (voc)
Sam Andrews (g)
Les Painter (g)
Mike Young (bg)
Jeff Hunter (dr)

THE YOUNG ONES
from Birkenhead (1962)
Allen Gaskell (g/voc)
Dennis Jeffcoate (g)
Alan Webster (g)
Les McFarlane (bg)
Kenny Webster (dr)

Z

THE ZEROS
from Liverpool (1964)
John Parry
David Skinner
John Kitson
David Brown
Kenny Webster (dr)

FINALLY

Here is a list of more than 350 further group names from Merseyside, not already named in the book but who were active in the Liverpool area in the time from 1957 until 1966. Some names may be confusing because there were also other groups from other places with identical names, but this list includes exceptional (non-recording) bands from Merseyside.

A big **THANK YOU** to them all for having been there at that time . . . .

A

The Abstract Minds
The Accoustics
The Ads
The Admins
The Advocats
Ahab & his Lot
The Aintree Four
The Alamos
The Albany Four
The Alibis
The Alligators
Annette & the Riverdales
Mark Anthony & the Alpha Beats
The Anzacs
The Apaches
The Approachers
Arrow & the Archers
The Astronaughts
The Atlantics
The Avalons

B

The Bachelor Boys
The Backbeats
The Banshees
The Doug Barry Sound
The Beat Cats
The Belltones
Bennie & the Jumping Beans
Bernadette & the Four Gents
Bernie & the Tornados
J.B. Bishop & the Curates
The Black Diamonds
The Blue Diamonds
The Blue Notes

The Doug Barry Sound 1967

The Blue Streaks
The Blues Giants
Bobby & the Be-Bops
Bobby & the Halers
The Boleros
The Boot Hill Billys
The Boys
The Breakdowns
The Broadways
Bruce & the Spiders
The Buccaneers
The Buffaloes
Johnny Burns & the Renegades

C

Cal's Combo
Carole & the Corvettes
Cash & the Cashmen
The Catalinas
The Cavaliers
The Cavels
The Cavemen
The Censors
The Centurians
The Champions
The Chandels
The Chee Syney Group
The Chequers
The Chicades
Chris & the Autocrats
The Cirques
The Clearways
The Climaks
The Clive Lord Five
The Cobblestones
The Cockroaches
The Collegians
The Conquerors
The Conspiratiors
The Contenders
The Cordelles
The Corvettes
The Countdowns
The Crackerjacks
The Mal Craig Trio
The Crestas
The Cross Rocks
The Crusaders

D

The Daleks
Danny & the Strollers
Eddie Danton & the Medics
The Dark Ages
The Dateliners
Dave & the Crusaders
The Daybreakers
The Dealers
Dean & the Capitols
The Decibels
Deek's Bohemians
The Deerstalkers
The Defiants
The Dekkas
The Delacardoes
The Dell Stars
The Delta Combo
The Deltics
The Demons
Dene & the Citizens
The Deputies
The Detroits
Dean Devlin & the Dynamites
The Diablos
The Downbeats
The Dresdens
The Drone Tones
The Druids
The Drumbeats
Duke Duval's Rockers
The Dynachords
The Dynamics
The Dynamites
The Dynamos

E

The Earthlings
Eddie & the Phantoms
Eddie & the Razers
The El Diablos
The Elks
The Billy Ellis Trio

F

The Fabz
The Factotums
The Falcons
The FBI
The Feelgoods
Pete Fenton & the Landsliders
The Fenton Weill Five
The Fire Flites
The Firebrands
The Flyaways
The Flyovers
The Forgers
The Four Quarters
The Fractions
The Steve Francis Four
Freddie & the Fireballs
Freddie & the Rousers

G

The Gay Tones
The Ghost Riders
The Gibsons
The Globetrotters
The Les Graham Five
The Group Five

H

The Hailers
The Hammers
Hank's Hoppers
The Harlequins
The Harpos
The Hellions
Roy Hepworth & the Hep Cats
The Heralds
The Hispanos
The Hoboes
The Hornets
The Hot Rocks
The Hungry 1's
Roy Hunter & the Falcons
The Huntsmen

I

The Illusions
The Impacts
The Informers
The Inner Circle
The Interludes

J

The Jackobeats
Al James & the Tornados
Jay & the Juniors
The J-Beats
The Jensons
The Jesters
Jimmy & the Teenbeats
The J.L.'s
Joey & the Kodaks
Johnny & the Semitones
The Jokers
Kenny Jordan & the Rousers

K

The Kandies
The Karacters
The Katz
The Keenbeats
Prince Khan & the Babes
The King Bee's
The Kingfishers
The Kingpins
The Kingstrums
The Kiwis
The Klaxons
The Ko-Dels
The Kobras
The Kommotions
The Konkers
The Kreeps

L

The Landslides
The Lawmen
The Lectrons
The Leemen
The Legends
Liam & the White Brothers
The Liberators
The Lidos
The Lincolns
Count Linsey & the Skeletons
The Little Boys Blue
The Live Jive Five

M

The Madcaps
The Mad Monks
The Mailmen
The Majestics
The Mal Craig Trio
Ray Malcolm & the Sunsets
The Managers
The Manhattans
The Marawacks
The Marlins

The Matchbox Five
The Megatones
The Meteors
Johnny Mika & the Shades
Mike & the Creoles
Mike & the Explorers
The Minutes
The Mission Men
The Mistake
The Mohawks
Roy Molloy & the Teenbeats
The Monarchs
The Moonrakers
The Mosquitos
The Music Students
The Musicians
The Mustangs
The Mysteries
The Mystics

N

The Chris Nava Combo
The Night Boppers

A Great Sound . . .
A Great Group
* * * THE * * *
MANAGERS
DAVE — JIMMY — PHIL — DAVE
Telephone : WAT 3517

THE GROUP WITH A STRIKING
DIFFERENCE!!
THE MATCHBOX 5
Manager: M. J. OWEN,
131 LIVERPOOL RD.,
SOUTHPORT.
Tel.: 65039

The CHRIS NAVA COMBO

432

O

Ogi & the Flintstones
Nick Olsen & the Four Aces
The 1-2-3-4-5
The Opals

P

The Page Boys
Paul & the Diamonds
The Pegasus Four
The Peppermint Twisters
Peter & the Sceptres
The Phantom Five
The Photons
The Plebs
The Plims
The Presidents
The Pretenders
The Problems
The Protests
The Prowlers
The Pyramids

Q

The Quiet Ones
The Quiet Three

R

The Rainmakers
The Ramblers
The Ramrods
The Rawhides
The Reason Why
The Reasons
The Red Diamonds
The Red Mountain Boys
The Red River Boys
The Regents
The Rembrants
The Renicks
Vince Reno & the Sabres
Ricky & the Vibrators
The Rigg
Rita & the Renegades
The Robettes
The Rockerfellers
The Rockin' Clippers
Dave Roman & the Chariots
The Rontons
The Bob Ross Group
Roy & the Falcons

S

The Sad Saks
Remo Sand & the Spinning Tops
The Sandgrounders
The Saracens
Satan & the Hellcats
Russ Saunders & the V-Tones
The Screaming Sculls
The Sentinals
The Sepias
The Shakespears
The Sheriffs
The Shimmy Shakers
The Shondells
The Silverstones
The Sinisters
The Skyliners
The Sleepwalkers
The Sneakers
Solomon's Mines
The Soul Seekers
The Soundsmen
The Spades
The Spectres
The Spekeasys
The Spitfires
The Sputnicks
The Statesmen
Wayne Stephens & the Vikings
The Steve Francis Four
Paul Stevens & the Emperors
Al Stone & the Earthquakes
The Sunnysides
The Swaydes

FOR THE BEST IN BEAT..

THE SARACENS

Phone: J. ARCHER .. BOO 3942

THE SOUL SEEKERS R & B.
WAT. 7554

T

The Tagg
J. Taylor & the Top Spots
The Team-Mates
The T-Beats
The Teddybears
The Teenage Rebels
The Teentones
The Tempos
Terry & the Zodiacs
The Three Deuces
Three Dots & A Dash
The Thrillers
The Thundermen
The Tigers
The Tomboys
Tommy & the Teenbeats
Tony & the Black Shadows

Tony & the Quandros
Tony & the Triads
Tony & the Tuxedos
The Traders
The Trakkers
The Travelons
The Trebletones
The Tremas
The Tremolos
The Tremors
The Trend-Setts
The Tributes
The Tudors
Mel Turner & the Souvenirs

U

The Unicorns
The US-Limited

V

The Vaders
The Vanguards
The Varasounds
The Vermont Quartet
The Vibrators
The Vibros
The Viceroys
The Victors
The Vikings
Vikki & the Moonlighters
Vince & the Hot Rods
The Vocanics

W

The Wayfarers
The Waysiders
The Wild Ones
The Wranglers
The Wyverns

X

The X-L's

Y

Cole Young & the Graduates
Dale Young & the Seminoles

Z

The Zef Four
The Zeniths
The Zwinging Coronets

. . . . and any other group that was around and sadly not included in this list

**More great books from
Mediaworld and Best Books Online
can be seen on our publishing web site at
www.bestbooksonline.co.uk**

Publish with us in electronic book form,
traditional form, or both, and
your work receives world-wide listings.

E-mail publishing@bestbooksonline.net
**or call us on
0845 6435483 within the United Kingdom, or
+447092103738 from outside
(24 hour voicemail facility)**

**Mediaworld PR Ltd,
PO Box 255, Yeadon,
Leeds, LS19 9AZ**

Words and people that mean business

We are a specialist company offering
much more than traditional publishers.
We deal with our authors personally
and provide all editing and marketing services
on a one to one basis.